Second Workshop on Evaluation and Comparison of NLP Systems (Eval4NLP 2021)

Online
10 November 2021

ISBN: 978-1-7138-9183-3

Printed from e-media with permission by:

Curran Associates, Inc.
57 Morehouse Lane
Red Hook, NY 12571

CURRAN ASSOCIATES INC.
proceedings
.com

Some format issues inherent in the e-media version may also appear in this print version.

Printed with permission by Curran Associates, Inc. (2024)

For permission requests, please contact the Association for Computational Linguistics at the address below.

Association for Computational Linguistics
209 N. Eighth Street
Stroudsburg, Pennsylvania 18360

Phone: 1-570-476-8006
Fax: 1-570-476-0860

acl@aclweb.org

Additional copies of this publication are available from:

Curran Associates, Inc.
57 Morehouse Lane
Red Hook, NY 12571 USA
Phone: 845-758-0400
Fax: 845-758-2633
Email: curran@proceedings.com
Web: www.proceedings.com

EMNLP 2021

Evaluation and Comparison of NLP Systems

Proceedings of the Second Workshop

November 10, 2021

The Eval4NLP 2021 organizers gratefully acknowledge the support from the following sponsors.

Introduction

Welcome to the Second Workshop on Evaluation and Comparison of NLP Systems (Eval4NLP 2021).

Undeniably, fair evaluations and comparisons are important to the NLP community for properly tracking progress and suggesting open problems in the field. In recent years, after the deep learning revolution, people are relying more and more on fine-tuning pre-trained language models to achieve downstream tasks, leading to significant growth in the number of published state-of-the-art results. Without appropriate evaluations (including methodologies, datasets, metrics, setups, reports, etc.), such results would be meaningless or even harmful to the community. Last year, the first workshop in the series, Eval4NLP 2020, was the first workshop to take a broad and unifying perspective on the subject matter. For this year, the goal of the second workshop is to continue the tradition by providing a platform for presenting and discussing the latest advances in NLP evaluation methods and resources.

The workshop has attracted lots of attention from the community with 36 research papers being submitted. After careful reviews by the program committee and the workshop organizers, 17 papers (including 14 long papers and 3 short papers) were accepted to present in the workshop. To increase the variety of the program, we additionally welcome 17 papers published recently elsewhere (i.e.,14 papers from the Findings of EMNLP 2021 and 3 papers from other prestigious publication venues in AI) to present in the workshop as well. Overall, our program covers a wide range of topics in NLP evaluation and comparison, including new evaluation metrics for different NLG tasks (e.g., summarization, translation, data-to-text, text-to-SQL) and NLP models (e.g., embeddings, user feedback predictions, maths word problem solvers, coreference resolution); new benchmark datasets for tasks like authorship attribution, multilingual narratives, gender bias, NER, subword segmentation, and open question answering; and critical analyses over existing evaluation benchmarks (e.g., SemEval) and paradigms (e.g., system comparison methods and statistical tests).

Moreover, we organized a shared task on explainable quality estimation. Given a pair of a source sentence and a machine-translated sentence, participants were asked to estimate the sentence-level quality score of the translation and explain the score by providing a continuous word-level score for each input word or token indicating its importance for the prediction. There were seven teams participating in the shared task and six of them submitted papers describing their systems. We, the organizers, also wrote a paper summarizing the competition and the lessons learned. All are included in the proceedings.

We would like to thank all of the authors and the shared task participants for their contributions, the program committee for their thoughtful reviews (especially those who kindly help conduct emergency reviews), the steering committee for their advice and selection of best research papers, the keynote speakers for sharing their vision and outlook, the sponsors (The Artificial Intelligence Journal and Salesforce Research) for their generous support, and all the attendees for their participation. We believe that all of these will contribute to a lively and successful workshop. Looking forward to meeting you all (virtually) at Eval4NLP 2021!

Eval4NLP 2021 Organization Team,
Yang Gao, Steffen Eger, Wei Zhao, Piyawat Lertvittayakumjorn, Marina Fomicheva

Organizers:

Yang Gao, Royal Holloway, University of London, UK
Steffen Eger, Technische Universität Darmstadt, Germany
Wei Zhao, Technische Universität Darmstadt, Germany
Piyawat Lertvittayakumjorn, Imperial College London, UK
Marina Fomicheva, University of Sheffield, UK

Steering Committee:

Ani Nenkova, University of Pennsylvania, US
Caiming Xiong, Salesforce, US
Ehud Reiter, University of Aberdeen, UK
Dan Roth, University of Pennsylvania, US
Sebastian Ruder, Google DeepMind, UK

Program Committee:

Jonas Belouadi (Technische Universität Darmstadt)
Prachya Boonkwan (NECTEC)
Daniel Cer (Google Research; University of California at Berkeley)
Elizabeth Clark (University of Washington)
Zi-Yi Dou (UCLA)
Rotem Dror (University of Pennsylvania)
Steffen Eger (Technische Universität Darmstadt)
Marina Fomicheva (University of Sheffield)
George Foster (Google)
Johannes Fürnkranz (JKU Linz)
Yang Gao (Royal Holloway, University of London)
Yanjun Gao (University of Wisconsin Madison)
Kyle Gorman (The Graduate Center, City University of New York)
Francisco Guzmán (Facebook)
Kornraphop Kawintiranon (Georgetown University)
Natthawut Kertkeidkachorn (Japan Advanced Institute of Science and Technology)
Douwe Kiela (Facebook)
Christoph Leiter (Technische Universität Darmstadt)
Piyawat Lertvittayakumjorn (Imperial College London)
Lucy Lin (University of Washington)
Chin-Yew Lin (Microsoft Research)
Maxime Peyrard (EPFL)
Roi Reichart (Technion - Israel Institute of Technology)
Leonardo F. R. Ribeiro (Technische Universität Darmstadt)
Stefan Riezler (Heidelberg University)
Horacio Saggion (Universitat Pompeu Fabra)
Yanchen Wang (Georgetown University)
Shiyue Zhang (The University of North Carolina at Chapel Hill)
Wei Zhao (Technische Universität Darmstadt)

Invited Speaker:

Ani Nenkova, University of Pennsylvania, US
Chien-Sheng Wu, Salesforce Research, US
Dan Roth, University of Pennsylvania, US Ehud Reiter, University of Aberdeen, UK
Sebastian Ruder, Google DeepMind, UK

Table of Contents

Conference Program

9:00–9:10 *Opening Remarks*

9:15–9:55 *Keynote Talk 1*

10:00–10:40 **Paper Presentation Session 1**

[Findings] *How Suitable Are Subword Segmentation Strategies for Translating Non-Concatenative Morphology?*
Chantal Amrhein and Rico Sennrich

[Findings] *AStitchInLanguageModels: Dataset and Methods for the Exploration of Idiomaticity in Pre-Trained Language Models*
Harish Tayyar Madabushi, Edward Gow-Smith, Carolina Scarton and Aline Villavicencio

[Findings] *Entity-Based Semantic Adequacy for Data-to-Text Generation*
Juliette Faille, Albert Gatt and Claire Gardent

Differential Evaluation: a Qualitative Analysis of Natural Language Processing System Behavior Based Upon Data Resistance to Processing
Lucie Gianola, Hicham El Boukkouri, Cyril Grouin, Thomas Lavergne, Patrick Paroubek and Pierre Zweigenbaum

Validating Label Consistency in NER Data Annotation
Qingkai Zeng, Mengxia Yu, Wenhao Yu, Tianwen Jiang and Meng Jiang

10:45–11:25 *Keynote Talk 2*

11:30–12:10 **Paper Presentation Session 2**

How Emotionally Stable is ALBERT? Testing Robustness with Stochastic Weight Averaging on a Sentiment Analysis Task
Urja Khurana, Eric Nalisnick and Antske Fokkens

[Findings] *Challenges in Detoxifying Language Models*
Johannes Welbl, Amelia Glaese, Jonathan Uesato, Sumanth Dathathri, John Mellor, Lisa Anne Hendricks, Kirsty Anderson, Pushmeet Kohli, Ben Coppin and Po-Sen Huang

[Findings] *Adversarial Examples for Evaluating Math Word Problem Solvers*
Vivek Kumar, Rishabh Maheshwary and Vikram Pudi

November 10, 2021 (continued)

[Findings] *Making Heads and Tails of Models with Marginal Calibration for Sparse Tagsets*
Michael Kranzlein, Nelson F. Liu and Nathan Schneider

[Findings] *TURINGBENCH: A Benchmark Environment for Turing Test in the Age of Neural Text Generation*
Adaku Uchendu, Zeyu Ma, Thai Le, Rui Zhang and Dongwon Lee

StoryDB: Broad Multi-language Narrative Dataset
Alexey Tikhonov, Igor Samenko and Ivan Yamshchikov

12:15–12:55 ***Keynote Talk 3***

13:00–14:00 **Lunch Break**

14:00–14:40 ***Keynote Talk 4***

14:45–15:25 **Paper Presentation Session 3**

SeqScore: Addressing Barriers to Reproducible Named Entity Recognition Evaluation
Chester Palen-Michel, Nolan Holley and Constantine Lignos

Trainable Ranking Models to Evaluate the Semantic Accuracy of Data-to-Text Neural Generator
Nicolas Garneau and Luc Lamontagne

[Findings] *TSDAE: Using Transformer-based Sequential Denoising Auto-Encoder for Unsupervised Sentence Embedding Learning*
Kexin Wang, Nils Reimers and Iryna Gurevych

Evaluation of Unsupervised Automatic Readability Assessors Using Rank Correlations
Yo Ehara

Testing Cross-Database Semantic Parsers With Canonical Utterances
Heather Lent, Semih Yavuz, Tao Yu, Tong Niu, Yingbo Zhou, Dragomir Radev and Xi Victoria Lin

Writing Style Author Embedding Evaluation
Enzo Terreau, Antoine Gourru and Julien Velcin

15:30–16:10 *Keynote Talk 5*

16:15–16:55 **Paper Presentation Session 4**

ESTIME: Estimation of Summary-to-Text Inconsistency by Mismatched Embeddings
Oleg Vasilyev and John Bohannon

[Findings] *Towards Realistic Single-Task Continuous Learning Research for NER*
Justin Payan, Yuval Merhav, He Xie, Satyapriya Krishna, Anil Ramakrishna, Mukund Sridhar and Rahul Gupta

Statistically Significant Detection of Semantic Shifts using Contextual Word Embeddings
Yang Liu, Alan Medlar and Dorota Glowacka

[Findings] *Benchmarking Meta-embeddings: What Works and What Does Not*
Iker García, Rodrigo Agerri and German Rigau

Referenceless Parsing-Based Evaluation of AMR-to-English Generation
Emma Manning and Nathan Schneider

MIPE: A Metric Independent Pipeline for Effective Code-Mixed NLG Evaluation
Ayush Garg, Sammed Kagi, Vivek Srivastava and Mayank Singh

17:00–17:45 **Shared Task Presentation & Award Announcement**

IST-Unbabel 2021 Submission for the Explainable Quality Estimation Shared Task
Marcos Treviso, Nuno M. Guerreiro, Ricardo Rei and André F. T. Martins

Error Identification for Machine Translation with Metric Embedding and Attention
Raphael Rubino, Atsushi Fujita and Benjamin Marie

Reference-Free Word- and Sentence-Level Translation Evaluation with Token-Matching Metrics
Christoph Wolfgang Leiter

The Eval4NLP Shared Task on Explainable Quality Estimation: Overview and Results
Marina Fomicheva, Piyawat Lertvittayakumjorn, Wei Zhao, Steffen Eger and Yang Gao

Award Announcement
Eval4NLP 2021 Organizers

November 10, 2021 (continued)

17:50–18:00 Concluding Remarks

Recordings/Posters

Developing a Benchmark for Reducing Data Bias in Authorship Attribution
Benjamin Murauer and Günther Specht

Error-Sensitive Evaluation for Ordinal Target Variables
David Chen, Maury Courtland, Adam Faulkner and Aysu Ezen-Can

HinGE: A Dataset for Generation and Evaluation of Code-Mixed Hinglish Text
Vivek Srivastava and Mayank Singh

What is SemEval evaluating? A Systematic Analysis of Evaluation Campaigns in NLP
Oskar Wysocki, Malina Florea, Dónal Landers and André Freitas

The UMD Submission to the Explainable MT Quality Estimation Shared Task: Combining Explanation Models with Sequence Labeling
Tasnim Kabir and Marine Carpuat

Explaining Errors in Machine Translation with Absolute Gradient Ensembles
Melda Eksi, Erik Gelbing, Jonathan Stieber and Chi Viet Vu

Explainable Quality Estimation: CUNI Eval4NLP Submission
Peter Polák, Muskaan Singh and Ondřej Bojar

[Non-archival] *How Robust are Model Rankings: A Leaderboard Customization Approach for Equitable Evaluation*
Swaroop Mishra and Anjana Arunkumar

[Non-archival] *AI as Author – Bridging the Gap Between Machine Learning and Literary Theory*
Imke van Heerden and Anil Bas

[Non-archival] *The statistical advantage of automatic NLG metrics at the system level*
Johnny Tian-Zheng Wei and Robin Jia

[Findings] *A Comprehensive Comparison of Word Embeddings in Event & Entity Coreference Resolution*
Judicael POUMAY and Ashwin Ittoo

[Findings] *Expected Validation Performance and Estimation of a Random Variable's Maximum*
Jesse Dodge, Suchin Gururangan, Dallas Card, Roy Schwartz and Noah A. Smith

[Findings] *GooAQ: Open Question Answering with Diverse Answer Types*
Daniel Khashabi, Amos Ng, Tushar Khot, Ashish Sabharwal, Hannaneh Hajishirzi and Chris Callison-Burch

[Findings] *Sometimes We Want Ungrammatical Translations*
Prasanna Parthasarathi, Koustuv Sinha, Joelle Pineau and Adina Williams

Differential Evaluation: a Qualitative Analysis of Natural Language Processing System Behavior Based Upon Data Resistance to Processing

Lucie Gianola, Hicham El Boukkouri, Cyril Grouin,
Thomas Lavergne, Patrick Paroubek, Pierre Zweigenbaum
Université Paris-Saclay, CNRS, LISN, 91405, Orsay, France
`firstname.lastname@lisn.fr`

Abstract

Most of the time, when dealing with a particular Natural Language Processing task, systems are compared on the basis of global statistics such as recall, precision, F1-score, etc. While such scores provide a general idea of the behavior of these systems, they ignore a key piece of information that can be useful for assessing progress and discerning remaining challenges: the relative difficulty of test instances. To address this shortcoming, we introduce the notion of *differential evaluation* which effectively defines a pragmatic partition of instances into gradually more difficult bins by leveraging the predictions made by a set of systems. Comparing systems along these difficulty bins enables us to produce a finer-grained analysis of their relative merits, which we illustrate on two use-cases: a comparison of systems participating in a multi-label text classification task (CLEF eHealth 2018 ICD-10 coding), and a comparison of neural models trained for biomedical entity detection (BioCreative V chemical-disease relations dataset).

1 Introduction

The analysis of NLP system results has mainly focused on evaluation scores meant to rank systems and feed leaderboards. In tasks such as information extraction, text classification, etc., evaluation generally relies on the comparison of a hypothesis (typically a system output) with a gold standard, generally produced through manual annotation. Since the MUC-6 conference (Grishman and Sundheim, 1996), the metrics used were created for information retrieval (Cleverdon, 1960): recall (true positive rate), precision (positive predictive value) and their harmonic (possibly weighted) mean, the F1-score. Evaluation scripts are widely available nowadays, for instance those of the CoNLL shared tasks (Tjong Kim Sang and De Meulder, 2003). These scripts rely on an annotation scheme based on the BIO prefix used to specify whether a token is at the beginning, inside or outside of an annotation span, making it a *de facto* standard for NER evaluation (Nadeau and Sekine, 2007). Many other NLP tasks have developed or used their own metrics, such as accuracy for classification, BLEU (Papineni et al., 2002) for machine translation, ROUGE for machine translation and text summarization (Lin, 2004), word error rate for automatic speech recognition, etc. While evaluation is the key step in shared tasks, developers also need to evaluate the performance of their systems for feature selection or architecture design choices, especially when several systems are combined (Jiang et al., 2016).

However, scores only are insufficient to capture the behavior of systems and to provide a finer-grained analysis of their pros and cons. Indeed, though widely used, scores are not free of imperfections, as demonstrated by Peyrard et al. (2021) who discuss the use of the average to aggregate evaluation scores. They show that very different system behaviors can yield similar scores when using the average and suggest an alternative aggregation mechanism. Some researchers also call for going beyond performance scores: Ethayarajh and Jurafsky (2020) suggest that performance-based evaluation (as promoted by leaderboards) overlooks aspects such as utility, prediction cost, and robustness of models. They recommend considering the point of view of the user of models rather than just performance scores to estimate their relevance.

Trying to provide a finer understanding of the issues raised by the input text and of the limitations of the evaluated systems, we propose a new qualitative analysis method that takes into account the observed relative difficulty of predicting gold labels for each input. This difficulty is assessed pragmatically based upon the number of systems that predict a gold label (a true positive) for a given input. As a qualitative method, its aim is not to compute an evaluation measure nor to rank systems, but

Proceedings of the 58th Annual Meeting of the Association for Computational Linguistics, pages 1–10

https://doi.org/10.26615/978-954-452-056-4_001

Input/Systems	A	B	C	D	E	F
[...]						
762_levodopa	1	1	1	1	1	1
1004_cyclophosphamide	1	1	1	1	1	1
1032_cyclophosphamide	1	1	1	1	1	1
1034_cyp	1	1	1	1	0	0
1105_cyp	1	0	1	1	0	0
1128_cyp	1	0	0	1	0	1
[...]						

Figure 1: Example input file for a set of six systems. 1 means the system yielded a true positive for the instance, and 0 means it did not (the instance was 'missed').

Input/Systems	A	B	C	D	E	F
Instance 1		x	x	x	x	x
Instance 2	x		x	x	x	x
Instance 3	x		x	x	x	x
Instance 4	x	x		x	x	x
Instance 5	x		x	x	x	x
Instance 6	x	x		x	x	x
Instance 7	x	x		x	x	x
Instance 8	x		x	x	x	x
Instance 9	x	x	x	x	x	
Instance 10	x		x	x	x	x
Instance 11	x	x	x		x	x
Instance 12	x		x	x	x	x
Instance 13	x	x		x	x	x
Instance 14	x	x	x		x	x
Total	**13** (93%)	**8** (57%)	**10** (71%)	**12** (86%)	**14** (100%)	**13** (93%)

Figure 2: Composition of bin-5 in the comparison of six systems. Each instance (row) is missed by exactly one system. Note that each system (column) may miss multiple instances in this bin.

instead to obtain an overview of *how* different systems achieve the task, and thus understand where their strengths and weaknesses are.

After explaining how the method works globally (Section 2), we illustrate it with data from two shared tasks from the biomedical domain, one for multi-label classification and another for named entity recognition (Section 3), then discuss a few points and directions for future investigation (Section 4).

2 Differential evaluation: highlighting the 'difficulty' of examples

Our qualitative analysis method, which we call *differential evaluation*[1], globally considers the various sets of correct instances ('true positives', or 'gold instances') that were discovered by a set of systems. Since the aim of the method is not to produce a ranking, the considered systems can be different systems performing the same task, as in a shared task for example, or different versions of the same system also performing a given task, as in a development context.

As input, the algorithm takes a matrix of instances and systems, as shown in Figure 1. For each instance, it then computes how many systems discovered it correctly (i.e., in Figure 1, '762_levodopa' has been discovered by 6 systems, '1034_cyp' has been discovered by 4 systems, etc.) This enables it to compute then how many instances have been detected by all systems, by all systems but one, by all systems but two, etc., and by no system at all. This yields a grouping of instances into *bins* depending on the number of systems that discovered them. There are as many bins as there are systems plus one for the set of instances that were discovered by none of the systems. Bin-1 is the set of instances detected by exactly one system, bin-2 the set of instances detected by exactly two systems, etc.; and bin-0, the set of instances that no system was able to detect (see Section 3 for illustrated examples). Figure 2 shows the composition of bin-5 in a case where six systems are compared, and displays the percentage coverage of the bin for each system. Figure 3 shows a schema of the global scenario of the method.

Instances in bin-N (where N is the number of considered systems), which holds the set of entities discovered by all systems, can be considered as the *easiest* to predict, while instances in bin-0, which holds the set of entities that no system was able to detect, can be seen as the *most difficult*. More-

[1]https://github.com/PierreZweigenbaum/differential-evaluation

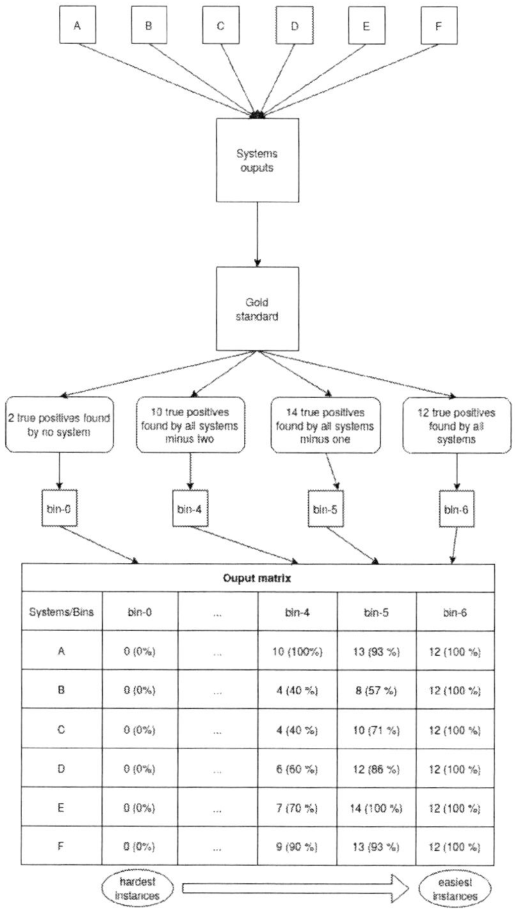

Figure 3: Differential evaluation scenario.
True positives (TPs) are displayed with absolute and relative values (percentage of the number of instances in the bin) in the output matrix, as in Table 1 and Figure 4 respectively. System contributions to a bin can have a null intersection: i.e. here, in bin-4, Systems B and C may be yielding TPs for totally different sets of instances. Bins 1, 2 and 3 omitted for conciseness.

over, bin-1, which holds instances discovered by a single system, can be seen as the bin holding the singular contribution of each system. As such, bin-1 is particularly interesting when considering system combination architectures or ROVER-like performance measures (Fiscus, 1997).

Figure 4 presents one of the outputs of the method, a heatmap of percentages of system TPs relative to the total number of instances in each bin, in this case for the CLEF eHealth 2018 ICD-10 coding task for Italian (we analyse this example in detail in Section 3.1.1). The first column on the left is bin-0, holding only 0 values as we have said that bin-0 is the bin of instances missed by all

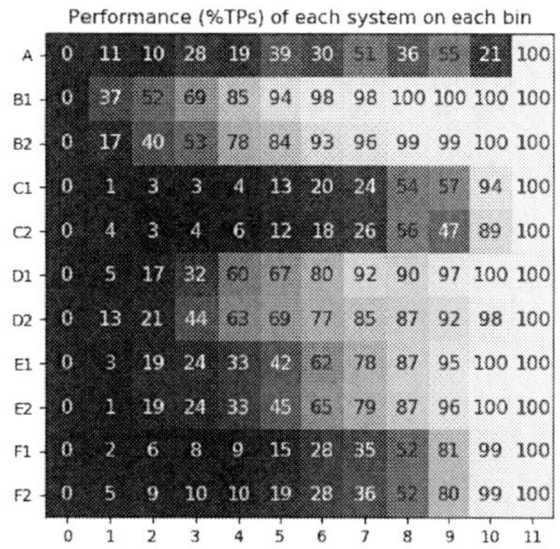

Figure 4: Percentage of labels (true positives) correctly found by each system in each bin for Italian in the CLEF eHealth 2018 ICD-10 coding task. Systems on x-axis and bins on y-axis.

systems (as shown by Table 1, here 305 instances were missed by all systems). The second column from the left holds bin-1, and so on. Another output of the method is the table of absolute values corresponding to the percentages heatmap, such as Table 1. It would then be interesting to investigate whether a pattern emerges concerning the linguistic nature of instances, which would help to chart the difficulty of the task, and complete the qualitative aspect of the analysis.

3 Experiments

In this section, we present insights that can be drawn from the use of differential evaluation on data related to two shared tasks addressing respectively multi-label text classification and named entity recognition, both in the biomedical domain. Note that our algorithm processes the systems in the order in which they are presented and that it is not intended to create a new ranking of the systems, but rather to provide more fine-grained information to analyze how a given system has performed or achieved its ranking.

3.1 CLEF eHealth 2018 ICD-10 coding

We show as an example the output obtained in the comparison of systems in a multi-label text classification task in Italian and Hungarian (Névéol et al., 2018). In the gold standard, each input text is associated to one or more true labels, i.e., codes in the International Classification of Diseases (ICD-10). A true positive system prediction is an association between a given input text and one of the true labels for this text in the gold standard. In this dataset,

Systems	bin-0	bin-1	bin-2	bin-3	bin-4	bin-5	bin-6	bin-7	bin-8	bin-9	bin-10	bin-11	Total TPs per system
A	0	21	33	93	104	271	311	652	*645*	765	*829*	3800	*7524*
B1	0	**69**	**163**	**224**	**472**	**648**	**1005**	**1245**	**1774**	**1390**	**3890**	3800	**14680**
B2	0	31	126	172	434	575	959	1211	1760	1373	3886	3800	14327
C1	0	*2*	*8*	*11*	*24*	89	208	*306*	958	813	3658	3800	9877
C2	0	7	11	14	31	*83*	*189*	327	1005	*660*	3445	3800	9572
D1	0	9	55	105	331	463	823	1168	1608	1344	3884	3800	13590
D2	0	24	67	143	351	474	795	1073	1543	1284	3827	3800	13381
E1	0	6	60	77	183	289	639	982	1549	1327	3886	3800	12798
E2	0	2	60	78	184	312	665	1003	1557	1337	3886	3800	12884
F1	0	4	20	27	49	105	291	444	919	1125	3854	3800	10638
F2	0	10	29	34	57	131	289	458	930	1110	3855	3800	10703
Total per bin	305	185	316	326	555	688	1029	1267	1781	1392	3890	3800	15534

Table 1: Number of labels (true positives) correctly found by each system in each bin for Italian: absolute values. Bin n contains the labels found by exactly n systems. Best performance in green, worst performance in red.

the evaluation method therefore compares label attribution rather than entities.

3.1.1 Italian

Eleven systems were examined for Italian, and 15,534 labels were to be discovered. Some of the teams that participated in the shared task submitted two runs for variants of their base system, hence names such as B1 and B2 when two systems are submitted by the same team in Figure 4 and other tables or figures. As shown in Table 1, bin-0 holds 305 labels found by none of the systems. Bin-1 holds 185 labels found by exactly one system, among which System A discovered 21 labels, System B1 discovered 69 labels, and so on. Bin-11 holds 3,800 labels found by all eleven systems. Figure 4 and Table 1 show bin repartition with percentages and absolute values. In Table 1, column "Total TPs per system" presents the total number of labels found per system, and row "Total per bin" contains the total number of labels to be found. We use color codes to highlight the best/worst system for each bin.

Performances are pretty steady, with System B1 outperforming all the others in every bin. The worst results are shared by Systems C1 and C2, and System A that performs badly for bins-8 and 10, which are among the "easiest" bins. As seen in Table 1, although System E2 scores the worst for bin-1 with only two labels discovered, it manages to keep up with the performances of the other systems in the other bins, and its global performance (12,884 total TPs discovered) is pretty average. On the other hand, Systems C1 and C2, which are the worst systems across all bins, are not so bad globally with 9,877 and 9,572 total TPs. In fact, System A achieves a very low performance on two of the

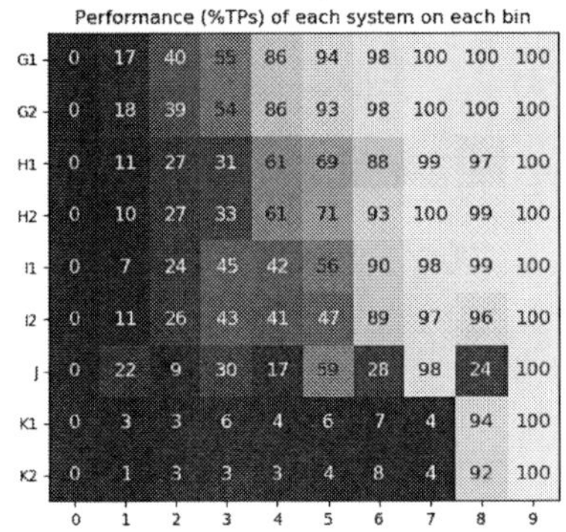

Figure 5: Percentage of labels (true positives) correctly found by each system in each bin for Hungarian. Systems on x-axis and bins on y-axis.

"easiest" bins, and thus yields less than half of the total labels, despite a not so bad performance on bin-1. Figure 4 shows that systems can be divided into groups of better and worse performances (B1, B2, D1, D2, E1, E2 vs. A, C1, C2, F1, F2). We can also see that System B1 reaches a perfect score over all easier bins up to bin-8, which hints at its being robust on easy instances.

3.1.2 Hungarian

Figure 5 and Table 2 show the proportion and number of detected labels per system within each bin for the Hungarian language[2].

As highlighted by colors in Table 2, we can see that globally, Systems G1 and G2 perform the best, and Systems K1 and K2 perform the worst.

Just above K1 and K2 in terms of Total TPs per system (Table 2), System J is the worst at detecting labels from bin-8 (see also Figure 5), which can

[2]The data are not the same as that for Italian, hence the different total values.

Systems	bin-0	bin-1	bin-2	bin-3	bin-4	bin-5	bin-6	bin-7	bin-8	bin-9	Total TPs per system
G1	0	104	**555**	**655**	**2855**	**4760**	**11246**	37654	**9034**	26324	**93187**
G2	0	116	542	642	2828	4700	11239	**37659**	9028	26324	93078
H1	0	72	381	375	2001	3471	10080	37367	8749	26324	88820
H2	0	62	380	394	2019	3606	10620	37525	8985	26324	89915
I1	0	45	333	538	1375	2877	10293	36748	8980	26324	87513
I2	0	67	366	519	1356	2400	10208	36575	8695	26324	86510
J	0	**136**	126	364	557	2986	3331	37024	*2134*	26324	72982
K1	0	19	46	73	140	285	*832*	1693	8460	26324	37872
K2	0	*7*	*45*	*40*	*89*	*215*	947	*1508*	8303	26324	*37478*
Total per bin	1442	628	1387	1200	3305	5060	11466	37679	9046	26324	97537

Table 2: Number of labels (true positives) correctly found by each system in each bin for Hungarian: absolute values. Bin n contains the labels found by exactly n systems. In this analysis, the systems are ordered in decreasing order of F1-score, determined prior to the present analysis.

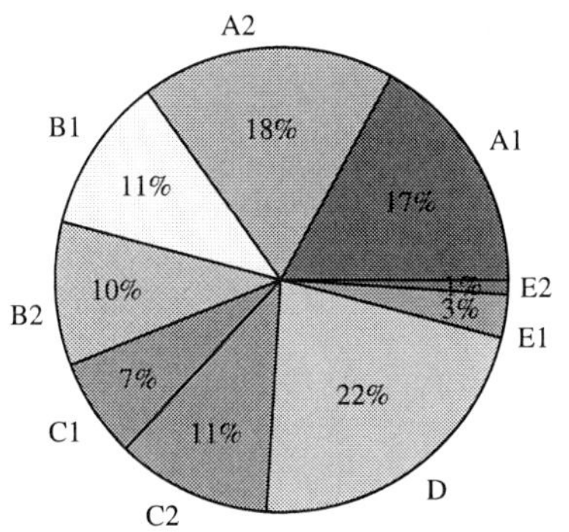

Figure 6: Proportion of labels discovered by exactly one system, per system for Hungarian.

be considered "easy" labels, with a very low proportion of 24% when all other systems are above 90%. In contrast however, it detects the largest number of labels in bin-1 (see also Figure 6). This is the only case where System G1 is significantly outperformed. System J is therefore good at detecting some "difficult" labels. This is a strong indicator that this system is likely to use a method that is quite different from the other systems and might bring complementary expertise on some inputs, which deserves further investigation.

Another perspective comes from looking at the overall performance for labels from bin-1, which, contrary to the example of Italian where most of bin-1 is yielded by four systems among eleven, is distributed in a more balanced way among systems. This means that labels from bin-1 are not yielded by one unique system that would be outperforming all the others, but that every system makes an important contribution to this bin (Figure 6).

3.2 BioCreative V CDR entities

The BioCreative V chemical-disease relation (CDR) task is originally a relation extraction task (Wei et al., 2016). Its data can also be used to train and evaluate entity-detection systems for chemical and disease entities, which is what we examine here. The dataset is made of 1,500 PubMed abstracts of scientific papers, divided equally into training, development and test. In the gold standard, each input token is associated to one true label and named entities are encoded according to the BIO (begin, inside, outside) scheme. In the present work we deal with tokens rather than entities, so that we can apply the presented method directly. We consider that 'O' labels are negatives and that all other labels are positives. A true positive system prediction is an association between an input token and a non-'O' label that is the gold-standard label for this token.

We are comparing entity detection systems that rely on word embeddings based upon CharacterBert (El Boukkouri et al., 2020) or fastText (Bojanowski et al., 2017), pre-trained on different corpora, either *as-is* or concatenated with knowledge embeddings learned using node2vec (Grover and Leskovec, 2016) on two biomedical vocabularies (the Medical Suject Headings (MeSH), and SNOMED CT). Moreover, we also consider a variant of CharacterBert where the node2vec embeddings are injected within the model architecture. The fastText embeddings are either randomly initialized, which we note "fastTextRandom"; pre-trained on a newswire corpus (Gigaword (Graff et al., 2007)), which we note "fastTextGigaword"; or on medical corpora (PubMed Central[3] and MIMIC-III (Johnson et al., 2016)), which

[3]https://www.ncbi.nlm.nih.gov/pmc/tools/openftlist/

Model	bin-0	bin-1	bin-2	bin-3	bin-4	bin-5	bin-6	bin-7	bin-8	bin-9	bin-10	bin-11	bin-12	Tot. TPs /system
Enh.CharBertFromGenN2V	0	**12**	65	72	**155**	**148**	156	**176**	223	**294**	465	852	3894	6512
CharBertFromGen	0	9	**70**	**75**	147	147	**158**	174	**228**	287	**477**	868	3894	**6534**
CharBertGenN2V	0	1	10	41	107	112	139	168	199	282	466	868	3894	6287
CharBertGen	0	3	7	41	103	113	131	163	205	285	463	853	3894	6261
fastTextGigawordN2V	0	6	7	7	28	61	77	110	164	244	446	**869**	3894	5913
fastTextGigaword	0	*0*	*3*	*7*	*19*	60	78	111	*106*	196	*343*	*812*	3894	*5629*
fastTextMimicN2V	0	*0*	9	14	29	*43*	59	91	165	235	450	862	3894	5851
fastTextMimic	0	2	10	9	20	53	*56*	*88*	128	*190*	413	830	3894	5693
fastTextPubMedN2V	0	4	12	21	47	51	87	113	190	254	453	830	3894	5956
fastTextPubMed	0	3	10	29	39	83	101	116	182	247	449	862	3894	6015
fastTextRandomN2V	0	0	5	11	28	39	39	77	106	161	322	792	3894	5474
fastTextRandom	0	1	2	9	18	30	41	62	56	106	143	338	3894	4700
Total TPs per bin	178	41	105	112	185	188	187	207	244	309	489	876	3894	7015

Table 3: Absolute values for chemical NER. Best performance in green, worst performance in red, orange when the random initialization is above one of the other initializations.

Models	bin-0	bin-1	bin-2	bin-3	bin-4	bin-5	bin-6	bin-7	bin-8	bin-9	bin-10	bin-11	bin-12	Tot. TPs /system
Enh.CharBertFromGenN2V	0	16	70	74	124	115	159	**181**	**256**	**296**	389	800	3617	6097
CharBertFromGen	0	**44**	**89**	**92**	**142**	**123**	**164**	179	247	289	389	791	3617	**6166**
CharBertGenN2V	0	14	29	66	106	110	137	166	238	278	378	795	3617	5934
CharBertGen	0	24	32	57	110	107	137	162	234	287	387	802	3617	5956
fastTextGigawordN2V	0	*3*	22	36	59	70	112	141	224	288	403	803	3617	5778
fastTextGigawordN2V	0	5	*7*	*17*	*25*	*50*	*72*	*91*	*126*	205	*311*	*730*	3617	*5256*
fastTextMimicN2V	0	6	12	25	39	54	103	144	207	257	359	791	3617	5614
fastTextMimic	0	13	12	29	33	51	85	94	145	*200*	325	746	3617	5350
fastTextPubMedN2V	0	6	15	32	64	65	141	162	236	292	**408**	**814**	3617	5852
fastTextPubMed	0	5	12	29	50	53	103	118	182	204	332	764	3617	5469
fastTextRandomN2V	0	10	27	41	52	52	85	112	177	223	314	717	3617	5427
fastTextRandom	0	10	9	24	28	40	58	60	96	124	195	489	3617	4750
Total TPs per bin	340	156	168	174	208	178	226	230	296	327	419	822	3617	7161

Table 4: Absolute values for disease NER. Best performance in green, worst performance in red, orange when the random initialization is above one of the other initializations.

we respectively note “fastTextPubMed” and “fastTextMimic”. The CharacterBert models are either pre-trained on general corpora (English Wikipedia and OpenWebText (Gokaslan and Cohen, 2019)), which we note “CharBertGen”; or pre-trained on general corpora then re-trained on PubMed and MIMIC-III, which we note “CharBertFromGen”. In all cases the suffix “N2V” refers to a concatenation with the node2vec knowledge representations, with the exception of “Enh.CharBertFromGenN2V” which refers to the variant of CharacterBERT where the node2vec vectors are injected directly within the architecture. This last model is pre-trained on the general corpus then re-trained on PubMed and MIMIC-III in order to be compared with “CharBertFromGen”.

Tables 3 and 4 respectively show absolute values for chemical and disease entity recognition, and Figures 7 and 8 the corresponding bin percentages.

3.2.1 Global performances and pairwise comparison of models

Overall, we can see that the contextual CharacterBert embeddings perform better than the static fastText vectors in both chemical and disease recognition, with the worst performances for randomly initialized fastText embeddings. Moreover, we see that the CharacterBert models trained on medical data perform better than their general versions (Tables 3 and 4, Figures 7 and 8), which confirms the interest of retraining the general models on in-domain data.

Chemical CharacterBert seems to perform rather similarly regardless of the combination with node2vec embeddings. For fastText models, pairwise comparison in Table 5 shows that the introduction of knowledge embeddings (node2vec) improves recall. Comparison of bins further confirms this observation: we can see that the im-

	bin-1	bin-2	bin-3	bin-4	bin-5	bin-6	bin-7	bin-8	bin-9	bin-10	bin-11	Recall
EnhancedCharBertFromGenN2V	**29**	62	64	**84**	**79**	83	**85**	91	**95**	95	97	92,83
CharBertFromGen	22	**67**	**67**	79	78	**84**	84	**93**	93	**98**	**99**	**93,14**
CharBertGenN2V	2	**10**	37	**58**	60	**74**	**81**	82	91	95	**99**	**89,62**
CharBertGen	**7**	7	37	56	60	70	79	**84**	**92**	95	97	89,25
fastTextGigawordN2V	**15**	**7**	6	**15**	32	41	53	**67**	**79**	**91**	**99**	**84,29**
fastTextGigaword	0	3	6	10	32	**42**	**54**	43	63	70	93	80,24
fastTextMimicN2V	0	9	**12**	**16**	23	**32**	**44**	**68**	**76**	**92**	**98**	**83,41**
fastTextMimic	**5**	**10**	8	11	**28**	30	43	52	61	84	95	81,15
fastTextPubMedN2V	**10**	**11**	19	**25**	27	47	55	**78**	**82**	**93**	95	84,90
fastTextPubMed	7	10	**26**	21	**44**	**54**	**56**	75	80	92	**98**	**85,74**
fastTextRandomN2V	0	**5**	**10**	**15**	**21**	21	**37**	**43**	**52**	**66**	**90**	**78,03**
fastTextRandom	**2**	2	8	10	16	**22**	30	23	34	29	39	67,0

Table 5: Pairwise comparison of systems with or without addition of Node2Vec embeddings for chemical NER (bin-0 and bin-12 are not considered). The best model for each bin is highlighted in green.

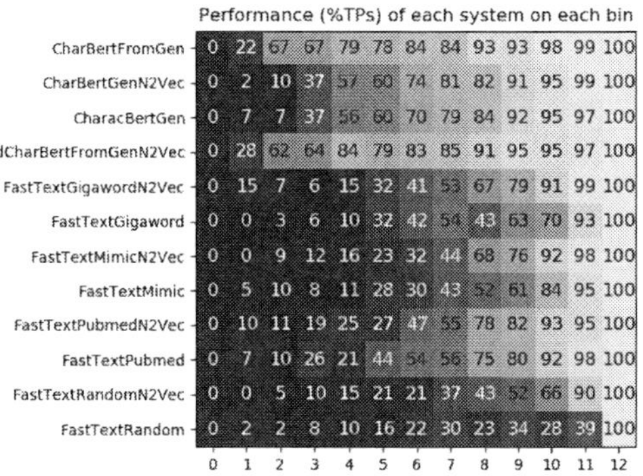

Figure 7: Percentage of labels (true positives) correctly found by each system in each bin for chemical substances.

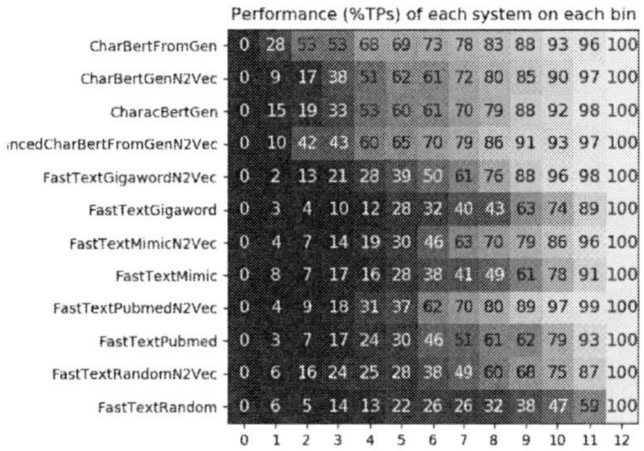

Figure 8: Percentage of labels (true positives) correctly found by each system in each bin for diseases.

provement is made on "easy" entities (bins 8 through 11). However, for "fastTextPubMed" the effect of node2vec is not so clear or even harmful (bins 5 and 6). This phenomenon could be explained by the fact that both PubMed and the BioCreative CDR task are from the biomedical domain while MIMIC-III and Gigaword are from somewhat different domains (clinical and newswire domains respectively). In the case of fastTextPubMed, adding medical knowledge embeddings seems to degrade performance.

Disease While node2vec has a strong positive effect on fastText models regardless of their source corpus, pairwise comparison of recall for disease NER in Table 6 shows that the addition of node2vec is detrimental to CharacterBert models. However, this analysis can be refined by comparing bin-wise performances: for CharacterBert models trained on medical data (top two lines), the versions that do not use node2vec embeddings are better on "more difficult" bins, while the enhanced version are actually better on "easier" bins.

3.2.2 Bin inspection

Browsing through the bins can give an idea of the kinds of entities they hold. This can be done in different ways.

Bin-0 exploration We inspect here the contents of bin-0 for both the chemical and disease recognition tasks, as this bin is supposed to hold false negatives that resist all systems, i.e. the most difficult entities.

Bin-0 for both chemical and disease contains occurrences of abbreviations, which occur quite frequently within parentheses in the context of their full form: for example "bs" for "bile salt" and "rd" (*sic*) for "lenalidomide and dexamethasone" for chemical, "mi" for "myocardial infarction" and "mb" for "microbleeds" for disease. We also spot

	bin-1	bin-2	bin-3	bin-4	bin-5	bin-6	bin-7	bin-8	bin-9	bin-10	bin-11	Recall
EnhancedCharBertFromGenN2V	10	42	43	60	65	70	**79**	**86**	**91**	93	**97**	85,14
CharBertFromGen	**28**	**53**	**53**	**68**	**69**	**73**	78	83	88	93	96	**86,11**
CharBertGenN2V	9	17	**38**	51	**62**	61	**72**	**80**	85	90	97	82,87
CharBertGen	**15**	**19**	33	**53**	60	61	70	79	**88**	**92**	**98**	**83,17**
fastTextGigawordN2V	2	**13**	**21**	**28**	**39**	**50**	**61**	**76**	**88**	**96**	**98**	**80,69**
fastTextGigaword	**3**	4	10	12	28	32	40	43	63	74	89	73,40
fastTextMimicN2V	4	7	14	**19**	**30**	**46**	**63**	**70**	**79**	**86**	**96**	**78,40**
fastTextMimic	**8**	7	**17**	16	29	38	41	49	61	78	91	74,71
fastTextPubMedN2V	**4**	**9**	**18**	**31**	**37**	**62**	**70**	**80**	**89**	**97**	**99**	**81,72**
fastTextPubMed	3	7	17	24	30	46	51	61	62	79	93	76,37
fastTextRandomN2V	6	**16**	**24**	**25**	**29**	**38**	**49**	**60**	**68**	**75**	**87**	**75,79**
fastTextRandom	6	5	14	13	22	26	26	32	38	47	59	66,33

Table 6: Pairwise comparison of systems with or without addition of Node2Vec embeddings for disease NER (bin-0 and bin-12 are not considered). The best model for each bin is highlighted in green.

expressions that should perhaps not be in the gold standard, such as "abuse of cocaine and ethanol" tagged as a disease, or typographic errors such as "antithyroidmedications".

Both bins also hold an important number of single-character tokens such as punctuation marks and digits. For disease recognition, these include the determiner "a", which occurs most of the time as a part of a multi-word entity. A similar phenomenon occurs with other tokens such as "of". Occurrences of these words seem to be due to multi-word entities referring to diseases and conditions such as "enlargement of pulse pressure", "occlusion of renal vessels", "thrombosis of a normal renal artery". It seems that multi-word entities account for a significant proportion of the generated errors, where systems only recover the first word of a multi-word entity. For example, chemical bin-0 holds all occurrences of "channel" and "blockers" from "calcium channel blockers", while occurrences of "calcium" in this context are always labelled correctly.

However, a quick inspection of other bins reveals that those part-of-speech and morphological characteristics (punctuation, single-character entities and abbreviations) are not specific to bin-0. For instance, punctuation marks make for 14% of chemical bin-0 tokens, and for 9 to 28% of bins 1 to 11 (0.07% for bin-12). In the case of disease recognition, punctuation represents 8.8% of bin-0, while ranging from 1.7% to 5.1% of bins 1 to 12 (this difference in proportions between chemical and disease can be explained by the nature of the entities, chemical entities often involving dots or hyphens). Further exploration of the distribution of part-of-speech and morphological categories may lead to some understanding of the bins' contents.

We also found two other phenomena both in chemical bin-0 and in disease bin-0: hapax legomena ('hapaxes') and ambiguous tokens.

Hapaxes are tokens that occur only once in the whole data. In bin-0 of the chemical NER task, examples include "adrenergic", "colony", "steroidal" or "agents". In disease bin-0, examples include "bacillary", "audiogenic", "choreic", "teratogenic".

Ambiguous tokens in bin-0 are due to their multiple or specific meanings in the corpus. This is the case for token "chinese" (note that the corpus is lower-cased), which occurs in "chinese herbal slimming pill", "chinese herbal", "chinese herbs", and is systematically missed in the chemical recognition tasks. We assume that this is probably because it is confused with "chinese" used as the nationality of patients. The same applies to hapax "philadelphia" from "philadelphia chromosome". These examples lead us to assume that specialized usage of "common" vocabulary terms in chemical or disease entities induces a difficulty for systems.

Distribution across bins Finally, another way to perform bin inspection is to look at the distribution of mentions of a same word across bins. As an illustration, we use the distribution of "calcium" in chemical bins (Table 7): one mention is in bin-1, no mention is in bin-2 and 3, one mention is in bin-4, etc. While most mentions of "calcium" are retrieved by all eleven systems (29 mentions precisely), a total of six of those mentions are individually discovered respectively by exactly one, four, five, nine, nine, and ten systems. This feedback is potentially very useful, since we can then rank every mention in ascending order of difficulty, and proceed to look for explanations for why those six mentions resist detection by a number of systems.

	bin-0	bin-1	bin-2	bin-3	bin-4	bin-5	bin-6	bin-7	bin-8	bin-9	bin-10	bin-11	bin-12
calcium	0	1	0	0	1	1	0	0	0	2	1	0	29

Table 7: Distribution of "calcium" occurrences through bins.

4 Discussion and future work

As we have seen, differential evaluation is a qualitative analysis method that allows for more in-depth evaluation when comparing the behavior of several systems with each other. Rather than relying only on the classical global metrics, it provides an insight into how the performance of each system is actually distributed in automatically-determined subsets of examples relative to other systems, and how systems contribute in their very own way.

As presented in the heatmap we used, harder elements to process are in the first column while easier elements are in the last column. This sorting into several columns allows us to rapidly overview how systems perform on a given task. Based on the analysis we made on the content of bins from several tasks and distinct domains, we observed that the first bin is generally composed of elements such as abbreviations and ambiguous words used in several contexts (some of these contexts are a part of an annotation while other contexts are not); moreover, these elements are often short (two or three characters long), which makes them difficult to process for statistical approaches. In the case of multi-label text classification for Hungarian (Section 3.1.2), differential analysis provided an insight that would have been overlooked by global scores.

Future directions include the following points. First, as we have seen in Section 3.2.2, in the case of named entity recognition, examples composed of several tokens are counted token per token and not as a whole entity. Including this dimension will give another insight into the behavior of models for named-entity recognition. A second direction is to extend the current approach, which focuses on recall, hence true positives against false negatives, to take into account other basic evaluation variables, namely false positives and true negatives. A third useful direction would be to retrieve information on the context of occurrence of examples and their global features: sentence length, direct context, average number of characters per token for each bin, etc. Finally, a fourth direction would be to automatically track the distribution of different mentions of a same word across bins, as we have done manually with "calcium" in the second paragraph of Section 3.2.2. Linked to the previous development regarding contextual information, this would allow us to understand precisely why one particular occurrence of a word is missed while the others are more easily spotted.

Acknowledgments

This work has been made possible by the resources of the MAPA project. The MAPA project is an INEA-funded Action for the European Commission under the Connecting Europe Facility (CEF) – Telecommunications Sector with Grant Agreement No INEA/CEF/ICT/A2019/1927065. https://mapa-project.eu/

References

Piotr Bojanowski, Edouard Grave, Armand Joulin, and Tomas Mikolov. 2017. Enriching word vectors with subword information. *Transactions of the Association for Computational Linguistics*, 5:135–146.

C.W. Cleverdon. 1960. The ASLIB Cranfield research project on the comparative efficiency of indexing systems. *ASLIB Proceedings*, 12:421–431. ISSN: 0001-253X.

Hicham El Boukkouri, Olivier Ferret, Thomas Lavergne, Hiroshi Noji, Pierre Zweigenbaum, and Jun'ichi Tsujii. 2020. CharacterBERT: Reconciling ELMo and BERT for word-level open-vocabulary representations from characters. In *Proceedings of the 28th International Conference on Computational Linguistics*, pages 6903–6915, Barcelona, Spain (Online). International Committee on Computational Linguistics.

Kawin Ethayarajh and Dan Jurafsky. 2020. Utility is in the eye of the user: A critique of NLP leaderboards. In *Proceedings of the 2020 Conference on Empirical Methods in Natural Language Processing (EMNLP)*, pages 4846–4853, Online. Association for Computational Linguistics.

Jonathan G Fiscus. 1997. A post-processing system to yield reduced word error rates: recognizer output voting error reduction (ROVER). In *Proceedings of the IEEE Workshop on Automatic Speech Recognition and Understanding*, pages 347–357, Santa Barbara, CA.

Aaron Gokaslan and Vanya Cohen. 2019. Openwebtext corpus. `http://Skylion007.github.io/OpenWebTextCorpus`.

David Graff, Junbo Kong, Ke Chen, and Kazuaki Maeda. 2007. *English Gigaword, LDC2007T07*. Linguistic Data Consortium, Philadelphia. Web Download.

Ralph Grishman and Beth Sundheim. 1996. Message Understanding Conference-6: A brief history. In *Proceedings of the 16th Conference on Computational Linguistics - Volume 1*, COLING '96, page 466–471, USA. Association for Computational Linguistics.

Aditya Grover and Jure Leskovec. 2016. Node2vec: Scalable feature learning for networks. In *Proceedings of the 22nd ACM SIGKDD International Conference on Knowledge Discovery and Data Mining*, KDD '16, page 855–864, New York, NY, USA. Association for Computing Machinery.

ICD-10. 2011. *ICD-10. International Statistical Classification of Diseases and Related Health Problems. 10th Revision. Volume 2. Instruction manual.* World Health Organization.

Ridong Jiang, Rafael E. Banchs, and Haizhou Li. 2016. Evaluating and combining name entity recognition systems. In *Proceedings of the Sixth Named Entity Workshop*, pages 21–27, Berlin, Germany. Association for Computational Linguistics.

Alistair E W Johnson, Tom J Pollard, Lu Shen, Li-Wei H Lehman, Mengling Feng, Mohammad Ghassemi, Benjamin Moody, Peter Szolovits, Leo Anthony Celi, and Roger G Mark. 2016. MIMIC-III, a freely accessible critical care database. *Sci Data*, 3:160035.

Chin-Yew Lin. 2004. ROUGE: A package for automatic evaluation of summaries. In *Text Summarization Branches Out*, pages 74–81, Barcelona, Spain. Association for Computational Linguistics.

David Nadeau and Satoshi Sekine. 2007. A survey of named entity recognition and classification. *Lingvisticae Investigationes*, 30:3–26.

Aurélie Névéol, Aude Robert, Francesco Grippo, Claire Morgand, Chiara Orsi, László Pelikán, Lionel Ramadier, Grégoire Rey, and Pierre Zweigenbaum. 2018. CLEF eHealth 2018 multilingual information extraction task overview: ICD10 coding of death certificates in French, Hungarian and Italian. In *CLEF 2017 Evaluation Labs and Workshop: Online Working Notes*.

Kishore Papineni, Salim Roukos, Todd Ward, and Wei-Jing Zhu. 2002. Bleu: a method for automatic evaluation of machine translation. In *Proceedings of the 40th Annual Meeting of the Association for Computational Linguistics*, pages 311–318, Philadelphia, Pennsylvania, USA. Association for Computational Linguistics.

Maxime Peyrard, Wei Zhao, Steffen Eger, and Robert West. 2021. Better than average: Paired evaluation of NLP systems. In *Proceedings of the 59th Annual Meeting of the Association for Computational Linguistics and the 11th International Joint Conference on Natural Language Processing (Volume 1: Long Papers)*, pages 2301–2315, Online. Association for Computational Linguistics.

Erik F. Tjong Kim Sang and Fien De Meulder. 2003. Introduction to the CoNLL-2003 shared task: Language-independent named entity recognition. In *Proceedings of the Seventh Conference on Natural Language Learning at HLT-NAACL 2003*, pages 142–147.

Chih-Hsuan Wei, Yifan Peng, Robert Leaman, Allan Peter Davis, Carolyn J. Mattingly, Jiao Li, Thomas C. Wiegers, and Zhiyong Lu. 2016. Assessing the state of the art in biomedical relation extraction: overview of the BioCreative V chemical-disease relation (CDR) task. *Database J. Biol. Databases Curation*, 2016.

Validating Label Consistency in NER Data Annotation

Qingkai Zeng[†], **Mengxia Yu**[†], **Wenhao Yu**[†], **Tianwen Jiang**[‡],
Meng Jiang[†]
†University of Notre Dame, Notre Dame, IN, USA
‡Harbin Institute of Technology, Harbin, Heilongjiang, China
†{qzeng, myu2, wyu1, mjiang2}@nd.edu
‡{twjiang}@ir.hit.edu.cn

Abstract

Data annotation plays a crucial role in ensuring your named entity recognition (NER) projects are trained with the correct information to learn from. Producing the most accurate labels is a challenge due to the complexity involved with annotation. Label inconsistency between multiple subsets of data annotation (e.g., training set and test set, or multiple training subsets) is an indicator of label mistakes. In this work, we present an empirical method to explore the relationship between label (in-)consistency and NER model performance. It can be used to validate the label consistency (or catch the inconsistency) in multiple sets of NER data annotation. In experiments, our method identified the label inconsistency of test data in SCIERC and CoNLL03 datasets (with 26.7% and 5.4% label mistakes). It validated the consistency in the corrected version of both datasets.

1 Introduction

Named entity recognition (NER) is one of the foundations of many downstream tasks such as relation extraction, event detection, and knowledge graph construction. NER models require vast amounts of labeled data to learn and identify patterns that humans cannot continuously. It is really about getting accurate data to train the models. When end-to-end neural models achieve excellent performance on NER in various domains (Lample et al., 2016; Liu et al., 2018; Luan et al., 2018; Zeng et al., 2020, 2021), building useful and challenging NER benchmarks, such as CoNLL03, WNUT16, and SCIERC, contributes significantly to the research community.

Data annotation plays a crucial role in building benchmarks and ensuring NLP models are trained with the correct information to learn from (Luan et al., 2018; Jiang et al., 2020; Yu et al., 2020). Producing the necessary annotation from any asset at scale is a challenge, mainly because of the complexity involved with annotation. Getting the most accurate labels demands time and expertise.

Label mistakes can hardly be avoided, especially when the labeling process splits the data into multiple sets for distributed annotation. The mistakes cause label inconsistency between subsets of annotated data (e.g., training set and test set or multiple training subsets). For example, in the CoNLL03 dataset (Sang and De Meulder, 2003), a standard NER benchmark that has been cited over 2,300 times, label mistakes were found in 5.38% of the test set (Wang et al., 2019). Note that the state-of-the-art results on CoNLL03 have achieved an F1 score of $\sim$ .93. So even if the label mistakes make up a tiny part, they cannot be negligible when researchers are trying to improve the results further. In the work of Wang *et al.*, five annotators were recruited to correct the label mistakes. Compared to the original test set results, the corrected test set results are more accurate and stable.

However, two critical issues were not resolved in this process: *i)* How to identify label inconsistency between the subsets of annotated data? *ii)* How to validate that the label consistency was recovered by the correction?

Another example is SCIERC (Luan et al., 2018) (cited $\sim$50 times) which is a multi-task (including NER) benchmark in AI domain. It has 1,861 sentences for training, 455 for dev, and 551 for test. When we looked at the false predictions given by SCIIE which was a multi-task model released along with the SCIERC dataset, we found that as many as 147 (26.7% of the test set) sentences were not properly annotated. (We also recruited five annotators and counted a mistake when all the annotators report it.) Three examples are given in Table 1: two of them have wrong entity types; the third has a wrong span boundary. As shown in the experiments section, after the correction, the NER performance becomes more accurate and stable.

Proceedings of the 58th Annual Meeting of the Association for Computational Linguistics, pages 11–15

https://doi.org/10.26615/978-954-452-056-4_002

Table 1: Three examples to compare original and corrected annotation in the test set of the SCIERC dataset. If the annotation on the test set consistently followed the "codebook" that was used to annotate training data, the entities in the first two examples would be labelled as "Task" (not "Method") for sure.

Original Examples	Corrected Examples
Starting from a DP-based solution to the [**traveling salesman problem**]Method, we present a novel technique ...	Starting from a DP-based solution to the [**traveling salesman problem**]Task, we present a novel technique ...
FERRET utilizes a novel approach to [**Q/A**]Method known as predictive questioning which attempts to identify ...	FERRET utilizes a novel approach to [**Q/A**]Task known as predictive questioning which attempts to identify ...
The goal of this work is the enrichment of [**human-machine interactions**]Task in a natural language environment.	The goal of this work is the [**enrichment of human-machine interactions**]Task in a natural language environment.

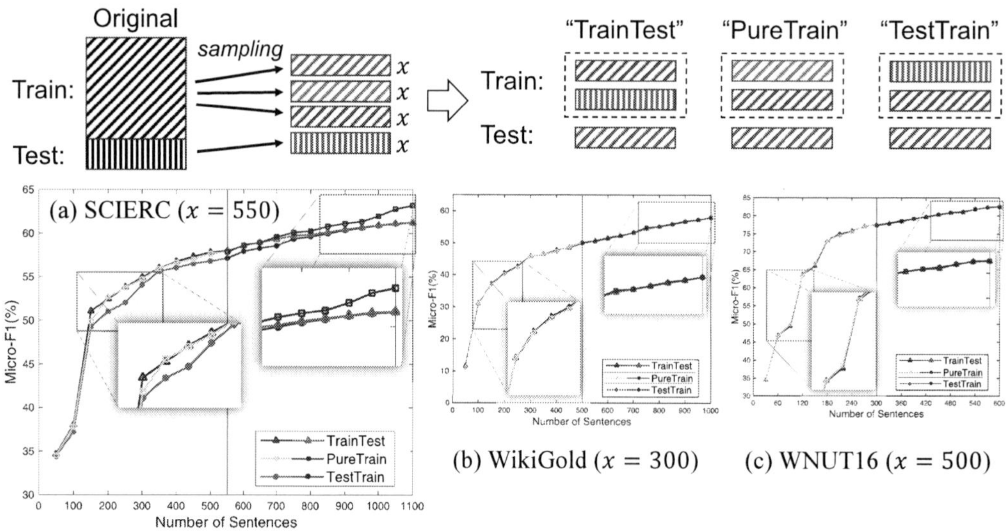

Figure 1: *Identifying label inconsistency of test set with training set:* We sample *three* exclusive subsets (of size x) from the training set (orange, green, and blue). We use one subset as the *new* test set (orange). We apply the SCIIE NER model on the new test set. We build three *new* training sets: *i)* "TrainTest" (blue-red), *ii)* "PureTrain" (green-blue), *iii)* "TestTrain" (red-blue). Results on SCIERC show that the test set (red) is *less predictive* of training samples (orange) than the training set itself (blue or green). This was not observed on two other datasets.

Besides the significant correction on the SCIERC dataset, our contributions in this work are as follows: *i)* an empirical, visual method to identify the label inconsistency between subsets of annotated data (see Figure 1), *ii)* a method to validate the label consistency of corrected data annotation (see Figure 2). Experiments show that they are effective on the CoNLL03 and SCIERC datasets.

2 Proposed Methods

2.1 A method to identify label inconsistency

Suppose the labeling processes on two parts of annotated data were consistent. They are likely to be equivalently predictive of each other. In other words, if we train a model with a set of samples from either part A or part B to predict a different set from part A, the performance should be similar.

Take SCIERC as an example. We were wondering whether the labels in the test set were consistent with those in the training set. Our method to identify the inconsistency is presented in Figure 1.

We sample *three* exclusive subsets (of size x) from the training set. We set $x = 550$ according to the size of the original test set. We use one of the subsets as the *new* test set. Then we train the SCIIE NER model (Luan et al., 2018) to perform on the new test set. We build three *new* training sets to feed into the model:

- "TrainTest": first fed with one training subset and then the original test set;
- "PureTrain": fed with two training subsets;
- "TestTrain": first fed with the original test set and then one of the training subsets.

Results show that "TestTrain" performed the worst at the early stage because the quality of the

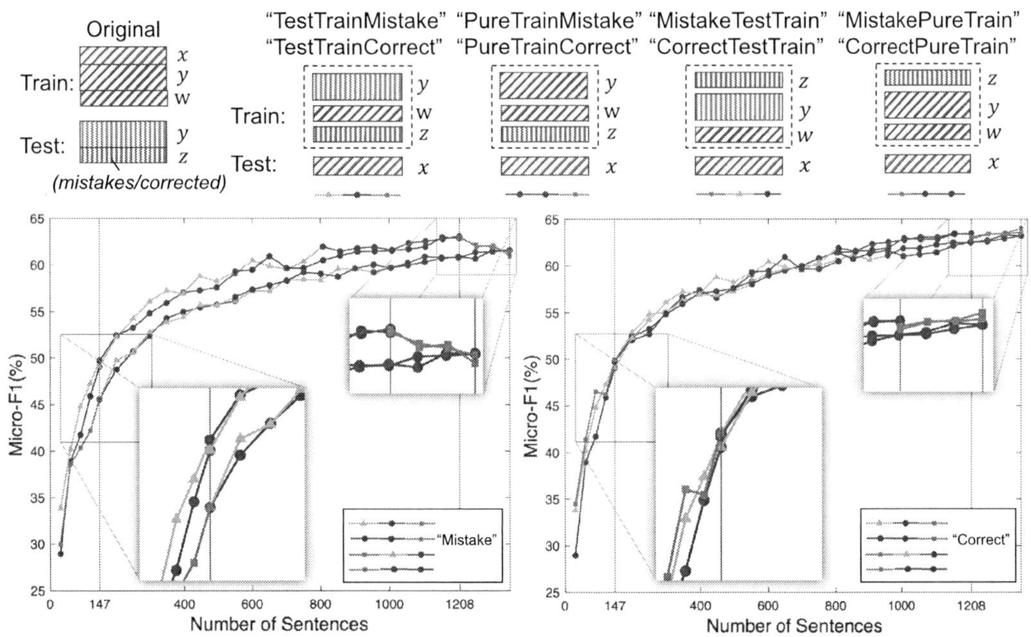

Figure 2: *Validating label consistency in corrected test set*: We corrected z of $y + z$ sentences in the test set. We sampled *three* exclusive subsets of size x, y, and w from the training set. We use the first subset (of size x) as the *new* test set. We build four *new* training sets as shown in the figure and feed them into the SCIIE model (at the top of the figure). Results show that the label mistakes (red parts of the curves on the left) do hurt the performance no matter fed at the beginning or later; and the corrected test set performs as well as the training set (on the right).

original test set is not reliable. In "TrainTest" the performance no longer improved when the model started being fed with the original test set. "PureTrain" performed the best. All the observations conclude that the original test set is less predictive of training samples than the training set itself. It may be due to the issue of label inconsistency. Moreover, we do not have such observations on two other datasets, WikiGold and WNUT16.

2.2 A method to validate label consistency after correction

After we corrected the label mistakes, how could we empirically validate the recovery of label consistency? Again, we use a subset of training data as the new test set. We evaluate the predictability of the original wrong test subset, the corrected test subset, and the rest of the training set. We expect to see that the wrong test subset delivers weaker performance and the other two sets make comparable good predictions. Figure 2 illustrates this idea.

Take SCIERC as an example. Suppose we corrected z of $y + z$ sentences in the test set. The original wrong test subset ("Mistake") and the corrected test subset ("Correct") are both of size z. Here $z = 147$ and the original good test subset $y = 404$ ("Test"). We sampled *three* exclusive subsets of size x, y, and $w = 804$ from the training set ("Train"). We use the first subset (of size x) as the *new* test set. We build four *new* training sets and feed into the SCIIE model. Each new training set has $y + w + z = 1,355$ sentences.

- "TestTrainMistake"/"TestTrainCorrect": the original good test subset, the third sampled training subset, and the original wrong test subset (or the corrected test subset);
- "PureTrainMistake"/"PureTrainCorrect": the second and third sampled training subsets and the original wrong test subset (or the corrected test subset);
- "MistakeTestTrain"/"CorrectTestTrain": the original wrong test subset (or the corrected test subset), the original good test subset, and the third sampled training subset;
- "MistakePureTrain"/"CorrectPureTrain": the original wrong test subset (or the corrected test subset) and the second and third sampled training subsets.

Results show that the label mistakes (i.e., original wrong test subset) hurt the model performance

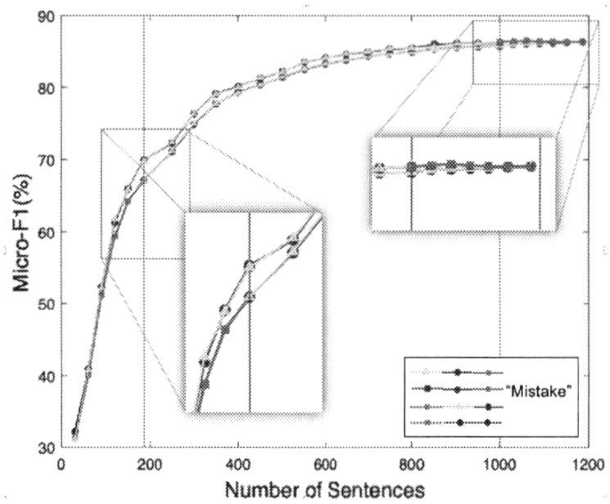

(a) Original with label mistakes

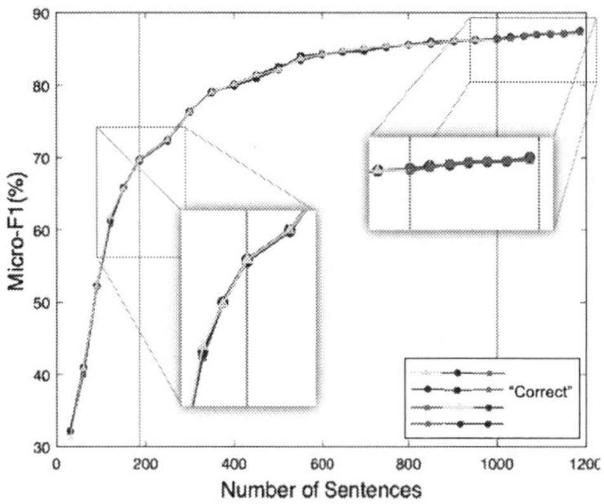

(b) Corrected

Figure 3: Identifying label inconsistency and validating the consistency in the original & corrected CoNLL03.

whenever being fed at the beginning or later. The corrected test subset delivers comparable performance with the original good test subset and the training set. This demonstrates the label consistency of the corrected test set with the training set.

3 Experiments

3.1 Results on SCIERC

The visual results of the proposed methods have been presented in Section 2. Here we deploy five state-of-the-art NER models to investigate their performance on the corrected SCIERC dataset. The NER models are BiLSTM-CRF (Lample et al., 2016), LM-BiLSTM-CRF (Liu et al., 2018), single-task and multi-task SCIIE (Luan et al., 2018), and multi-task DyGIE (Luan et al., 2019).

As shown in Table 2, all NER models deliver better performance on the corrected SCIERC than the original dataset. So the training set is more consistent with the fixed test set than the original wrong test set. In future work, we will explore more baselines in the leaderboard.

Table 2: Five NER models perform consistently better on the corrected SCIERC than on the original dataset.

Method	Corrected SCIERC			Original SCIERC		
	P	R	F1	P	R	F1
BiLSTM-CRF	58.35	47.95	**52.64**	56.13	48.07	51.79
LM-BiLSTM-CRF	62.78	58.20	**60.40**	59.15	57.15	58.13
SCIIE-single	71.20	62.88	**66.79**	65.77	60.90	63.24
SCIIE-multi	72.66	63.22	**67.61**	67.66	61.72	64.56
DyGIE-multi	69.64	67.02	**68.31**	65.09	65.28	65.18

3.2 Results on CoNLL03

Based on the correction contributed by (Wang et al., 2019), we use the proposed method to justify label inconsistency though the label mistakes take "only" 5.38%. It also validates the label consistency after recovery. Figure 3(a) shows that starting with the wrong labels in the original test set makes the performance worse than starting with the training set or the good test subset. After label correction, this issue is fixed in Figure 3(b).

4 Related Work

NER is typically cast as a sequence labeling problem and solved by models integrate LSTMs, CRF, and language models (Lample et al., 2016; Liu et al., 2018; Zeng et al., 2019, 2020). Another idea is to generate span candidates and predict their type. Span-based models have been proposed with multi-task learning strategies (Luan et al., 2018, 2019). The multiple tasks include concept recognition, relation extraction, and co-reference resolution.

Researchers notice label mistakes in many NLP tasks (Manning, 2011; Wang et al., 2019; Eskin, 2000; Květoň and Oliva, 2002). For instance, it is reported that the bottleneck of the POS tagging task is the consistency of the annotation result (Manning, 2011). People tried to detect label mistakes automatically and minimize the influence of noise in training. The mistake re-weighting mechanism is effective in the NER task (Wang et al., 2019). We focus on visually evaluating the label consistency.

5 Conclusion

We presented an empirical method to explore the relationship between label consistency and NER model performance. It identified the label inconsistency of test data in SCIERC and CoNLL03 datasets (with 26.7% and 5.4% label mistakes). It validated the label consistency in multiple sets of NER data annotation on two benchmarks, CoNLL03 and SCIERC.

Acknowledgements

This work is supported by National Science Foundation IIS-1849816 and CCF-1901059.

References

Eleazar Eskin. 2000. Detecting errors within a corpus using anomaly detection. In *Proceedings of the 1st North American chapter of the Association for Computational Linguistics conference*, pages 148–153. Association for Computational Linguistics.

Tianwen Jiang, Qingkai Zeng, Tong Zhao, Bing Qin, Ting Liu, Nitesh V Chawla, and Meng Jiang. 2020. Biomedical knowledge graphs construction from conditional statements. *IEEE/ACM transactions on computational biology and bioinformatics*, 18(3):823–835.

Pavel Květoň and Karel Oliva. 2002. (semi-)automatic detection of errors in PoS-tagged corpora. In *COLING 2002: The 19th International Conference on Computational Linguistics*.

Guillaume Lample, Miguel Ballesteros, Sandeep Subramanian, Kazuya Kawakami, and Chris Dyer. 2016. Neural architectures for named entity recognition. *arXiv preprint arXiv:1603.01360*.

Liyuan Liu, Jingbo Shang, Xiang Ren, Frank Fangzheng Xu, Huan Gui, Jian Peng, and Jiawei Han. 2018. Empower sequence labeling with task-aware neural language model. In *Thirty-Second AAAI Conference on Artificial Intelligence*.

Yi Luan, Luheng He, Mari Ostendorf, and Hannaneh Hajishirzi. 2018. Multi-task identification of entities, relations, and coreference for scientific knowledge graph construction. *Proceedings of the 2018 Conference on Empirical Methods in Natural Language Processing (EMNLP)*.

Yi Luan, Dave Wadden, Luheng He, Amy Shah, Mari Ostendorf, and Hannaneh Hajishirzi. 2019. A general framework for information extraction using dynamic span graphs. *Proceedings of the 2019 Conference of the North American Chapter of the Association for Computational Linguistics: Human Language Technologies*.

Christopher D Manning. 2011. Part-of-speech tagging from 97% to 100%: is it time for some linguistics? In *International conference on intelligent text processing and computational linguistics*.

Erik F Sang and Fien De Meulder. 2003. Introduction to the conll-2003 shared task: Language-independent named entity recognition. *arXiv preprint cs/0306050*.

Zihan Wang, Jingbo Shang, Liyuan Liu, Lihao Lu, Jiacheng Liu, and Jiawei Han. 2019. Crossweigh: Training named entity tagger from imperfect annotations. In *Proceedings of the 2019 Conference on Empirical Methods in Natural Language Processing and the 9th International Joint Conference on Natural Language Processing (EMNLP-IJCNLP)*.

Wenhao Yu, Mengxia Yu, Tong Zhao, and Meng Jiang. 2020. Identifying referential intention with heterogeneous contexts. In *Proceedings of The Web Conference 2020*.

Qingkai Zeng, Jinfeng Lin, Wenhao Yu, Jane Cleland-Huang, and Meng Jiang. 2021. Enhancing taxonomy completion with concept generation via fusing relational representations. In *ACM SIGKDD International Conference on Knowledge Discovery & Data Mining (KDD)*.

Qingkai Zeng, Mengxia Yu, Wenhao Yu, Jinjun Xiong, Yiyu Shi, and Meng Jiang. 2019. Faceted hierarchy: A new graph type to organize scientific concepts and a construction method. In *Proceedings of the Thirteenth Workshop on Graph-Based Methods for Natural Language Processing (TextGraphs-13)*.

Qingkai Zeng, Wenhao Yu, Mengxia Yu, Tianwen Jiang, Tim Weninger, and Meng Jiang. 2020. Tri-train: Automatic pre-fine tuning between pre-training and fine-tuning for sciner. In *Proceedings of the 2020 Conference on Empirical Methods in Natural Language Processing: Findings*.

How Emotionally Stable is ALBERT? Testing Robustness with Stochastic Weight Averaging on a Sentiment Analysis Task

Urja Khurana[♡] and **Eric Nalisnick**[◇] and **Antske Fokkens**[♡♣]
♡ CLTL, Dept. of Language, Literature & Communication, Vrije Universiteit Amsterdam
◇ Informatics Institute, University of Amsterdam
♣ Dept. of Mathematics and Computerscience, Eindhoven University of Technology
{u.khurana,antske.fokkens}@vu.nl
e.t.nalisnick@uva.nl

Abstract

Despite their success, modern language models are fragile. Even small changes in their training pipeline can lead to unexpected results. We study this phenomenon by examining the robustness of ALBERT (Lan et al., 2020) in combination with Stochastic Weight Averaging (SWA)—a cheap way of ensembling—on a sentiment analysis task (SST-2). In particular, we analyze SWA's stability via CheckList criteria (Ribeiro et al., 2020), examining the agreement on errors made by models differing only in their random seed. We hypothesize that SWA is more stable because it ensembles model snapshots taken along the gradient descent trajectory. We quantify stability by comparing the models' mistakes with Fleiss' Kappa (Fleiss, 1971) and overlap ratio scores. We find that SWA reduces error rates in general; yet the models still suffer from their own distinct biases (according to CheckList).

1 Introduction

Current language models perform well on data that resemble the distribution they are trained on, but even a slight variation in the model training setup can lead to results that diverge from what is originally reported (Fokkens et al., 2013; Sellam et al., 2021). Furthermore, when the model relies on spurious correlations for decision making, it then contains biases that are not represented by real world data. Ideally a model should be robust to data that has (slightly) different characteristics from the data it was trained on. Accuracy and related metrics, despite their popularity, are usually not sufficient to identify these frailties. This is known as *underspecification* (D'Amour et al., 2020): different predictors can achieve similar results on a specific task, but exhibit diverging performance on other tasks due to different induced biases.

Stress tests are an increasingly popular method for exposing biases of a model. To test the linguistic capabilities and robustness of models, Ribeiro et al. (2020) introduce *CheckList*, an evaluation methodology that is comparable to the aforementioned *stress tests* for robustness. CheckList can be used to investigate which linguistic phenomena are fully captured by a model and for which the model is thus expected to be robust across datasets.

Robustness and generalization can be improved by ensembling multiple models. Training different models, however, is expensive. *Stochastic Weight Averaging* (SWA) (Izmailov et al., 2018) is a way of ensembling without the need to train different models. During training, the weights of the model at specific timepoints are averaged, avoiding the need to keep track of several models. The idea is that SWA explores different solutions close to a high performing minimum.

In this paper, we study the effect of SWA on the robustness to both a standard sentiment analysis dataset and different CheckList capabilities. We investigate if models varying only in their random seeds still have different behavior on the same data when trained using SWA. Specifically, we train ALBERT-large (Lan et al., 2020) on SST-2 (Socher et al., 2013), a sentiment analysis dataset, with 10 random seeds. We perform one run with SWA turned off (termed *vanilla models*) and repeat the procedure with SWA turned on (termed *SWA models*). We explore the robustness of the trained models using the CheckList methodology by looking at the stability of mistakes. We quantify this stability to measure the agreement in mistakes between the different models and compare the resulting values between the vanilla and SWA models.

Our main hypothesis is that **using SWA leads to more stable models**. We therefore expect more overlap across random seeds in the results on the SST-2 evaluation data. We also expect SWA to lead to more overlap in mistakes for CheckList items that are captured by part of the vanilla models. We also anticipate (minor) improvements of general

Proceedings of the 58th Annual Meeting of the Association for Computational Linguistics, pages 16–31

https://doi.org/10.26615/978-954-452-056-4_003

performance in both cases. For CheckList phenomena that are already largely captured or not at all, on the other hand, we do not expect to see major differences between vanilla models and SWA in terms of general performance or overlap.

We make the following contributions:

- We explore the effects of SWA on the stability and robustness of ALBERT-large that stem from underspecification.
- We perform the, to our knowledge, first joint study of SWA and CheckList.
- We provide an in-depth analysis of results by going beyond accuracy to look at overlap and agreement between random seeds and CheckList.
- We quantify agreement between different models by calculating overlap ratio and Fleiss' Kappa score on their mistakes.

We find that SWA improves on error rates in general, but results on increased stability are mixed: models with different random seeds still hold onto their own distinct induced biases on linguistic information captured by part of the models in our CheckList evaluation. There is minor improvement in stability on the Fleiss' Kappa score on the development set of SST-2, but results are not conclusive. Finally, we observe a large error rate for one of the random seeds on both SST-2 and CheckList, which also leads to a less strong result on increasing agreement between models.

2 Related Work

To the best of our knowledge, we are the first to combine SWA with CheckList and apply it to a BERT-based model to understand its effect on robustness with different random seeds. The work closest to ours has used variations of SWA for investigating the differences in interpretability on CNNs and LSTMs among different random seeds (Madhyastha and Jain, 2019). A similar method to Stochastic Weight Averaging was employed by Xu et al. (2020) with a different objective: improving the fine-tuning process of BERT. They propose to average the BERT model at each time-step and two types of knowledge distillation to improve fine-tuning of the model. The averaging receives slightly better results and their variant of knowledge distillation works the best. However, it is unclear what the effect of this is on different random seeds.

Instead of looking at a form of ensembling, Hua et al. (2021) investigate the effect of injecting noise in BERT as a regularizer on the stability (sensitivity to input perturbation) of the models and show that fine-tuning performance improves. They point out that this improves generalizability as well, by looking at the difference in accuracy on the training and test set. However, training and test set might contain the same biases and hence might not reveal generalization issues (Elangovan et al., 2021).

Varying Performance Most work until now has focused on behavioral changes of models on train and test data when changing an arbitrary choice of the pipeline, such as the random seed (Zhong et al., 2021; Sellam et al., 2021). Investigating the behavior of language models with different pre-training and fine-tuning random seeds on an instance-level, Zhong et al. (2021) find that the fine-tuning random seed is influential for the variation in performance on an instance-level. This contrast in performance is also highlighted by Sellam et al. (2021); they release multiple BERT checkpoints with a different weight initialization and show diverging performance between similarly trained models. Such behavior has also been observed for out-of-distribution samples (McCoy et al., 2020; D'Amour et al., 2020; Amir et al., 2021), where different induced biases are found when the random seed is modified and checkpoints behave differently on unseen data, even when evaluation performance is similar. (D'Amour et al., 2020; Amir et al., 2021). Watson et al. (2021) show that outputs from explainability methods also vary when changing hyperparameters, e.g. the random seed.

Model Evaluation Evaluating models on a development set might not expose certain biases or weaknesses a model has acquired due to the possibility of the same biases occurring in the training set. Hence, scalable diagnostic methodologies are useful to investigate a model's capabilities (Wu et al., 2019; Ribeiro et al., 2020; Wu et al., 2021; Goel et al., 2021). Even though these methodologies all focus on evaluation, the approach can vary between the methods. Wu et al. (2021) tackle evaluation from a counterfactual point of view. Wu et al. (2019) not only examine counterfactuals but also grouping queries to ensure that error analysis is scaled to all instances. Likewise, Goel et al. (2021)

exploit such subpopulation grouping, in addition to adversarial attacks, perturbations, and evaluation sets. It is possible to be unaware of certain subpopulations for which the model is weak, and therefore d'Eon et al. (2021) introduce a method that looks for such weak groups. Ribeiro et al. (2020) provide a methodology to analyze robustness toward basic capabilities and operationalize this with different test types (e.g. invariance to specific perturbations, basic capabilities). There are also more task specific efforts for evaluation, such as perturbations for robustness in task-oriented dialog (Liu et al., 2021) and evaluation of bias in a sentiment analysis setting (Asyrofi et al., 2021).

3 Method

To examine *Stochastic Weight Averaging*'s effect on model stability due to *underspecification*, we finetune a pretrained ALBERT-large version 2 on the SST-2 dataset. We train two types of models 10 times:[1]

- *Vanilla model*: Model finetuned with the hyperparameter values from Lan et al. (2020)
- *SWA model*: Model finetuned for the first few epochs with the hyperparameter values from Lan et al. (2020) and then switching to a SWA training schedule

For all models, we keep the training protocol the same except for the random seed. We train 10 models with a different random seed per model type. This gives us 20 different models: 10 *vanilla models* and 10 *SWA models*.[2] We then investigate the robustness of each model on CheckList tests and compare the performance of *vanilla models* with *SWA models*.

Due to *underspecification*, the vanilla models are expected to have deviating performances on the tests across different random seeds, while the SWA models are expected to dampen this effect. We make a distinction between the following scenarios and what we expect:

1. **Linguistic information captured by all of the models**: We expect all of the models, regardless of the random seed, to be able to perform well on basic capabilities. Hence, we do not expect SWA to make much improvement, as there should not be a different behavior across random seeds. Stability will stay consistent here.

2. **Linguistic information captured by a part of the models**: This type of linguistic information is only captured by a part of the models due to their own induced biases. Hence, we expect that not all vanilla models behave similarly on such instances. With the introduction of SWA, more stability thus more overlap between mistakes is expected.

3. **Linguistic information captured by none of the models**: Some information cannot be captured by the model at all or it is unlikely that the model will be able to handle such information properly. In such cases, we do not expect SWA models to have an increase in performance, though that cannot be ruled out since it is possible that the weight space averaged by SWA is able to capture it. For the former, we do expect a large overlap of mistakes with SWA models since such information is not captured by any of the models.

3.1 Stochastic Weight Averaging

Stochastic Weight Averaging (SWA) is a cheap approach to create ensembles by averaging over different snapshots over the SGD trajectory, in contrast to the widely used approach of training different models (Izmailov et al., 2018). In essence, SWA ensembles in weight space instead of the usual model space. Due to the ensembling nature of correlated members from the same trajectory, we expect better generalization; a reduction in error rate and more stability in mistakes on unseen data.

We employ a strategy where the SWA models are trained in the same manner as the vanilla models for the first two epochs. This cut-off epoch is chosen empirically, by observing that the vanilla models start converging around 2-3 epochs. We make use of the Adam optimizer instead of the SGD optimizer since the former optimizer is used for the training of ALBERT. From the third epoch, the learning rate drops to a constant learning rate and at every end of the epoch, the model weights are

[1] We provide all code at `https://github.com/cltl/robustness-albert`

[2] The experiments originally contained five random seeds, of which *Random Seed 0* had exceptionally poor performance of 90.83 accuracy on the development set. This was far from the reported validation accuracy of 94.9 (`https://github.com/google-research/albert#albert`). For the camera-ready version, we trained an additional five seeds, which confirmed that the anomalous one is indeed an outlier.

averaged with the running average weights. With a high constant learning rate, the model is able to explore other solutions that are close to the local minimum that was found after two epochs and close to convergence. The respective constant learning rates of each random seed can be found in Table 1. The values for the learning rates are found empirically on the development set with the following candidate learning rates: {6e-06, 7.5e-06}.[3]

	SWA Learning Rate
Random Seed 0	6e-06
Random Seed 1	7.5e-06
Random Seed 2	6e-06
Random Seed 3	6e-06
Random Seed 4	7.5e-06
Random Seed 5	6e-06
Random Seed 6	6e-06
Random Seed 7	6e-06
Random Seed 8	6e-06
Random Seed 9	7.5e-06

Table 1: The constant SWA learning rates for each random seed.

3.2 SST-2 Dataset

We use the binary version of the Stanford Sentiment Treebank dataset[4] (Socher et al., 2013), which consists of human-annotated sentences from movie reviews originating from `rottentomatoes.com` for a sentiment classification task. This version of the dataset is also included in the GLUE task (Wang et al., 2018). We use this dataset since sentiment analysis is an interesting task to study underspecification as it is a more subjective task, making rigorous, multifaceted evaluation even more important. The training set consists of 67349 phrases, while the validation and test dataset consist of 872 and 1821 sentences respectively. We use the training and validation set for the training procedure, while the test set is used for the generation of specific CheckList items.

[3]We looked at the learning rates in examples from the original paper at `https://github.com/timgaripov/swa#examples` where some SWA learning rates are half of the original learning rate and explored close candidate learning rates. From previous initial experiments learning rate $5e-06$ did not work and was thus left out in these sets of experiments.

[4]`https://nlp.stanford.edu/sentiment/index.html`

3.3 Checklist Evaluation

CheckList is a methodology to test basic and linguistic capabilities of a model, similar to behavioral testing in software engineering (Ribeiro et al., 2020). They make a distinction between three types of tests:

Minimum Functionality Test (MFT): Small examples to test for basic capabilities. We test if each instance has the specified label.

Invariance Test (INV): Tests that apply perturbations to the input and expect the prediction to stay consistent, *regardless of the correctness of the prediction*. The original input together with its perturbations is seen as one test case.

Directional Expectation Tests (DIR): Tests where the output is expected to change in a specific way, when the input is modified: the confidence is expected to change in a specific direction. Similar to INV tests, the original input with modifications is seen as a test case.

In this paper, we consider different MFTs, INVs, and DIRs tests for sentiment analysis. We check for basic capabilities and robustness. Each trained model is evaluated on our CheckList set up and their performances are compared. We expect that vanilla models make more mistakes than SWA models and qualitatively make less overlapping mistakes due to each model having their own different induced biases. On the other hand, SWA models are expected to have more overlapping mistakes, due to its ensembling and explorative nature in the weight space.

We created 18 CheckList capability tests by adapting tests from the CheckList GitHub repository[5] to the use-case in this paper. For reasons of space, we refer to individual capability tests with transparent names followed by the test size, only using short explanations when the name by itself is not sufficiently clear. For tests that perturb the input and are not created from scratch, we use the test set from SST-2. Each original input can be augmented more than once, depending on the capability. These tests are followed by two numbers when introduced: the number of original items and total items with perturbations included. A full overview of the CheckList capabilities and their sizes can be found in Table 7 in Appendix D.

[5]`https://github.com/marcotcr/checklist/blob/master/notebooks/Sentiment.ipynb`

4 Results

This section presents the outcome of our experiments. We first provide results on the original dataset and then the results on CheckList items. Lastly we examine how stable vanilla and SWA models are by looking at the label agreement between models trained from different seeds.

4.1 Stochastic Weight Averaging

As mentioned in the previous section, we originally ran our experiments on five random seeds and added five additional seeds after observing that one seed performed lower than all others. When we compare the accuracy of the vanilla models with the SWA models on the validation set of SST-2 in Table 2, it is evident that most of the SWA models perform slightly better than the vanilla models. The only exceptions are *Random Seed 0, 7,* and *8*. Upon running our experiments on five additional seeds, *Random Seed 0* remains the only seed that has an accuracy around 0.90, confirming that it is an outlier. The SWA versions of the other two random seeds might not outperform their vanilla counterparts but achieve a close accuracy.

Due to the outlying behavior of *Random Seed 0*, we leave its results out of the rest of the analysis, to avoid noise from this model influencing the analysis. We present the complete results with *Random Seed 0* included in Appendix C.

	Vanilla	SWA
Random Seed 0	**0.9083**	0.8991
Random Seed 1	0.9507	**0.9541**
Random Seed 2	0.9450	**0.9495**
Random Seed 3	0.9507	**0.9541**
Random Seed 4	0.9450	**0.9461**
Random Seed 5	0.9495	**0.9507**
Random Seed 6	0.9450	**0.9472**
Random Seed 7	**0.9438**	0.9392
Random Seed 8	**0.9461**	0.9450
Random Seed 9	0.9415	**0.9461**

Table 2: Accuracy on the validation set of SST-2 for the vanilla and SWA models of the different random seeds.

4.2 CheckList Evaluation

4.2.1 Vanilla Model Results

Error Rates We show the failure rate for each capability per vanilla model in Figure 1a. For the *Movie Sentiments* (n=58), *Single Positive Words* (n=22), *Single Negative Words* (n=14), and *Sentiment-laden Words in Context* (n=1350) capabilities there are no mistakes made by any of the vanilla models. On *Add Positive Phrases* (n=500, m=5500), only *Random Seed 8* makes mistakes with a very small error rate. Similarly, on *Movie Industries Sentiments* (n=1200) only *Random Seed 8* and *Random Seed 2* make mistakes, again with very small error rates that would not be visible on the plot. Hence for clarity, these capabilities are left out of the plot.

There is not much variation in the error rate for most of the capabilities. The most variation in performance among the random seeds can be observed for the capability that tests negations of positive sentences, with a neutral sentiment in the middle of the sentence: *Negation of Positive, neutral words in the middle* (D) (n=500). Interestingly, it is evident that particular random seeds can deal with negation better than others: *Random Seed 1, 4,* and *5*. These random seeds have the lowest error rate for both *Negation of Positive Sentences* (C) (n=1350) and *Negation of Positive, neutral words in the middle.*

Overlap Ratios A similar error rate, however, does not mean that the errors occur for the same instances. Hence, we analyze the overlap of errors of the vanilla models per capability. We calculate an overlap ratio by dividing the intersection of the failures of two random seeds by the union of those same failures. In contrast to the error rates, the overlap ratios are on an instance-level instead of case-level. There is no overlap of errors between the models for the capability *Add Positive Phrases*. The capability with the highest overlap ratio is *Movie Genre Specific Sentiments* (A) (n=736), which checks for sentiments that are fitting or not for specific genres: e.g. a scared feeling after watching a horror movie. This indicates that most of the models make similar mistakes for this capability. When looking at the mistakes, all the models misclassify sentences about horror movies being terrifying, scary, frightening or calming, a comedy movie being serious and a drama movie being funny instead of serious. In general, most of the vanilla models have a low overlap ratio, with the only exceptions being *Negation of Positive, neutral words in the middle* (D) and *Temporal Sentiment Change* (B) (n=2152). The latter capability contains sentences where the sentiment changes over time. These two contain certain random seeds that

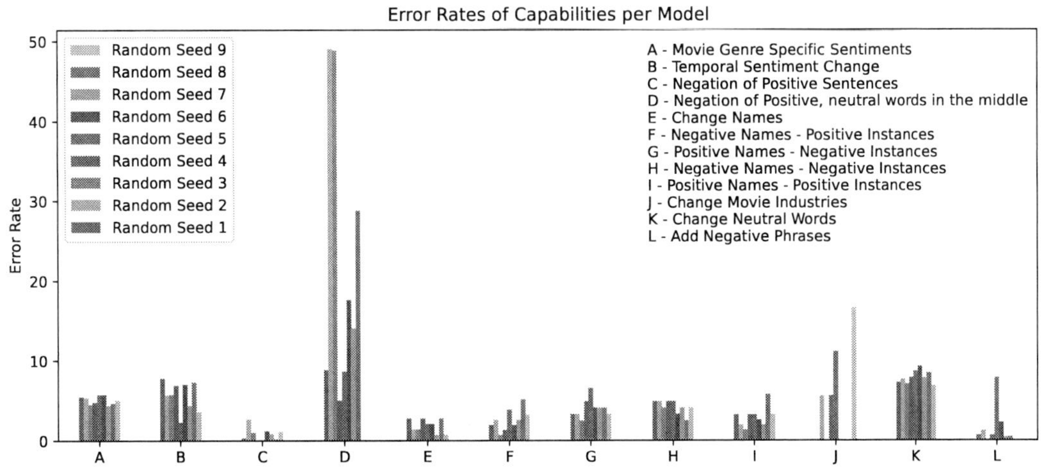

(a) Error rates of each vanilla random seed for each CheckList capability.

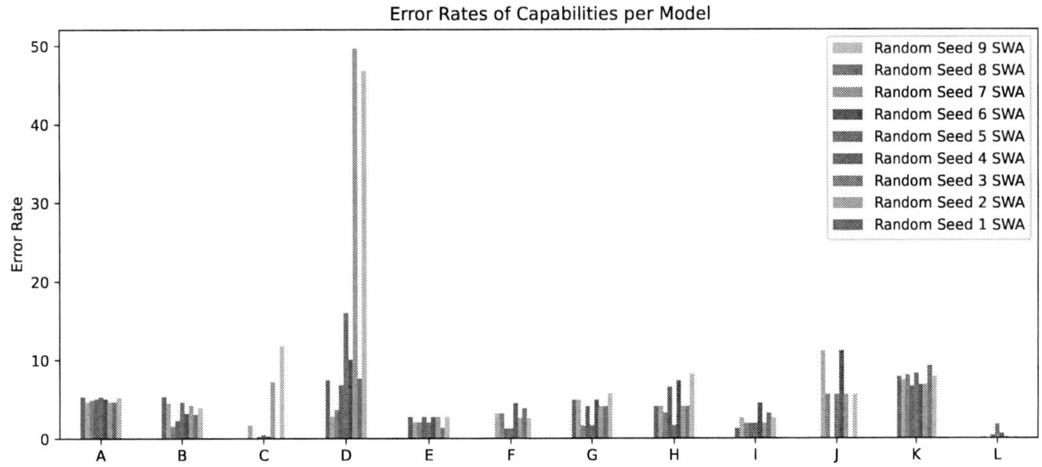

(b) Error rates of each SWA random seed for each CheckList capability.

Figure 1: Comparison of error rates per capability of vanilla and SWA models.

achieve a higher overlap ratio, as we can see in the spread of the box for these capabilities.

4.2.2 SWA Model Results

Error Rates Error rates for the SWA models per capability can be found in Figure 1b. In general, we can observe a (slight) reduction in error rate with SWA models compared to vanilla models. On *Add Positive Phrases*, only *Random Seed 5* and *Random Seed 6* have a slight increase in error rate. The latter is also the only one to make a mistake on *Movie Industries Sentiments*[6]. The largest drop can be seen for *Negation of Positive, neutral words in the middle* (D), where the diverging performance seen for the vanilla models has been reduced for most random seeds, except for *Random Seed 7* and *Random Seed 9*, whose error rates increase significantly. Similar behavior can be observed for *Negation of Positive Sentences* (C), where only the SWA versions of *Random Seed 7* and *9* have an increase in error rate. This suggests that the SWA solution for these two random seeds is worse in handling negation than their corresponding vanilla versions. For other capabilities, the error rate mostly reduces slightly or stays the same. The only exceptions are *Positive Names - Negative Instances* (G) (n=123, m=1353) and *Negative Names - Negative Instances* (H) (n=123, m=1353), where Negative Names are names that tend to occur in negative reviews in the training data, similarly for positive names, and we

[6]These error rates are too low (0.2% - 0.35%) to be visible in the plot, hence left out.

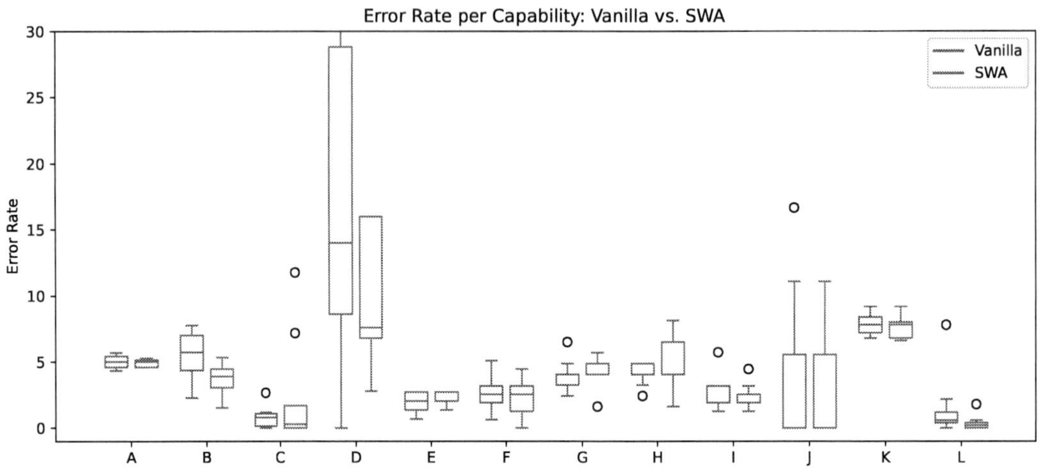

(a) Comparison of variation in error rates between vanilla (red boxes) and SWA models (blue boxes), showcased per CheckList capability. Outliers are indicated with a circle.

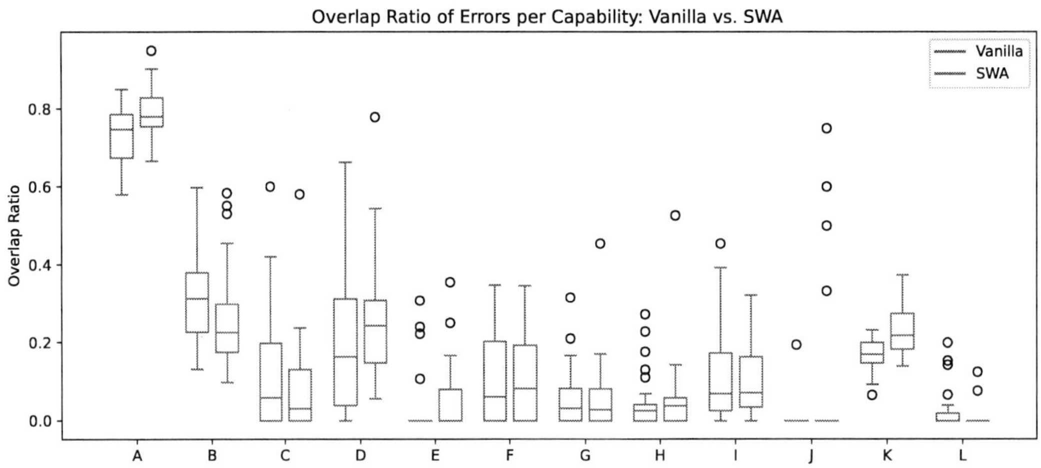

(b) Comparison of variation in overlap ratios between vanilla (red boxes) and SWA models (blue boxes), showcased per CheckList capability. Outliers are indicated with a circle.

Figure 2: Comparing the variation of error rates and overlap ratios per capability for vanilla and SWA models. Legend for the x-axis can be found in Figure 1

insert these names in negative instances of the test set. More details are provided in Appendix D.

Overlap Ratios The overlap ratio for most capabilities remains low. Notably, the spread of overlap ratio for *Movie Genre Specific Sentiments* (A) increases from the vanilla models. All of the models still struggle with understanding that horror movies being terrifying, scary or frightening is positive, and calming is negative. This is in line with the expectations of SWA not improving (much) on capabilities that are not captured by any of the models. We find increase in overlap for *Change Names* (E) (n=147, m=1617), *Negative Names - Negative Instances* (H), and *Change Neutral Words* (K) (n=500, m=3846), in accordance with our expectation of SWA bringing more stability. There is a different trend, against expectations, for *Add Negative Phrases* (L), *Negation of Positive Sentences* (C), and *Temporal Sentiment Change* (B), where the large variation of overlap of vanilla models is reduced significantly. For the rest of the capabilities, the overlap ratio appears to stay somewhat the same.

Overall, there are three different outcomes when comparing stability with SWA to vanilla models: (1) Good performance of vanilla models stays consistent for the SWA models. (2) Large variations in error rates with vanilla models are reduced with SWA, but the overlap of mistakes does not increase and might decrease for some cases. (3) Overlap ratio with SWA does not necessarily increase, when error rates of the vanilla models are somewhat similar and remain the same for the SWA models. As such, we do not find evidence to confirm our hypothesis based on overlap between the outcomes on CheckList items.

4.3 Fleiss' Kappa

To further investigate the stability of SWA models, we measure the inter-model agreement on the misclassifications with the use of Fleiss' Kappa (Fleiss, 1971). This measure is used for inter-annotator agreement which can be related to the nine random seeds. In our case the annotators and the predictions being their annotations, used for both the vanilla and SWA models. Negative values or values close to zero are considered to indicate a rather low agreement, while the higher the value, the more agreement there is.

	Vanilla	SWA	Difference
With Random Seed 0	0.205964	0.247299	0.041335
Without Random Seed 0	0.226725	0.360317	0.133592
With Random Seed 0	0.3984	0.4381	0.03967
Without Random Seed 0	0.3881	0.4106	0.0225

Table 3: Fleiss' Kappa values of the vanilla and SWA models on the agreement on the misclassifications on the development set. The upper block is with the first five random seeds and the lower is with all 10.

The results on the development set in Table 3 illustrate a significant increase in agreement for SWA models, when considering the initial four random seeds, without outlier *Random Seed 0*. While the agreement is still on the lower side, hinting at the presence of induced biases, the increase indicates more agreement on errors between the models and lesser distinct mistakes. We hence look at the Fleiss' Kappa values with the additional five random seeds incorporated. The Fleiss' Kappa agreement increases significantly in general for both the vanilla and SWA models. We now only observe a small increase in agreement when applying SWA compared to the vanilla models.

	Vanilla	SWA	Difference
Negation of Positive Sentences	0.029640	0.020448	-0.009192
Negation of Positive, neutral words in the middle	0.107637	0.142219	0.034582
Movie Genre Specific Sentiments	0.581853	0.660138	0.078285
Temporal Sentiment Change	0.248653	0.290926	0.042273
Change Names	-0.091694	-0.084096	0.007598
Negative Names - Positive Instances	0.006975	0.006021	-0.000954
Positive Names - Negative Instances	-0.069162	-0.076226	-0.007064
Negative Names - Negative Instances	-0.082486	-0.069141	0.013346
Positive Names - Positive Instances	0.012704	0.035196	0.022492
Change Movie Industries	-0.072503	-0.052239	0.020264
Change Neutral Words	0.087306	0.135759	0.048453
Add Negative Phrases	-0.031328	-0.062053	-0.030724

Table 4: Fleiss' Kappa values of the vanilla and SWA models on the agreement on CheckList mistakes per capability. The first part of the table shows the MFT capabilities, the second part are the INV capabilities, and the third part are the DIR capabilities.

We calculate the Kappa measure on the predictions of all the random seeds on the CheckList items as well. For the tests that measure basic capabilities (MFTs), we look at the agreement on predictions of errors. With tests that perturb an input (INVs), the instances that flip the output prediction are considered as a failure, so we check for model agreement on flipping for an instance. Similarly, for capabilities that test a directional change in confidence (DIRs), instances that go against the expected direction are considered failures and we compare model agreement on if they change in the same direction.

The Kappa values for the CheckList mistakes in Table 4 stay mostly unchanged with slight increases or decreases in agreement. This is in accordance with the results observed for the development set mistakes: it appears that SWA does not provide the stability across random seeds and still suffers from its own induced biases. Generally, the agreement is on the lower side. The Kappa values for *Movie Industries Sentiments* and *Add Positive Phrases* were 0.0 for both vanilla and SWA models and hence left out of the table. For *Movie Genre Specific Sentiments* we see a large agreement and the biggest increase in agreement with SWA. This corresponds to the high overlap ratio for the same capability.

While SWA globally cuts down on error rate, it appears that this does not necessarily translate to improvement in stability: there is still disagreement in the labels assigned by individual models. Even with SWA, the models appear to make different errors on CheckList as confirmed by the low Kappa values and overlap ratio. For some capabilities the spread of the overlap ratio is on the higher side, indicating that *some* random seed models are closer to each other in terms of decision making, but this does not hold for *all*.

5 Discussion

This research illustrates the potential impact of random seeds. First, our original sample of 5 seeds contained an outlier that performed far worse than the other seeds (as well as the original study). Second, while initial results on the SST-2 development set were promising when looking at the 4 random seeds that showed normal behavior, these results did not hold when adding 5 additional random seeds. This highlights the necessity for proper analysis and the fragility of deep language models. Possibly, the initial random seeds were closer to each other in the weight space and hence SWA appeared to increase the agreement significantly. The additional random seeds could lie farther away, thus subsiding the increased agreement. In the future, more comprehensive research on the proximity and behavior of different random seeds could therefore be useful.

Even though CheckList provides an easy way to investigate the capabilities of a model, automatizing some tests can be hard. There can be situations in which labels indicated for a specific capability might not hold for a certain test case. For instance, negating a negative sentence might not always lead to a positive sentence, it can also be neutral. Similarly, we applied negations on some instances from the test set but the label is not required to flip, depending on the placement of the negation. Therefore, we leave out the results in our conclusions as the labels did not always make sense upon investigation. In some instances, it is also unclear what the resulting label should be. We have added the results for these specific capabilities in Appendix B for completeness. For further experiments, we would like to manually generate some CheckList capabilities to ensure validity of the labels. This will also enable us to focus on the creation of more subjective tests, cases that are less black-and-white than the tests conducted in this research. We can then gain more insights into the fragility of models when it comes to border cases.

6 Conclusion

We combine SWA with the CheckList methodology to explore the effects of SWA on the robustness of a BERT-based model (ALBERT-large) on different random seeds and apply it to a sentiment analysis task. To understand how SWA affects the stability amongst different random seeds, we analyze in-depth the results and mistakes made on the development set and CheckList test items and provide error rates, overlap ratios, and Fleiss' Kappa agreement values. While SWA is able to reduce the error rate in general amongst most of the random seeds, on the CheckList tests, there are still some capabilities that models make their own distinct mistakes on with SWA incorporated. The stability on the development set also improves only slightly. In the future, we would like to create more hand-crafted CheckList capabilities for further rigorous study. Furthermore, it could be useful to thoroughly investigate the impact of adjacency of random seeds on their error agreement.

Acknowledgements

This research was (partially) funded by the Hybrid Intelligence Center, a 10-year programme funded by the Dutch Ministry of Education, Culture and Science through the Netherlands Organisation for Scientific Research.

References

Silvio Amir, Jan-Willem van de Meent, and Byron Wallace. 2021. On the impact of random seeds on the fairness of clinical classifiers. In *Proceedings of the 2021 Conference of the North American Chapter of the Association for Computational Linguistics: Human Language Technologies*, pages 3808–3823, Online. Association for Computational Linguistics.

Muhammad Hilmi Asyrofi, Imam Nur Bani Yusuf, Hong Jin Kang, Ferdian Thung, Zhou Yang, and David Lo. 2021. Biasfinder: Metamorphic test generation to uncover bias for sentiment analysis systems. *arXiv preprint arXiv:2102.01859*.

Alexander D'Amour, Katherine Heller, Dan Moldovan, Ben Adlam, Babak Alipanahi, Alex Beutel,

Christina Chen, Jonathan Deaton, Jacob Eisenstein, Matthew D Hoffman, et al. 2020. Underspecification presents challenges for credibility in modern machine learning. *arXiv preprint arXiv:2011.03395*.

Greg d'Eon, Jason d'Eon, James R. Wright, and Kevin Leyton-Brown. 2021. The spotlight: A general method for discovering systematic errors in deep learning models.

Aparna Elangovan, Jiayuan He, and Karin Verspoor. 2021. Memorization vs. generalization : Quantifying data leakage in NLP performance evaluation. In *Proceedings of the 16th Conference of the European Chapter of the Association for Computational Linguistics: Main Volume*, pages 1325–1335, Online. Association for Computational Linguistics.

Joseph L Fleiss. 1971. Measuring nominal scale agreement among many raters. *Psychological bulletin*, 76(5):378.

Antske Fokkens, Marieke van Erp, Marten Postma, Ted Pedersen, Piek Vossen, and Nuno Freire. 2013. Offspring from reproduction problems: What replication failure teaches us. In *Proceedings of the 51st Annual Meeting of the Association for Computational Linguistics (Volume 1: Long Papers)*, pages 1691–1701, Sofia, Bulgaria. Association for Computational Linguistics.

Karan Goel, Nazneen Fatema Rajani, Jesse Vig, Zachary Taschdjian, Mohit Bansal, and Christopher Ré. 2021. Robustness gym: Unifying the NLP evaluation landscape. In *Proceedings of the 2021 Conference of the North American Chapter of the Association for Computational Linguistics: Human Language Technologies: Demonstrations*, pages 42–55, Online. Association for Computational Linguistics.

Matthew Honnibal, Ines Montani, Sofie Van Landeghem, and Adriane Boyd. 2020. spaCy: Industrial-strength Natural Language Processing in Python.

Hang Hua, Xingjian Li, Dejing Dou, Chengzhong Xu, and Jiebo Luo. 2021. Noise stability regularization for improving BERT fine-tuning. In *Proceedings of the 2021 Conference of the North American Chapter of the Association for Computational Linguistics: Human Language Technologies*, pages 3229–3241, Online. Association for Computational Linguistics.

Pavel Izmailov, Dmitrii Podoprikhin, Timur Garipov, Dmitry Vetrov, and Andrew Gordon Wilson. 2018. Averaging weights leads to wider optima and better generalization. In *34th Conference on Uncertainty in Artificial Intelligence 2018, UAI 2018*, 34th Conference on Uncertainty in Artificial Intelligence 2018, UAI 2018, pages 876–885. Association For Uncertainty in Artificial Intelligence (AUAI).

Zhenzhong Lan, Mingda Chen, Sebastian Goodman, Kevin Gimpel, Piyush Sharma, and Radu Soricut. 2020. ALBERT: A lite BERT for self-supervised learning of language representations. In *8th International Conference on Learning Representations, ICLR 2020, Addis Ababa, Ethiopia, April 26-30, 2020*. OpenReview.net.

Jiexi Liu, Ryuichi Takanobu, Jiaxin Wen, Dazhen Wan, Hongguang Li, Weiran Nie, Cheng Li, Wei Peng, and Minlie Huang. 2021. Robustness testing of language understanding in task-oriented dialog. In *Proceedings of the 59th Annual Meeting of the Association for Computational Linguistics and the 11th International Joint Conference on Natural Language Processing (Volume 1: Long Papers)*, pages 2467–2480, Online. Association for Computational Linguistics.

Pranava Madhyastha and Rishabh Jain. 2019. On model stability as a function of random seed. In *Proceedings of the 23rd Conference on Computational Natural Language Learning (CoNLL)*, pages 929–939, Hong Kong, China. Association for Computational Linguistics.

R. Thomas McCoy, Junghyun Min, and Tal Linzen. 2020. BERTs of a feather do not generalize together: Large variability in generalization across models with similar test set performance. In *Proceedings of the Third BlackboxNLP Workshop on Analyzing and Interpreting Neural Networks for NLP*, pages 217–227, Online. Association for Computational Linguistics.

Marco Tulio Ribeiro, Tongshuang Wu, Carlos Guestrin, and Sameer Singh. 2020. Beyond accuracy: Behavioral testing of NLP models with CheckList. In *Proceedings of the 58th Annual Meeting of the Association for Computational Linguistics*, pages 4902–4912, Online. Association for Computational Linguistics.

Thibault Sellam, Steve Yadlowsky, Jason Wei, Naomi Saphra, Alexander D'Amour, Tal Linzen, Jasmijn Bastings, Iulia Turc, Jacob Eisenstein, Dipanjan Das, et al. 2021. The multiberts: Bert reproductions for robustness analysis. *arXiv preprint arXiv:2106.16163*.

Richard Socher, Alex Perelygin, Jean Wu, Jason Chuang, Christopher D Manning, Andrew Y Ng, and Christopher Potts. 2013. Recursive deep models for semantic compositionality over a sentiment treebank. In *Proceedings of the 2013 conference on empirical methods in natural language processing*, pages 1631–1642.

Alex Wang, Amanpreet Singh, Julian Michael, Felix Hill, Omer Levy, and Samuel Bowman. 2018. GLUE: A multi-task benchmark and analysis platform for natural language understanding. In *Proceedings of the 2018 EMNLP Workshop BlackboxNLP: Analyzing and Interpreting Neural Networks for NLP*, pages 353–355, Brussels, Belgium. Association for Computational Linguistics.

Matthew Watson, Bashar Awwad Shiekh Hasan, and Noura Al Moubayed. 2021. Agree to disagree: When deep learning models with identical architectures produce distinct explanations. *arXiv preprint arXiv:2105.06791*.

Thomas Wolf, Lysandre Debut, Victor Sanh, Julien Chaumond, Clement Delangue, Anthony Moi, Pierric Cistac, Tim Rault, Rémi Louf, Morgan Funtowicz, et al. 2019. Huggingface's transformers: State-of-the-art natural language processing. *arXiv preprint arXiv:1910.03771*.

Tongshuang Wu, Marco Tulio Ribeiro, Jeffrey Heer, and Daniel Weld. 2019. Errudite: Scalable, reproducible, and testable error analysis. In *Proceedings of the 57th Annual Meeting of the Association for Computational Linguistics*, pages 747–763, Florence, Italy. Association for Computational Linguistics.

Tongshuang Wu, Marco Tulio Ribeiro, Jeffrey Heer, and Daniel S Weld. 2021. Polyjuice: Generating counterfactuals for explaining, evaluating, and improving models. In *Proceedings of the 59th Annual Meeting of the Association for Computational Linguistics*.

Yige Xu, Xipeng Qiu, Ligao Zhou, and Xuanjing Huang. 2020. Improving bert fine-tuning via self-ensemble and self-distillation. *arXiv preprint arXiv:2002.10345*.

Ruiqi Zhong, Dhruba Ghosh, Dan Klein, and Jacob Steinhardt. 2021. Are larger pretrained language models uniformly better? comparing performance at the instance level. In *Findings of the Association for Computational Linguistics: ACL-IJCNLP 2021*, pages 3813–3827, Online. Association for Computational Linguistics.

A Technical Details

For model training, we make use of the HuggingFace (Wolf et al., 2019) pipeline and train the models on a single GeForce RTX 2080 Ti. We use the same hyperparameter settings as reported by Lan et al. (2020). The visualization of the learning rate schedules can be seen in Figure 3.

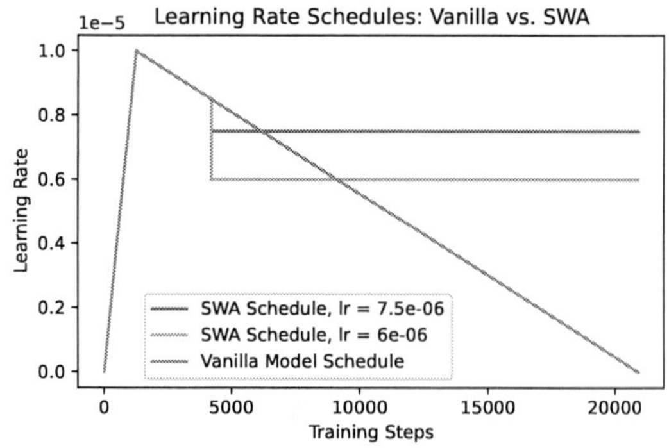

Figure 3: All the different learning rate schedules start identically with 1256 warmup steps to 1e-5. For the vanilla models (the green line) the learning rate anneals linearly to 0 till the 20935th step. This is in accordance with the hyperparameters reported in Lan et al. (2020). For the SWA models, after the second epoch, the learning rate drops to one of the specified learning rates (blue or orange lines) and stays constant.

As the HuggingFace pipeline does not provide the labels for the test set of SST-2, we match the phrases of the test set in HuggingFace with the phrases in the SST-2 dataset from the *dictionary.txt* file, downloaded from GLUE,[7] to get their phrase IDs. Then we use those IDs to extract the labels from *sentiment_labels.txt*. Every label above 0.6 is mapped to *positive* and equal to or lower than 0.4 is mapped to *negative*, as mentioned in the instructions of the *README.md* file. Some sentences are matched manually as they differ only in British vs. American English spelling.

B Results of Excluded Capabilities

For completeness, we also show the results for capabilities excluded from our analysis. For *Add Negations* and *Negation of Negative Sentences* we generated automatic test cases but the labels were not always correct upon investigation. Hence, we left these two capabilities out of the analysis.

In Table 5 we show the Fleiss' Kappa values, the error rates per capability for the vanilla and SWA models can be found in Figure 4a and Figure 4b, respectively. The variation in error rates and overlap ratios between vanilla and SWA models can be found in the Figures 5a and 5b respectively. All the results are with the five initial random seeds, *Random Seed 0* included.

[7] `https://gluebenchmark.com/tasks`

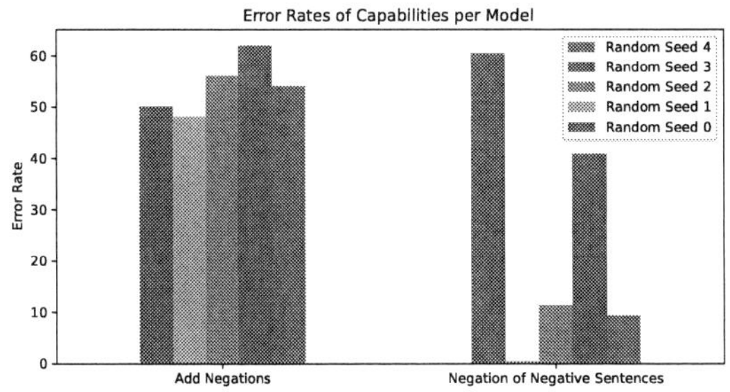

(a) Error rates of each vanilla random seed for the excluded capabilities.

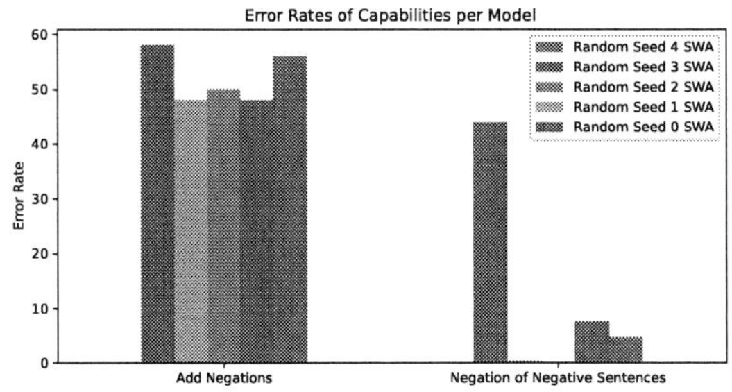

(b) Error rates of each SWA random seed for the excluded capabilities.

Figure 4: Comparison of error rates of vanilla and SWA models for the excluded capabilities.

	Vanilla	SWA	Difference
Add Negations	0.475553	0.470416	-0.005136
Negation of Negative Sentences	-0.025882	-0.066728	-0.040845

Table 5: Fleiss' Kappa values of the excluded capabilities.

C CheckList Results with Random Seed 0

We present our results on CheckList with *Random Seed 0* as well for transparency. We again present the Fleiss' Kappa values for the CheckList capabilities in Table 6. The error rates of each capability per vanilla and SWA models can be found in Figures 6a and 6b. We also plot the variation in error rates (Figure 7a) and overlap ratios (Figure 7b).

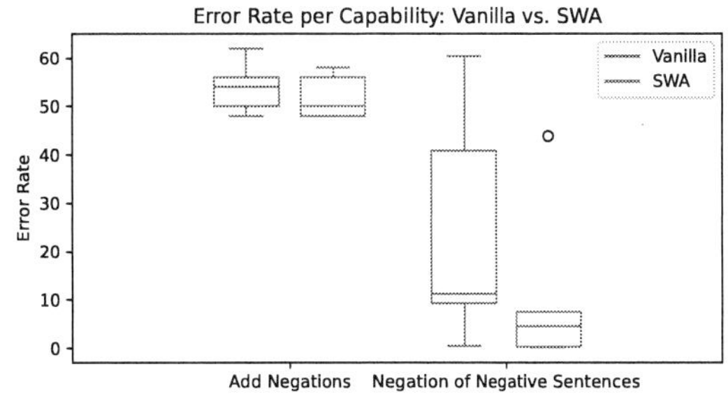

(a) Comparison of variation in error rates between vanilla (red boxes) and SWA models (blue boxes), for the excluded capabilities.

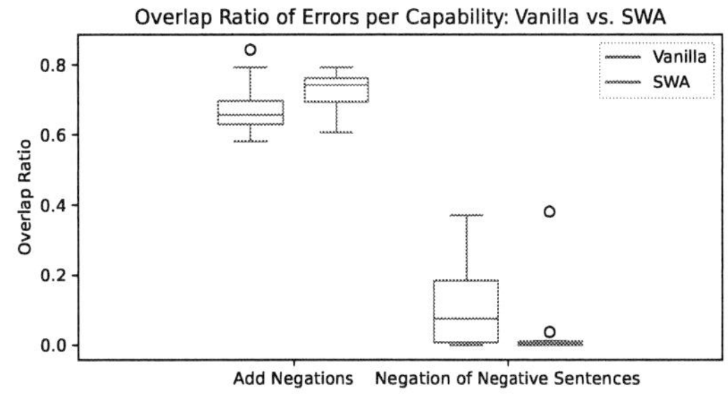

(b) Comparison of variation in overlap ratios between vanilla (red boxes) and SWA models (blue boxes), for the excluded capabilities.

Figure 5: Comparing the variation of error rates and overlap ratios for the excluded capabilities.

D CheckList Capabilities

In Table 7 we describe each CheckList capability that we test for. For perturbing capabilities such as *Negative names, Positive instances* and its other variants, we extract names from the SST-2 training set with Spacy (Honnibal et al., 2020). Due to false positives, we manually remove names that do not refer to a person, such as movie names and historical figures. Per name, we calculate the mean of labels of the instances it occurs in. This way, we can select positive and negative names to perturb test set instances with.

As reviews were predominantly about Hollywood, we also perturbed instances talking specifically about it. We compile a list of around 10 other movie industries,[8] based on how many movies are produced[9] and revenue.

[8] https://en.wikipedia.org/wiki/List_of_Hollywood-inspired_nicknames

[9] https://en.wikipedia.org/wiki/Film_industry#Statistics

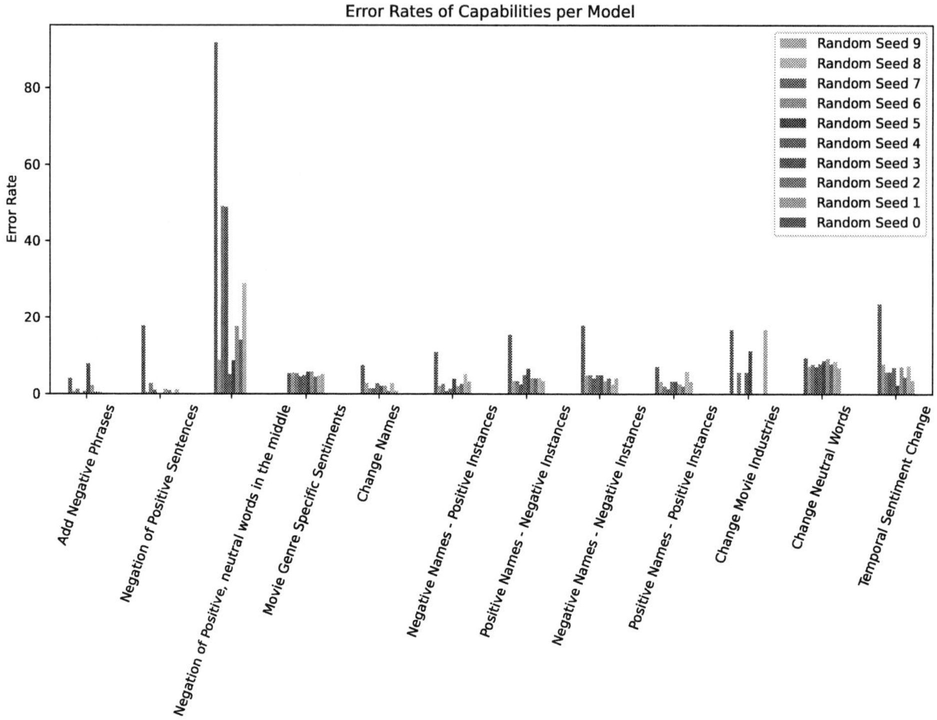

(a) Error rates of each vanilla random seed for each CheckList capability.

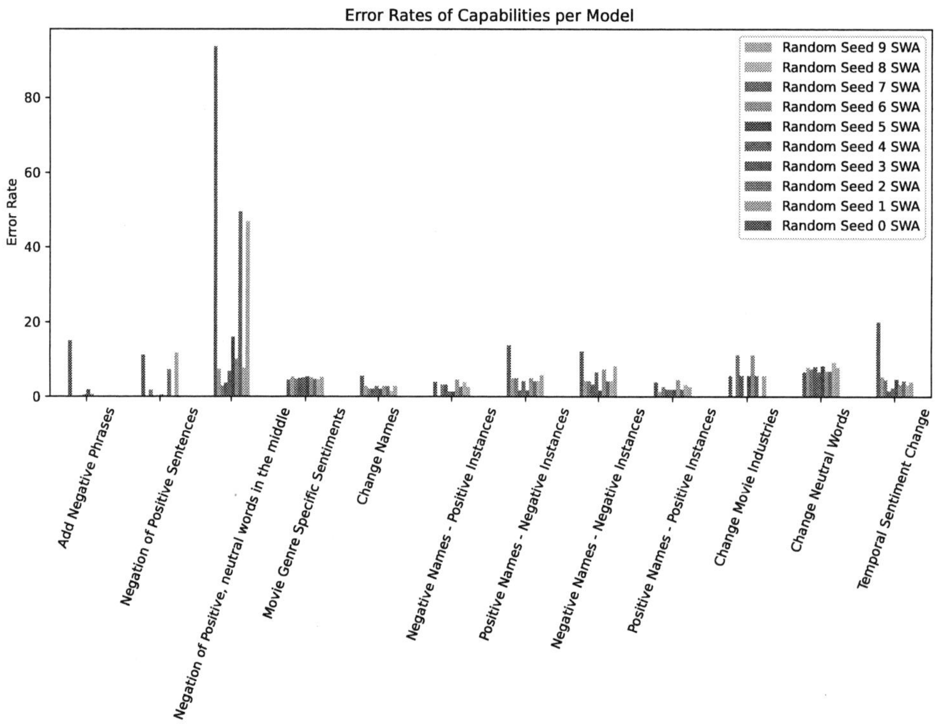

(b) Error rates of each SWA random seed for each CheckList capability.

Figure 6: Comparison of error rates per capability of vanilla and SWA models with all the 10 random seeds.

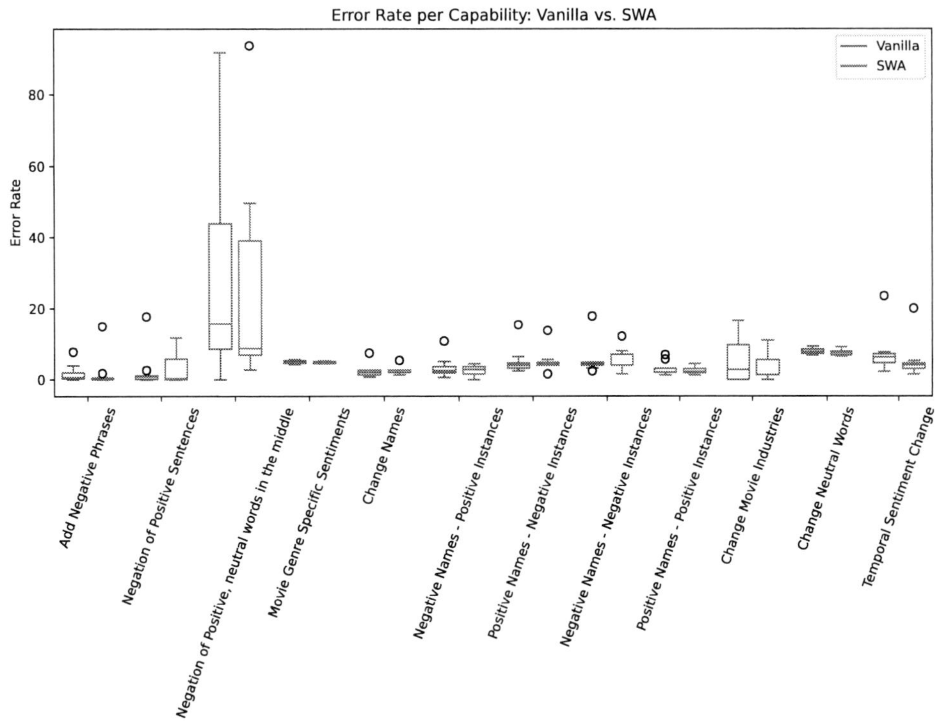

(a) Comparison of variation in error rates between vanilla (red boxes) and SWA models (blue boxes), showcased per CheckList capability. Outliers are indicated with a circle.

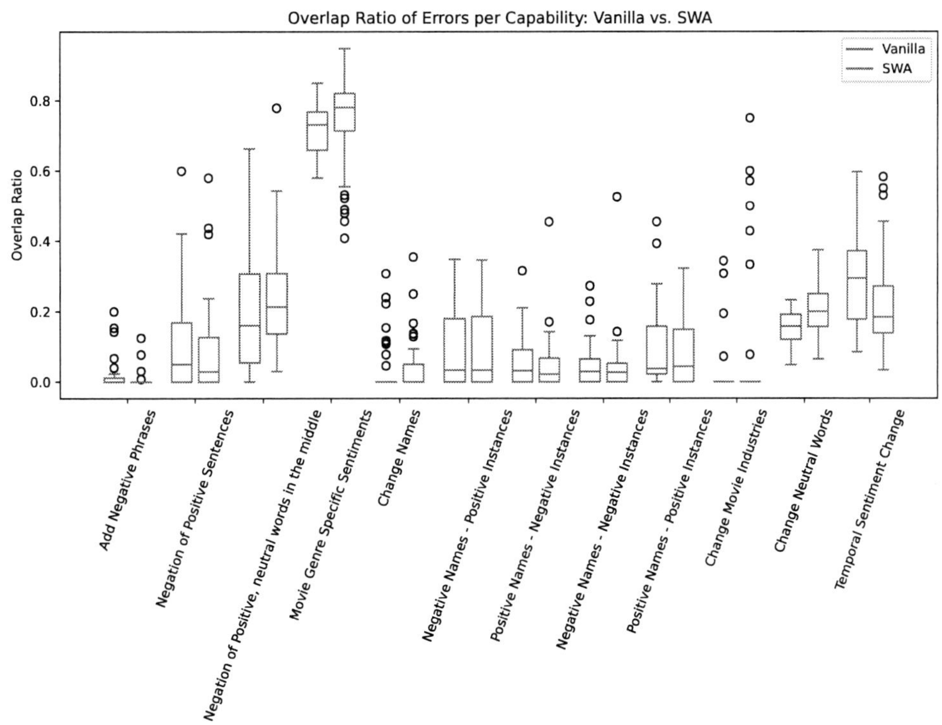

(b) Comparison of variation in overlap ratios between vanilla (red boxes) and SWA models (blue boxes), showcased per CheckList capability. Outliers are indicated with a circle.

Figure 7: Comparing the variation of error rates and overlap ratios per capability for vanilla and SWA models, including results from *Random Seed 0*.

	Vanilla	**SWA**	**Difference**
Negation of Positive Sentences	0.048956	0.031777	-0.017179
Negation of Positive, neutral words in the middle	0.132425	0.150507	0.018082
Movie Genre Specific Sentiments	0.583256	0.590209	0.006952
Sentiment-laden Words in Context	0.000000	0.000000	0.000000
Temporal Sentiment Change	0.335020	0.428743	0.093723
Movie Industries Sentiments	-0.048387	-0.036866	0.011521
Change Names	-0.046527	-0.074413	-0.027887
Negative Names - Positive Instances	-0.007656	-0.007270	0.000386
Positive Names - Negative Instances	-0.044586	-0.067630	-0.023044
Negative Names - Negative Instances	-0.046272	-0.061678	-0.015406
Positive Names - Positive Instances	0.001146	0.017189	0.016043
Change Movie Industries	-0.041426	-0.042046	-0.000620
Change Neutral Words	0.072667	0.124769	0.052101
Add Positive Phrases	-0.058824	-0.043796	0.015028
Add Negative Phrases	-0.051318	-0.021295	0.030023

Table 6: Fleiss' Kappa values of the vanilla and SWA models on the misclassifications on the CheckList tests separately, all the 10 random seeds, including outlier *Random Seed 0*. The first part of the table shows the MFT capabilities, the second part are the INV capabilities, and the third part are the DIR capabilities.

Capability	Test Type	#Examples	Description	Original CheckList Name
Single Positive Words	MFT	22	Positive words that should be predicted *positive* (e.g. beautiful, brilliant, enjoyed).	
Single Negative Words	MFT	14	Negative words that should be predicted *negative* (e.g. hate, disliked, dreaded).	
Sentiment-laden Words in Context	MFT	1350	Sentences that contain positive or negative words about movie-related sentiments (e.g. "I despise that director").	
Temporal Sentiment Change	MFT	2152	Sentences that contain a change in sentiment over time regarding movies. Expectations are that depending on the final sentiment, the predictions are positive or negative.	used to, but now
Negation of Positive Sentences	MFT	1350	Sentences with a negation of a positive sentiment. Predictions should be negative.	Simple negations: negative
Negation of Positive, neutral words in the middle	MFT	500	Negation of a positive sentence, with a neutral sentiment in the middle. Should be negative.	Simple negations: not negative
Movie Genre Specific Sentiments	MFT	736	Sentences with sentiments that are specific for a movie genre, such as horror movies being scary (positive). Based on the sentiment, prediction should be negative or positive.	
Movie Sentiments	MFT	58	Simple sentences about movies. Based on the sentiment, could be predicted as negative or positive.	
Movie Industries Sentiments	MFT	1200	Sentences that talk about movie industries in a positive and negative way and the predictions should be accordingly.	
Change Neutral Words	INV	500 / 3846	Neutral words are changed with BERT, such as "that", "this", "of", etc. Expect the prediction to stay the same.	change neutral words with BERT
Change Names	INV	147 / 1617	Changes the name in a review. Expectation is that the prediction stays the same.	
Negative names - Positive instances	INV	157 / 1727	Change names in positive reviews with names from training set that were only in negative reviews. Expectation is that predictions stay the same.	Polarizing Negative Names - Positive Instances
Positive names - Negative instances	INV	123 / 1353	Change names in negative reviews with names from training set that were only in positive reviews. Expectation is that predictions stay the same.	Polarizing Positive names - Negative instances
Negative names - Negative instances	INV	123 / 1353	Change names in negative reviews with names from training set that were only in negative reviews. Expectation is that predictions stay the same.	Polarizing Negative names - Negative instances
Positive names - Positive instances	INV	157 / 1727	Change names in positive reviews with names from training set that were only in positive reviews. Expectation is that predictions stay the same.	Polarizing Positive names - Positive instances
Change Movie Industries	INV	18 / 252	Changes a movie industry (Hollywood) to another one in movie reviews. After changing, the prediction should stay the same.	
Add Positive Phrases	DIR	500 / 5500	Add a positive phrase to a review, expecting the prediction confidence for positive to go up.	
Add Negative Phrases	DIR	500 / 5000	Add a negative phrase to a review, expecting the prediction confidence for negative to go up.	

Table 7: Overview of all the CheckList capabilities, with the test type, amount of examples, and a description of the capability provided. For clarity, we also provide the name of the capabilities originally used in the code, if they are not the same.

StoryDB: Broad Multi-language Narrative Dataset

Alexey Tikhonov
Yandex
Berlin, Germany
altsoph@gmail.com

Igor Samenko
ICT RAS
Novosibirsk, Russia

Ivan P. Yamshchikov
LEYA Laboratory
Yandex and
Higher School of Economincs
St. Petersburg, Russia
ivan@yamshchikov.info

Abstract

This paper presents StoryDB — a broad multi-language dataset of narratives. StoryDB is a corpus of texts that includes stories in 42 different languages. Every language includes 500+ stories. Some of the languages include more than 20 000 stories. Every story is indexed across languages and labeled with tags such as a genre or a topic. The corpus shows rich topical and language variation and can serve as a resource for the study of the role of narrative in natural language processing across various languages including low resource ones. We also demonstrate how the dataset could be used to benchmark three modern multilanguage models, namely, mDistillBERT, mBERT, and XLM-RoBERTa.

1 Introduction

Stories are central to human culture and communication. However, it seems that stories are easier said than generated. Despite incredible recent progress in natural language processing generation of longer texts is still a challenge (van Stegeren and Theune, 2019; Rashkin et al., 2020). Ostermann et al. (2019) present a machine comprehension corpus for the end-to-end evaluation of script knowledge with 50% of the questions in the corpus that require script knowledge for the correct answer. The authors demonstrate that though the task is not challenging to humans, existing machine comprehension models fail to perform well on the data, even if they make use of a commonsense knowledge base.

Partially, this challenge could be attributed to the lack of adequate memory models. Longer texts demand better memory mechanisms and possible ways to construct such mechanisms are discussed in the literature for the last 25 years. Long short-term memory networks (Hochreiter and Schmidhuber, 1997), Neural Turing Machines (Graves et al., 2014), memory networks (Weston et al., 2014) and many other architectures try to tackle this problem. Attempts to introduce some form of memory in transformers, such as (Guo et al., 2019) or (Burtsev and Sapunov, 2020), could be regarded as the next steps in this long line of work.

There are some interesting recent attempts to generate long texts using some form that makes such longer text feasible for a human reader. For example, Agafonova et al. (2020) generate a diary of a neural network. Yet the generation of a narrative is still challenging. For a detailed review of earlier approaches to narrative generation, we address the reader to (Kybartas and Bidarra, 2016). Even modern models for narrative generation rely heavily on some form of expert knowledge or some type of hierarchical structure of the narrative. For example, Fan et al. (2019) first generate the predicate-argument structure of the text, then generate a surface realization of the predicate-argument structure, finally replace the entity placeholders with context-sensitive names and references. Fan et al. (2019); Ammanabrolu et al. (2020) propose a hierarchical generation framework that first plans a storyline, and then generate a story based on it. present a technique for preprocessing textual story data into event sequences. Xu et al. (2018) develop a model that first generates the most critical phrases, called skeleton, and then expands the skeleton to a complete and fluent sentence. Similarly, Martin et al. (2018) provide a mid-level of abstraction between words and a sentence to minimize event sparsity and present a technique for automated story generation whereby the problem is decomposed into the generation of successive events and the generation of natural language sentences from events. Finally, Brahman et al. (2020) develop an approach, where the user provides the model with such mid-level sentence abstractions in the form of cue phrases during the generation process.

However, we should take into consideration that modern Natural Language Processing (NLP) is fun-

Proceedings of the 58th Annual Meeting of the Association for Computational Linguistics, pages 32–39

https://doi.org/10.26615/978-954-452-056-4_004

damentally an experimental discipline, so the lack of dedicated data could be another bottleneck for the development of narrative generation. This paper tries to amend this problem.

Unfortunately, the majority of available narrative datasets deal with some constrained form of a short plot that is usually called *scenario*. These scenarios are centered around common activities, i.e. going grocery shopping or taking a shower. These narrative datasets available in the literature are also extremely small and could not be used with the most advanced modern NLP models. Regneri et al. (2010) collect 493 event sequence descriptions for 22 behavior scenarios. Modi et al. (2016) present InScript dataset that consists of 1,000 stories centered around 10 different scenarios. Wanzare et al. (2019) provide 200 scenarios and attempt to identify all references to them in a collection of narrative texts. Mostafazadeh et al. (2016) present a corpus of 50k five-sentence commonsense stories. Finally, there is an MPST dataset that contains 14K movie plot synopses, (Kar et al., 2018), and WikiPlots[1] that contains 112 936 story plots extracted from English language Wikipedia. Recently Malysheva et al. (2021) provided a dataset of TV series along with an instrument for narrative arc analysis. These datasets are useful yet as well as a vast majority of the narrative datasets they are only available in English.

This paper provides a large multi-language dataset of stories in natural language. The stories have a cross-language index and every story and character are cross-linked if they occur in different languages. Additionally, the texts have tags such as a genre or a topic. This is the first story dataset of such magnitude that we know of. We hope that a large dataset of long storylines could be used for various aspects of narrative research as well as to facilitate experiments with end-to-end narrative generation.

2 Data

StoryDB is motivated by several interesting experiments that used WikiPlots — one of the larger English datasets of narratives available for all-purpose narrative research that we have mentioned earlier. Seeing various applications that Wikiplots dataset found in the NLP community, we believe, that Sto ryDB would be even more useful due to multiple languages, advanced filtering that guarantees higher quality of obtained data, and genre tagging. To improve reproducibility and make StoryDB usable as Wikipedia is further updated we publish the data as well as the code for the filtering pipeline[2]. The stories that form StoryDB are extracted from any Wikipedia article that contains a sub-header that contains the word "plot" (e.g., "Plot", "Plot Summary", etc.) in a corresponding language.

2.1 Dataset structure

The dataset consists of several index files and includes a directory `plots`. Every file in the directory has a similar structure. Two first letters of the filename stand for the ISO 639-1[3] code of the language for the texts presented in the file. For example, `hy_plots.tsv` contains 4 861 plots in Armenian language. The file `simple_plots.tsv` contains stories in Simple English. Every entry in the plots file has a similar structure and includes the following fields:

- ID — the unique number of a plot that is the same across every language in the dataset;
- Lang — the language of this particular entry;
- Link — a link to the Wikipedia page containing the plot;
- Title — the title of the story;
- Text — the text of the story;
- Categories — the categories that Wikipedia assigns to this story.

One can navigate across plot files using StoryDB's Index file `plot_matrix.tsv`. The rows of the file stand for languages. If a given plot is available in a given language then the title of this plot stands in the corresponding cell of the `plot_matrix.tsv`. For example, if "Wee free men" is available in Simple English it could be found by its title in the corresponding `simple_plots.tsv`. StoryDB also includes `plot_rake.tsv` that contains keywords extracted with RAKE algorithm (Rose et al., 2010) for every story.

Finally, the files `ID_lang_tag.tsv` and `ID_tag_average.tsv` include information about tags that correspond to the given story. We discuss tagging procedure in detail later.

[1] https://github.com/markriedl/WikiPlots

[2] https://drive.google.com/drive/folders/1RCWk7pyvIpubtsf-f2pIsfqTkvtV80Yv

[3] https://en.wikipedia.org/wiki/ISO_639-1

2.2 Preprocessing

Our motivation is to provide a dataset of storylines for various languages including the low-resource ones. Roughly speaking, we want to be sure that every story that ends up in StoryDB is a legitimate storyline description in the corresponding natural language. Thus we are more interested in the precision of the dataset rather than in the recall. To guarantee a higher quality of the obtained stories we implemented several heuristical filters that we briefly describe here.

English Wikipedia is an order of magnitude bigger than any other Wikipedia both in terms of users and in terms of admins[4]. This makes the English list of storylines to be the most extensive one. We regard it as the least noisy one and use it as a reference source for the filtering procedure. We exclude every page that includes a plot yet has no plot section in English Wikipedia for the same entry.

If Wikipedia in language X has a page with title A and this page is also available in language Y under title B, we list such pair of stories as `[language_X, title_A, language_Y, title_B]`". Every entry in this list is an edge in a graph of stories. Every vertex in this graph has a corresponding name `language, title`. Unlike connected stories from different languages that usually contain similar storylines, the stories listed under the same name in the same language might differ significantly. Say, two stories in language X `[language_X, title_A]` and `[language_X, title_B]` are both linked to one story in another language Y `[language_Y, title_C]`. To avoid such ambiguities we exclude fully connected components that contain more than one entry in the same language. Obtained list of stories ends up in the resulting matrix of stories to navigate the dataset. We experimented with various filtering procedures and found this combination to produce a sufficiently rich dataset with a minimum amount of duplicates.

StoryDB is also equipped with a catalog of characters. If a given character that has an individual Wikipedia page is mentioned in a story, its description in the original language is saved into the corresponding tsv-file alongside the ID of a story and the language of the description.

[4]https://meta.wikimedia.org/wiki/List_of_Wikipedias

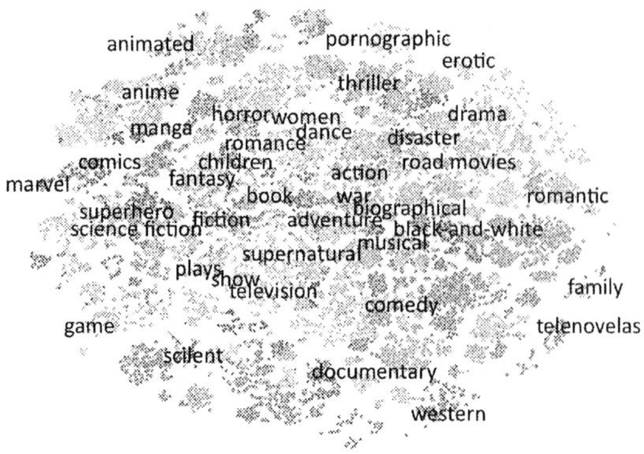

Figure 1: t-SNE visualisation for plots in StoryDB clustered according to their tags. Figure shows centroids of the tags with higher variance across the dataset.

2.3 Tagging

We annotate the resulting stories using meta-information on categories from Wiki API[5]. For every plot, we list all translated categories marked in every language in which this plot is available. Then we search these category lists for substrings that include tags from the manually created list of tags[6]. This allows us to proved language-specific tags for every language, that are listed in `ID_lang_tag.tsv`. For example, Czech version of Black Night has tags `action; crime; drama; superhero; comics;` and `thriller`, while the same story in Persian has no tag `comics`, but has additional tags `neo-noir; psychological; epic;` and `screenplays;`.

File `ID_tag_average.tsv` includes the scores of the tags available for every story. The scores are calculated as follows: we count the number of times that a given tag is associated with a given story. Then we divide this number over the total number of languages in which the story is represented. The obtained space of tags could be useful for narrative exploration. Every story becomes a vector with every coordinate on the interval $[0, 1]$. Figure 1 shows a t-SNE visualisation of this space (Van der Maaten and Hinton, 2008) alongside the centroids of the more distinctive tags.

2.4 StoryDB

Figure 2 shows the relative size of the datasets in every language presented in StoryDB. English

[5]https://www.mediawiki.org/w/api.php?action=help&modules=query%2Bcategories

[6]The list of tags is published with the dataset.

heavily dominates followed by Italian, French, Russian, and German.

There are more than 20 languages that have three thousand or more stories available, including such languages as Finnish, Hungarian, or Persian. Table 1 summarises some of the resulting parameters of the obtained dataset.

Story DB	
Number of languages	42
Median # of stories in a language	2 772
Maximal # of stories in a language	63 756
Minimum # of stories in a language	568

Table 1: Some resulting parameters of the StoryDB.

3 Evaluation

We have used three modern transformer-based architectures for the evaluation:

- mBERT[7] (Devlin et al., 2018) — a multi-language version of BERT;
- mDistilBERT[8] (Sanh et al., 2019) — a distilled version of multi-language BERT;
- XLM-Roberta[9] (Conneau et al., 2020) — a model that is two times larger than BERT in terms of the number of parameters.

These models are the most widely used multi-language models to date. The results of the experiments are publicly available at Weights and Biases[10], see (Biewald, 2020). The evaluation was performed on ten largest languages in StoryDB, namely: English — 'en', French — 'fr', Italian — 'it', Russian — 'ru', German — 'de', Dutch — 'nl', Ukrainian — 'uk', Portuguese — 'pt', Polish — 'pl', and Spanish — 'es'.

We evaluated three tasks:

- Task A. Multilabel classification for tags on a multilanguage corpus of plots;
- Task B. Multilabel classification for tags in cross-lingual learning;
- Task C. Multilabel classification for tags in cross-lingual learning with a corpus of overlapping plots that occur in every language.

	Hamming Score	Multilabel Accuracy
mDistillBERT	0.47	0.31
mBERT	0.50	0.33
XLM-RoBERTa	0.50	0.33

Table 2: Task A. Hamming score and multilabel accuracy for the vector of predicted tags on a validation set. Training data consists of sixteen thousand plots in ten languages, with one tenth of the dataset in every language.

Let us now describe every task in detail.

3.1 Task A

We have sampled the ten most frequents tags out of StoryDB (tag 'film' was the most frequent yet was excluded as a somewhat redundant one). These tags were: 'drama', 'comedy', 'television', 'fiction', 'series', 'action', 'thriller', 'black-and-white', 'science fiction', 'horror'. These ten tags form a vector, where every dimension corresponds to one particular tag. '1' encodes the presence of the tag and '0' stands for the absence of it.

For every language out of the top ten in StoryDB, we have sampled 2000 plots such that every plot has at least one tag out of the list of the ten most popular tags. In Task A the plots were sampled randomly for every language, so there is some overlap between languages. On average, 2% of the plots in one language reoccur in another one. It is important to note that the set of tags for a given plot might differ across languages and one plot could have several tags simultaneously. Thus, multilabel classification is a natural evaluation task under these circumstances.

Since the dataset is not balanced with respect to tags we used the binary cross-entropy loss[11] over the vector of tags. Table 2 and Table 3 sum up the results of three models on a multilanguage dataset of plots. Further details across languages and tags are available online[12].

3.2 Task B

Now let us do a similar setup yet train every model on one language in StoryDB and test its accuracy

[7] https://huggingface.co/bert-base-multilingual-cased

[8] https://huggingface.co/distilbert-base-multilingual-cased

[9] https://huggingface.co/xlm-roberta-base

[10] https://wandb.ai/altsoph/storydb _eval.task1
https://wandb.ai/altsoph/storydb_eval.task3
https://wandb.ai/altsoph/storydb_eval.task3

[11] https://pytorch.org/docs/stable/generated/torch.nn.BCELoss.html

[12] https://wandb.ai/altsoph/storydb_eval.task1

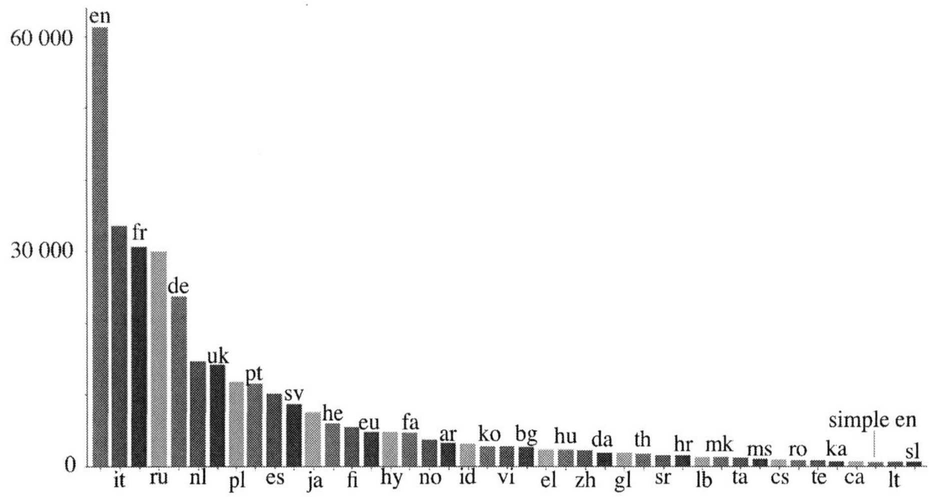

Figure 2: Number of stories in every language that has more that five hundred entries in StoryDB.

	mD-BERT	mBERT	XLM-R
Comedy	0.69	0.67	0.69
Action	0.67	0.70	0.67
Fiction	0.78	0.80	0.81
Thriller	0.67	0.63	0.64
Horror	0.70	0.76	0.75
Drama	0.73	0.74	0.74
Series	0.77	0.78	0.78
Television	0.74	0.76	0.76
Science Fiction	0.78	0.80	0.81
Black and White	0.68	0.65	0.62

Table 3: Task A. AUC-ROC for binary tag classifiers on a validation set. Training data consists of sixteen thousand plots in ten languages, with one tenth of the dataset in every language.

on another language. The parameters of the training datasets and labels are the same as in Task A above but every model is trained on one dataset and is then tested on other languages. Table 4 show the performance of mBERT, yet mDistillBERT and XLM-RoBERTa demonstrate similar behavior. The detailed results could be found online[13].

Table 4 demonstrates that if we train the model on one language and validate it on the other the quality of the multilabel tag classification drops. This drop varies across languages and tends to be smaller for the languages that belong to the same language family.

3.3 Task C

The last validation is similar to Task B, yet now we sample plots that overlap in every language. This limits us to 1500 plots in six languages that we split into train and test. Now every plot occurs in every language. Table 5 shows the model manages to recover certain tags in one language after the pre-training on the other. Table 5 shows the performance of XLM-RoBERTa, yet mDistillBERT and mBERT demonstrate similar behavior. The performance of the models tends to be better on overlapping plots if we compare it to Task B. The detailed results could be found online[14].

The multilabel accuracy for tag prediction declines further yet it can neither be attributed to specific lexical properties of a particular language nor any form of overlap of plots across languages.

[13]https://wandb.ai/altsoph/storydb_eval.task2

[14]https://wandb.ai/altsoph/storydb_eval.task3

	en	de	nl	fr	it	es	pt	ru	uk	pl
en	0.36	0.16	0.14	0.16	0.10	0.17	0.15	0.13	0.12	0.15
de	0.15	0.40	0.16	0.18	0.12	0.16	0.20	0.19	0.18	0.21
nl	0.20	0.33	0.41	0.20	0.22	0.32	0.29	0.31	0.25	0.30
fr	0.16	0.20	0.16	0.51	0.13	0.18	0.18	0.16	0.14	0.19
it	0.19	0.30	0.24	0.21	0.21	0.26	0.28	0.27	0.24	0.30
es	0.23	0.24	0.20	0.22	0.18	0.45	0.27	0.22	0.22	0.23
pt	0.15	0.21	0.17	0.22	0.10	0.19	0.44	0.19	0.14	0.23
ru	0.12	0.21	0.16	0.13	0.12	0.20	0.22	0.45	0.16	0.20
uk	0.10	0.20	0.16	0.14	0.09	0.19	0.19	0.23	0.25	0.20
pl	0.19	0.27	0.19	0.21	0.11	0.20	0.24	0.24	0.20	0.48

Table 4: Task B. Multilabel accuracy for the vector of predicted tags by mBERT. Training data consists of one thousand six hundred plots in one language. Every row shows validation accuracy of a model pretrained on the corresponding language and validated on the plots in a language from the corresponding column.

	en	de	nl	fr	it	es
en	0.29	0.16	0.12	0.12	0.10	0.08
de	0.27	0.31	0.18	0.19	0.15	0.11
nl	0.34	0.30	0.32	0.17	0.13	0.17
fr	0.22	0.20	0.16	0.27	0.15	0.10
it	0.34	0.29	0.23	0.25	0.25	0.16
ru	0.25	0.21	0.18	0.18	0.18	0.13

Table 5: Task C. Multilabel accuracy for the vector of predicted tags by XLM-RoBERTa across the dataset of plots withour cross-language overlaps. Training data consists of one thousand two hundred plots in one language. Every row shows validation accuracy of a model pretrained on the corresponding language and validated on the plots in a language from the corresponding column.

This series of evaluation tasks demonstrates two crucial properties of StoryDB:

- StoryDB could be used to work with narrative structures on the most abstract cross-lingual level;
- StoryDB allows controlling for various cross-lingual similarities of plots during ablation experiments with models of narrative.

4 Discussion

We believe that a broad multilanguage dataset of narratives can facilitate several areas of narrative research.

- Cross-cultural research of narrative structure. StoryDB provides possibilities to compare the structure of narrative in various languages. Since StoryDB includes every story in its original language and is equipped with a universal system of tags it is a natural source for such cross-cultural research.
- Classification of narratives. StoryDB includes an extensive amount of narratives for various languages alongside their genre tags. This allows to develop new methods for narrative classification as well as extensively test the ones that already exist, see for example (Reiter et al., 2014).
- Quantitative research of the narrative structure. (y Pérez, 2007) represents a story as a cluster of emotional links and tensions between characters that progress over storytime. StoryDB includes the description of the plots alongside the key characters. Such information could be insightful for a deeper quantitative understanding of narrative as a by-product of character interaction.
- Summarization of narrative. Parallel corpora in different languages contain similar descriptions of the narrative that could vary in terms of details and length. That makes StoryDB a useful tool for potential narrative summarization research such as (Barros et al., 2019).
- End-to-end narrative generation. StoryDB is the first dataset of narratives that we know of that contains narrative descriptions in various natural languages.

5 Conclusion

This paper presents StoryDB — a broad multi-language dataset of narratives. We describe the construction of the dataset, provide the code for the whole pipeline, list the parameters of the resulting dataset, and briefly discuss several areas of natural language processing research, where StoryDB could be useful for the community.

We hope that StoryDB could be broadened as more plot descriptions are added to various languages. These considerations make StoryDB a flexible resource that would be relevant for the NLP community as the subfield of quantitative narrative research moves on.

References

Yana Agafonova, Alexey Tikhonov, and Ivan P Yamshchikov. 2020. Paranoid transformer: Reading narrative of madness as computational approach to creativity. *Future Internet*, 12(11):182.

Prithviraj Ammanabrolu, Ethan Tien, Wesley Cheung, Zhaochen Luo, William Ma, Lara J Martin, and Mark O Riedl. 2020. Story realization: Expanding plot events into sentences. In *Proceedings of the AAAI Conference on Artificial Intelligence*, volume 34, pages 7375–7382.

Cristina Barros, Elena Lloret, Estela Saquete, and Borja Navarro-Colorado. 2019. Natsum: Narrative abstractive summarization through cross-document timeline generation. *Information Processing & Management*, 56(5):1775–1793.

Lukas Biewald. 2020. Experiment tracking with weights and biases. Software available from wandb.com.

Faeze Brahman, Alexandru Petrusca, and Snigdha Chaturvedi. 2020. Cue me in: Content-inducing approaches to interactive story generation. In *Proceedings of the 1st Conference of the Asia-Pacific Chapter of the Association for Computational Linguistics and the 10th International Joint Conference on Natural Language Processing*, pages 588–597.

Mikhail S Burtsev and Grigory V Sapunov. 2020. Memory transformer. *arXiv preprint arXiv:2006.11527*.

Alexis Conneau, Kartikay Khandelwal, Naman Goyal, Vishrav Chaudhary, Guillaume Wenzek, Francisco Guzmán, Édouard Grave, Myle Ott, Luke Zettlemoyer, and Veselin Stoyanov. 2020. Unsupervised cross-lingual representation learning at scale. In *Proceedings of the 58th Annual Meeting of the Association for Computational Linguistics*, pages 8440–8451.

Jacob Devlin, Ming-Wei Chang, Kenton Lee, and Kristina Toutanova. 2018. BERT: pre-training of deep bidirectional transformers for language understanding. *CoRR*, abs/1810.04805.

Angela Fan, Mike Lewis, and Yann Dauphin. 2019. Strategies for structuring story generation. In *Proceedings of the 57th Annual Meeting of the Association for Computational Linguistics*, pages 2650–2660.

Alex Graves, Greg Wayne, and Ivo Danihelka. 2014. Neural turing machines. *arXiv preprint arXiv:1410.5401*.

Qipeng Guo, Xipeng Qiu, Pengfei Liu, Yunfan Shao, Xiangyang Xue, and Zheng Zhang. 2019. Star-transformer. In *Proceedings of the 2019 Conference of the North American Chapter of the Association for Computational Linguistics: Human Language Technologies, Volume 1 (Long and Short Papers)*, pages 1315–1325.

Sepp Hochreiter and Jürgen Schmidhuber. 1997. Long short-term memory. *Neural computation*, 9(8):1735–1780.

Sudipta Kar, Suraj Maharjan, A Pastor López-Monroy, and Thamar Solorio. 2018. Mpst: A corpus of movie plot synopses with tags. In *Proceedings of the Eleventh International Conference on Language Resources and Evaluation (LREC 2018)*.

Ben Kybartas and Rafael Bidarra. 2016. A survey on story generation techniques for authoring computational narratives. *IEEE Transactions on Computational Intelligence and AI in Games*, 9(3):239–253.

Laurens Van der Maaten and Geoffrey Hinton. 2008. Visualizing data using t-sne. *Journal of machine learning research*, 9(11).

Anastasia Malysheva, Alexey Tikhonov, and Ivan P Yamshchikov. 2021. Dyplodoc: Dynamic plots for document classification. *arXiv preprint arXiv:2107.12226*.

Lara J Martin, Srijan Sood, and Mark Riedl. 2018. Dungeons and dqns: Toward reinforcement learning agents that play tabletop roleplaying games. In *INT/WICED@ AIIDE*.

Ashutosh Modi, Tatjana Anikina, Simon Ostermann, and Manfred Pinkal. 2016. Inscript: Narrative texts annotated with script information. In *Proceedings of the Tenth International Conference on Language Resources and Evaluation (LREC'16)*, pages 3485–3493.

Nasrin Mostafazadeh, Nathanael Chambers, Xiaodong He, Devi Parikh, Dhruv Batra, Lucy Vanderwende, Pushmeet Kohli, and James Allen. 2016. A corpus and cloze evaluation for deeper understanding of commonsense stories. In *Proceedings of the 2016 Conference of the North American Chapter of the Association for Computational Linguistics: Human Language Technologies*, pages 839–849.

Simon Ostermann, Michael Roth, and Manfred Pinkal. 2019. Mcscript2. 0: A machine comprehension corpus focused on script events and participants. In *Proceedings of the Eighth Joint Conference on Lexical* *and Computational Semantics (* SEM 2019)*, pages 103–117.

Rafael Pérez y Pérez. 2007. Employing emotions to drive plot generation in a computer-based storyteller. *Cognitive Systems Research*, 8(2):89–109.

Hannah Rashkin, Asli Celikyilmaz, Yejin Choi, and Jianfeng Gao. 2020. Plotmachines: Outline-conditioned generation with dynamic plot state tracking. In *Proceedings of the 2020 Conference on Empirical Methods in Natural Language Processing (EMNLP)*, pages 4274–4295.

Michaela Regneri, Alexander Koller, and Manfred Pinkal. 2010. Learning script knowledge with web experiments. In *Proceedings of the 48th Annual Meeting of the Association for Computational Linguistics*, pages 979–988.

Nils Reiter, Anette Frank, and Oliver Hellwig. 2014. An nlp-based cross-document approach to narrative structure discovery. *Literary and Linguistic Computing*, 29(4):583–605.

Stuart Rose, Dave Engel, Nick Cramer, and Wendy Cowley. 2010. Automatic keyword extraction from individual documents. *Text Mining: Applications and Theory*, pages 1–20.

Victor Sanh, Lysandre Debut, Julien Chaumond, and Thomas Wolf. 2019. Distilbert, a distilled version of bert: smaller, faster, cheaper and lighter. *ArXiv*, abs/1910.01108.

Judith van Stegeren and Mariët Theune. 2019. Narrative generation in the wild: Methods from nanogenmo. In *Proceedings of the Second Workshop on Storytelling*, pages 65–74.

Lilian Diana Awuor Wanzare, Michael Roth, and Manfred Pinkal. 2019. Detecting everyday scenarios in narrative texts. In *Proceedings of the Second Workshop on Storytelling*, pages 90–106.

Jason Weston, Sumit Chopra, and Antoine Bordes. 2014. Memory networks. *arXiv preprint arXiv:1410.3916*.

Jingjing Xu, Xuancheng Ren, Yi Zhang, Qi Zeng, Xiaoyan Cai, and Xu Sun. 2018. A skeleton-based model for promoting coherence among sentences in narrative story generation. In *Proceedings of the 2018 Conference on Empirical Methods in Natural Language Processing*, pages 4306–4315.

SeqScore: Addressing Barriers to Reproducible Named Entity Recognition Evaluation

Chester Palen-Michel and **Nolan Holley** and **Constantine Lignos**
{cpalenmichel, lignos}@brandeis.edu
nrh2@williams.edu
Michtom School of Computer Science
Brandeis University

Abstract

To address a looming crisis of unreproducible evaluation for named entity recognition, we propose guidelines and introduce SeqScore, a software package to improve reproducibility. The guidelines we propose are extremely simple and center around transparency regarding how chunks are encoded and scored. We demonstrate that despite the apparent simplicity of NER evaluation, unreported differences in the scoring procedure can result in changes to scores that are both of noticeable magnitude and statistically significant. We describe SeqScore, which addresses many of the issues that cause replication failures.

1 Introduction

There are many complex tasks in natural language processing (NLP) where current evaluation standards are based around evolving metrics designed to correlate well with human judgments, some complex and some simple. For example, every year sees the introduction and careful evaluation of new metrics for machine translation, summarization, and natural language generation.

However, named entity recognition (NER) and other chunk extraction tasks have largely been evaluated the same way since the CoNLL shared tasks of the early 2000s (Tjong Kim Sang and Buchholz, 2000; Tjong Kim Sang, 2002; Tjong Kim Sang and De Meulder, 2003). Following the CoNLL chunking and NER shared tasks, a true positive prediction typically requires exact matches[1] in span (the tokens or characters in a chunk) and the type assigned to the chunk (e.g., person).

With such a simple metric, it would seem that performing exact match NER evaluation would be trivially simple. Precision, recall, and F1 are easy to compute; all that is required is to count true positives, false positives, and false negatives. But when it comes to evaluation, challenges emerge in how evaluation is actually implemented. In the case of NER, as we will demonstrate these challenges emerge in the process of converting token-level annotations and system predictions into spans.

We do not think it is sufficient to point out these issues without attempting to provide a solution. Inspired by successful efforts in the machine translation community to address similar issues (Post, 2018), we began developing a toolkit and set of practices in summer 2020 to improve the replicability of experiments for NER. Our toolkit, SeqScore, provides researchers the necessary tools to score, validate, and examine both system outputs and annotation. SeqScore is open source and has been publicly released.[2]

This paper provides clear, easy-to-follow guidelines that facilitate reproducibility for NER (and other chunking task) experiments, explains them, provides a toolkit for easily following them, and then presents experiments using SeqScore that shows the impact of following them. The contribution of this paper is that it introduces and justifies guidelines for NER experiment reproducibility and provides a toolkit that makes them easy to follow.

2 Guidelines for reproducibility

We propose that in order to have sound and reproducible NER evaluation, the following guidelines should be followed:

1. Report what chunk encoding scheme was used (e.g. BIO).
2. Use an external scorer—not one internal to the system—and report which scorer was used.
3. Be explicit regarding what form of invalid label sequence repair was used.

[1] While there have been efforts to promote partial matching (Chinchor, 1998; Segura-Bedmar et al., 2013) and focusing on rarer entities (Derczynski et al., 2017), micro-averaaged exact match F1 is still the most common metric in use for NER.

[2] https://github.com/bltlab/seqscore

Proceedings of the 58th Annual Meeting of the Association for Computational Linguistics, pages 40–50

https://doi.org/10.26615/978-954-452-056-4_005

4. Only score against a gold standard that faithfully follows the chunk encoding scheme (e.g. BIO) in use.

5. Use good statistical practices when reporting results.

Many of these will seem like obvious ideas or practices that should be taken as a given. However, we have found almost no papers provide enough information to determine whether they are compliant with all of these guidelines specifically, very few papers report what scorer was used to produce the reported scores, and many that provide accompanying code do not include any evaluation code.

We examined several papers with state of the art NER results on the CoNLL 2003 dataset considering guidelines 1, 2, and 3. Of these papers Liu et al. (2019) follow 1, 2, and 3. Yamada et al. (2020) explicitly follows guidelines 2 and 3. Luoma and Pyysalo (2020) met guideline 1. Akbik et al. (2019) give details of their scoring decision for a previous paper, Akbik et al. (2018), mentioning they fixed an prior error in scoring, but do not explicitly detail how they fixed their scoring procedure for the baseline in Akbik et al. (2019). All other papers we surveyed did not explicitly satisfy guidelines 1, 2, and 3 (Wang et al., 2020, 2021; Shahzad et al., 2021; Baevski et al., 2019; Yu et al., 2020; Jiang et al., 2019; Li et al., 2020; Devlin et al., 2019).

As an example of a common departure from these practices, many papers that perform NER experiments publish the scores produced by NCRF++ (Yang et al., 2018). As previously detailed by Lignos and Kamyab (2020), NCRF++ uses an internal scorer with an undocumented label sequence repair method, so reporting any numbers from it would be contrary to guidelines 2 and 3. As Lignos and Kamyab demonstrated, on a specific subset of models that produce a high number of invalid transitions, that scorer produces F1 scores approximately half a point higher than the most commonly-used external scorer.

Guideline 4, which requires that the annotation precisely follow the chunk encoding scheme, also seems obvious. However, it was not actually followed for 2 of the 4 datasets for the CoNLL NER evaluations in 2002–3, as only the English and Dutch data were free of errors of this type (see Section 3.4). As these datasets are arguably the most famous NER datasets in existence, this is surprising. While this would only have a very minor impact on evaluation results, an evaluation cannot be reproducible if different scorers might interpret the gold standard differently due to differences in how invalid label sequences are handled (see Section 3.2). When examining other NER datasets, we have found more pervasive occurrences of invalid label sequences.

We will not discuss guideline 5 in any detail as practices change over time, but we will highlight the need to report a distribution of scores, rather than a single score. Reimers and Gurevych (2017) demonstrate this clearly for NER specifically, and SeqScore supports aggregating scoring across multiple runs and reporting summary statistics.

Many of these rules may seem like common sense, but by enumerating them, we provide a published "checklist" for researchers to follow.

3 The mechanics of NER evaluation

We now turn to explaining the mechanics of NER evaluation to explain why following these guidelines is important. In this section, we explain the subtleties of working with chunk encodings, which will reinforce the importance of following the first three guidelines.

3.1 The CoNLL tradition

Evaluating named entity recognition (NER) and similar chunking tasks is conceptually straightforward. The primary metrics are the precision, recall, and F1 of the extracted chunks, often called phrases, or for NER specifically, entities or mentions. The CoNLL-2000 shared task on chunking (Tjong Kim Sang and Buchholz, 2000) set the first and most long-lasting standard for distributing data for and evaluating chunking tasks.

Briefly, this standard—which we will call "CoNLL-style"—is that each dataset (train, etc.) is represented in a sentence-split, tokenized, delimited format. Each sentence consists of a sequence of lines, and each line contains at least a token and a label for that token. This format was accompanied by a scoring script, `conlleval`.[3] The labels give information about the spans of the chunks, using encoding schemes that have developed from the original IOB representation of Ramshaw and Marcus (1995).

While some models may use more complex encodings, the current standard for datasets is that

[3] `https://www.clips.uantwerpen.be/conll2000/chunking/conlleval.txt`

chunks are encoded using BIO (begin, inside, outside), where the first token of each chunk receives a B- label, any following tokens in the chunk receive an I- label, and any tokens not contained in a chunk receive O label. This standard format, albeit with minor variations, has been used continuously for NER datasets (Tjong Kim Sang, 2002; Tjong Kim Sang and De Meulder, 2003; Benikova et al., 2014; Derczynski et al., 2017, among others).

Not every evaluation of these type of tasks has used this structure. Many datasets (e.g., Doddington et al., 2004; Hovy et al., 2006; Strassel and Tracey, 2016) use start and end offsets as the primary method of identifying spans, which can avoid issues related to tokenization and completely dissociates the annotation from the encoding of chunks using labels. As we show later, this dissociation automatically removes a major source of non-reproducibility in evaluation.

3.2 Scoring and repair

When it comes to evaluating system output, while the CoNLL-style format is truly simple, the process of using it for evaluation only *seems* simple.

The fundamental problem is that there is generally nothing that forces a system's output—or even the annotation (see Section 3.4)—to follow the intended state machine of the scheme for encoding chunks. While using a CRF may reduce—and constrained decoding (Lester et al., 2020) can eliminate—invalid label transitions, we must still be able to provide reproducible scoring methods for models that do not use these approaches.

As shown in Table 1, if we are using BIO encoding, a system could produce the sequence `O I-ORG`, illegally entering the "inside" state without going through "begin." Similarly, we might encounter a `B-MISC I-ORG` transition, beginning a chunk of type MISC but then continuing into an ORG chunk. Handling these invalid transitions requires an implicit or explicit *repair* method.

3.3 Repairs in practice

Since the `conlleval` scoring script, scoring predicted labels and repairing the invalid sequences that they contain have gone hand in hand. SeqScore follows this tradition, allowing for scoring labels that contain invalid sequences, but unlike `conlleval`, its repair methods are configurable, and unlike any other scorer we are aware of it supports inspecting the repaired label sequences through writing them to a file. By requiring the user to select the repair method and making a previously invisible feature visible, we are making it easy for users to follow guideline 3.

The user can specify whether to perform `conlleval`-style repair, to *discard* invalid sequences, or to make no repairs (*none*), which will raise an error if any invalid sequences are encountered. The differences between these repair methods are show in Table 1. Due to the complexities of attempting to repair invalid label sequences in BIOES,[4] repair is only supported for BIO and IOB encodings.

For example, given an I- followed by another I- of differing type such as `I-ORG I-LOC`, one could coerce either the first or second tag to match the other and maintain that this is all one mention. Another option is to treat the second tag as B- and begin a new mention. The latter is what most scorers do, but it should be noted that this is not *a priori* the correct choice.

As we describe each repair method in more detail, we will use examples from actual output on the CoNLL 2003 English data. We used SeqScore to find the invalid transitions in the BERT (Devlin et al., 2019) model output from Tu and Lignos (2021) and selected examples of each type.

For BIO, the possible invalid transitions are an I- preceded by O (Table 2), an I- preceded by an I- of a different type (Table 3), and an I- preceded by a B- of a different type (Table 4). `conlleval`-style scorers take the approach of changing any unexpected I- to a B- (thus our name "begin repair"), while discard-style scorers discard tokens started by an invalid sequence.

While begin and discard are the dominant repair methods in use, other methods are possible. Stanza's (Qi et al., 2020) undocumented approach (shown in Table 1) most closely resembles the discard repair method but does not discard all invalid sequences. For invalid sequences caused by a type mismatch, Stanza uses the type of the last token as the type for the whole mention, and unlike begin or discard, keeps the entire span as a single mention. For example, `B-ORG I-ORG E-LOC` would be decoded as one mention of type LOC, since LOC is the type of the last token. While we have described the repair methods that we are aware of, others may exist whether intentionally or as accidental deviations from more common repair methods.

[4]See Kroutikov (2019) for a discussion of the large number of ways to score invalid BIOES sequences.

Encoding	his	Liberal	Democratic	party	and	the	Russian	Duma
Valid	O	B-ORG	I-ORG	I-ORG	O	O	B-MISC	B-ORG
Invalid	O	**I-ORG**	I-ORG	I-ORG	O	O	B-MISC	**I-ORG**
Begin Repair	O	B-ORG	I-ORG	I-ORG	O	O	B-MISC	B-ORG
Discard Repair	O	O	O	O	O	O	B-MISC	O
Stanza Repair	O	O	O	O	O	O	B-ORG	I-ORG

Table 1: Valid and invalid BIO label sequences and repairs of the invalid sequence for the sentence fragment *his Liberal Democratic party and the Russian Duma* from the CoNLL-03 English training data (lines 3633–40). Labels that cause invalid transitions are bolded.

Repair	Labels					
None	O	**I-ORG**	I-ORG	O	B-PER	I-PER
Begin	O	**B-ORG**	I-ORG	O	B-PER	I-PER
Discard	O	**O**	O	O	B-PER	I-PER

Table 2: Original and repaired labels for *Trade and Industry Secretary Ian Lang* (CoNLL-03 English)

Repair	Labels				
None	O	B-ORG	I-ORG	**I-LOC**	O
Begin	O	B-ORG	I-ORG	**B-LOC**	O
Discard	O	B-ORG	I-ORG	**O**	O

Table 3: Original and repaired labels for *the Oceanic Control Center in* (CoNLL-03 English)

Lignos and Kamyab (2020) demonstrate the variation that occurs due to different repair methods for invalid label transitions, finding that at least one NER toolkit takes an alternate approach to handling invalid transitions that consistently produces higher F1 scores for some models than scoring with `conlleval`. Its approach is not incorrect; these "edge cases" can be interpreted different ways. However, the result is that different scorers can produce different scores for the same output, even though they claim to measure the same thing.

With these facts in mind, we believe that we are approaching a replicability crisis for NER and other chunking tasks, as scores cannot reliably be compared across papers, and replications can fail due to lack of information about the scoring procedure.

Repair	Labels				
None	O	B-LOC	**I-ORG**	I-ORG	O
Begin	O	B-LOC	**B-ORG**	I-ORG	O
Discard	O	B-LOC	**O**	O	O

Table 4: Original and repaired labels for *(Rangoon) University early* (CoNLL-03 English)

3.4 Invalid transitions in gold standards

Most discussions of invalid label sequences focus on the system output, but widely-used annotated data often contains invalid sequences as well. For example, the CoNLL-02 Spanish data is BIO-encoded but contains three invalid O to I- transitions, one in each of the train, testa, and testb subsets. The original IOB-encoded CoNLL-03 German data contains 10 invalid transitions.[5]

While they may not have major impacts on scores, these invalid sequences represent a replication issue. Any scorer using the discard repair can *remove mentions from the gold standard*; even if the number of mentions removed is small, it is not an acceptable evaluation practice for the scorer to effectively change the gold standard. If two researchers use different repair methods and the annotation contains invalid transitions, they are not only evaluating their system output differently but also not evaluating against the same gold standard.

One of the design tenets of SeqScore is that the detection and repair of invalid label sequences is *explicit* and *configurable*. SeqScore supports validating IO, IOB (IOB1), BIO (IOB2), and the isomorphic BIOES, BILOU, BMES, and BMEOW (Radford et al., 2015) encodings.

Here is an example of validating the CoNLL-02 Spanish training data using SeqScore:

```
$ seqscore validate --labels BIO
esp.train
Encountered 1 errors in 1 tokens, 8323
sequences, and 1 documents in esp.train
Invalid transition O -> I-LOC for token
'San' on line 221619
```

Our recommendation is that validation (and if

[5]We validated the CoNLL-02 Dutch, CoNLL-03 English, GermEval 2014 (Benikova et al., 2014), and W-NUT 2017 Emerging and Rare Entities (Derczynski et al., 2017) data sets and found no issues. The CoNLL-03 German data was corrected in a later BIO-encoded release.

needed, repair) be run on any invalid gold standards before scoring. Doing so guarantees that the gold standard faithfully follows the chunk encoding and has no invalid transitions, so regardless of the repair method used, the gold standard will be interpreted the same way. This practice satisfies guideline 4.

3.5 Label conversion

SeqScore also supports conversion between valid IO, IOB, BIO, BIOES, BMES, and BMEOW encodings using the `convert` subcommand. To prevent malformed output, it raises an error if the input contains any invalid sequences. The input can be repaired using the `repair` subcommand if it is IOB or BIO encoded. By separating repair and conversion, there are no "hidden" changes.

Many other label scheme converters convert labels at the token (rather than mention) level, which allows invalid sequences to propagate from the input to the output, sometimes with unexpected results. For example, Stanza converts to BIOES before scoring, passing along invalid label sequences from BIO to BIOES. While in BIO invalid transitions are limited to invalid I- labels, when invalid BIO sequences are converted to BIOES, there are many potential ways to convert them depending on how the input was interpreted.

4 Experiments

Our paper so far has discussed the importance of following the proposed guidelines but has not quantified the impact of doing so. We conducted a series of experiments on NER datasets to examine the extent to which the variations in scores from different repair methods applied to system outputs could lead to different results. These experiments also demonstrate the usefulness of SeqScore as a package for producing a reproducible and complete set of results for sequence labeling tasks.

As we show in the following experiments, NER using large multilingual models fine-tuned on lower-resourced datasets can show significant variation due to the scoring method used. We selected lower-resourced datasets for two reasons. First, we believe that this a major frontier for innovation in NER, and many new results will be reported in this area for years to come. Second, unlike higher-resourced datasets, the current state of the art for these datasets involves the application of large language models, which are particularly prone to producing invalid transitions.

Lang.	Begin	Discard	Δ	p-value
amh	71.19 ±1.20	**71.87** ±1.11	0.69	0.15
hau	89.78 ±0.41	**90.12** ±0.47	0.34	0.19
ibo	84.18 ±0.94	**84.57** ±0.86	0.39	0.33
kin	73.29 ±1.39	**74.51** ±1.26	1.22	0.06
lug	80.02 ±0.90	**80.32** ±0.85	0.30	0.29
luo	74.43 ±1.60	**74.96** ±1.56	0.53	0.27
pcm	87.89 ±0.72	**88.48** ±0.71	0.59	**0.03**
swa	87.43 ±0.55	**87.79** ±0.62	0.36	0.17
wol	64.74 ±1.82	**65.19** ±1.70	0.45	0.50
yor	77.63 ±0.17	**78.40** ±1.04	0.77	0.07

Table 5: Comparison of F1 scores across repair methods using XLM-R and MasakhaNER data.

Lang.	Begin	Discard	Δ	p-value
hau	86.87 ±0.38	**87.36** ±0.32	0.49	**0.01**
ibo	84.82 ±0.77	**85.14** ±0.72	0.32	0.32
kin	72.14 ±1.07	**73.41** ±1.00	1.27	**0.02**
lug	80.42 ±1.04	**80.83** ±1.05	0.41	0.29
luo	73.37 ±1.52	**74.18** ±1.53	0.81	0.15
pcm	87.97 ±0.62	**88.47** ±0.52	0.50	0.10
swa	86.73 ±0.49	**87.12** ±0.52	0.39	0.13
wol	65.35 ±1.58	**66.29** ±1.58	0.94	0.26
yor	78.96 ±0.86	**79.87** ±0.75	0.91	**0.03**

Table 6: Comparison of F1 scores across repair methods using mBERT and MasakhaNER data.

4.1 Comparing repair methods

We evaluated two multilingual models, multilingual BERT (Devlin et al., 2019) and XLM-R (Conneau et al., 2020), on the MasakhaNER datasets (Adelani et al., 2021) which cover 10 African languages. Both of the models were trained for 50 epochs, using 10 different random seeds; we report the mean and standard deviation (as mean ± std. deviation) of F1 across the seeds. Amharic was excluded from the mBERT experiments, as mBERT was not trained on its character set and thus predicts no names. XLM-R was trained on all 10 MasakhaNER languages.

For each language, we report the difference in mean F1 score between the begin and discard repair methods for all languages except Amharic. We also examine the difference in mean F1 score between two models that are scored using different repair methods. We provide statistical significance of each comparison using the Wilcoxon rank-sum test, which is computed using the ten F1 scores for each configuration. We use the Wilcoxon rank-sum test as it provides a robust comparison between two distributions without assuming that the scores are normally distributed, as there is no guarantee that scores follow such a distribution.

As shown in Tables 5 and 6, the discard repair method universally produces higher F1 scores. Using the significance threshold of $p < 0.05$ (bolded), a handful of the comparisons between repair methods are statistically significant, specifically the mBERT scores for Hausa, Kinyarwanda, and Yoruba and the XLM-R scores for Nigerian Pidgin. The results that are not statistically significant still demonstrate a noteworthy difference in F1, with the discard score being 0.61 points higher than begin on average across all comparisons, statistically significant or not.

It is not obvious why some models show a statistically significant difference with the discard repair method while others do not. Table 7 shows the average count of invalid label sequences across models and languages. While it is notable that Kinyarwanda and Yoruba have higher counts and happen to be significant in experiments using mBERT, Hausa has a comparatively low count as does Nigerian Pidgin which also had significant results (see Tables 5 and 6).

We also performed a small qualitative exploration of invalid transitions. We classified the invalid transitions in three ways: the begin strategy repairs in such a way that the repaired entity is correct, discard correctly discards a system predicted entity where there should be none, or neither correctly repairs the predicted entity. In the case that neither repair method is correct, discard favors a higher F1 since the begin strategy creates a false negative and false positive, while discard creates only a false negative.

We examined the invalid transitions for XLM-R Nigerian Pidgin and Wolof—selected due to having the lowest and highest p-values, respectively—in the test set output from the runs with the median scores.[6] Wolof had 3 of 13 invalid transitions correctly repaired by begin, while discard correctly repaired only 2. For Nigerian Pidgin, begin correctly repaired only 1 of 12 while discard correctly repaired 4 of 12.

While Nigerian Pidgin shows a larger gap between the effectiveness of the two repair methods, ultimately the number of repaired transitions is quite small due to their relative rarity and the small size of data sets for lower-resourced languages and thus it is difficult to draw conclusions. Our analysis could not identify a simple explanation for the differences observed across languages, and this merits further examination in future work.

Lang.	XLM-R	mBERT
amh	13.9 ±4.33	-
hau	11.5 ±3.27	15.7 ±4.06
ibo	19.8 ±6.64	18.8 ±3.80
kin	39.3 ±7.04	40.3 ±8.87
lug	14.9 ±3.92	15.5 ±4.50
luo	12.7 ±5.01	14.9 ±3.93
pcm	17.8 ±6.81	12.9 ±5.59
swa	15.0 ±3.23	15.9 ±3.00
wol	10.8 ±4.07	17.3 ±5.36
yor	32.4 ±6.92	29.6 ±7.88

Table 7: Means and standard deviations of across runs of the number of invalid transitions repaired for system output for each model and language.

4.2 Simulating a real scenario

While we have shown that using a different repair method can sometimes lead to significant differences in F1 scores, using different repair methods on the exact same system output is not what happens in practice. Instead, the current situation is more likely to be that two different system outputs are unknowingly evaluated using differing repair methods by different authors.

To simulate a more likely situation, suppose one researcher has trained an mBERT model and another has trained an XLM-R model but neither explicitly mentions what repair strategy was used while scoring. We will now explore how the use of different repair methods would affect the conclusions drawn from researchers unknowingly using different scoring procedures when comparing their models.

In Table 8, we compare XLM-R using the begin repair to mBERT using discard and XLM-R using the discard repair to mBERT using begin. Suppose one team used XLM-R with the discard method to evaluate on Kinyarwanda while the other used mBERT and begin. The team using XLM-R with discard for scoring would have a score of 74.51 compared with the other team's score of 72.14, for a statistically significant difference in F1 of 2.37. If the teams switched scoring methods, the mean scores are much closer at 73.29 compared with 73.41, reducing the difference between the score to 0.12, which is statistically indistinguishable.

While Kinyarwanda is the most dramatic example, the difference in F1 changes considerably depending on the combination of repair methods used. Of the 9 language datasets, 7 show a change in

[6]As there were an even number of runs (10), we used the higher of the two median runs for each language.

Lang.	XLM-R Begin	mBERT Discard	Δ	p-value	XLM-R Discard	mBERT Begin	Δ	p-value
hau	89.78	87.36	2.42	**0.0002**	90.12	86.87	3.25	**0.0002**
ibo	84.18	85.14	0.96	**0.0233**	84.57	84.82	0.25	0.5708
kin	73.29	73.41	0.12	0.9397	74.51	72.12	2.37	**0.0012**
lug	80.02	80.83	0.81	**0.0494**	80.32	80.42	0.10	0.8206
luo	74.43	74.18	0.25	0.8206	74.96	73.37	1.59	**0.0257**
pcm	87.89	88.47	0.58	**0.0452**	88.48	87.97	0.51	0.1306
swa	87.43	87.12	0.31	0.2265	87.79	86.73	1.06	**0.0012**
wol	64.74	66.29	1.55	0.0696	65.19	65.35	0.16	0.8206
yor	77.63	79.87	2.42	**0.0002**	78.40	78.96	0.56	0.3447

Table 8: Comparison crossing models and repair methods.

whether the difference between models is statistically significant depending on which repair method is used with each model, highlighting the importunt of guideline 3. If in addition to using different repair methods, if one researcher reported their best test set score with no information about the distribution—as we have discovered a recent state of the art NER paper did—there would likely be even larger differences.

These experiments show that if researchers do not report their full scoring procedure, they may inadvertently obfuscate which models actually perform better and their claims of improvement may just be statistical noise. However, if researchers use SeqScore, they can evaluate their system using multiple repair techniques without the risk of using two entirely different scorers, and their evaluations will be replicable by other researchers.

5 Comparison with other toolkits

To place SeqScore in the context of other work and to address the question of novelty, we compare SeqScore to other similar tools.

5.1 Design Considerations

The primary goal of SeqScore is to provide a highly usable scorer for chunk extraction sequence labeling tasks such as NER. But SeqScore is not just a scorer; it is designed to address the entire lifecycle of working with data: validating and examining annotation, converting between various chunk encodings, identifying and repairing invalid label sequences, and finally producing scores. SeqScore is implemented in Python, and like Git it uses subcommands to perform each task, for example `score` to score, and `validate` to validate files. While other packages exist for scoring and handling invalid label sequences, no other package has the convenience of everything in one place.

We believe this convenience lessens the barriers to providing more detailed reporting of scoring methods, and that this convenience and packaging together of all of these features is a novelty of SeqScore. For example, unlike `conlleval` and every other NER scorer we examined, SeqScore supports aggregating scores across multiple prediction files for the same reference. This enables the now-common practice of reporting the mean and standard deviation across runs, aiding in following guideline 5. While this is a simple feature, by reducing the effort required to report these scores, we believe we can help improve adoption of this practice. Of the papers we surveyed, only about two-thirds were clear about how many runs they used and whether their reported score was an average or a best run.

Table 9 compares the features of SeqScore against other packages for scoring and working with sequence labeling data for chunking tasks. While SeqScore is designed to include as many features as possible, there are some features it does not implement. One is partial match scoring, which is implemented in nervaluate (Segura-Bedmar et al., 2013)[7] following the MUC scoring approach (Chinchor and Sundheim, 1993). Also, SeqScore only processes CoNLL-style file formats.

NER scorers can broadly be grouped in terms of how closely they resemble the `conlleval` Perl script. There are direct re-implementations, those that score in the same spirit as `conlleval` but have additional features, and those that take a different approach to invalid labels. The set of scorers we examine is not exhaustive but covers the most widely-used ones.

[7] `https://github.com/ivyleavedtoadflax/nervaluate`

	SeqScore	Stanza	NCRF++	iobes	sighsmile	spyysalo	wnuteval	seqeval	conlleval
Warns for invalid label seqs.	✓			✓			✓		
begin repair	✓				✓	✓	✓	✓	✓
Discard repair	✓	✓	✓	✓				✓	
Converts label schemes	✓	✓	✓	✓					
Scoring	✓	✓	✓		✓	✓	✓	✓	✓
Aggregation across runs	✓								

Table 9: Comparison of package features

5.2 `conlleval` reimplementations

To the best of our knowledge after testing on a number of datasets and edge cases, each of these is a faithful replication of the original `conlleval` Perl script: spyysalo `conlleval.py`[8], and sighsmile `conlleval.py`[9]. The spyysalo and sighsmile re-implimentations differ from the original `conlleval` script mainly in that they have support for BIOES and are written in Python instead of Perl.

5.3 `conlleval`-style scorers

`wnuteval`[10] `wnuteval` is limited to the entity types used in the shared task it was developed for. It raises warnings about invalid transitions. However, it does not handle multiple mention encoding schemes. We also found that it does not raise any warnings or errors about uneven document lengths between system and gold files; while this seems like an unusual case to test, with the use of models set maximum sequence lengths as a decoding hyperparameter, it is common to accidentally truncate sentences when producing system output for evaluation.

seqeval seqeval (Nakayama, 2018) can score on many different label schemes. It is unique in being one of the only scorers we examined that has more than one approach to invalid label sequences, a feature added concurrently with the development of SeqScore. Seqeval refers to them as *default* and *strict* modes. *Default* is `conlleval`-style (begin), while *strict* is what we refer to as *discard*.

5.4 Internal scorers

There are also numerous internal scorers that are part of larger NLP toolkits and packages. Though there are certainly plenty of others, we examine evaluation methods found in NCRF++ and Stanza. Neither of the approaches of these internal scorers follow `conlleval`-style handling of invalid label sequences.

Stanza Stanza (Qi et al., 2020) is a collection of models and tools for NLP. It supports NER in multiple languages and includes its own scorer implementation. Stanza's scorer is similar to *discard* or seqeval's strict mode, with a few exceptions. Stanza also includes a number of tools for converting between schemes.

NCRF++ NCRF++ (Yang et al., 2018) is a framework for doing neural sequence labeling tasks in a highly configurable way. It implements its own scorer with an approach to invalid sequences using the *discard* method.

5.5 Handling invalid label transitions

Lester (2020) provides a library for parsing label schemes, identifying invalid label sequences, converting between label schemes, and enumerating the legality of possible transitions. While this library is very useful for handling label schemes and invalid transitions, it does not address what we believe is a necessary decoupling of the scorer from the handling of invalid label sequences. While it is capable of identifying invalid transitions and supporting one's own implementation to constrain or repair invalid sequences, it does not provide common methods for repairing invalid sequences.

Lignos and Kamyab (2020) demonstrate the difference that can occur when two scorers handle invalid label sequences differently. However, they do not provide any software to evaluate these differences and only test using CoNLL-03 English data with older neural models.

6 Conclusion

This paper has provided guidelines for reproducible NER research and demonstrated the importance of

[8] `https://github.com/spyysalo/conlleval.py`

[9] `https://github.com/sighsmile/conlleval`

[10] `http://noisy-text.github.io/2017/files/wnuteval.py`

following them, both by describing the principles behind them and demonstrating the impact on actual scores. Ultimately, researchers can choose to either accept the status quo—which for NER is non-reproducible research due to both a lack of standard practices and a lack of standard tools—or attempt to elevate the practice in the field to higher standards. We hope that by providing a software toolkit to help follow these guidelines, we have substantially reduced the barriers to performing reproducible research for this task.

While we have created a software package to accompany our recommendations—one that makes following them extremely simple—we do not claim that using SeqScore is necessary for reproducible results. Just like sacreBLEU is not the only way to produce a reproducible MT score, SeqScore is not the only reproducible way to score NER output. However, as it is actively maintained, well-tested, and it can handle multiple repair methods, we strongly encourage its use. By focusing on transparency and prioritizing supporting reproducible research in the design of SeqScore, we believe we have produced a toolkit that can have substantial positive impact on the field.

Adoption of this paper's recommendations by researchers will increase transparency in the scoring process and enable standardization of scoring methods in a field we believe is approaching a reproducibility crisis.

Acknowledgments

We would like to thank David Adelani for helping us work with the MasakhaNER data. We would also like to thank two anonymous reviewers for their useful feedback on the paper. Chester Palen-Michel was supported by the Alfred Schonwalter Graduate Computer Science Summer Fellowship through a gift from a generous donor to Brandeis University.

References

David Ifeoluwa Adelani, Jade Abbott, Graham Neubig, Daniel D'souza, Julia Kreutzer, Constantine Lignos, Chester Palen-Michel, Happy Buzaaba, Shruti Rijhwani, Sebastian Ruder, Stephen Mayhew, Israel Abebe Azime, Shamsuddeen Muhammad, Chris Chinenye Emezue, Joyce Nakatumba-Nabende, Perez Ogayo, Anuoluwapo Aremu, Catherine Gitau, Derguene Mbaye, Jesujoba Alabi, Seid Muhie Yimam, Tajuddeen Gwadabe, Ignatius Ezeani, Rubungo Andre Niyongabo, Jonathan Mukiibi, Verrah Otiende, Iroro Orife, Davis David, Samba Ngom, Tosin Adewumi, Paul Rayson, Mofetoluwa Adeyemi, Gerald Muriuki, Emmanuel Anebi, Chiamaka Chukwuneke, Nkiruka Odu, Eric Peter Wairagala, Samuel Oyerinde, Clemencia Siro, Tobius Saul Bateesa, Temilola Oloyede, Yvonne Wambui, Victor Akinode, Deborah Nabagereka, Maurice Katusiime, Ayodele Awokoya, Mouhamadane MBOUP, Dibora Gebreyohannes, Henok Tilaye, Kelechi Nwaike, Degaga Wolde, Abdoulaye Faye, Blessing Sibanda, Orevaoghene Ahia, Bonaventure F. P. Dossou, Kelechi Ogueji, Thierno Ibrahima DIOP, Abdoulaye Diallo, Adewale Akinfaderin, Tendai Marengereke, and Salomey Osei. 2021. MasakhaNER: Named entity recognition for african languages. *Transactions of the Association for Computational Linguistics (TACL)*. In press.

Alan Akbik, Tanja Bergmann, and Roland Vollgraf. 2019. Pooled contextualized embeddings for named entity recognition. In *Proceedings of the 2019 Conference of the North American Chapter of the Association for Computational Linguistics: Human Language Technologies, Volume 1 (Long and Short Papers)*, pages 724–728, Minneapolis, Minnesota. Association for Computational Linguistics.

Alan Akbik, Duncan Blythe, and Roland Vollgraf. 2018. Contextual string embeddings for sequence labeling. In *Proceedings of the 27th International Conference on Computational Linguistics*, pages 1638–1649, Santa Fe, New Mexico, USA. Association for Computational Linguistics.

Alexei Baevski, Sergey Edunov, Yinhan Liu, Luke Zettlemoyer, and Michael Auli. 2019. Cloze-driven pretraining of self-attention networks. In *Proceedings of the 2019 Conference on Empirical Methods in Natural Language Processing and the 9th International Joint Conference on Natural Language Processing (EMNLP-IJCNLP)*, pages 5360–5369, Hong Kong, China. Association for Computational Linguistics.

Darina Benikova, Chris Biemann, Max Kisselew, and Sebastian Padó. 2014. GermEval 2014 named entity recognition shared task: Companion paper.

Nancy Chinchor and Beth Sundheim. 1993. MUC-5 evaluation metrics. In *Fifth Message Understanding Conference (MUC-5): Proceedings of a Conference Held in Baltimore, Maryland, August 25-27, 1993*.

Nancy A. Chinchor. 1998. Overview of MUC-7. In *Seventh Message Understanding Conference (MUC-7): Proceedings of a Conference Held in Fairfax, Virginia, April 29 - May 1, 1998*.

Alexis Conneau, Kartikay Khandelwal, Naman Goyal, Vishrav Chaudhary, Guillaume Wenzek, Francisco Guzmán, Edouard Grave, Myle Ott, Luke Zettlemoyer, and Veselin Stoyanov. 2020. Unsupervised cross-lingual representation learning at scale. In

Proceedings of the 58th Annual Meeting of the Association for Computational Linguistics, pages 8440–8451, Online. Association for Computational Linguistics.

Leon Derczynski, Eric Nichols, Marieke van Erp, and Nut Limsopatham. 2017. Results of the WNUT2017 shared task on novel and emerging entity recognition. In *Proceedings of the 3rd Workshop on Noisy User-generated Text*, pages 140–147, Copenhagen, Denmark. Association for Computational Linguistics.

Jacob Devlin, Ming-Wei Chang, Kenton Lee, and Kristina Toutanova. 2019. BERT: Pre-training of deep bidirectional transformers for language understanding. In *Proceedings of the 2019 Conference of the North American Chapter of the Association for Computational Linguistics: Human Language Technologies, Volume 1 (Long and Short Papers)*, pages 4171–4186, Minneapolis, Minnesota. Association for Computational Linguistics.

George Doddington, Alexis Mitchell, Mark Przybocki, Lance Ramshaw, Stephanie Strassel, and Ralph Weischedel. 2004. The automatic content extraction (ACE) program – tasks, data, and evaluation. In *Proceedings of the Fourth International Conference on Language Resources and Evaluation (LREC'04)*, Lisbon, Portugal. European Language Resources Association (ELRA).

Eduard Hovy, Mitchell Marcus, Martha Palmer, Lance Ramshaw, and Ralph Weischedel. 2006. OntoNotes: The 90% solution. In *Proceedings of the Human Language Technology Conference of the NAACL, Companion Volume: Short Papers*, pages 57–60, New York City, USA. Association for Computational Linguistics.

Yufan Jiang, Chi Hu, Tong Xiao, Chunliang Zhang, and Jingbo Zhu. 2019. Improved differentiable architecture search for language modeling and named entity recognition. In *Proceedings of the 2019 Conference on Empirical Methods in Natural Language Processing and the 9th International Joint Conference on Natural Language Processing (EMNLP-IJCNLP)*, pages 3585–3590, Hong Kong, China. Association for Computational Linguistics.

Mike Kroutikov. 2019. 7776 ways to compute F1 for an NER task. `http://blog.innodatalabs.com/7776_ways_to_compute_f1_for_ner_task/`.

Brian Lester. 2020. iobes: Library for span level processing. In *Proceedings of Second Workshop for NLP Open Source Software (NLP-OSS)*, pages 115–119, Online. Association for Computational Linguistics.

Brian Lester, Daniel Pressel, Amy Hemmeter, Sagnik Ray Choudhury, and Srinivas Bangalore. 2020. Constrained decoding for computationally efficient named entity recognition taggers. In *Findings of the Association for Computational Linguistics: EMNLP 2020*, pages 1841–1848, Online. Association for Computational Linguistics.

Xiaoya Li, Jingrong Feng, Yuxian Meng, Qinghong Han, Fei Wu, and Jiwei Li. 2020. A unified MRC framework for named entity recognition. In *Proceedings of the 58th Annual Meeting of the Association for Computational Linguistics*, pages 5849–5859, Online. Association for Computational Linguistics.

Constantine Lignos and Marjan Kamyab. 2020. If you build your own NER scorer, non-replicable results will come. In *Proceedings of the First Workshop on Insights from Negative Results in NLP*, pages 94–99, Online. Association for Computational Linguistics.

Yijin Liu, Fandong Meng, Jinchao Zhang, Jinan Xu, Yufeng Chen, and Jie Zhou. 2019. GCDT: A global context enhanced deep transition architecture for sequence labeling. In *Proceedings of the 57th Annual Meeting of the Association for Computational Linguistics*, pages 2431–2441, Florence, Italy. Association for Computational Linguistics.

Jouni Luoma and Sampo Pyysalo. 2020. Exploring cross-sentence contexts for named entity recognition with BERT. In *Proceedings of the 28th International Conference on Computational Linguistics*, pages 904–914, Barcelona, Spain (Online). International Committee on Computational Linguistics.

Hiroki Nakayama. 2018. seqeval: A python framework for sequence labeling evaluation. Software available from https://github.com/chakki-works/seqeval.

Matt Post. 2018. A call for clarity in reporting BLEU scores. In *Proceedings of the Third Conference on Machine Translation: Research Papers*, pages 186–191, Brussels, Belgium. Association for Computational Linguistics.

Peng Qi, Yuhao Zhang, Yuhui Zhang, Jason Bolton, and Christopher D. Manning. 2020. Stanza: A python natural language processing toolkit for many human languages. In *Proceedings of the 58th Annual Meeting of the Association for Computational Linguistics: System Demonstrations*, pages 101–108, Online. Association for Computational Linguistics.

Will Radford, Xavier Carreras, and James Henderson. 2015. Named entity recognition with document-specific KB tag gazetteers. In *Proceedings of the 2015 Conference on Empirical Methods in Natural Language Processing*, pages 512–517, Lisbon, Portugal. Association for Computational Linguistics.

Lance Ramshaw and Mitch Marcus. 1995. Text chunking using transformation-based learning. In *Third Workshop on Very Large Corpora*.

Nils Reimers and Iryna Gurevych. 2017. Reporting score distributions makes a difference: Performance study of LSTM-networks for sequence tagging. In

Proceedings of the 2017 Conference on Empirical Methods in Natural Language Processing, pages 338–348, Copenhagen, Denmark. Association for Computational Linguistics.

Isabel Segura-Bedmar, Paloma Martínez, and María Herrero-Zazo. 2013. SemEval-2013 task 9 : Extraction of drug-drug interactions from biomedical texts (DDIExtraction 2013). In *Second Joint Conference on Lexical and Computational Semantics (*SEM), Volume 2: Proceedings of the Seventh International Workshop on Semantic Evaluation (SemEval 2013)*, pages 341–350, Atlanta, Georgia, USA. Association for Computational Linguistics.

Moemmur Shahzad, Ayesha Amin, Diego Esteves, and Axel-Cyrille Ngonga Ngomo. 2021. Inferner: an attentive model leveraging the sentence-level information for named entity recognition in microblogs. In *The International FLAIRS Conference Proceedings*, volume 34.

Stephanie Strassel and Jennifer Tracey. 2016. LORELEI language packs: Data, tools, and resources for technology development in low resource languages. In *Proceedings of the Tenth International Conference on Language Resources and Evaluation (LREC'16)*, pages 3273–3280, Portorož, Slovenia. European Language Resources Association (ELRA).

Erik F. Tjong Kim Sang. 2002. Introduction to the CoNLL-2002 shared task: Language-independent named entity recognition. In *COLING-02: The 6th Conference on Natural Language Learning 2002 (CoNLL-2002)*.

Erik F. Tjong Kim Sang and Sabine Buchholz. 2000. Introduction to the CoNLL-2000 shared task chunking. In *Fourth Conference on Computational Natural Language Learning and the Second Learning Language in Logic Workshop*.

Erik F. Tjong Kim Sang and Fien De Meulder. 2003. Introduction to the CoNLL-2003 shared task: Language-independent named entity recognition. In *Proceedings of the Seventh Conference on Natural Language Learning at HLT-NAACL 2003*, pages 142–147.

Jingxuan Tu and Constantine Lignos. 2021. TMR: Evaluating NER recall on tough mentions. In *Proceedings of the 16th Conference of the European Chapter of the Association for Computational Linguistics: Student Research Workshop*, pages 155–163, Online. Association for Computational Linguistics.

Xinyu Wang, Yong Jiang, Nguyen Bach, Tao Wang, Zhongqiang Huang, Fei Huang, and Kewei Tu. 2021. Improving named entity recognition by external context retrieving and cooperative learning. In *Proceedings of the 59th Annual Meeting of the Association for Computational Linguistics and the 11th International Joint Conference on Natural Language Processing (Volume 1: Long Papers)*, pages 1800–1812, Online. Association for Computational Linguistics.

Yiyi Wang, Emily Prud'hommeaux, Meysam Asgari, and Jill Dolata. 2020. Automated scoring of clinical expressive language evaluation tasks. In *Proceedings of the Fifteenth Workshop on Innovative Use of NLP for Building Educational Applications*, pages 177–185, Seattle, WA, USA → Online. Association for Computational Linguistics.

Ikuya Yamada, Akari Asai, Hiroyuki Shindo, Hideaki Takeda, and Yuji Matsumoto. 2020. LUKE: Deep contextualized entity representations with entity-aware self-attention. In *Proceedings of the 2020 Conference on Empirical Methods in Natural Language Processing (EMNLP)*, pages 6442–6454, Online. Association for Computational Linguistics.

Jie Yang, Shuailong Liang, and Yue Zhang. 2018. Design challenges and misconceptions in neural sequence labeling. In *Proceedings of the 27th International Conference on Computational Linguistics*, pages 3879–3889, Santa Fe, New Mexico, USA. Association for Computational Linguistics.

Juntao Yu, Bernd Bohnet, and Massimo Poesio. 2020. Named entity recognition as dependency parsing. In *Proceedings of the 58th Annual Meeting of the Association for Computational Linguistics*, pages 6470–6476, Online. Association for Computational Linguistics.

Trainable Ranking Models to Evaluate the Semantic Accuracy of Data-to-Text Neural Generator

Nicolas Garneau and Luc Lamontagne
Université Laval, Québec, Canada
Computer Science Department
{first.last}@ift.ulaval.ca

Abstract

In this paper, we introduce a new embedding-based metric relying on trainable ranking models to evaluate the semantic accuracy of neural data-to-text generators. This metric is especially well suited to semantically and factually assess the performance of a text generator when tables can be associated with multiple references and table values contain textual utterances. We first present how one can implement and further *specialize* the metric by training the underlying ranking models on a legal Data-to-Text dataset. We show how it may provide a more robust evaluation than other evaluation schemes in challenging settings using a dataset comprising paraphrases between the table values and their respective references. Finally, we evaluate its generalization capabilities on a well-known dataset, WebNLG, by comparing it with human evaluation and a metric recently introduced based on natural language inference. We then illustrate how it naturally characterizes, both quantitatively and qualitatively, omissions and hallucinations.

1 Introduction

Data-to-Text (D2T) generation (Kukich, 1983; McKeown, 1985; Reiter and Dale, 1997) is a specialized task of natural language generation (NLG) where a model takes as input (semi)-structured data (e.g. a table) and generates a textual utterance that is both syntactical and semantically faithful to the input. Several architectures were proposed to solve this task. They may rely strictly on templates (Gatti et al., 2018; Puzikov and Gurevych, 2018; Wiseman et al., 2018), separate planning (what to say) from generation (how to say it) (Puduppully et al., 2019; Moryossef et al., 2019) or be a fully derivable neural architecture (Lebret et al., 2016; Wiseman et al., 2017; Gehrmann et al., 2018). While achieving interesting performance at natural language generation tasks (Lewis et al., 2020; Gehrmann et al., 2021), pre-trained neural language models

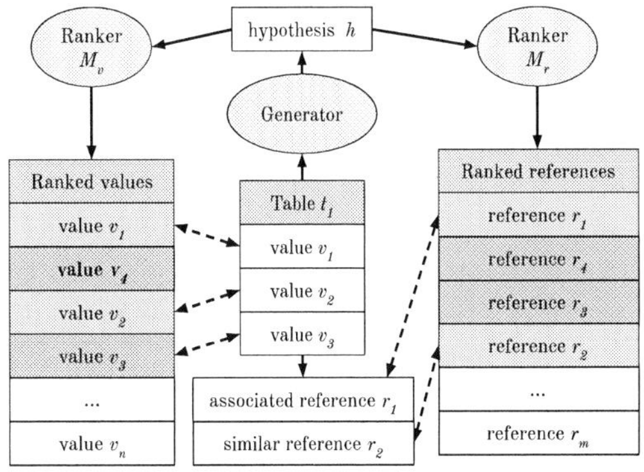

Figure 1: Round-trip evaluation in the table–hypothesis setting (left) and reference–hypothesis setting (right).

(hence neural architectures in general), are prone to hallucinate facts (Dušek et al., 2018) which brings their usability at stake in sensitive domains such as the legal one.

In this paper, we wish to promote the usability of neural architecture by proposing a new trainable automatic evaluation metric well suited to evaluate the semantic accuracy of such D2T generator. This metric is designed as a two factor "round-trip evaluation" in order to assess the accuracy a given generated hypothesis. First, we use the hypothesis to try to recreate the original table by ranking its values amongst all other values in the dataset. Then, we retrieve similar references amongst all other references in the dataset by ranking them still using that same hypothesis. We illustrate both round-trip evaluation scheme (table reconstruction and reference ranking) in Figure 1.

Our approach is well suited to semantically and factually assess a generator's performance in cases where the tables can be associated with multiple references, and the tables' values contain textual utterances. We present how one can further *specialize* the proposed evaluation metric by training the underlying ranking models on the target dataset, hence providing a more robust evaluation. Re-

Proceedings of the 58th Annual Meeting of the Association for Computational Linguistics, pages 51–61
https://doi.org/10.26615/978-954-452-056-4_006

lying on the mean average precision, we present how it naturally characterizes, both quantitatively and qualitatively, omissions and hallucinations of a given generator. This framework offers great flexibility in how it can be implemented and further improved. We identify two main components that can be tuned to improve the efficiency of our proposed metric when evaluating NLG systems; a similarity function between reference texts and the underlying ranking models.

However, having a metric where the efficiency is highly dependent on how it is implemented is highly problematic for an absolute comparison against other metrics or evaluation methodologies. This is why we propose a way to "fix a metric" i.e. how good, on the gold annotations, one implementation of the metric can be? Having a "fixed metric" then allows us to evaluate NLG systems against each other properly.

In our experiments, we first apply our metric on a challenging dataset in the legal domain, *Plum2Text* (Garneau et al., 2021). We show how the specialization of the ranking models can be beneficial or even necessary. More precisely, we illustrate these benefits when paraphrasing between the data (i.e. table) and the reference text highly characterizes the dataset in hand. Then, we illustrate its generalization capabilities even in simpler settings on a well-known D2T dataset, WebNLG (Gardent et al., 2017). We show how it is able to discriminate a set of generators, and correlates positively with human judgment. Our contribution is thus a new trainable automatic D2T evaluation metric that naturally characterizes both omissions and hallucinations of neural architectures.

2 Evaluating Data-to-Text Generation

Evaluating natural language generated text is a very hard task. Reiter and Belz (2009) and Reiter (2018) question the validity of widely used metrics. Sai et al. (2020) provide an extensive survey of the field, and more precisely separate the D2T evaluation metrics along 2 dimensions: either they use the table t or not (i.e. Table-Free), and either they are trained or untrained metrics. For instance, automatic evaluation metrics such as BLEU (Papineni et al., 2002), ROUGE (Lin, 2004) or METEOR (Banerjee and Lavie, 2005) are not trained and neither use the table t. They only partially account for the faithfulness of a given generated hypothesis w.r.t its associated references. Even though these metrics are widely used, they fall short to capture factual aspects in a D2T setting, and correlate poorly with human judgment (Liu et al., 2016; Novikova et al., 2017).

BLEURT (Sellam et al., 2020) is a metric trained on English texts that is designed to better model human judgment on generated texts. However, it does not take into account the input table. Sun and Zhou (2012) proposed iBLEU for paraphrase generation, an adaptation of the BLEU score that takes into account the context (the original phrase), the generated hypothesis and the reference. Its variant, BLEU-T, rewards an hypothesis h that overlaps with the content of the input table t as follows;

$$\text{BLEU-T} = \alpha\text{BLEU}(h,t) + (1-\alpha)\text{BLEU}(h,r)$$

where α is a parameter that balances faithfulness between the table t and the reference r.

	Table-Free	**Table**
Untrained	BLEU, ROUGE, METEOR	PARENT, BLEU-T/iBLEU, NLI, **Ours**
Trained	BLEURT	**Ours**

Table 1: Different metrics and their position in the evaluation spectrum, including the two variants of our proposed metric which can be trained or not.

Wiseman et al. (2017) proposed an extractive evaluation scheme where a model tries to identify relations in h between a pair of entities in order to recreate the table t that was used for the generation. Matching between the extracted entities and the table values is simply done via string-to-string comparison since the values in their dataset are short textual utterance of up to a few tokens. Dhingra et al. (2019) extended this metric (PARENT) by considering overlapping n-grams in the generated hypothesis h with both the table t and the reference text r. More recently, Dušek and Kasner (2020) proposed a metric that relies strictly on a pre-trained version of a natural language inference model (which will be referenced as "NLI" from now on) that verifies if a given hypothesis is entailed or not by the input table. They framed the evaluation as a categorical result given an hypothesis h (e.g. as being "Correct" or "Incorrect") but one can also use the underlying NLI model's confidence score for a softer evaluation. Using ranking models supplement their approach by identifying hallucinations *and* omissions (to some extent) and quantitatively characterizes both phenomena.

Trained metrics using the context (in our case t) have been proposed for dialogue generation tasks (Lowe et al., 2017; Tao et al., 2018). However none of them is suitable for a D2T setting where the characterization of hallucinations (and to some extent omissions) are required in order to use a neural D2T generator in production. We thus wish to fill in this gap by presenting in the following section a new evaluation scheme. This scheme offers the advantage to exploit both the table t and the reference r, to be based on ranking models, and to be either trained or not. We illustrate in Table 1 where the metrics discussed in this section lie in the table–table-free and trained–untrained spectrum.

3 Data-to-Text Evaluation through Ranking

To assess the accuracy of a generated hypothesis h, it can be useful to consider both the input table t and the target reference r, i.e. validate the correctness of h according to its table and its reference. We thus propose a way to assess the fidelity of h by reconstructing the table t ($h \nrightarrow t$) and by retrieving its corresponding reference(s) r ($h \nrightarrow r$) using ranking models. This premise is highly motivated by the fact that similar text descriptions should be associated to semantically similar table contents. In both settings, the ranking models are evaluated using the Average Precision (AP), which we describe next.

3.1 Table Reconstruction

Borrowing from information retrieval terminology, in the context of $h \nrightarrow t$, we treat every value v in the table t as a document and h as a query. Different from the information extraction method proposed by Wiseman et al. (2017)[1], we wish to recreate t by finding the corresponding set of values $\mathbf{v}_i$ amongst the set of possible table values V, given a ranker $\mathcal{M}_v$ and the query h_i. To do so, we retrieve a ranked list of all the possible values $\hat{V} = \mathcal{M}_v(h_i)$ and compute the Precision at k (P@k) of the query h_i in the following way;

$$\text{P@}k_i = \frac{|\mathbf{v}_i@k \cap \hat{V}@k|}{|\hat{V}@k|} \tag{1}$$

We can then compute the Average Precision of the table reconstruction ($\text{AP}^{h \nrightarrow t}$) given the following formula;

$$\text{AP}^{h \nrightarrow t} = \frac{1}{|\mathbf{v}_i|} \sum_{k=1}^{|\hat{V}|} \text{P@}k_i, \tag{2}$$

giving us a sense of how well the ranker $\mathcal{M}_v$ is able to retrieve the set of table values $\mathbf{v}_i$ corresponding to the hypothesis h_i.

3.2 Reference Ranking

In the context of $h \nrightarrow r$, we still treat h as the query, but r as the document. In a case where multiple references can be deduced by the same table (or similar ones), it makes sense to take into consideration other references that share some similarities with the real reference. More precisely, a table t could refer to multiple references with a certain degree of correspondence, hence these references can be seen as similar documents. We can even push this further by assuming that if two tables t_i and t_j share similarities amongst their values, their corresponding references r_i and r_j will be semantically similar.

Given t_i, r_i and t_j, r_j, we define the following similarity function;

$$f : (t_i, t_j) \rightarrow d_{i,j} \tag{3}$$

such that $d_{i,j}$ is the degree of similarity between between two tables t_i and t_j. This similarity function is a proxy to the semantic similarity between r_i and r_j. For instance, by using the intersection over union of t_i and t_j table values, we use the following function; $f = (t_i \cap t_j)/(t_i \cup t_j)$. We thus consider, for a given r_i and its associated table t_i, the set of references where $d_{i,*} > \delta$ as being relevant references[2]. Given an hypothesis h_i, we can then query the set of references R in order to get a ranked list of references $\hat{R}_i = \mathcal{M}_r(h_i)$ where $\mathcal{M}_r$ is a ranking model for the references. We define R_i^* as being the ordered gold set of references according to f.

Let the Cumulative Relevance Score (CRS) of h_i be $\sum_{j=1}^{k} d_{i,j}$. We define the *estimated* and

[1]The information extraction scheme is relevant where the table values can be framed as triplets, where a model tries to put the different extracted entities into relation (e.g. the Rotowire dataset). Our method generalizes the table reconstruction step whereas one can freely design its own ranker model.

[2]We use $\delta > 0$ in our experiments.

true CRS at k being CRS applied on $\hat{R}_i$ and R_i^*, yielding $\hat{R}_i$-CRS@k and R_i^*-CRS@k respectively. Formally, $\hat{R}_i$-CRS@$k = \sum_{j=1}^{k} f(h_i, \hat{r}_j)$ and R_i^*-CRS@$k = \sum_{j=1}^{k} f(h_i, r_j^*)$. We thus compute Precision at k in the following way;

$$\text{P@}k_i = \frac{\hat{R}_i\text{-CRS@}k_i}{R_i^*\text{-CRS@}k_i} \tag{4}$$

obtaining the $\text{AP}^{h \rightarrow r}$ of h_i with the following formula;

$$\text{AP}^{h \rightarrow r} = \frac{1}{R_i^*\text{-CRS}} \sum_{k=1}^{|R|} \text{P@}k_i \times d_{i,k} \tag{5}$$

where $d_{i,k}$, properly scales $\text{P@}k_i$ so that $\text{AP}^{h \rightarrow r}$ is between 0 and 1.

Finally, in both settings, we respectively compute the mean Average Precision (mAP) over the set of Hypotheses H;

$$\text{mAP}^{h \rightarrow t} = \frac{1}{|H|} \sum_{i=1}^{|H|} \text{AP}_i^{h \rightarrow t} \tag{6}$$

$$\text{mAP}^{h \rightarrow r} = \frac{1}{|H|} \sum_{i=1}^{|H|} \text{AP}_i^{h \rightarrow r} \tag{7}$$

where $\text{mAP}^{h \rightarrow t}$ illustrate the capacity of $\mathcal{M}_v$ to rank the hypotheses H accordingly to their respective table values, and $\text{mAP}^{h \rightarrow r}$ the capacity of $\mathcal{M}_r$ to rank the hypotheses H according to their similar references (and implicitly their respective tables).

In an ideal world, evaluating on gold annotations, both ranking models $\mathcal{M}_v$ and $\mathcal{M}_r$ should obtain a mAP of 1. In practice, however, we can only hope that each model will be as close as possible to 1, mostly due to noise in the data, annotation errors, or to the distribution of the data itself. In the next section, we introduce a robust ranking model based on sentence embeddings applied in both $h \rightarrow t$ and $h \rightarrow r$ settings. We also introduce how this model can be trained on the dataset in hand.

3.3 Training Ranking Models

We consider the embedding-based ranking models using the information retrieval version of Sentence-BERT (SBERT) (Reimers and Gurevych, 2019), based on the BERT architecture (Devlin et al., 2019)[3]. More concretely, we use SBERT to encode both the set of possible table values V and the set of references R into a list of vector representations (i.e. matrices) $\mathbf{V}$ and $\mathbf{R}$. We then encode the hypothesis h into its respective vector representation $\mathbf{h}$. The models $\mathcal{M}_v$ and $\mathcal{M}_r$ re-order the vectors in $\mathbf{V}$ and $\mathbf{R}$ according to the cosine similarity with $\mathbf{h}$, yielding $\hat{V}$ and $\hat{R}$ needed for the computation of our metric.

Reimers and Gurevych (2019) showed that fine-tuning SBERT on the downstream task's dataset can lead to substantial improvements. To this end, we propose to fine-tune SBERT in both settings, $h \rightarrow t$ and $h \rightarrow r$, by creating their very specific training datasets. In our experiments, we used the multilingual version of BERT (Devlin et al., 2019) as the base model, XLM-R (Conneau et al., 2020; Reimers and Gurevych, 2020).

In the $h \rightarrow t$ setting, for every value $v_{i,j}$ in table t_i with its corresponding reference r_i, we create a positive pair $(v_{i,j}, r_i, 1)$. We then randomly sample negative examples such that $(v_{i,j}, r_m)$ is not within the original dataset and fine-tune SBERT to discriminate positive from negative pairs, $(v_{i,j}, r_m, 0)$.

In the $h \rightarrow r$ setting, we use Equation 3 to determine the similarity between two given references r_i and r_j. Using the cartesian product of $R \times R$, we thus generate every possible reference pairs with their respective similarity value, $(r_i, r_j, d_{i,j})$ and fine-tune SBERT to maximize the similarity between similar pairs, and minimize it between dissimilar pairs. In practice, we down sample pairs where $d_{i,j} = 0$ since it corresponds to 80% of the generated pairs. While this training procedure is very generic an applicable to most D2T datasets, it can be modified to suit one's specifics.

In both settings, we split the training data in a train and validation sets of 80% and 20% respectively. We fine-tuned SBERT for 4 epochs, keeping only the best performing model on the validation set. Regardless of the downstream dataset used, using a GeForce 2080 graphic card, this process took 4 hours for each setting.

3.4 Characterizing omissions and hallucinations

An insightful way of qualitatively analyzing the capacity of a given neural D2T generator is by characterizing omissions and hallucinations. More precisely, we want to know which element from the table may have been forgotten by the generator and which element in the generated text may be consid-

[3]In our experiments, we also tested a word co-occrurrence ranking, Elasticsearch (`https://www.elastic.co/`), as explained in Section 4.1.

ered as hallucinations (Dušek et al., 2018; Dušek and Kasner, 2020). We acknowledge the fact that characterizing omissions may not be relevant in cases we would only like to describe highlights of a basketball game (Wiseman et al., 2017), especially when there is a seperate planning step (Puduppully et al., 2019; Moryossef et al., 2019). However, in the legal domain, describing a semi-structured document in its whole (omissions), and solely this document (hallucinations), is of high importance to foster a truthful view of a legal system (Beauchemin et al., 2020).

Using a ranking-based metric, we can potentially identify which elements from the table are considered as omissions and what has been hallucinated in the hypothesis. Intuitively, ranking models basically offer this characterization for free. Indeed, on the table reconstruction side, considering the gold set of n values v and the set of top n returned values $\hat{v}$ from $\mathcal{M}_t$, we obtain the omissions by computing the set difference of $o_t = v - \hat{v}$. As per the implicit definition of hallucinations and assuming a neural generator has been trained on a training set, we define hallucinations as being values from the training set that have been highly ranked. Therefore, we compute hallucinations as $a_t = \hat{v} - v$ such that $a_t \in V_{train}$. On the reference retrieval side, we consider the first retrieved reference and its associated table (or set of values), $\hat{v}$. We can similarly compute omissions and hallucinations as on the table reconstruction side, obtaining o_r and a_r. A given value $v_i \in v$ will considered omitted if it is present in o_t and o_r (i.e. 1.0), partially omitted if it is present in either o_t or o_r (i.e. 0.5) and not omitted if it is not present in any of the sets (i.e. 0.0). The same logic applies to hallucinations.

Roughly speaking, the mean average precision is a quantitative proxy loosely characterizing the omissions and hallucinations. Indeed, the average precision will consider not only the top n, but up to the last value that should have been retrieve in the list, thus making it an optimistic approximation of omissions and hallucinations. On the reference side, then again our metric is an optimistic approximation of omissions and hallucination in the sense that we consider every other references having a similarity score > 0. One could design a more exact quantitative approximation of omissions and hallucinations by only considering the first returned reference by the ranking model and analyzing its table with the corresponding true table t, as previously proposed.

	$h \rightarrow t$	$h \rightarrow r$	**Avg.**
Elasticsearch	0.588	0.596	0.592
SBERT Untrained	0.274	0.584	0.429
SBERT Trained	**0.831**	**0.871**	**0.851**

Table 2: Results of "fixing the metric" on *Plum2Text* using Elasticsearch, SBERT Untrained and SBERT Trained as different ranking models.

4 Experiments

In this section, we first illustrate the benefits of fine-tuning our proposed metric on the *Plum2Text* target dataset (Garneau et al., 2021). We then show how our metric can discriminate generators, and analyze omission and hallucination rates using WebNLG (Gardent et al., 2017).

4.1 Experiments with *Plum2Text*

In this section, we apply our metric on a challenging French dataset in the legal field, *Plum2Text* (Garneau et al., 2021), comprising references being a paraphrase of the table's values. It is composed of pairs of *plumitif*–description. A plumitif is a structured document containing all the key steps of a judicial case. The purpose of this dataset is to make the *plumitifs* more understandable to the population by generating a description from the input data.

There is an interesting exercise when comes the time to evaluate the effectiveness of a metric, especially when it is embedding-based. We dub this exercise as "fixing the metric", whereas we apply it on the gold annotations, i.e. $h = r$. This exercise tells us, to some extent, "how far we can go" with a given generator w.r.t the evaluation metric in the case we would know the answer. Using metrics based on word overlap would obviously yield a perfect score in the reference ranking setting. In these experiments, we thus only consider "fixing the metric" on the *Plum2Text* dataset since we do not have access to human evaluation over systems' outputs. This illustrates the challenge posed by the *Plum2Text* dataset (paraphrasing) as well as the benefits of fine-tuning our metric. As a baseline, we use Elasticsearch's ranking model (ES) based on word co-occurrence.

We can see from Table 2 that, on the Gold annotations, ES has decent performance on both $h \rightarrow t$ and $h \rightarrow r$. Supporting the findings of Reimers and

h →	t	Rank of v	
Reference r_i	**A Table t_i's Value v**	**ES**	**SBERT**
the accused is charged with **sexual touching** of his stepdaughter when she was between 10 and 15 years old.	*Section 151* – **Sexual interference**; Any person who, for a sexual purpose, directly or indirectly touches, with any part of the body or with any object, any part of the body of a child under the age of sixteen years	20	1
the accused pleaded guilty to the following charges : to have, on #DATE, in its possession 0,61 gram of cannabis	*Section 4* – **Possession of substance**. Except as authorized by the regulations, the **possession** of any **substance** listed in Appendix I, II or III is prohibited.	27	1

Table 3: Qualitative results of ES and SBERT fine-tuned model in the $h \rightarrow t$ setting. We illustrate the ability of a fine-tuned ranking model to properly rank a particular value v in the table t_i given the hypothesis h_i (in the case of Gold annotations, r_i).

h →	r	Rank of r_j	
Reference r_i	**Paraphrased Reference $r_j \vert d_{i,j} = 1.0$**	**ES**	**SBERT**
he **denies** any sexual act committed.	the accused states that **he has nothing to reproach himself for**.	N/A	3
PER **pleaded guilty** to **computer luring** of six teenage girls **between the ages of 13 and 17**.	a **guilty plea** [...] to **communicating by means of a computer** with x, a person **under the age of sixteen** [...]	N/A	4

Table 4: Qualitative results of both ES and SBERT fine-tuned in the $h \rightarrow r$ setting. We show the ranking of a paraphrased reference r_j according to the hypothesis h_i (in the case of Gold annotations, r_i).

Gurevych (2019), a pre-trained version of SBERT applied without fine-tuning on *Plum2Text* struggles at ranking, especially in the $h \rightarrow t$ setting (comprising a lot of paraphrasing). However a fine-tuned version of SBERT on *Plum2Text* yields strong performance, achieving a score of 0.851. There is inevitably a trade-off between using an untrained or trained version of our metric. From the results shown in Table 2 and in the context of paraphrases and synonyms, an embedding-based ranking model is definitely improving the evaluation.

4.1.1 Rankers' Behavior on Paraphrases and Synonyms

Supporting our claim that an embedding-based ranking model would be better at evaluating the generated hypotheses, especially when paraphrases characterize the dataset in hand, we qualitatively compare the ranking capabilities of the ES ranker and SBERT fine-tuned model.

In the $h \rightarrow t$ setting, we extract references r that are a paraphrased version of a given table value v. As illustrated in Table 3[4], SBERT learned synonyms such as "sexual *contacts*" and "sexual *touching*". SBERT also learned that "possession of *substance*" is related to drugs like *cannabis* or *cocaïne*, and is thus able to properly rank the associated reference even though there are different types of "possessions" (e.g. child pornography, illegal firearms). As illustrated in the results, simply relying on word co-occurrences yields poor ranking in cases where synonyms are used and shows that an embedding-based ranking model is clearly providing a better performance.

In the $h \rightarrow r$ setting, we analyze again the ranking behaviour of both rankers on paraphrased references. We can see in Table 4 that SBERT learned the various ways "pleading guilty" can be expressed (rows 1 and 2). It also learned that "communicating with people of 16 years and under using a computer" is similar to "computer luring of people between 13 and 17 years old". In most cases, we did not see the paraphrased reference among the top 200 results the ES ranker returned (N/A).

4.1.2 Motivation over a metric based on word overlap

To motivate the need to fine-tune rankers (hence the metric) for specific types of D2T datasets, we illustrate the performance of the recently introduced metric PARENT (Dhingra et al., 2019) on the gold annotations of *Plum2Text*, referred to as "Original" in Table 5. Without any surprises, the precision is 1.0 when $h = r$. The lower performance on the recall (and thus F1-Score) is due to paraphrasing, an inherent problem Dhingra et al. (2019) raised

[4]Note that all examples have been translated from French to facilitate the comprehension of the reader.

when they introduced their metric. To better illustrate this problem, we evaluate PARENT on a augmented version of *Plum2Text* i.e. for every pair r_i, r_j where $d_{i,j} = 1.0$ and $r_i \neq r_j$, we create a paraphrased example (t_i, r_j, r_i) where t_i is the table, r_i the hypothesis and r_j its associated reference. We can see in Table 5 that the results drop significantly due to the word overlap evaluation behavior, even though they should be similar to the Original Dataset.

Dataset	Precision	Recall	F1-Score
Original	1.0	0.565	0.673
Augmented	**0.355**	**0.24**	**0.191**

Table 5: Evaluation of PARENT on the Original and a Augmented version of *Plum2Text* (Garneau et al., 2021)

4.2 Experiments with WebNLG

In this section, we show that, even if our metric is well-suited for D2T dataset comprising textual utterance as table values, it generalizes to more common D2T settings as in WebNLG (Gardent et al., 2017). Shimorina et al. (2018) provide human evaluation on the different systems' outputs (listed in Figure 2, as well as on the gold annotations (`webnlg`). They considered three evaluation dimensions; Fluency, Grammar, and Semantic. In our case, we consider only the Semantic dimension.

First, we simply consider "fixing the metric", i.e. we apply our metric on the `webnlg` team's outputs (i.e. the gold annotations) and compare its values against the human evaluation[5] and the recently introduced metric by Dušek and Kasner (2020) (NLI). Results can be found in Figure 2. Intuitively, human evaluation should be very close to one (0.92)[6], and our trained metric achieves 0.88, which is close to human evaluation. The NLI metric average score is 0.73.

We then run the same experiment on a set of generators' outputs (Shimorina et al., 2018) in order to assess the capabilities of our proposed metric to discriminate amongst systems (i.e. teams). By looking at Figure 2, we can see that there is an agreement on the macro level between the human evaluation, our metric, and NLI in order to discriminate between the teams that performed well from the teams that did not. While the sample size is rather small (10 teams), the Pearson correlation score between human evaluation and our metric, human evaluation and NLI, are both 0.92 ($\rho < 0.005$). The average difference between human evaluation and our metric is 0.09 while human evaluation and NLI is 0.26. On the micro level, correlation scores show another story; human evaluation and our metric yield a Pearson correlation score of 0.47, human evaluation and NLI 0.59, our metric and NLI 0.43 ($\rho < 0.005$ in every cases). While there is a slight correlation between the different evaluation scheme, it seems that they do not always agree at the utterance level, contradicting one another in some cases. This point has already been raised by Dušek and Kasner (2020), suggesting that in some cases, the human evaluation is not accurate. However we decide to leave this specific analysis for future work.

4.2.1 Analysis of omissions and hallucinations

We further analyze the capacity of our metric to characterize omissions and hallucinations on the systems' outputs. To this end, we follow the methodology introduced in Section 3.4 and compute the *estimated* omission and hallucination rates w.r.t to the capacity of underlying rankers. Omission rate is the number of times an input value v was considered omitted by our metric, over the set of n input values. Hallucinations rate is the number of times a value v from the training set has been improperly ranked at the top n expected values[7]. We thus average the rates per system overall 223 examples for the WebNLG's test set.

In this experiment, we are interested in comparing Neural vs Non-Neural architectures, and see if our metric captures the implicit omission/hallucination behavior of neural generators. Results are displayed in Table 6. On the gold annotations, we obtained 0.41 and 0.37 omission and hallucination rates respectively. This is expected mostly because the underlying rankers are not perfect. While achieving 0.88 average precision on the gold annotations, this is an optimistic estimation of the ranking capabilities (see Section 3.4

[5]Human annotators used a three-point Likert scale (1 = Incorrect, 2 = Medium, 3 = Correct) and answers are averaged over multiple annotators. We normalized the scores between 0–1 for an easier comparison

[6]Out of the 224 human evaluation on the gold annotations, 38 have a score below or equal to 0.77.

[7]Rates are computed w.r.t the hypotheses produced by a given system. For example, Vietnam only produced 55 hypotheses given 223 input tables. We thus considered the input values of the 55 input tables for the calculation.

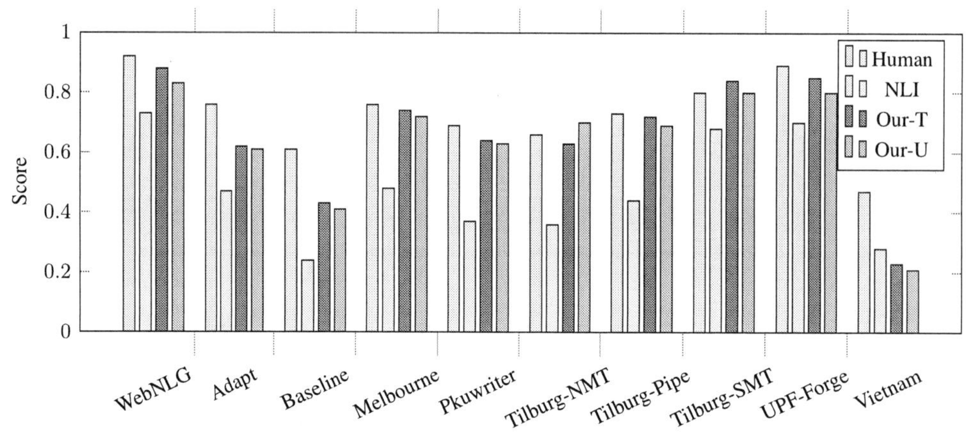

Figure 2: A comparison across human evaluation (semantic) on systems' outputs of Shimorina et al. (2018), the NLI metric proposed by Dušek and Kasner (2020), our metric trained and untrained. Our proposed metric, in every cases except one, is closer to human evaluation than the NLI metric.

for a discussion on this topic). Also, according to Dušek and Kasner (2020), there is some noise in the human evaluation.

Regarding the teams' statistics, we denote higher omission and hallucination rates for 3 out 5 neural systems. Interestingly, the estimated omission and hallucination rates of Adapt are quite high, while having a high semantic score from the human evaluation. On the contrary, Tilburg-NMT has low omission and hallucination rates while having a low human evaluation score. Melbourne has low omission and hallucination rates, which corroborates the fact that it was a good system. Non-Neural systems tend to be more stable on omissions and hallucinations, which is expected. In future experiments, we would like to compute the exact omission and hallucination rates of each team. While being a very time-consuming task, this evaluation will enable an in-depth analysis of omissions and hallucinations per system. This leads to the conclusion that, while being a first step at characterizing/quantifying omissions and hallucinations, more work has to be done towards this direction since it is a crucial evaluation aspect in D2T evaluation.

4.3 Is Fine-Tuning Worth the Shot?

In an era where deep learning models seem to be the norm, it is nonetheless legitimate to ask ourselves if training such a metric is worth the shot. In the case of WebNLG, where the data is extracted from Wikidata (Vrandečić and Krötzsch, 2014), a proxy of Wikipedia, and the underlying transformer models of the metric have been pre-trained on Wikipedia, we see a negligible gain from fine-tuning the metric. The lexical field is pretty much the same, and the reference text does not show many signs of paraphrasing.

	Team	Omission	Hallucination
	WebNLG	0.41	0.37
NEURAL	Adapt	**0.55**	**0.47**
	Baseline	**0.65**	**0.61**
	Melbourne	0.44	0.38
	Pkuwriter	**0.53**	**0.50**
	Tilburg-NMT	0.43	0.36
NON-NEURAL	Tilburg-pipe	0.45	0.38
	Tilburg-SMT	0.40	0.35
	UPF-Forge	0.41	0.35
	Vietnam	0.33	0.33

Table 6: Omission and Hallucination rates per team. We compare the omission and hallucination rates between WebNLG (the gold standard), Neural and Non-Neural architectures.

5 Conclusion

In this paper, we introduced a new trainable automation evaluation metric relying on ranking models which is specific to the D2T setting. To the best of our knowledge, this is the first metric that naturally quantifies omissions and hallucinations of neural textual generators that can also handle paraphrases. Characterizing omissions and hallucinations are of important matter in a sensitive area such as the legal domain. This lack of characterization is often a blocker to the use of recent neural generator models in the legal field. We hope that this metric will also promote the use of recent advances in neural textual generation in sensitive domains such as the medical field.

In our future works, we would like to use our metric to guide the decoding steps of neural D2T generators in order to produce faithful textual descriptions. As previously mentioned, the metric that we proposed is well suited to semantically and factually assess a generator's performance in cases where the tables can be associated with multiple references, and the tables' values contain textual utterances. We wish to generalize the way our method ranks table values through relevance matching (Guo et al., 2016). This would be highly desirable in cases where table values are only up to a few tokens.

Acknowledgments

We thank the reviewers for their thoughtful comments and suggestions. Nicolas is funded by the Natural Sciences and Engineering Research Council of Canada (NSERC).

References

Satanjeev Banerjee and Alon Lavie. 2005. METEOR: An automatic metric for MT evaluation with improved correlation with human judgments. In *Proceedings of the ACL Workshop on Intrinsic and Extrinsic Evaluation Measures for Machine Translation and/or Summarization*, pages 65–72, Ann Arbor, Michigan. Association for Computational Linguistics.

David Beauchemin, Nicolas Garneau, Eve Gaumond, Pierre-Luc Déziel, Richard Khoury, and Luc Lamontagne. 2020. Generating intelligible plumitifs descriptions: Use case application with ethical considerations. In *Proceedings of the 13th International Conference on Natural Language Generation*, pages 15–21, Dublin, Ireland. Association for Computational Linguistics.

Alexis Conneau, Kartikay Khandelwal, Naman Goyal, Vishrav Chaudhary, Guillaume Wenzek, Francisco Guzmán, Edouard Grave, Myle Ott, Luke Zettlemoyer, and Veselin Stoyanov. 2020. Unsupervised cross-lingual representation learning at scale. In *Proceedings of the 58th Annual Meeting of the Association for Computational Linguistics*, pages 8440–8451, Online. Association for Computational Linguistics.

Jacob Devlin, Ming-Wei Chang, Kenton Lee, and Kristina Toutanova. 2019. BERT: Pre-training of deep bidirectional transformers for language understanding. In *Proceedings of the 2019 Conference of the North American Chapter of the Association for Computational Linguistics: Human Language Technologies, Volume 1 (Long and Short Papers)*, pages 4171–4186, Minneapolis, Minnesota. Association for Computational Linguistics.

Bhuwan Dhingra, Manaal Faruqui, Ankur Parikh, Ming-Wei Chang, Dipanjan Das, and William Cohen. 2019. Handling divergent reference texts when evaluating table-to-text generation. In *Proceedings of the 57th Annual Meeting of the Association for Computational Linguistics*, pages 4884–4895, Florence, Italy. Association for Computational Linguistics.

Ondřej Dušek and Zdeněk Kasner. 2020. Evaluating semantic accuracy of data-to-text generation with natural language inference. In *Proceedings of the 13th International Conference on Natural Language Generation*, pages 131–137, Dublin, Ireland. Association for Computational Linguistics.

Ondřej Dušek, Jekaterina Novikova, and Verena Rieser. 2018. Findings of the E2E NLG challenge. In *Proceedings of the 11th International Conference on Natural Language Generation*, pages 322–328, Tilburg University, The Netherlands. Association for Computational Linguistics.

Claire Gardent, Anastasia Shimorina, Shashi Narayan, and Laura Perez-Beltrachini. 2017. Creating training corpora for NLG micro-planners. In *Proceedings of the 55th Annual Meeting of the Association for Computational Linguistics (Volume 1: Long Papers)*, pages 179–188, Vancouver, Canada. Association for Computational Linguistics.

Nicolas Garneau, Eve Gaumond, Luc Lamontagne, and Pierre-Luc Déziel. 2021. Plum2text: A french plumitifs–descriptions data-to-text dataset for natural language generation. In *Proceedings of the 18th International Conference on Artificial Intelligence and Law*, Sao Paulo, Brazil. International Association for Artificial Intelligence and Law.

Lorenzo Gatti, Chris van der Lee, and Mariët Theune. 2018. Template-based multilingual football reports generation using Wikidata as a knowledge base. In *Proceedings of the 11th International Conference on Natural Language Generation*, pages 183–188, Tilburg University, The Netherlands. Association for Computational Linguistics.

Sebastian Gehrmann, Tosin Adewumi, Karmanya Aggarwal, Pawan Sasanka Ammanamanchi, Anuoluwapo Aremu, Antoine Bosselut, Khyathi Raghavi Chandu, Miruna-Adriana Clinciu, Dipanjan Das, Kaustubh Dhole, Wanyu Du, Esin Durmus, Ondřej Dušek, Chris Chinenye Emezue, Varun Gangal, Cristina Garbacea, Tatsunori Hashimoto, Yufang Hou, Yacine Jernite, Harsh Jhamtani, Yangfeng Ji, Shailza Jolly, Mihir Kale, Dhruv Kumar, Faisal Ladhak, Aman

Madaan, Mounica Maddela, Khyati Mahajan, Saad Mahamood, Bodhisattwa Prasad Majumder, Pedro Henrique Martins, Angelina McMillan-Major, Simon Mille, Emiel van Miltenburg, Moin Nadeem, Shashi Narayan, Vitaly Nikolaev, Andre Niyongabo Rubungo, Salomey Osei, Ankur Parikh, Laura Perez-Beltrachini, Niranjan Ramesh Rao, Vikas Raunak, Juan Diego Rodriguez, Sashank Santhanam, João Sedoc, Thibault Sellam, Samira Shaikh, Anastasia Shimorina, Marco Antonio Sobrevilla Cabezudo, Hendrik Strobelt, Nishant Subramani, Wei Xu, Diyi Yang, Akhila Yerukola, and Jiawei Zhou. 2021. The GEM benchmark: Natural language generation, its evaluation and metrics. In *Proceedings of the 1st Workshop on Natural Language Generation, Evaluation, and Metrics (GEM 2021)*, pages 96–120, Online. Association for Computational Linguistics.

Sebastian Gehrmann, Falcon Dai, Henry Elder, and Alexander Rush. 2018. End-to-end content and plan selection for data-to-text generation. In *Proceedings of the 11th International Conference on Natural Language Generation*, pages 46–56, Tilburg University, The Netherlands. Association for Computational Linguistics.

Jiafeng Guo, Yixing Fan, Qingyao Ai, and W. Bruce Croft. 2016. A deep relevance matching model for ad-hoc retrieval. In *Proceedings of the 25th ACM International on Conference on Information and Knowledge Management*, CIKM '16, page 55–64, New York, NY, USA. Association for Computing Machinery.

Karen Kukich. 1983. Design of a knowledge-based report generator. In *21st Annual Meeting of the Association for Computational Linguistics*, pages 145–150, Cambridge, Massachusetts, USA. Association for Computational Linguistics.

Rémi Lebret, David Grangier, and Michael Auli. 2016. Neural text generation from structured data with application to the biography domain. In *Proceedings of the 2016 Conference on Empirical Methods in Natural Language Processing*, pages 1203–1213, Austin, Texas. Association for Computational Linguistics.

Mike Lewis, Yinhan Liu, Naman Goyal, Marjan Ghazvininejad, Abdelrahman Mohamed, Omer Levy, Veselin Stoyanov, and Luke Zettlemoyer. 2020. BART: Denoising sequence-to-sequence pre-training for natural language generation, translation, and comprehension. In *Proceedings of the 58th Annual Meeting of the Association for Computational Linguistics*, pages 7871–7880, Online. Association for Computational Linguistics.

Chin-Yew Lin. 2004. ROUGE: A package for automatic evaluation of summaries. In *Text Summarization Branches Out*, pages 74–81, Barcelona, Spain. Association for Computational Linguistics.

Chia-Wei Liu, Ryan Lowe, Iulian Serban, Mike Noseworthy, Laurent Charlin, and Joelle Pineau. 2016. How NOT to evaluate your dialogue system: An empirical study of unsupervised evaluation metrics for dialogue response generation. In *Proceedings of the 2016 Conference on Empirical Methods in Natural Language Processing*, pages 2122–2132, Austin, Texas. Association for Computational Linguistics.

Ryan Lowe, Michael Noseworthy, Iulian Vlad Serban, Nicolas Angelard-Gontier, Yoshua Bengio, and Joelle Pineau. 2017. Towards an automatic Turing test: Learning to evaluate dialogue responses. In *Proceedings of the 55th Annual Meeting of the Association for Computational Linguistics (Volume 1: Long Papers)*, pages 1116–1126, Vancouver, Canada. Association for Computational Linguistics.

Kathleen R. McKeown. 1985. *Text Generation: Using Discourse Strategies and Focus Constraints to Generate Natural Language Text*. Cambridge University Press, USA.

Amit Moryossef, Yoav Goldberg, and Ido Dagan. 2019. Step-by-step: Separating planning from realization in neural data-to-text generation. In *Proceedings of the 2019 Conference of the North American Chapter of the Association for Computational Linguistics: Human Language Technologies, Volume 1 (Long and Short Papers)*, pages 2267–2277, Minneapolis, Minnesota. Association for Computational Linguistics.

Jekaterina Novikova, Ondřej Dušek, Amanda Cercas Curry, and Verena Rieser. 2017. Why we need new evaluation metrics for NLG. In *Proceedings of the 2017 Conference on Empirical Methods in Natural Language Processing*, pages 2241–2252, Copenhagen, Denmark. Association for Computational Linguistics.

Kishore Papineni, Salim Roukos, Todd Ward, and Wei-Jing Zhu. 2002. Bleu: a method for automatic evaluation of machine translation. In *Proceedings of the 40th Annual Meeting of the Association for Computational Linguistics*, pages 311–318, Philadelphia, Pennsylvania, USA. Association for Computational Linguistics.

Ratish Puduppully, Li Dong, and Mirella Lapata. 2019. Data-to-text generation with content selection and planning. *Proceedings of the AAAI Conference on Artificial Intelligence*, 33(01):6908–6915.

Yevgeniy Puzikov and Iryna Gurevych. 2018. E2E NLG challenge: Neural models vs. templates. In *Proceedings of the 11th International Conference on Natural Language Generation*, pages 463–471, Tilburg University, The Netherlands. Association for Computational Linguistics.

Nils Reimers and Iryna Gurevych. 2019. Sentence-BERT: Sentence embeddings using Siamese BERT-networks. In *Proceedings of the 2019 Conference on Empirical Methods in Natural Language Processing* and the 9th International Joint Conference on Natural Language Processing (EMNLP-IJCNLP), pages 3982–3992, Hong Kong, China. Association for Computational Linguistics.

Nils Reimers and Iryna Gurevych. 2020. Making monolingual sentence embeddings multilingual using knowledge distillation. In *Proceedings of the 2019 Conference on Empirical Methods in Natural Language Processing*. Association for Computational Linguistics.

Ehud Reiter. 2018. A structured review of the validity of BLEU. *Computational Linguistics*, 44(3):393–401.

Ehud Reiter and Anja Belz. 2009. An investigation into the validity of some metrics for automatically evaluating natural language generation systems. *Computational Linguistics*, 35(4):529–558.

Ehud Reiter and Robert Dale. 1997. Building applied natural language generation systems. *Natural Language Engineering*, 3(1):57–87.

Ananya B. Sai, Akash Kumar Mohankumar, and Mitesh M. Khapra. 2020. A survey of evaluation metrics used for nlg systems. *ArXiv*, abs/2008.12009.

Thibault Sellam, Dipanjan Das, and Ankur Parikh. 2020. BLEURT: Learning robust metrics for text generation. In *Proceedings of the 58th Annual Meeting of the Association for Computational Linguistics*, pages 7881–7892, Online. Association for Computational Linguistics.

Anastasia Shimorina, Claire Gardent, Shashi Narayan, and Laura Perez-Beltrachini. 2018. WebNLG Challenge: Human Evaluation Results. Technical report, Loria & Inria Grand Est.

Hong Sun and Ming Zhou. 2012. Joint learning of a dual SMT system for paraphrase generation. In *Proceedings of the 50th Annual Meeting of the Association for Computational Linguistics (Volume 2: Short Papers)*, pages 38–42, Jeju Island, Korea. Association for Computational Linguistics.

Chongyang Tao, Lili Mou, Dongyan Zhao, and Rui Yan. 2018. Ruber: An unsupervised method for automatic evaluation of open-domain dialog systems. *AAAI Conference on Artificial Intelligence*.

Denny Vrandečić and Markus Krötzsch. 2014. Wikidata: A free collaborative knowledgebase. *Commun. ACM*, 57(10):78–85.

Sam Wiseman, Stuart Shieber, and Alexander Rush. 2017. Challenges in data-to-document generation. In *Proceedings of the 2017 Conference on Empirical Methods in Natural Language Processing*, pages 2253–2263, Copenhagen, Denmark. Association for Computational Linguistics.

Sam Wiseman, Stuart Shieber, and Alexander Rush. 2018. Learning neural templates for text generation. In *Proceedings of the 2018 Conference on Empirical Methods in Natural Language Processing*, pages 3174–3187, Brussels, Belgium. Association for Computational Linguistics.

Evaluation of Unsupervised Automatic Readability Assessors Using Rank Correlations

Yo Ehara
Tokyo Gakugei University
4-1-1 Nukuikita-machi, Koganei-shi, Tokyo 184-8501 Japan
ehara@u-gakugei.ac.jp

Abstract

Automatic readability assessment (ARA) is the task of automatically assessing readability with little or no human supervision. ARA is essential for many second language acquisition applications to reduce the workload of annotators, who are usually language teachers. Previous unsupervised approaches manually searched textual features that correlated well with readability labels, such as perplexity scores of large language models. This paper argues that, to evaluate an assessors' performance, rank-correlation coefficients should be used instead of Pearson's correlation coefficient (ρ). In the experiments, we show that its performance can be easily underestimated using Pearson's ρ, which is significantly affected by the linearity of the output readability scores. We also propose a lightweight unsupervised readability assessor that achieved the best performance in both the rank correlations and Pearson's ρ among all unsupervised assessors compared.

1 Introduction

Assessing readability plays an essential role in second language acquisition; it can be used for many educational applications such as intelligent reading support systems and placement tests for language classes. Readability assessment is a costly task for educational experts and language teachers. To perform it, they must read a text and assess its readability by guessing how difficult the text is for target learning readers. Hence, to reduce the cost of the labor required by educational experts, the task of automatically identifying the readability of texts for language learners, known as automatic readability assessment (ARA), has been extensively studied in the field of artificial intelligence (AI).

Unsupervised automatic readability assessment appeared early but has recently been reexamined as a research focus. Early studies such as the Dale-Chall formula (1948) (Dale and Chall, 1948), the Flesch Reading Ease formula (Flesch, 1948) (1948), and the Flesch-Kincaid readability formula (1975) (Kincaid et al., 1975) were *unsupervised*, as they did not use costly annotated readability labels. Given a text, these formulae calculate its readability score based on simple superficial textual features such as the average length of a word in the given text. However, most of these early formulae are designed to assess readability for children who are native speakers. Evaluation datasets with readability labels annotated by language teachers targeting second language learners appeared much later, in the 2010s (Feng et al., 2010; Xia et al., 2016; Vajjala and Lučić, 2018). In these works, automatic readability assessment tasks using these evaluation datasets were formalized as a supervised document classification problem, and substantial research efforts were invested into the construction of classifiers by feature engineering to find complicated textual features that correlate well with readability labels.

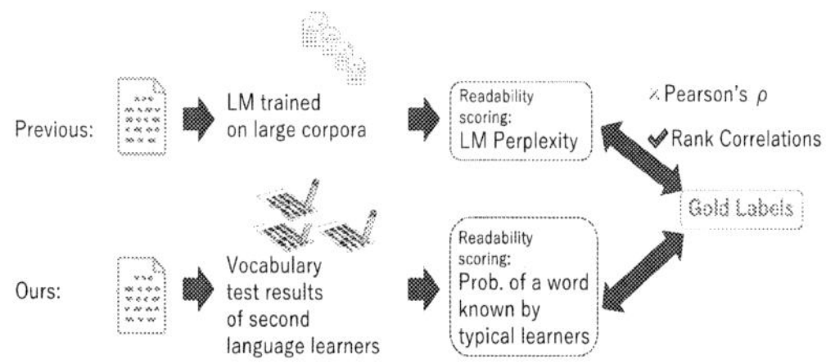

Figure 1: Overview of the previous and our approaches.

Recently, Martinc et al. (2021) revisited the unsupervised approach. They proposed that the perplexity scores of neural language models can also be used to represent the readability of text for second language learners and proposed to use them for unsupervised automatic readability assessment. The upper part of Fig. 1 show their approach. Given a text, their method uses no valuable readability label for training but uses only the language model trained on other large corpora, their method pre-

Proceedings of the 58th Annual Meeting of the Association for Computational Linguistics, pages 62–72

https://doi.org/10.26615/978-954-452-056-4_007

dicts the text's readability score as an output.

While this idea is sound, however, their evaluation is validated using the correlation coefficient, or Pearson's ρ, as illustrated on the right-hand side of Fig. 1. Pearson's ρ measures the degree of *linear* correlation between two random variables (Mukaka, 2012). As neither the readability levels of the evaluation corpora nor the readability scores output by unsupervised readability assessors are necessarily linear, the use of Pearson's ρ can lead to inaccurate evaluation.

This study investigates how the use of Pearson's ρ affects the evaluation of unsupervised readability assessors. We analyze how unsupervised assessors' performance can be easily underestimated if the readability scores are not linear. For this purpose, we also build a lightweight unsupervised readability assessor, denoted by the lower part of Fig. 1. We show that, alternatively, rank-correlation coefficients are more robust to the linearity and appropriate for this evaluation.

The contributions of this paper are summarized as follows.

- We indicate that the previous evaluation of unsupervised readability assessors by using Pearson's ρ is problematic.
- We demonstrate the degree by which Pearson's ρ underestimates the readability score without linearity on a publicly available reliable evaluation dataset.
- We show that, instead of Pearson's ρ, the use of rank-correlation coefficients is appropriate.
- We propose a novel lightweight unsupervised readability assessor that achieves best performance in terms of both Pearson's ρ and rank-correlation coefficients.

2 Automatic Readability Assessment

This section formalizes the problem of automatic readability assessment. Let us suppose that we have N texts to assess: we write the set of texts as $\{\mathcal{T}_i | i \in \{1, \dots, N\}\}$. Let $\mathcal{Y}$ be the set of readability labels. Labels are typically ordered in the order of difficulty. For example, in the *OneStopEnglish* dataset (Vajjala and Lučić, 2018), we can set $\mathcal{Y} = \{0, 1, 2\}$, where 0 is elementary, 1 is intermediate, and 2 is advanced. The number of levels depends on the evaluation corpus. Using $\mathcal{Y}$, we write the label for $\mathcal{T}_i$ as $y_i \in \mathcal{Y}$.

2.1 Goal in Unsupervised Setting

Given each text $\mathcal{T}_i$, an *assessor* outputs its readability score s_i. In a supervised setting, the *assessor* knows the number of levels in the evaluation corpus from training examples. Hence, s_i ranges within $\mathcal{Y}$: $s_i \in \mathcal{Y}$. However, in an unsupervised setting, it is noteworthy that the assessor does not know $\mathcal{Y}$, or how many levels the evaluation corpus has, because no label is given. Hence, even if only integers are allowed for y_i, s_i can be a real value.

Throughout this paper, we write arrays using [and]. Given N texts $[\mathcal{T}_i | i \in \{1, \dots, N\}]$, our goal is to make an assessor output arrays of readability scores $[s_i | i \in \{1, \dots, N\}]$ that *correlate well* with the array of labels $[y_i | i \in \{1, \dots, N\}]$. Here, there are multiple types of correlation coefficients between the array of scores and the array of labels, which we explain in the later sections. Typically, we should use *rank coefficients* when s_i is real-valued.

2.2 Evaluation and Correlation coefficients

In most evaluation datasets, educational experts are asked to assess text readability by choosing a label from the set of predefined readability labels, $\mathcal{Y}$. In contrast, automatic readability assessors output real-valued scores in an unsupervised setting. How do we compare readability level labels and real-valued scores?

A simple but naïve way to make this comparison is to use the Pearson correlation coefficient $\rho_{y,s}$, which is defined as follows:

$$\rho_{y,s} = \frac{cov(y, s)}{\sigma_y \sigma_s} \qquad (1)$$

In Eq. 1, $cov(y, s)$ denotes the covariance between y and s, σ_y denotes the standard deviation of y, and σ_s denotes the standard deviation of s. Eq. 1 ranges $[-1, 1]$, where 1 is the perfect correlation.

However, the Pearson correlation coefficient measures the degree of *linear* correlation between two random variables (Mukaka, 2012). The readability levels of evaluation corpora are not necessarily linearly distributed. Readability scores that the assessors output are also not necessarily linear. In these cases, it is usually more appropriate to focus on the correlation between the *rankings* of the readability label y_is and scores s_is. *Rank correlation coefficients* measure the correlation between two rankings with the range of $[-1, 1]$. Two types of them are notable: Spearman's ρ and Kendall's τ (Alvo and Philip, 2014).

Spearman's ρ is defined as the Pearson's ρ between two rankings. We first convert labels into rankings: rg_y, and convert scores into rankings: rg_s. Then, using Eq. 1, Spearman's ρ is defined as $\rho_{\text{rg}_y \text{rg}_s}$. When converting labels into rankings, texts that have the same level are regarded as *ties* in a ranking. While there are many ways to handle ties, the *mid-rank* method is usually used in calculating Spearman's ρ (Amerise and Tarsitano, 2015). This method simply uses the average of ranks for the rank of a tie. For example, let us consider an array of labels $[2, 1, 1, 0]$. The two 1s in this array are ties taking the 2nd and 3rd ranks. As the average of 2 and 3 is 2.5, the *mid-rank* ranking of this array is $[4, 2.5, 2.5, 1]$.

We first introduce the definition of Kendall's τ when there are no ties as follows.

$$\tau = \frac{n_c - n_d}{\text{Num. of all pairs}} \tag{2}$$

Kendall's τ focuses on the pairs of the given arrays: in our setting, (y_i, s_i) and $(y_{i'}, s_{i'})$ where $i < i'$. n_c denotes the number of concordant pairs, n_d denotes the number of discordant pairs. The pair is said to be concordant if either both $y_i < y_{i'}$ and $s_i < s_{i'}$ hold or $y_i > y_{i'}$ and $s_i > s_{i'}$; otherwise, the pair is said to be discordant. If $y_i = y_{i'}$, we call y_i and $y_{i'}$ ties. The same holds for s. Num. of all pairs $= \frac{1}{2}N(N-1)$ when there are no ties.

In reality, y has many ties, so Eq. 2 cannot be used for the evaluation.. There are multiple correction methods to account for ties in Kendall's τ; they are named τ-a, τ-b, and τ-c. In our setting, namely unsupervised readability assessment, tau-c should be used because y and s may have different scales.

τ-b can be described as follows [1].

$$\tau_b = \frac{n_c - n_d}{\sqrt{(n_0 - n_1)(n_0 - n_2)}} \tag{3}$$

n_c denotes the number of concordant pairs, n_d denotes the number of discordant pairs. $n_0 = N(N-1)/2$, n_1 is the sum of all possible pairs within each tied group for the first quantity, n_2 is the sum of all possible pairs within each tied group for the second quantity.

τ-c can be written as follows[2]. To obtain m, we first construct the contingency table made from the first and second quantity. Using the rows and columns of the table, m is defined as $\min(\text{num. of rows}, \text{num. of columns})$.

$$\tau_c = \frac{2(n_c - n_d)}{N^2 \frac{m-1}{m}} \tag{4}$$

[1] https://en.wikipedia.org/wiki/Kendall_rank_correlation_coefficient#Tau-b

[2] https://en.wikipedia.org/wiki/Kendall_rank_correlation_coefficient#Tau-c

```
15. deficit:
The company <had a large deficit>.
a: spent a lot more money than it earned
b: went down a lot in value
c: had a plan for its spending
                that used a lot of money
d: had a lot of money stored in the bank

26. malign:
His <malign> influence is still felt.
a: good
b: evil
c: very important
d: secret
```

Figure 2: Examples of the Vocabulary Size Test. Test-takers are asked to choose the option that paraphrases the part between "$<$" and "$>$" from a, b, c, and d.

3 Proposed Method: Vocabulary Testing

This section describes our unsupervised readability assessor that employs a novel approach: instead of using valuable readability labels as the source of text difficulty for typical second language learners, our proposed method uses vocabulary tests as the source of word difficulty for typical second language learners and obtains readability scores based on accurately estimated word difficulty. To this end, this section explains how to analyze vocabulary test result data to obtain word difficulty.

Fig. 2 shows example questions from the vocabulary size test, a widely used vocabulary test in applied linguistics (Beglar and Nation, 2007). Each question asks about a word in a multiple-choice question format. The test consists of 100 questions like those shown in Fig. 2. Ehara (2018) used this test to have 100 second-language learners take the test and to collect their responses. Their data were published and made publicly available. We used their dataset to train our classifiers.

3.1 Evaluating vocabulary test results: Item Response Theory

We want to analyze vocabulary test results to obtain word difficulty values encoding learners' language knowledge. To this end, we employed the idea of *item response theory* (Baker, 2004), a statistical model that can estimate learners' abilities and test questions' difficulties from the learners' responses to the questions.

Let $\mathcal{V}$ be the set of vocabulary, and let $\mathcal{L}$ be the set of learners. Let $z_{v,l} \in \{0,1\}$ be the result of whether learner $l \in \mathcal{L}$ correctly answered the question for word $v \in \mathcal{V}$: $z_{l,v} = 1$ if l answered correctly for word v; otherwise, $z_{l,v} = 0$. Correct answers usually imply that l knows word v.

Then, by using $\{z_{v,l}\}$ as the training data, we train the following model:

$$p(z = 1|v, l) = \text{sigmoid}(a_l - d_v) \qquad (5)$$

In Eq. 5, a_l is the ability parameter of learner l, d_v is the difficulty of word w, and sigmoid denotes the logistic sigmoid function, i.e., $\text{sigmoid}(x) = \frac{1}{1+\exp(-x)}$. The logistic sigmoid function is the binary version of the softmax function, which is frequently used in neural classifiers. It is a monotonously increasing function ranging within $(0,1)$. As $\text{sigmoid}(0) = \frac{1}{1+1} = \frac{1}{2}$, when a learner's ability a_l is larger than the word difficulty d_v, the probability that learner l knows word v can be written as follows: $p(z = 1|v, l) > \frac{1}{2}$ in Eq. 5. Likewise, by using Eq. 5, we can compare a learner's ability and word difficulty in the same dimension.

To estimate learner ability and word difficulty, $z_{v,l}$ is given as z in Eq. 5 in the training phase. In this way, in *item response theory*, learner ability and word difficulty are comparable, and these parameters are to be estimated from the test result data.

3.2 Obtaining difficulty of words not in the vocabulary test

In Eq. 5, d_v denotes the word difficulty estimated from the vocabulary tests. Here, in addition to the word difficulty for the words within the vocabulary test, we also want to obtain word difficulty values for all words that may appear in the target language. To this end, we calculate d_v from the word frequency in large balanced corpora as follows:

$$d_v = -\sum_{k=1}^{K} w_k \log(\text{freq}_k(v) + 1) \qquad (6)$$

In Eq. 6, K is the number of corpora to use, $\text{freq}_k(v)$ denotes the frequency of word v in the k-th corpus, and w_k is the weight parameter of the k-th corpus.

In summary, given the vocabulary test results $\{z_{v,l}\}$ and corpus frequency features $\text{freq}_k(v)$, we can estimate the parameters: namely, the weight of the k-th corpus w_k and learner l's ability a_l. By putting Eq. 5 and Eq. 6 together, we can see that the inside formula of the sigmoid function is linear with respect to the parameters to be estimated because all terms consist of a product of a parameter and a constant calculated from features, and no term has a product of two or more parameters. As the sigmoid function of a linear combination of parameters can be reformulated as a logistic regression, we can implement Eq. 5 and Eq. 6 by using typical logistic regression classifiers such as scikit-learn [3] and LIBLINEAR [4]. We will release our code upon the acceptance of the paper.

Note that we do not use the valuable readability label $\{y_i\}$ in the training phase; hence, our method is categorized as an unsupervised method.

3.3 Proposed Automatic Readability Assessor

After estimating the parameters using the above-mentioned procedure, we use the following formula to obtain the readability of given $\mathcal{T}_i$. Here, l_{avg} denotes the test-taker whose estimated ability parameter is closest to the average of the estimated ability parameter values $\{a_l\}$s. Intuitively, the following equation calculates the probability that the average learner knows all the words that appear in $\mathcal{T}_i$ and uses it as the readability score:

$$\begin{aligned} s_i &= score(\mathcal{T}_i) \\ &= -\frac{1}{|\mathcal{T}_i|} \log \left(\prod_{v \in \mathcal{T}_i} p(z = 1|v, l_{\text{avg}}) \right). \quad (7) \end{aligned}$$

4 Experimental Settings

4.1 Choice of Dataset

We used the OneStopEnglish dataset (Vajjala and Lučić, 2018) for our evaluation because of the following reasons. First, it is one of the newest datasets. Second, it is publicly available and downloadable. Third, it is a reliable dataset in the sense that it has no known pitfalls when used as a corpus for evaluation.

While Martinc et al. (2021) uses other corpora such as the WeeBit corpus (Xia et al., 2016) and the Newsela corpus (Xu et al., 2015), both have known pitfalls when used for the evaluation of automatic readability assessment. The WeeBit corpus is not a *parallel corpus*, which is explained in the next

[3] `https://scikit-learn.org/stable/`

[4] `https://www.csie.ntu.edu.tw/~cjlin/liblinear/`

subsection. This means that each level consists of totally different articles covering different topics. As some topics such as politics tend to use more difficult phrases than other topics, it is difficult to see how the topic of content influences the resulting performance values. The Newsela corpus is a parallel corpus, which removes the influence caused by topics. However, according to Martinc et al. (2021), its readability labels can be easily identified from the average sentence length in a text: the average sentence length achieved 0.906 in the Pearson's ρ correlation. Hence, even if a method works well on the Newsela corpus, it could be possible that the method merely inherently calculates and uses average sentence length.

4.2 OneStopEnglish dataset

Regarding the source of the dataset, Vajjala and Lučić (2018) says that "onestopenglish.com is an English language learning resources website run by MacMillan Education, with over 700,000 users across 100 countries."

The dataset has three levels: elementary, intermediate, and advanced. According to Vajjala and Lučić (2018), the original articles were taken from the Guardian newspaper. The OneStopEnglish dataset is a parallel corpus, i.e, language teachers manually rewrote the original articles into the three aforementioned readability levels. Hence, one notable characteristic of this dataset is that all three levels have the same content with different readability levels. Hence, by using this dataset, we can avoid having classifiers learn differences in content or topic rather than readability levels.

All three levels have 189 texts each, 567 texts in total. We split these texts into a *training set* consisting of 339 texts, a *validation* set consisting of 114 texts, and a *test* set consisting of 114 texts. The *training set* and *validation* sets were used to train solely supervised methods for comparison. Unsupervised methods did not use the training and validation sets; they used only the test set.

4.3 Baseline Methods

4.3.1 Supervised methods

First, we introduce the supervised methods that we used for comparison because it involves the training data mentioned right above. As the BERT-based sequence classification has been reported to achieve excellent results (Devlin et al., 2019), we applied the standard BERT-based sequence classification approach involving pretraining and fine-tuning. For the pretrained model, we used **bert-large-cased-whole-word-masking** in the Huggingface models [5].

Then, we fine-tuned the model using the aforementioned 339 training texts. For this fine-tuning, we used a GeForce RTX 3090 board that has 24 GiB of Graphical Processing Unit (GPU) memory. The fine-tuning and resulting model took up 16 GiB of GPU memory. This means that it is difficult to achieve similar performance without GPUs with large memory. We named this fine-tuned model **spvBERT**, in which "spv" denotes being supervised. In order to see how the size of training data has an influence on the performance, we also conducted experiments with 168 training texts, which amounted to almost half of the total 339 training texts. We named this model **spvBERT_half**.

All the fine-tuning procedures were conducted using the Adam optimizer (Kingma and Ba, 2015) with a setting of 10 epochs and a 0.00001 training rate.

4.3.2 Unsupervised methods

For the implementation of conventional readability formulae, we used the **readability** PyPI package [6]. We used almost all readability formulae implemented in this package for our experiments: namely, **Flesch-Kincaid** (Flesch-Kincaid Grade Level, FKGL) (Kincaid et al., 1975), **ARI** (Automated Readability Index) (Senter and Smith, 1967), the **Coleman-Liau** Index (Coleman and Liau, 1975), **Flesch Reading Ease** (Flesch, 1948), the **Gunning Fog Index** (Gunning, 1952), **LIX** (Björnsson, 1968), the **SMOG Index** (Mc Laughlin, 1969), the RIX index (Anderson, 1983), and the **Dale-Chall Index** (Dale and Chall, 1948). Among these methods, notably, some formulae such as the Dale-Chall Index depend on their own list of easy/difficult words. Others, such as the Flesch-Kincaid grade level (FKGL), do not require such a list of difficult words but use superficial features such as the total number of syllables in a text. For space limitation, we do not cite all equations, however, we only cite FKGL as being famous and cite Dale-Chall as showing good performance in our evaluation.

$$\text{FKGL} = 0.39\frac{\text{total words}}{\text{total sentences}} \qquad (8)$$

[5]https://huggingface.co/models

[6]https://pypi.org/project/readability/

$$+ \quad 11.8\frac{\text{total syllables}}{\text{total sentences}} - 15.59$$

$$\text{Dale-Chall} \quad = \quad 15.79 \times \left(\frac{\text{difficult words}}{\text{words}}\right) \quad (9)$$
$$+ \quad 0.0496\left(\frac{\text{words}}{\text{sentences}}\right)$$

More details of these formulae and their implementation are described on the project page. All of these readability formulae are *unsupervised* in the sense that they do not require any training data.

For the unsupervised neural language model, we also used the **bert-large-cased-whole-word-masking** pretraining model and used the **BertForMaskedLM** function to obtain the perplexity of each sentence of the text of interest. We chose this pretraining model because Martinc et al. (2021) reported that they used **bert-base-uncased** and reported not so good performance, so we chose a BERT-based model larger than the one that they used. Note that, unlike neural sequence classification, language models are designed to be unsupervised and thus do not require any training data to fine-tune. All we need to do for the neural language model is to input each sentence in the text of interest and calculate the perplexity score of the inputted sentence.

For splitting a text into sentences, we used the **sent_tokenize** function in the **nltk** Python package [7]. After the split, we simply used the average of the perplexity scores of each sentence in a text as the readability score. As the perplexity score of a sentence encodes the fluency of the inputted sentence, this roughly measures the overall fluency of the inputted sentence. We call this method **BERTLMavg**, where LM denotes a *language model*.

As **BERTLMavg** does not use fine-tuning, it uses less GPU memory compared to **spvBERT**. However, **BERTLMavg** uses 1,793 MiB of GPU memory to output perplexity scores, which is still impractical in a low-computational-resource environment.

According to Martinc et al. (2021), BERT language models do not perform good results. Hence, while not directly comparable because we could not obtain their test set, for a rough comparison, we cited their best model on the OneStopEnglish dataset, **TCN RSRS-simple**. The model is temporal convolutional network (TCN) trained on the Simplified Wikipedia corpus. For space limitations, refer to Martinc et al. (2021) for the details of this method.

Proposed model was trained on a previously published and publicly available vocabulary dataset (Ehara, 2018). For the corpus word frequency, we used the frequencies taken from the British National Corpus (BNC Consortium, 2007) and the Corpus of Contemporary American English (COCA) (Davies, 2008). Both corpora are balanced general corpora used extensively in English education (Nation, 2006). Especially, the word frequencies of these corpora are important resources for determining word difficulty in English education. For counting text frequencies, we used **nltk.stem.WordNetLemmatizer** in the **nltk** package to lemmatize words appearing in running texts.

Our **Proposed** model uses the average of the negative log likelihood that an average learner knows each word in the text as presented in Eq. 7. As our **Proposed** model uses the BNC and COCA word frequencies, it could be possible that these word frequencies have an essential influence on the performance of the **Proposed** model. To check this, we also measured the correlation between the gold labels and the average negative log of the unigram probability values of the given text in each corpus. We name these feature-based methods as **BNC** and **COCA**.

4.4 Experimental Results: Pearson's ρ and performance

This subsection describes the experimental results showing the problem of using Pearson's ρ in evaluation.

Tab. 1 shows the experimental results. The columns of Tab. 1 show the rank correlation coefficients introduced in the previous sections. Namely, they are Spearman's ρ, Kendall's τ with tie correction type b (τ-b), and Kendall's τ with tie correction type c (τ-c). Pearson's ρ is shown in the rightmost column. As we explained in previous sections, Pearson's ρ is affected by the linearity of scores. To see how Pearson's ρ is affected by the linearity of scores, below each unsupervised method **M**, we show $exp(\mathbf{M})$ to indicate the resulting performance values when we replaced the scores of M with the exponentilized the scores of M, i.e, exp(the score of M) to remove linearity. The distinction of "unsupervised" and "supervised" is clearly marked in the leftmost column.

In Tab. 1, we can easily see that, for all unsuper-

[7] nltk.org

Supervision	Method	Spearman's ρ	Kendall's τ-b	Kendall's τ-c	Pearson's ρ
Unsupervised	**Flesch-Kincaid**	0.324	0.253	0.308	0.359
	exp(**Flesch-Kincaid**)	0.324	0.253	0.308	0.149
	ARI	0.317	0.248	0.302	0.351
	exp(**ARI**)	0.317	0.248	0.302	0.136
	Coleman-Liau	0.373	0.295	0.359	0.372
	exp(**Coleman-Liau**)	0.373	0.295	0.359	0.185
	FleschReadingEase	-0.387	-0.301	-0.366	-0.426
	exp(**FleschReadingEase**)	-0.387	-0.301	-0.366	-0.169
	GunningFogIndex	0.331	0.257	0.313	0.362
	exp(**GunningFogIndex**)	0.331	0.257	0.313	0.151
	LIX	0.348	0.273	0.332	0.383
	exp(**LIX**)	0.348	0.273	0.332	0.129
	SMOGIndex	0.456	0.360	0.438	0.479
	exp(**SMOGIndex**)	0.456	0.360	0.438	0.306
	RIX	0.437	0.340	0.414	0.462
	exp(**RIX**)	0.437	0.340	0.414	0.181
	DaleChallIndex	0.495	0.387	0.472	0.506
	exp(**DaleChallIndex**)	0.495	0.387	0.472	0.431
	TCN RSRS-simple	-	-	-	0.615(*)
	BERTLMavg	-0.220	-0.173	-0.210	-0.040
	exp(**BERTLMavg**)	-0.220	-0.173	-0.210	-0.005
	BNC	-0.012	-0.009	-0.010	-0.006
	exp(**BNC**)	-0.012	-0.009	-0.010	-0.123
	COCA	-0.018	-0.016	-0.020	-0.039
	exp(**COCA**)	-0.018	-0.016	-0.020	-0.121
	Proposed	**0.730**	**0.592**	**0.709**	**0.715**
	exp(**Proposed**)	**0.730**	**0.592**	**0.709**	0.260
Supervised	**spvBERT_half**	0.751	0.729	0.725	0.747
	spvBERT	**0.866**	**0.856**	**0.854**	**0.864**

Table 1: Experimental Results on the OneStopEnglish Dataset. For a method M, exp(M) denotes the correlations between the array of exp(M's score) and the gold labels. (*) denotes that the value is cited from other papers.

vised methods except for **BNC** and **COCA**, the correlations of the exponentialized scores measured by Pearson's ρ are closer to 0 than their original scores. In contrast, the rank correlation coefficient values are kept unchanged because exp is a monotonous function and hence the ranking is not altered by the use of exp. The reason why the performance values of **BNC** and **COCA** seem slightly increased is presumably because of noise: **BNC** and **COCA** did not correlate with the readability labels statistically significantly in the first place. Neither did exp(**BNC**) and exp(**COCA**).

The drop in performance scores is enormous for some methods such as **Proposed**: its performance was originally 0.715 but plunges to 0.260 by using exp. This result indicates the vulnerability of using Pearson's ρ in the evaluation: the evaluation by Pearson's ρ is strongly affected by how linear the scores are, suggesting the use of rank correlation for better evaluation.

TCN RSRS-simple is the best model using the same dataset in Martinc et al. (2021). As they show only the performance measured by the Pearson correlation, we wrote – for other rank correlation coefficients. Also note that we cannot make direct comparison as we could not obtain their test set used for their experiments. This is marked by the (*) after the value. While we can see that **Proposed** achieved better correlation than **TCN RSRS-simple**, we are not sure if this result indicates the linearity of the methods or the superiority of **Proposed** against **TCN RSRS-simple**. Likewise, the use of Pearson's ρ only makes followup papers' efforts to compare results difficult.

4.5 Performance Comparison

In all unsupervised methods, our **Proposed** method achieved the best results in all rank correlation coefficients and Pearson's ρ, although we need to be careful with the interpretation of Pearson's rho as explained in Sec. 2.2. These results were statistically significant ($p < 0.01$): all correlation coefficients can also be used for statistical testing. In each of the statistical tests, the null hypothesis is that no association exists between the scores and the gold labels. When measured using Spearman's ρ, **Proposed** achieved a value of 0.730, which is close to 0.751, the performance achieved by *supervised* BERT using half of the training data.

BERTLMavg did not achieve good results in predicting readability labels. This result suggests that perplexity and readability are different measures and that, to measure readability, we need to obtain and make use of the information about what a typical language learner knows about the target second language.

Interestingly, **BNC** and **COCA** achieved poor results in predicting readability labels. This result shows that the reason that **Proposed** method outperformed the others is not merely because the features that **Proposed** used are excellent. A good combination of the two features results in significant results. The use of only one of the two does not achieve good results. Hence, we can see that **Proposed** works excellently for making the combination of the two corpus-based features.

For a comparison with supervised models, Tab. 1 shows their performances: **spvBERT** and **spvBERT_half**. Supervised models output labels rather than scores in their prediction phase: we directly used these labels to calculate rank correlation coefficients for a fair comparison with unsupervised models. Leveraging the supervision, they outperformed most of the unsupervised methods in all rank correlation coefficients. This means that using valuable supervision yields great improvement in the predictive performance of readability.

The performance differences among **spvBERT**, **BERTLMavg**, and **Proposed** can be interpreted as follows. BERT is a large model trying to use as much information as possible from a sentence, such as syntactic structure. Hence, it is difficult for the model to find useful information contributing to readability without supervision. **Proposed** is a bag-of-words model that is designed to be lightweight by sacrificing such complicated factors. Hence, the performance difference between **spvBERT** and **Proposed** can be regarded as a degree that information beyond word difficulty – such as syntactic information or sentence context – accounts for readability. While this is beyond the focus of this paper, a detailed error analysis between **spvBERT** and **Proposed** may lead to understanding what kind of syntactic information or contexts in a sentence contribute to readability.

4.6 Memory and Speed

We used a Core i7-10700K (3.80 GHz) machine with a GeForce RTX 3090 board for all experiments. The **BERTLMavg**, which is an unsupervised BERT language model, uses $1,793$ MiB GPU memory. In contrast, **Proposed** is merely a logistic regression and does not require as GPU for practical use. In addition, the model's features are smaller than those of the BERT models. **Proposed** uses the BNC and COCA frequencies, which amount to 10 MiB of CPU memory, which is roughly $\frac{1}{100}$ of that used by the unsupervised BERT models. In terms of speed, to classify all texts in the test set, while **BERTLMavg** utilizes 368 s, **Proposed** utilizes only 5.37 s. This indicates that the **Proposed** is 68.5 times faster than **BERTLMavg**.

5 Discussion

In this paper, we discussed the necessity to use rank correlation coefficients to evaluate automatic readability assessment. The problem that Pearson correlation coefficients reflect not only the correlation between two scores but also the linearity of the scores is not particularly novel and has been pointed out for a long time. This study showed that this problem has a significant impact in the evaluation of the ARA task. In fact, in the recent evaluation of the ARA task (Martinc et al., 2021), the problem of linearity in the Pearson coefficients was *not* addressed and its evaluation simply uses the Pearson correlation coefficients. To the best of our knowledge, this is the first study to demonstrate the effect of this problem on the performance values in the ARA task and examine the extent to which the linearity of the scores affects the scores in Tab. 1.

In this paper, we termed the **Proposed** method as

"unsupervised," according to (Martinc et al., 2021). They termed methods that do not use manually annotated readability labels as "unsupervised" even if the methods use supervised machine learning. In fact, the proposed method is trained using the vocabulary test dataset (Ehara, 2018). Phrases, such as "the most average learner" and "learner ability, all refer to the learners on this vocabulary test dataset. In this study, knowing that the term supervised/unsupervised is misleading, we deliberately described the proposed method as "unsupervised" for easy comparison with previous studies.

In NLP, the **Proposed** method is closely related to complex word identification (CWI) tasks (Yimam et al., 2018; Paetzold and Specia, 2016). CWI is a task that aims to discover difficult words in a text. The relationship between CWI and personalized text readability was previously studied in (Ehara, 2019). The task of obtaining the difficulty of an English word for each individual ESL learner, as we did in this study, can be regarded as personalized CWI (Ehara et al., 2012, 2014) [8]. Personalized CWI has many downstream applications in NLP such as lexical simplification (Lee and Yeung, 2018, 2019), text recommendation for language learners (Ehara et al., 2013; Yeung and Lee, 2018; Lee, 2021), and translator selection in crowdsourcing (Ehara et al., 2016). Some studies focus on the relationship between word semantics and word difficulty (Ehara et al., 2014; Beinborn et al., 2016; Ehara, 2020b). Regarding the interpretability of CWI classifiers, Ehara (2020a) studied the relationship CWI classifiers' weights and vocabulary sizes.

6 Conclusions

In this paper, we investigated the correlation coefficients to evaluate the performance of unsupervised automatic readability assessors. The experimental results showed that the readability performances measured by Pearson's ρ are strongly affected by the linearity of the output scores, whereas those measured by rank correlations are not affected. This indicates the appropriateness of using rank correlation coefficients to evaluate unsupervised automatic readability assessors. We also proposed a lightweight unsupervised assessor based on word difficulty for typical second language learners calculated from a vocabulary test result dataset. This assessor could achieve the best score among all the compared unsupervised assessors.

In the future, we plan to conduct a more detailed analysis to investigate which rank correlations, including those not introduced in this paper, are more appropriate for the evaluation.

[8]The journal version of (Ehara et al., 2012) is (Ehara et al., 2018).

Acknowledgment

This study was supported by JST ACT-X Grant Number JPMJAX2006 and JSPS KAKENHI Grant Number 18K18118. We used the ABCI infrastructure from AIST for the computational resources. We appreciate anonymous reviewers for their valuable comments.

References

Mayer Alvo and LH Philip. 2014. *Statistical methods for ranking data*, volume 1341. Springer.

Ilaria L Amerise and Agostino Tarsitano. 2015. Correction methods for ties in rank correlations. *Journal of Applied Statistics*, 42(12):2584–2596.

Jonathan Anderson. 1983. Lix and rix: Variations on a little-known readability index. *Journal of Reading*, 26(6):490–496.

Frank B. Baker. 2004. *Item Response Theory : Parameter Estimation Techniques, Second Edition.* CRC Press.

David Beglar and Paul Nation. 2007. A vocabulary size test. *The Language Teacher*, 31(7):9–13.

Lisa Beinborn, Torsten Zesch, and Iryna Gurevych. 2016. Predicting the Spelling Difficulty of Words for Language Learners. In *Proceedings of the 11th Workshop on Innovative Use of NLP for Building Educational Applications*, pages 73–83, San Diego, CA. Association for Computational Linguistics.

C. H. Björnsson. 1968. Läsbarhet, Stockholm.

BNC Consortium. 2007. The british national corpus, version 3 (bnc xml edition). Distributed by Bodleian Libraries, University of Oxford, on behalf of the BNC Consortium `http://www.natcorp.ox.ac.uk/`.

Meri Coleman and Ta Lin Liau. 1975. A computer readability formula designed for machine scoring. *Journal of Applied Psychology*, 60(2):283.

Edgar Dale and Jeanne S Chall. 1948. A formula for predicting readability: Instructions. *Educational research bulletin*, pages 37–54.

Mark Davies. 2008. The corpus of contemporary american english (coca). Available online at `https://www.english-corpora.org/coca/`.

Jacob Devlin, Ming-Wei Chang, Kenton Lee, and Kristina Toutanova. 2019. BERT: Pre-training of Deep Bidirectional Transformers for Language Understanding. In *Proc. of NAACL*, pages 4171–4186, Minneapolis, Minnesota.

Yo Ehara. 2018. Building an English Vocabulary Knowledge Dataset of Japanese English-as-a-Second-Language Learners Using Crowdsourcing. In *Proc. of LREC*.

Yo Ehara. 2019. Uncertainty-Aware Personalized Readability Assessments for Second Language Learners. In *2019 18th IEEE International Conference On Machine Learning And Applications (ICMLA)*, pages 1909–1916.

Yo Ehara. 2020a. Interpreting neural CWI classifiers' weights as vocabulary size. In *Proceedings of the Fifteenth Workshop on Innovative Use of NLP for Building Educational Applications*, pages 171–176, Seattle, WA, USA → Online. Association for Computational Linguistics.

Yo Ehara. 2020b. Neural rasch model: How do word embeddings adjust word difficulty? In *Computational Linguistics – 16th International Conference of the Pacific Association for Computational Linguistics, PACLING 2019, Hanoi, Vietnam, October 11–13, 2019, Revised Selected Papers*, pages 88–96, Singapore. Springer Singapore.

Yo Ehara, Yukino Baba, Masao Utiyama, and Eiichiro Sumita. 2016. Assessing Translation Ability through Vocabulary Ability Assessment. In *Proc. of IJCAI*.

Yo Ehara, Yusuke Miyao, Hidekazu Oiwa, Issei Sato, and Hiroshi Nakagawa. 2014. Formalizing Word Sampling for Vocabulary Prediction as Graph-based Active Learning. In *Proc. of EMNLP*, pages 1374–1384.

Yo Ehara, Issei Sato, Hidekazu Oiwa, and Hiroshi Nakagawa. 2012. Mining Words in the Minds of Second Language Learners: Learner-Specific Word Difficulty. In *Proceedings of COLING 2012*, pages 799–814, Mumbai, India. The COLING 2012 Organizing Committee.

Yo Ehara, Issei Sato, Hidekazu Oiwa, and Hiroshi Nakagawa. 2018. Mining Words in the Minds of Second Language Learners for Learner-specific Word Difficulty. *Journal of Information Processing*, 26:267–275.

Yo Ehara, Nobuyuki Shimizu, Takashi Ninomiya, and Hiroshi Nakagawa. 2013. Personalized Reading Support for Second-language Web Documents. *ACM Trans. Intell. Syst. Technol.*, 4(2):31:1–31:19.

Lijun Feng, Martin Jansche, Matt Huenerfauth, and Noémie Elhadad. 2010. A Comparison of Features for Automatic Readability Assessment. pages 276–284.

Rudolf Flesch. 1948. A new readability yardstick. *Journal of Applied Psychology*, 32(3):221–233.

Robert Gunning. 1952. *The Technique of Clear Writing*. McGraw-Hill.

J Peter Kincaid, Robert P Fishburne Jr, Richard L Rogers, and Brad S Chissom. 1975. Derivation of new readability formulas (automated readability index, fog count and flesch reading ease formula) for navy enlisted personnel. Technical report, Naval Technical Training Command Millington TN Research Branch.

Diederik P Kingma and Jimmy Ba. 2015. Adam: A method for stochastic optimization. In *Proc. of ICLR*.

John Lee and Chak Yan Yeung. 2018. Personalizing Lexical Simplification. In *Proceedings of the 27th International Conference on Computational Linguistics*, pages 224–232, Santa Fe, New Mexico, USA. Association for Computational Linguistics.

John Lee and Chak Yan Yeung. 2019. Personalized Substitution Ranking for Lexical Simplification. In *Proceedings of the 12th International Conference on Natural Language Generation*, pages 258–267, Tokyo, Japan. Association for Computational Linguistics.

John SY Lee. 2021. An editable learner model for text recommendation for language learning. *ReCALL*, pages 1–15.

Matej Martinc, Senja Pollak, and Marko Robnik-Šikonja. 2021. Supervised and Unsupervised Neural Approaches to Text Readability. *Computational Linguistics*, 47(1):141–179.

G Harry Mc Laughlin. 1969. Smog grading-a new readability formula. *Journal of reading*, 12(8):639–646.

Mavuto M Mukaka. 2012. A guide to appropriate use of correlation coefficient in medical research. *Malawi medical journal*, 24(3):69–71.

I. Nation. 2006. How Large a Vocabulary is Needed For Reading and Listening? *Canadian Modern Language Review*, 63(1):59–82.

Gustavo Paetzold and Lucia Specia. 2016. Collecting and Exploring Everyday Language for Predicting Psycholinguistic Properties of Words. In *Proceedings of COLING 2016, the 26th International Conference on Computational Linguistics: Technical Papers*, pages 1669–1679, Osaka, Japan. The COLING 2016 Organizing Committee.

RJ Senter and Edgar A Smith. 1967. Automated readability index. Technical report, CINCINNATI UNIV OH.

Sowmya Vajjala and Ivana Lučić. 2018. OneStopEnglish corpus: A new corpus for automatic readability assessment and text simplification. In

Proceedings of the Thirteenth Workshop on Innovative Use of NLP for Building Educational Applications, pages 297–304, New Orleans, Louisiana. Association for Computational Linguistics.

Menglin Xia, Ekaterina Kochmar, and Ted Briscoe. 2016. Text Readability Assessment for Second Language Learners. In *Proceedings of the 11th Workshop on Innovative Use of NLP for Building Educational Applications*, pages 12–22, San Diego, CA. Association for Computational Linguistics.

Wei Xu, Chris Callison-Burch, and Courtney Napoles. 2015. Problems in Current Text Simplification Research: New Data Can Help. *Transactions of the Association for Computational Linguistics*, 3:283–297.

Chak Yan Yeung and John Lee. 2018. Personalized Text Retrieval for Learners of Chinese as a Foreign Language. In *Proc. of COLING*, pages 3448–3455.

Seid Muhie Yimam, Chris Biemann, Shervin Malmasi, Gustavo H. Paetzold, Lucia Specia, Sanja Štajner, Anaïs Tack, and Marcos Zampieri. 2018. A Report on the Complex Word Identification Shared Task 2018. *arXiv:1804.09132 [cs]*. ArXiv: 1804.09132.

Testing Cross-Database Semantic Parsers Using Canonical Utterances

Heather Lent[ç]* **Semih Yavuz**[ʃ] **Tao Yu**[fi]
Tong Niu[ʃ] **Yingbo Zhou**[ʃ] **Dragomir Radev**[Y] **Xi Victoria Lin**[Φ]
[ç] University of Copenhagen, [ʃ] Salesforce Research
[fi] Hong Kong University, [Y] Yale University, [Φ] Facebook AI Research
hcl@di.ku.dk, tyu@cs.hku.hk
{syavuz, tniu, yingbo.zhou}@salesforce.com
dragomir.radev@yale.edu, victorialin@fb.com

Abstract

The benchmark performance of cross-database semantic parsing has climbed steadily in recent years, catalyzed by the wide adoption of pre-trained language models. Yet existing work have shown that state-of-the-art cross-database semantic parsers struggle to generalize to novel user utterances, databases and query structures. To obtain transparent details on the strengths and limitation of these models, we propose a diagnostic testing approach based on controlled synthesis of canonical natural language and SQL pairs. Inspired by the CheckList (Ribeiro et al., 2020), we characterize a set of essential capabilities for cross-database semantic parsing models, and detailed the method for synthesizing the corresponding test data. We evaluated a variety of high performing models using the proposed approach, and identified several non-obvious weaknesses across models (e.g. unable to correctly select many columns). Our dataset and code are released as a test suite at http://github.com/hclent/BehaviorCheckingSemPar.

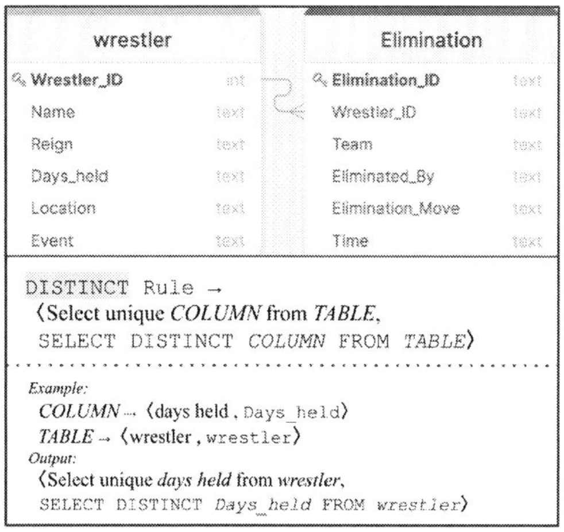

Figure 1: The database (top) is applied to our SCFG production rule (middle) to produce a new example for the DISTINCT category (bottom). See Appendix B for production rules of other categories.

1 Introduction

Cross-database semantic parsing, the task of mapping natural language utterances to SQL queries for any database, has attracted increasing attention since the introduction of benchmarks like WikiSQL (Zhong et al., 2017) and Spider (Yu et al., 2018). The advent of pre-trained language models (Peters et al., 2018; Devlin et al., 2019; Liu et al., 2019; Lewis et al., 2020) has further accelerated the progress in this area (Lin et al., 2020; Yu et al., 2020; Shi et al., 2020; Wang et al., 2020; Choi et al., 2020).

Despite impressive gains on standard benchmarks, studies on cross-database semantic parsing models show that they still suffer from out-of-distribution (OOD) generalization when presented with novel user utterances (Suhr et al., 2020; Radhakrishnan et al., 2020; Shaw et al., 2021), databases (Suhr et al., 2020) and SQL query structures (Finegan-Dollak et al., 2018; Suhr et al., 2020; Shaw et al., 2021). As baseline performance climbs ever upward, at what point can we confidently deploy our models to end users, and how will we know we have reached this point?

Inspired by Ribeiro et al. (2020), which has shown the effectiveness of simple, systematic, and heuristic behavior checking strategies for evaluating the robustness of NLP models, we propose a controllable, non-adversarial unit testing approach to shed more light on the capabilities of cross-database semantic parsers. We implement a synchronous context-free grammar (SCFG) to generate natural language questions based on SQL queries (Figure 1). This grammar features production rules that evaluate important categories of SQL element types such as clauses (e.g. SELECT and WHERE), as well as commonly used operators including aggre-

*Work done during an internship at Salesforce Research.

Proceedings of the 58th Annual Meeting of the Association for Computational Linguistics, pages 73–83

https://doi.org/10.26615/978-954-452-056-4_008

gators (MAX), conditionals (BETWEEN), and logical operators (OR). We handcraft the rules for these categories to ensure that the generated question-query pairs are simple, natural, unambiguous, and with minimal cross-category overlap.

We apply our evaluation framework to four state-of-the-art text-to-SQL models, namely BRIDGE (Lin et al., 2020), RATSQL-RoBERTa and RATSQL-GraPPa (Yu et al., 2020), and RATSQL-GAP (Shi et al., 2020), and observe that these models struggle to extend their success on the Spider dev set consistently to our evaluation data, with the exception of a few categories. Further analysis of the fine grained categories shows that they also fail on many rudimentary test cases (e.g., selecting multiple columns and properly producing conjunctions). While existing studies show that the models tend to fail on challenging cases that involve novel user expression (Suhr et al., 2020) and SQL structures (Suhr et al., 2020; Shaw et al., 2021), our diagnosis exposes more robustness issues in their surface form understanding (even with seemingly simple inputs), and highlights the importance of addressing such issues in the modeling foundation (Bommasani et al., 2021). Our dataset and code are released as an extensible test suite.

2 Related Work

Paraphrasing A number of augmentation methods have been made to create paraphrases of the input query, with methods such as synonym replacement (Kwiatkowski et al., 2013), use of a paraphrase model (Berant and Liang, 2014), and backwards utterance generation (Zhong et al., 2020). While these approaches ensure the creation of additional examples with more variation on the natural language side, they can be vulnerable to error, when a wrong synonym or paraphrase is chosen by a model. Although such errors may amount to just noise when used as additional training data in conjunction with a benchmark dataset, they make evaluation on such generated sets impossible, unless examples with errors are manually removed from the dataset.

Canonical Utterances Wang et al. (2015) demonstrated that it is possible to lessen the reliance on humans for creating a dataset by first generating logical forms and canonical utterances, and then use crowdsourcing to create more natural-sounding paraphrases of the questions. They note that this method is particularly effective when you seek to quickly create data for creating a *domain specific* parser. Iyer et al. (2017) also demonstrated that crowdsourced annotations from such approaches, as in turn user feedback in an online setting, can be used improve parses and detect incorrect queries. Although originally designed in the context of transfer-based machine translation to generate translation pairs (Chiang, 2005), SCFG's have also been adapted in previous semantic parsing work (Wong and Mooney, 2006, 2007) for generating new sentence-parse pairs. More recent utilization's of SCFG's for semantic parsing induce the grammar and use the resulting data for additional training and pre-training (Jia and Liang, 2016; Yu et al., 2020).

Robustness Testing Finally, Ribeiro et al. (2020) has demonstrated the efficacy of handcrafting templates for generating data points to "unit test" the models. We design synchronous context-free grammar (SCFG) production rules to generate test data for specific cross-database semantic parsing capabilities. Other NLP evaluation frameworks that look beyond accuracy and target a more general set of NLP tasks have also been proposed (Goel et al., 2021; Liu et al., 2021; Kiela et al., 2021).

3 Generating Canonical Natural Language Utterances Using SCFG

Motivation There are in general two ways to perform behavior testing on a model: one with automatically generated data, the other with manually curated data. In this work we focus on the former because it not only scales with almost no additional cost, but also serves as a pre-filtering mechanism before we test it further with human-in-the-loop. The input to text-to-SQL models is a *natural* question. However, generating natural language has two challenges: (i) it is difficult to automatically produce novel human-like utterances with high-fidelity; (ii) natural language is inherently ambiguous, while input to text-to-SQL models is required to be accurate enough to have a one-to-one mapping between the natural question and the SQL query. Motivated by the above requirements, we propose using the inherently non-ambiguous Synchronous context-free grammar (SCFG) for generating canonical natural language utterances in English[1].

[1]This method is also extendable to other languages.

Details of SCFG SCFG is a type of formal grammar which produce pairs of utterances that share a meaning with each other. There are two key components of a context-free grammar: *symbols* and *production rules* that connect them. In our case, the symbols correspond to the SQL elements, which are presented in the first column of Table 1.[2] The production rules are mappings between SQL elements and natural language words. In Figure 1 we provide such an example where SCFG maps the SQL element `DISTINCT` to the word *"unique"*, hence converting the SQL query "SELECT DISTINCT Column FROM Table" to the natural language question "Select unique Column from Table". The mappings between symbols and query words are intentionally designed to mimic the language in the Spider dataset (Yu et al., 2018), which ensures that the generated examples remain close to the training distribution.[3]

Intuitively, questions produced by the SCFG lie somewhere in-between natural language and SQL: they are not as natural as real human questions, but are much more human-like than the SQL queries. Accommodating such a trade-off ensures that the generated queries are both natural and accurate. More examples of SCFG rules can be found in Appendix C.

Generation of evaluation data To thoroughly evaluate each SQL element, we create as many valid question-query pairs as possible for each database in Spider, so that there is adequate representation for infrequent categories. Note that many databases have tables that only correspond to a subset of elements.[4] Consequently the number of collected examples in Table 1 (second column) are not evenly distributed.[5]

When generating examples for a given SQL element, the example operates over only one table, and we only introduce the minimum amount of other elements to make the generation grammatical and uncompounded. For example, the operator `BETWEEN` necessitates `SELECT` and `WHERE` clauses to generate a coherent query, but any additional operators, even if they can make the query more compositional, are excluded, as our goal is to unit test each SQL element individually. In turn, our generated data are also intended to be as easy as possible for models to succeed on.

			Exact Set Match Acc.			
	Target SQL Element	**#**	BRIDGE†	RATSQL+ RoBERTa	RATSQL+ GraPPa	RATSQL+ GAP
	Spider Dev	1034	68.2	69.6	73.4	71.8
Basic Clauses	`SELECT`	1700	53.6	46.5	62.6	73.5
	`DISTINCT`	850	86.4	86.6	94.5	88.3
	`WHERE`	1003	73.2	70.3	84.4	82.1
	`ORDER BY`	1946	51.0	54.7	71.4	76.5
	`GROUP BY`	653	35.5	51.3	45.9	5.7
	`HAVING`	604	0.1	0.0	0.0	0.0
	Cat. Avg.		53.4	53.7	**65.7**	64.4
Aggregate Ops	`MIN`	794	74.5	59.1	93.7	83.2
	`MAX`	794	75.3	17.5	85.9	47.4
	`SUM`	794	66.0	71.1	52.2	52.1
	`COUNT`	850	34.4	56.3	70.3	66.8
	`AVG`	794	56.7	58.1	81.8	79.7
	Cat. Avg.		61.0	52.5	**76.7**	65.9
Condition Ops	$\leqslant, <, >, \geqslant$	440	55.2	37.9	61.3	88.6
	$!=$	397	27.2	68.3	62.4	92.4
	`BETWEEN`	256	65.9	26.7	34.9	51.0
	Cat. Avg.		49.4	44.3	52.9	**77.3**
Logic Ops	`AND`	401	3.2	4.5	7.2	16.2
	`OR`	401	5.1	5.0	8.2	17.1
	`AND & OR`	369	4.1	4.3	8.6	18.1
	Cat. Avg.		4.1	4.6	8.0	**17.1**
	Overall Avg.		45.0	42.9	55.3	**55.6**

Table 1: Results on the models per our SCFG categories. # shows the number of test examples present. Cat. Avg. reflects the category average weighted by the number of examples per each target SQL element. †BRIDGE results are averaged across three checkpoints with different random initializations, while the RAT-SQL results are based on the best checkpoints according to the dev set evaluation.

Human verification of evaluation data To verify that our generated examples are indeed human-like and accurate, we recruited volunteers[6] who are proficient in SQL to label a subset of 40 randomly chosen question-query pairs, and rate each pair on its "readability" and "semantic equality". The question-query pairs are chosen such that all cate-

[2]We collected the SQL elements from `https://www.w3schools.com/sql/` and `https://www.techonthenet.com/sqlite/`.

[3]Competent performance across categories in Table 1 demonstrate our data overlap with the training distribution.

[4]For example, a table with only text-type columns can not be used to generate pairs with mathematical concepts *minimum* or *less than*.

[5]To have a uniform distribution, one may perform sub-sampling (which wastes valuable data), or design a model to automatically generate new tables – we leave the latter as future work.

[6]Our annotation task posed no risk or harm to annotators, and required 30 minutes of the volunteers' time.

	Target SQL Element and Example	Model Predictions with Highlighted Errors
SELECT	*NL:* Select name, id, department name, total credits from student *SQL:*`SELECT name, ID, dept_name, tot_cred FROM student`	*BRIDGE:*`SELECT student.ID, student.name, student.dept_name, student.tot_cred FROM student` *RS+RoB:*`SELECT student.name, student.ID, student.dept_name, Sum(student.tot_cred) FROM student GROUP BY student.ID` *RS+GraPPa:*`SELECT student.name, student.ID, student.dept_name, Sum(student.tot_cred) FROM student` *RS+GAP:*`SELECT student.name, student.ID, student.dept_name, Sum(student.tot_cred) FROM student`

Table 2: Model predictions on a randomly chosen SELECT example. See Appendix B for additional qualitative examples of model predictions on different categories.

Columns	#	Exact Set Match Acc.			
		BRIDGE	RATSQL+ RoBERTa	RATSQL+ GraPPa	RATSQL+ GAP
1	852	69.1	52.3	70.8	**85.4**
2	253	60.9	68.8	81.0	**88.9**
3	191	68.3	63.4	**85.9**	**85.9**
4	154	21.0	32.5	61.0	**81.8**
5	122	0.0	0.0	0.0	0.0
6	69	0.0	0.0	0.0	0.0

Table 3: Performance of models on SELECT clauses by number of columns being selected.

gories are represented at least twice. Each question-query pair was annotated by three annotators and we take their majority vote. An example given to annotators can be found in Appendix B.

For readability, 77.5% of generated questions were labeled by annotators to be "easily understandable"; 17.5% were labeled "understandable with some effort" and 5% were labeled "not understandable". We obtain this statistics by taking the majority vote of the three annotations for each question and counting a tie as "not understandable". In the same manner, annotators also identified 97.5% of questions were "semantically equivalent" to their SQL counterpart and 2.5% were "not equivalent".

We computed Fleiss' Kappa to measure inter-annotator agreement for both readability and equivalency. The results were 0.19 and 0.04, respectively, which are generally considered insufficient to claim there is strong agreement. However, we find the low scores a result of the limitation of Fleiss' Kappa, which is more reliable when each example is annotated by more annotators (we have only 3). Reviewing the annotations for readability reveals that there were 14 examples without perfect agreement for readability. For equivalency, there were only 4 of them.

4 Experiments

4.1 Experiment Setup

Models We evaluate four leading models on the Spider challenge (Yu et al., 2018) on our generated question-query pairs: BRIDGE (Lin et al., 2020), RATSQL-RoBERTa and RATSQL-GraPPa (Yu et al., 2020) and RATSQL-GAP (Shi et al., 2020). With the exception of BRIDGE, the other models were developed upon the original RATSQL model (Wang et al., 2020), which was notable for introducing a *relation-aware self-attention mechanism* for schema linking. Yu et al. (2020) extended the RATSQL framework by adding pre-training into their setup, and Shi et al. (2020) also incorporates supplementary pre-training triplet data generated by another model. The BRIDGE model is fundamentally different from the others, as it consists of a sequentially-driven architecture, rather than operating over graphs. For schema-linking, BRIDGE uses a custom encoder powered by BERT (Devlin et al., 2019) with attention over the sequences.

Evaluation Methodology Our experiments consist of evaluating each model on the generated set of question-query pairs with the canonical language questions as inputs. We evaluate Exact Set Match Accuracy for subsets of the data pertaining to each target SQL element, and then calculate the average score for each SQL token category weighted by number of examples.

4.2 Results

Main Results Table 1 highlights several interesting observations.[7] Most models only perform on par with their baseline (or better) on a few target SQL elements (e.g. `DISTINCT`, `WHERE`). More

[7]The metrics in Table 1 are diagnostic instead of explanatory. There can be multiple factors affecting the model performance on an evaluation point and our tests cannot isolate them.

often they perform below the baseline on most elements, with a few extreme outliers for total or near total failure (e.g. `HAVING`, `AND`).

Controlled Evaluation All models perform below their own baseline accuracies for simple examples that test the `SELECT` clause. We present an example of such model predictions in Table 2. One contributing factor to these low scores is the number of columns being selected. Table 3 shows that SQL models are only able to successfully produce queries with a limited number of columns, although basic column selection should not be such a difficult task for these models. While it is not surprising that models show difficulty generalizing to unseen length or structures (Lake and Baroni, 2017), this finding is concerning because there are many practical use cases where users will need to select more than four columns.[8]

5 Conclusion

We propose a simple and controllable approach for synthesizing text-to-SQL pairs for unit testing model performance on various semantic categories. Our controlled test suites allow for more extensive and fine-grained evaluation of state-of-the-art text-to-SQL models, which reveal a general lack of robustness in generalizing beyond the benchmark examples across several categories such as `SELECT` and `WHERE`. More importantly, our study highlights the importance of developing evaluation strategies beyond fixed test and dev set accuracy for understanding real progress made by the state-of-the-art text-to-SQL models and the remaining key challenges.

6 Acknowledgments

We would like to thank our reviewers for their helpful feedback. Heather Lent received funding from the European Union's Horizon 2020 research and innovation programme under the Marie Skłodowska-Curie grant agreement No 801199.

References

Jonathan Berant and Percy Liang. 2014. Semantic parsing via paraphrasing. In *Proceedings of the 52nd Annual Meeting of the Association for Computational Linguistics (Volume 1: Long Papers)*, pages 1415–1425, Baltimore, Maryland. Association for Computational Linguistics.

Rishi Bommasani, Drew A. Hudson, Ehsan Adeli, Russ Altman, Simran Arora, Sydney von Arx, Michael S. Bernstein, Jeannette Bohg, Antoine Bosselut, Emma Brunskill, Erik Brynjolfsson, Shyamal Buch, Dallas Card, Rodrigo Castellon, Niladri Chatterji, Annie S. Chen, Kathleen Creel, Jared Quincy Davis, Dorottya Demszky, Chris Donahue, Moussa Doumbouya, Esin Durmus, Stefano Ermon, John Etchemendy, Kawin Ethayarajh, Li Fei-Fei, Chelsea Finn, Trevor Gale, Lauren Gillespie, Karan Goel, Noah D. Goodman, Shelby Grossman, Neel Guha, Tatsunori Hashimoto, Peter Henderson, John Hewitt, Daniel E. Ho, Jenny Hong, Kyle Hsu, Jing Huang, Thomas Icard, Saahil Jain, Dan Jurafsky, Pratyusha Kalluri, Siddharth Karamcheti, Geoff Keeling, Fereshte Khani, Omar Khattab, Pang Wei Koh, Mark S. Krass, Ranjay Krishna, Rohith Kuditipudi, and et al. 2021. On the opportunities and risks of foundation models. *CoRR*, abs/2108.07258.

David Chiang. 2005. A hierarchical phrase-based model for statistical machine translation. In *Proceedings of the 43rd Annual Meeting of the Association for Computational Linguistics (ACL'05)*, pages 263–270, Ann Arbor, Michigan. Association for Computational Linguistics.

DongHyun Choi, Myeong Cheol Shin, EungGyun Kim, and Dong Ryeol Shin. 2020. Ryansql: Recursively applying sketch-based slot fillings for complex text-to-sql in cross-domain databases.

Jacob Devlin, Ming-Wei Chang, Kenton Lee, and Kristina Toutanova. 2019. BERT: Pre-training of deep bidirectional transformers for language understanding. In *Proceedings of the 2019 Conference of the North American Chapter of the Association for Computational Linguistics: Human Language Technologies, Volume 1 (Long and Short Papers)*, pages 4171–4186, Minneapolis, Minnesota. Association for Computational Linguistics.

Catherine Finegan-Dollak, Jonathan K. Kummerfeld, Li Zhang, Karthik Ramanathan, Sesh Sadasivam, Rui Zhang, and Dragomir Radev. 2018. Improving text-to-SQL evaluation methodology. In *Proceedings of the 56th Annual Meeting of the Association for Computational Linguistics (Volume 1: Long Papers)*, pages 351–360, Melbourne, Australia. Association for Computational Linguistics.

Karan Goel, Nazneen Fatema Rajani, Jesse Vig, Samson Tan, Jason Wu, Stephan Zheng, Caiming Xiong, Mohit Bansal, and Christopher Ré. 2021. Robustness gym: Unifying the NLP evaluation landscape. *CoRR*, abs/2101.04840.

Srinivasan Iyer, Ioannis Konstas, Alvin Cheung, Jayant Krishnamurthy, and Luke Zettlemoyer. 2017. Learning a neural semantic parser from user feedback. In *Proceedings of the 55th Annual Meeting of the Association for Computational Linguistics (Volume 1: Long Papers)*, pages 963–973, Vancouver, Canada. Association for Computational Linguistics.

[8]For example, the large tables in Spider's *soccer_1* database

Robin Jia and Percy Liang. 2016. Data recombination for neural semantic parsing. In *Proceedings of the 54th Annual Meeting of the Association for Computational Linguistics (Volume 1: Long Papers)*, pages 12–22, Berlin, Germany. Association for Computational Linguistics.

Douwe Kiela, Max Bartolo, Yixin Nie, Divyansh Kaushik, Atticus Geiger, Zhengxuan Wu, Bertie Vidgen, Grusha Prasad, Amanpreet Singh, Pratik Ringshia, Zhiyi Ma, Tristan Thrush, Sebastian Riedel, Zeerak Waseem, Pontus Stenetorp, Robin Jia, Mohit Bansal, Christopher Potts, and Adina Williams. 2021. Dynabench: Rethinking benchmarking in NLP. In *Proceedings of the 2021 Conference of the North American Chapter of the Association for Computational Linguistics: Human Language Technologies, NAACL-HLT 2021, Online, June 6-11, 2021*, pages 4110–4124. Association for Computational Linguistics.

Tom Kwiatkowski, Eunsol Choi, Yoav Artzi, and Luke Zettlemoyer. 2013. Scaling semantic parsers with on-the-fly ontology matching. In *Proceedings of the 2013 Conference on Empirical Methods in Natural Language Processing*, pages 1545–1556, Seattle, Washington, USA. Association for Computational Linguistics.

Brenden M. Lake and Marco Baroni. 2017. Still not systematic after all these years: On the compositional skills of sequence-to-sequence recurrent networks. *CoRR*, abs/1711.00350.

Mike Lewis, Yinhan Liu, Naman Goyal, Marjan Ghazvininejad, Abdelrahman Mohamed, Omer Levy, Veselin Stoyanov, and Luke Zettlemoyer. 2020. BART: Denoising sequence-to-sequence pretraining for natural language generation, translation, and comprehension. In *Proceedings of the 58th Annual Meeting of the Association for Computational Linguistics*, pages 7871–7880, Online. Association for Computational Linguistics.

Xi Victoria Lin, Richard Socher, and Caiming Xiong. 2020. Bridging textual and tabular data for cross-domain text-to-SQL semantic parsing. In *Findings of the Association for Computational Linguistics: EMNLP 2020*, pages 4870–4888, Online. Association for Computational Linguistics.

Pengfei Liu, Jinlan Fu, Yang Xiao, Weizhe Yuan, Shuaichen Chang, Junqi Dai, Yixin Liu, Zihuiwen Ye, and Graham Neubig. 2021. EXPLAINABOARD: an explainable leaderboard for NLP. *CoRR*, abs/2104.06387.

Yinhan Liu, Myle Ott, Naman Goyal, Jingfei Du, Mandar Joshi, Danqi Chen, Omer Levy, Mike Lewis, Luke Zettlemoyer, and Veselin Stoyanov. 2019. Roberta: A robustly optimized bert pretraining approach.

Matthew Peters, Mark Neumann, Mohit Iyyer, Matt Gardner, Christopher Clark, Kenton Lee, and Luke Zettlemoyer. 2018. Deep contextualized word representations. In *Proceedings of the 2018 Conference of the North American Chapter of the Association for Computational Linguistics: Human Language Technologies, Volume 1 (Long Papers)*, pages 2227–2237, New Orleans, Louisiana. Association for Computational Linguistics.

Karthik Radhakrishnan, Arvind Srikantan, and Xi Victoria Lin. 2020. Colloql: Robust cross-domain text-to-sql over search queries. *CoRR*, abs/2010.09927.

Marco Tulio Ribeiro, Tongshuang Wu, Carlos Guestrin, and Sameer Singh. 2020. Beyond accuracy: Behavioral testing of NLP models with CheckList. In *Proceedings of the 58th Annual Meeting of the Association for Computational Linguistics*, pages 4902–4912, Online. Association for Computational Linguistics.

Peter Shaw, Ming-Wei Chang, Panupong Pasupat, and Kristina Toutanova. 2021. Compositional generalization and natural language variation: Can a semantic parsing approach handle both? In *Proceedings of the 59th Annual Meeting of the Association for Computational Linguistics and the 11th International Joint Conference on Natural Language Processing, ACL/IJCNLP 2021, (Volume 1: Long Papers), Virtual Event, August 1-6, 2021*, pages 922–938. Association for Computational Linguistics.

Peng Shi, Patrick Ng, Zhiguo Wang, Henghui Zhu, Alexander Hanbo Li, Jun Wang, Cicero Nogueira dos Santos, and Bing Xiang. 2020. Learning contextual representations for semantic parsing with generation-augmented pre-training.

Alane Suhr, Ming-Wei Chang, Peter Shaw, and Kenton Lee. 2020. Exploring unexplored generalization challenges for cross-database semantic parsing. In *Proceedings of the 58th Annual Meeting of the Association for Computational Linguistics*, pages 8372–8388, Online. Association for Computational Linguistics.

Bailin Wang, Richard Shin, Xiaodong Liu, Oleksandr Polozov, and Matthew Richardson. 2020. RAT-SQL: Relation-aware schema encoding and linking for text-to-SQL parsers. In *Proceedings of the 58th Annual Meeting of the Association for Computational Linguistics*, pages 7567–7578, Online. Association for Computational Linguistics.

Yushi Wang, Jonathan Berant, and Percy Liang. 2015. Building a semantic parser overnight. In *Proceedings of the 53rd Annual Meeting of the Association for Computational Linguistics and the 7th International Joint Conference on Natural Language Processing (Volume 1: Long Papers)*, pages 1332–1342, Beijing, China. Association for Computational Linguistics.

Yuk Wah Wong and Raymond Mooney. 2006. Learning for semantic parsing with statistical machine translation. In *Proceedings of the Human Language*

Technology Conference of the NAACL, Main Conference, pages 439–446.

Yuk Wah Wong and Raymond Mooney. 2007. Learning synchronous grammars for semantic parsing with lambda calculus. In *Proceedings of the 45th Annual Meeting of the Association of Computational Linguistics*, pages 960–967.

Tao Yu, Chien-Sheng Wu, Xi Victoria Lin, Bailin Wang, Yi Chern Tan, Xinyi Yang, Dragomir Radev, Richard Socher, and Caiming Xiong. 2020. Grappa: Grammar-augmented pre-training for table semantic parsing.

Tao Yu, Rui Zhang, Kai Yang, Michihiro Yasunaga, Dongxu Wang, Zifan Li, James Ma, Irene Li, Qingning Yao, Shanelle Roman, Zilin Zhang, and Dragomir Radev. 2018. Spider: A large-scale human-labeled dataset for complex and cross-domain semantic parsing and text-to-SQL task. In *Proceedings of the 2018 Conference on Empirical Methods in Natural Language Processing*, pages 3911–3921, Brussels, Belgium. Association for Computational Linguistics.

Victor Zhong, Mike Lewis, Sida I. Wang, and Luke Zettlemoyer. 2020. Grounded adaptation for zero-shot executable semantic parsing. In *Proceedings of the 2020 Conference on Empirical Methods in Natural Language Processing (EMNLP)*, pages 6869–6882, Online. Association for Computational Linguistics.

Victor Zhong, Caiming Xiong, and Richard Socher. 2017. Seq2sql: Generating structured queries from natural language using reinforcement learning. *CoRR*, abs/1709.00103.

A Model Performance on Dev Examples Corresponding to Categories

			Exact Set Match Acc.			
				RATSQL+		
Target SQL Element	#train	#dev	BRIDGE	RoBERTa	GraPPa	GAP
SELECT	213	32	82.3	90.6	96.9	81.2
DISTINCT	113	5	86.7	100	100	60.0
WHERE	343	61	77.2	83.6	83.6	100
ORDER BY	560	83	78.3	88.0	90.4	78.3
GROUP BY	16	8	83.3	50.0	50.0	75.0
MIN	2	4	16.7	0.0	50.0	0.0
MAX	10	5	0.0	0.0	0.0	0.0
SUM	25	2	100	100	100	100
COUNT	245	40	99.2	100	97.5	97.5
<=, <, >, >=	70	6	77.8	66.7	100	100
! =	14	52	83.3	85.7	85.7	100
AND	50	5	66.7	60.0	100	60.0
OR	54	10	100	88.0	100	78.3

Table 4: Performance of models on Spider Dev by our categories. SCFG elements that had zero corresponding examples are removed from the table. Here we include the number of examples in Spider training and Spider dev to demonstrate the underlying training and development distributions. Examples counted here are strictly relate to the chosen category. (i.e. examples with multiple SQL elements that do not pertain exactly to the categories are excluded from these counts).

B Example of Annotation Task

Example database schema given to annotators:

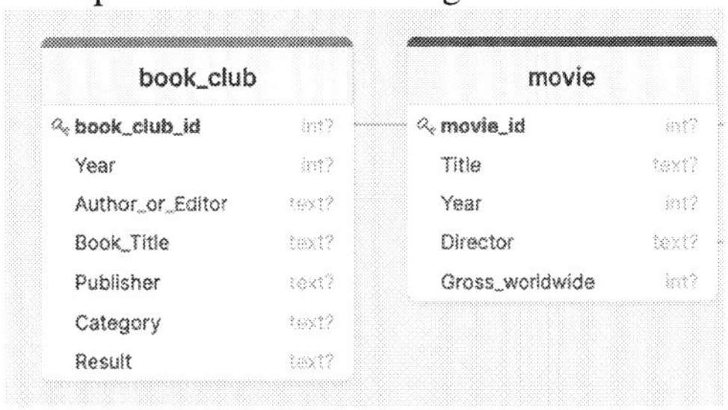

Example question-query pair given to annotators:
/**Question:** Select year from movie when movie id is greater than 1
Query: `SELECT Year FROM movie WHERE movie_id > 1 ;`

Annotators are asked to choose one answer from the list below, to describe the readability and equivalency of the question-query pair, above:

1. **Readability**:
   - I can easily understand the question

- I have some problems understanding the question, but I can understand with some effort
- I do not understand the question after trying my best to interpret it

2. **Equivalency**:

   - The question and the SQL query match perfectly
   - The question and SQL query do not fully match, but the answer to the question can be inferred from the SQL query results
   - The SQL query does not return the answer to the question

C Example Model Predictions and SCFG Production Rules

See Table 5 for model predictions, and Figures 2 and 3 for example SCFG production rules.

	Target SQL Element and Example	Model Predictions with Highlighted Errors & Highlighted Missing Elements
GROUP_BY	*NL:* Select time slot id and minimum end minute from time slot grouped by time slot id *SQL:* `SELECT time_slot_id, MIN(end_min) FROM time_slot GROUP BY time_slot_id`	*BRIDGE:* `SELECT time_slot.time_slot_id, MIN(time_slot.end_hr) FROM time_slot GROUP BY time_slot.time_slot_id` *RS+RoB:* `SELECT time_slot.time_slot_id, MIN(time_slot.end_min) FROM time_slot GROUP BY time_slot.time_slot_id` *RS+GraPPa:* `SELECT time_slot.time_slot_id, Min(time_slot.end_min) FROM time_slot GROUP BY time_slot.time_slot_id` *RS+GAP:* `SELECT time_slot.time_slot_id, Min(time_slot.end_min), Min(time_slot.end_min) FROM time_slot GROUP BY time_slot.time_slot_id`
HAVING	*NL:* Select name from people grouped by name with maximum people id equal to 2 *SQL:* `SELECT Name FROM people GROUP BY Name HAVING MAX(People_ID) = 2`	*BRIDGE:* `SELECT people.Name, MAX(people.Height) FROM people JOIN perpetrator ON people.People_ID = perpetrator.People_ID WHERE people.People_ID = 2 GROUP BY people.People_ID people.Name HAVING MAX(people.People_ID) =2)` *RS+RoB:* `SELECT people.Name FROM people GROUP BY people.Name HAVING Count(*) >= MAX(people.People_ID =) 'terminal'` *RS+GraPPa:* `SELECT people.Name, Max(people.People_ID) FROM perpetrator JOIN people ON perpetrator.People_ID = people.People_ID GROUP BY people.Name HAVING Count(*) >= MAX(people.People_ID) = 'terminal'` *RS+GAP:* `SELECT people.Name FROM people JOIN perpetrator WHERE GROUP BY Name HAVING MAX people.People_ID = 'terminal'`
OR	*NL:* Select building from classroom when building equals Stabler or capacity equals 115 or room number equals 261 *SQL:* `SELECT building FROM classroom WHERE building = 'Stabler' OR capacity = 115 OR room_numer = 261`	*BRIDGE:* `SELECT classroom.building FROM classroom WHERE classroom.building = 'Stabler' OR classroom.capacity = 115 UNION SELECT * FROM classroom WHERE classroom.building = 'Stabler' OR classroom.room_numer = 261` *RS+RoB:* `SELECT classroom.building FROM classroom WHERE classroom.building = 'terminal' OR classroom.capacity = 'terminal' OR classroom.room_number = 261` *RS+GraPPa:* `SELECT classroom.building FROM classroom WHERE classroom.building = 'terminal' OR classroom.capacity = 'terminal' OR classroom.room_numer = 261` *RS+GAP:* `SELECT classroom.building FROM classroom WHERE classroom.building = 'terminal' OR classroom.capacity = 'terminal' AND OR classroom.room_number = 'terminal' AND classroom.room_number = 'terminal'`

Table 5: Example predictions on selected target SQL elements from the BRIDGE, and RATSQL (RS) based models using RoBERTa (+RoB), GraPPa, and GAP.

SELECT
RULE → ⟨ Select COLUMN from TABLE, SELECT COLUMN FROM TABLE⟩

Example:
TABLE → ⟨ school performance , school_performance ⟩
COLUMN → ⟨ class a , Class_A ⟩
Output Production:
NL: Select class a from school performance
SQL: SELECT Class_A FROM school_performance

RULE → ⟨ Select COLUMNS from TABLE, SELECT COLUMNS FROM TABLE⟩

Example:
TABLE → ⟨ people , people ⟩
COLUMNS → ⟨ (height, name, weight, people id) , (Height, Name, Weight, People_ID) ⟩
Output Production:
NL: Select height, name, weight, people id from people
SQL: SELECT Height, Name, Weight, People_ID FROM people

ORDER_BY
RULE → ⟨ Select COLUMN1 from TABLE sorted by COLUMN2,
SELECT COLUMN1 FROM TABLE ORDER BYCOLUMN2⟩

Example:
TABLE → ⟨ circuits , circuits ⟩
COLUMN1 → ⟨ longitude, lng ⟩
COLUMN2 → ⟨ latitude, lat ⟩
Output Production:
/ **NL:** Select longitude from circuits sorted by latitude
SQL: SELECT lng FROM circuits ORDER BY lat

RULE → ⟨ Select COLUMN1 from TABLE sorted by COLUMN2 ORDER,
SELECT COLUMN1 FROM TABLE ORDER BY COLUMN2 ORDER⟩

Example:
TABLE → ⟨ debate people , debate_people ⟩
COLUMN1 → ⟨ debate id, debate_id ⟩
COLUMN2 → ⟨ negative, Negativ ⟩
ORDER → ⟨ in ascending order , ASC ⟩
Output Production:
/ **NL:** Select debate id from debate people sorted by negative in ascending order
SQL: SELECT Debate_ID FROM debate_people ORDER BY Negative ASC

HAVING
RULE → ⟨ Select COLUMN1 from TABLE grouped by COLUMN1 with DEGREE imum COLUMN2 equal to COLUMNVALUE,
SELECT COLUMN1 FROM TABLE GROUP BY COLUMN1 HAVING DEGREE COLUMN2 = COLUMNVALUE ⟩

Example:
TABLE → ⟨ climber , climber ⟩
COLUMN1 → ⟨ name, Name ⟩
COLUMN2 → ⟨ points, Points ⟩
DEGREE → ⟨ min , MIN ⟩
COLUMNVALUE → ⟨ 6.0, 6.0 ⟩
Output Production:
/ **NL:** Select name from climber grouped by name with minimum points equal to 6.0
SQL: SELECT Name FROM climber GROUP BY Name HAVING MIN(Points) = 6.0

Figure 2: Example SCFG Production Rules for selected SQL Clauses

MIN

RULE → ⟨ Select minimum COLUMN from TABLE, SELECT MIN(COLUMN) FROM TABLE⟩

Example:
TABLE → ⟨ student addresses , Student_Addresses ⟩
COLUMN → ⟨ monthly rental , monthly_rental ⟩
Output Production:
/ NL: Select minimum monthly rental from student addresses
\SQL: SELECT MIN(monthly_rental) FROM Student_Addresses

<=, <,>,>=

RULE → ⟨ Select COLUMN1 from TABLE when COLUMN2 EQUALITY COLUMNVALUE, SELECT COLUMN1 FROM TABLE WHERE COLUMN2 EQUALITY COLUMNVALUE⟩

Example:
TABLE → ⟨ faculty , faculty ⟩
COLUMN1 → ⟨ faculty, Faculty ⟩
COLUMN2 → ⟨ campus, Campus ⟩
EQUALITY → ⟨ greater than, > ⟩
COLUMNVALUE → ⟨ 20 , 20 ⟩
Output Production:
/ NL: Select faculty from faculty when campus is greater than 20
\SQL: SELECT Faculty FROM faculty WHERE Campus > 20

AND

RULE → ⟨ BASE CONJUNCTIONPHRASE CONJUNCTIONPHRASE COLEQUALITYVALUE, BASE CONJUNCTIONPHRASE CONJUNCTIONPHRASE COLEQUALITYVALUE⟩

Example:
BASE → ⟨ Select all columns from parties in events when, SELECT * FROM Parties_in_Events WHERE ⟩
CONJUNCTIONPHRASE → ⟨ COLEQUALITYVALUE and , COLEQUALITYVALUE AND ⟩
COLEQUALITYVALUE → ⟨ event id equals 9, Event_ID = 9 ⟩
COLEQUALITYVALUE → ⟨ role code equals Organizer, Role_Code = 'Organizer' ⟩
COLEQUALITYVALUE → ⟨ party id equals 4, Party_ID = 4 ⟩
Output Production:
/ NL:
Select all columns from parties in events when event id equals 9 and role code equals Organizer and party id equals 4
\SQL: SELECT * FROM Parties_in_Events WHERE Event_ID = 9 AND Role_Code = 'Organizer' AND Party_ID = 4

Figure 3: Example SCFG Production rules for other selected SQL operators

Writing Style Author Embedding Evaluation

Enzo Terreau **Antoine Gourru** **Julien Velcin**
Université de Lyon, Lyon 2, ERIC UR3083
{enzo.terreau, antoine.gourru, julien.velcin}@univ-lyon2.fr

Abstract

Learning authors representations from their textual productions is now widely used to solve multiple downstream tasks, such as classification, link prediction or user recommendation. Author embedding methods are often built on top of either Doc2Vec (Le and Mikolov, 2014) or the Transformer architecture (Devlin et al., 2019). Evaluating the quality of these embeddings and what they capture is a difficult task. Most articles use either classification accuracy or authorship attribution, which does not clearly measure the quality of the representation space, if it really captures what it has been built for. In this paper, we propose a novel evaluation framework of author embedding methods based on the writing style. It allows to quantify if the embedding space effectively captures a set of stylistic features, chosen to be the best proxy of an author writing style. This approach gives less importance to the topics conveyed by the documents. It turns out that recent models are mostly driven by the inner semantic of authors' production. They are outperformed by simple baselines, based on state-of-the-art pretrained sentence embedding models, on several linguistic axes. These baselines can grasp complex linguistic phenomena and writing style more efficiently, paving the way for designing new style-driven author embedding models.

1 Introduction

Since the early work of Mikolov et al. 2013a, and more recent models based on the Transformer architecture (Devlin et al., 2019), continuous word representations have been key in processing and analyzing textual data. It led to a prolific research on learning meaningful representations of larger-scale textual entities, such as paragraph, document or even authors. Learning author embeddings can be used to solve several downstream tasks, such as user recommendation (Nayyeri et al., 2020) and classification (Benton and Dredze, 2018). Additionally, metadata (e.g., graph structure (Gourru et al., 2020), timestamp (Delasalles et al., 2019)) are often used to guide the representation learning process, in particular with application to social media. This is referred as user embedding, while author embedding only focuses on the textual production of users.

Despite a growing literature in both author and user embedding (Maharjan et al., 2019; Wu et al., 2020), it is usually difficult to tell what these representations really capture from its textual production. Although most recent models reach more than 90% accuracy in authorship attribution on several datasets (Maharjan et al., 2019), none of the existing works tried to determine if the embedding space captures topic preferences, topological information, sentiment or stylistic features. Getting a better understanding of what these spaces really capture can be a real asset to design new machine learning models.

For instance, one could be interested in linking several authors with similar writing style even though they deal with different topics. It is even more important with literacy data or for specific tasks such as authorship attribution for forensic investigation (Amir et al., 2017; Ganguly et al., 2016; Kumar et al., 2019). Being able to compare and determine which embedding methods are the more relevant in such a context is essential. Unfortunately, in most previous works, the evaluation of author embedding relies solely on classification accuracy, which demonstrates the need for a more robust and richer evaluation framework. As stated in (Conneau et al., 2018), most evaluation methods for embedding are based on downstream tasks, which does not fully assess the quality of the embedding space, if it really captures what is has been built for.

To tackle this issue, we propose a novel experimental scheme to evaluate author representations based on her writing style. Even though there is no

Proceedings of the 58th Annual Meeting of the Association for Computational Linguistics, pages 84–93

https://doi.org/10.26615/978-954-452-056-4_009

consensual definition of what the writing style is, many works have tried to identify the most relevant features to characterize it. In this article, we consider low-level structural and syntactical features uncorrelated with topics, and we show that most author embedding methods are in fact essentially driven by semantic. The code is made available at the following address: Style Embedding Evaluation

2 Related Works

In this section, we present an overview of existing author embedding models and evaluation frameworks. We also briefly review prior works on stylistic features selection through authorship attribution.

Author embedding consists in learning, for each author, a vector representation in a low dimensional space. In this space, the proximity between two vectors should relate to the similarity in authors' textual production.

Part of the literature focuses on user embedding. While works on author and user embedding may look similar, they should not be mistaken. User embedding usually refers to the context of social media where, in addition to the user textual production, several metadata (e.g., retweet, likes, links) are used to guide the learning process. Here, we mostly focus on methods that leverage the textual content only. Nevertheless, our experimental protocol method can be used to evaluate user embedding models in a stylistic way, in combination with other metrics. We leave this perspective to future work.

2.1 Author Embedding models

Representation learning in NLP took a huge step forward with (Mikolov et al., 2013b) and (Mikolov et al., 2013a) who proposed two neural models to learn word vectors, based on the distributional hypothesis. Each word embedding is learnt by solving a word co-occurrence prediction task. The Doc2Vec model (Le and Mikolov, 2014) extends these models to document embedding by adding a document id to the word context. More recently, Devlin et al. (2019) proposed another word representation method, the BERT model, that reaches state-of-the-art in various downstream tasks. Based on the Transformer architecture, each word representation is contextualized and thus different given the sentence in which it occurs. Today, Doc2Vec and BERT methods and their extensions constitute the basic bricks of every author embedding method.

Recent works apply representation learning to authors by solving several downstream tasks, such as author classification and link prediction. For example, the Aut2Vec model (Ganguly et al., 2016) is built on top of (Le and Mikolov, 2014). Document and author embeddings are initialized using Doc2Vec. Then, they train a single hidden layer model to perform authorship prediction (the Content Info model). The idea is to bring author representation closer to the content she/he produced. This simple model is paired with a link-info model using the same idea for co-authorship graph, which we do not develop here. Maharjan et al. (2019) use Doc2Vec formulation on documents of character trigrams. According to them, character trigrams should better capture both semantic content and writing style, as it was shown by previous studies (Sapkota et al., 2015; Stamatatos, 2013; Schwartz et al., 2013). The trigrams are also annotated according to their position in a given word or if they contain punctuation or not, following the idea of Sapkota et al. (2015). A few BERT-based methods recently emerged. Wu et al. (2020) use BERT to build representations of each author's posts. They are then aggregated using a bidirectionnal GRU. It allows to tackle authors with a various number of posts. This architecture is trained on authorship classification with a Multi-Layer Perceptron on top. One can also mention several methods dealing with dynamic author embedding (Kumar et al. (2019), Delasalles et al. (2019)). While our metric can also be applied to such contexts, we choose to work first in a static setting.

2.2 Author Embedding evaluation

Previous works use different strategies to evaluate the quality of author representations. Ganguly et al. (2016) perform link prediction (predicting if two authors have already co-authored a paper based on their embedding) and clustering. The latter requires an annotated dataset, the final metric being the Normalized Mutual Information after simple clustering through K-Means for example. Link prediction supposes we have additional information to text content if we want to build the author network. Maharjan et al. (2019) and Wu et al. (2020) also evaluate their models using an annotated dataset, through user depression prediction and gender prediction (Reddit MBTI9k dataset) for the first one, and book likeability prediction for the second one

(Goodread corpus). A simple classification model (e.g., SVM, MLP) is trained to predict the class for each author through its embedding. The accuracy score then allows to compare each method.

Maharjan et al. (2019) use authorship attribution to evaluate the quality of their model. Authorship attribution consists in predicting the author of a given document. It requires that document and author representations lie in the same space. It is performed either by clustering or simply by computing the cosine similarity between a document embedding and each author's embeddings to get either an accuracy score or a coverage error. This task could be a reference to evaluate author embedding. Being able to perfectly associate an author with its production ensures that the method efficiently captures each author's writing habits and characteristics. However, one of the biggest issues of authorship attribution is the lack of interpretability. It fails to reveal if a given author embedding method is more based on the content/topics or on the author writing style. To fully understand the distinction between writing style and content we can mention the book *Exercises in Style* of French author Raymond Queneau, who wrote the same story 99 times, but in 99 different ways (see Table 1). Although the story which is told remains the same, the choice of words and complexity of each sentence strongly differs. A way to get around this issue is to evaluate one's method on at least two datasets with various profiles. Sari et al. (2018) show that the decisive features to discriminate the author of a document can either be topic based or style based, depending on the dataset under study. Using at least two datasets when evaluating author embedding methods is a good step to better understand the model capacities.

Finally, author embedding evaluation methods are mostly centered on narrow downstream tasks and do not fully quantify the quality of the embedding space. For example, likeability prediction in (Maharjan et al., 2019) only measures one precise aspect of what the embedding space can capture. Conneau et al. (2018) therefore propose a large range of probing tasks to evaluate sentence embeddings. Following their idea, we propose an evaluation method for author embedding strictly based on writing style.

2.3 Stylometric Analysis

In this section we detailed which textual features are the most used to efficiently characterize an author's style. Authorship attribution is commonly used to identify an author way of writing and the most relevant features related to it. (Juola and Stamatatos, 2013; Stamatatos, 2013; Sapkota et al., 2015; Sari et al., 2018) propose a huge variety of textual extracted properties to tackle the problem of authorship attribution. The main breakthrough is that character n-grams are one of the most efficient and versatile features. It provides insight on both writing style and topic content of a given document. Sapkota et al. (2015) even show that character n-grams can be enhanced with position based affixes and punctuation n-grams.

More classic features (e.g., word and punctuation frequencies, hapax legomena, dislegomena) are also used with good efficiency since the 19th century (Mendenhall, 1887). They are often combined with function word frequencies (Zhao and Zobel (2005)) as they improve the performance of classifiers in authorship detection. Sari et al. (2018) performed ablation study on the authorship attribution problem, with style features (punctuation, function words, word length, etc.), topical features (frequencies of most common word n-grams) and hybrid variables (frequencies of most common character n-grams). Doing so, they reach state-of-the-art performance on two out of four datasets. They allow to identify the most useful and easily retrievable stylometric features to identify an author writing style without topic information. However, they do not rely on author embedding and cannot evaluate whether the embedding captures the writing style or not.

3 New proposed framework for author embedding evaluation

A classification model usually evaluates whether an embedding method successfully captures an author's topic preferences. Here, we want to evaluate how well the embedding captures its way of writing. As stated earlier, simple stylistic features are a good proxy of the authors' writing style. These features can easily be extracted from a corpus and aggregated by author. Training a simple regression model (typically linear regression or more complex methods, such as support vector regression) using author embedding to predict these features would allow to compare these representations in their abil-

Writing style	Extract
Notation	*Two hours later, I meet him in the Cour de Rome, in front of the gare Saint-Lazare.*
Litotes	*Two hours later I met him again;*
Metaphorically	*In a bleak, urban desert, I saw it again that self-same day, ...*
Retrograde	*I met him in the middle of the Cour de Rome, after having left him rushin avidly towards a seat.*
Surprises	*Two hours after, guess whom I met in front of the gare Saint-Lazare!*

Table 1: We illustrate here the distinction between writing style and semantic thanks to Raymond Queneau. For each writing style the same passage of the story is shown.

ity to separate writing styles. Even better, it would show if the representation space effectively captures each stylistic feature. Figures 1 and 2 show the intuition behind this simple idea. To the best of our knowledge, this method is the first to evaluate this aspect of author embedding. At the opposite of classification tasks, there is no metric such as accuracy for regression that gives an absolute measure of performance. Here, we propose to use the Mean Square Error as regression score, in a 10-fold cross validation scheme. First results show how poorly current author embedding method capture writing style and thus set a new goal for new methods to come.

3.1 Selection of key stylistic features

The selection of the stylistic features to retrieve from the corpus is key. It needs to fully embrace each author's writing style and specificity, whether it is based on phonetic, syntax, or structural. It should not be topic related. Based on (Zhao and Zobel, 2005), (Elahi and Muneer, 2018), (Sari et al., 2018), we choose a total of 301 stylistic features that are summed up in Table 3. Each of these features are aggregated into categories extracted from the aforementioned references according to their nature. Although none of the aforementioned works study POS and NER tags as stylistic features, (Szwed, 2017) shows that it can be used for authorship attribution with good results. (Feng et al., 2012; Ganjigunte Ashok et al., 2013) demonstrate that they are effective markers of the syntactic structure of a text, performing sentence type identification with POS tags. We therefore incorporate these features in our metric. As a test, we perform authorship attribution using these variables on the Project Gutenberg dataset with a simple logistic regression and a various number of authors. Results are shown in Table 2. We use two metrics, accuracy, and coverage error. Coverage error computes how far we need to go through the ranked scores to cover the true labels. Using style-based features only, we are able to reach an accuracy of 96% with 10 authors and 88% with 50 authors. The averaged coverage error is always near 2 (correct author has the second highest score in average in prediction). Best authorship attribution methods reach accuracy score between 90% and 95% (Sari et al., 2018; Ruder et al., 2016), depending on the dataset and the number of authors. These features are thus a good proxy of an author writing style as no topic information directly flows through the selected variables. Of course, there are correlation between style and topics. Strong line break frequency attest of poetry, strong PERSON NER-tag frequency attest of novels and so on. Are writing style and topics strictly separable remains an open question (Subramanian et al., 2018). Here, we tried to keep variables with least topic information possible.

Authorship Attribution scores		
Number of authors	**Accuracy**	**Coverage error**
10	0.96	1.04
50	0.88	1.80
100	0.79	2.28

Table 2: Authorship attribution with logistic regression using only stylistic features. With no direct topic information, we are able to reach 96% accuracy with only 10 authors. These was performed on the full Project Gutenberg dataset with a random authors sample.

4 Evaluation

4.1 Competitors

To test our metric, we select several author embedding methods among the ones presented in Section 2.1. The Content Info model of Ganguly et al. (2016) (embedding size 512) and the annotated ngram based Doc2Vec model of Maharjan et al. (2019), with embedding size fixed to 300 (referred

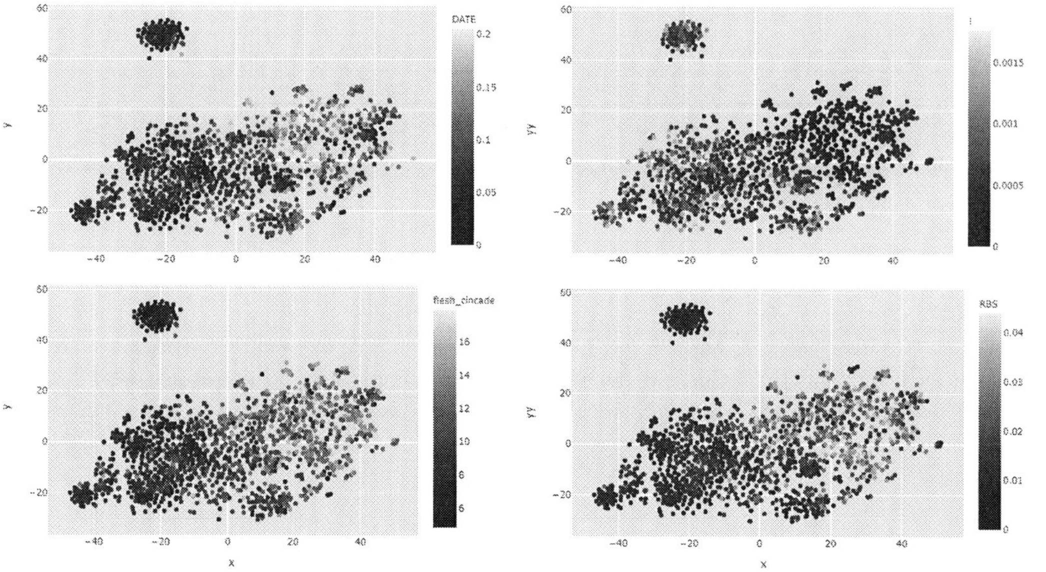

Figure 1: We project NGRAM DOC2VEC embeddings on the full Gutenberg dataset into a 2D space with t-SNE and we represent the gradient of 4 selected stylistic features (before standardization): DATE entity frequency, Exclamation mark frequency, Flesh-Cincade readability index and superlative adverb frequency - RBS. Clear tendencies appear, which motivates our method.

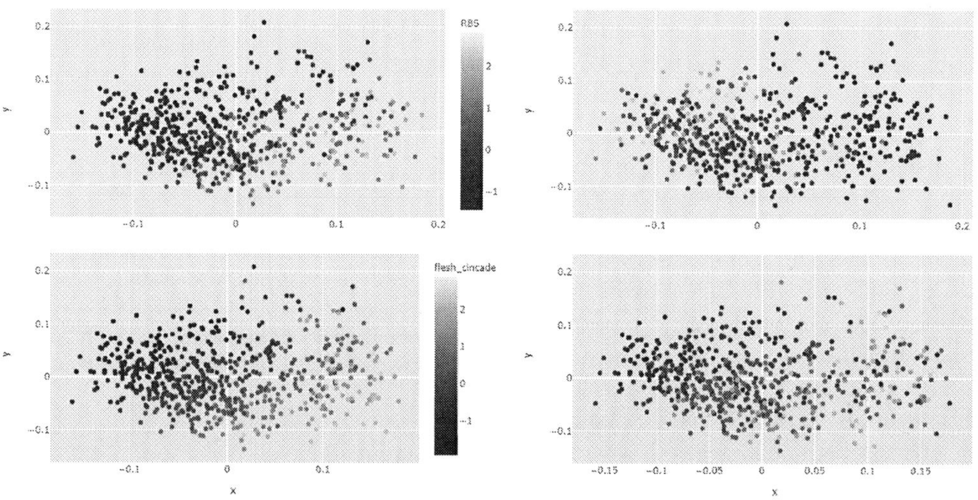

Figure 2: We project USE embeddings on the reduced Gutenberg dataset into a 2D space with t-SNE and we represent the gradient of 4 selected stylistic features (before standardization): DATE entity frequency, Exclamation mark frequency, Flesh-Cincade readability index and superlative adverb frequency - RBS. Clear tendencies appear, which motivates our method.

Type of features	Examples	Number of features
Letters	Letters frequencies	26
Numbers	Numbers frequencies	10
Structural	Avg word length, Hapax Legomena, Syllable count, ...	9
Punctuation	Punctuation sign frequencies	16
Function words	Function words (does, once, doing, ...) frequencies	174
Tag	Pos tag frequencies	43
Ner	Name Entity Recognition tag frequencies	18
Indexes	Complexity and readability indexes	7

Table 3: List of stylistic features selected and their categories. Frequencies are computed by sentence.

as NGRAM Doc2Vec in this paper). We also add two state-of-the-art sentence embedding methods: a) Universal Sentence Encoder (USE) (Cer et al., 2018), based on a Deep Averaging Network (DAN) built on top of a Bag Of Word (BOW) vector, and b) Sentence BERT (Reimers and Gurevych, 2019), built on top of BERT. Author embedding is then calculated by simply averaging every sentence representation of an author (embedding size 512 for USE and 768 for SBERT). Whereas it performs well on several downstream tasks for sentence embedding, we expect lower results in author embedding, both because of the averaging of full documents, and as it is not trained specifically to retrieve writing style. We choose not to test the most recent (Wu et al., 2020), which is closer to user embedding, and to focus on well-established method.

4.2 Datasets & framework

For the stylistic features extraction, we use spacy word and sentence tokenizer, POS-tagger and NER. We use nltk set of English stopwords and nltk CMU Dictionary for syllable count. Each feature is standardized before regression. The regression algorithm used is an SVR with Radial Basis Function (rbf) kernel as it offers both quick training time and best results among other kernels in our experiments.

We apply our evaluation protocol to datasets of different natures, using most recent author embedding approaches. First, we experiment with a Lyrics dataset [1], consisting in a set of 47 singers from various music genre (Bob Dylan to Eminem, including Prince and Radiohead). There are around 2,300 verses by author. This dataset is rather small and unusual but is a good illustration of our approach. Nevertheless, poetry and by extension song lyrics are the type of document where one could expect literary style to express the most.

We also experiment on a Project Gutenberg dataset extracted following (Gerlach and Font-Clos, 2018) paper. The Project Gutenberg is a multilingual library of more than 60,000 e-books for which U.S. copyright has expired. It is freely available and started in 1971. This dataset is often used in NLP, whether for its literacy aspect or for automatic translation. Here, we focus on the texts written in English, randomly sampling 10 books for each author. As most of the books are novels, we only take the 200 first sentences of each book, to eventually obtain 664 authors with 2,000 sentences by author. We refer to this subset as the "reduced Project Gutenberg dataset" in the upcoming paragraphs.

Finally, we use part of the Blog Authorship Corpus. This dataset is composed of 681,288 posts from 19,320 authors gathered in the early 2000s. There are approximately 35 posts and 7,250 words by user. We only take 500 bloggers with at least 50 blogposts to build our reduced dataset of the BlogAuthorshipCorpus.

These three datasets allow to cover different aspect of writing style, from pure literature to social media. To compare how well each embedding also captures content, we extract the 10 most relevant topics using LDA from the reduced version of project Gutenberg. We then perform a topic prediction task based on embeddings with an SVM. Results are presented in Table 4.

4.3 Results

All results are presented in Table 5, 6 and 7. For the Gutenberg and Blog Authorship datasets, they are summed up in Figure 3. Although smaller, the Lyrics dataset gives clear tendencies which are confirmed by the results on Blog Authorship and Gutenberg. The Content Info and NGRAM

[1] https://www.kaggle.com/paultimothymooney/poetry

Topic prediction on Gutenberg dataset		
Embedding method	**Accuracy**	**Coverage error**
Content-Info	0.81	1.32
SBERT	0.76	1.38
USE	0.74	1.43
NGRAM Doc2Vec	0.73	1.44

Table 4: Topic prediction from author embeddings with an SVM. Topic are retrieved with an LDA with 10 topics. We see that each model efficiently captures each author's topic preferences, Content-Info model being the best at this task.

Doc2Vec models designed to build consistent author embeddings both obtain the worst MSE scores. USE and SBERT outperform them on almost every axis defined among our stylistic features. USE and SBERT are powerful models, pretrained on huge corpora with multitask training. It seems that they are able to capture linguistic notions, which is not achievable by current author embedding models.

As expected, the Content Info model performs poorly. It is based on BOW representations thus unable to grasp any structural, syntactic or punctuation-based information such as TAG or NER, even more after word tokenization. This model strictly focuses on topic preferences, as shown in Table 4, reaching top accuracy on topic prediction.

Character n-grams are known as the best features to capture both style and content, even more when they are annotated regarding their position in a word or if they contain punctuation as in (Sapkota et al., 2015). Here we show that Maharjan et al. (2019)'s method does not properly capture complex syntactic notions, suffering from the reduced window size in Doc2Vec formulation. Similarly to the Content Info model, it cannot detect TAG or NER, but grasps punctuation with ease. As function words are not filtered during preprocessing, all the tested models perform equally well along this axis.

The real surprise here is how well SBERT and USE perform in capturing complex grammatical and linguistic notions such as TAG, readability and complexity indexes. They also perform well along the structural axis (e.g., average word/sentence length, hapax legomena, short words frequency). Clark et al. (2019) show that each BERT attention head naturally focuses on different linguistic phenomena in a sentence. For example, in some heads, direct objects attend to their verbs. In others, auxiliary verbs mostly put attention to the verb they modify, and so on. Our experiment seems to show that this information is propagated to the author embedding. This is why transformer-based models, not even fine-tuned on a specific author-based downstream task, capture writing style notions so well. For USE, we use the DAN version, which performs non-linear transformations on word and bigram embedding averages over sentences. Despite the BOW assumption made in the model, it is the best embedding model regarding our metric. The DAN model successfully retrieves complex linguistic information, showing that a syntactic treatment of sentences is not a prerequisite to effectively represent them, as stated in the original paper (Iyyer et al., 2015). This gives a huge improvement in terms of computation time against costly transformer-based models. Training models on multiple tasks with a huge corpus allows to skip the need to process semantically sentences and documents. USE is trained on question answering, next and previous sentence prediction, and the SNLI task. We could expect the Transformer version of USE to have even better results, at the cost of a higher computation time. Relying on these pretrained models seems to be the path to develop new author embedding methods to better capture the writing style, as improvements can still be done on several axes.

5 Conclusion

We presented a new evaluation framework for author embedding focusing on the writing style. This evaluation scheme is based on the extraction of stylistic features which represent a good proxy of an author way of writing. We show that simple baselines outperform recent author embedding models in predicting most of those stylistic features. These baselines rely on state-of-the-art sentence embedding models which capture complex linguistic notion thanks to multitask training on several big corpora. This demonstrates the need to develop new author embedding models that can grasp the author writing style. If models relying on Doc2Vec show clear limit in this task, USE with a DAN architecture seems to be a way to go.

References

Silvio Amir, Glen Coppersmith, Paula Carvalho, Mario J Silva, and Byron C Wallace. 2017. Quan-

Embedding	Average MSE Regression Score along with standard deviation (SVR Model) on Lyrics Dataset							
	Letters	Numbers	Structural	Punctuation	Func. words	TAG	NER	Indexes
USE	**0.78 (0.21)**	**0.84 (0.08)**	**0.56 (0.28)**	**0.73 (0.24)**	**0.93 (0.17)**	**0.43 (0.31)**	**0.58 (0.26)**	**0.32 (0.24)**
Content Info	0.81 (0.21)	1.08 (0.10)	0.78 (0.21)	0.96 (0.14)	0.94 (0.15)	0.98 (0.06)	0.99 (0.07)	0.90 (0.12)
Ngram Doc2Vec	1.00 (0.08)	1.07 (0.06)	1.01 (0.04)	1.01 (0.03)	1.04 (0.06)	1.00 (0.04)	0.99 (0.04)	0.98 (0.018)
SBERT	0.79 (0.20)	1.12 (0.10)	0.77 (0.22)	0.97 (0.11)	0.94 (0.12)	0.97 (0.06)	0.96 (0.09)	0.82 (0.21)

Table 5: MSE score (standard deviation in parenthesis) on the prediction of stylistic features from author embedding on the Lyrics dataset using SVR. In bold the best score for every axis. Surprisingly, both author embedding methods are outperformed by simply averaging USE Embeddings when it comes to writing style representation.

Embedding	Average MSE Regression Score along with standard deviation (SVR Model) on Gutenberg dataset							
	Letters	Numbers	Structural	Punctuation	Func. words	TAG	NER	Indexes
USE	**0.61 (0.27)**	**0.86 (0.09)**	**0.34 (0.18)**	0.59 (0.26)	**0.65 (0.24)**	**0.45 (0.29)**	**0.65 (0.17)**	**0.27 (0.15)**
Content Info	0.67 (0.22)	0.87 (0.12)	0.54 (0.18)	0.67 (0.16)	0.71 (0.19)	0.65 (0.17)	0.74 (0.13)	0.50 (0.15)
Ngram Doc2Vec	0.63 (0.20)	0.88 (0.12)	0.51 (0.20)	**0.58 (0.21)**	0.68 (0.19)	0.59 (0.19)	0.71 (0.14)	0.45 (0.15)
SBERT	0.67 (0.27)	0.90 (0.07)	0.41 (0.19)	0.62 (0.26)	0.71 (0.21)	0.51 (0.27)	0.69 (0.18)	0.32 (0.18)

Table 6: MSE score (standard deviation in parenthesis) on the prediction of stylistic features from author embedding on the Gutenberg dataset using SVR. In bold, the best scores for each axis.

Embedding	Average MSE Regression Score along with standard deviation (SVR Model) on Blog Authorship Corpus dataset							
	Letters	Numbers	Structural	Punctuation	Func. words	TAG	NER	Indexes
USE	**0.67 (0.25)**	**0.83 (0.05)**	**0.45 (0.20)**	0.78 (0.17)	**0.81 (0.17)**	**0.63 (0.21)**	**0.80 (0.17)**	**0.38 (0.18)**
Content Info	0.80 (0.15)	0.85 (0.07)	0.62 (0.23)	0.92 (0.09)	0.87 (0.12)	0.90 (0.05)	0.93 (0.07)	0.70 (0.29))
Ngram Doc2Vec	0.77 (0.16)	0.88 (0.05)	0.67 (0.16)	**0.78 (0.13)**	0.84 (0.12)	0.82 (0.09)	0.86 (0.11)	0.67 (0.13)
SBERT	0.68 (0.28)	0.85 (0.03)	0.48 (0.19)	0.80 (0.12)	0.85 (0.16)	0.66 (0.20)	0.82 (0.18)	0.41 (0.16)

Table 7: MSE score (standard deviation in parenthesis) on the prediction of stylistic features from author embedding on the Blog Authorship Corpus dataset using SVR. In bold the best scores for each axis.

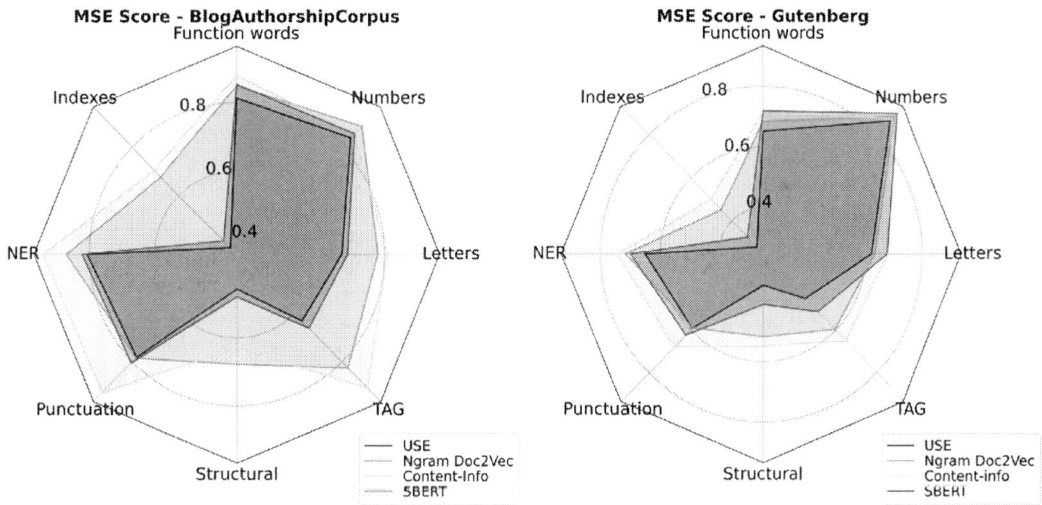

Figure 3: We represent previous regression results on spider charts to better visualize on which axis each embedding method performs the best.

tifying mental health from social media with neural user embeddings. In *Proceedings of the Machine Learning for Healthcare Conference*, pages 306–321.

Adrian Benton and Mark Dredze. 2018. Using author embeddings to improve tweet stance classification. In *Proceedings of the 2018 EMNLP Workshop W-NUT: The 4th Workshop on Noisy User-generated Text*, pages 184–194, Brussels, Belgium. Association for Computational Linguistics.

Daniel Cer, Yinfei Yang, Sheng-yi Kong, Nan Hua, Nicole Limtiaco, Rhomni St. John, Noah Constant, Mario Guajardo-Cespedes, Steve Yuan, Chris Tar, Yun-Hsuan Sung, Brian Strope, and Ray Kurzweil. 2018. Universal sentence encoder. *CoRR*, abs/1803.11175.

Kevin Clark, Urvashi Khandelwal, Omer Levy, and Christopher D. Manning. 2019. What does BERT look at? an analysis of bert's attention. In *Proceedings of the 2019 ACL Workshop BlackboxNLP: Analyzing and Interpreting Neural Networks for NLP*, volume abs/1906.04341.

Alexis Conneau, German Kruszewski, Guillaume Lample, Loïc Barrault, and Marco Baroni. 2018. What you can cram into a single $&!#* vector: Probing sentence embeddings for linguistic properties. In *Proceedings of the 56th Annual Meeting of the Association for Computational Linguistics (Volume 1: Long Papers)*, pages 2126–2136, Melbourne, Australia. Association for Computational Linguistics.

Edouard Delasalles, Sylvain Lamprier, and Ludovic Denoyer. 2019. Learning Dynamic Author Representations with Temporal Language Models. *CoRR*, abs/1909.04985.

Jacob Devlin, Ming-Wei Chang, Kenton Lee, and Kristina Toutanova. 2019. Bert: Pre-training of deep bidirectional transformers for language understanding. In *Proceedings of the 2019 Conference of the North American Chapter of the Association for Computational Linguistics: Human Language Technologies, Volume 1 (Long and Short Papers)*, pages 4171–4186.

Hassaan Elahi and Haris Muneer. 2018. Identifying Different Writing Styles in a Document Intrinsically using Stylometric Analysis. The complete code and detailed documentation is available on the attached Github Link: https://github.com/harismuneer/Writing-Styles-Classification-Using-Stylometric-Analysis.

Song Feng, Ritwik Banerjee, and Yejin Choi. 2012. Characterizing stylistic elements in syntactic structure. *EMNLP-CoNLL 2012 - 2012 Joint Conference on Empirical Methods in Natural Language Processing and Computational Natural Language Learning, Proceedings of the Conference*, (July):1522–1533.

Soumyajit Ganguly, Manish Gupta, Vasudeva Varma, Vikram Pudi, et al. 2016. Author2vec: Learning author representations by combining content and link information. In *Proceedings of the 25th International Conference Companion on World Wide Web*, pages 49–50. International World Wide Web Conferences Steering Committee.

Vikas Ganjigunte Ashok, Song Feng, and Yejin Choi. 2013. Success with style: Using writing style to predict the success of novels. In *Proceedings of the 2013 Conference on Empirical Methods in Natural Language Processing*, pages 1753–1764, Seattle, Washington, USA. Association for Computational Linguistics.

Martin Gerlach and Francesc Font-Clos. 2018. A standardized project gutenberg corpus for statistical analysis of natural language and quantitative linguistics. *CoRR*, abs/1812.08092.

Antoine Gourru, Julien Velcin, and Julien Jacques. 2020. Gaussian embedding of linked documents from a pretrained semantic space. In *IJCAI*, pages 3912–3918.

Mohit Iyyer, Varun Manjunatha, Jordan Boyd-Graber, and Hal Daumé III. 2015. Deep unordered composition rivals syntactic methods for text classification. In *Proceedings of the 53rd Annual Meeting of the Association for Computational Linguistics and the 7th International Joint Conference on Natural Language Processing (Volume 1: Long Papers)*, pages 1681–1691, Beijing, China. Association for Computational Linguistics.

Patrick Juola and Efstathios Stamatatos. 2013. Overview of the author identification task at pan 2013. *CEUR Workshop Proceedings*, 1179.

Srijan Kumar, Xikun Zhang, and Jure Leskovec. 2019. Predicting dynamic embedding trajectory in temporal interaction networks. *CoRR*, abs/1908.01207.

Quoc V. Le and Tomás Mikolov. 2014. Distributed representations of sentences and documents. In *Proceedings of the 31st International Conference on Machine Learning*, volume 32(2), pages 1188–1196.

Suraj Maharjan, Deepthi Mave, Prasha Shrestha, Manuel Montes-Y-Gómez, Fabio A. González, and Thamar Solorio. 2019. Jointly learning author and annotated character N-gram embeddings: A case study in literary text. *International Conference Recent Advances in Natural Language Processing, RANLP*, 2019-Septe.

T. C. Mendenhall. 1887. The characteristic curves of composition. *Science*, ns-9(214S):237–246.

Tomas Mikolov, Kai Chen, Greg Corrado, and Jeffrey Dean. 2013a. Efficient estimation of word representations in vector space. *arXiv preprint arXiv:1301.3781*.

Tomas Mikolov, Ilya Sutskever, Kai Chen, Greg S Corrado, and Jeff Dean. 2013b. Distributed representations of words and phrases and their compositionality. In *Advances in neural information processing systems*, pages 3111–3119.

Mojtaba Nayyeri, Sahar Vahdati, Xiaotian Zhou, Hamed Shariat Yazdi, and Jens Lehmann. 2020. Embedding-based recommendations on scholarly knowledge graphs. In *The Semantic Web*, pages 255–270, Cham. Springer International Publishing.

Nils Reimers and Iryna Gurevych. 2019. Sentence-bert: Sentence embeddings using siamese bert-networks. *CoRR*, abs/1908.10084.

Sebastian Ruder, Parsa Ghaffari, and John G. Breslin. 2016. Character-level and multi-channel convolutional neural networks for large-scale authorship attribution. *CoRR*, abs/1609.06686.

Upendra Sapkota, Steven Bethard, Manuel Montes, and Thamar Solorio. 2015. Not all character n-grams are created equal: A study in authorship attribution. In *Proceedings of the 2015 Conference of the North American Chapter of the Association for Computational Linguistics: Human Language Technologies*, pages 93–102, Denver, Colorado. Association for Computational Linguistics.

Yunita Sari, Mark Stevenson, and Andreas Vlachos. 2018. Topic or Style ? Exploring the Most Useful Features for Authorship Attribution. *27th International conference on computational lingustics*, pages 343–353.

Roy Schwartz, Oren Tsur, Ari Rappoport, and Moshe Koppel. 2013. Authorship attribution of micro-messages. In *Proceedings of the 2013 Conference on Empirical Methods in Natural Language Processing*, pages 1880–1891, Seattle, Washington, USA. Association for Computational Linguistics.

Efstathios Stamatatos. 2013. On the robustness of authorship attribution based on character n-gram features. *Journal of Law and Policy*, 21:421–439.

Sandeep Subramanian, Guillaume Lample, Eric Michael Smith, Ludovic Denoyer, Marc'Aurelio Ranzato, and Y-Lan Boureau. 2018. Multiple-attribute text style transfer. *CoRR*, abs/1811.00552.

Piotr Szwed. 2017. Authorship attribution for polish texts based on part of speech tagging. pages 316–328.

Xiaodong Wu, Weizhe Lin, Zhilin Wang, and Elena Rastorgueva. 2020. Author2vec: A framework for generating user embedding. *CoRR*, abs/2003.11627.

Ying Zhao and Justin Zobel. 2005. Effective and scalable authorship attribution using function words. In *Information Retrieval Technology*, pages 174–189, Berlin, Heidelberg. Springer Berlin Heidelberg.

ESTIME: Estimation of Summary-to-Text Inconsistency by Mismatched Embeddings

Oleg Vasilyev, John Bohannon
Primer Technologies Inc.
San Francisco, California
oleg, john@primer.ai

Abstract

We propose a new reference-free summary quality evaluation measure, with emphasis on the faithfulness. The measure is based on finding and counting all probable potential inconsistencies of the summary with respect to the source document. The proposed ESTIME, Estimator of Summary-to-Text Inconsistency by Mismatched Embeddings, correlates with expert scores in summary-level SummEval dataset stronger than other common evaluation measures not only in Consistency but also in Fluency. We also introduce a method of generating subtle factual errors in human summaries. We show that ESTIME is more sensitive to subtle errors than other common evaluation measures.

1 Introduction

Summarization must preserve the factual consistency of the summary with the text. Human annotation of factual consistency can be accompanied with detailed classification of factual errors, thus giving a hope that the annotation scores are reasonably objective (Kryscinski et al., 2020; Huang et al., 2020; Vasilyev et al., 2020b; Gabriel et al., 2020; Maynez et al., 2020).

Factual consistency of a summary is one of several summary qualities; for the purpose of human annotation these qualities can be specified in different ways (Xenouleas et al., 2019; Kryscinski et al., 2020; Fan et al., 2018; Vasilyev et al., 2020b; Fabbri et al., 2020). Summarization models nowadays create satisfactorily fluent, coherent and informative summaries, but the factual consistency suffers from hallucinations, entity swaps and other errors. Some factual errors are easily noticeable; other factual errors could be hardly noticeable even for annotators (Lux et al., 2020; Vasilyev et al., 2020b) - which is arguably even worse.

Existing summary evaluation measures are based on several approaches, which may be sensitive to some qualities more than to others. A question-answering based evaluation estimates how helpful is the summary in answering questions about the source text (Xenouleas et al., 2019; Eyal et al., 2019; Scialom et al., 2019; Deutsch et al., 2020; Durmus et al., 2020; Wang et al., 2020). A text reconstruction approach estimates how helpful is the summary in guessing parts of the source text (Vasilyev et al., 2020a,b; Egan et al., 2021). Evaluation measures that use some kind of text similarity can estimate how similar is the summary to special human-written reference summaries (Zhang et al., 2020; Zhao et al., 2019; Lin, 2004), or, more realistically, how similar is the summary to the source text (Gao et al., 2020; Louis and Nenkova, 2009).

In order to assess how well an evaluation measure works for factual consistency, it is necessary either to have a dataset of human-annotated imperfect machine-generated summaries (Bhandari et al., 2020; Fabbri et al., 2020), or to have a dataset of artificially introduced factual errors in originally factually correct human-written summaries (Kryscinski et al., 2020).

In this paper we focus on presenting a new evaluation measure with emphasis on factual consistency. Our contribution:

1. We introduce **ESTIME**: Estimator of Summary-to-Text Inconsistency by Mismatched Embeddings[1]. Using human-annotated machine-generated summaries of SummEval (Fabbri et al., 2020), we compare ESTIME with other evaluation measures.
2. We introduce a natural method of generating subtle factual errors. We use it here to compare the performance of ESTIME with other measures on human-written summaries with generated subtle errors.

[1] https://github.com/PrimerAI/blanc/tree/master/estime

Proceedings of the 58th Annual Meeting of the Association for Computational Linguistics, pages 94–103

https://doi.org/10.26615/978-954-452-056-4_010

2 Methods

The motivations for our estimator:

1. Any location in a summary has a context that loosely corresponds to a context in one or more locations in the text.
2. In the most similar context, the summary would normally use the same word that was used in the text.
3. Summary generation models produce very few new (not from the text) words per summary.
4. Transformer-made token embeddings are highly contextual (Ethayarajh, 2019).

In order to estimate the consistency of a summary with the text, we attempt to count all the summary tokens that could be potentially related to a factual error. To this end, we check embeddings of all the tokens of the summary that have one or more occurrences in the text. For each embedding we find its match: the most similar embedding in the text. If the corresponding tokens are not the same, we add up such mismatch into our score of inconsistency. Our goal is not an error correction or precise location of errors, but a score estimating the summary consistency quality. The algorithm is simple:

1. Obtain embeddings for all tokens in the text. In the summary, obtain embeddings only for the tokens that occur at least once in the text. To obtain an embedding of a token, mask the token, run a token-prediction transformer model on the context surrounding the token, and take the embedding of the token from a hidden layer.
2. For each of the obtained embeddings of the summary tokens, find the most similar embedding in the text. If the corresponding tokens do not coincide, count this as a potential inconsistency. The total number of such inconsistencies is our score, ESTIME.

We measure 'similarity' of embeddings by their scalar product. Thus, ESTIME score is the number N_a of 'alarms':

$$N_a = \sum_{i:t_i \in T} H(\max_{\beta:t'_\beta \neq t_i} (e_i e'_\beta) - s(i)) \quad (1)$$

$$s(i) \equiv \max_{\alpha:t'_\alpha = t_i} (e_i e'_\alpha) \quad (2)$$

Here H is Heaviside function; the summary is a sequence of tokens t_i, each having embedding e_i; the text T is a sequence of tokens t'_α, having embeddings e'_α. The summation in Equation 1 is over all the summary tokens t_i that exist in the text T. The count N_a gets added $+1$ whenever the best match to e_i from the embeddings of unequal tokens e'_β exceeds the best match from the embeddings of occurrences of the same token $t_\alpha = t_i$ in the text.

The tokens are obtained by the tokenizer corresponding to the token-prediction transformer model. Notice that we do not verify the summary tokens that do not occur in the text. Such tokens still can influence the context used for embeddings of other tokens. The algorithm is asymmetric with respect to the summary and the text: it is supposed to estimate summary-to-text inconsistency.

This approach is different from matching embeddings for sake of measuring similarity (e.g. similarity between a summary and a reference summary in BERTScore (Zhang et al., 2020)), and from using a model trained to replace wrong tokens with correct ones (Cao et al., 2020; Kryscinski et al., 2020).

The embeddings are taken using the pretrained BERT model (Devlin et al., 2019) bert-large-uncased-whole-word-masking of Transformers library (Wolf et al., 2020). While there is no crucial difference with other varieties of BERT, ALBERT and RoBERTa, this model showed a better overall performance, and we used it for evaluations in the next sections. For the sake of faster processing, we do not run the model separately for each token, but at a single run obtain embeddings for all tokens separated by the distance of 8 tokens. This means that the context for each masked token is a little muddied by masking of a few other tokens, but the distance of 8 tokens is large enough for the effect to be negligible. The results of the next sections are obtained with input size of 450 tokens (close to max BERT input length). Finally, when input window does not touch the beginning or end of the text, we do not mask the tokens too close to the edge of the window: no masking within the margin of 50 tokens at the edges of the input window. The algorithm is simple, but for convenience we provide the code[2].

In the next sections we present results for the versions ESTIME-12 and ESTIME-24, corresponding to the embeddings from the middle (12th layer) and from the top (24th layer) of the large BERT; as explained later we also consider ESTIME-21.

[2]https://github.com/PrimerAI/blanc/tree/master/estime

measure	consistency		relevance		coherence		fluency	
	ρ	τ	ρ	τ	ρ	τ	ρ	τ
BLANC-AXXL	0.200	0.098	0.246	0.179	0.127	0.093	0.115	0.066
BLANC-BLU	0.207	0.102	0.217	0.156	0.116	0.085	0.112	0.065
(-)ESTIME-12	0.374	0.184	0.140	0.100	0.238	0.173	0.343	0.198
(-)ESTIME-21	**0.404**	**0.200**	0.188	0.134	0.300	0.217	**0.399**	**0.232**
(-)ESTIME-24	0.358	0.176	0.117	0.084	0.187	0.134	0.363	0.209
(-)J-Shannon	0.193	0.095	0.406	0.298	0.289	0.213	0.125	0.072
SummaQA-F1	0.174	0.085	0.16	0.113	0.089	0.065	0.12	0.069
SummaQA-P	0.197	0.097	0.179	0.127	0.112	0.082	0.133	0.076
SUPERT	0.297	0.147	0.306	0.222	0.236	0.175	0.175	0.101
BERTScore-F1	0.109	0.053	0.371	0.273	**0.377**	**0.277**	0.142	0.082
BERTScore-P	0.055	0.027	0.268	0.196	0.323	0.238	0.126	0.072
BERTScore-R	0.164	0.081	**0.423**	**0.309**	0.345	0.253	0.12	0.069
BLEU	0.095	0.047	0.213	0.153	0.176	0.128	0.140	0.080
ROUGE-L	0.115	0.057	0.241	0.174	0.170	0.124	0.079	0.045
ROUGE-1	0.137	0.067	0.302	0.220	0.184	0.134	0.080	0.046
ROUGE-2	0.129	0.063	0.245	0.177	0.146	0.105	0.063	0.036
ROUGE-3	0.149	0.073	0.251	0.180	0.160	0.116	0.066	0.038

Table 1: Summary level correlations ρ (Spearman) and τ (Kendall Tau-c) of quality estimators with human experts scores. The top rows evaluation measures are reference-free, separated from the lower rows evaluation measures, which need human references. In each column the highest correlation is bold-typed. The only p-values above 0.01 in this table are p=0.03 for BERTScore-P and p=0.01 for ROUGE-2.

3 Performance on human-annotated machine-generated summaries

3.1 Correlations with expert scores

We used SummEval dataset [3] (Fabbri et al., 2020) for comparing ESTIME with a few well known or promising evaluation measures. The part of SummEval dataset that we use consists of 100 texts, each text is accompanied by 16 summaries generated by 16 different models, making altogether 1600 text-summary pairs. Each text-summary pair is annotated (on scale 1 to 5) by 3 experts for 4 qualities: consistency, relevance, coherence and fluency. We took average of the expert scores for each quality of a text-summary pair. Each text is also accompanied by 11 human-written reference summaries, for the measures that need them. (In latest version of (Fabbri et al., 2020) a 17th model - Pegasus dynamic mix - is added to the annotations.)

We calculated scores of ESTIME and other measures for all the 1600 summaries, and presented their correlations with the average expert scores in Table 1. The measures in Table 1 are split into the group of reference-free measures (top) and the measures requiring human-written references (bottom). All the measures are based on certain principles rather than on finetuning on some human-annotated datasets. Here BLANC-help (Vasilyev et al., 2020a) is calculated in two versions[4], which differ by the underlying models: BLU - bert-large-uncased, and AXXL - albert-xxlarge-v2. ESTIME and Jensen-Shannon (Louis and Nenkova, 2009) values are negated. SummaQA (Scialom et al., 2019) is represented by SummaQA-P (prob) and SummaQA-F1 (F1 score)[5]. SUPERT (Gao et al., 2020) is calculated as single-doc with 20 reference sentences 'top20'[6] (using bert-large-nli-stsb-mean-tokens). BLEU (Papineni et al., 2002) is calculated with NLTK. BERTScore (Zhang et al., 2020) (by default [7] using roberta-large) is represented by F1, precision (P) and recall (R). For ROUGE (Lin, 2004) the ROUGE-L is calculated as rougeLsum[8].

By design ESTIME should perform well for consistency, and indeed it beats other measures in the table. Being a one-sided summary-to-text estimator

[3] https://github.com/Yale-LILY/SummEval

[4] https://github.com/PrimerAI/blanc#blanc-on-summeval-dataset

[5] https://github.com/recitalAI/summa-qa

[6] https://github.com/yg211/acl20-ref-free-eval

[7] https://github.com/Tiiiger/bert_score

[8] https://github.com/google-research/google-research/tree/master/rouge

of inconsistencies, ESTIME should not and does not perform well for relevance. ESTIME performs better than other measures for fluency, and reasonably well for coherence (ESTIME-21 is better for coherence than the rest of the reference-free metrics). Interestingly, a comparison of ESTIME-12 vs ESTIME-24 shows that the middle of the transformer knows better than the top about all the summary qualities except the fluency. In Appendix A we show and discuss a curious pattern of dependency of correlations on the embeddings layer. Correlations with all qualities peak around the layer 21, then sharply drop by the top layer 24. This is the reason we added ESTIME-21 to the table. While ESTIME-21 is the best choice, each of the three shown ESTIME versions is better than the rest of the measures for consistency and fluency.

3.2 System level correlations

measure	ρ	τ
BLANC-AXXL	0.812	0.617
BLANC-BLU	0.724	0.567
(-)ESTIME-12	0.756	0.583
(-)ESTIME-21	0.821	0.633
(-)ESTIME-24	0.815	0.633
(-)J-Shannon	0.753	0.533
SummaQA-F1	0.862	0.667
SummaQA-P	**0.912**	**0.750**
SUPERT	0.832	0.633
BERTscore-F1	-0.029	-0.017
BERTscore-P	-0.329	-0.217
BERTscore-R	0.885	0.733
BLEU	-0.150	-0.017
ROUGE-L	0.376	0.283
ROUGE-1	0.694	0.517
ROUGE-2	0.779	0.600
ROUGE-3	0.888	0.717

Table 2: System level correlation ρ (Spearman) and τ (Kendall Tau-c) of quality estimators with human experts scores of consistency. Top rows show reference-free evaluation measures.

In Table 2 we show correlations on system level, meaning that the scores (of automated measures and of human experts) are averaged over the 100 texts, so that each array of scores has length only 16 rather than 1600 (Fabbri et al., 2020). The purpose of this would be a comparison of the summarization models. The results are shown for consistency only; for other qualities some measures have p-value higher than 0.05. The ranking of the measures changes with averaging over the texts (Table 2 vs Table 1). We may speculate that some measures may be more sensitive to the model generation style which can lead to less errors or more errors on average; other measures may be more sensitive to specific factual errors in each summary. If it is true, we would have to be cautious about the measures that do well on the system level and do not do well on the summary level.

3.3 Discussion

While we must be cautious about picking evaluation measure version most fitting human scores (Vasilyev and Bohannon, 2021), using ESTIME-21 is probably justified by simultaneous maximum at level 21 for all four summary qualities, as shown in Figures 1 and 2 in Appendix A. For our definition of ESTIME we preferred N_a of Equation 1 rather than the alternative definition N_w of Equation 3 in Appendix B. N_w is counting all the text tokens that managed to 'win', i.e. to be closer to a summary token than any text occurrence of the summary token. We are concerned that if the summary token is bad (inconsistent with its context), the number of the 'winners' is large and might be fairly arbitrary.

We defined ESTIME in Equations 1 and 2 by using simple scalar product of embeddings. In Appendix C we show that using normalized embeddings only makes the correlations worse, by almost fully erasing the 'Layer-21 maximum'.

In Appendix D we give an example of switching to a simpler underlying model: bert-base-uncased. This slightly weakens the correlations, and makes the dependency on the layer id less sharp.

In Appendix E we give an example of excluding part of speech tokens from consideration by ESTIME. This means that the summation in Equation 1 will use only tokens t_i of some parts of speech, and that the max will similarly restrict the tokens t'_β. Despite high frequency of determiners in texts, the omission of the determiners from ESTIME makes almost no difference.

As explained in Section 2, in obtaining embeddings we are using a somewhat spoiled context, because we mask many tokens in a single input (albeit requiring the masks to be reasonably separated). In Appendix F we show that our separation requirements are indeed reasonable, and making them twice more strict barely change the correlations.

4 Performance on human summaries with generated subtle errors

Machine-generated summaries, even by abstractive summarization models, generally follow the source text by frequently reproducing large spans from it. Human summaries are more varied in describing the source text, and it is interesting how useful can be ESTIME for evaluating them. Fundamentally, we are asking how flexible are the embeddings in understanding the context. In order to answer this question, we made random selection of 2000 text-summary pairs from CNN/Daily Mail dataset (Hermann et al., 2015). For each human-written summary we then added the same summary modified by generated factual errors. We thus made 4000 text-summary pairs. We assigned the 'golden' scores as 1 to each clean summary, and 0 to each summary with errors.

Our 'subtle errors' generation method is simple, heuristic-free and easily reproducible. In order to generate an error, we randomly select a whole-word token in the summary, mask and predict it by an LM model (we used bert-base-cased). We then select the top predicted candidate that is not equal to the real token, and substitute it for the real token. The resulting *subtle errors* are similar to real machine-generated mishaps and hallucinations, with the fluency preserved.

The evaluation task is now more difficult: the summaries are human-written, and the errors are subtle. Without labeling of the generated errors, we cannot be confident of always having real factual errors: large part of the generated errors are indeed truly factual errors, but the rest disturb coherence or fluency, or make synonyms. For purposes of a preliminary simple evaluation here, and to ensure high probability of having true errors, we generated 3 random errors in each 'score=0' summary. Table 3 shows that ESTIME is more sensitive to the generated errors than other measures. Only reference-free measures could be applied in this situation. All p-values in the table are less than 10^{-3}, except 0.023 for BLANC-AXXL, 0.002 for Jensen-Shannon and 0.001 for SummaQA-P.

In Table 3 the correlation of ESTIME-21 with generated errors turns out to be lower than the correlation of ESTIME-24. If we guessed correctly in Apendix A about the reasons for the drop of the correlations between the layers 21 and 24 in Figures 1 and 2, then the relatively high value of ESTIME-24 indicates that it may have additionally benefited from an information relevant to predicting tokens, even when the generated token replacements are not factual errors. In the near future we plan to follow up these evaluations on a large fully labeled dataset of 'subtle errors'.

measure	ρ	τ
BLANC-AXXL	0.036	0.042
BLANC-BLU	0.076	0.087
(-)ESTIME-12	0.138	0.159
(-)ESTIME-21	0.163	0.188
(-)ESTIME-24	**0.169**	**0.195**
(-)J-Shannon	0.048	0.055
SummaQA-F1	0.055	0.064
SummaQA-P	0.054	0.062
SUPERT	0.107	0.123

Table 3: Correlation ρ (Spearman) and τ (Kendall Tau-c) of quality estimators with the presence of generated subtle errors in human summary. The dataset of 4000 text-summary pairs was created by random pick of 2000 test-summary pairs from CNN / Daily Mail dataset, duplicating these 2000 pairs, and by generating subtle errors in the 2000 duplicated summaries.

5 Conclusion

We introduced ESTIME: estimator of summary-to-text inconsistency by mismatched embeddings, - a measure of summary quality with emphasis on measuring factual inconsistency between the summary and the text. The fact that this simple measure correlates with human-labeled consistency and fluency much better than more complex measures tells us about the current state of summary evaluation, and about the power of contextual embeddings.

We also introduced a method for generating *subtle errors*; the method has a potential for creating consistent and realistic benchmark datasets for factual consistency. In the near future we intend to release such fully labeled flexible dataset.

Acknowledgments

We thank Nidhi Vyas and anonymous reviewers for review of the paper and valuable feedback.

References

Manik Bhandari, Pranav Narayan Gour, Atabak Ashfaq, Pengfei Liu, and Graham Neubig. 2020. Re-evaluating evaluation in text summarization. In *Proceedings of the 2020 Conference on Empirical Meth-*

ods in Natural Language Processing, pages 9347–9359. Association for Computational Linguistics.

Meng Cao, Yue Dong, Jiapeng Wu, and Jackie Chi Kit Cheung. 2020. Factual error correction for abstractive summarization models. In *Proceedings of the 2020 Conference on Empirical Methods in Natural Language Processing*, pages 6251–6258. Association for Computational Linguistics (2020).

Daniel Deutsch, Tania Bedrax-Weiss, and Dan Roth. 2020. Towards question-answering as an automatic metric for evaluating the content quality of a summary. *arXiv*, arXiv:2010.00490.

Jacob Devlin, Ming-Wei Chang, Kenton Lee, and Kristina Toutanova. 2019. BERT: Pre-training of deep bidirectional transformers for language understanding. In *Proceedings of the 2019 Conference of the North American Chapter of the Association for Computational Linguistics: Human Language Technologies, Volume 1 (Long and Short Papers)*, pages 4171–4186, Minneapolis, Minnesota. Association for Computational Linguistics.

Esin Durmus, He He, and Mona Diab. 2020. FEQA: A question answering evaluation framework for faithfulness assessment in abstractive summarization. In *Proceedings of the 58th Annual Meeting of the Association for Computational Linguistics*, pages 5055–5070. Association for Computational Linguistics.

Nicholas Egan, Oleg Vasilyev, and John Bohannon. 2021. Play the Shannon game with language models: A human-free approach to summary evaluation. *arXiv*, arXiv:2103.10918.

Kawin Ethayarajh. 2019. How contextual are contextualized word representations? Comparing the geometry of BERT, ELMo, and GPT-2 embeddings. In *Proceedings of the 2019 Conference on Empirical Methods in Natural Language Processing and the 9th International Joint Conference on Natural Language Processing*, pages 55–65. Association for Computational Linguistics (Hong Kong, China, 2019).

Matan Eyal, Tal Baumel, and Michael Elhadad. 2019. Question answering as an automatic evaluation metric for news article summarization. In *Proceedings of the 2019 Conference of the North American Chapter of the Association for Computational Linguistics: Human Language Technologies, Volume 1*, pages 3938–3948. Association for Computational Linguistics.

Alexander R. Fabbri, Wojciech Kryściński, Bryan McCann, Caiming Xiong, Richard Socher, and Dragomir Radev. 2020. SummEval: Re-evaluating summarization evaluation. *arXiv*, arXiv:2007.12626v4.

Lisa Fan, Dong Yu, and Lu Wang. 2018. Robust neural abstractive summarization systems and evaluation against adversarial information. *arXiv*, arXiv:1810.06065.

Saadia Gabriel, Asli Celikyilmaz, Rahul Jha, Yejin Choi, and Jianfeng Gao. 2020. Go figure! A meta evaluation of factuality in summarization. *arXiv*, arXiv:2010.12834.

Yang Gao, Wei Zhao, and Steffen Eger. 2020. SUPERT: Towards new frontiers in unsupervised evaluation metrics for multi-document summarization. In *Proceedings of the 58th Annual Meeting of the Association for Computational Linguistics*, pages 1347–1354. Association for Computational Linguistics.

Karl Moritz Hermann, Tomáš Kočiský, Edward Grefenstette, Lasse Espeholt, Will Kay, Mustafa Suleyman, and Phil Blunsom. 2015. Teaching machines to read and comprehend. In *Advances in Neural Information Processing Systems 28*, pages 1693–1701. Curran Associates, Inc.

Dandan Huang, Leyang Cui, Sen Yang, Guangsheng Bao, Kun Wang, Jun Xie, and Yue Zhang. 2020. What have we achieved on text summarization? In *Proceedings of the 2020 Conference on Empirical Methods in Natural Language Processing*, pages 446–469. Association for Computational Linguistics.

Wojciech Kryscinski, Bryan McCann, Caiming Xiong, and Richard Socher. 2020. Evaluating the factual consistency of abstractive text summarization. In *Proceedings of the 2020 Conference on Empirical Methods in Natural Language Processing*, pages 9332–9346. Association for Computational Linguistics.

Chin-Yew Lin. 2004. ROUGE: A package for automatic evaluation of summaries. In *Proceedings of Workshop on Text Summarization Branches Out*, pages 74–81. Association for Computational Linguistics.

Annie Louis and Ani Nenkova. 2009. Automatically evaluating content selection in summarization without human models. In *Proceedings of the 2009 Conference on Empirical Methods in Natural Language Processing*, pages 306–314. Association for Computational Linguistics.

Klaus-Michael Lux, Maya Sappelli, and Martha Larson. 2020. Truth or error? Towards systematic analysis of factual errors in abstractive summaries. In *Proceedings of the First Workshop on Evaluation and Comparison of NLP Systems (Eval4NLP)*, pages 1–10. Association for Computational Linguistics (2020).

Joshua Maynez, Shashi Narayan, Bernd Bohnet, and Ryan McDonald. 2020. On faithfulness and factuality in abstractive summarization. In *Proceedings of the 58th Annual Meeting of the Association for Computational Linguistics*, pages 1906–1919. Association for Computational Linguistics (2020).

Kishore Papineni, Salim Roukos, Todd Ward, and Wei-Jing Zhu. 2002. BLEU: a method for automatic evaluation of machine translation. In *Proceedings of the*

40th Annual Meeting of the Association for Computational Linguistics (ACL), pages 311–318, Philadelphia. Association for Computational Linguistics.

Thomas Scialom, Sylvain Lamprier, Benjamin Piwowarski, and Jacopo Staiano. 2019. Answers unite! Unsupervised metrics for reinforced summarization models. In *Proceedings of the 2019 Conference on Empirical Methods in Natural Language Processing and the 9th International Joint Conference on Natural Language Processing*, pages 3246–3256, Hong Kong, China. Association for Computational Linguistics.

Oleg Vasilyev and John Bohannon. 2021. Is human scoring the best criteria for summary evaluation? In *Findings of the Association for Computational Linguistics: ACL-IJCNLP 2021*, pages 2184–2191. Association for Computational Linguistics.

Oleg Vasilyev, Vedant Dharnidharka, and John Bohannon. 2020a. Fill in the BLANC: Human-free quality estimation of document summaries. In *Proceedings of the First Workshop on Evaluation and Comparison of NLP Systems*, pages 11–20. Association for Computational Linguistics.

Oleg Vasilyev, Vedant Dharnidharka, Nicholas Egan, Charlene Chambliss, and John Bohannon. 2020b. Sensitivity of BLANC to human-scored qualities of text summaries. *arXiv*, arXiv:2010.06716.

Alex Wang, Kyunghyun Cho, and Mike Lewis. 2020. Asking and answering questions to evaluate the factual consistency of summaries. In *Proceedings of the 58th Annual Meeting of the Association for Computational Linguistics*, pages s 5008–5020. Association for Computational Linguistics (2020).

Thomas Wolf, Lysandre Debut, Victor Sanh, Julien Chaumond, Clement Delangue, Anthony Moi, Pierric Cistac, Tim Rault, Remi Louf, Morgan Funtowicz, Joe Davison, Sam Shleifer, Patrick von Platen, Clara Ma, Yacine Jernite, Julien Plu, Canwen Xu, Teven Le Scao, Sylvain Gugger, Mariama Drame, Quentin Lhoest, and Alexander Rush. 2020. Transformers: State-of-the-art natural language processing. In *Proceedings of the 2020 Conference on Empirical Methods in Natural Language Processing: System Demonstrations*, pages 38–45. Association for Computational Linguistics (2020).

Stratos Xenouleas, Prodromos Malakasiotis, Marianna Apidianaki, and Ion Androutsopoulos. 2019. SUM-QE: a BERT-based summary quality estimation model. In *Proceedings of the 2019 Conference on Empirical Methods in Natural Language Processing and the 9th International Joint Conference on Natural Language Processing*, pages 6005–6011, Hong Kong, China. Association for Computational Linguistics.

Tianyi Zhang, Varsha Kishore, Felix Wu, Kilian Q. Weinberger, and Yoav Artzi. 2020. BERTScore: Evaluating text generation with BERT. *arXiv*, arXiv:1904.09675v3.

Wei Zhao, Maxime Peyrard, Fei Liu, Yang Gao, Christian M. Meyer, and Steffen Eger. 2019. MoverScore: Text generation evaluating with contextualized embeddings and earth mover distance. In *Proceedings of the 2019 Conference on Empirical Methods in Natural Language Processing and the 9th International Joint Conference on Natural Language Processing*, pages 563–578. Association for Computational Linguistics.

A Dependency on layers

It is natural to expect that embeddings from top layer would be good in characterizing context for a token. In Figures 1 and 2 we show correlations of SummEval expert scores with ESTIME versions that are defined by a model layer from which the embeddings are taken. (The model is bert-large-uncased-whole-word-masking.) Immediate observation about the dependency of the correlation value on the model layer is that after reaching maximum around layer 21, the correlation value quickly drops at higher layers. At low levels the correlation value increases fast by layer 5 (for coherence and relevance or 7 (for consistency and fluency) and then grows much slower, sometimes going flat or even dropping down.

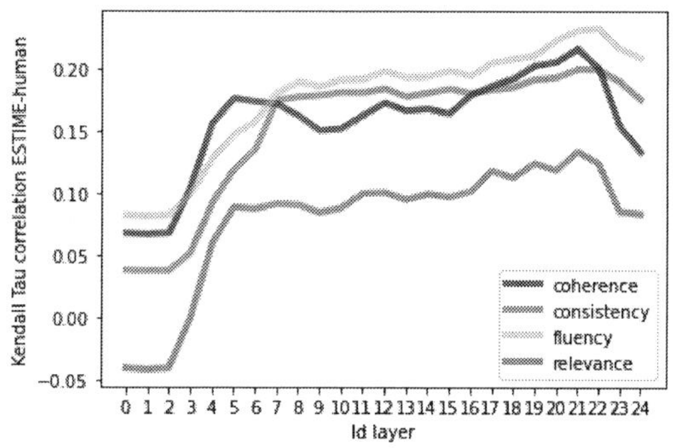

Figure 1: Kandall Tau-c correlation between SummEval experts scores and ESTIME using embeddings taken from different layers of the model.

We have no guess why the dependency of the correlations on the layer Id is so strong immediately after the layer #2 and why it is weak further in the wide range of the middle layers. However, we can speculate about the sharp drop after the 'layer #21 peak'. It may be that below the layer #21 peak, the BERT model keeps a lot of generic contextual information for two reasons: it is trained for two tasks (next sentence prediction and masked token prediction), and each node has to be useful for all or for the most of the nodes above. But after

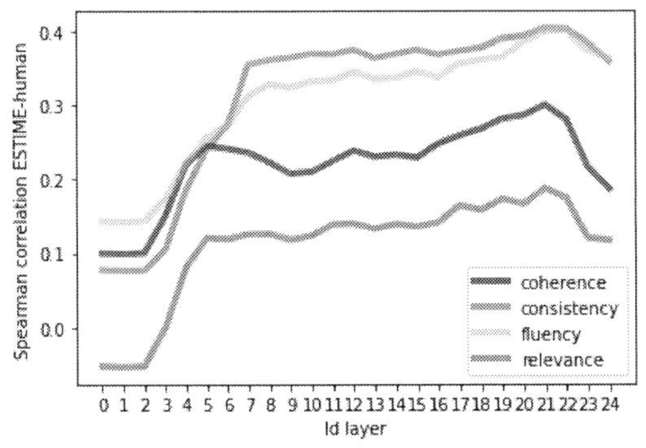

Figure 2: Spearman correlation between SummEval experts scores and ESTIME using embeddings taken from different layers of the model.

the peak, the last few layers at positions close to each text token are strongly influenced by the token prediction task.

In the plots shown in this Appendix, as well as in all other plots through the paper, the correlations p-values are below 0.05 (mostly far below). Unlike the summary level correlations, the system level correlations have not much data. This is why, keeping only the correlations with p-values below 0.05, we can show in Figure 3 only the consistency quality, and even for the consistency we have less range of layers.

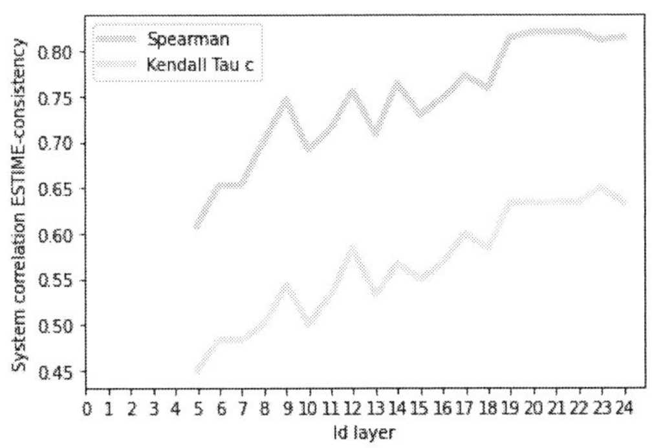

Figure 3: Spearman and Kendall Tau-c correlations - system level - between SummEval experts scores of consistency and ESTIME using embeddings taken from different layers of the model.

B Count of winning tokens in text

ESTIME is defined in Equation 1 and is considered through the paper as a count of 'alarming' summary tokens. It could be alternatively defined as a count of all winner-tokens from the text, as defined in Equation 3.

$$N_w = \sum_{i:t_i \in T} \sum_{\beta:t'_\beta \neq t_i} H((e_i e'_\beta) - s(i)) \quad (3)$$

In Figures 4 and 5 we see how N_w differs from ESTIME (N_a).

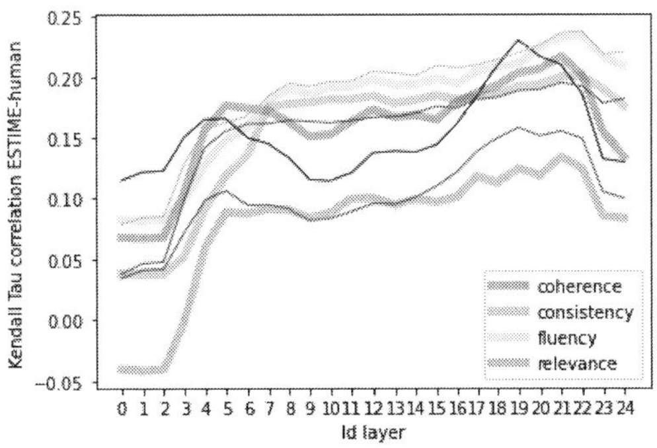

Figure 4: Kandall Tau-c correlation between SummEval experts scores and ESTIME by embeddings from different layers of the model. Thick lines: ESTIME (as defined by Equation 1 and considered through the paper). Thin lines: N_w as defined by Equation 3.

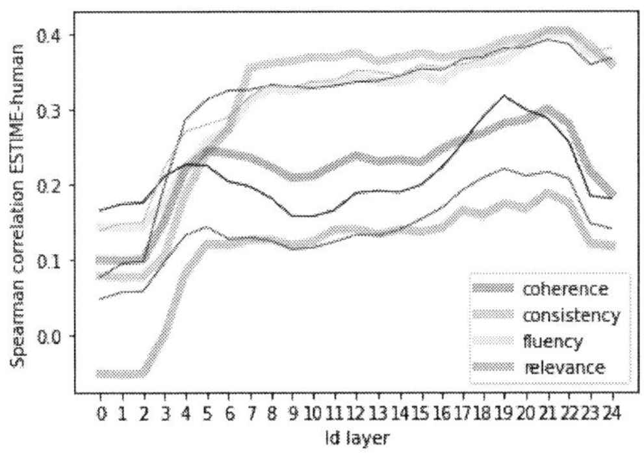

Figure 5: Spearman correlation between SummEval experts scores and ESTIME by embeddings from different layers of the model. Thick lines: ESTIME (as defined by Equation 1 and considered through the paper). Thin lines: N_w as defined by Equation 3.

C Normalization of embeddings

We used unnormalized embeddings for ESTIME. From Figures 6 and 7 it is clear that normalizing embeddings does not improve ESTIME. Curiously, the effect of the normalization on the correlations is in destroying the peak around the layer 21.

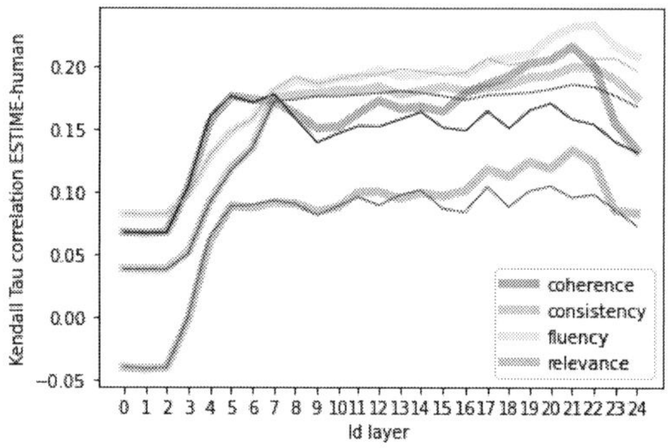

Figure 6: Kandall Tau-c correlation between SummEval experts scores and ESTIME by embeddings from different layers of the model. Thick lines: unnormalized embeddings (as used through the paper). Thin lines: normalized embeddings.

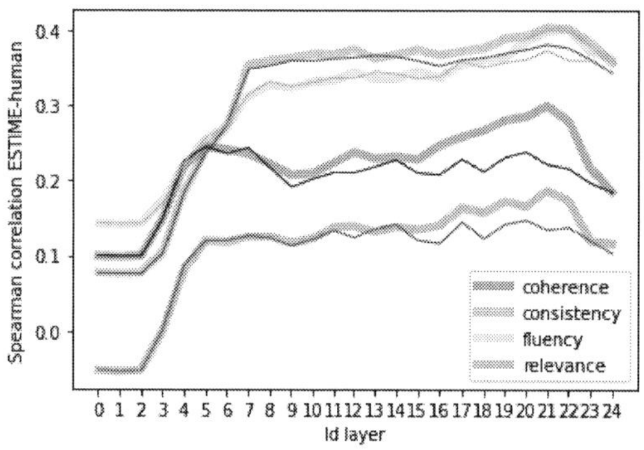

Figure 7: Spearman correlation between SummEval experts scores and ESTIME by embeddings from different layers of the model. Thick lines: unnormalized embeddings (as used through the paper). Thin lines: normalized embeddings.

This could mean that the lengths of the embeddings carry all the information necessary for creating the peak at the layer 21.

D Comparison with base BERT

As default and through the paper ESTIME uses the model bert-large-uncased-whole-word-masking. In Figures 8 and 9 we show an example of a comparison with another model - bert-base-uncased. Unlike the large model, the bert-base-uncased has 0-12 range of its layers, and in the plots here we rescaled them by x2, interpolating in between for odd layer Ids. This allows to compare the trends of the correlations along the relative depth of the transformer. We observe the familiar quick rise at low depth, a drop at high levels close to the output, and a slow growth or plateau in between, - but all these features are less sharp for the bert-base-uncased. It is puzzling that a larger transformer, with twice longer 'distance' for backpropagation to travel from the top to the bottom, has more distinct features of quick rise, plateau, peak and drop, with exact locations of the end of the quick rise and of the peak.

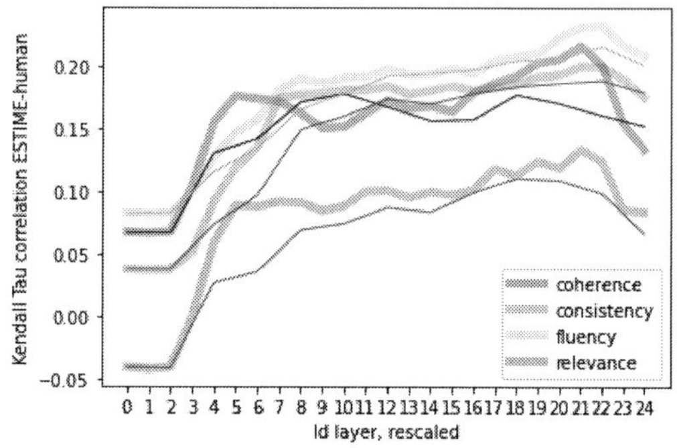

Figure 8: Kandall Tau-c correlation between SummEval experts scores and ESTIME by embeddings from different layers of the model. Thick lines: the model is bert-large-uncased-whole-word-masking. Thin lines: the model is bert-base-uncased.

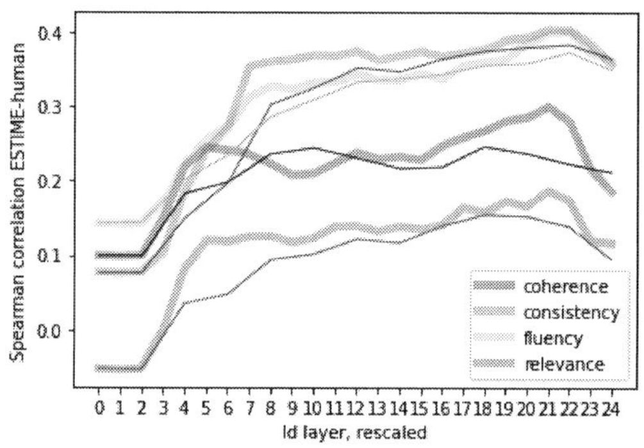

Figure 9: Spearman correlation between SummEval experts scores and EESTIME by embeddings from different layers of the model. Thick lines: the model is bert-large-uncased-whole-word-masking. Thin lines: the model is bert-base-uncased.

E Example of excluding a part of speech

Throughout the paper we used all text tokens for ESTIME. In Figures 10 and 11 we show an example of excluding from consideration a part of speech: determiners. Determiners occur very frequently in the text, but exclusion of them does not make much difference in the resulting correlations with human scores, especially for the quality we are most interested in: consistency.

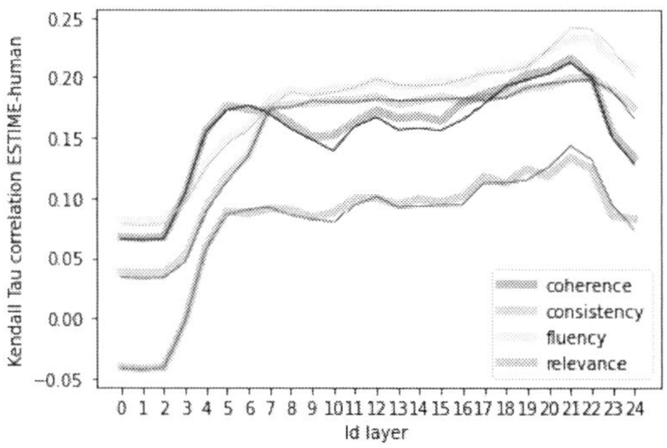

Figure 10: Kandall Tau-c correlation between SummEval experts scores and ESTIME by embeddings from different layers of the model. Thick lines: all tokens are used, as is done throughout the paper. Thin lines: tokens of determiners (part of speech) are not used.

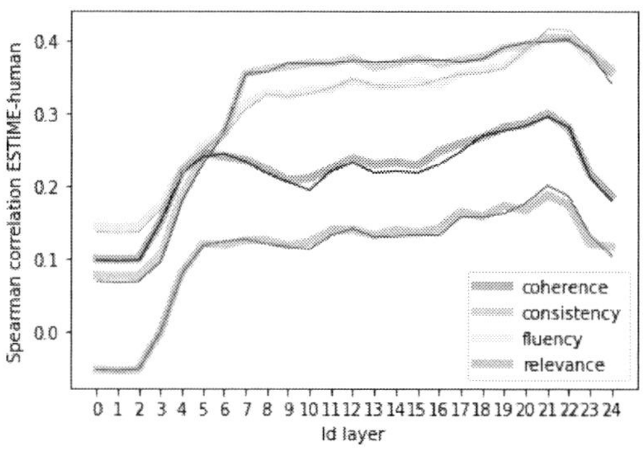

Figure 11: Spearman correlation between SummEval experts scores and EESTIME by embeddings from different layers of the model. Thick lines: all tokens are used, as is done throughout the paper. Thin lines: tokens of determiners (part of speech) are not used.

F Parameters for sparse masking

In Section 2 we explained that for faster processing we take embeddings not one at a time, but as much as fit into an input window, as long as the masking is done with 8 tokens separation, and within the margin 50 tokens from the input edges (unless input edge touches the edge of the text). In Figures 12 and 13 we compare our default parameters with a twice more sparse version: 16 tokens separation, and 100 tokens margin. The sparser version should be better, but slower to run. From the figures it is clear that the sparser version has almost the same correlations; our default sparsity is good enough.

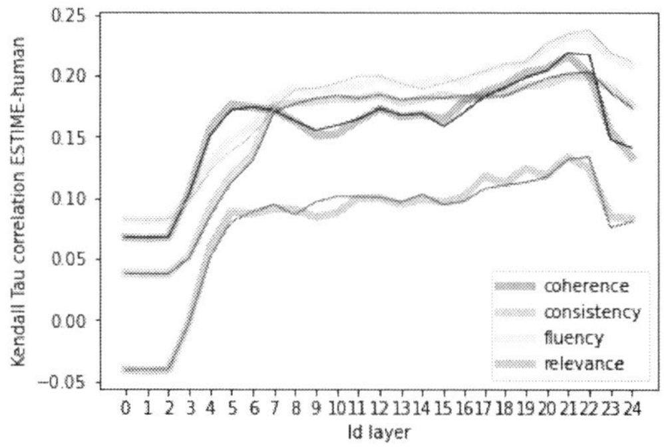

Figure 12: Kandall Tau-c correlation between SummEval experts scores and ESTIME by embeddings from different layers of the model. Thick lines: sparsity of the masking is defined by the distance 8 and the margin 50 (see Section 2), as used through the paper. Thin lines: Distance 8, margin 100.

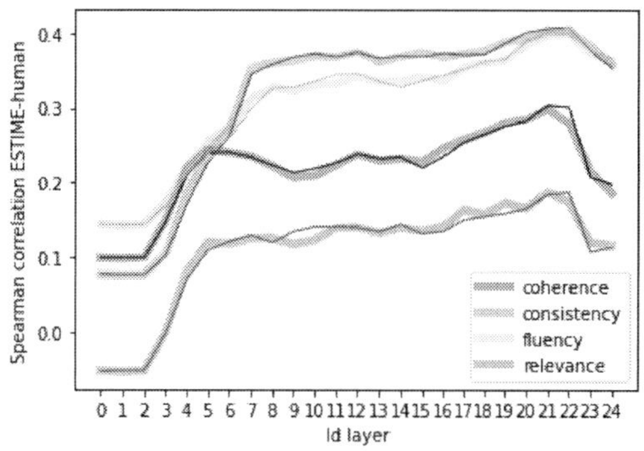

Figure 13: Spearman correlation between SummEval experts scores and EESTIME by embeddings from different layers of the model. Thick lines: sparsity of the masking is defined by the distance 8 and the margin 50 (see Section 2), as used through the paper. Thin lines: Distance 8, margin 100.

Statistically Significant Detection of Semantic Shifts using Contextual Word Embeddings

Yang Liu
University of Helsinki
yang.liu@helsinki.fi

Alan Medlar
University of Helsinki
alan.j.medlar@helsinki.fi

Dorota Głowacka
University of Helsinki
dorota.glowacka@helsinki.fi

Abstract

Detecting lexical semantic change in smaller data sets, e.g. in historical linguistics and digital humanities, is challenging due to a lack of statistical power. This issue is exacerbated by non-contextual embedding models that produce one embedding per word and, therefore, mask the variability present in the data. In this article, we propose an approach to estimate semantic shift by combining contextual word embeddings with permutation-based statistical tests. We use the false discovery rate procedure to address the large number of hypothesis tests being conducted simultaneously. We demonstrate the performance of this approach in simulation where it achieves consistently high precision by suppressing false positives. We additionally analyze real-world data from SemEval-2020 Task 1 and the Liverpool FC subreddit corpus. We show that by taking sample variation into account, we can improve the robustness of individual semantic shift estimates without degrading overall performance.

1 Introduction

Semantic change detection methods are used in historical linguistics and digital humanities to study the evolution of word meaning over time and in different domains (Kutuzov et al., 2018). While semantic shift estimates have been shown to correlate with simulated (Schlechtweg et al., 2019; Shoemark et al., 2019) and manual (Schlechtweg et al., 2020) annotations of meaning change, to our knowledge, no existing methods attempt to characterize the uncertainty of the estimated semantic shift for each individual word. This is especially problematic because semantic change detection is usually based on word embeddings (Kutuzov et al., 2018) and recently it has been observed that their stability can vary widely across term frequencies (Wendlandt et al., 2018; Antoniak and Mimno, 2018), implying that many semantic shift estimates are erroneously inflated or underestimated. Prior studies have addressed this issue by filtering out words that fall below a term frequency threshold. While this approach can remove a majority of false positives, it risks the introduction of false negatives. A more robust approach would take into account the sample variation to determine whether there is evidence that an estimated semantic shift is sufficiently different from zero to be considered statistically significant. Unfortunately, non-contextual word embeddings lose this information, flattening all instances of the same term into a single word embedding.

In this paper, we focus on the problem of robust semantic change detection in scenarios where there is either limited data or low frequency terms of interest (e.g. Del Tredici et al. (2019)). Our approach is based on contextual word embeddings, such as those produced by BERT (Devlin et al., 2019), and permutation-based statistical tests. Contextual word embeddings have several advantages over non-contextual embeddings for inferring semantic shift when there is limited data. First, we can leverage pre-trained models that were trained on large-scale data, encoding prior knowledge of the language. Second, as contextual word embeddings are generated for every instance of a given word, there is an opportunity to characterize the strength of evidence for each semantic shift using statistical testing.

The approach we propose in this paper focuses on the application and evaluation of statistical testing in semantic change detection. Our contributions are as follows:

- We show how to apply statistical significance tests to any semantic change detection method based on contextual word embeddings. To our knowledge, this is the first paper to use statistical testing in the context of individual words in semantic change detection.
- We show in simulation that using permutation tests while controlling the false discovery rate

Proceedings of the 58th Annual Meeting of the Association for Computational Linguistics, pages 104–113

https://doi.org/10.26615/978-954-452-056-4_011

improves precision and scales to estimating the uncertainty for all words in a vocabulary.

- We evaluate the impact of statistical testing on overall performance using manually annotated data sets in multiple languages. In a majority of cases, our approach improves performance, resulting in higher Spearman correlations between estimated semantic shifts and annotations.

2 Related Work

Computational methods for semantic change detection are used to compare corpora spanning decades or even centuries. They have been used, for example, to analyze historical word usage (Hamilton et al., 2016a) and to identify statistical laws of language change (Hamilton et al., 2016b). More recently, there has been increased interest in detecting short-term meaning change, such as novel slang terms, in Amazon reviews (Kulkarni et al., 2015), Twitter data (Shoemark et al., 2019) and specialist online communities (Del Tredici et al., 2019).

Prior to the wide-spread use of word embeddings, numerous methods were developed to detect semantic change, including dynamic topic models (Blei and Lafferty, 2006), word co-occurrence statistics (Gulordava and Baroni, 2011) and graph-based methods (Mitra et al., 2014). Methods for semantic change detection based on word embeddings exploit their distributional properties to identify words whose relative position in the embedding space has changed over time, implying a concordant change in meaning (Kutuzov et al., 2018). The earliest work in this area was based on continuous training, initializing each embedding model with embeddings from the previous time step (Kim et al., 2014). Subsequent methods improved performance by training independent embedding models for each corpus (Kulkarni et al., 2015; Hamilton et al., 2016b). Embeddings are invariant under rotation and therefore need to be aligned by solving the orthogonal Procrustes problem (Hamilton et al., 2016b). This alignment step can be avoided altogether by, for example, comparing word neighborhoods (Hamilton et al., 2016a) or using temporal referencing (Dubossarsky et al., 2019).

Semantic shift detection with contextual word embeddings is becoming increasingly popular. Hu et al. (2019) used BERT embeddings to define exemplar representations for pre-defined word senses to track usage over time. Several methods have side-stepped the need for known word senses by clustering BERT embeddings (Giulianelli et al., 2020; Martinc et al., 2020b) and shown that clustering-based approaches can scale to the whole vocabulary (Montariol et al., 2021). Another benefit of using contextual word embeddings is that pre-trained models are widely available for many different languages. These models can be used for fine-tuning to perform semantic change detection using more limited data (Martinc et al., 2020a). Lastly, researchers have started to experiment with ensembling multiple types of word embeddings and distance metrics to improve overall performance (Kutuzov and Giulianelli, 2020; Martinc et al., 2020b).

Recently, there have been several benchmarking studies of semantic change detection methods using simulated data (Shoemark et al., 2019; Schlechtweg et al., 2019) and manually annotated data sets (Schlechtweg et al., 2020). These studies found that variations on the method proposed by Hamilton et al. (2016b) performed best, however, methods based on contextual word embeddings were either absent or the study was based on data where contextual information was partially lost due to shuffling the order of sentences in the corpus (Schlechtweg et al., 2020).

In this paper, we use contextual word embeddings to identify statistically significant semantic shifts. Statistical significance has not been the subject of much investigation in the semantic shift literature. Indeed, the only approach we are aware of was proposed by Kulkarni et al. (2015), which used bootstrapping to perform change-point detection in time series. However, their method is not applicable to scenarios where there is only two time points nor does it take into account the sample variance within each corpus. Our approach addresses both of these issues and can be applied to any semantic change detection method based on contextual word embeddings.

3 Data

Table 1 lists the data sets used in this article. The Liverpool FC corpus collects data from the Liverpool Football Club subreddit from the Reddit online discussion forum. The corpus is in English and split into two time periods from 2011-2013 and 2017 (Del Tredici et al., 2019). SemEval-2020 Task 1 was created to benchmark semantic change detection methods using two subtasks: binary classifica-

	Target words	Corpus size (million tokens)	
		C1	C2
Liverpool FC	97	8.5	11.9
SemEval-2020 English	37	6.5	6.7
SemEval-2020 German	48	70.2	72.3
SemEval-2020 Latin	40	1.7	9.4
SemEval-2020 Swedish	31	71.0	110.0

Table 1: Number of annotated words and corpus sizes for Liverpool FC and SemEval-2020 Task 1 corpora.

tion of whether a word sense has been gained or lost (subtask 1) and ranking words according to their degree of semantic change (subtask 2). The data set contains English, German, Latin and Swedish corpora, all of which contain data from two time periods. All sentences were shuffled and the words lemmatized. We only used the manual annotations from subtask 2 (Schlechtweg et al., 2020).

4 Methodology

Our approach uses contextual word embeddings and permutation-based statistical testing to detect semantic shifts in scenarios where data is limited. While our approach can be applied to any method based on contextual embeddings, we used the method proposed by Martinc et al. (2020a) because of its conceptual simplicity and faster runtime compared to other methods. We generated all contextual word embeddings with BERT (Devlin et al., 2019) using the implementation from HuggingFace's Transformers library (Wolf et al., 2019). In all experiments, we used a base version of BERT (the exact pre-trained models used are specified in later sections) with 12 attention layers and a hidden layer size of 768. All parameters were set to the default values used in the Transformers library ver. 2.5.0, unless stated otherwise.

4.1 Estimating Semantic Shifts

Following the approach outlined by Martinc et al. (2020a), we fine-tune a pre-trained BERT model for each data set, combining both time periods. After fine-tuning, we use the following procedure to generate word representations: we feed sentences of up to 512 tokens into BERT and extract contextual embeddings for each token in the sequence. Following Devlin et al. (2019), we extract embeddings by summing the last 4 encoder layers in the model. As BERT uses byte-pair input encoding, not all tokens correspond to individual words (Kudo and Richardson, 2018). We therefore create contextual embeddings for each word by averaging the embeddings of its constituent tokens.

For each word, we create a non-contextual embedding for each time period by averaging over all contexts for that word. We estimate semantic shift using the cosine distance between these two non-contextual embeddings. To assess the uncertainty in these estimates, we calculate p-values using permutation tests, which are adjusted for multiple comparisons using a false discovery rate procedure (described below). If the p-value is greater than 0.05, there is insufficient evidence to reject the null hypothesis of no difference in meaning between time periods and, therefore, any observed differences can be attributed to random sample variation.

4.2 Permutation Tests

Permutation tests are non-parametric significance tests. Non-parametric tests make no assumptions with respect to the underlying sampling distribution of the data. The goal of the permutation test is to determine whether the observed test statistic (i.e. the cosine distance) is significantly different from zero (the null hypothesis being that there is no semantic shift between the two time periods). Permutation tests generate the sampling distribution by reassigning group labels (i.e. time periods) to all observations by sampling without replacement. We then recalculate the test statistic between the two randomized groups. This procedure is repeated many times, either by enumerating all possible combinations of group assignments or by randomly sampling n permutations. We calculate the p-value as the proportion of the sampling distribution that is greater than or equal to the observed test statistic and reject the null hypothesis for all p-values $< \alpha$, where α, the significance threshold, is usually set to 0.05. Clearly, this procedure limits the smallest non-zero p-value to $\frac{1}{n}$. When we cannot calculate the p-value exactly (i.e. if all combinations cannot be enumerated), we first use $n = 10^3$. If the p-value is < 0.05, we increase n to 10^4. Finally, if the p-value is < 0.005, we increase n to 10^5. P-values with a value of 0.0 are reported as $\frac{1}{n}$.

For example, from the Liverpool FC data set, the word *shovel* appears 5 and 35 times in the 2011-2013 and 2017 corpora, respectively. The number of combinations, $\binom{40}{5}$, is too large to enumerate exhaustively, forcing us to use random sampling. Figure 1 shows the sampling distribution together

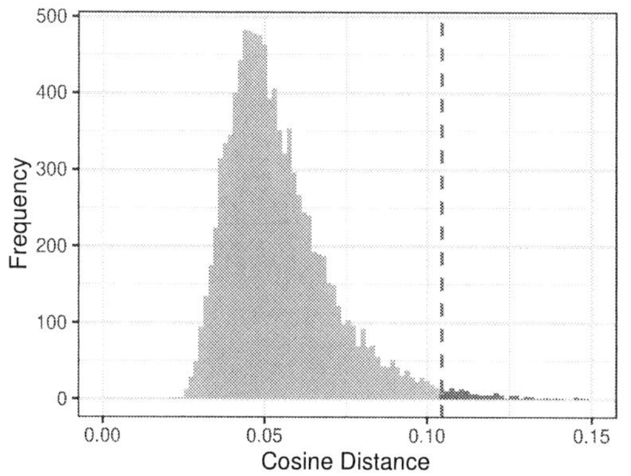

Figure 1: Histogram of the sampling distribution for *shovel* from the Liverpool FC data set. The red dashed line at $x = 0.104$ is the observed cosine distance between average BERT embeddings. The p-value is 0.0212 (the proportion of the histogram colored red).

with the observed distance of 0.104 (dashed red line). As 2.12% of the sampling distribution is greater than or equal to 0.104, the p-value is 0.0212 and, therefore, statistically significant.

If we want to investigate many words in the same experiment, however, then we need to consider the issue of multiple comparisons (Hsu, 1996). In brief, the multiple comparisons problem is where we reject the null hypothesis too often due to the number of simultaneous independent hypothesis tests performed. It is, therefore, desirable to set a lower (more stringent) significance threshold for the set of simultaneous significance tests. We do this in a principled way using a false discovery rate procedure.

4.3 False Discovery Rate

We use the Benjamini-Hochberg procedure to adjust p-values for multiple comparisons (Benjamini and Hochberg, 1995). In doing so, we are limiting the false discovery rate (FDR), i.e. the proportion of false positives, which can potentially be very large if we perform a significance test for every word in the vocabulary.

The Benjamini-Hochberg procedure assumes that we perform m significance tests producing a list of p-values, $P_1, P_2 \dots P_m$, ranked into ascending order. We control the FDR at the significance threshold, α, by finding the largest value of k, such that $P_{(k)} \leq \frac{k}{m}\alpha$. We reject the null hypothesis for all p-values less than P_k (Benjamini and Hochberg, 1995). The implementation of FDR that we use additionally makes the corresponding corrections to all other p-values, allowing for any α to be used post-correction.

Returning to our previous example, the significance test for *shovel* was only one of 97 tests performed to analyze the Liverpool FC data set. Controlling for FDR adjusts the original (significant) p-value of 0.0212 to 0.0605, suggesting there is insufficient evidence, given the number of independent significance tests performed, to believe the observed distance of 0.104 is different from zero. We, therefore, attribute the observed difference between time periods to random variation.

5 Synthetic Evaluation

We created multiple simulated data sets to highlight the importance of significance testing when performing semantic change detection across the whole vocabulary. Previous work also used simulated data to compare methods (Kulkarni et al., 2015; Shoemark et al., 2019), however, they focused on simulating time series, whereas we only simulate two time periods.

5.1 Synthetic Data Set Construction

We create synthetic data sets using a method similar to Shoemark et al. (2019). For each simulation run, we create two synthetic corpora: $C1$ and $C2$. Each synthetic corpus is created by randomly sampling with replacement 70% of the sentences from the Liverpool FC 2017 corpus (the larger of the two time periods). $C1$ and $C2$ have the same distributional characteristics, but vary due to sampling noise. We insert controlled shifts by copying and editing sentences in the data set, altering both the term frequency and co-occurrence distributions of shifted words (described below). Finally, we fine-tune the English `BERT-base-uncased` model for 5 epochs using all unique sentences from $C1$ and $C2$, before calculating cosine distances, permutation tests and FDR correction.

Our procedure for inserting semantic shifts is as follows. We select n pairs of words: an acceptor word, that gains new meanings, and a donor word, where these new meanings come from. We pick word pairs by (i) filtering out words with low (< 5) or high (> 500) term frequencies and those with > 5 word senses according to WordNet (very few words in WordNet have only a single word sense, the threshold was chosen to limit the number of word senses without being too restrictive), (ii) we then sort words into descending order by term frequency, (iii) we pair up consecutive words and, (iv) randomly select word pairs. For each word pair, we randomly generate a proportion, p, and sample p of the sentences containing the donor word from $C2$ and replaced the donor word with the acceptor word. We only simulated gains in word meaning because they are equivalent to losses with only two time points, i.e. a gain from $C1 \rightarrow C2$ is equivalent to a loss from $C2 \rightarrow C1$. To ensure that we do not create any unintentional changes in the meaning of the donor words, these changes were made to copies of the sampled sentences, i.e. the term frequency of donor words is unchanged.

We created 10 data sets using this procedure, each simulating 500 semantic shifts. Given that p is randomly generated, these shifts can result in anything from a term frequency gain of 1 (which is undetectable due to sampling variation) to the term frequency approximately doubling. As a result of the initial random sampling to create the corpora, the number of non-artificially shifted words with a difference in term frequency of at least +50% was ~1200 and +100% was ~150. The size of the shared vocabulary between $C1$ and $C2$ was ~31,000 words in all simulation runs.

Model fine-tuning took < 2 hours on an Nvidia Volta V100 GPU with 32GB of RAM. *P*-value calculations were parallelized, taking a total of 170 CPU hours per simulation run on Intel Xeon CPUs running at 2.1 GHz.

5.2 Baseline Optimization

As a baseline, we compared our approach to the method proposed by Martinc et al. (2020a), described in Section 4.1, i.e. cosine distance between average embeddings without significance testing. To set the term frequency threshold to even consider a word for semantic shift detection, we found the optimal threshold that maximised precision@500. This baseline represents the best-case scenario and is, therefore, impossible to replicate in real-world settings as we would not know *a priori* which words have undergone semantic shift. The optimal term frequency threshold varied for each simulation run, ranging between 19–25. We refer to this method as *Optimal TF*.

5.3 Results

We evaluated how well FDR adjusted p-values compare with those from the permutation tests and the baseline. We used precision@K averaged over the 10 simulation runs. Precision@$K = TP(K)/K$,

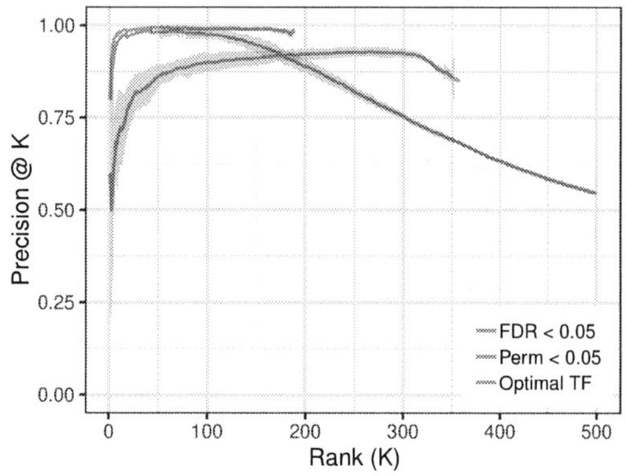

Figure 2: Precision@K averaged over 10 simulation runs. Perm and FDR were filtered using the p-values from permutation tests and FDR correction, respectively. Optimal TF filters at the optimal term frequency threshold to maximise precision@500.

where K is the rank and $TP(K)$ is the count of true positives found in the top-K ranks. We used all values of K from 1–500.

5.3.1 Precision@K

Figure 2 shows how precision@K varied for the three methods tested. FDR outperformed TF Optimal for all values of K where there was at least K significant results, with the exception of precision@1, where they were equal. FDR output the fewest results of all three methods, ranging from 177 to 189 words across the 10 simulation runs. For precision@177 (the last rank with FDR results in all 10 simulation runs), the lowest precision for FDR was 0.96 compared to 0.86 for TF Optimal, an improvement of 11.6%. For TF Optimal, performance starts to drop from around rank 100, falling to 0.55 at rank 500.

We additionally included the p-values from the permutation tests without FDR correction (*Perm* in Figure 2). Overall, the permutation tests had the highest precision lower in the ranking, but suffered from more false positives at the top of the ranking compared to the more conservative FDR. While FDR and Optimal TF had an average precision@10 close to 1.0, the unadjusted p-values from the permutation test had an average precision@10 of 0.71. For precision@335 (the last rank with permutation test results in all simulation runs), the lowest precision was 0.86.

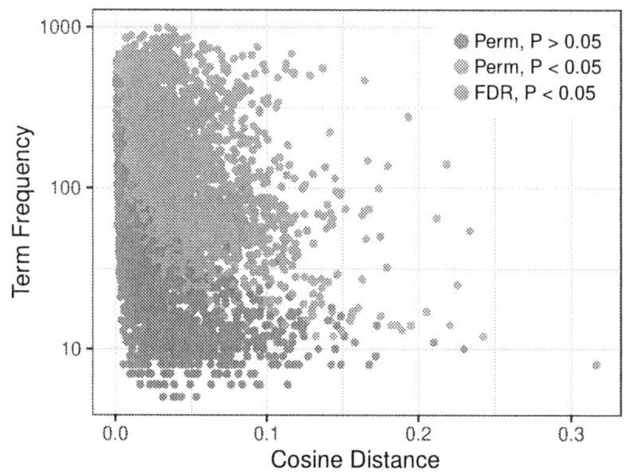

Figure 3: Cosine distance between average BERT embeddings vs term frequency (log scaled). Colors show whether $P < 0.05$ for permutation test and FDR (yellow and blue dots, respectively).

5.3.2 Issues with Term Frequency Thresholds

Figure 3 shows the cosine distance for each word with a simulated semantic shift across all 10 simulation runs versus term frequency on a log scale. The colors indicate whether the distance was not statistically significant (gray), significant for the permutation test, but not after FDR correction (yellow) or significant after FDR correction (blue). Significance testing makes a complex trade-off between the effect size (cosine distance), sample size (term frequency) and the number of significance tests performed. Semantic shift studies usually threshold on term frequency, however, it is clear from Figure 3 that thresholding on any combination of term frequency or cosine distance will filter out words where the estimated semantic shift achieves statistical significance, unnecessarily introducing false negatives and potentially omitting important results.

5.3.3 Factors Influencing Detection

We hypothesized that confounding factors, such as the distance between acceptor and donor words in the embedding space, could spuriously influence whether a semantic shift estimate achieves significance. To investigate this concern, we created a logistic regression model with a binary response variable of whether the FDR p-value was < 0.05. We used the following explanatory variables from the simulations: gain in term frequency of the acceptor word and two confounding variables (i) the final term frequency of the acceptor word and (ii) the original cosine distance between donor and acceptor words. We standardized all explanatory variables so we could rank them by their relative effect size. All regression coefficients were highly significant ($P < 2 \times 10^{-16}$).

The gain in term frequency from donor to acceptor word had the strongest effect on whether semantic change could be detected by FDR ($\beta = 10.7$). The confounding variables, however, had a comparatively modest effect. The term frequency of the acceptor word had a negative effect (-1.52) and the distance between acceptor and donor words had a small positive effect (0.53). These findings suggest that significance testing supports semantic change detection and is not strongly biased towards potential confounders.

6 Empirical Evaluation

We used five manually annotated data sets (see Table 1) to evaluate whether our approach impacts overall performance. We hypothesized that erroneous estimates of semantic change will have a negative impact on the Spearman correlation between cosine distance and manual annotations.

6.1 Experimental Setup

Each corpus from SemEval-2020 and Liverpool FC was composed of data from two time periods. As in our simulations, we fine-tuned a single BERT model on the entire corpus (i.e. the concatenation of both time periods) for 5 epochs. We used the `BERT-base-uncased` pre-trained BERT model for English, `bert-base-german-dbmdz-uncased` for German, Latin BERT (Bamman and Burns, 2020) for Latin and `af-ai-center/bert-base-swedish-uncased` for Swedish. As each corpus provides a list of target words with known semantic shift, we calculated cosine distances, permutation tests and FDR correction for only these words. We evaluated performance with the Spearman correlation between the estimated semantic shifts and the ground truth. We did this between (i) all target words (the baseline), (ii) words where the p-value from the permutation test was < 0.05 and (iii) words where the FDR corrected p-value was < 0.05. We note that our chosen baseline Martinc et al. (2020a) does not have state-of-the-art performance on SemEval-2020, however, we are only concerned with the relative differences in performance from applying significance testing.

	English			German			Latin			Swedish	
	0.2	0.15	0.1	0.2	0.15	0.1	0.2	0.15	0.1	0.1	0.05
Baseline	0.287	0.312	0.332	**0.512**	0.481	0.419	0.302	0.272	0.240	**0.134**	0.141
+ Permutation Tests	**0.301**	0.330	**0.341**	0.502	0.496	0.460	**0.304**	**0.285**	0.273	0.127	**0.162**
+ False Discovery Rate	**0.301**	**0.332**	0.339	0.502	**0.498**	**0.467**	**0.304**	**0.285**	**0.286**	0.127	**0.162**

Table 2: Spearman correlations of cosine distance vs. semantic shift for English, German, Latin and Swedish from SemEval-2020. Data sets were randomly sampled without replacement using sampling rates of 0.2, 0.15 and 0.1 (with the exception of Swedish, which was subsampled to 0.1 and 0.05). Each result is the mean over 100 runs.

6.2 SemEval-2020

Many of the target words in SemEval-2020 have high term frequencies of up to several thousand per time period. Given that words with high term frequencies will be highly significant, we created artificially smaller data sets using random subsampling. For English, German and Latin, we randomly sampled without replacement using sampling rates of 0.2, 0.15 and 0.1. For Swedish, we used sampling rates of 0.1 and 0.05. These sampling rates were chosen to cover the range of almost all words achieving significance to only $\sim$30 achieving significance (below which, the Spearman correlation was often not statistically significant). Swedish has only 31 words in the target set and the highest term frequencies, necessitating lower sampling rates. We created 100 randomly subsampled data sets per sampling rate for each language. Model fine-tuning took approximately $1, 24, 2.5$ and 36 hours for English, German, Latin and Swedish, respectively, using the same computing resources as previously. P-value calculation varied per language and sampling rate from 25 minutes to 2 hours.

6.2.1 Results

Table 2 shows the average Spearman correlation for each data set in SemEval-2020 for each sampling rate tested. Despite the small size of the target sets, significance testing generally had a positive impact on Spearman correlation. FDR correction had the highest or joint highest correlation in 8/11 experiments. The baseline outperformed both permutation tests and FDR correction in two experiments, however, the difference was at most only 0.01. At the lowest sampling rates, the margin by which our approach outperformed the baseline varied widely: with a sampling rate of 0.1 there was an improvement of 11.5% and 19.2%, for German and Latin, respectively. However, for English the improvement was only 2.5%.

In these experiments, performing FDR correction, compared to permutation tests, made a minimal difference to correlation because there were only 31-48 significance tests compared to $\sim 31,000$ simultaneous tests performed in Section 5.

6.3 Liverpool FC Subreddit

Compared to SemEval-2020, words in the Liverpool FC corpus tend to have lower term frequencies. Additionally, the Liverpool FC corpus had a higher proportion of words with a ground truth semantic shift of zero (40/97). The Liverpool FC corpus better represents the kind of observational studies we focus on with our approach, where data is sparse and therefore noisier. Model fine-tuning and p-value calculation took < 3 hours in total.

6.3.1 Results

Figure 4 shows a scatter plot of the cosine distance versus semantic shift index for the 97 words in the target set. Each word is colored by p-value: gray were not statistically significant (57/97), yellow were significant for the permutation test, but not after FDR correction (10/97) and blue were significant after FDR correction (30/97). For a majority of words, there is insufficient evidence to reject the null hypothesis that the semantic change is zero.

Some words failed to achieve significance due to low term frequency: *dank* and *roast*, for example, only occur once in the 2011-2013 corpus. Other words had a high term frequency, but a low estimated shift – requiring substantial evidence to be considered significantly different from zero. Of the 40 target words with a ground truth semantic shift of zero, FDR correction found that 35 were not significantly different from zero (compared to 32 using raw p-values from the permutation test).

The number of words filtered out by significance testing is so great that it negatively impacts correlation. Table 3 shows the Spearman correlations. The method with the highest correlation was using permutation tests without FDR correction, outperforming the baseline by 4.7%. The loss in correlation in FDR correction is caused by three outliers (*clench,*

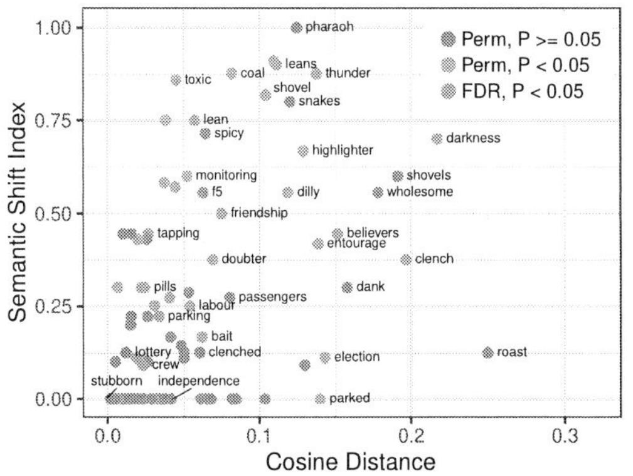

Figure 4: Cosine distance vs. semantic shift index for Liverpool FC data set. Colors show whether $P < 0.05$ for permutation test and FDR (yellow and blue dots).

election and *parked*). The negative influence of these words would be lessened if more words had achieved statistical significance, as was the case with using just permutation tests.

Significance testing highlights how we can be misled by randomness. Del Tredici et al. (2019) stated that false positives with a semantic shift index of zero may be caused by a referential effect, i.e. words that refer to different people or events in different time periods, such as *independence* which referred to events in Catalonia (Figure 4, bottom left). However, a simpler explanation is that there is insufficient evidence to support the cosine distance being significantly different from zero. Similarly, the estimates for *pharaoh* and *shovel* are not too low because they are being used metaphorically (Del Tredici et al., 2019), but because the estimated semantic shift is not statistically significant.

7 Conclusions

We presented an approach to identify statistically significant semantic change using contextual word embeddings, permutation tests and false discovery rate. Our work was motivated by the fact that while there are many methods for semantic change detection, they only estimate the magnitude of a given shift and ignore the uncertainty in their estimates. As a result, existing semantic change detection methods are problematic to apply if (i) the data set is of limited size or (ii) you need to estimate the semantic shift for words with low term frequencies.

In simulation, we demonstrated that using a combination of permutation tests and false discovery rate allows us to scale semantic shift estimation to every word in the vocabulary while avoiding false positives and achieving high precision (Figure 2). In our analysis of the SemEval-2020 data sets, we showed that significance testing has a generally positive impact on Spearman correlation (Table 2). In these examples, the false discovery rate procedure made less of a difference due to the limited number of significance tests performed. In the Liverpool FC corpus, less than a third of target words achieved significance with FDR correction, causing outliers to have a greater influence on correlation than they did on permutation tests (Table 3). However, we were able to highlight how conclusions from Del Tredici et al. (2019) could be more easily explained by semantic shift estimates not being statistically significant due to insufficient evidence.

	Liverpool FC
Baseline	0.536
+ Permutation Tests	**0.561**
+ False Discovery Rate	0.478

Table 3: Spearman correlations of cosine distance vs. semantic shift for the Liverpool FC corpus.

Our work has several limitations. First, the need to recalculate semantic shifts for each permutation increases computational requirements substantially. While this did not prevent us from calculating *p*-values for the whole vocabulary in our simulations, it will be challenging to scale to more complex methods that are based on, for example, clustering. Second, false discovery rate assumes that simultaneous significance tests are independent, which is not the case for word usage. A better approach would account for correlations in usage between words to calibrate the significance threshold more appropriately.

In this paper, we used a semantic shift method which did not exploit the full potential of contextual word embeddings, i.e. to disambiguate between word senses. In future work, we are going to investigate whether more scalable techniques (e.g. Dwass (1957)) could be applied at the word sense level, where even large data sets could potentially start to suffer from the small data problems we focused on in this article.

Acknowledgements

The authors were supported by a grant from Business Finland grant number 3283/31/2019. The authors wish to acknowledge CSC – IT Center for Science, Finland, for computational resources.

References

Maria Antoniak and David Mimno. 2018. Evaluating the stability of embedding-based word similarities. *Transactions of the Association for Computational Linguistics*, 6:107–119.

David Bamman and Patrick J Burns. 2020. Latin bert: A contextual language model for classical philology. *arXiv preprint arXiv:2009.10053*.

Yoav Benjamini and Yosef Hochberg. 1995. Controlling the false discovery rate: a practical and powerful approach to multiple testing. *Journal of the Royal statistical society: series B (Methodological)*, 57(1):289–300.

David M. Blei and John D. Lafferty. 2006. Dynamic topic models. In *Machine Learning, Proceedings of the Twenty-Third International Conference (ICML 2006), Pittsburgh, Pennsylvania, USA, June 25-29, 2006*, volume 148 of *ACM International Conference Proceeding Series*, pages 113–120. ACM.

Marco Del Tredici, Raquel Fernández, and Gemma Boleda. 2019. Short-term meaning shift: A distributional exploration. In *Proceedings of the 2019 Conference of the North American Chapter of the Association for Computational Linguistics: Human Language Technologies, Volume 1 (Long and Short Papers)*, pages 2069–2075, Minneapolis, Minnesota. Association for Computational Linguistics.

Jacob Devlin, Ming-Wei Chang, Kenton Lee, and Kristina Toutanova. 2019. BERT: Pre-training of deep bidirectional transformers for language understanding. In *Proceedings of the 2019 Conference of the North American Chapter of the Association for Computational Linguistics: Human Language Technologies, Volume 1 (Long and Short Papers)*, pages 4171–4186, Minneapolis, Minnesota. Association for Computational Linguistics.

Haim Dubossarsky, Simon Hengchen, Nina Tahmasebi, and Dominik Schlechtweg. 2019. Time-out: Temporal referencing for robust modeling of lexical semantic change. In *Proceedings of the 57th Annual Meeting of the Association for Computational Linguistics*, pages 457–470, Florence, Italy. Association for Computational Linguistics.

Meyer Dwass. 1957. Modified randomization tests for nonparametric hypotheses. *The Annals of Mathematical Statistics*, pages 181–187.

Mario Giulianelli, Marco Del Tredici, and Raquel Fernández. 2020. Analysing lexical semantic change with contextualised word representations. In *Proceedings of the 58th Annual Meeting of the Association for Computational Linguistics*, pages 3960–3973, Online. Association for Computational Linguistics.

Kristina Gulordava and Marco Baroni. 2011. A distributional similarity approach to the detection of semantic change in the Google Books ngram corpus. In *Proceedings of the GEMS 2011 Workshop on GEometrical Models of Natural Language Semantics*, pages 67–71, Edinburgh, UK. Association for Computational Linguistics.

William L. Hamilton, Jure Leskovec, and Dan Jurafsky. 2016a. Cultural shift or linguistic drift? comparing two computational measures of semantic change. In *Proceedings of the 2016 Conference on Empirical Methods in Natural Language Processing*, pages 2116–2121, Austin, Texas. Association for Computational Linguistics.

William L. Hamilton, Jure Leskovec, and Dan Jurafsky. 2016b. Diachronic word embeddings reveal statistical laws of semantic change. In *Proceedings of the 54th Annual Meeting of the Association for Computational Linguistics (Volume 1: Long Papers)*, pages 1489–1501, Berlin, Germany. Association for Computational Linguistics.

Jason Hsu. 1996. *Multiple comparisons: theory and methods*. CRC Press.

Renfen Hu, Shen Li, and Shichen Liang. 2019. Diachronic sense modeling with deep contextualized word embeddings: An ecological view. In *Proceedings of the 57th Annual Meeting of the Association for Computational Linguistics*, pages 3899–3908, Florence, Italy. Association for Computational Linguistics.

Yoon Kim, Yi-I Chiu, Kentaro Hanaki, Darshan Hegde, and Slav Petrov. 2014. Temporal analysis of language through neural language models. In *Proceedings of the ACL 2014 Workshop on Language Technologies and Computational Social Science*, pages 61–65, Baltimore, MD, USA. Association for Computational Linguistics.

Taku Kudo and John Richardson. 2018. SentencePiece: A simple and language independent subword tokenizer and detokenizer for neural text processing. In *Proceedings of the 2018 Conference on Empirical Methods in Natural Language Processing: System Demonstrations*, pages 66–71, Brussels, Belgium. Association for Computational Linguistics.

Vivek Kulkarni, Rami Al-Rfou, Bryan Perozzi, and Steven Skiena. 2015. Statistically significant detection of linguistic change. In *Proceedings of the 24th International Conference on World Wide Web, WWW 2015, Florence, Italy, May 18-22, 2015*, pages 625–635. ACM.

Andrey Kutuzov and Mario Giulianelli. 2020. UiO-UvA at SemEval-2020 task 1: Contextualised embeddings for lexical semantic change detection. In *Proceedings of the Fourteenth Workshop on Semantic Evaluation*, pages 126–134, Barcelona (online). International Committee for Computational Linguistics.

Andrey Kutuzov, Lilja Øvrelid, Terrence Szymanski, and Erik Velldal. 2018. Diachronic word embeddings and semantic shifts: a survey. In *Proceedings of the 27th International Conference on Computational Linguistics*, pages 1384–1397, Santa Fe, New Mexico, USA. Association for Computational Linguistics.

Matej Martinc, Petra Kralj Novak, and Senja Pollak. 2020a. Leveraging contextual embeddings for detecting diachronic semantic shift. In *Proceedings of the 12th Language Resources and Evaluation Conference*, pages 4811–4819, Marseille, France. European Language Resources Association.

Matej Martinc, Syrielle Montariol, Elaine Zosa, and Lidia Pivovarova. 2020b. Discovery team at SemEval-2020 task 1: Context-sensitive embeddings not always better than static for semantic change detection. In *Proceedings of the Fourteenth Workshop on Semantic Evaluation*, pages 67–73, Barcelona (online). International Committee for Computational Linguistics.

Sunny Mitra, Ritwik Mitra, Martin Riedl, Chris Biemann, Animesh Mukherjee, and Pawan Goyal. 2014. That's sick dude!: Automatic identification of word sense change across different timescales. In *Proceedings of the 52nd Annual Meeting of the Association for Computational Linguistics (Volume 1: Long Papers)*, pages 1020–1029, Baltimore, Maryland. Association for Computational Linguistics.

Syrielle Montariol, Matej Martinc, and Lidia Pivovarova. 2021. Scalable and interpretable semantic change detection. In *Proceedings of the 2021 Conference of the North American Chapter of the Association for Computational Linguistics: Human Language Technologies*, pages 4642–4652, Online. Association for Computational Linguistics.

Dominik Schlechtweg, Anna Hätty, Marco Del Tredici, and Sabine Schulte im Walde. 2019. A wind of change: Detecting and evaluating lexical semantic change across times and domains. In *Proceedings of the 57th Annual Meeting of the Association for Computational Linguistics*, pages 732–746, Florence, Italy. Association for Computational Linguistics.

Dominik Schlechtweg, Barbara McGillivray, Simon Hengchen, Haim Dubossarsky, and Nina Tahmasebi. 2020. SemEval-2020 task 1: Unsupervised lexical semantic change detection. In *Proceedings of the Fourteenth Workshop on Semantic Evaluation*, pages 1–23, Barcelona (online). International Committee for Computational Linguistics.

Philippa Shoemark, Farhana Ferdousi Liza, Dong Nguyen, Scott Hale, and Barbara McGillivray. 2019. Room to Glo: A systematic comparison of semantic change detection approaches with word embeddings. In *Proceedings of the 2019 Conference on Empirical Methods in Natural Language Processing and the 9th International Joint Conference on Natural Language Processing (EMNLP-IJCNLP)*, pages 66–76, Hong Kong, China. Association for Computational Linguistics.

Laura Wendlandt, Jonathan K. Kummerfeld, and Rada Mihalcea. 2018. Factors influencing the surprising instability of word embeddings. In *Proceedings of the 2018 Conference of the North American Chapter of the Association for Computational Linguistics: Human Language Technologies, Volume 1 (Long Papers)*, pages 2092–2102, New Orleans, Louisiana. Association for Computational Linguistics.

Thomas Wolf, L Debut, V Sanh, J Chaumond, C Delangue, A Moi, P Cistac, T Rault, R Louf, M Funtowicz, et al. 2019. Huggingface's transformers: State-of-the-art natural language processing. *ArXiv, abs/1910.03771*.

Referenceless Parsing-Based Evaluation of AMR-to-English Generation

Emma Manning **Nathan Schneider**
Georgetown University
{esm76, nathan.schneider}@georgetown.edu

Abstract

Reference-based automatic evaluation metrics are notoriously limited for NLG due to their inability to fully capture the range of possible outputs. We examine a referenceless alternative: evaluating the adequacy of English sentences generated from Abstract Meaning Representation (AMR) graphs by parsing into AMR and comparing the parse directly to the input. We find that the errors introduced by automatic AMR parsing substantially limit the effectiveness of this approach, but a manual editing study indicates that as parsing improves, parsing-based evaluation has the potential to outperform most reference-based metrics.

1 Introduction

Natural language generation (NLG) is notoriously difficult to evaluate well due to its one-to-many nature: thanks to the infinite capacity of human language, any given meaning can be expressed in a potentially unlimited number of ways. Thus, listing the 'right answer(s)' and comparing a system's output against such a list, which is a possible evaluation method for many other tasks, is fundamentally limited for NLG. Nevertheless, automatic evaluation of NLG has traditionally been dominated by reference-based metrics like BLEU (Papineni et al., 2002).

In recent years, however, referenceless evaluation metrics have been gaining popularity in NLG and related fields. In this paper we examine the potential and limitations of one such approach: using semantic parsing to compare a generated sentence to a meaning representation from which it was generated, in order to measure semantic adequacy. We focus on generation of English text from Abstract Meaning Representation graphs ("AMRs"; Banarescu et al., 2013). Figure 1 shows an example of an AMR, which represents the meaning of a sentence. AMR does not represent certain morphological and syntactic details such as tense, number,

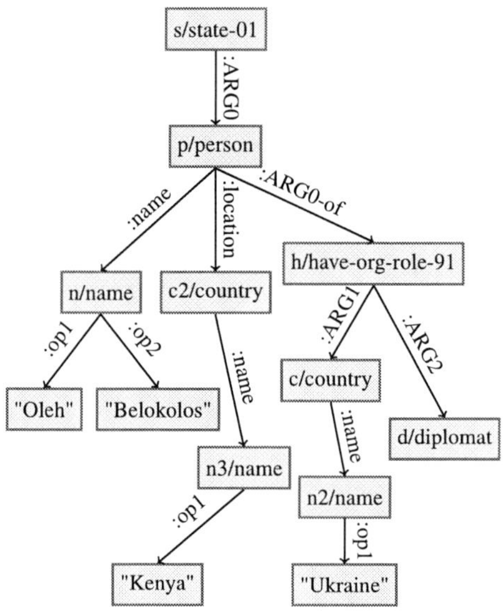

Figure 1: AMR graph for the sentence "Ukrainian diplomat in Kenya oleh belokolos stated –"

definiteness, and word order, so the graph shown could represent a number of alternate sentences, such as:

- Oleh Belokolos, the Ukrainian diplomat in Kenya, states:
- A Ukrainian diplomat in Kenya named Oleh Belokolos has made a statement.

Ideally, then, a sentence generated from an AMR graph should be judged on how well it expresses the elements of meaning given in the graph, ignoring the details that are not included.

We examine the hypothesis that we can measure the semantic adequacy of a sentence *generated* from an AMR by performing the reverse operation—namely, *parsing* the generated sentence into AMR—and measuring the similarity of the parsed AMR graph to the original. In essence, this idea exploits complementarity of English-to-AMR parsers and AMR-to-English generators being evaluated. Assuming an accurate parse, we would ex-

Proceedings of the 58th Annual Meeting of the Association for Computational Linguistics, pages 114–122

https://doi.org/10.26615/978-954-452-056-4_012

Var	Description
r	Reference sentence
a	Gold AMR, created from r
g	Sentence automatically generated from a
p	AMR automatically parsed from g
p'	Manually-corrected version of automatic parses p

Table 1: Summary of notation used in this paper, with a description of each type of sentence and AMR used.

pect this to be a good measure of the adequacy of the generated sentence, since a sentence that accurately expresses the meaning in the original AMR should have the same AMR. We further formalize this approach in §2. As discussed in §3, this method has also been suggested by Opitz and Frank (2021); we contribute new analyses of its validity, in particular by measuring its correlation with human adequacy judgments collected by Manning et al. (2020). We find that errors made by an automatic AMR parser substantially limit the quality of parsing-based evaluation as a proxy for human evaluation, resulting in a lower correlation with adequacy scores than many reference-based metrics (§5). To approximate an upper bound for the potential of this evaluation approach with improved parsing, we conduct an additional study using manually-corrected AMR parses; we find that this substantially improves the quality of the metric (§6).

2 Parsing-Based Evaluation

AMR-to-English generation is the task of taking an input AMR graph a and generating a sentence g expressing the meaning content of the AMR in English. Ideally, we would evaluate generation by comparing g directly to a to determine how well g expresses the meaning in a; this is what the human annotators whose judgments we use (see §4) did. However, we don't know of an existing way to directly compare a sentence to an AMR graph; instead, our metrics tend to compare two items of the same type. Reference-based metrics compare the generated sentence g to r, the English sentence for which the AMR was created, and which is typically used as the sole reference in evaluation. We analyze the hypothesis that we can more accurately capture the details relevant to AMR by comparing AMRs to each other: specifically, comparing a to either p, an automatic parse of g, or to p', a manually-corrected version of p. Our notation is summarized in table 1.

3 Background

The evaluation method we analyze in this paper is closely related to the $\mathcal{MF}_\beta$ metric suggested by Opitz and Frank (2021), which combines a measure of meaning preservation, $\mathcal{M}$, with a language model–based measure of grammatical form, $\mathcal{F}$. Their meaning preservation metric, $\mathcal{M}$, assigns a score to a generated sentence by parsing it into AMR and computing the parse's similarity to the gold AMR. They use the AMR parser by Cai and Lam (2020) and the S^2match similarity metric; we experiment with these as well as other options for both parser and metric. While they perform a number of pilot experiments to test the robustness of $\mathcal{MF}_\beta$, such as its performance with different parsers, Opitz and Frank do not test the correlation of their metric with human judgments; thus, the work presented here adds to our understanding of the validity of this type of metric as a proxy for human evaluation.

As a baseline, we also compare the results of parsing-based evaluation with several reference-based metrics, including those that have traditionally been used to evaluate AMR generation as well as newer metrics that have shown promising results for NLG.

4 Data

We use human judgment data from Manning et al. (2020), consisting of judgments on a total of 600 sentences: 100 human-authored reference sentences and their corresponding AMRs, and 500 sentences automatically generated from these AMRs by 5 different systems. When comparing to reference-based automatic metrics, we do not score the reference sentences themselves since, with only one reference per AMR, these would trivially receive perfect scores on such metrics.

Each sentence has a score on a scale of 0–100, for each of fluency and adequacy, averaged over two annotators. We compare automatic metrics to these judgments, and particularly to the adequacy judgments, since we are primarily interested in parsing-based evaluation as a proxy for adequacy evaluation.

Annotators additionally provided binary judgments on whether information was added or omitted, and whether the sentence was incomprehensible; we use the latter of these judgments in §6 to determine which generated sentences to manually edit the parses of.

5 Experiment 1: Automatic Metrics

This section describes experiments with variations on the automatic version of the parsing based metric; that is, the use of similarity metrics comparing the automatic parse p to the gold AMR a. We experiment with different AMR parsers (§5.1) and variations on the Smatch similarity metric (§5.2) and measure the correlation to human judgments of adequacy (§5.3).

5.1 Parsers

We compare gold AMRs to AMR parses of the generated sentences. This includes using three different automatic English-to-AMR parsers, described below.

JAMR. The JAMR parser[1] (Flanigan et al., 2014, 2016) is an early AMR parser; we use it as a baseline to compare against the more recent, higher-accuracy parsers. The JAMR parser uses a semi-Markov model to identify concepts, followed by a graph variant on Maximum Spanning Tree algorithms to identify the relations between concepts. We used the 2016 version, which achieved a Smatch score of 67 on the LDC2015E86 dataset.

LYU-TITOV. While most AMR parsers first train an aligner to align AMR nodes with words in a sentence prior to training the parser itself, Lyu and Titov (2018)[2] treat alignments as latent variables in a joint probabilistic model for identifying concepts, relations, and alignments. This parser achieved a Smatch score of 73.7 on LDC2015E86 and 74.4 on LDC2016E25, which at the time was state-of-the-art.

CAI-LAM. Cai and Lam (2020)[3] was the state of the art in AMR parsing as of 2020, with a Smatch score of 80.2 on LDC2017T10. This transformer-based parser uses iterative inference to determine which part of the input sentence to parse and where to add it to the output graph, without requiring explicit alignments.

Parser performance. We evaluate each parser's accuracy on our sample of 100 sentences by computing $Smatch(a, p(r))$, i.e., the similarity between the gold AMRs in the sample and their corresponding parsed references. We find that CAI-LAM performs the best with a Smatch score of 84.9, followed by 76.3 for LYU-TITOV and 71.1 for JAMR.

[1]Code: `https://github.com/jflanigan/jamr`

[2]Code: `https://github.com/ChunchuanLv/AMR_AS_GRAPH_PREDICTION`

[3]Code: `https://github.com/jcyk/AMR-gs`

5.2 Similarity Metrics

The second piece needed for parsing-based evaluation is a way to quantify the similarity of an AMR parse to the original AMR.

The standard metric for comparing two AMRs—such as to evaluate the quality of an AMR parser or inter-annotator-agreement between human parses—is Smatch (Cai and Knight, 2013). The Smatch score compares triples between two AMR graphs, where each triple is an edge of the graph (a semantic relationship) combined with each of the nodes it connects. For a given pair of AMRs, the Smatch score is the maximum F1-score of triples which can be obtained with a one-to-one mapping of variables between the two graphs.[4]

We also experimented with a small variation on the original Smatch. Smatch computes the similarity between two different AMR graphs based on inferred alignments between the two graphs' concepts. Since checking all possible mappings is computationally intractable, it starts with one 'smart' initialization, then retries with random initializations; the default is four random restarts. This means that Smatch scores are nondeterministic; when running twice on the same pair of AMRs, we sometimes got different scores. To mitigate this effect, we made two changes: First, we increased the number of restarts to 100 to increase the chance that the best mapping would be found, while still maintaining a reasonable runtime. Second, we seeded the random function in the Smatch script to make the results reproducible. In table 3, we refer to the default Smatch as 'Smatch_4', while the variation with a seed and 100 restarts is 'Smatch_{100}+seed'.

More recently, Opitz et al. (2020) analyzed both Smatch and an alternative metric, SemBleu (Song and Gildea, 2019), and proposed a new variant of Smatch, S^2match, which conforms to desirable principles better than either previous metric. In particular, S^2match introduces the concept of embedding-based semantic gradable semantic similarity by allowing for soft matches between concepts. While the primary advantage of this variant is for tasks with more variation in wording, such as measuring the similarity of paraphrases, it could also be advantageous in our setting—for example, to penalize AMR generation systems that represent a concept with the wrong word less if it is a se-

[4]We compute Smatch using the `smatch.py` script found at `https://github.com/jflanigan/jamr/tree/Semeval-2016/scripts/smatch_2.0.2`.

	Fluency	Adequacy
$BLEU_\uparrow$	0.40	0.52
$METEOR_\uparrow$	0.41	0.57
$TER_\downarrow$	−0.33	−0.43
$CHRF{+}{+}_\uparrow$	0.32	0.47
$BERTScore_\uparrow$	0.47	0.60
$BLEURT_\uparrow$	**0.60**	**0.69**

Table 2: Sentence-level correlations with human judgments for **reference-based** metrics.

	$Smatch_4$	$Smatch_{100}$+seed	S^2match
JAMR	0.358	0.356	0.362
LYU-TITOV	0.462	0.460	0.465
CAI-LAM	0.495	0.492	0.494

Table 3: Sentence-level correlations with human judgments for **parsing-based** metrics, with different choices of parser and similarity metric.

mantically related one, or to mitigate the effects of certain parser errors. Thus, we also experiment with computing the S^2match similarity of parsed sentences to the original AMRs.[5]

5.3 Results

The primary statistic of interest for this study is the sentence-level correlation between a proposed metric and human judgments, particularly those for adequacy. We measure this with Spearman's Rho correlation. Following Manning et al. (2020), we compare several popular reference-based metrics; table 2 reports the correlations for the 5 metrics they used: BLEU (Papineni et al., 2002), METEOR (Banerjee and Lavie, 2005), TER (Snover et al., 2006), ChrF++ (Popović, 2017), and BERTScore (Zhang et al., 2020). We add the results of one newer metric, BLEURT (Sellam et al., 2020). Of these, BLEURT performs the best by this measure with a correlation of 0.69. BLEU, the most popular metric for this task, has a correlation of 0.52.

Table 3 shows the correlation with adequacy for each variant of the parser-based metric, combining the three AMR parsers and three similarity metrics used. Notably, even the highest correlations here underperform those achieved by BLEU, METEOR, BERTScore, and BLEURT.

As expected, the correlation increases with parser quality, indicating that parsers that have higher accuracy on human-authored sentences also do better with generated sentences.

For each parser, there is very little difference between the different similarity metrics. The similarity between $Smatch_4$ and $Smatch_{100}$+seed is expected, since these are separated only by minor implementation differences. The lack of substantial improvement when using S^2match is probably because it is rare for the generated sentences to contain concepts that are different but semantically similar to those in the gold AMR.

Since none of the similarity metrics are clearly stronger than the others based on correlations, we choose $Smatch_{100}$+seed as the best for more conceptual reasons: it is more reproducible, and unlike S^2match, does not rely on embeddings. The use of additional resources seems unjustified in this case if it does not improve performance, especially given concerns that using embeddings in an evaluation metric makes it less transparent and more arbitrary (results can vary depending on specific choice of language model) than a simpler method.

Thus, for the following experiments, we use the CAI-LAM parser combined with $Smatch_{100}$+seed.

6 Experiment 2: Manually-Edited Parses

Even a state-of-the-art AMR parser is of course not perfect, and may struggle more with parsing automatically-generated sentences than the human-authored ones it is designed for. The potential for parser error is a major limitation of the proposed approach; evaluating the parse p against gold AMR a can only be a good measure of g's relationship to a if p is a sufficiently accurate parse of g. Thus, to get a better sense of the effect that parsing errors can have on this metric even when using a SOTA parser, and of a rough upper bound for how well the metric could work in the future as parsing improves, we also manually edited a sample of the parses p to create alternate parses, p', which better reflect the meaning expressed in the generated sentences g, and use Smatch to compare p' to a.

6.1 Methods

Since the CAI-LAM parser is the strongest automatic parser, we used its parses as a starting point. For a given generated sentence g or reference sentence r, we compared the sentence to the automatic parse $p(g)$ or $p(r)$, and edited the parse to represent, as accurately as possible, the meaning expressed in the sentence. This sometimes included referring to the gold AMR a to ensure consistency between our annotations and the canonical representation of the same meanings. All edits were performed by the first author.

[5]We calculate S^2match using https://github.com/Heidelberg-NLP/amr-metric-suite.

System	Edited Parses
Guo	65
Konstas	83
Manning	25
Ribeiro	70
Zhu	73
Reference	90
Total	406

Table 4: Number of sentences (out of 100) from each generation system that were not marked as incomprehensible by either annotator, and whose AMRs were manually edited.

However, this approach is limited by an assumption that the generated sentences *have* meanings in the same way that human-authored sentences do. In fact, many of the generated sentences in this dataset do not clearly and unambiguously express a particular meaning. Since it is essentially impossible to 'accurately' parse an incoherent sentence, we only edited the parses of sentences which were not marked as incomprehensible by either annotator in the human evaluation. Table 4 shows how many sentences from each system fit this criterion. Overall, we edited parses for 406 sentences, or 67.7% of the total sample of 600 sentences used in the human evaluation. Excluding references, we edited parses for 316 of the 500 automatically-generated sentences, or 63.2%. For the remaining sentences, we use the unedited automatic parse.

Even after filtering out those marked incomprehensible, we encountered many sentences that we found unclear or highly ambiguous; perhaps there were so many unclear sentences in the data that annotators reserved the annotation only for the most egregious cases. We did our best to interpret these sentences as well as we could, erring on the side of preserving the automatic parse's interpretation when it seemed as reasonable as an alternative. Nevertheless, this required some subjective judgment calls. An example of a difficult-to-annotate case is shown in table 5. The generated sentence, "ukraine and ukraine in kenya stated –", would probably never be produced by a human author, and it is difficult to assign a precise meaning to it. In this case, we decided to preserve the automatic parser's interpretation that it describes a statement being made by two entities: the country Ukraine, and a separate location, also known as Ukraine, that is in Kenya.

<table>
<tr><td>r</td><td>Ukrainian diplomat in Kenya oleh belokolos stated –</td></tr>
<tr><td>g</td><td>ukraine and ukraine in kenya stated –</td></tr>
<tr><td>p</td><td><pre>(c0 / state-01
    :ARG0 (c1 / and
        :op1 (c2 / ukraine)
        :op2 (c3 / ukraine
            :location (c4 / country
                :name (c5 / name
                    :op1 "Kenya")
                :wiki "Kenya"))))</pre></td></tr>
<tr><td>p'</td><td><pre>(c0 / state-01
    :ARG0 (c1 / and
        :op1 (c2 / country
            :wiki "Ukraine"
            :name (n2 / name
                :op1 "Ukraine"))
        :op2 (c3 / location
            :name (n3 / name
                :op1 "Ukraine")
            :location (c4 / country
                :name (c5 / name
                    :op1 "Kenya")
                :wiki "Kenya"))))</pre></td></tr>
</table>

Table 5: An example of a generated sentence with unclear meaning.

	Full Sample	INC0
Automatic Parses	0.49	0.35
Edited Parses	**0.66**	**0.46**

Table 6: Sentence-level Spearman's correlation of Smatch with human adequacy scores, when using edited parses vs. automatic ones. INC0 indicates the subset of AMRs that were edited.

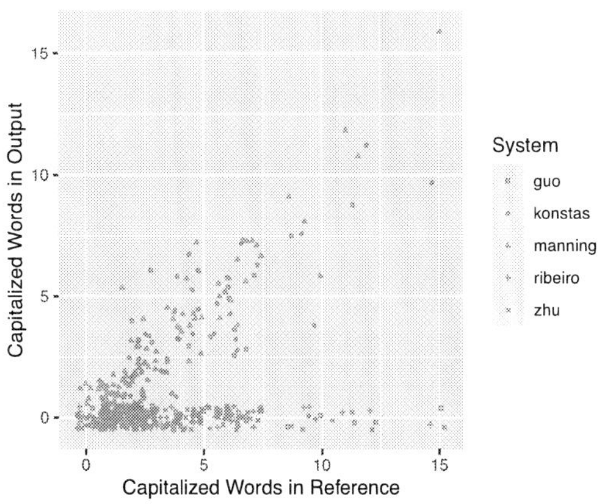

Figure 2: Scatterplot of number of capitalized words in the output compared to the reference for each system (jitter=0.5).

6.2 Results

As table 6 shows, the correlation of Smatch with adequacy improves substantially when using the edited parses, as opposed to the purely automatic ones. With edits, the correlation over all data increases to 0.66, better than most of the automatic metrics—the only exception is BLEURT, with a correlation of 0.69 (see table 2). It seemed possible that this improvement occurred simply because the edited sample of sentences, which generally received stronger human scores, largely had their Smatch scores improved by the editing process. Thus we also include the correlations on only the edited sample (INC0); the fact that the correlation improves within this sample demonstrates that editing does help distinguish better and worse sentences.

Table 7 shows an example where editing helped substantially. The generated sentence fully expresses the information in the gold AMR, and received fluency and adequacy scores of 100—in fact, it differs from the reference only in capitalization—but the automatic parse differs greatly from the gold AMR, resulting in a low Smatch score of 0.222. Parser errors in this case include a failure to recognize the two named entities in the sentence, as well as misidentifying the root concept as `be-located-at-91` rather than `organization`. While the edited parse doesn't perfectly match the gold AMR, it corrects these major errors, resulting in a much higher Smatch score of 0.875.

<table>
<tr><td>r</td><td>The Institute for Science and International Security is a private research organization located in Washington.</td></tr>
<tr><td>g</td><td>the institute for science and international security is a private research organization located in washington .</td></tr>
<tr><td>a</td><td><pre>(o / organization
    :mod (r / research-01)
    :ARG1-of (p / private-03)
    :domain (o2 / organization
        :wiki "Institute_for_Science_and_
            International_Security"
        :name (n / name
        :op1 "Institute" :op2 "for"
        :op3 "Science" :op4 "and"
        :op5 "International"
        :op6 "Security"))
    :ARG1-of (l / locate-01
        :location (c / city
            :wiki "Washington,_D.C."
            :name (n2 / name
                :op1 "Washington"))))</pre></td></tr>
<tr><td>p</td><td><pre>(c0 / be-located-at-91
    :ARG1 (c1 / institute
        :mod (c3 / organization
            :ARG1-of (c6 / private-03)
            :mod (c5 / research-01))
        :topic (c4 / and
            :op1 (c7 / science)
            :op2 (c8 / security
                :mod (c9 / international))))
    :ARG2 (c2 / washington))</pre></td></tr>
<tr><td>p'</td><td><pre>(c0 / organization
    :domain (c4 / organization
        :name (c6 / name
            :op1 "Institute" :op2 "for"
            :op3 "Science" :op4 "and"
            :op5 "International"
            :op6 "Security")
        :wiki "Institute_for_Science_and_
        International_Security")
    :location (c3 / city
        :name (c5 / name
            :op1 "Washington")
        :wiki "Washington,_D.C.")
    :mod (c1 / private-03)
    :mod (c2 / research-01))</pre></td></tr>
</table>

Table 7: An example where parser error led to a low Smatch score on a high-adequacy sentence, which is improved substantially in the edited parse.

r	A US-endorsed package of incentives to cease enriched uranium production
g	the us endorsed package of incentives to cease enriched uranium production .

a	<pre>(p / package
	    :consist-of (t / thing
	        :ARG0-of (i / incentivize-01
	            :ARG2 (c2 / cease-01
	                :ARG1 (p2 / produce-01
	                    :ARG1 (u / uranium
	                      :ARG1-of
	                      (e2 / enrich-01))))))
	    :ARG1-of (e / endorse-01
	        :ARG0 (c / country
	            :wiki "United_States"
	            :name (n / name :op1 "US"))))</pre>

p	<pre>(c0 / endorse-01
	    :ARG0 (c2 / we)
	    :ARG1 (c1 / package-01
	        :ARG1 (c3 / incentivize-01
	            :ARG2 (c4 / cease-01
	                :ARG1 (c5 / produce-01
	                    :ARG1 (c6 / uranium)
	                    :ARG1-of
	                    (c7 / enrich-01))))))</pre>

p'	<pre>(c0 / endorse-01
	    :ARG0 (c2 / country
	        :name (c5 / name :op1 "US")
	        :wiki "United_States")
	    :ARG1 (c1 / package-01
	        :ARG1 (c3 / incentivize-01
	            :ARG2 (c4 / cease-01
	                :ARG1 (p1 / produce-01
	                   :ARG1 (c6 / uranium
	                     :ARG1-of
	                     (c7 / enrich-01)))))))</pre>

Table 8: An example of a parser error due to lack of capitalization in the generated sentence. 'US', written as 'us' by the system, is treated as a form of the pronoun 'we' by the parser.

System	Unedited ρ	Edited ρ	Improvement
Konstas	0.53	0.59	0.05
Manning	0.44	0.57	0.12
Guo	0.44	0.59	0.14
Ribeiro	0.53	0.72	0.19
Zhu	0.35	0.59	0.24
Overall	0.49	0.66	0.17

Table 9: Spearman's correlation of adequacy scores with Smatch scores based on unedited and edited parses. The two systems that produce capitalization are shown above the line; the three below output only lowercase.

7 Analysis

A common parser error was failure to recognize named entities when they were not capitalized; examples of this are given in tables 7 and 8. As figure 2 shows, three of the systems never produce capitals in their output, while those of Konstas and Manning typically produce about as many capitals as are present in the reference. Thus, it seems likely that the systems that never produce capitals may be unfairly penalized by a parsing-based metric.

Table 9 shows that when separating the data by system, there is no clear difference in the degree to which Smatch correlates with adequacy for systems that capitalize compared to those that do not. However, the *difference* between $Smatch(a, p')$ and $Smatch(a, p)$ is greater for the systems that do not produce capitals; that is, manual editing had a greater effect on the reliability of the parser-based metric on the systems which do not produce capitals than those that do.

It may be possible to overcome this particular limitation of the automatic parser by adding a preprocessing step that recognizes and capitalizes named entities, or by training the parser on more all-lowercase examples.

8 Conclusion

In this paper, we have explored the idea of evaluating AMR generation via AMR parsing and similarity metrics, using the human judgments of adequacy collected by Manning et al. (2020) to test the validity of possible variants of the parsing-based metric approach and compare them to existing reference-based metrics. We found that parser quality is a major factor affecting the performance of this evaluation approach: the better the AMR parser, the better the evaluation; however, even a state-of-the-art parser with an accuracy of 80+% on standard human-authored data has significant limitations for evaluating generated sentences, including a failure to recognize named entities in the absence of capitalization. We showed that when automatic AMR parses are manually edited to better reflect the meaning in generated sentences, this referenceless metric outperforms most popular automatic reference-based metrics, including BLEU and BERTScore (but not BLEURT).

While the current reliance on manual editing for more reliable results may not be practical for evaluation, the results of this experiment indicate that fully-automatic parser-based metrics are likely to prove more reliable in the future as the state of the art in AMR parsing continues to improve, especially if newer AMR generation systems also more closely replicate human-authored data, such as by producing more human-like capitalization than the majority of systems tested here did.

References

Laura Banarescu, Claire Bonial, Shu Cai, Madalina Georgescu, Kira Griffitt, Ulf Hermjakob, Kevin Knight, Philipp Koehn, Martha Palmer, and Nathan Schneider. 2013. Abstract Meaning Representation for sembanking. In *Proceedings of the 7th Linguistic Annotation Workshop and Interoperability with Discourse*, pages 178–186, Sofia, Bulgaria. Association for Computational Linguistics.

Satanjeev Banerjee and Alon Lavie. 2005. METEOR: An automatic metric for MT evaluation with improved correlation with human judgments. In *Proceedings of the ACL Workshop on Intrinsic and Extrinsic Evaluation Measures for Machine Translation and/or Summarization*, pages 65–72, Ann Arbor, Michigan. Association for Computational Linguistics.

Deng Cai and Wai Lam. 2020. AMR parsing via graph-sequence iterative inference. In *Proceedings of the 58th Annual Meeting of the Association for Computational Linguistics*, pages 1290–1301, Online. Association for Computational Linguistics.

Shu Cai and Kevin Knight. 2013. Smatch: an evaluation metric for semantic feature structures. In *Proceedings of the 51st Annual Meeting of the Association for Computational Linguistics (Volume 2: Short Papers)*, pages 748–752, Sofia, Bulgaria. Association for Computational Linguistics.

Jeffrey Flanigan, Chris Dyer, Noah A. Smith, and Jaime Carbonell. 2016. CMU at SemEval-2016 task 8: Graph-based AMR parsing with infinite ramp loss. In *Proceedings of the 10th International Workshop on Semantic Evaluation (SemEval-2016)*, pages 1202–1206, San Diego, California. Association for Computational Linguistics.

Jeffrey Flanigan, Sam Thomson, Jaime Carbonell, Chris Dyer, and Noah A. Smith. 2014. A discriminative graph-based parser for the Abstract Meaning Representation. In *Proceedings of the 52nd Annual Meeting of the Association for Computational Linguistics (Volume 1: Long Papers)*, pages 1426–1436, Baltimore, Maryland. Association for Computational Linguistics.

Chunchuan Lyu and Ivan Titov. 2018. AMR parsing as graph prediction with latent alignment. In *Proceedings of the 56th Annual Meeting of the Association for Computational Linguistics (Volume 1: Long Papers)*, pages 397–407, Melbourne, Australia. Association for Computational Linguistics.

Emma Manning, Shira Wein, and Nathan Schneider. 2020. A human evaluation of AMR-to-English generation systems. In *Proceedings of the 28th International Conference on Computational Linguistics*, pages 4773–4786, Barcelona, Spain (Online). International Committee on Computational Linguistics.

Juri Opitz and Anette Frank. 2021. Towards a decomposable metric for explainable evaluation of text generation from AMR. In *Proceedings of the 16th Conference of the European Chapter of the Association for Computational Linguistics: Main Volume*, pages 1504–1518, Online. Association for Computational Linguistics.

Juri Opitz, Letitia Parcalabescu, and Anette Frank. 2020. AMR similarity metrics from principles. *Transactions of the Association for Computational Linguistics*, 8:522–538.

Kishore Papineni, Salim Roukos, Todd Ward, and Wei-Jing Zhu. 2002. Bleu: a method for automatic evaluation of machine translation. In *Proceedings of the 40th Annual Meeting of the Association for Computational Linguistics*, pages 311–318, Philadelphia, Pennsylvania, USA. Association for Computational Linguistics.

Maja Popović. 2017. chrF++: words helping character n-grams. In *Proceedings of the Second Conference on Machine Translation*, pages 612–618, Copenhagen, Denmark. Association for Computational Linguistics.

Thibault Sellam, Dipanjan Das, and Ankur Parikh. 2020. BLEURT: Learning robust metrics for text generation. In *Proceedings of the 58th Annual Meeting of the Association for Computational Linguistics*, pages 7881–7892, Online. Association for Computational Linguistics.

Matthew Snover, Bonnie Dorr, Richard Schwartz, Linnea Micciulla, and John Makhoul. 2006. A Study of Translation Edit Rate with Targeted Human Annotation. In *Proceedings of the 7th Conference of the Association for Machine Translation in the Americas*, pages 223–231, Cambridge.

Linfeng Song and Daniel Gildea. 2019. SemBleu: A robust metric for AMR parsing evaluation. In *Proceedings of the 57th Annual Meeting of the Association for Computational Linguistics*, pages 4547–4552, Florence, Italy. Association for Computational Linguistics.

Tianyi Zhang, Varsha Kishore, Felix Wu, Kilian Q. Weinberger, and Yoav Artzi. 2020. BERTScore: Evaluating Text Generation with BERT. In *ICLR*.

MIPE: A Metric Independent Pipeline for Effective Code-Mixed NLG Evaluation

Ayush Garg*, **Sammed S Kagi***
IIT Gandhinagar, India
{ayush.g,sammed.shantinath}@alumni.iitgn.ac.in

Vivek Srivastava
TCS Research, India
srivastava.vivek2@tcs.com

Mayank Singh
IIT Gandhinagar, India
singh.mayank@iitgn.ac.in

Abstract

Code-mixing is a phenomenon of mixing words and phrases from two or more languages in a single utterance of speech and text. Due to the high linguistic diversity, code-mixing presents several challenges in evaluating standard natural language generation (NLG) tasks. Various widely popular metrics perform poorly with the code-mixed NLG tasks. To address this challenge, we present a metric independent evaluation pipeline *MIPE* that significantly improves the correlation between evaluation metrics and human judgments on the generated code-mixed text. As a use case, we demonstrate the performance of *MIPE* on the machine-generated Hinglish (code-mixing of Hindi and English languages) sentences from the *HinGE* corpus. We can extend the proposed evaluation strategy to other code-mixed language pairs, NLG tasks, and evaluation metrics with minimal to no effort.

1 Introduction

Code-mixing (hereafter '*CM*') is a commonly observed communication pattern for a multilingual speaker to mix words and phrases from multiple languages. CM is widespread across various language pairs across the globe, such as Spanish-English (Spanglish) and Hindi-English (Hinglish). Various studies (Baldauf, 2004) have predicted the high growth in the number of CM speakers, which would surpass the number of native speakers in various globally popular languages (e.g., English).

With the advent of social-media platforms (e.g., Twitter, Facebook, etc.), we observe a manifold increase in the CM communication by multilingual speakers. This leads to a large scale availability of CM data for various NLP tasks. Recently, we witness magnitude of work to address various CM NLP tasks such as language identification (Shekhar et al., 2020; Singh et al., 2018a; Ramanarayanan et al., 2019; Barman et al., 2014; Gundapu and Mamidi, 2018), POS tagging (Singh et al., 2018b; Vyas et al., 2014; Pratapa et al., 2018), named entity recognition (Singh et al., 2018a; Priyadharshini et al., 2020; Winata et al., 2019), word normalisation (Singh et al., 2018c; Parikh and Solorio, 2021), CM metrics (Guzmán et al., 2017; Srivastava and Singh, 2021a), sentiment analysis (Patwa et al., 2020; Joshi et al., 2016), stance detection (Utsav et al., 2020; Sane et al., 2019), natural language inference (Khanuja et al., 2020), machine translation (Srivastava and Singh, 2020; Dhar et al., 2018), and question-answering (Chandu et al., 2019; Thara et al., 2020).

We observe a growing interest in the computational linguistic community to study the CM NLG tasks. Recently, various resources and systems have been proposed that explore different dimensions of the CM NLG (Yang et al., 2020; Gautam et al., 2021; Gupta et al., 2021; Rizvi et al., 2021; Gupta et al., 2020; Jawahar et al., 2021). Evaluation of the CM NLG tasks is challenging due to the high linguistic diversity and lack of standardization. To address this challenge, Srivastava and Singh (2021b) has proposed *HinGE* corpus for the Hinglish CM text generation and evaluation (see Section 2 for details). *HinGE* corpus demonstrates the inefficacy of various widely popular metrics on the CM dataset.

In this paper, we choose five evaluation metrics (see Section 3 for details) as discussed in (Srivastava and Singh, 2021b) to demonstrate the efficacy of *MIPE*. Our proposed metric independent pipeline (*MIPE*) augments these metrics and addresses four major linguistic bottlenecks: (i) spelling variations, (ii) language switching, (iii) missing words, and (iv) the limited number of reference sentences associated with the CM NLG systems. The main contributions are:

- We identify four major reasons for the poor

* equal contribution

Proceedings of the 58th Annual Meeting of the Association for Computational Linguistics, pages 123–132

https://doi.org/10.26615/978-954-452-056-4_013

quality performance of various widely popular evaluation metrics for the code-mixed NLG evaluation.

- We propose a metric independent evaluation pipeline *MIPE* that addresses the identified bottlenecks in CM NLG evaluation. Furthermore, we show its efficacy in generating highly correlated metric scores against human scores.

The rest of the paper is organized as follows. In Section 2, we discuss the dataset for the CM NLG evaluation task. In Section 3, we present the *MIPE* pipeline addressing the four major bottlenecks for effective CM NLG evaluation. We discuss the results in Section 4. In Section 5, we discuss the current state and future direction. We conclude the discussion in Section 6.

ENGLISH: is another human being saying, "Do you understand this?"
HINDI: कोई दूसरा मनुष्य ये कहे, "क्या आपको समझ आया?"
HUMAN-GENERATED 1: is another human being saying, "kya aapko samaj aaya?"
HUMAN-GENERATED 2: koi dusra human being yeh kahe, "Do you understand this?"

WAC GENERATED: koee doosra human ye kahe, kya aapko samajh aaya
RATING 1: 9
RATING 2: 8

PAC GENERATED: koee doosra manushy ye kahe, kya aapko samajh understand
RATING 1: 7
RATING 2: 8

Figure 1: Example of the CM sentences generated by the annotator along with WAC and PAC generated CM sentence from the parallel English-Hindi sentence pair. Two human annotators rate the machine-generated sentence on a scale of 1–10.

2 Dataset

Recently, we observe various works to address the underlying challenges with the CM NLG. Numerous resources and systems have been proposed recently to advance the field. In our experiments, we use the *HinGE* corpus proposed in (Srivastava and Singh, 2021b). The *HinGE* corpus contains 1,976 English-Hindi parallel sentences from the IIT-B parallel corpus (Kunchukuttan et al., 2018). Corresponding to each of the English-Hindi parallel sentences, *HinGE* has two variants of CM Hinglish sentences:

- Human-generated Hinglish sentences: (Srivastava and Singh, 2021b) have employed eight human annotators to generate the Hinglish sentences. Each parallel sentence pair is annotated by a single human annotator. Human annotators have generated at least two Hinglish sentences corresponding to each parallel sentence pair. On average, 2.5 Hinglish sentences are generated for each parallel sentence pair.

- Machine-generated Hinglish sentences: Srivastava and Singh (2021b) proposes two rule-based algorithms to generate the CM sentences. They leverage the matrix-frame theory to generate the Hinglish sentences where Hindi is the matrix language and English tokens are embedded. The proposed algorithms differ significantly at the level of granularity (i.e., word and phrase). We will use the acronyms WAC (word-aligned code-mixing) and PAC (phrase-aligned code-mixing) for the two algorithm variants in the rest of the paper.

In addition to the machine-generated Hinglish sentences, *HinGE* has a human rating corresponding to each generated sentence. The human rating varies between 1–10, indicating low to high generation quality. Two human annotators have rated each of the machine-generated CM sentences. Figure 1 shows the example CM sentences generated by humans and two rule-based algorithms along with the rating to the machine-generated CM sentences. Figure 2 shows the distribution of the human ratings to the machine-generated Hinglish sentences. WAC-generated sentences receive a relatively high rating ($>$ 6) as compared to PAC. In addition, WAC showed a low degree of human disagreements than PAC.

Efficacy of NLG Evaluation Metrics: Srivastava and Singh (2021b) present a study demonstrating the inefficacy of five widely popular NLG evaluation metric on the *HinGE* corpus. The five metrics are: (i) Bilingual Evaluation Understudy Score (**BLEU**, Papineni et al. (2002)), (ii) **NIST** (Doddington, 2002), (iii) BERTScore (**BS**, Zhang et al. (2019)), (iv) Word Error Rate (**WER**, Levenshtein (1966)), and (v) Translator Error Rate (**TER**, Snover et al. (2006)). Higher BLEU, NIST, or BS values and lower WER or

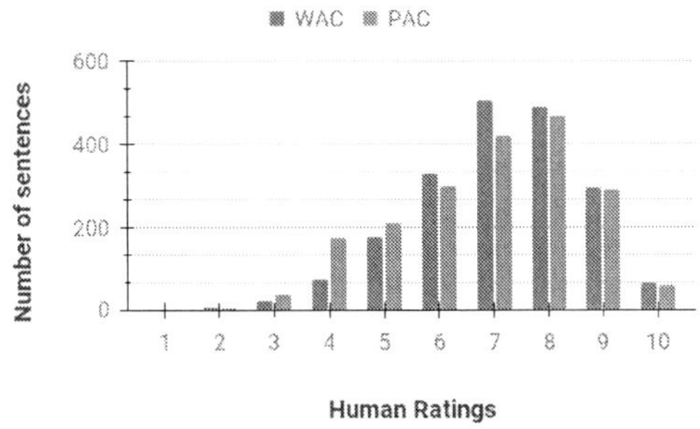

Figure 2: Distribution of human ratings on the generated Hinglish sentences using WAC and PAC. The figure is taken from Srivastava and Singh (2021b).

TER values represent better generation performance. Tables 1 and 2 show the comparison of five metric scores against the human ratings against WAC and PAC (see scores present in columns with heading *'Without MIPE'*). In addition, (Srivastava and Singh, 2021b) present a correlation study between the human ratings and the metric scores. For this purpose they divide the ratings into three buckets:

- Bucket 1: Human rating between 2–10.
- Bucket 2: Human rating between 2–5.
- Bucket 3: Human rating between 6–10.

Table 4 shows the correlation between the human ratings and the metric scores for WAC and PAC (see scores present in columns with heading *'Without MIPE'*). The correlation scores show a scope to build systems that shows a high correlation with human judgment.

3 MIPE

As discussed in the previous section, the widely used evaluation metrics fail to capture the linguistic diversity of the CM data. Based on the empirical observation on the 10 datasets used in (Srivastava and Singh, 2021a), we identify four major reasons for the failure of NLG evaluation metrics on the CM data. We propose a metric independent evaluation pipeline *MIPE*, for effective evaluation. Using *MIPE*, we first reduce the spelling variations (see Section 3.1) and the language switching (see Section 3.2) in the candidate Hinglish sentence. Next, we introduce a penalty (see Section 3.3) on the evaluation score based on the degree of importance of the missing words in the candidate Hinglish sentence. Finally, we address the challenge of a limited number of reference sentences (see Section 3.4) by segmenting the candidate and the reference sentences into phrases and leveraging the paraphrasing capability. Figure 3 shows the architecture of the proposed evaluation pipeline.

3.1 Spelling variations

The first challenge to effective evaluation is the non-standard spellings of the code-mixed words. E.g., words *kanekt*, *connect*, and *connekt* conveys the same meaning in a Hinglish sentence. Due to a lack of writing standards for the code-mixed languages, the speakers often use their phonetic understanding of the source languages to write the CM sentences. Hence, in most spelling variations, the addition, omission, and substitution of letters indicate that the phonetics remains almost the same. Specifically, we observe three major reasons for spelling variations,

- $R1$: character repetition
- $R2$: replacement with similar-sounding character
- $R3$: vowel omission

To address these problems, we normalize words such that similar-sounding words are grouped. We leverage the concept of Phonetic Dissimilarity (PDS, Toutanova and Moore (2002)) to address the spelling variations in the CM language. Our proposed PDS algorithm is a variant of the popular dynamic programming-based edit distance algorithm. Similar to edit distance, PDS quantifies the dissimilarity between two strings by counting the minimum number of edit operations (addition, deletion, and substitution) required to transform one string into the other. In PDS, we assign different costs to each edit operation based on the phonetic characteristics of the corresponding characters of the two words and the edit operation under consideration. To access the phonetic characteristics, we use a corpus of all possible pronunciations of the English alphabets[1]. Algorithm 1describes PDS between a word w_1 (in candidate CM sentence) and w_2 (in reference CM sentences). To address $R1$, we remove repeating characters from both words. By default, we keep addition and

[1]https://www.speakmethod.com/alphabet_sounds.html

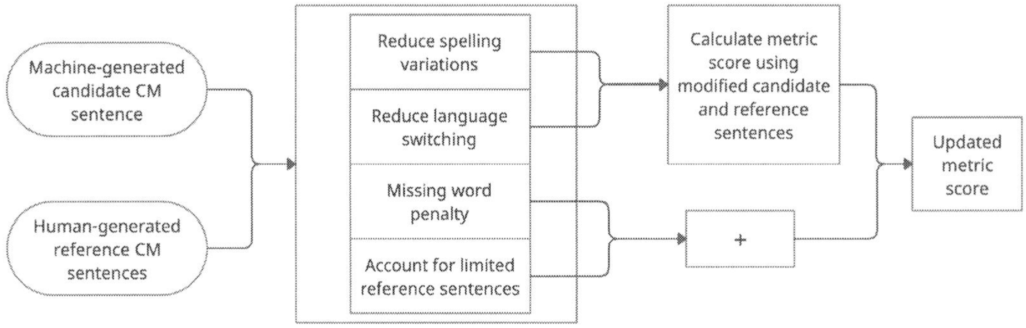

Figure 3: The architecture of the proposed CM NLG evaluation system *MIPE*. Machine-generated candidate CM sentences are generated by two rule-based algorithms (WAC and PAC). We reduce the spelling variation and language switching for both the candidate and reference sentences based on phonetics. A penalty is applied to the words in the candidate sentence which are not present in any of the reference sentences. We account for limited reference sentences by chunking the candidate and reference sentences into trigram phrases. The words in the candidate trigram phrases are assigned a score based on their presence in the reference phrases. The candidate phrase score is used to account for the limited reference sentences. Metric score is calculated based on the modified reference and candidate sentences. A missing word penalty and a penalty for limited reference sentences is added (or subtracted) from the modified metric score. It should be noted that the penalty is subtracted from the modified metric score if the lower metric score shows better performance (e.g., WER and TER.).

deletion cost = 1 and substitution cost = 2. To address $R2$, we decrease the substitution cost to ρ_{sub} for similar-sounding characters as substitution of one of these characters is highly likely. To address $R3$, we decrease the addition cost of vowels to ρ_{add} and the deletion cost of vowels to ρ_{del}, where $\rho_{add} > \rho_{del}$. This is due to the empirical observation that the omission of vowels is much more likely than an addition. Further, we decrease the addition and deletion costs of a possible silent character to ρ_{sil}. We consider the minimum of PDS($w1$, $w2$) and PDS($w2$, $w1$) as the final PDS score to identify the spelling variation between words $w1$ and $w2$. In our experiments, we keep $\rho_{sub} = \rho_{add} = \rho_{sil} = 0.75$, and $\rho_{del} = 0.25$.

3.2 Similar Words

Identifying similar words in the same or different languages is a challenging task in the CM languages. For example, two phrases *"in the market"* and *"in the bazaar"* convey the same semantics, but most automatic evaluation metrics will fail to identify the semantic similarity. To address the challenge of token-level similarity, we need a common representation of words across the source languages. To mitigate this problem, we propose a Similar Word Search (SWS) procedure. Algorithm 2 shows the description of the SWS procedure. Given a word from the candidate CM sentence as an input, the SWS procedure returns all similar words from the corresponding reference sentences. We select that word from the reference sentences, which yields the minimum PDS value. The SWS procedure returns a word from the reference set if the minimum PDS value is less than σ_{thres}. Otherwise, it computes pairwise cosine distance (in the cross-lingual word embedding space) between each word in a set of reference words and the input word. To create the cross-lingual embedding space, we use the pre-trained word vectors of dimension 300 for English and Hindi from fastText (Bojanowski et al., 2017). For the shared representation, we use VecMap (Artetxe et al., 2018) to learn the mapping in an unsupervised fashion with the default settings. We use the English and Hindi sentences from the IIT-B parallel corpus (Kunchukuttan et al., 2018). In case the cosine similarity is greater than σ_{cos}, the SWS procedure returns the word from the reference set; else, we assume that no similar word exists in the reference set. In our experiments, we keep $\sigma_{thres} = 2$, and $\sigma_{cos} = 0.5$.

3.3 Missing words

Generally, the generated candidate sentence misses some words resulting in a significant impact on the automatic evaluation scores. Some words are more important than others, but most

Algorithm 2: Similar Word Search

Def SWS(*references, word, distance*=σ_{thres}):
- $R=\{r_1, r_2, ..., r_m\}$ be the set of sentences in *references*. Covert each r_i to lowercase and remove all special characters.
- Make a set W of words for each r_i in R.
- PDS_{min}←*distance*, $cand \leftarrow None$
- **for** *each word* w_i *in* W **do**
  - **if** $PDS(w_i, word) <= PDS_{min}$ **then**
    - $PDS_{min} \leftarrow PDS(w_i, word)$
    - *cand* ← w_i
- **if** *cand != None* **then**
  - **return** cand
- **else**
  - word_emb ← CLWE(word) , $max_{sim} \leftarrow \sigma_{cos}$
  - **for** *each word* w_i *in* W **do**
    - sim ← cos_sim(word_emb, CLWE(w_i))
    - **if** *sim* >= max_{sim} **then**
      - $max_{sim} \leftarrow sim, cand \leftarrow w_i$
  - **if** *candidate != None* **then**
    - **return** cand
  - **else**
    - **return** word

metrics consider them equal ($M1$). Furthermore, most metrics match exact words with no flexibility in spelling variations and language switching ($M2$). Here, we address both these problems to apply a missing word penalty to the metric score with some writing style flexibility. To address $M1$, we use WAC procedure[2] to generate a large Hinglish corpus (hereafter *'ParallelCorp'*) of 2,132,184 sentences. For creating the parallel corpus, we collect English sentences from multiple sources[3,4,5,6] and translate them (if not already translated) into Hindi language using Google Translate API. We calculate IDF-values (Inverse Document Frequency) of each word in the Hinglish corpus. The words with low IDF values occur rarely and hence carry more semantic information. If a word is not present in the *ParallelCorp*, we consider it semantically important. To address $M2$, we relax the exact match condition by postulating that either the word is present in the candidate sentence or its variant is present in the sentence. Here, we allow two types of variations (i) minor spelling variations and (ii) language switch (for more details, see Sections 3.1 and 3.2). We use the SWS procedure to find a word variant keeping a maximum distance value of 1. Algorithm 3 shows the description of the missing word penalty (MWP) in detail. For each word w in a reference sentence, we check the presence of w and its variants in the candidate sentence. In case w is not present, we add w's IDF value as the penalty for the absence. We repeat the procedure for each reference sentence and take the minimum penalty among all reference sentences. We reduce the MWP score from the metric score for a given evaluation metric.

Algorithm 3: Missing Words Penalty

Def MWPenalty(*references, sentence*):
- Set min_penalty ← 1
- **for** *each* r_i *in references* **do**
  - Set penalty ← 0
  - Set total_imp ← 0
  - Create a set W of words in r_i
  - **for** *each word* w_i *in* W **do**
    - total_imp += IDF(w_i)
    - **if** w_i *not in sentence and SWS([sentence],* w_i*, 1) ==* w_i **then**
      - penalty += IDF(w_i)
  - penalty /= total_imp
  - **if** *penalty < min_penalty* **then**
    - min_penalty ← penalty
- **return** min_penalty

3.4 Limited Reference Sentences

A sentence can be paraphrased in numerous ways by interchanging subject and predicate, active and passive voice, and first, second, and third-person perspectives. With the code-mixed text, the paraphrasing possibilities significantly increase. For an automatic evaluation, it is infeasible to generate all possible paraphrases as reference sentences. Even though *HinGE* dataset has at least two reference sentences against a candidate sentence but it is insufficient to include all the possibilities. Thus, paraphrasing drastically limits the evaluation capabilities of various metrics. To address this problem, we present an algorithm *PhraseScore*. Algorithm 4 shows the description of the *PhraseScore* method. We split the candidate sentence and the set of reference sentences into trigram phrases. If word *w* in the candidate phrase exists in one of

[2]We employ WAC due to its capability to generate high-quality sentences (as shown in (Srivastava and Singh, 2021b)). Also, the Hinglish sentence generated by WAC has words from only the source English and Hindi sentences which in turn doesn't influence the IDF values of the generated words to a large extent.

[3]https://www.kaggle.com/kazanova/sentiment140

[4]https://www.kaggle.com/arkhoshghalb/twitter-sentiment-analysis-hatred-speech

[5]http://www.cfilt.iitb.ac.in/iitb_parallel/

[6]https://bit.ly/2XQjrU6

Algorithm 1: Phonetic Dissimilarity

```
Def PDS(w1, w2):
  • Remove consecutive duplicate characters
    from both the words w1 and w2
  • Set dp[len(w1)+1][len(w2)+1] = {0}
  • for i ← 0 to len(w1) do
    • for j ← 0 to len(w2) do
      • if i == 0 then
        • dp[i][j] ← j
        • continue
      • if j == 0 then
        • dp[i][j] ← i
        • continue
      • if w1[i-1] == w2[j-1] then
        • dp[i][j] ← dp[i-1][j-1]
      • else
        • sub ← 2, add ← 1, del ← 1
        • if w1[i-1] and w2[j-1] are
          similar sounding then
          • sub ← ρsub
        • if w1[i-1] can be silent then
          • delete ← ρsil
        • if w1[i-1] is a vowel then
          • delete ← ρdel
        • if w2[j-1] can be silent or a
          vowel then
          • add ← ρadd
        • dp[i][j] ← min(dp[i][j-1]+add,
          dp[i-1][j]+del, dp[i-1][j-1]+sub)
  • Return dp[len(w1)][len(w2)]
```

the reference phrases, we add the IDF value of the w in the phrase score for that phrase. Else, we subtract the IDF value as a penalty. This phrase score is aggregated, normalized over the number of phrases in the candidate sentence, and divided by the penalty of missing words in the candidate sentence. To prevent division by zero, we add 0.0001 to the penalty. In case a word is not present in the IDF dictionary, we assign it a relatively high value (μ_{miss}) to indicate that it is a rare word of high importance. Finally, we increase the metric score by adding the candidate sentence's *PhraseScore*. In our experiments, we keep μ_{miss}=20. Due to the unavailability of a paraphrasing system for a code-mixed language, the formulation of *PhraseScore* algorithm depends on the assumption that the trigram phrases in a sentence can be reordered to create new sentences.

4 Results and Evaluation

We evaluate WAC and PAC procedures augmented with *MIPE* pipeline against all the five metrics (as discussed in Section 2). Table 1 and 2 shows the effect of *MIPE* against the five metrics. As expected, all metrics show better scores with the *MIPE* augmentation. The metric scores after the *MIPE* shows a high correlation[7] against the metric scores without *MIPE* (see Table 3). This shows that improvements in the metric scores is constant throughout and are not by chance.

Algorithm 4: Limited Reference Sentences

```
Def PhraseScore(references, candidate,
penalty, idf):
  • Let R={r1, r2, ..., rm} be the set of
    sentences in references. Tokenize the
    candidate and the references and convert it
    into a list of phrases of 3 tokens. Let the
    lists be sent_phrase and ref_phrase
    respectively.
  • Set sent_score ← 0
  • for each s_phrase in sent_phrase do
    • score ← 0
    • for each r_phrase in ref_phrase do
      • t_score ← 0
      • for each word wi in s_phrase do
        • if wi in r_phrase then
          • if wi in idf.keys() then
            • t_score += idf[wi]
          • else
            • t_score += μmiss
        • else
          • if wi in idf.keys() then
            • t_score -= idf[wi]
          • else
            • t_score -= μmiss
      • score = max(score, t_score)
    • sent_score += score
  • sent_score = sent_score / (len(sent_phrase)
    * (penalty + 0.0001))
  • return sent_score
```

Table 4 shows the effect of *MIPE* on the correlation with the human scores. We use the same criteria to bucket the human ratings as discussed in Section 2. We observe a higher correlation in all the three buckets for WAC augmented with *MIPE*. This improvement is consistent throughout all the metrics. For PAC augmented with *MIPE*, we observe a decrease in correlation in the second bucket, which can be attributed to (i) a relatively large number of poor quality (low human scores) sentences generated by PAC, and (ii) rating poor quality CM sentence is a challenging task for humans due to lower readability of the sentence. For the rest of the buckets, PAC with *MIPE* shows a higher correlation with the human scores.

5 Current State and Future Directions

The results discussed in Section 4 demonstrate a need to build metrics, theories, and experiments for better CM NLG evaluation. Some of the

[7] We experiment with Pearson Correlation Coefficient.

Human score	Without *MIPE*					With *MIPE*				
	BLEU	WER	TER	NIST	BS	BLEU	WER	TER	NIST	BS
2	0.144	0.741	0.667	0.092	0.851	0.238	0.651	0.544	0.140	0.860
3	0.138	0.735	0.708	0.070	0.852	0.323	0.625	0.569	0.133	0.860
4	0.133	0.695	0.666	0.103	0.849	0.391	0.536	0.480	0.184	0.906
5	0.135	0.711	0.681	0.110	0.853	0.380	0.556	0.494	0.172	0.985
6	0.141	0.697	0.670	0.102	0.852	0.361	0.560	0.502	0.144	0.967
7	0.161	0.663	0.630	0.111	0.856	0.398	0.522	0.453	0.168	0.947
8	0.177	0.621	0.589	0.127	0.859	0.465	0.445	0.377	0.204	0.976
9	0.212	0.571	0.538	0.150	0.865	0.531	0.387	0.313	0.242	1.000
10	0.291	0.509	0.493	0.157	0.878	0.572	0.318	0.252	0.291	1.000

Table 1: Comparison of metric scores with and without using *MIPE* for WAC.

Human score	Without *MIPE*					With *MIPE*				
	BLEU	WER	TER	NIST	BS	BLEU	WER	TER	NIST	BS
2	0.126	0.672	0.698	0.176	0.8603	0.338	0.474	0.500	0.318	0.997
3	0.146	0.765	0.696	0.086	0.851	0.425	0.603	0.526	0.120	0.883
4	0.143	0.744	0.703	0.100	0.8464	0.419	0.598	0.523	0.130	0.888
5	0.153	0.726	0.680	0.114	0.8515	0.407	0.589	0.508	0.154	0.894
6	0.164	0.689	0.646	0.124	0.8558	0.449	0.525	0.456	0.171	0.912
7	0.176	0.661	0.618	0.121	0.8581	0.475	0.485	0.411	0.198	0.936
8	0.177	0.639	0.605	0.128	0.8598	0.498	0.437	0.370	0.200	0.938
9	0.184	0.614	0.590	0.129	0.8638	0.545	0.387	0.321	0.230	0.967
10	0.242	0.551	0.543	0.146	0.8731	0.600	0.314	0.262	0.280	0.997

Table 2: Comparison of metric scores with and without using *MIPE* for PAC.

	BLEU	WER	TER	NIST	BS
WAC	0.948	0.988	0.984	0.961	0.8326
PAC	0.830	0.986	0.982	0.944	0.8843

Table 3: Correlation between the evaluation metric scores with and without using *MIPE* pipeline.

	Correlation with human scores (Without MIPE)						Correlation with human scores (With MIPE)					
	Bucket 1		Bucket 2		Bucket 3		Bucket 1		Bucket 2		Bucket 3	
	WAC	PAC	WAC	PAC	WAC	PAC	WAC	PAC	WAC	PAC	WAC	PAC
BLEU	0.810	0.910	-0.861	**0.878**	0.941	0.844	**0.942**	**0.950**	**0.910**	0.643	**0.994**	**0.981**
WER	-0.936	**-0.822**	-0.785	**0.457**	-0.993	-0.973	**-0.949**	-0.780	**-0.880**	0.713	**-0.995**	**-0.993**
TER	-0.891	**-0.963**	0.000	**-0.610**	-0.998	-0.970	**-0.932**	-0.937	**-0.737**	0.229	**-0.998**	**-0.997**
NIST	**0.913**	0.127	0.642	**-0.559**	0.986	0.846	0.851	**0.246**	**0.769**	-0.671	**0.993**	**0.952**
BS	0.844	**0.710**	0.227	**-0.689**	**0.953**	0.937	**0.924**	0.400	**0.922**	-0.720	0.895	**0.972**

Table 4: Comparison of correlation between evaluation metrics and human scores for WAC and PAC with and without *MIPE* pipeline. The bold numbers indicate a better correlation in the respective bucket. A high positive correlation is preferred for BLEU and NIST whereas a negative correlation is preferred for WER and TER.

challenges and limitations of the proposed *MIPE* pipeline for effective CM NLG includes:

- Due to the unavailability of resources in other CM language pairs, the *MIPE* pipeline is tested on a single CM language. We need to extend the proposed evaluation strategy to other CM language pairs.
- The presence of two different languages in a single CM sentence increases the paraphrasing possibility to a much larger extent. We need metrics that attend to the CM sentences beyond the bag of words model. These metrics should also be able to account for paraphrasing.
- There are various other reasons (beyond the four reasons discussed in this paper) that influence the evaluation of CM NLG tasks such as named-entities, transliteration, etc. The *MIPE* pipeline doesn't currently account for these limitations.

- The code-mixed sentences in the *HinGE* dataset are not collected from the social media platforms. The code-mixed data from the social media platform tends to be more noisy and distorted which could influence the performance of *MIPE* pipeline.

As discussed, currently there are several limitations with the CM NLG evaluation which need to be addressed in order to build effective CM NLG systems for multilingual societies. Some of the lessons learned and the future directions for the CM NLG evaluations are:

- The limited resource availability is one of the major bottlenecks in the CM NLG tasks and evaluation. Currently, the available resources are smaller in size compared to the monolingual NLG tasks.
- In contrast to the *MIPE* augmentation pipeline, we need systems that can leverage the noisy nature of the code-mixed text. The currently proposed *MIPE* pipeline addresses the various challenges independently and attempts to reconstruct the noisy CM text for effective evaluation.
- The two languages participating in CM influence the various constructs of the target CM sentence such as grammar, syntax, etc. The current experimentation with only one CM language needs to be explored with other CM languages.
- Recently, we observe a rise in the availability of multilingual language models (LMs). These LMs could be used to build effective CM NLG evaluation systems.
- The current evaluation metrics seem to perform poorly with the CM languages. We need to build dedicated metrics for the CM NLG evaluation tasks that can leverage the linguistic diversity of the CM data.

6 Conclusion

In this paper, we present a metric independent evaluation pipeline for efficient code-mixed NLG evaluation. The proposed pipeline shows a high correlation between the human scores and the underlying evaluation metrics. Besides the four significant challenges to CM NLG evaluation, in the future, we also plan to address other challenges such as code-mixed existence of named-entities, informal writing style, and missing context.

References

Mikel Artetxe, Gorka Labaka, and Eneko Agirre. 2018. A robust self-learning method for fully unsupervised cross-lingual mappings of word embeddings. In *Proceedings of the 56th Annual Meeting of the Association for Computational Linguistics (Volume 1: Long Papers)*, pages 789–798.

Scott Baldauf. 2004. A hindi-english jumble, spoken by 350 million. [Online; accessed 23-May-2020].

Utsab Barman, Amitava Das, Joachim Wagner, and Jennifer Foster. 2014. Code mixing: A challenge for language identification in the language of social media. In *Proceedings of the first workshop on computational approaches to code switching*, pages 13–23.

Piotr Bojanowski, Edouard Grave, Armand Joulin, and Tomas Mikolov. 2017. Enriching word vectors with subword information. *Transactions of the Association for Computational Linguistics*, 5:135–146.

Khyathi Chandu, Ekaterina Loginova, Vishal Gupta, Josef van Genabith, Günter Neumann, Manoj Chinnakotla, Eric Nyberg, and Alan W Black. 2019. Code-mixed question answering challenge: Crowd-sourcing data and techniques. In *Third Workshop on Computational Approaches to Linguistic Code-Switching*, pages 29–38. Association for Computational Linguistics (ACL).

Mrinal Dhar, Vaibhav Kumar, and Manish Shrivastava. 2018. Enabling code-mixed translation: Parallel corpus creation and mt augmentation approach. In *Proceedings of the First Workshop on Linguistic Resources for Natural Language Processing*, pages 131–140.

George Doddington. 2002. Automatic evaluation of machine translation quality using n-gram co-occurrence statistics. In *Proceedings of the second international conference on Human Language Technology Research*, pages 138–145.

Devansh Gautam, Prashant Kodali, Kshitij Gupta, Anmol Goel, Manish Shrivastava, and Ponnurangam Kumaraguru. 2021. Comet: Towards code-mixed translation using parallel monolingual sentences. In *Proceedings of the Fifth Workshop on Computational Approaches to Linguistic Code-Switching*, pages 47–55.

Sunil Gundapu and Radhika Mamidi. 2018. Word level language identification in english telugu code mixed data. In *Proceedings of the 32nd Pacific Asia Conference on Language, Information and Computation*.

Abhirut Gupta, Aditya Vavre, and Sunita Sarawagi. 2021. Training data augmentation for code-mixed translation. In *Proceedings of the 2021 Conference of the North American Chapter of the Association for Computational Linguistics: Human Language Technologies*, pages 5760–5766.

Deepak Gupta, Asif Ekbal, and Pushpak Bhattacharyya. 2020. A semi-supervised approach to generate the code-mixed text using pre-trained encoder and transfer learning. In *Proceedings of the 2020 Conference on Empirical Methods in Natural Language Processing: Findings*, pages 2267–2280.

Gualberto A Guzmán, Joseph Ricard, Jacqueline Serigos, Barbara E Bullock, and Almeida Jacqueline Toribio. 2017. Metrics for modeling code-switching across corpora. In *INTERSPEECH*, pages 67–71.

Ganesh Jawahar, Muhammad Abdul-Mageed, VS Laks Lakshmanan, et al. 2021. Exploring text-to-text transformers for english to hinglish machine translation with synthetic code-mixing. In *Proceedings of the Fifth Workshop on Computational Approaches to Linguistic Code-Switching*, pages 36–46.

Aditya Joshi, Ameya Prabhu, Manish Shrivastava, and Vasudeva Varma. 2016. Towards sub-word level compositions for sentiment analysis of hindi-english code mixed text. In *Proceedings of COLING 2016, the 26th International Conference on Computational Linguistics: Technical Papers*, pages 2482–2491.

Simran Khanuja, Sandipan Dandapat, Sunayana Sitaram, and Monojit Choudhury. 2020. A new dataset for natural language inference from code-mixed conversations. In *Proceedings of the The 4th Workshop on Computational Approaches to Code Switching*, pages 9–16.

Anoop Kunchukuttan, Pratik Mehta, and Pushpak Bhattacharyya. 2018. The iit bombay english-hindi parallel corpus. In *Proceedings of the Eleventh International Conference on Language Resources and Evaluation (LREC 2018)*.

Vladimir I Levenshtein. 1966. Binary codes capable of correcting deletions, insertions, and reversals. In *Soviet physics doklady*, volume 10, pages 707–710.

Kishore Papineni, Salim Roukos, Todd Ward, and Wei-Jing Zhu. 2002. Bleu: a method for automatic evaluation of machine translation. In *Proceedings of the 40th annual meeting on association for computational linguistics*, pages 311–318. Association for Computational Linguistics.

Dwija Parikh and Thamar Solorio. 2021. Normalization and back-transliteration for code-switched data. In *Proceedings of the Fifth Workshop on Computational Approaches to Linguistic Code-Switching*, pages 119–124.

Parth Patwa, Gustavo Aguilar, Sudipta Kar, Suraj Pandey, PYKL Srinivas, Björn Gambäck, Tanmoy Chakraborty, Thamar Solorio, and Amitava Das. 2020. Semeval-2020 task 9: Overview of sentiment analysis of code-mixed tweets. In *Proceedings of the Fourteenth Workshop on Semantic Evaluation*, pages 774–790.

Adithya Pratapa, Monojit Choudhury, and Sunayana Sitaram. 2018. Word embeddings for code-mixed language processing. In *Proceedings of the 2018 conference on empirical methods in natural language processing*, pages 3067–3072.

Ruba Priyadharshini, Bharathi Raja Chakravarthi, Mani Vegupatti, and John P McCrae. 2020. Named entity recognition for code-mixed indian corpus using meta embedding. In *2020 6th International Conference on Advanced Computing and Communication Systems (ICACCS)*, pages 68–72. IEEE.

Vikram Ramanarayanan, Robert Pugh, Yao Qian, and David Suendermann-Oeft. 2019. Automatic turn-level language identification for code-switched spanish–english dialog. In *9th International Workshop on Spoken Dialogue System Technology*, pages 51–61. Springer.

Mohd Sanad Zaki Rizvi, Anirudh Srinivasan, Tanuja Ganu, Monojit Choudhury, and Sunayana Sitaram. 2021. Gcm: A toolkit for generating synthetic code-mixed text. In *Proceedings of the 16th Conference of the European Chapter of the Association for Computational Linguistics: System Demonstrations*, pages 205–211.

Sushmitha Reddy Sane, Suraj Tripathi, Koushik Reddy Sane, and Radhika Mamidi. 2019. Stance detection in code-mixed hindi-english social media data using multi-task learning. In *Proceedings of the Tenth Workshop on Computational Approaches to Subjectivity, Sentiment and Social Media Analysis*, pages 1–5.

Shashi Shekhar, Dilip Kumar Sharma, and MM Sufyan Beg. 2020. Language identification framework in code-mixed social media text based on quantum lstm—the word belongs to which language? *Modern Physics Letters B*, 34(06):2050086.

Kushagra Singh, Indira Sen, and Ponnurangam Kumaraguru. 2018a. Language identification and named entity recognition in hinglish code mixed tweets. In *Proceedings of ACL 2018, Student Research Workshop*, pages 52–58.

Kushagra Singh, Indira Sen, and Ponnurangam Kumaraguru. 2018b. A twitter corpus for hindi-english code mixed pos tagging. In *Proceedings of the Sixth International Workshop on Natural Language Processing for Social Media*, pages 12–17.

Rajat Singh, Nurendra Choudhary, and Manish Shrivastava. 2018c. Automatic normalization of word variations in code-mixed social media text. *arXiv preprint arXiv:1804.00804*.

Matthew Snover, Bonnie Dorr, Richard Schwartz, Linnea Micciulla, and John Makhoul. 2006. A study of translation edit rate with targeted human annotation. In *Proceedings of association for machine translation in the Americas*, volume 200. Cambridge, MA.

Vivek Srivastava and Mayank Singh. 2020. Phinc: a parallel hinglish social media code-mixed corpus for machine translation. *arXiv preprint arXiv:2004.09447*.

Vivek Srivastava and Mayank Singh. 2021a. Challenges and limitations with the metrics measuring the complexity of code-mixed text. In *Proceedings of the Fifth Workshop on Computational Approaches to Linguistic Code-Switching*, pages 6–14.

Vivek Srivastava and Mayank Singh. 2021b. Hinge: A dataset for generation and evaluation of code-mixed hinglish text. *arXiv preprint arXiv:2107.03760*.

S Thara, E Sampath, Phanindra Reddy, et al. 2020. Code mixed question answering challenge using deep learning methods. In *2020 5th International Conference on Communication and Electronics Systems (ICCES)*, pages 1331–1337. IEEE.

Kristina Toutanova and Robert C Moore. 2002. Pronunciation modeling for improved spelling correction. In *Proceedings of the 40th Annual Meeting on Association for Computational Linguistics*, pages 144–151.

Jethva Utsav, Dhaiwat Kabaria, Ribhu Vajpeyi, Mohit Mina, and Vivek Srivastava. 2020. Stance detection in hindi-english code-mixed data. In *Proceedings of the 7th ACM IKDD CoDS and 25th COMAD*, CoDS COMAD 2020, page 359–360, New York, NY, USA. Association for Computing Machinery.

Yogarshi Vyas, Spandana Gella, Jatin Sharma, Kalika Bali, and Monojit Choudhury. 2014. Pos tagging of english-hindi code-mixed social media content. In *Proceedings of the 2014 Conference on Empirical Methods in Natural Language Processing (EMNLP)*, pages 974–979.

Genta Indra Winata, Zhaojiang Lin, and Pascale Fung. 2019. Learning multilingual meta-embeddings for code-switching named entity recognition. In *Proceedings of the 4th Workshop on Representation Learning for NLP (RepL4NLP-2019)*, pages 181–186.

Zhen Yang, Bojie Hu, Ambyera Han, Shen Huang, and Qi Ju. 2020. Csp: Code-switching pre-training for neural machine translation. In *Proceedings of the 2020 Conference on Empirical Methods in Natural Language Processing (EMNLP)*, pages 2624–2636.

Tianyi Zhang, Varsha Kishore, Felix Wu, Kilian Q Weinberger, and Yoav Artzi. 2019. Bertscore: Evaluating text generation with bert. *arXiv preprint arXiv:1904.09675*.

IST-Unbabel 2021 Submission for the Explainable Quality Estimation Shared Task

Marcos V. Treviso[1,2], **Nuno M. Guerreiro**[1,2], **Ricardo Rei**[2,3,4], **André F. T. Martins**[1,2,3]
[1]Instituto de Telecomunicações, Lisbon, Portugal
[2]Instituto Superior Técnico, Lisbon, Portugal
[3]Unbabel, Lisbon, Portugal
[4]INESC-ID, Lisbon, Portugal

Abstract

We present the joint contribution of Instituto Superior Técnico (IST) and Unbabel to the Explainable Quality Estimation (QE) shared task, where systems were submitted to two tracks: constrained (without word-level supervision) and unconstrained (with word-level supervision). For the constrained track, we experimented with several explainability methods to extract the relevance of input tokens from sentence-level QE models built on top of multilingual pre-trained transformers. Among the different tested methods, composing explanations in the form of attention weights scaled by the norm of value vectors yielded the best results. When word-level labels are used during training, our best results were obtained by using word-level predicted probabilities. We further improve the performance of our methods on the two tracks by ensembling explanation scores extracted from models trained with different pre-trained transformers, achieving strong results for in-domain and zero-shot language pairs.

1 Introduction

Quality estimation (QE) aims at assessing the quality of a translation system without relying on reference translations (Blatz et al., 2004; Specia et al., 2018). This paper describes the joint contribution of Instituto Superior Técnico (IST) and Unbabel to the Explainable Quality Estimation shared task (Fomicheva et al., 2021a). The goal of the shared task is to identify translation errors without direct word-level supervision (constrained track) or with access to word-level labels (unconstrained track).

Recent advances in QE have led to consistent improvements at predicting quality assessments such as *Direct Assessments* (DAs, Graham et al. 2013). Traditional QE systems had to predict *Human Translation Error Rate* (HTER, Snover et al. 2006), yet with the advent of neural machine translation, we observed a shift from fluency into adequacy errors (Martindale and Carpuat, 2018). For that reason, DAs started getting used as the ground-truth score for assessing the quality of translations (Specia et al., 2020). However, with DAs we lose the ability to generate word-level supervision, impacting the interpretability of sentence-level predictions in terms of lower granularity elements such as word-level translation errors.

At the same time, state-of-the-art QE systems such as OpenKiwi (Kepler et al., 2019b) and TransQuest (Ranasinghe et al., 2020b) build on top of multilingual pre-trained models such as BERT (Devlin et al., 2019) and XLM-RoBERTa (Conneau et al., 2020), which are largely responsible for the performance boost we have observed in the last two editions of the WMT QE shared task (Fonseca et al., 2019; Specia et al., 2020). Due to the usage of such overparametrized black-box models, this performance boost also comes at the cost of efficiency and interpretability.

Research in explainable NLP uncovered several strategies to interpret models' decisions, either in a post-hoc manner by querying a trained model for extracting perturbation or gradient measures (Ribeiro et al., 2016; Arras et al., 2016), or by building models that are inherently interpretable (Lei et al., 2016; Chang et al., 2020). Recent works have also put transformers under the lens of explainability, aiming at unraveling interpretable patterns that clarify how decisions emerge from attention heads and across hidden states at each layer (De Cao et al., 2020; Abnar and Zuidema, 2020; Voita et al., 2021).

In this shared task, we experiment with several of these methods to extract the relevance of input tokens from sentence-level QE models built on top of multilingual pre-trained transformers[1]. For the constrained track, where models are unaware of word-level supervision, our best results were de-

[1]Our code can be found at: `https://github.com/deep-spin/explainable_qe_shared_task/`.

Proceedings of the 58th Annual Meeting of the Association for Computational Linguistics, pages 133–145

https://doi.org/10.26615/978-954-452-056-4_014

rived from attention-based explanations. When we used word-level labels during training, the best results were obtained by using word-level predicted probabilities. Furthermore, we were able to push the performance further by ensembling explanations for both tracks.

2 Background

Quality Estimation. QE systems are usually designed according to the granularity in which predictions are made: word, sentence, or document-level. The goal of word-level QE is to assign quality labels (OK or BAD) to each *machine-translated word*, indicating whether that word is a translation error or not. Additionally, current systems also classify *source words* to denote words in the original sentence that have been mistranslated or omitted in the target. On the other hand, sentence-level QE aims at predicting the quality of the whole translated sentence, either in terms of how many edit operations are required to fix it (HTER) or in terms of human judgments (DA). Similarly, document-level QE systems predict a single outcome (a real score or a ranking index) for an entire document.

Transformers. The multi-head attention mechanism is the bedrock on which transformers are built. They are responsible for contextualizing the information within and across input sentences dynamically (Vaswani et al., 2017). Concretely, given as input a matrix $\boldsymbol{Q} \in \mathbb{R}^{n \times d}$ containing d-dimensional representations for n queries, and matrices $\boldsymbol{K}, \boldsymbol{V} \in \mathbb{R}^{m \times d}$ for m keys and values, the *scaled dot-product attention* at a single head is computed as:

$$\text{att}(\boldsymbol{Q}, \boldsymbol{K}, \boldsymbol{V}) = \pi \underbrace{\left(\frac{\boldsymbol{Q}\boldsymbol{K}^\top}{\sqrt{d}} \right)}_{\boldsymbol{Z} \in \mathbb{R}^{n \times m}} \boldsymbol{V} \in \mathbb{R}^{n \times d}. \quad (1)$$

The π transformation maps rows to distributions, with softmax being the most common choice, $\pi(\boldsymbol{Z})_{ij} = \text{softmax}(\boldsymbol{z}_i)_j$. Multi-head attention is computed by evoking Eq. 1 in parallel for each head h:

$$\text{head}_h(\boldsymbol{Q}, \boldsymbol{K}, \boldsymbol{V}) = \text{att}(\boldsymbol{Q}\boldsymbol{W}_h^Q, \boldsymbol{K}\boldsymbol{W}_h^K, \boldsymbol{V}\boldsymbol{W}_h^V),$$

where $\boldsymbol{W}_h^Q$, $\boldsymbol{W}_h^K$, $\boldsymbol{W}_h^V$ are learned linear transformations. The output of the multi-head attention module is the concatenation of all k heads followed by a learnable linear transformation $\boldsymbol{W}^O$:

$$\text{mh-att}(\boldsymbol{Q}, \boldsymbol{K}, \boldsymbol{V}) = \text{concat}(\text{head}_1, ..., \text{head}_k)\boldsymbol{W}^O.$$

This way, heads have the capability of learning specialized phenomena. Transformers with only encoder-blocks, such as BERT (Devlin et al., 2019) and XLM-RoBERTa (Conneau et al., 2020), have only the encoder self-attention, and thus $m = n$.

Explainability in NLP. There is a large body of work on the analysis and interpretation of models in NLP. Some of these models are built on top of attention mechanisms, which automatically learn a weighted representation of input features. Attention weights provide plausible, but not always faithful, explanations (Jain and Wallace, 2019; Wiegreffe and Pinter, 2019). In contrast, rationalizers with hard attention are arguably more faithful but require stochastic networks (Lei et al., 2016; Bastings et al., 2019), with recent works avoiding stochasticity via sparse deterministic selections (Guerreiro and Martins, 2021). Other approaches seek local explanations by considering gradient measures (Arras et al., 2016; Bastings and Filippova, 2020), or by perturbing the input and querying the classifier in a post-hoc manner (Ribeiro et al., 2016; Kim et al., 2020). Since transformers are composed of several layers and attention heads, many works analyze and improve the multi-head attention mechanism directly to produce better explanations (Kobayashi et al., 2020; Hao et al., 2021). More elaborated methods consider the entire flow of information coming from attention weights, hidden states, or gradients to interpret the model's decision (De Cao et al., 2020; Abnar and Zuidema, 2020; Voita et al., 2021).

3 Constrained Track

The goal of the constrained track is to identify machine translation errors without explicit word-level annotation. More precisely, it aims at performing word-level quality estimation by casting the task as a prediction explainability problem. In the context of QE, explanations can be seen as highlights, representing the relevance of input words w.r.t. the model's prediction via continuous scores. We next describe the datasets, models, and explainability methods that we used for this track.

3.1 Datasets

Seeking to improve the performance of our models on the zero-shot language pairs (LPs), we used all language pairs from the MLQE-PE dataset (Fomicheva et al., 2020) to train our models

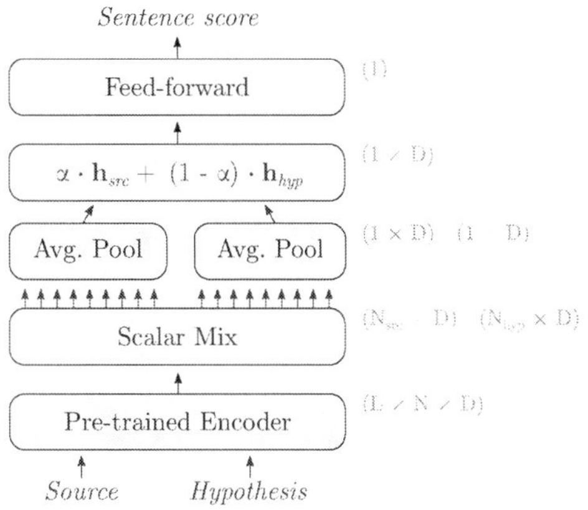

Figure 1: General architecture of our models for the constrained track. L represents the number of layers. N_{src} and N_{hyp} represent the number of words in the source and hypothesis sentences, respectively. $N = N_{\text{src}} + N_{\text{hyp}}$ is the number of words after concatenating the two sentences. D is the size of hidden vectors.

for both tracks. For RO-EN and ET-EN, we evaluated our models on the validation set of these LPs. For the two zero-shot LPs, DE-ZH and RU-DE, we used the 20 sentences made available by the shared task and the validation sets of EN-ZH and EN-DE to improve the robustness of the evaluation of explanations w.r.t. the target language. We used word-level labels to train word-level models for the unconstrained track only. For sentence-level models, we supervise our models using DA scores.

3.2 Sentence-level Models

Since QE is a fundamental tool in many MT pipelines, we focus our efforts on designing and explaining QE systems with high sentence-level performance. Therefore, we opted to follow the recent trend in this area (Kepler et al., 2019b; Ranasinghe et al., 2020a) and employed two pre-trained multilingual language models as the feature extractors for our models: XLM-RoBERTa and RemBERT.

The overall architecture of our models is shown in Figure 1. The tokenized source $\boldsymbol{s} = \langle s_1, ..., s_N \rangle$ and hypothesis $\boldsymbol{t} = \langle t_1, ..., t_M \rangle$ sentences are concatenated and passed as input to the encoder, which produces hidden state vectors $\boldsymbol{H}_0, ..., \boldsymbol{H}_L$ for each layer $0 \leq \ell \leq L$, where $\boldsymbol{H}_i \in \mathbb{R}^{(N+M)\times d}$. Next, all hidden states are fed to a scalar mix module (Peters et al., 2018) that learns a weighted sum of the hidden states of each layer of the encoder, producing a new sequence of aggregated hidden states $\boldsymbol{H}_{L+1}$. We split $\boldsymbol{H}_{L+1}$ into source $\boldsymbol{H}_{src} \in \mathbb{R}^{N\times d}$ and hypothesis hidden states $\boldsymbol{H}_{hyp} \in \mathbb{R}^{M\times d}$, which are independently passed to an average pooling layer to get their sentence representations $\boldsymbol{h}_{src}$ and $\boldsymbol{h}_{hyp}$. We merge both representations via a convex combination with $\alpha = 0.5$ to encourage the model to use both source and hypothesis contexts. Finally, we pass the combined vector to a 2-layered feed-forward module in order to get a sentence score prediction $\hat{y} \in \mathbb{R}$. Moreover, attention matrices $\boldsymbol{A}_1, ..., \boldsymbol{A}_L$ are also recovered as a by-product of the forward propagation, where $\boldsymbol{A}_i \in \mathbb{R}^{(N+M)\times(N+M)}$. The hyperparameters used for training can be found in §B.

XLM-RoBERTa as encoder. We set a XLM-RoBERTa Large (XLM-R, Conneau et al. 2020) as the encoder layer.[2] XLM-R is a cross-lingual transformer pre-trained on massive amounts of multilingual data. It consists of 24 encoder blocks with 16 attention heads each. Following (Zerva et al., 2021) we train our complete model on DAs by using adapters for the XLM-R encoder (Houlsby et al., 2019; Pfeiffer et al., 2020) to adapt it to the domain specific data of the QE task with minimal training effort.

XLM-RoBERTa for zero-shot LPs. To improve the robustness of XLM-R on out-of-domain data, we used an XLM-RoBERTa Large model that was trained with DA's from the metrics shared task.[3] Next, we set it as the encoder layer, and adapted it for predicting DAs from the MLQE corpus as in (Zerva et al., 2021). Altogether, the data from the Metrics shared task encompasses 30 language pairs from the news domain—yet, the zero-shot LPs are not included in this set. The hyperparameters and the training regime of this model are the same as the previously described XLM-R. We denote this model as XLM-R-M from here on.

RemBERT as encoder. We replace the XLM-R by a RemBERT model as the encoder layer (Chung et al., 2021).[4] Multilingual BERT (Devlin et al., 2019) has been shown to provide complementary performance to XLM-based models for sentence-level and word-level QE (Kepler et al., 2019a). We opted to use RemBERT since it can be seen as a larger multilingual BERT with decoupled input and output embeddings, which helps to accelerate

[2] https://huggingface.co/xlm-roberta-large

[3] https://huggingface.co/Unbabel/xlm-roberta-wmt-metrics-da

[4] https://huggingface.co/google/rembert

ENCODER	RO-EN	ET-EN	DE-ZH	RU-DE
OpenKiwi	0.820	0.757	0.395	0.176
XLM-R	0.878	0.756	0.521	**0.563**
XLM-R-M	0.877	**0.780**	**0.797**	0.352
RemBERT	**0.883**	0.762	-0.002	0.505

Table 1: Pearson correlation of our sentence-level QE systems by varying the model used as the encoder layer.

training. It consists of 32 encoder blocks with 18 attention heads each. Rather than aggregating layers with the scalar mix layer, we perform average pooling over the hidden states of the last layer of RemBERT. For training, we simply finetune the whole model with small learning rates.

Results. Table 1 summarizes the performance of our sentence-level models on the validation set in terms of Pearson correlation for each language pair evaluated in the shared task. For completeness, we show results for the 20 sentences made available by the shared task for DE-ZH and RU-DE. We also include OpenKiwi with a XLM-R Large as the encoder for comparison. We note that results for DE-ZH and RU-DE are noisy due to the small amount of validation data available for these LPs.

3.3 Explainability Methods

Several explainability methods can be used to extract highlights from a trained model in a post-hoc fashion. It is also possible to design a model that is explainable by construction, such as rationalizers (Lei et al., 2016; Bastings et al., 2019). We investigate rationalizers, attention, gradient, and perturbation-based methods for this shared task.

Attention-based methods. Since the backbone of our models consists of pre-trained multilingual transformers, we studied their main component—the multi-head attention mechanism—expecting to find interpretability patterns that assign higher scores to words associated with translation errors. We extracted the following explanations from the multi-head attention mechanism:

- **Attention weights:** average the attention matrix $\mathbf{A}$ row-wise for all heads in all layers, amounting to a total of $24 \times 16 = 384$ and $32 \times 18 = 576$ explanation vectors $\boldsymbol{a} \in \mathbb{R}^{N+M}$ for XLM-R and RemBERT-based models, respectively.
- **Cross-attention weights:** by manual inspection of attention weights, we noticed that some attention heads learn plausible connections from source-to-hypothesis and hypothesis-to-source. Therefore, instead of computing a row-wise average of the entire attention matrix, we average only cross-alignment rows.[5]
- **Attention $\times$ Norm:** following the findings of Kobayashi et al. (2020), we scale attention weights by the norm of value vectors $\|\boldsymbol{V}\boldsymbol{W}_h^V\|_2$.

Gradient-based methods. Explanations extracted by storing gradients computed during the backward propagation is a standard tool used to interpret NLP models. For this shared task, we investigate the following gradient-based methods:[6]

- **Gradient $\times$ Hidden States:** we compute gradients w.r.t. the hidden states of each layer, and multiply the resultant vectors by the hidden state vectors themselves: $\nabla_{\boldsymbol{H}_i} \times \boldsymbol{H}_i \in \mathbb{R}^{N+M}$, for $0 \leq i \leq L+1$.
- **Gradient $\times$ Attention:** the same as before, but we use the output of the multi-head attention module instead of the hidden states.
- **Integrated Gradients**: we extract integrated gradient explanations w.r.t. the hidden states of each layer. We use a zero-vector as the baseline. We map gradients to explainability scores by normalizing them by their L2 norm and summing the hidden dimensions: $\mathbf{1}^\top \nabla_{\boldsymbol{H}_i} / \|\nabla_{\boldsymbol{H}_i}\|_2$.

Perturbation-based methods. As baselines, we also extracted explanations using **LIME** (Ribeiro et al., 2016) and a **leave-one-out** strategy, where we replace the "erased" token by the `<mask>` token, which is used for the masked-language model training of XLM-R and RemBERT.

Rationalizers. We append a differentiable binary mask layer (Bastings et al., 2019) on top of the XLM-R model in order to select which tokens are passed on for an estimator for the prediction of a sentence-level score. For each instance, we take the model representations from the scalar-mix layer and pass it to an encoder module, in which we sample a binary mask $\boldsymbol{z} \in [0, 1]^{N+M}$ from a relaxed Bernoulli distribution (Maddison et al., 2017; Jang et al., 2017), and pass $\boldsymbol{z} \odot [\boldsymbol{s}; \boldsymbol{t}]$ to an estimator module, which re-embeds the masked input and

[5]Note that we can get cross-attentions from XLM-R and RemBERT by selecting only the words of the source that attend to the hypothesis and vice-versa.

[6]Our implementation is based on Captum: `https://captum.ai/`

ENCODER	RO-EN Source	RO-EN Target	ET-EN Source	ET-EN Target
OpenKiwi	0.581	0.620	0.488	0.554
XLM-R	0.610	0.644	**0.503**	**0.559**
XLM-R-M	**0.636**	**0.667**	0.464	0.530
RemBERT	0.624	0.659	0.474	0.555
ENCODER	DE-ZH Source	DE-ZH Target	RU-DE Source	RU-DE Target
OpenKiwi	**0.271**	0.184	0.243	0.029
XLM-R	0.230	0.312	0.273	0.061
XLM-R-M	0.262	**0.336**	**0.343**	0.179
RemBERT	0.173	0.211	0.247	**0.201**

Table 2: Source and target MCC results of our word-level QE systems by varying the model used as the encoder layer. The values of λ for each model are: $10^3, 10^4, 10^4, 10^4$.

pass it to a linear output layer. Therefore, good explanations z will aid the estimator in producing good sentence-level scores. In training time, the parameters of the encoder and the estimator are jointly trained. In test time, we do not sample the binary masks. Instead, we use the relaxed Bernoulli distribution probabilities as explanations.

4 Unconstrained Track

In this track, we opted to use word-level annotation by incorporating a word-level loss to our previous models. To do this, we apply a map from word pieces to tokens after the scalar mix layer and pass the hidden vectors of each token through a feed-forward layer with a sigmoid activation to predict scores $\hat{y}_i \in [0, 1]$. We weight the word-level loss by λ and sum it with the sentence-level loss. As baseline, we train a XLM-R Large model using OpenKiwi with the default hyperparameters. For all word-level models, we train with $\lambda \in \{10^3, 10^4, 10^5\}$ and save the checkpoint with the best performance on the validation set.

Results. Table 2 shows the results of our word-level models on the validation set in terms of Matthews correlation coefficient (MCC) for each LP evaluated in the shared task. For completeness, we include the results for the 20 available sentences for DE-ZH and RU-DE.

5 Experimental Results

Although we can regard the extracted explanations as errors in the translation output, an analogous evaluation of word-level QE is not straightforward since the standard metrics require binary labels rather than continuous scores. Therefore, the explanations are evaluated against the ground-truth word-level labels in terms of the Area Under the Curve (AUC), Average Precision (AP), and Recall at Top-K (R@K) metrics only on the subset of translations that contain errors.

Furthermore, since all of our models use subword tokenization, to get explanations for an entire word, we tried aggregating the scores of its word pieces by taking the sum, mean, or max, and we found that taking the sum performs better overall.

5.1 Constrained Track

Attention heads are better alone. We found that some attention heads (mostly at upper layers) learned to focus on words associated with BAD tags, achieving great performance in terms of AUC and AP on the validation set. We show in Figure 2 the target AUC of different attention heads per layer as a heatmap for RO-EN, with darker colors indicating higher results.[7] We can see that attention heads in layers 18 and 19 perform better than other layers in general, and that some attention heads solely outperform the average of all attention heads for all respective layers. For example, the attention head 3 at layer 18 achieves an AUC score of 0.79, while the average of all attention heads from layer 18 gets an AUC score of 0.74 (5 points difference). The findings are similar for source AUC, with the exception that attention heads at lower layers also seem to achieve comparable, yet not better, results. This behavior was also noted by Fomicheva et al. (2021b), with the difference that we analyzed attention heads independently rather than averaging them at each layer. Kobayashi et al. (2020) also arrive at similar findings but in terms of alignment error rate in a neural machine translation context.

Attention $\times$ Norm outperforms other explainers. By scaling attention probabilities by the L2 norm of value vectors, we improved the performance further. All of our best results consist of attention-based explainers, with the majority being the explanations that consider the norm of value vectors. We show the results of our best explainers on the validation set of RO-EN in Table 3 using XLM-R as encoder.[8] When using XLM-R-M or RemBERT as encoder the results are similar, except that the best explainer comes from different attention heads at different upper layers.

[7] We got similar findings for ET-EN.

[8] Results for ET-EN follow the same trend (see §C).

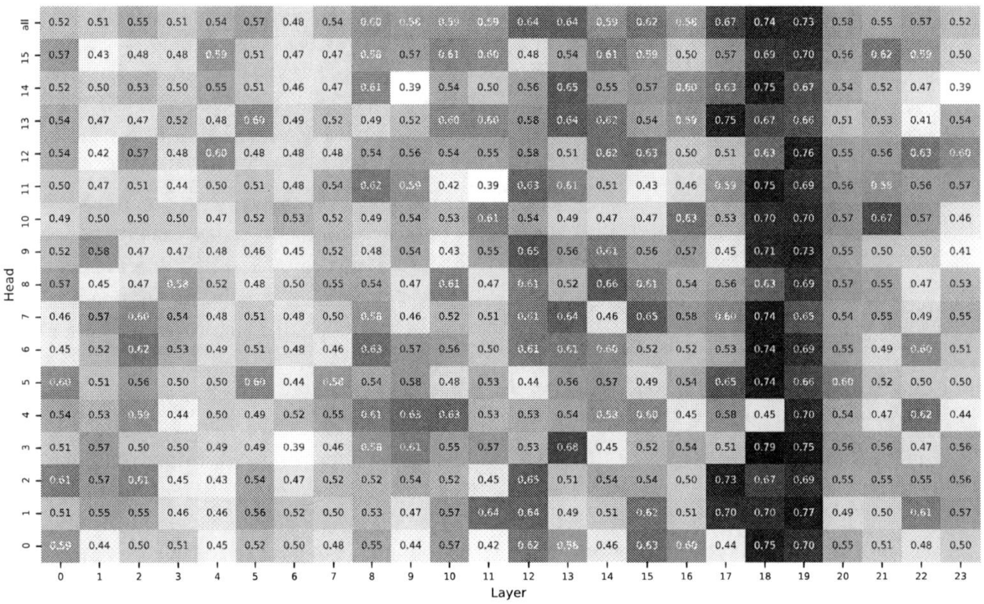

Figure 2: Target AUC of different attention heads at each layer of our XLM-R model for RO-EN. The last tick on the y-axis represents the average of all attention heads.

EXPLAINER	Source			Target		
	AUC	AP	R@K	AUC	AP	R@K
Attention	0.7445	0.6353	0.5164	0.7894	0.7189	0.6054
Cross-attention	0.7514	0.6345	0.5170	0.8066	0.7378	0.6293
Attention × Norm	**0.7851**	**0.6875**	**0.5701**	**0.8136**	**0.7432**	**0.6342**
Gradient × Hidden States	0.6949	0.5629	0.4399	0.6780	0.5388	0.4044
Gradient × Attention	0.7104	0.5942	0.4913	0.7618	0.6747	0.5628
Integrated Gradients	0.6539	0.5251	0.4059	0.6560	0.5148	0.3853
LIME	0.6470	0.5160	0.3922	0.5892	0.4576	0.3300
Leave-one-out	0.6970	0.5673	0.4409	0.5921	0.4752	0.3567
Relaxed-Bernoulli Rationalizer	0.4803	0.3638	0.2483	0.5434	0.4043	0.2914

Table 3: Constrained track results for different explainability methods on the validation set of RO-EN using XLM-R as encoder.

Overall, we observed that attention methods outperform gradient and perturbation methods by a considerable margin, and gradients w.r.t. attention outputs yield better results than gradients w.r.t. hidden states, indicating that the information stored in attention heads is valuable. In Figure 3 we show the attention map of two attention heads that perform well in terms of source AUC and target AUC on the validation set of RO-EN. We noted qualitatively that attention-heads that perform well on source AUC usually focus on cross-sentence tokens,[9] whereas attention-heads that have good results in terms of target AUC usually focus on hypothesis tokens. Lastly, our strategy of appending a bottleneck layer acting as rationalizer did not work well, achieving worse results than perturbation-based methods.

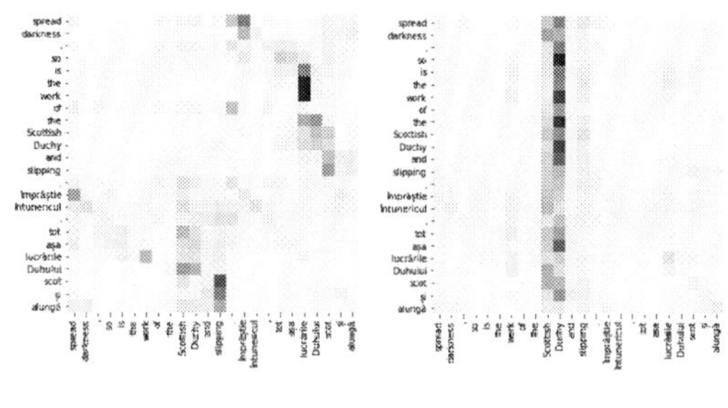

Figure 3: Example of two attention maps from particular heads that perform well on source AUC (left) and target AUC (right) for RO-EN.

[9]Cross-sentence tokens are hypoehsis tokens attended by source tokens and also source tokens attended by hypoehsis tokens.

LP	ENCODER	Source (constrained)			Target (constrained)			Source (unconstrained)			Target (unconstrained)		
		AUC	AP	R@K	AUC	AP	R@K	AUC	AP	R@K	AUC	AP	R@K
RO-EN	OpenKiwi	-	-	-	-	-	-	0.907	0.811	0.704	0.921	0.826	0.718
	XLM-R	0.785	0.687	0.570	0.814	0.743	0.634	0.914	0.825	0.722	0.928	0.851	0.764
	XLM-R-M	0.753	0.661	0.548	0.769	0.693	0.593	0.913	0.826	0.724	0.926	0.851	0.761
	RemBERT	0.784	0.699	0.590	0.790	0.686	0.572	0.918	0.831	0.731	0.934	0.862	0.769
	Ensemble	**0.807**	**0.720**	**0.607**	**0.842**	**0.772**	**0.662**	**0.927**	**0.844**	**0.744**	**0.942**	**0.874**	**0.786**
ET-EN	OpenKiwi	-	-	-	-	-	-	0.848	0.749	0.635	0.873	0.798	0.692
	XLM-R	0.733	0.618	0.486	0.740	0.648	0.530	0.858	0.768	0.656	0.881	0.814	0.711
	XLM-R-M	0.623	0.504	0.367	0.712	0.625	0.513	0.854	0.751	0.630	0.875	0.804	0.704
	RemBERT	**0.750**	**0.638**	**0.523**	0.708	0.595	0.476	0.851	0.747	0.631	0.881	0.806	0.703
	Ensemble	0.744	0.637	0.509	**0.764**	**0.680**	**0.569**	**0.870**	**0.778**	**0.668**	**0.896**	**0.832**	**0.735**
DE-ZH	OpenKiwi	-	-	-	-	-	-	0.721	0.616	0.545	0.648	0.483	0.356
	XLM-R	0.720	0.465	0.288	0.683	0.542	0.406	0.674	0.486	0.298	0.650	0.511	0.352
	XLM-R-M	0.773	**0.609**	**0.454**	0.697	0.545	0.427	0.711	0.574	0.463	**0.712**	**0.595**	**0.468**
	RemBERT	0.762	0.579	0.405	0.692	0.470	0.358	0.619	0.443	0.341	0.585	0.445	0.354
	Ensemble	**0.792**	0.581	0.440	**0.711**	**0.575**	**0.477**	**0.745**	**0.635**	**0.548**	0.705	0.575	0.418
RU-DE	OpenKiwi	-	-	-	-	-	-	0.727	0.620	0.559	0.620	0.409	0.359
	XLM-R	0.719	0.400	0.316	0.822	0.500	0.335	0.729	0.604	0.485	0.623	0.369	0.282
	XLM-R-M	0.743	0.529	0.425	0.838	0.532	0.369	0.740	0.645	0.545	0.640	0.470	**0.447**
	RemBERT	0.776	**0.646**	**0.550**	0.826	0.537	0.418	**0.802**	0.712	0.607	**0.721**	0.504	0.393
	Ensemble	**0.804**	0.604	0.459	**0.855**	**0.628**	**0.514**	0.799	**0.716**	**0.616**	0.719	**0.521**	0.439

Table 4: Constrained (left) and unconstrained (right) track results on the validation set for all LPs using the Attention × Norm explainer.

Results for all LPs. We show the results on the validation set for all LPs in Table 4 (left) with the best Attention × Norm explanations for each tested encoder. We also report results of ensembled explanations, which are obtained by simply averaging selected Attention × Norm explanations from models with different encoders. When comparing single encoders for in-domain LPs, we see that explanations from our XLM-R-based model achieved the best results for source and target metrics on RO-EN, with competitive results on ET-EN, for which explanations from a RemBERT-based model ranked first for source metrics. Despite being a simple strategy, we usually got ∼2 more points of AUC, AP, and R@K by averaging attention explanations. We note that explanations from XLM-R-M and RemBERT perform well on the 20 sentences made available by the shared task for zero-shot LPs. Between XLM-R and XLM-R-M, explanations from the latter lead to better results for both DE-ZH and RU-DE, suggesting that the additional data from the Metrics shared task might help to improve the robustness for zero-shot LPs. Ensembling explanations also leads to higher performance for zero-shot LPs. However, we note that results for DE-ZH and RU-DE are noisy due to the small amount of validation data.

5.2 Unconstrained Track

In this track, we used the predicted probabilities of BAD tags from supervised word-level QE models

LP	Source			Target		
	AUC	AP	R@K	AUC	AP	R@K
RO-EN	0.856	0.727	0.621	0.881	0.783	0.678
ET-EN	0.863	0.757	0.640	0.824	0.740	0.630
DE-ZH	0.731	0.495	0.356	0.707	0.475	0.336
RU-DE	0.770	0.626	0.518	0.755	0.581	0.468
RO-EN	0.934	0.813	0.708	0.940	0.844	0.745
ET-EN	0.935	0.854	0.768	0.922	0.851	0.762
DE-ZH	0.668	0.468	0.322	0.673	0.500	0.369
RU-DE	0.848	0.709	0.593	0.806	0.633	0.515

Table 5: Official test set results for constrained (top) and unconstrained (bottom) tracks.

as explanation scores. The results are shown in Table 4 (right). As found in the constrained track, XLM-R and RemBERT-based models perform better for in-domain LPs, while XLM-R-M and RemBERT lead to better results for zero-shot LPs. Consistent with our findings in the constrained track, ensembling explanations also reflects in improvements in this track.

6 Official results

The official results of the shared task are shown in Table 5 for all LPs. Our final submissions consist of ensembled explanations since they proved to perform better for all LPs in both tracks. More specifically, we ensembled Attention × Norm explainers from the models shown in Table 4 (left) for the constrained track; and we ensembled the predicted probabilities of BAD tags from the models shown in Table 4 (right) for the unconstrained track. Overall, results for the unconstrained track are superior to those obtained in the constrained track. However, the opposite is true for DE-ZH, suggesting that extracting rationales from a sentence-level QE model is a promising weak-supervised strategy to identify translation errors.

7 Conclusion

Final remarks. We have shown that the multi-head mechanism—the bedrock on which transformers are built—is able to learn the importance of tokens associated with BAD tags. Furthermore, composing explanations in the form of attention probabilities scaled by the norm of value vectors leads to further improvements (Kobayashi et al., 2020). Ensembling these explanations yields the best results overall for all tested metrics on all LPs, including zero-shot ones.

Future work. Transformers are composed of many parameters across a vast amount of heads and layers. Strategies that explore how explanations are formed as we move to upper layers are promising, such as computing attention flows and differentiable binary masks per layer (Abnar and Zuidema, 2020; De Cao et al., 2020). Moreover, as shown in Figure 4, we noticed that our best explainers suffer on sentences with higher quality, likely due to the low number of translation errors for those sentences. A simple way to circumvent this problem is to force the explainer to "focus" on words associated with lower scores (or to the BAD class in a classification setting). Thus, strategies such as framing the prediction of DA scores as a classification problem or inducing class-wise rationalizers (Chang et al., 2019) can be helpful.

This shared task focused only on the intersection between explainability and Quality Estimation, yet for future work we plan to apply explainability methods to recent MT metrics such as COMET (Rei et al., 2020a,b; Glushkova et al., 2021) and BLEURT (Sellam et al., 2020a,b).

Acknowledgements

This work was supported by the P2020 programs MAIA (contract 045909) and Unbabel4EU (contract 042671), by the European Research Council (ERC StG DeepSPIN 758969), and by the Fundação para a Ciência e Tecnologia through contract UIDB/50008/2020.

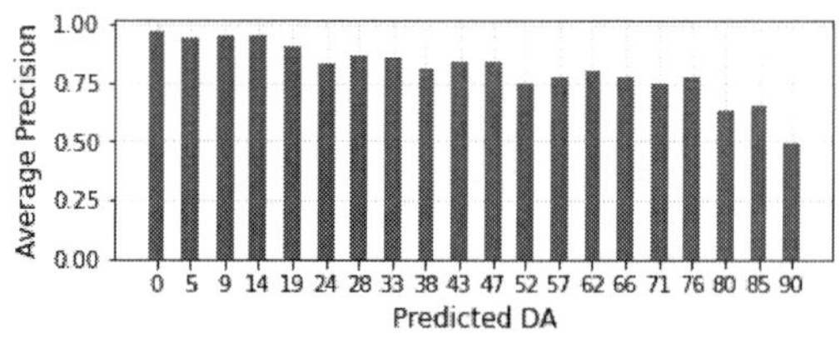

Figure 4: Predicted DAs vs. the average precision of our best explainer on the validation set of RO-EN.

References

Samira Abnar and Willem Zuidema. 2020. Quantifying attention flow in transformers. In *Proceedings of the 58th Annual Meeting of the Association for Computational Linguistics*, pages 4190–4197, Online. Association for Computational Linguistics.

Leila Arras, Franziska Horn, Grégoire Montavon, Klaus-Robert Müller, and Wojciech Samek. 2016. Explaining predictions of non-linear classifiers in NLP. In *Proceedings of the 1st Workshop on Representation Learning for NLP*, pages 1–7, Berlin, Germany. Association for Computational Linguistics.

Jasmijn Bastings, Wilker Aziz, and Ivan Titov. 2019. Interpretable neural predictions with differentiable binary variables. In *Proceedings of the 57th Annual Meeting of the Association for Computational Linguistics*, pages 2963–2977, Florence, Italy. Association for Computational Linguistics.

Jasmijn Bastings and Katja Filippova. 2020. The elephant in the interpretability room: Why use attention as explanation when we have saliency methods? In *Proceedings of the Third BlackboxNLP Workshop on Analyzing and Interpreting Neural Networks for NLP*, pages 149–155, Online. Association for Computational Linguistics.

John Blatz, Erin Fitzgerald, George Foster, Simona Gandrabur, Cyril Goutte, Alex Kulesza, Alberto Sanchis, and Nicola Ueffing. 2004. Confidence estimation for machine translation. In *COLING 2004: Proceedings of the 20th International Conference on Computational Linguistics*, pages 315–321, Geneva, Switzerland. COLING.

Shiyu Chang, Yang Zhang, Mo Yu, and Tommi Jaakkola. 2019. A Game Theoretic Approach to Class-wise Selective Rationalization. In *Advances in Neural Information Processing Systems*, volume 32. Curran Associates, Inc.

Shiyu Chang, Yang Zhang, Mo Yu, and Tommi Jaakkola. 2020. Invariant rationalization. In *International Conference on Machine Learning*, pages 1448–1458. PMLR.

Hyung Won Chung, Thibault Fevry, Henry Tsai, Melvin Johnson, and Sebastian Ruder. 2021. Rethinking Embedding Coupling in Pre-trained Language Models. In *International Conference on Learning Representations*.

Alexis Conneau, Kartikay Khandelwal, Naman Goyal, Vishrav Chaudhary, Guillaume Wenzek, Francisco Guzmán, Edouard Grave, Myle Ott, Luke Zettlemoyer, and Veselin Stoyanov. 2020. Unsupervised cross-lingual representation learning at scale. In *Proceedings of the 58th Annual Meeting of the Association for Computational Linguistics*, pages 8440–8451, Online. Association for Computational Linguistics.

Nicola De Cao, Michael Sejr Schlichtkrull, Wilker Aziz, and Ivan Titov. 2020. How do decisions emerge across layers in neural models? interpretation with differentiable masking. In *Proceedings of the 2020 Conference on Empirical Methods in Natural Language Processing (EMNLP)*, pages 3243–3255, Online. Association for Computational Linguistics.

Jacob Devlin, Ming-Wei Chang, Kenton Lee, and Kristina Toutanova. 2019. BERT: Pre-training of deep bidirectional transformers for language understanding. In *Proceedings of the 2019 Conference of the North American Chapter of the Association for Computational Linguistics: Human Language Technologies, Volume 1 (Long and Short Papers)*, pages 4171–4186, Minneapolis, Minnesota. Association for Computational Linguistics.

Marina Fomicheva, Piyawat Lertvittayakumjorn, Wei Zhao, Steffen Eger, and Yang Gao. 2021a. The Eval4NLP Shared Task on Explainable Quality Estimation: Overview and Results. In *Proceedings of the 2nd Workshop on Evaluation and Comparison of NLP Systems*.

Marina Fomicheva, Lucia Specia, and Nikolaos Aletras. 2021b. Translation Error Detection as Rationale Extraction. *arXiv preprint arXiv:2108.12197*.

Marina Fomicheva, Shuo Sun, Erick Fonseca, Frédéric Blain, Vishrav Chaudhary, Francisco Guzmán, Nina Lopatina, Lucia Specia, and André F. T. Martins. 2020. MLQE-PE: A Multilingual Quality Estimation and Post-Editing Dataset. *arXiv preprint arXiv:2010.04480*.

Erick Fonseca, Lisa Yankovskaya, André F. T. Martins, Mark Fishel, and Christian Federmann. 2019. Findings of the WMT 2019 shared tasks on quality estimation. In *Proceedings of the Fourth Conference on Machine Translation (Volume 3: Shared Task Papers, Day 2)*, pages 1–10, Florence, Italy. Association for Computational Linguistics.

Taisiya Glushkova, Chrysoula Zerva, Ricardo Rei, and André F. T. Martins. 2021. Uncertainty-Aware Machine Translation Evaluation. In *Findings of the Association for Computational Linguistics: EMNLP 2021*, Online. Association for Computational Linguistics.

Yvette Graham, Timothy Baldwin, Alistair Moffat, and Justin Zobel. 2013. Continuous measurement scales in human evaluation of machine translation. In *Proceedings of the 7th Linguistic Annotation Workshop and Interoperability with Discourse*, pages 33–41, Sofia, Bulgaria. Association for Computational Linguistics.

Nuno Miguel Guerreiro and André F. T. Martins. 2021. SPECTRA: Sparse Structured Text Rationalization. In *Proceedings of the 2021 Conference on Empirical Methods in Natural Language Processing (EMNLP)*, Online. Association for Computational Linguistics.

Yaru Hao, Li Dong, Furu Wei, and Ke Xu. 2021. Self-Attention Attribution: Interpreting Information Interactions Inside Transformer. *Proceedings of the AAAI Conference on Artificial Intelligence*, 35(14):12963–12971.

Neil Houlsby, Andrei Giurgiu, Stanislaw Jastrzebski, Bruna Morrone, Quentin De Laroussilhe, Andrea Gesmundo, Mona Attariyan, and Sylvain Gelly. 2019. Parameter-efficient transfer learning for NLP. In *International Conference on Machine Learning*, pages 2790–2799. PMLR.

Sarthak Jain and Byron C. Wallace. 2019. Attention is not Explanation. In *Proceedings of the 2019 Conference of the North American Chapter of the Association for Computational Linguistics: Human Language Technologies, Volume 1 (Long and Short Papers)*, pages 3543–3556, Minneapolis, Minnesota. Association for Computational Linguistics.

Eric Jang, Shixiang Gu, and Ben Poole. 2017. Categorical Reparameterization with Gumbel-Softmax.

Fabio Kepler, Jonay Trénous, Marcos Treviso, Miguel Vera, António Góis, M. Amin Farajian, António V. Lopes, and André F. T. Martins. 2019a. Unbabel's participation in the WMT19 translation quality estimation shared task. In *Proceedings of the Fourth Conference on Machine Translation (Volume 3: Shared Task Papers, Day 2)*, pages 78–84, Florence, Italy. Association for Computational Linguistics.

Fabio Kepler, Jonay Trénous, Marcos Treviso, Miguel Vera, and André F. T. Martins. 2019b. OpenKiwi: An open source framework for quality estimation. In *Proceedings of the 57th Annual Meeting of the Association for Computational Linguistics: System Demonstrations*, pages 117–122, Florence, Italy. Association for Computational Linguistics.

Siwon Kim, Jihun Yi, Eunji Kim, and Sungroh Yoon. 2020. Interpretation of NLP models through input marginalization. In *Proceedings of the 2020 Conference on Empirical Methods in Natural Language Processing (EMNLP)*, pages 3154–3167, Online. Association for Computational Linguistics.

Goro Kobayashi, Tatsuki Kuribayashi, Sho Yokoi, and Kentaro Inui. 2020. Attention is not only a weight:

Analyzing transformers with vector norms. In *Proceedings of the 2020 Conference on Empirical Methods in Natural Language Processing (EMNLP)*, pages 7057–7075, Online. Association for Computational Linguistics.

Tao Lei, Regina Barzilay, and Tommi Jaakkola. 2016. Rationalizing neural predictions. In *Proceedings of the 2016 Conference on Empirical Methods in Natural Language Processing*, pages 107–117, Austin, Texas. Association for Computational Linguistics.

Chris J. Maddison, Andriy Mnih, and Yee Whye Teh. 2017. The Concrete Distribution: A Continuous Relaxation of Discrete Random Variables.

Marianna Martindale and Marine Carpuat. 2018. Fluency over adequacy: A pilot study in measuring user trust in imperfect MT. In *Proceedings of the 13th Conference of the Association for Machine Translation in the Americas (Volume 1: Research Track)*, pages 13–25, Boston, MA. Association for Machine Translation in the Americas.

Matthew E. Peters, Mark Neumann, Mohit Iyyer, Matt Gardner, Christopher Clark, Kenton Lee, and Luke Zettlemoyer. 2018. Deep contextualized word representations. In *Proceedings of the 2018 Conference of the North American Chapter of the Association for Computational Linguistics: Human Language Technologies, Volume 1 (Long Papers)*, pages 2227–2237, New Orleans, Louisiana. Association for Computational Linguistics.

Jonas Pfeiffer, Andreas Rücklé, Clifton Poth, Aishwarya Kamath, Ivan Vulić, Sebastian Ruder, Kyunghyun Cho, and Iryna Gurevych. 2020. AdapterHub: A framework for adapting transformers. In *Proceedings of the 2020 Conference on Empirical Methods in Natural Language Processing: System Demonstrations*, pages 46–54, Online. Association for Computational Linguistics.

Tharindu Ranasinghe, Constantin Orasan, and Ruslan Mitkov. 2020a. TransQuest at WMT2020: Sentence-level direct assessment. In *Proceedings of the Fifth Conference on Machine Translation*, pages 1049–1055, Online. Association for Computational Linguistics.

Tharindu Ranasinghe, Constantin Orasan, and Ruslan Mitkov. 2020b. TransQuest: Translation quality estimation with cross-lingual transformers. In *Proceedings of the 28th International Conference on Computational Linguistics*, pages 5070–5081, Barcelona, Spain (Online). International Committee on Computational Linguistics.

Ricardo Rei, Craig Stewart, Ana C Farinha, and Alon Lavie. 2020a. COMET: A neural framework for MT evaluation. In *Proceedings of the 2020 Conference on Empirical Methods in Natural Language Processing (EMNLP)*, pages 2685–2702, Online. Association for Computational Linguistics.

Ricardo Rei, Craig Stewart, Ana C Farinha, and Alon Lavie. 2020b. Unbabel's participation in the WMT20 metrics shared task. In *Proceedings of the Fifth Conference on Machine Translation*, pages 911–920, Online. Association for Computational Linguistics.

Marco Tulio Ribeiro, Sameer Singh, and Carlos Guestrin. 2016. Why should i trust you?: Explaining the predictions of any classifier. In *Proc. ACM SIGKDD*, pages 1135–1144. ACM.

Thibault Sellam, Dipanjan Das, and Ankur Parikh. 2020a. BLEURT: Learning robust metrics for text generation. In *Proceedings of the 58th Annual Meeting of the Association for Computational Linguistics*, pages 7881–7892, Online. Association for Computational Linguistics.

Thibault Sellam, Amy Pu, Hyung Won Chung, Sebastian Gehrmann, Qijun Tan, Markus Freitag, Dipanjan Das, and Ankur Parikh. 2020b. Learning to evaluate translation beyond English: BLEURT submissions to the WMT metrics 2020 shared task. In *Proceedings of the Fifth Conference on Machine Translation*, pages 921–927, Online. Association for Computational Linguistics.

Matthew Snover, Bonnie Dorr, Richard Schwartz, Linnea Micciulla, and John Makhoul. 2006. A study of translation edit rate with targeted human annotation. In *In Proceedings of Association for Machine Translation in the Americas*, pages 223–231.

Lucia Specia, Frédéric Blain, Marina Fomicheva, Erick Fonseca, Vishrav Chaudhary, Francisco Guzmán, and André F. T. Martins. 2020. Findings of the WMT 2020 shared task on quality estimation. In *Proceedings of the Fifth Conference on Machine Translation*, pages 743–764, Online. Association for Computational Linguistics.

Lucia Specia, Carolina Scarton, and Gustavo Henrique Paetzold. 2018. Quality estimation for machine translation. *Synthesis Lectures on Human Language Technologies*, 11(1):1–162.

Ashish Vaswani, Noam Shazeer, Niki Parmar, Jakob Uszkoreit, Llion Jones, Aidan N Gomez, Ł ukasz Kaiser, and Illia Polosukhin. 2017. Attention is All you Need. In *Advances in Neural Information Processing Systems (NeurIPS)*, volume 30, pages 5998–6008. Curran Associates, Inc.

Elena Voita, Rico Sennrich, and Ivan Titov. 2021. Analyzing the source and target contributions to predictions in neural machine translation. In *Proceedings of the 59th Annual Meeting of the Association for Computational Linguistics and the 11th International Joint Conference on Natural Language Processing (Volume 1: Long Papers)*, pages 1126–1140, Online. Association for Computational Linguistics.

Sarah Wiegreffe and Yuval Pinter. 2019. Attention is not not explanation. In *Proceedings of the 2019 Conference on Empirical Methods in Natural Language*

Processing and the 9th International Joint Conference on Natural Language Processing (EMNLP-IJCNLP), pages 11–20, Hong Kong, China. Association for Computational Linguistics.

Chrysoula Zerva, Daan van Stigt, Ricardo Rei, Ana C Farinha, José G. C. de Souza, Taisiya Glushkova, Miguel Vera, Fabio Kepler, and André Martins. 2021. IST-Unbabel 2021 Submission for the Quality Estimation Shared Task. In *Proceedings of the Fifth Conference on Machine Translation*, Online. Association for Computational Linguistics.

A Computing infrastructure

Our infrastructure consists of 5 machines with the specifications shown in Table 6. The machines were used interchangeably, and all experiments were executed in a single GPU. Despite having machines with different specifications, we did not observe large differences in the execution time of our models across distinct machines.

#	GPU	CPU
1	4 × Titan Xp - 12GB	16 × AMD Ryzen 1950X @ 3.40GHz - 128GB
2	4 × GTX 1080 Ti - 12GB	8 × Intel i7-9800X @ 3.80GHz - 128GB
3	3 × RTX 2080 Ti - 12GB	12 × AMD Ryzen 2920X @ 3.50GHz - 128GB
4	3 × RTX 2080 Ti - 12GB	12 × AMD Ryzen 2920X @ 3.50GHz - 128GB
5.1	4 × Quadro RTX 6000 - 24GB	12 × Intel Xeon Silver 4214 @ 2.20GHz - 256GB
5.2	4 × RTX 2080 Ti - 12GB	12 × Intel Xeon Silver 4214 @ 2.20GHz - 256GB

Table 6: Computing infrastructure.

B Training hyperparameters

The hyperparameters used for training are shown in Table 7.

HYPERPARAM.	XLM-R	XLM-R-M	REMBERT
Feed-forward size	1024	1024	1024
Batch size	2	2	1
Optimizer	Adam	Adam	Adam
Number of epochs	10	10	10
Early stopping patience	3	3	3
Encoder learning rate	1×10^{-4}	1×10^{-4}	3×10^{-5}
Feed-forward learning rate	1×10^{-4}	1×10^{-4}	1×10^{-5}
Gradient accumulation	4	4	8
Dropout	0.05	0.05	0.05

Table 7: Hyperparmeters used for training sentence (constrained) and word-level (unconstrained) QE systems.

C Full results for the constrained track

Following the analysis described in §5.1, we report the best results for each explainability method for XLM-R-based models in Table 8 on the validation set of RO-EN and Table 9 on the validation set of ET-EN. We also report the best explainers based on Attention × Norm for XLM-R-M and RemBERT-based models. For explainability methods based on attention weights, we show two attention heads: one with the best performance on source AUC and another with the best performance on target AUC. Besides submitting ensembled explanations, we also made submissions with Attention × Norm heads that achieve the top performance on the validation set of RO-EN and ET-EN.

#	ENCODER	EXPLAINER	Source			Target		
			AUC	AP	R@K	AUC	AP	R@K
1	XLM-R	Attention - Layer 18 - Head 3	0.6555	0.4569	0.3509	0.7894	0.7189	0.6054
2	XLM-R	Attention - Layer 18 - Head 0	0.7445	0.6353	0.5164	0.7462	0.6488	0.5197
3	XLM-R	Cross-attention - Layer 18 - Head 3	0.7092	0.5461	0.4139	0.8066	0.7378	0.6293
4	XLM-R	Cross-attention - Layer 18 - Head 0	0.7514	0.6345	0.5170	0.7374	0.6254	0.4883
5	XLM-R	Attention × Norm - Layer 18 - Head 3	0.7178	0.5686	0.4372	**0.8136**	**0.7432**	**0.6342**
6	XLM-R	Attention × Norm - Layer 19 - Head 2	**0.7851**	**0.6875**	**0.5701**	0.8099	0.7301	0.6153
7	XLM-R	Gradient × Hidden States - Layer 15	0.6949	0.5629	0.4399	0.6780	0.5388	0.4044
8	XLM-R	Gradient × Attention - Layer 17	0.7104	0.5942	0.4913	0.7618	0.6747	0.5628
9	XLM-R	Integrated Gradients - Layer 15	0.6539	0.5251	0.4059	0.6560	0.5148	0.3853
10	XLM-R	LIME	0.6470	0.5160	0.3922	0.5892	0.4576	0.3300
11	XLM-R	Leave-one-out	0.6970	0.5673	0.4409	0.5921	0.4752	0.3567
12	XLM-R	Relaxed-Bernoulli Rationalizer	0.4803	0.3638	0.2483	0.5434	0.4043	0.2914
13	XLM-R-M	Attention × Norm - Layer 23 - Head 3	0.6993	0.5824	0.4571	0.7686	0.6932	0.5932
14	XLM-R-M	Attention × Norm - Layer 23 - Head 1	0.7530	0.6612	0.5479	0.7612	0.6841	0.5802
15	RemBERT	Attention × Norm - Layer 23	0.7824	0.6987	0.5901	0.7904	0.6865	0.5723
16	RemBERT	Attention × Norm - Layer 22 - Head 5	0.7842	0.6822	0.5752	0.7167	0.5549	0.4278
1	Ensemble	(5) + (6) + (15)	0.8043	0.7137	0.5970	0.8398	0.7695	0.6606
2	Ensemble	(5) + (6) + (14) + (15)	**0.8074**	**0.7203**	**0.6071**	**0.8421**	**0.7725**	**0.6624**

Table 8: Full constrained track results on the validation set of RO-EN.

#	ENCODER	EXPLAINER	Source			Target		
			AUC	AP	R@K	AUC	AP	R@K
1	XLM-R	Attention - Layer 18 - Head 3	0.6406	0.5205	0.3811	0.7094	0.6210	0.5037
2	XLM-R	Attention - Layer 18 - Head 0	0.6656	0.5619	0.4438	0.7055	0.6011	0.4779
3	XLM-R	Cross-attention - Layer 18 - Head 3	0.6587	0.5335	0.3947	0.7270	0.6396	0.5226
4	XLM-R	Cross-attention - Layer 17 - Head 13	0.7090	0.5927	0.4673	0.6788	0.5760	0.4599
5	XLM-R	Attention × Norm - Layer 18 - Head 3	0.6697	0.5540	0.4228	0.7257	0.6373	0.5200
6	XLM-R	Attention × Norm - Layer 19 - Head 2	0.7335	0.6181	0.4857	**0.7404**	**0.6477**	**0.5303**
7	XLM-R	Gradient × Hidden States - Layer 14	0.6567	0.5403	0.4156	0.6041	0.4837	0.3619
8	XLM-R	Gradient × Attention - Layer 17	0.6613	0.5597	0.4322	0.6891	0.5983	0.4798
9	XLM-R	Integrated Gradients - Layer 15	0.6194	0.4995	0.3699	0.5705	0.4649	0.3489
10	XLM-R	LIME	0.6221	0.4968	0.3606	0.5405	0.4297	0.3222
11	XLM-R	Leave-one-out	0.6584	0.5375	0.4082	0.5493	0.4494	0.3412
12	XLM-R	Relaxed-Bernoulli Rationalizer	0.4933	0.3794	0.2481	0.5406	0.4277	0.3211
13	XLM-R-M	Attention × Norm - Layer 21 - Head 8	0.6235	0.5041	0.3670	0.7122	0.6254	0.5133
14	XLM-R-M	Attention × Norm - Layer 21 - Head 9	0.5510	0.4106	0.2738	0.7068	0.6175	0.5059
15	RemBERT	Attention × Norm - Layer 23	0.7465	**0.6382**	**0.5229**	0.7085	0.5954	0.4756
16	RemBERT	Attention × Norm - Layer 23 - Head 8	**0.7501**	0.6203	0.4912	0.6758	0.5486	0.4418
1	Ensemble	(5) + (6) + (15)	**0.7467**	**0.6368**	**0.5113**	0.7545	0.6662	0.5512
2	Ensemble	(5) + (6) + (14) + (15)	0.7441	0.6366	0.5089	**0.7639**	**0.6805**	**0.5688**

Table 9: Full constrained track results on the validation set of ET-EN.

Error Identification for Machine Translation with Metric Embedding and Attention

Raphael Rubino and **Atsushi Fujita** and **Benjamin Marie**
National Institute of Information and Communications Technology
3-5 Hikaridai, Seika-cho, Soraku-gun, Kyoto, 619-0289, Japan
raphael.rubino,atsushi.fujita,bmarie@nict.go.jp

Abstract

Quality Estimation (QE) for Machine Translation has been shown to reach relatively high accuracy in predicting sentence-level scores, relying on pretrained contextual embeddings and human-produced quality scores. However, the lack of explanations along with decisions made by end-to-end neural models makes the results difficult to interpret. Furthermore, word-level annotated datasets are rare due to the prohibitive effort required to perform this task, while they could provide interpretable signals in addition to sentence-level QE outputs. In this paper, we propose a novel QE architecture which tackles both the word-level data scarcity and the interpretability limitations of recent approaches. Sentence-level and word-level components are jointly pretrained through an attention mechanism based on synthetic data and a set of MT metrics embedded in a common space. Our approach is evaluated on the *Eval4NLP* 2021 shared task and our submissions reach the first position in all language pairs. The extraction of metric-to-input attention weights show that different metrics focus on different parts of the source and target text, providing strong rationales in the decision-making process of the QE model.

1 Introduction

Quality Estimation (QE) for Machine Translation (MT) (Blatz et al., 2004; Quirk, 2004; Specia et al., 2009) aims at providing quality scores or labels to MT output when translation references are not available. Sentence-level QE is usually conducted using human produced direct assessments (DA) (Graham et al., 2013) or post-edits. The latter allows to derive token-level quality indicators such as *good* and *bad* tags (Fonseca et al., 2019; Specia et al., 2020). Token-level QE is particularly useful for applications such as source pre-editing or focused MT post-editing, but requires high-quality fine-grained annotated data for supervised learning. Furthermore, token-level quality indicators can be seen as explanations for sentence-level scores, whether given by humans or automatically produced. However, explainability of QE models decisions is obscured by contemporary approaches relying on large data-driven neural-based models, making use of pretrained contextual language models (LM) such as BERT (Devlin et al., 2019) and XLM (Conneau and Lample, 2019), albeit showing steady performance increase as reported in the QE shared tasks (Fonseca et al., 2019; Specia et al., 2020). Yet, the QE layers and architectures are rarely investigated, neither for performance nor for interpretability purposes, and the center of attention is mainly on large pretrained models and generating additional (synthetic) training corpora.

In this paper, we present a novel QE architecture which encompasses a metric-to-input attention mechanism allowing for several extensions of the habitual QE approach. First, since sentence-level QE scores are usually obtained with surface-level MT metrics computed between translation outputs and human produced references or post-edits such as HTER (Snover et al., 2006), we propose to make use of several metrics simultaneously in order to model translation errors at various granularities, i.e. at the character, token, and phrase levels. Second, we design a *metric embeddings model* which represents metrics in their own space through a dedicated set of learnable parameters, allowing for straightforward extensions of the number and type of metrics. Third, by employing an attention mechanism between metric embeddings and bilingual input representations, the metric-to-input attention weights indicate where each metric focuses given an input sequence, increasing the interpretability of the QE components. We conduct a set of experiments on the *Eval4NLP* 2021 shared task dataset (Fomicheva et al., 2021) using only the training data along with sentence-level scores officially released for the tasks (illustrated in Figure 1). In addition, we

Proceedings of the 58th Annual Meeting of the Association for Computational Linguistics, pages 146–156

https://doi.org/10.26615/978-954-452-056-4_015

Source	Religioon pakub vaimu puhastamiseks teatud vahendeid .
MT	Religion offers certain means of cleansing the spirit .
PE	Religion offers certain means of cleansing the spirit .
Sentence-level scores: DA 0.905 – chrF 1.0 – TER 0.0 – BLEU 1.0	
Source	Tänu Uku kalastamiskirele pääseb Õnne 13 maja põlengust .
MT	Thanks to the breath of fresh fishing , 13 houses are escaped from contempt .
PE	Thanks to Uku 's passion for fishing, the house at Õnne 13 is saved from fire.
Sentence-level scores: DA 0.132 – chrF 0.366 – TER 0.667 – BLEU 0.0	

Figure 1: Samples of source sentences, automatic translations and human post-editions, along with direct assessment (DA) scores, taken from the *Eval4NLP* 2021 shared task Estonian–English validation set representing high and low quality translations. Additional metrics are presented, namely chrF, TER and BLEU, to illustrate variations related to metrics granularity. Green and red colors are tokens annotated with classes 0 and 1 respectively.

produce a large synthetic corpus for QE pretraining using publicly available resources.

The contributions of our work are the following: *(i)* a novel QE architecture using metric embeddings and attention-based interpretable neural components allowing for unsupervised token-level quality indicators, *(ii)* an extensible framework designed for unrestricted sentence-level QE scores or labels where new metrics can be added through finetuning, *(iii)* the reproducibility guaranteed by the use of publicly available datasets, tools, and models, and *(iv)* word and sentence-level QE results on par or outperforming top-ranked approaches based on the official *Eval4NLP* 2021 shared task results.

The remainder of this paper is organized as follows. In Section 2, we introduce some background in QE based on contextual language model, followed in Section 3 with the detailed implementation of the proposed model using metric embedding and attention. In Section 4, the experimental setup is presented, including the data and tools used, as well as the training procedure of our models. Section 5 contains the results obtained in our experiments along with their analysis and interpretation. A comparison of our method and results with previous work is made in Section 6. Finally, we conclude and suggest future research directions in Section 7.

2 Background

Current state-of-the-art QE approaches are commonly based on sentence encoders taking as input source–translation pairs (Ranasinghe et al., 2020a; Wang et al., 2020; Rubino, 2020). Encoders are usually contextual LMs pretrained on large amount of multilingual data. Existing QE implementations commonly rely on additional layers added on top of a pretrained LM, which enables multi-task learning for word and sentence-level QE.

Pretraining of contextual LMs is done by optimizing a prediction function given input sequences of tokens containing randomly masked tokens, or tokens randomly replaced by other tokens sampled from the vocabulary. Formally, given an input sequence Z of n tokens $z_{1:n}$, corresponding word (or subword) embeddings $x_{1:n}$ with dimension d ($x_{1:n} \in \mathbb{R}^{n \times d}$) are learned, and output contextual embeddings $h^l_{1:n} \in \mathbb{R}^{n \times d}$ are computed at each layer $l \in [1, L] \subset \mathbb{N}$ of a Transformer encoder (Vaswani et al., 2017). Usually based on the output of the last encoder layer, the model optimizes the following loss function: $\ell(s,t) = -\mathbb{E}_{r \sim [1,n]} \log P(z_r | \bar{z}_r)$, where z_r are randomly sampled tokens from z to be masked or replaced and $\bar{z}_r$ are the remaining tokens from z with $r \in [1, n] \subset \mathbb{N}$. To perform QE, QE-specific layers are commonly added on top of pretrained contextual LMs, being fed with contextual token embeddings from the topmost (i.e., L-th) layer of the LM.

For sentence-level QE the specific component is a regression head formalized by $y^s = \sigma(\phi(h^L_{1:n}) \cdot W^s + b^s)$, where $y^s \in [0, 1] \subset \mathbb{R}$. W^s and b^s are trainable parameters of the linear output layer, ϕ is a pooling function, and σ is the sigmoid function. The output y^s of this QE component is a score indicating the sentence-level translation quality.

For token-level QE a classification head is implemented as $y^t_{1:n} = softmax(h^L_{1:n} \cdot W^t + b^t)$, where $y^t_{1:n} \in \mathbb{R}^{n \times |C|}$ with C the set of word-level QE classes, W^t and b^t are trainable parameters of the linear output layer. The output $y^t_{1:n}$ of this QE component is a vector of labels indicating the translation quality of corresponding input tokens. Source tokens are annotated according to the accuracy of their translation, while annotations of target tokens also take into account their position in the target sequence.

Multiple losses are then computed, one for the sentence-level and one for each word-level outputs (source and target tokens), based on gold labels to train (or finetune) the contextual LM and the QE model in an end-to-end fashion using back-propagation (Kim et al., 2017; Lee, 2020; Rubino and Sumita, 2020). Commonly used losses are cross-entropy and mean-squared error for classification and regression respectively.

However, this approach has limitations While the token-level QE implementation makes use of each input token representation in context thanks to the pretrained LM, the sentence-level QE components relies only on the pooled representation of the input sequence. This approach drastically limits the amount of information flowing through the sentence-level specific set of layers and may force the network to focus more on cues and data artifacts which correlate with QE scores, instead of encoding translation-related features from source and target inputs (Sun et al., 2020). These findings corroborate with the empirical observation made by Kepler et al. (2019), where the authors obtained the best word-level QE results using BERT and ignoring target language features when predicting source quality labels and vice-versa. Additionally, most recent QE approaches do not allow for the interpretability of sentence-level QE predictions at test time and leads to the current state of QE as a set of *black-box* components. Furthermore, token-level error annotations is costly to produce.

3 Metric Embedding and Attention

Motivated by the limitations to contextual LM based QE, we propose a novel architecture employing metric embeddings and attention, which is computed between the contextual embeddings and the embedded QE criteria of the supervised learning task, namely MT automatic metrics or direct assessment scores provided by human annotators.

The metric embedding matrix $E \in \mathbb{R}^{g \times d}$, randomly initialized at the beginning of training, is added on top of the pretrained LM to model metrics in their own space, with a predefined set of sentence-level metrics $M = \{m_1, \ldots, m_g\}$. Each metric is initially represented as a one-hot vector, noted $m_j \in \mathbb{R}^g$ with $j \in [1, g] \subset \mathbb{N}$. Its corresponding embedding is retrieved with $m_j \cdot E$, forming the query used in the attention mechanism (eqn. 1):

$$Q_{i,j} = (m_j \cdot E) \cdot W_i^Q \tag{1}$$

where $i \in [1, u] \subset \mathbb{N}$ is the head index from a predefined number of heads, $Q_{i,j} \in \mathbb{R}^d$ is the metric embedding corresponding to the one-hot vector m_j, $W_i^Q \in \mathbb{R}^{d \times (d/u)}$ is a matrix of learnable parameters projecting the metric embedding into the dimensionality of the attention head (d/u). Note that we present the query computation for a single metric but our implementation allows several metrics to be packed into a single query, sharing the parameter matrix W_i^Q (biases are omitted for the sake of simplicity).

Keys and values which are the two other components of the attention mechanism, noted K_i and V_i respectively, are computed based on the output of the topmost layer of the pretrained LM, which is first fed into a position-wise feed-forward layer following (eqn. 2):

$$\begin{aligned} ff_{1:n} &= ReLU(h_{1:n}^L \cdot W^{s,D_1}) \cdot W^{s,D_2} \\ K_i &= ff_{1:n} \cdot W_i^K \ , \ V_i = ff_{1:n} \cdot W_i^V \end{aligned} \tag{2}$$

where W_i^K and $W_i^V \in \mathbb{R}^{d \times (d/u)}$ are the parameter matrices for the keys and values respectively, $W^{s,D_1} \in \mathbb{R}^{d \times b}$ and $W^{s,D_2} \in \mathbb{R}^{b \times d}$ are parameter matrices of the linear layers with dimensionality b and a $ReLU$ activation function in between, leading to $ff_{1:n} \in \mathbb{R}^{n \times d}$.

Metrics to tokens attention weights aim to represent the focus made by a given metric on specific parts of the input sequences. These attention weights are computed between the embedding of a metric and the contextually encoded input tokens (eqn. 3):

$$\alpha_{i,j,1:n} = \sigma\left(\frac{Q_{i,j} K_i^T}{\sqrt{d/u}}\right) \tag{3}$$

where σ is the sigmoid function. Note that the common way to compute attention weights, as presented in Vaswani et al. (2017), relies on $softmax$ which is based on the exponential function, well-suited for tasks such as machine translation as it results in few *alignments* between tokens involved in the attention mechanism. However, in the case of unsupervised sequence labeling such as token-level QE without annotated data, zero to many tokens may influence sentence-level scores given a metric. Thus, to allow more flexibility in the distribution of attention weights over input tokens and following the approach presented in (Rei and Søgaard, 2018), we replaced $softmax$ by $sigmoid$.

Sentence-level scores are obtained for each metric with the weighted sum of value vectors for each attention head (eqn. 4):

$$attn_{i,j} = \sum \alpha_{i,j,1:n} V_i, \quad (4)$$

where $attn_{i,j} \in \mathbb{R}^{(d/u)}$, before concatenating the output of each head and projecting the result back in the dimensionality of the model (eqn. 5):

$$y_j^{s'} = (attn_{1,j} \oplus \ldots \oplus attn_{u,j}) \cdot W^O \quad (5)$$

with $W^O \in \mathbb{R}^{d \times d}$. Finally, we project $y_j^{s'}$ from the model dimensionality to a single score through a metric specific linear layer: $y_j^s = y_j^{s'} \cdot W_j^s$ with $W_j^s \in \mathbb{R}^{d \times 1}$ and $y_j^s \in [0,1] \subset \mathbb{R}$.

Token-level QE scores are computed by using the attention weights (see eqn. 3) followed by three transformations: attention heads combination through a linear transformation, concatenation of token embeddings and combined attention heads, combination of metrics through a final linear transformation (eqn. 6):

$$\begin{aligned} y_{j,1:n}^{t'} &= \alpha_{j,1:n} \cdot W^{t,H} \\ y_{1:n}^{t} &= (y_{1:n}^{t'} \oplus h_{1:n}^{L}) \cdot W^{t,O} \end{aligned} \quad (6)$$

where $\alpha_{j,1:n} = (\alpha_{1,j,1:n} \oplus \ldots \oplus \alpha_{u,j,1:n})$, $y_{1:n}^{t'} = (y_{1,1:n}^{t'} \oplus \ldots \oplus y_{g,1:n}^{t'})$, $W^{t,H} \in \mathbb{R}^{u \times 1}$ and $W^{t,O} \in \mathbb{R}^{(d+g) \times 1}$ are parameter matrices of linear layers, leading to $y^t \in [0,1] \subset \mathbb{R}$ for each token in the input sequence $z_{1:n}$.

The learning process allows for supervised or unsupervised token-level QE. Note that all learnable parameters for the sentence-level QE components except W_j^s are shared between metrics, including the metric embeddings matrix E. We believe that such an approach enables to capture translation errors at different granularities according to the specificity of each metric, e.g., characters, tokens and phrases, while keeping a reasonable total amount of learnable parameters. The loss functions for sentence-level QE are mean-squared error while the losses for token-level QE are cross-entropy. The final loss is obtained by linearly combining all losses computed for each output of the model. The general architecture of our QE model is illustrated in Figure 2.

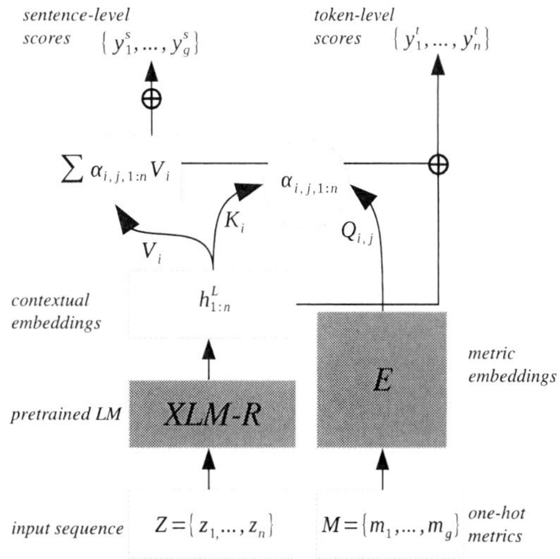

Figure 2: Architecture of the metric embeddings and attention mechanism. Shaded elements, curved arrows and $\oplus$ are parameters of the model, i and j are the attention head and the metric indexes respectively.

Supervised learning is conducted by computing losses according to each output of the model and their corresponding gold labels from the training data. Thus, for the sentence-level QE layers, we compute one loss per metric (Mean Squared Error), while for the token-level QE layers, if token-level annotations are available, two losses allow to optimize the model for source and target tokens separately (Cross-entropy).

Unsupervised learning is conducted when token-level annotations are not available, which is one of the objectives in the constrained task of *Eval4NLP* 2021. In this case, only sentence-level losses are used to optimize the parameter of the model through backpropagation. Following the guidelines of the shared task, we do not use the direct assessment annotations made by humans at the word-level.

4 Experimental Setup

This section presents our experimental setup, including the pretrained models, the datasets and the training procedure. All pretrained models and scripts used in our experiments are based on PyTorch (Paszke et al., 2019) and all computations are conducted on NVIDIA V100 GPUs with CUDA v10.2.

4.1 Pretrained Models

Two types of pretrained models were necessary to conduct our experiments: contextual embedding LMs to encode bilingual input sequences and MT models to produce synthetic data required for QE pretraining.

Contextual embedding LMs used in our experiments are based on a pretrained XLM-R checkpoint, namely *xlm-roberta-large* from the HuggingFace Transformers library (Wolf et al., 2020). This model, initially introduced in (Conneau et al., 2020), was pretrained on 2.5TB of filtered CommonCrawl data, covering 100 languages with a vocabulary of $250k$ BPE tokens (Sennrich et al., 2016), $1,024$ embedding and hidden-state dimensions, $4,096$-dimensional feed-forward layers and 16 attention heads.

MT models used in our experiments are transformer-based neural MT (NMT) models. For two language pairs and translation directions of the *Eval4NLP* 2021 shared task, namely Estonian→English (ET–EN) and Romanian→English (RO–EN), we used pretrained NMT models made available by the WMT'20 QE shared task organizers (Specia et al., 2020).[1] For German→Chinese (DE–ZH) and Russian→German (RU–DE), the two zero-shot pairs of the shared task, we used the mBART50 model (Liu et al., 2020; Tang et al., 2020).[2] All NMT models are based on the fairseq library (Ott et al., 2019).

4.2 Datasets

Two datasets were used in our experiments: a synthetic dataset for QE pretraining, and the shared task dataset consisting of training, validation and test sets. Details of the latter dataset are presented in Table 1 while we give more information about the synthetic data in this section.

	Lang.	Sent.	Tokens	Types
Train	ET–EN	7.0k	98.1k / 136.6k	28.9k / 14.6k
	RO–EN	7.0k	120.2k / 123.3k	23.5k / 15.2k
Valid	ET–EN	1.0k	14.4k / 20.1k	6.9k / 4.7k
	RO–EN	1.0k	17.3k / 17.7k	6.4k / 4.8k
Test	ET–EN	1.0k	14.0k / 19.6k	6.9k / 4.7k
	RO–EN	1.0k	17.4k / 17.8k	6.3k / 4.8k
	DE–ZH	1.4k	24.9k / 52.8k	8.4k / 2.2k
	RU–DE	1.2k	25.4k / 28.8k	10.2k / 7.5k

Table 1: Official training, validation and test data released for the *Eval4NLP* 2021 shared task. DE–ZH and RU–DE are zero-shot language pairs thus have neither training nor validation corpora. Tokens and types columns contain source / MT counts, *k* stands for thousands, Chinese tokens and types are characters.

Lang.	Sent.	Tokens	Types
ET–EN	24.9M	322.5M / 411.0M	4.8M / 2.8M
RO–EN	42.1M	600.5M / 601.2M	4.0M / 3.6M
DE–ZH	19.8M	422.8M / 708.1M	4.5M / 3.3k
RU–DE	19.5M	256.9M / 262.7M	4.4M / 4.4M

Table 2: Synthetic data produced for QE pretraining. Tokens and types columns contain source / MT counts, *M* stands for millions and *k* for thousands, Chinese tokens and types are characters.

Synthetic data generation was based on gathered parallel corpora translated by the NMT systems presented in Section 4.1. The translated sentences were compared to the target side of the parallel corpora to produce sentence-level scores based on chrF (Popović, 2016), TER (Snover et al., 2006) and BLEU (Papineni et al., 2002) metrics. Additionally, only for the synthetic data, we produced token-level scores following the usual procedure to determine post-editing effort (Specia et al., 2020).[3] For this step, word alignments were required to obtain source-side token-level quality indicators. We used the same parallel corpora to produce synthetic data and to train word alignments based on the IBM 2 model (Brown et al., 1993) and trained using *fast_align* (Dyer et al., 2013). Details about the synthetic data are presented in Table 2.[4]

The special case of DE–ZH resulting from preliminary experiments, we noticed for this language pair that the translation quality of the synthetic data was low compared to the three other language pairs. We assumed that it was due to two issues:

[1]Models available at https://github.com/facebookresearch/mlqe/blob/master/nmt_models/README-models.md

[2]Model available at https://github.com/pytorch/fairseq/tree/master/examples/multilingual

[3]Scripts and procedure available at https://github.com/deep-spin/qe-corpus-builder

[4]Parallel corpora were collected from the WMT news translation task (Tiedemann, 2016) and OPUS (Tiedemann, 2016).

the quality of the DE–ZH parallel corpora and the performance of the NMT model. To tackle the first issue, we generated our own DE–ZH parallel corpora by pivot-based (back-) translation, starting from a monolingual Chinese corpus composed of CommonCrawl and NewsCrawl 2018 to 2020, translating it into English using an in-house NMT model trained with Marian (Junczys-Dowmunt et al., 2018) on the WMT'21 QE ZH–EN parallel corpus, then translating the English output into German using the EN–DE NMT model released by the WMT'20 QE shared task organizers, resulting in a synthetic DE–ZH parallel corpus. To tackle the second issue, we finetuned mBART50 using NewsCommentary and MultiUN DE–ZH retrieved from OPUS, as these two corpora appeared to be the cleanest among the available ones.

4.3 Training Procedure

We detail in this section the training procedures employed for QE pretraining on the synthetic data and finetuning on the officially released training data.

QE pretraining was conducted per language pair starting from the XLM-R checkpoint presented in Section 4.1 using two different random seeds and learning rates. Additionally, four QE pretraining were conducted on the concatenation of all synthetic data using four different random seeds and two learning rates. Training was ran for two epochs for the language specific models and for a single epoch for the remaining ones. We restricted the length of training samples to a minimum of 5 and a maximum of 128 subword tokens for the bilingual models and a maximum of 96 subword tokens for the multilingual ones. Training was conducted with batches of 128 source and target sequences with the AdamW optimizer (Loshchilov and Hutter, 2019) (parameters $\beta_1 = 0.9$, $\beta_2 = 0.999$ and $\epsilon = 1 \times 10^{-6}$). A linear learning rate warmup was employed during the first 50k updates to reach a maximum value of 5×10^{-6} or 2×10^{-6} depending on the model and random seed, which remained without decay until the end of the first epoch. The dropout rates were set to 0.1 for both the embeddings and the transformer blocks (feed-forward and attention layers), the model dimensionality and embedding size was 1,024, feed-forward layers had a dimensionality of 4,096 and the numbers of attention heads were set to 16 for the language model and 8 for the metric attention block.

Finetuning was conducted using the officially released data presented in Table 1 during 20 epochs, monitoring the performance of each model using the validation set. No length restriction was applied on these corpora. In addition to the three automatic metrics used during QE pretraining, namely chrF, TER and BLEU, the direct assessment scores provided by the shared task organizers were used by simply adding an entry in the metric embeddings matrix. A few hyperparameters, namely the batch size, learning rate, as well as embedding and Transformer dropout rates, were optimized in a grid-search manner. The best resulting models according to token-level source and target performances based on the official metrics (Area Under the Curve, AUC, and Average Precision, AP) were kept for ensembling and predicting scores on the validation and test sets.

5 Results and Analysis

We present in Table 3 the results obtained on the *Eval4NLP* 2021 shared task as reported by the organizers, including our baselines and final submissions along with the three baselines proposed by the organizers, namely random scores, TransQuest (Ranasinghe et al., 2020b) combined with LIME (Ribeiro et al., 2016) (noted *Official baseline 1*), and XMoverScore (Zhao et al., 2020) combined with SHAP (Lundberg and Lee, 2017) (noted *Official baseline 2*). Our baselines are composed of ensembles of two finetuned language-specific QE pretrained models while our final submissions are composed of ensembles of eight finetuned models for each of token-level tasks (source and target) and eight models for sentence-level tasks. The eight token-level models are, for each random seed, the best language-specific finetuned models according to source or target AUC and AP, and the best multilingual models according to source or target AUC. The eight sentence-level models are the best direct assessment Pearson's ρ for both bilingual and multilingual models, as well as the best direct assessment RMSE for the bilingual model.

Results show that our baselines and final submissions largely outperform the organizer's baselines on the four language pairs, while our final submissions reach higher source and target token-level performances compared to our baselines. Except for the DE–ZH pair, our final submissions are outperforming our baselines on the sentence-level Pearson's ρ evaluation. Because the main objec-

Lang.	Model	Source Token AUC	Source Token AP	Source Token top-K R	Target Token AUC	Target Token AP	Target Token top-K R	Sentence Pearson's ρ
ET–EN	Random baseline	0.488	0.338	0.193	0.496	0.358	0.247	-0.029
	Official baseline 1	0.545	0.440	0.309	0.624	0.536	0.426	0.772
	Official baseline 2	0.535	0.370	0.231	0.616	0.441	0.339	0.494
	Our baseline	0.926	0.848	0.761	0.887	0.808	0.714	0.793
	Our submission	**0.932**	**0.852**	**0.771**	**0.896**	**0.824**	**0.734**	**0.845**
RO–EN	Random baseline	0.501	0.281	0.149	0.515	0.312	0.188	0.017
	Official baseline 1	0.478	0.351	0.243	0.635	0.523	0.415	0.899
	Official baseline 2	0.535	0.293	0.148	0.667	0.536	0.437	0.695
	Our baseline	0.937	0.826	0.727	0.942	0.860	0.770	0.855
	Our submission	**0.947**	**0.851**	**0.752**	**0.946**	**0.869**	**0.778**	**0.918**
DE–ZH	Random baseline	0.499	0.300	0.172	0.495	0.293	0.172	0.000
	Official baseline 1	0.486	0.317	0.196	0.461	0.271	0.145	**0.335**
	Official baseline 2	0.474	0.288	0.158	0.545	0.333	0.220	0.176
	Our submission	**0.847**	**0.645**	**0.509**	**0.849**	**0.679**	**0.571**	0.286
RU–DE	Random baseline	0.506	0.340	0.238	0.494	0.309	0.217	-0.017
	Official baseline 1	0.535	0.427	0.320	0.403	0.263	0.165	0.498
	Official baseline 2	0.522	0.356	0.261	0.523	0.329	0.227	0.252
	Our submission	**0.922**	**0.804**	**0.709**	**0.927**	**0.829**	**0.736**	**0.679**

Table 3: Official test results of the *Eval4NLP* 2021 shared task, according to three metrics for source and target token-level QE (AUC, AP and Recall at top-K), and one metric for sentence-level QE (Pearson's ρ).

tives of the shared task was token-level evaluation, we did not focus on improving the sentence-level scores. We assume that further improvements are achievable on this aspect of QE. Additionally, due to the lack of validation sets for the zero-shot language pairs, we could not try to improve over a baseline and thus only provided a unique and final submission. Note that we did not use the official word-level training data at all, neither during pretraining nor during finetuning of our models. Only the provided validation set was used for monitoring purposes.

Lang.	Model	Source Token AUC	Source Token AP	Target Token AUC	Target Token AP
ET–EN	Submission	0.876	0.781	0.904	0.843
	- Ensemble	0.869	0.773	0.898	0.831
	- Bilingual	0.869	0.771	0.898	0.831
	- Finetuning	0.856	0.752	0.875	0.791
	- Pretraining	0.633	0.515	0.631	0.513
RO–EN	Submission	0.928	0.860	0.950	0.891
	- Ensemble	0.918	0.843	0.941	0.873
	- Bilingual	0.916	0.839	0.937	0.866
	- Finetuning	0.903	0.815	0.925	0.835
	- Pretraining	0.582	0.350	0.573	0.417

Table 4: Results of the ablation study on non zero-shot pairs obtained on the validation set for token-level QE.

In order to evaluate the impact of QE pretraining and finetuning, as well as the difference in performance between ensemble and single models trained using language pair specific (bilingual) and multilingual datasets, we present an ablation study conducted on the word-level QE in Table 4 for the two non zero-shot language pairs. The results obtained without ensemble models are the average of results from individual models. The ablation study shows that individual models (- *Ensemble*) are outperformed by the ensemble (*Submission*), while removing language pair specific training data (- *Bilingual*) has limited impact on performances for ET–EN, which motivates the use of multilingual pretrained models and ensembling. Comparing removing finetuning and QE pretraining, the latter leads to the largest performance drop while the former has a relatively limited impact. This indicates that large amount of synthetic data combined with our approach performs well even without using any of the provided manually annotated data for the shared task.

As an explanation of sentence-level scores predicted by our model, we propose to extract the attention weights computed between the metric embeddings and the contextually encoded input sequences. A few samples extracted from the validation set are presented in Figure 3. We can see on these examples that individual metrics do not correlate with human annotations. However, the multimetric approach, which relies on heads and metrics combination through linear layers, provides a potential error identification method.

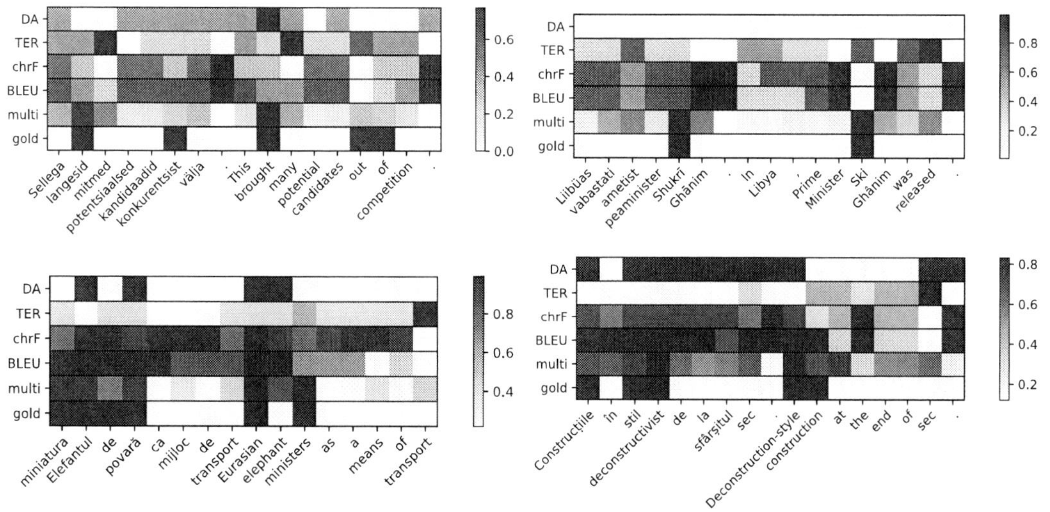

Figure 3: Attention weights computed between individual metric embeddings, namely DA, TER, chrF and BLEU, along with the multimetric approach (see eqn. 6) and the human annotations (noted *gold*). Samples extracted from the ET–EN and RO–EN validation sets (top and bottom respectively).

6 Previous Work

Since the shift of most NLP tasks towards using large pretrained contextual LMs as basis for task-specific finetuning, the research community working on QE for MT moved from a classic two-step process of feature engineering followed by machine learning (Blatz et al., 2004; Quirk, 2004; Specia et al., 2009) to an end-to-end training neural-based paradigm. First attempts in this direction were conducted by Kim et al. (2017) with the predictor-estimator, which inspired further work in using various types of encoders (Wang et al., 2020), enriching the model with features extracted from NMT models (Moura et al., 2020; Fomicheva et al., 2020a) or modifying the pretraining objective of contextual LMs for QE adaptation (Rubino and Sumita, 2020).

More recently, due to the costly nature of data acquisition for supervised learning of QE models, unsupervised approaches were proposed by relying mostly on signals given by NMT systems when translating source sentences (Fomicheva et al., 2020b), the so-called *glass-box* features. Alternatively, when the NMT systems which produced data to perform QE on are not available (i.e. *black-box* setting), relying on large amount of synthetic data for contextual LM continued training prior to finetuning appears to be an effective way to approximate human judgments of translation quality (Lee, 2020; Tuan et al., 2021).

7 Conclusion

This paper presented a novel QE architecture for unsupervised token-level quality prediction providing sentence-level explainable decisions from the model. We implemented a metric embeddings and attention mechanism on top of a widely used pretrained contextual LM, allowing to add metrics during finetuning and enabling high performance QE both at the levels of token and sentence. This extensible framework was shown to produce results on par or outperforming state-of-the-art QE approaches without relying on human-produced token-level annotations, which could be approximated with the use of relatively cost-effective synthetic data and automatic metrics. Our pivot-based translation approach also tackled a recurrent issue in MT when parallel data are scarce and final results for zero-shot language pairs validated this method.

Acknowledgements

We would like to thank the reviewers for their insightful comments and suggestions. A part of this work was conducted under the commissioned research program "Research and Development of Advanced Multilingual Translation Technology" in the "R&D Project for Information and Communications Technology (JPMI00316)" of the Ministry of Internal Affairs and Communications (MIC), Japan, and supported by JSPS KAKENHI grant numbers 20K19879 and 19H05660.

References

John Blatz, Erin Fitzgerald, George Foster, Simona Gandrabur, Cyril Goutte, Alex Kulesza, Alberto Sanchis, and Nicola Ueffing. 2004. Confidence Estimation for Machine Translation. In *Proceedings of the 20th International Conference on Computational Linguistics*, pages 315–321. International Committee on Computational Linguistics.

Peter F Brown, Stephen A Della Pietra, Vincent J Della Pietra, and Robert L Mercer. 1993. The Mathematics of Statistical Machine Translation: Parameter Estimation. *Computational linguistics*, 19(2):263–311.

Alexis Conneau, Kartikay Khandelwal, Naman Goyal, Vishrav Chaudhary, Guillaume Wenzek, Francisco Guzmán, Edouard Grave, Myle Ott, Luke Zettlemoyer, and Veselin Stoyanov. 2020. Unsupervised Cross-lingual Representation Learning at Scale. In *Proceedings of the 58th Annual Meeting of the Association for Computational Linguistics*, pages 8440–8451. Association for Computational Linguistics.

Alexis Conneau and Guillaume Lample. 2019. Cross-lingual Language Model Pretraining. In *Advances in Neural Information Processing Systems*, pages 7057–7067. Curran Associates, Inc.

Jacob Devlin, Ming-Wei Chang, Kenton Lee, and Kristina Toutanova. 2019. BERT: Pre-training of Deep Bidirectional Transformers for Language Understanding. In *Proceedings of the 2019 Conference of the North American Chapter of the Association for Computational Linguistics: Human Language Technologies, Volume 1 (Long and Short Papers)*, pages 4171–4186. Association for Computational Linguistics.

Chris Dyer, Victor Chahuneau, and Noah A. Smith. 2013. A Simple, Fast, and Effective Reparameterization of IBM Model 2. In *Proceedings of the 2013 Conference of the North American Chapter of the Association for Computational Linguistics: Human Language Technologies*, pages 644–648. Association for Computational Linguistics.

Marina Fomicheva, Piyawat Lertvittayakumjorn, Wei Zhao, Steffen Eger, and Yang Gao. 2021. The eval4nlp shared task on explainable quality estimation: Overview and results. In *Proceedings of the 2nd Workshop on Evaluation and Comparison of NLP Systems*.

Marina Fomicheva, Shuo Sun, Lisa Yankovskaya, Frédéric Blain, Vishrav Chaudhary, Mark Fishel, Francisco Guzmán, and Lucia Specia. 2020a. BERGAMOT-LATTE Submissions for the WMT20 Quality Estimation Shared Task. In *Proceedings of the Fifth Conference on Machine Translation*, pages 1010–1017. Association for Computational Linguistics.

Marina Fomicheva, Shuo Sun, Lisa Yankovskaya, Frédéric Blain, Francisco Guzmán, Mark Fishel, Nikolaos Aletras, Vishrav Chaudhary, and Lucia Specia. 2020b. Unsupervised Quality Estimation for Neural Machine Translation. *Transactions of the Association for Computational Linguistics*, 8:539–555.

Erick Fonseca, Lisa Yankovskaya, André F. T. Martins, Mark Fishel, and Christian Federmann. 2019. Findings of the WMT 2019 Shared Tasks on Quality Estimation. In *Proceedings of the Fourth Conference on Machine Translation (Volume 3: Shared Task Papers, Day 2)*, pages 1–12, Florence, Italy. Association for Computational Linguistics.

Yvette Graham, Timothy Baldwin, Alistair Moffat, and Justin Zobel. 2013. Continuous Measurement Scales in Human Evaluation of Machine Translation. In *Proceedings of the 7th Linguistic Annotation Workshop and Interoperability with Discourse*, pages 33–41. Association for Computational Linguistics.

Marcin Junczys-Dowmunt, Roman Grundkiewicz, Tomasz Dwojak, Hieu Hoang, Kenneth Heafield, Tom Neckermann, Frank Seide, Ulrich Germann, Alham Fikri Aji, Nikolay Bogoychev, et al. 2018. Marian: Fast Neural Machine Translation in C++. In *Proceedings of ACL 2018, System Demonstrations*, pages 116–121. Association for Computational Linguistics.

Fábio Kepler, Jonay Trénous, Marcos Treviso, Miguel Vera, António Góis, M Amin Farajian, António V Lopes, and André FT Martins. 2019. Unbabel's Participation in the WMT19 Translation Quality Estimation Shared Task. In *Proceedings of the Fourth Conference on Machine Translation (Volume 3: Shared Task Papers, Day 2)*, pages 80–86. Association for Computational Linguistics.

Hyun Kim, Jong-Hyeok Lee, and Seung-Hoon Na. 2017. Predictor-Estimator using Multilevel Task Learning with Stack Propagation for Neural Quality Estimation. In *Proceedings of the Second Conference on Machine Translation*, pages 562–568. Association for Computational Linguistics.

Dongjun Lee. 2020. Two-Phase Cross-Lingual Language Model Fine-Tuning for Machine Translation Quality Estimation. In *Proceedings of the Fifth Conference on Machine Translation*, pages 1024–1028. Association for Computational Linguistics.

Yinhan Liu, Jiatao Gu, Naman Goyal, Xian Li, Sergey Edunov, Marjan Ghazvininejad, Mike Lewis, and Luke Zettlemoyer. 2020. Multilingual Denoising Pre-training for Neural Machine Translation. *Transactions of the Association for Computational Linguistics*, 8:726–742.

Ilya Loshchilov and Frank Hutter. 2019. Decoupled Weight Decay Regularization. In *Proceedings of the Seventh International Conference on Learning Representations*.

Scott M Lundberg and Su-In Lee. 2017. A Unified Approach to Interpreting Model Predictions. In I. Guyon, U. V. Luxburg, S. Bengio, H. Wallach, R. Fergus, S. Vishwanathan, and R. Garnett, editors, *Advances in Neural Information Processing Systems 30*, pages 4765–4774. Curran Associates, Inc.

João Moura, miguel vera, Daan van Stigt, Fabio Kepler, and André F. T. Martins. 2020. IST-Unbabel Participation in the WMT20 Quality Estimation Shared Task. In *Proceedings of the Fifth Conference on Machine Translation*, pages 1029–1036. Association for Computational Linguistics.

Myle Ott, Sergey Edunov, Alexei Baevski, Angela Fan, Sam Gross, Nathan Ng, David Grangier, and Michael Auli. 2019. fairseq: A Fast, Extensible Toolkit for Sequence Modeling. In *Proceedings of the 2019 Conference of the North American Chapter of the Association for Computational Linguistics (Demonstrations)*, pages 48–53. Association for Computational Linguistics.

Kishore Papineni, Salim Roukos, Todd Ward, and Wei-Jing Zhu. 2002. BLEU: A Method for Automatic Evaluation of Machine Translation. In *Proceedings of ACL*, pages 311–318. Association for Computational Linguistics.

Adam Paszke, Sam Gross, Francisco Massa, Adam Lerer, James Bradbury, Gregory Chanan, Trevor Killeen, Zeming Lin, Natalia Gimelshein, Luca Antiga, et al. 2019. PyTorch: An Imperative Style, High-Performance Deep Learning Library. In *Advances in Neural Information Processing Systems*, pages 8026–8037. Curran Associates, Inc.

Maja Popović. 2016. chrF Deconstructed: β Parameters and n-gram Weights. In *Proceedings of the First Conference on Machine Translation*, pages 499–504. Association for Computational Linguistics.

Christopher Quirk. 2004. Training a Sentence-Level Machine Translation Confidence Measure. In *Proceedings of the Fourth International Conference on Language Resources and Evaluation*, pages 825–828. European Language Resources Association (ELRA).

Tharindu Ranasinghe, Constantin Orasan, and Ruslan Mitkov. 2020a. TransQuest at WMT2020: Sentence-Level Direct Assessment. In *Proceedings of the Fifth Conference on Machine Translation*, pages 1049–1055. Association for Computational Linguistics.

Tharindu Ranasinghe, Constantin Orasan, and Ruslan Mitkov. 2020b. TransQuest: Translation Quality Estimation with Cross-lingual Transformers. In *Proceedings of the 28th International Conference on Computational Linguistics*, pages 5070–5081. International Committee on Computational Linguistics.

Marek Rei and Anders Søgaard. 2018. Zero-shot sequence labeling: Transferring knowledge from sentences to tokens. In *Proceedings of the 2018 Conference of the North American Chapter of the Association for Computational Linguistics: Human Language Technologies, Volume 1 (Long Papers)*, pages 293–302. Association for Computational Linguistics.

Marco Tulio Ribeiro, Sameer Singh, and Carlos Guestrin. 2016. "Why Should I Trust You?" Explaining the Predictions of Any Classifier. In *Proceedings of the 22nd ACM SIGKDD International Conference on Knowledge Discovery and Data Mining*, pages 1135–1144. Association for Computing Machinery.

Raphael Rubino. 2020. NICT Kyoto Submission for the WMT'20 Quality Estimation Task: Intermediate Training for Domain and Task Adaptation. In *Proceedings of the Fifth Conference on Machine Translation*, pages 1042–1048. Association for Computational Linguistics.

Raphael Rubino and Eiichiro Sumita. 2020. Intermediate Self-supervised Learning for Machine Translation Quality Estimation. In *Proceedings of the 28th International Conference on Computational Linguistics*, pages 4355–4360. International Committee on Computational Linguistics.

Rico Sennrich, Barry Haddow, and Alexandra Birch. 2016. Neural Machine Translation of Rare Words with Subword Units. In *Proceedings of the 54th Annual Meeting of the Association for Computational Linguistics (Volume 1: Long Papers)*, pages 1715–1725. Association for Computational Linguistics.

Matthew Snover, Bonnie Dorr, Richard Schwartz, Linnea Micciulla, and John Makhoul. 2006. A Study of Translation Edit Rate with Targeted Human Annotation. In *Proceedings of the 7th Conference of the Association for Machine Translation in the Americas: Technical Papers*, pages 223–231. Association for Machine Translation in the Americas.

Lucia Specia, Frédéric Blain, Marina Fomicheva, Erick Fonseca, Vishrav Chaudhary, Francisco Guzmán, and André F. T. Martins. 2020. Findings of the WMT 2020 Shared Task on Quality Estimation. In *Proceedings of the Fifth Conference on Machine Translation*, pages 743–764. Association for Computational Linguistics.

Lucia Specia, Nicola Cancedda, Marc Dymetman, Marco Turchi, and Nello Cristianini. 2009. Estimating the Sentence-Level Quality of Machine Translation Systems. In *Proceedings of the 13th Annual conference of the European Association for Machine Translation*, pages 28–35. European Association for Machine Translation.

Shuo Sun, Francisco Guzmán, and Lucia Specia. 2020. Are we Estimating or Guesstimating Translation Quality? In *Proceedings of the 58th Annual Meeting of the Association for Computational Linguistics*, pages 6262–6267. Association for Computational Linguistics.

Yuqing Tang, Chau Tran, Xian Li, Peng-Jen Chen, Naman Goyal, Vishrav Chaudhary, Jiatao Gu, and Angela Fan. 2020. Multilingual Translation with Extensible Multilingual Pretraining and Finetuning. *arXiv preprint arXiv:2008.00401*.

Jörg Tiedemann. 2016. OPUS – Parallel Corpora for Everyone. In *Proceedings of the 19th Annual Conference of the European Association for Machine Translation: Projects/Products*. Baltic Journal of Modern Computing.

Yi-Lin Tuan, Ahmed El-Kishky, Adithya Renduchintala, Vishrav Chaudhary, Francisco Guzmán, and Lucia Specia. 2021. Quality Estimation without Human-labeled Data. In *Proceedings of the 16th Conference of the European Chapter of the Association for Computational Linguistics: Main Volume*, pages 619–625. Association for Computational Linguistics.

Ashish Vaswani, Noam Shazeer, Niki Parmar, Jakob Uszkoreit, Llion Jones, Aidan N Gomez, Łukasz Kaiser, and Illia Polosukhin. 2017. Attention is All You Need. In *Advances in Neural Information Processing Systems*, pages 5998–6008. Curran Associates, Inc.

Minghan Wang, Hao Yang, Hengchao Shang, Daimeng Wei, Jiaxin Guo, Lizhi Lei, Ying Qin, Shimin Tao, Shiliang Sun, Yimeng Chen, et al. 2020. HW-TSC's Participation at WMT 2020 Quality Estimation Shared Task. In *Proceedings of the Fifth Conference on Machine Translation*, pages 1056–1061. Association for Computational Linguistics.

Thomas Wolf, Lysandre Debut, Victor Sanh, Julien Chaumond, Clement Delangue, Anthony Moi, Pierric Cistac, Tim Rault, Remi Louf, Morgan Funtowicz, Joe Davison, Sam Shleifer, Patrick von Platen, Clara Ma, Yacine Jernite, Julien Plu, Canwen Xu, Teven Le Scao, Sylvain Gugger, Mariama Drame, Quentin Lhoest, and Alexander Rush. 2020. Transformers: State-of-the-Art Natural Language Processing. In *Proceedings of the 2020 Conference on Empirical Methods in Natural Language Processing: System Demonstrations*, pages 38–45. Association for Computational Linguistics.

Wei Zhao, Goran Glavaš, Maxime Peyrard, Yang Gao, Robert West, and Steffen Eger. 2020. On the Limitations of Cross-lingual Encoders as Exposed by Reference-Free Machine Translation Evaluation. In *Proceedings of the 58th Annual Meeting of the Association for Computational Linguistics*, pages 1656–1671. Association for Computational Linguistics.

Reference-Free Word- and Sentence-Level Translation Evaluation with Token-Matching Metrics

Christoph Wolfgang Leiter
CS Department, TU Darmstadt
christoph.leiter@stud.tu-darmstadt.de

Abstract

Many modern machine translation evaluation metrics like BERTScore, BLEURT, COMET, MonoTransquest or XMoverScore are based on black-box language models. Hence, it is difficult to explain why these metrics return certain scores. This year's Eval4NLP shared task tackles this challenge by searching for methods that can extract feature importance scores that correlate well with human word-level error annotations. In this paper we show that unsupervised metrics that are based on token-matching can intrinsically provide such scores. The submitted system interprets the similarities of the contextualized word-embeddings that are used to compute (X)BERTScore as word-level importance scores. We make our code available[1].

1 Introduction

In recent years, machine translation evaluation metrics constantly improved in their correlation with human judgements (e.g. Mathur et al., 2020; Specia et al., 2020). However, this improvement comes at a loss of understandability. Early metrics such as BLEU (Papineni et al., 2002) and METEOR (Lavie et al., 2004; Banerjee and Lavie, 2005) follow a clearly defined algorithm without learnable weights. Therefore, these metrics are interpretable by design and could even be computed per hand. Newer metrics such BERTScore (Zhang et al., 2020), BLEURT (Sellam et al., 2020), COMET (Rei et al., 2020a), MonoTransquest (Ranasinghe et al., 2020a,b), MoverScore (Zhao et al., 2019) or XMoverScore (Zhao et al., 2020) instead leverage transformer (Vaswani et al., 2017) based language models. As these base their predictions on thousands of learned parameters, they are too complex to understand without employing further techniques. Such techniques that aim to support the understanding of black-box models are the scope of XAI (eXplainable Artificial Intelligence) (e.g. Carvalho et al., 2019; Bodria et al., 2021).

This year's Eval4NLP shared task (Fomicheva et al., 2021a) considers to what extend XAI techniques extract feature importance scores from metrics that correlate with word-level error annotations. Some embedding based metrics, such as MoverScore, XMoverScore and BERTScore can be categorized as *unsupervised matching* (Yuan et al., 2021). These metrics are unsupervised, as they are not fine-tuned on human annotated translation scores. And they perform *matching*, as the sentence-level score is calculated based on how well each token in one sentence matches to tokens in the other sentence.

This work evaluates the usage of the token-level matches of BERTScore and XMoverScore as feature-importance explanation of the sentence-level score. It was conducted as part of a master thesis by Leiter (2021).

2 Related Work

This system paper is related to work in the fields of machine translation evaluation metrics and explainable artificial intelligence.

2.1 Metrics

A large number of metrics has been proposed to grade the quality of machine translations (e.g. Mathur et al., 2020; Specia et al., 2020). Reference-based metrics grade machine translations based on one or more reference translations. Reference-free metrics grade machine translations based on the source sentence. Due to the structure of the shared task this paper considers reference-free metrics, in specific BERTScore (Zhang et al., 2020) with multilingual language embeddings (reference-free usage is proposed by Zhou et al., 2020; Song et al., 2021) and XMoverScore (Zhao et al., 2020). To differentiate, we will refer to the reference-free BERTScore

[1] https://github.com/Gringham/WordAndSentScoresFromTokenMatching

Proceedings of the 58th Annual Meeting of the Association for Computational Linguistics, pages 157–164

https://doi.org/10.26615/978-954-452-056-4_016

as *XBERTScore*. Other reference-free metrics are for example MonoTransquest (Ranasinghe et al., 2020a,b) and COMET for quality estimation (Rei et al., 2020b). Many reference-free metrics have been enabled by the pre-training of multilingual language models on large scale datasets. Examples are multilingual BERT (Devlin et al., 2018) and XLM-Roberta (Conneau et al., 2020). The discussed metrics produce a single score per translation. In contrast, word-level metrics such as the metrics by Lee (2020) and Ranasinghe et al. (2021) predict word-level errors. Word-level metrics are closely related to the goal of the Eval4NLP shared task, as the extracted feature importance scores are evaluated with word-level error annotations (Fomicheva et al., 2021a).

2.2 Explainable Artificial Intelligence

As summarized in related surveys (e.g. Carvalho et al., 2019; Lertvittayakumjorn and Toni, 2021; Linardatos et al., 2021), explainability techniques can be categorized along several dimensions. Intrinsic (self-explaining) models explain their output during the original computation, while post-hoc methods are applied afterwards. Model-agnostic techniques can be applied to any model, while model-specific techniques are specific to certain architectures. Also, global methods try to explain a model as a whole, while local methods give insights into single pairs of input/output.

The goal of the Eval4NLP shared task is the extraction of feature importance scores as word-level error indications (Fomicheva et al., 2021a), i.e. each input feature (here tokens) should be assigned a score of how important it is for a predicted output. As these are assigned per input, they can be counted towards the local techniques. Further, the methods proposed in this paper are intrinsic and model specific. Note that even though the model itself produces the explanation, i.e. a token level output, the approaches we present do not explain the internal workings of the underlying language model.

Other model-specific post-hoc feature importance methods are, for example, Integrated Gradients (Sundararajan et al., 2017), DiffMask (De Cao et al., 2020) and (Guan et al., 2019). Model-agnostic post-hoc feature importance methods are for example LIME (Ribeiro et al., 2016), SHAP (Lundberg and Lee, 2017) and Input Marginalization (Kim et al., 2020). Fomicheva et al. (2021b) present the first evaluation of explainabilitiy techniques in the same context as the shared task.

3 Feature Importance from Token-Matching

In this section we describe the extraction of word-level importance scores from XBERTScore and XMoverScore. In specific, we consider that words that are well aligned between source and translation are important for the sentence-level score and are likely to be correct translations. If a word does not align well, it is likely to be an error. Hence, the maximal similarity (or minimal dissimilarity) of each word between source and translation can be interpreted as word-level (importance) score. We choose $x = (x_1, ..., x_n)$ to represent a source sentence and $y = (y_1, ..., y_m)$ to represent a translation where x_i and y_j refer to arbitrary token embeddings in x and y.

3.1 XBERTScore

XBERTScore computes a reference-free sentence score as follows (Zhang et al., 2020; Zhou et al., 2020; Song et al., 2021):

1. A multilingual pre-trained transformer model is chosen and contextualized embeddings are extracted for each word in translation and source. These are obtained by performing a forward pass and extracting the hidden states at a layer of choice.

2. A matrix $S \in \mathbb{R}^{n \times m}$ of cosine similarities between each embedding of source and translation is constructed. In other words, entries in S are computed as $S_{ij} = \frac{x_i^T y_j}{||x_i|| \, ||y_j||}$.

3. Two vectors x_{max} and y_{max} are determined. x_{max} contains the maximum similarity of each token in x to tokens in y:

   $$x_{max} = (\max\ S_{1,*}, ..., \max\ S_{n,*})$$

   Respectively y_{max} contains the maximum similarity to each token in y to tokens in x:

   $$y_{max} = (\max\ S_{*,1}, ..., \max\ S_{*,m})$$

4. Zhang et al. (2020) propose three different scores: R_{BERT}, P_{BERT} and F_{BERT}. R_{BERT} computes the recall $R_{BERT} = mean(x_{max})$. P_{BERT} computes the precision $P_{BERT} = mean(y_{max})$. The F_{BERT}-Score is computed as $2\frac{P_{BERT} * R_{BERT}}{P_{BERT} + R_{BERT}}$.

System	Hypothesis AUC	AP	RtopK	Source AUC	AP	RtopK	Pearson
XBERTScore(XLMR)	0.741	0.600	0.485	0.734	0.579	0.448	0.520
XBERTScore(XLMR$_{NLI1}$)	0.772	0.640	0.523	0.753	0.606	0.475	0.575
XBERTScore(XLMR$_{NLI2}$)	0.757	0.628	0.518	0.747	0.597	0.464	0.575
XBERTScore(XLMR$_{Ensemble}$)	0.778	0.655	0.540	0.755	0.608	**0.481**	**0.582**
XBERTScore(mBERT)	0.673	0.506	0.396	0.683	0.514	0.377	0.303
XBERTScore(mBART)	0.648	0.504	0.392	0.664	0.503	0.378	0.255
XMoverScore(mBERT)	0.676	0.528	0.425	0.660	0.503	0.372	0.530
XMoverScore(mBERT)-KEEP	0.746	0.608	0.497	0.731	0.571	0.432	0.52
XMoverScore(XLMR$_{Ensemble}$)-KEEP	**0.781**	**0.658**	**0.544**	**0.759**	**0.609**	0.479	0.543
XMoverScore + SHAP (Baseline)	0.593	0.444	0.338	0.513	0.394	0.262	0.415

Table 1: Results on the et-en dev set of the shared task. Metrics for word level outputs are Area Under the Curve, Average Precision and Recall at top K. The sentence-level correlation to human judgements is denoted as Pearson.

System	Hypothesis AUC	AP	RtopK	Source AUC	AP	RtopK	Pearson
XBERTScore(XLMR)	0.818	0.685	0.507	0.779	0.599	0.466	0.742
XBERTScore(XLMR$_{NLI1}$)	0.837	0.710	0.584	0.798	0.632	0.514	0.765
XBERTScore(XLMR$_{NLI2}$)	0.828	0.705	0.589	0.801	**0.658**	**0.531**	0.763
XBERTScore(XLMR$_{Ensemble}$)	**0.848**	**0.730**	**0.615**	**0.808**	0.652	0.525	**0.770**
XBERTScore(mBERT)	0.777	0.613	0.491	0.749	0.567	0.433	0.645
XBERTScore(mBART)	0.738	0.587	0.473	0.738	0.591	0.474	0.556
XMoverScore(mBERT)	0.719	0.562	0.450	0.705	0.537	0.427	0.634
XMoverScore(mBERT)-KEEP	0.790	0.636	0.505	0.759	0.584	0.461	0.623
XMoverScore(XLMR$_{Ensemble}$)-KEEP	0.842	0.721	0.607	0.794	0.624	0.497	0.725
XMoverScore + SHAP (Baseline)	0.641	0.462	0.341	0.541	0.384	0.265	0.638

Table 2: Results on the ro-en dev set of the shared task. Metrics for word level outputs are Area Under the Curve, Average Precision and Recall at top K. The sentence-level correlation to human judgements is denoted as Pearson.

5. They describe further steps such as idf-weighting and rescaling of scores, which we don't apply in this paper. Idf-weighting over many sentences potentially increases the sentence level scores.

Zhang et al. (2020) compute R_{BERT} and P_{BERT} from embeddings in a single formula. In above's description we describe the construction of the matrix S and the vectors x_{max} and y_{max} as extra steps, as we interpret these vectors as token-level importance scores. To explain, we treat x_{max_i} as the importance score for embedding x_i in x (and the token at the i-th position of x), the same applying for y.

Many language-models use sub-word tokenization (e.g. Sentencepiece (Kudo and Richardson, 2018)), so that the importance-scores are at a sub-word level. To receive word-level scores, we parse the scored tokens to be aligned with the input sentences. Multiple scores that belong to a single word are averaged. If a token did not receive a score, e.g. as punctuation was dropped (see XMoverScore(mBERT) in section 4), we assign the score of the previous token.

To further improve the correlation to word-level error annotations, we ensemble word-level and sentence-level (F_{BERT}) scores by summing them across different models:

$$F_{ensemble} = \sum_{i=1}^{z} F_{BERT_i}$$

$$x_{max_{ensemble}} = \sum_{i=1}^{z} x_{max_i}$$

Here, F_{BERT_i} denotes the XBERTScore returned by using the i-th of z models to extract contextualized embeddings and $x_{max_{ensemble}}$ describes the element-wise sum of respective x_{max} vectors. Again, $x_{max_{ensemble_i}}$ is treated as importance score for embedding x_i in x. $y_{max_{ensemble}}$ is calculated analogous.

In section 4, the F-Score is evaluated in terms of its pearson correlation to sentence-level scores. $x_{max_{ensemble}}$ is evaluated in terms of its correlation to word-level error annotations of the source and $y_{max_{ensemble}}$ is evaluated in terms of its correlation to word-level error annotations of the hypothesis.

3.2 XMoverScore

Zhao et al. (2020) propose XMoverScore (XMS), a metric that matches n-grams of tokens based on the word mover's distance (WMD) (Kusner et al., 2015). In the case of unigrams, they first compute a matrix $C \in \mathbb{R}^{n \times m}$, with $C_{ij} = ||x_i - y_j||_2$. Then, based on C, they minimize the WMD to determine the optimal alignment between the two sentences.

Using the same notation as for XBERTScore, we obtain token-level scores as follows:

$$x_{min} = (\min\ C_{1,*}, ..., \min\ C_{n,*})$$

$$y_{min} = (\min\ C_{*,1}, ..., \min\ C_{*,m})$$

As for XBERTScore, we obtain word-level scores by aligning the token-level scores based on the input sentences. Again, word- and sentence-level scores can be ensembled via summation.

Zhao et al. (2020) further improve the sentence-level score by remapping the token-embeddings and employing a target-side language model. The remapping assumes that tokens in the cross-lingual embedding space are not fully aligned between languages. They propose two techniques for mitigation. Linear cross-lingual projection (CLP) learns a projection matrix that projects tokens of the source language such that the distance to tokens of the target language is minimized. Universal language mismatch-direction (UMD) determines a global direction along which the embeddings of two languages are misaligned. Then the projection along this direction is subtracted form each embedding. Both techniques use embeddings that were aligned using small parallel corpora. Zhao et al. (2020) employ the target-side language model as an additional measure of fluency of translations. In our experiments we do not use this model, as it might lower the degree to which the word-level scores explain the sentence-level scores.

3.3 Inversion

In the Eval4NLP shared task errors are considered as important for the sentence-level score (Fomicheva et al., 2021a), i.e. they should receive a higher feature-importance than correct words. Hence, we invert the word-level scores and use $-x_{max}$ and $-y_{max}$ for XBERTScore (likewise $-x_{min}$ and $-y_{min}$ for XMoverScore).

4 Experiment Setup

We calculate word- and sentence- level scores for the dev sets[2] of the Eval4NLP shared task (Fomicheva et al., 2021a), which are a subset of the MLQE-PE corpus by Fomicheva et al. (2020b,a). The organizers provide 1000 samples for the *ro-en* (Romanian-English) and *et-en* (Estonian-English) language pairs each. For every sample they provide a source sentence, a translation, a sentence-level ground truth score and word-level ground truth labels for source and translation. On the word-level they label a word with 1 if it is erroneous and 0 if it is correct.

Zhao et al. (2019) show that the usage of language models fine-tuned for Natural Language Inference (NLI) improves the results of MoverScore. Therefore, we evaluate models fine-tuned for NLI for XBertScore and XMoverScore. The results of the following configurations are reported:

- **XBERTScore(XLMR):** XBERTScore using the pre-trained XLMR-large model (Conneau et al., 2020).
- **XBERTScore(XLMR$_{NLI1}$):** XBERTScore using an XLMR-large model fine-tuned on XNLI (Conneau et al., 2018) from the Huggingface model hub[3].
- **XBERTScore(XLMR$_{NLI2}$):** XBERTScore using another XLMR-large model fine-tuned on XNLI (Conneau et al., 2018) and ANLI (Nie et al., 2020) from the Huggingface model hub[4].
- **XBERTScore(XLMR$_{Ensemble}$):** An ensemble version of the three models above that uses the ensembling step described in section 3.1.
- **XBERTScore(mBERT):** XBERTScore using multilingual BERT (Devlin et al., 2018) to extract contextualized embeddings.

[2] https://github.com/eval4nlp/SharedTask2021/tree/main/data/dev

[3] https://huggingface.co/joeddav/xlm-roberta-large-xnli

[4] https://huggingface.co/vicgalle/xlm-roberta-large-xnli-anli

- **XBERTScore(mBART):** XBERTScore using mBart-large 50 many-to-many (Tang et al., 2020).

- **XMoverScore(mBERT):** We report the scores for XMS[5] with unigrams and CLP remapping mode. XMS is based on the 12th layer of multilingual BERT.

- **XMoverScore(mBERT)-KEEP:** The original implementation of XMS by Zhao et al. (2020) drops embeddings of sub-words that are not the start of a word as well as punctuation. This configuration keeps them during the computation.

- **XMoverScore(XLMR$_{Ensemble}$)-KEEP:** XMS using the ensemble configuration described for XBERTScore above. Additionally, CLP and UMD mappings were trained on 30k sentences for each ensembled model and respective layer. The scores were summed across CLP and UMD mappings. Embeddings of punctuation and sub-words were kept.

- **XMoverScore+SHAP (Baseline):** A baseline copied from the shared task (Fomicheva et al., 2021a). The output score of XMS is explained with SHAP (Lundberg and Lee, 2017).

The result of (X)BERTScore by Zhang et al. (2020) depends on the choice of the layer to extract embeddings from. For the models already included in their library[6], we use the layers they tested perform best in a reference-based setting. For XLMR-NLI1 we choose layer 16 and for XMLR-NLI2 we choose layer 17, which we determined to perform best on a small subset of *et-en* data from the MLQE-PE corpus. Appendix A lists hashes produced by the BERTScore library that summarize the configurations. For XMoverScore(XLMR$_{Ensemble}$)-KEEP we choose the same layers.

The word-level scores are evaluated with Area Under the Curve (AUC), Recall at top K (RtopK) and Average Precision (AP) using the implementation by the organizers of the Eval4NLP shared task[7].

[5]https://github.com/AIPHES/ACL20-Reference-Free-MT-Evaluation/blob/master/score_utils.py

[6]https://github.com/Tiiiger/bert_score

[7]https://github.com/eval4nlp/SharedTask2021/blob/main/scripts/evaluate.py

5 Results

Table 1 and 2 show the results for the different configurations and language pairs. Metrics based on XLMR-large achieve the highest correlations. This is expected as it uses 24 layers in contrast to mBERT and mBART (encoder) with 12 layers. Also, the models fine-tuned for NLI perform better than the pre-trained XLMR model. Amongst all configurations, the XLMR-Ensembles perform best. Only for the AP and RtopK of the source in ro-en a single NLI model performed better. XMoverScore(mBERT)-KEEP achieves higher word-level scores than XBERTScore(mBERT), which indicates the successfulness of the applied remapping of embeddings. XMoverScore(mBERT) is worse at the word-level, as the scores of the dropped punctuation are inferred from the previous token. Further, XMoverScore(mBERT) being worse than XBERTScore(mBERT) on sentence-level might be caused by XMS using the 12th layer instead of the 9th. XMoverScore(XLMR$_{Ensemble}$)-KEEP, which also uses remappings, achieves slightly higher word-level correlations than XBERTScore(mBERT) for et-en but not for ro-en. This indicates that the applied remapping techniques are less effective for XLMR-large. Another interesting observation is that the sentence-level scores of XBERTScore with mBERT and mBART are much lower than the others for et-en, suggesting a weakness of these embeddings when compared with greedy matching rather than XMS's word mover's distance.

In the test-phase of the shared task we submitted XBERTScore(XLMR$_{Ensemble}$), which achieved its highest rank for the zero-shot language pair *ru-de* (Russian-German) and its lowest rank for *de-zh* (German-Chinese). For the latter one, the sentence scores even had a negative correlation. The cause of this remains to be investigated in the future.

6 Conclusion

In this paper we have evaluated XBERTScore and XMoverScore for word-level error annotations in a reference-free setup. The best reported configurations are based on multiple XLMR models. For future work it might be interesting to apply XLMR models that are remapped with novel cross-lingual alignment techniques. Also, it could be considered to incorporate the token-probabilities of the target-side language model of XMS into the word-level scores.

References

Satanjeev Banerjee and Alon Lavie. 2005. METEOR: An automatic metric for MT evaluation with improved correlation with human judgments. In *Proceedings of the ACL Workshop on Intrinsic and Extrinsic Evaluation Measures for Machine Translation and/or Summarization*, pages 65–72, Ann Arbor, Michigan. Association for Computational Linguistics.

Francesco Bodria, Fosca Giannotti, Riccardo Guidotti, Francesca Naretto, Dino Pedreschi, and Salvatore Rinzivillo. 2021. Benchmarking and survey of explanation methods for black box models.

Diogo V. Carvalho, Eduardo M. Pereira, and Jaime S. Cardoso. 2019. Machine learning interpretability: A survey on methods and metrics. *Electronics*, 8(8).

Alexis Conneau, Kartikay Khandelwal, Naman Goyal, Vishrav Chaudhary, Guillaume Wenzek, Francisco Guzmán, Edouard Grave, Myle Ott, Luke Zettlemoyer, and Veselin Stoyanov. 2020. Unsupervised cross-lingual representation learning at scale. In *Proceedings of the 58th Annual Meeting of the Association for Computational Linguistics*, pages 8440–8451, Online. Association for Computational Linguistics.

Alexis Conneau, Ruty Rinott, Guillaume Lample, Adina Williams, Samuel Bowman, Holger Schwenk, and Veselin Stoyanov. 2018. XNLI: Evaluating cross-lingual sentence representations. In *Proceedings of the 2018 Conference on Empirical Methods in Natural Language Processing*, pages 2475–2485, Brussels, Belgium. Association for Computational Linguistics.

Nicola De Cao, Michael Sejr Schlichtkrull, Wilker Aziz, and Ivan Titov. 2020. How do decisions emerge across layers in neural models? interpretation with differentiable masking. In *Proceedings of the 2020 Conference on Empirical Methods in Natural Language Processing (EMNLP)*, pages 3243–3255, Online. Association for Computational Linguistics.

Jacob Devlin, Ming-Wei Chang, Kenton Lee, and Kristina Toutanova. 2018. BERT: pre-training of deep bidirectional transformers for language understanding. *CoRR*, abs/1810.04805.

Marina Fomicheva, Piyawat Lertvittayakumjorn, Wei Zhao, Steffen Eger, and Yang Gao. 2021a. The eval4nlp shared task on explainable quality estimation: Overview and results. In *Proceedings of the 2nd Workshop on Evaluation and Comparison of NLP Systems*.

Marina Fomicheva, Lucia Specia, and Nikolaos Aletras. 2021b. Translation error detection as rationale extraction.

Marina Fomicheva, Shuo Sun, Erick Fonseca, Frédéric Blain, Vishrav Chaudhary, Francisco Guzmán, Nina Lopatina, Lucia Specia, and André F. T. Martins. 2020a. MLQE-PE: A multilingual quality estimation and post-editing dataset. *arXiv preprint arXiv:2010.04480*.

Marina Fomicheva, Shuo Sun, Lisa Yankovskaya, Frédéric Blain, Francisco Guzmán, Mark Fishel, Nikolaos Aletras, Vishrav Chaudhary, and Lucia Specia. 2020b. Unsupervised quality estimation for neural machine translation. *Transactions of the Association for Computational Linguistics*, 8:539–555.

Chaoyu Guan, Xiting Wang, Quanshi Zhang, Runjin Chen, Di He, and Xing Xie. 2019. Towards a deep and unified understanding of deep neural models in NLP. In *Proceedings of the 36th International Conference on Machine Learning*, volume 97 of *Proceedings of Machine Learning Research*, pages 2454–2463. Pmlr.

Siwon Kim, Jihun Yi, Eunji Kim, and Sungroh Yoon. 2020. Interpretation of NLP models through input marginalization. In *Proceedings of the 2020 Conference on Empirical Methods in Natural Language Processing (EMNLP)*, pages 3154–3167, Online. Association for Computational Linguistics.

Taku Kudo and John Richardson. 2018. SentencePiece: A simple and language independent subword tokenizer and detokenizer for neural text processing. In *Proceedings of the 2018 Conference on Empirical Methods in Natural Language Processing: System Demonstrations*, pages 66–71, Brussels, Belgium. Association for Computational Linguistics.

Matt Kusner, Yu Sun, Nicholas Kolkin, and Kilian Weinberger. 2015. From word embeddings to document distances. In *Proceedings of the 32nd International Conference on Machine Learning*, volume 37 of *Proceedings of Machine Learning Research*, pages 957–966, Lille, France. Pmlr.

Alon Lavie, Kenji Sagae, and Shyamsundar Jayaraman. 2004. The significance of recall in automatic metrics for mt evaluation. In *Machine Translation: From Real Users to Research*, pages 134–143, Berlin, Heidelberg. Springer Berlin Heidelberg.

Dongjun Lee. 2020. Two-phase cross-lingual language model fine-tuning for machine translation quality estimation. In *Proceedings of the Fifth Conference on Machine Translation*, pages 1024–1028, Online. Association for Computational Linguistics.

Christoph Wolfgang Leiter. 2021. Explaining machine translation metrics - application and assessment of explainability techniques in the domain of machine translation evaluation. Unpublished thesis. TU Darmstadt.

Piyawat Lertvittayakumjorn and Francesca Toni. 2021. Explanation-based human debugging of nlp models: A survey. *arXiv preprint arXiv:2104.15135*.

Pantelis Linardatos, Vasilis Papastefanopoulos, and Sotiris Kotsiantis. 2021. Explainable ai: A review of machine learning interpretability methods. *Entropy*, 23(1).

Scott M Lundberg and Su-In Lee. 2017. A unified approach to interpreting model predictions. In *Advances in Neural Information Processing Systems*, volume 30. Curran Associates, Inc.

Nitika Mathur, Johnny Wei, Markus Freitag, Qingsong Ma, and Ondřej Bojar. 2020. Results of the WMT20 metrics shared task. In *Proceedings of the Fifth Conference on Machine Translation*, pages 688–725, Online. Association for Computational Linguistics.

Yixin Nie, Adina Williams, Emily Dinan, Mohit Bansal, Jason Weston, and Douwe Kiela. 2020. Adversarial NLI: A new benchmark for natural language understanding. In *Proceedings of the 58th Annual Meeting of the Association for Computational Linguistics*, pages 4885–4901, Online. Association for Computational Linguistics.

Kishore Papineni, Salim Roukos, Todd Ward, and Wei-Jing Zhu. 2002. Bleu: a method for automatic evaluation of machine translation. In *Proceedings of the 40th Annual Meeting of the Association for Computational Linguistics*, pages 311–318, Philadelphia, Pennsylvania, USA. Association for Computational Linguistics.

Tharindu Ranasinghe, Constantin Orasan, and Ruslan Mitkov. 2020a. TransQuest at WMT2020: Sentence-level direct assessment. In *Proceedings of the Fifth Conference on Machine Translation*, pages 1049–1055, Online. Association for Computational Linguistics.

Tharindu Ranasinghe, Constantin Orasan, and Ruslan Mitkov. 2020b. TransQuest: Translation quality estimation with cross-lingual transformers. In *Proceedings of the 28th International Conference on Computational Linguistics*, pages 5070–5081, Barcelona, Spain (Online). International Committee on Computational Linguistics.

Tharindu Ranasinghe, Constantin Orasan, and Ruslan Mitkov. 2021. An exploratory analysis of multilingual word-level quality estimation with cross-lingual transformers. In *Proceedings of the 59th Annual Meeting of the Association for Computational Linguistics and the 11th International Joint Conference on Natural Language Processing (Volume 2: Short Papers)*, pages 434–440, Online. Association for Computational Linguistics.

Ricardo Rei, Craig Stewart, Ana C Farinha, and Alon Lavie. 2020a. COMET: A neural framework for MT evaluation. In *Proceedings of the 2020 Conference on Empirical Methods in Natural Language Processing (EMNLP)*, pages 2685–2702, Online. Association for Computational Linguistics.

Ricardo Rei, Craig Stewart, Ana C Farinha, and Alon Lavie. 2020b. Unbabel's participation in the WMT20 metrics shared task. In *Proceedings of the Fifth Conference on Machine Translation*, pages 911–920, Online. Association for Computational Linguistics.

Marco Tulio Ribeiro, Sameer Singh, and Carlos Guestrin. 2016. "why should i trust you?": Explaining the predictions of any classifier. In *Proceedings of the 22nd ACM SIGKDD International Conference on Knowledge Discovery and Data Mining*, Kdd '16, page 1135ÔÇô1144, New York, NY, USA. Association for Computing Machinery.

Thibault Sellam, Dipanjan Das, and Ankur Parikh. 2020. BLEURT: Learning robust metrics for text generation. In *Proceedings of the 58th Annual Meeting of the Association for Computational Linguistics*, pages 7881–7892, Online. Association for Computational Linguistics.

Yurun Song, Junchen Zhao, and Lucia Specia. 2021. SentSim: Crosslingual semantic evaluation of machine translation. In *Proceedings of the 2021 Conference of the North American Chapter of the Association for Computational Linguistics: Human Language Technologies*, pages 3143–3156, Online. Association for Computational Linguistics.

Lucia Specia, Frédéric Blain, Marina Fomicheva, Erick Fonseca, Vishrav Chaudhary, Francisco Guzmán, and André F. T. Martins. 2020. Findings of the WMT 2020 shared task on quality estimation. In *Proceedings of the Fifth Conference on Machine Translation*, pages 743–764, Online. Association for Computational Linguistics.

Mukund Sundararajan, Ankur Taly, and Qiqi Yan. 2017. Axiomatic attribution for deep networks. In *Proceedings of the 34th International Conference on Machine Learning - Volume 70*, ICML'17, page 3319–3328. JMLR.org.

Yuqing Tang, Chau Tran, Xian Li, Peng-Jen Chen, Naman Goyal, Vishrav Chaudhary, Jiatao Gu, and Angela Fan. 2020. Multilingual translation with extensible multilingual pretraining and finetuning. *CoRR*, abs/2008.00401.

Ashish Vaswani, Noam Shazeer, Niki Parmar, Jakob Uszkoreit, Llion Jones, Aidan N Gomez, Ł ukasz Kaiser, and Illia Polosukhin. 2017. Attention is all you need. In *Advances in Neural Information Processing Systems*, volume 30. Curran Associates, Inc.

Weizhe Yuan, Graham Neubig, and Pengfei Liu. 2021. Bartscore: Evaluating generated text as text generation.

Tianyi Zhang, Varsha Kishore, Felix Wu, Kilian Q. Weinberger, and Yoav Artzi. 2020. Bertscore: Evaluating text generation with bert. In *International Conference on Learning Representations*.

Wei Zhao, Goran Glavaš, Maxime Peyrard, Yang Gao, Robert West, and Steffen Eger. 2020. On the limitations of cross-lingual encoders as exposed by reference-free machine translation evaluation. In *Proceedings of the 58th Annual Meeting of the Association for Computational Linguistics*, pages 1656–1671, Online. Association for Computational Linguistics.

Wei Zhao, Maxime Peyrard, Fei Liu, Yang Gao, Christian M. Meyer, and Steffen Eger. 2019. MoverScore: Text generation evaluating with contextualized embeddings and earth mover distance. In *Proceedings of the 2019 Conference on Empirical Methods in Natural Language Processing and the 9th International Joint Conference on Natural Language Processing (EMNLP-IJCNLP)*, pages 563–578, Hong Kong, China. Association for Computational Linguistics.

Lei Zhou, Liang Ding, and Koichi Takeda. 2020. Zero-shot translation quality estimation with explicit cross-lingual patterns. In *Proceedings of the Fifth Conference on Machine Translation*, pages 1068–1074, Online. Association for Computational Linguistics.

A BERTScore Hashes

The BERTScore library by Zhang et al. (2020) provides a function to generate hashes of the metric's configuration to allow better reproducibility[8]. Here we list the hashes of the configurations we used:

- **XBERTScore(XLMR):** xlm-roberta-large_L17_no-idf_version=0.3.10(hug_trans=4.4.0)
- **XBERTScore(XLMR_$NLI1$):** joeddav/xlm-roberta-large-xnli_L16_no-idf_version=0.3.10(hug_trans=4.4.0)
- **XBERTScore(XLMR_$NLI2$):** vicgalle/xlm-roberta-large-xnli-anli_L17_no-idf_version=0.3.10(hug_trans=4.4.0)
- **XBERTScore(XLMR_$Ensemble$):**
  - xlm-roberta-large_L17_no-idf_version=0.3.10(hug_trans=4.4.0)
  - joeddav/xlm-roberta-large-xnli_L16_no-idf_version=0.3.10(hug_trans=4.4.0)
  - vicgalle/xlm-roberta-large-xnli-anli_L17_no-idf_version=0.3.10(hug_trans=4.4.0)
- **XBERTScore(mBERT):** bert-base-multilingual-cased_L9_no-idf_version=0.3.10(hug_trans=4.4.0)
- **XBERTScore(mBART):** facebook/mbart-large-50-many-to-many-mmt_L12_no-idf_version=0.3.10(hug_trans=4.4.0)

[8] `https://github.com/Tiiiger/bert_score`

The Eval4NLP Shared Task on Explainable Quality Estimation: Overview and Results

Marina Fomicheva*, **Piyawat Lertvittayakumjorn**†, **Wei Zhao**‡, **Steffen Eger**‡, **Yang Gao**◇

∗ University of Sheffield, UK † Imperial College London, UK
‡ TU Darmstadt, Germany ◇ Royal Holloway, University of London, UK
m.fomicheva@sheffield.ac.uk pl1515@imperial.ac.uk
wei.zhao@h-its.org eger@aiphes.tu-darmstadt.de
yang.gao@rhul.ac.uk

Abstract

In this paper, we introduce the Eval4NLP-2021 shared task on explainable quality estimation. Given a source-translation pair, this shared task requires not only to provide a sentence-level score indicating the overall quality of the translation, but also to *explain* this score by identifying the words that negatively impact translation quality. We present the data, annotation guidelines and evaluation setup of the shared task, describe the six participating systems, and analyze the results. To the best of our knowledge, this is the first shared task on explainable NLP evaluation metrics. Datasets and results are available at `https://github.com/eval4nlp/SharedTask2021`.

1 Introduction

Recent Natural Language Processing (NLP) systems based on pre-trained representations from Transformer language models, such as BERT (Devlin et al., 2019) and XLM-Roberta (Conneau et al., 2020), have achieved outstanding results in a variety of tasks. This boost in performance, however, comes at the cost of efficiency and interpretability. Interpretability is a major concern in modern Artificial Intelligence (AI) and NLP research (Doshi-Velez and Kim, 2017; Danilevsky et al., 2020), as black-box models undermine users' trust in new technologies (Mercado et al., 2016; Toreini et al., 2020).

In the Eval4NLP 2021 shared task, we focus on evaluating machine translation (MT) as an example of this problem. Specifically, we look at the task of *quality estimation* (QE), where the aim is to predict the quality of MT output at inference time without access to reference translations (Blatz et al., 2004; Specia et al., 2018b).[1] Translation quality can be assessed at different levels of granularity: *sentence-level*, i.e. predicting the overall quality of translated sentences, and *word-level*, i.e. highlighting specific errors in the MT output. Those have traditionally been treated as two separate tasks, each one requiring dedicated training data.

In this shared task, we propose to address word-level translation error identification as an explainability task.[2] Explainability is a broad area aimed at explaining predictions of machine learning models. Rationale extraction methods achieve this by selecting a portion of the input that justifies model output for a given data point (Lei et al., 2016; Jain et al., 2020). A natural way to explain sentence-level quality assessment is to identify translation errors. Hence, we frame **error identification as a task of providing explanations for the predictions of sentence-level QE models**. We claim that this task represents a challenging new benchmark for testing explainability for NLP and provides a new way of addressing word-level QE.

On the one hand, QE is different from other explainable NLP tasks with existing datasets (DeYoung et al., 2020) in various important aspects. First, it is a regression task, as opposed to binary or multiclass text classification explored in previous work. Second, it is a multilingual task where the output score captures the relationship between source and target sentences. Finally, QE is fundamentally different from e.g. text classification, where clues are typically separate words or phrases (Zaidan et al., 2007) that can often be considered

[1] While QE is typically treated as a supervised task, a related research direction is *reference-free* evaluation, which refers to unsupervised cross-lingual metrics that assess MT quality by computing distances between cross-lingual semantic representations of the source and target sentences (Zhao et al., 2020; Song et al., 2021).

[2] A study on *global explainability* of MT evaluation metrics, disentangling them along linguistic factors such as syntax and semantics, has recently been conducted in Kaster et al. (2021). In contrast, our shared task addresses *local explainability* of individual input instances.

Proceedings of the 58th Annual Meeting of the Association for Computational Linguistics, pages 165–178

https://doi.org/10.26615/978-954-452-056-4_017

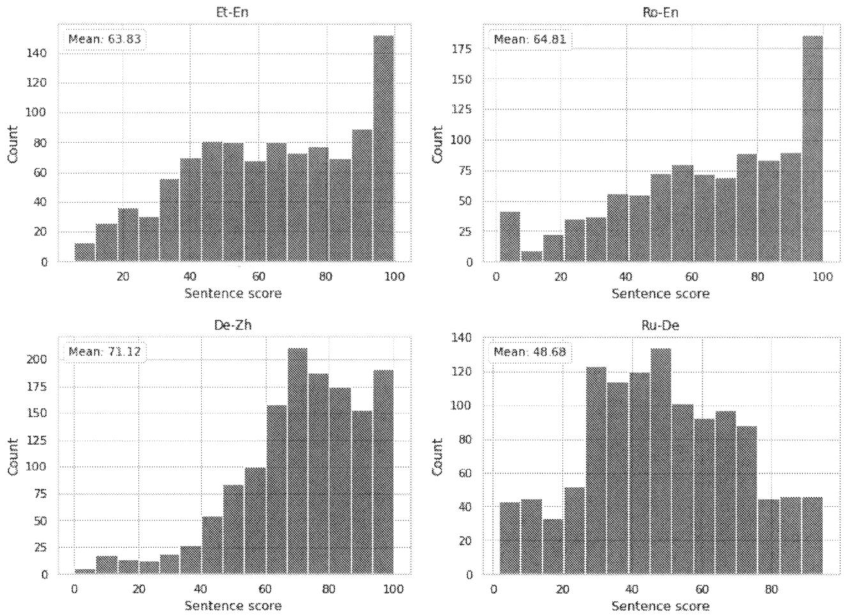

Figure 1: Distribution of sentence-level scores for each language pair.

independently of the rest of the text. By contrast, translation errors can only be identified given the context of the source and target sentences. Thus, this shared task provides a new benchmark for testing explainability methods in NLP.

On the other hand, treating word-level QE as an explainability problem offers some advantages compared to the current approaches. First, we can potentially avoid the need for supervised data at word level. Second, gold standard test sets can be made less expensive and more reliable. As we will show in Section 2, rationalized sentence-level evaluation can be a middle ground between relatively cheap but noisy annotations derived from post-editing (Fomicheva et al., 2020) and very informative but expensive explicit error annotation based on error taxonomies, such as the Multidimensional Quality Metrics (MQM) framework (Lommel et al., 2014b). For this shared task, we build a new test set with manually annotated explanations for sentence-level quality ratings. To the best of our knowledge, this is the first MT evaluation dataset annotated with human rationales.

The **main objective** of the shared task is threefold. First, it aims to explore the plausibility of explainable evaluation metrics (Wiegreffe and Pinter, 2019), by proposing a test set with manually annotated rationales. It helps the community better understand how similar the generated explanations are to the human explanations. Second, the shared task encourages research on unsupervised or semi-supervised methods for error identification, so as to reduce the cost on word-level MT error annotation. Last but not least, the shared task sheds light on how current NLP evaluation systems arrive at their predictions and to what extent this process is aligned with human reasoning.

2 Data

For this shared task, we collected a new test set with (i) manual assessment of translation quality at sentence level and (ii) word-level rationales that explain the sentence-level scores (Section 2.1). For training and development purposes, the participants were advised to use existing resources, which are briefly discussed in Section 2.2.

2.1 Eval4NLP Test Set

Language pairs and MT systems The test set contains four language pairs: Estonian-English (Et-En), Romanian-English (Ro-En), Russian-German (Ru-De) and German-Chinese (De-Zh). For Et-En and Ro-En, we use the source and translated sentences from the test21 partition of the MLQE-PE dataset (Fomicheva et al., 2020). For Ru-De, the source sentences were extracted from Wikipedia following the procedure described in Guzmán et al. (2019) and translated using the ML50 fairseq (Ott et al., 2019) multilingual Transformer model (Tang et al., 2020). For De-Zh, the translations were produced using the Google Translate API, as the MT quality of the ML50 model was too low for this language pair according to our preliminary experiments.

Language pair	Tokens Source/Target	Sentences All/With rationales
Et-En	14,044/19,576	1,000/718
Ro-En	17,359/17,770	1,000/665
De-Zh	24,903/27,027	1,410/911
Ru-De	25,383/28,802	1,180/1,061

Table 1: Total number of source tokens, target tokens, sentences and sentences with lower-than-perfect sentence score (i.e. sentences with rationales) in the Eval4NLP 2021 test set.

Sentence- and word-level annotation For this annotation effort, we adapted the *Appraise* manual evaluation interface (Federmann, 2012). For sentence-level annotation, we follow the guidelines from the MLQE-PE dataset (Fomicheva et al., 2020), a variant of the so called *direct assessment* (DA) scores proposed by Graham et al. (2016). As illustrated in Figure 2, the annotators were asked to provide a sentence rating by moving a slider on the quality scale from left (worse) to right (best). They were additionally provided with instructions on what specific quality ranges represent. Following Graham et al. (2016), the numeric values were not visible to the annotators, but the scale is interpreted numerically as follows: *1-10* range represents a completely incorrect translation; *11-30*, a translation that contains a few correct keywords, but the overall meaning is different or lost; *31-50*, a translation that preserves parts of the original meaning; *51-70*, a translation which is understandable and conveys the overall meaning of the source but contains a few errors; *71-90*, a translation that closely preserves the semantics of the source and has only minor mistakes; and *91-100*, a perfect translation.

Crucially, besides the sentence-level rating, the annotators were asked to provide a rationale for their decisions. Specifically, for all translations except those they considered perfect, the annotators were required to highlight the words in the MT sentence corresponding to translation errors that would explain the assigned sentence score.[3] They were also asked to highlight the source words that caused the errors in the MT output, as shown in Figure 2. The missing contents was annotated by highlighting the source words that were not translated, whereas for the added (hallucinated) contents the annotators were only required to highlight the corresponding target words. We interpreted the highlighting as binary labels, indicating whether a given word is part of the rationale (positive class), or not (negative class). The annotators were provided with detailed annotation guidelines, which are available at `https://github.com/eval4nlp/SharedTask2021/tree/main/annotation-guidelines`.

The annotation was conducted by 3 annotators for Et-En and Ro-En, and by (up to) 4 annotators for Ru-De and De-Zh.[4] Et-En and Ro-En data was annotated by Estonian and Romanian native speakers with near native proficiency in English. De-Zh data was annotated by Chinese native speakers with strong proficiency in German. Finally, Ru-De data was annotated by native speakers of Russian with near native proficiency in German. The annotators for Ro-En, Et-En, and Ru-De are students specializing in Linguistics and Translation or are professional translators; the annotators for De-Zh are students specializing in computer science. The cost of annotation was approximately 4,000 Euro, with working times of 15 to 25 hours per annotator for De-Zh and Ru-De (Et-En and Ro-En annotators were compensated for the whole work, instead of on an hourly basis, and not all of them noted down their working times).

To produce a single sentence-level score, we take an average across the scores from individual annotators. To obtain a single binary label for each token, we use a majority voting mechanism, where the token is considered as part of the rationale if it was highlighted by the majority of the annotators.[5]

Inter-annotator agreement Table 2 shows average agreement levels between our annotators (on common sets of annotated data instances). We use Pearson correlation for sentence-level scores and

[3]For all languages except for Chinese, the source sentences and MT outputs were tokenized with Moses tokenizer available at `https://github.com/moses-smt/mosesdecoder`. For Chinese, the jieba tokenizer was used: `https://github.com/fxsjy/jieba`.

[4]Not all annotators annotated all sentences for Ru-De and De-Zh. Individual annotators did 1411, 871, 1101, 1026 sentences for De-Zh, and 601, 1002, 1181, 1001 sentences for Ru-De.

[5]When there is an even number of annotators, we weight the annotations by annotator reliability measured using their average agreement with the other annotators.

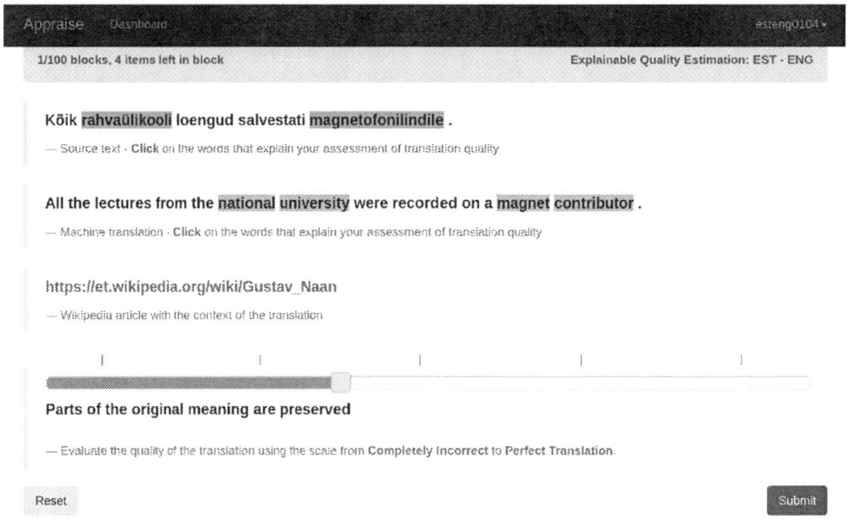

Figure 2: Screenshot of the annotation interface.

Cohen's kappa coefficient for word-level annotations. To be more precise, we measure Pearson correlation among all common instances between two annotators and then report the average across annotators; we measure average kappa agreement (averaged over all sentences) between any two annotators and then report the average across all annotators. We observe that Ro-En and Ru-De are most consistently annotated and De-Zh and Et-En have least agreement on average. Overall, our agreements are acceptable, however, in all cases, ranging from 0.42 to 0.67 kappa on word-level and ~0.6 to 0.8 Pearson on sentence-level. For comparison, the average kappa reported by Lommel et al. (2014a) for the fine-grained MQM error annotation ranges from 0.25 to 0.34.

	Sentence-Level	Word-Level	
		Source	Target
De-Zh	0.59	0.48	0.55
Ru-De	0.71	0.56	0.59
Ro-En	0.81	0.54	0.67
Et-En	0.68	0.42	0.45

Table 2: Sentence-level (Pearson) and word-level (kappa) agreements for different language pairs.

Data statistics The number of annotated sentences, as well as the number of the source and target tokens in the test set are shown in Table 1. In addition, we show the number of sentences with lower-than-perfect translation quality. This is the final subset of sentences that was used to evaluate the submissions to the shared task, since in our manual evaluation setup no rationales were required for the MT outputs with perfect quality. As shown in Table 1, for all the language pairs the vast majority of translations has a lower-than-perfect score, where the percentage of such sentences is the lowest for De-Zh (65%) and the highest for Ru-De (90%).

Figure 1 shows the distribution of sentence-level scores for each language pair. The language pair with the highest average quality is De-Zh, whereas Ru-De has the lowest average score. For Et-En, Ro-En and Ru-De, the scores cover the whole quality range, while the distribution for De-Zh is highly skewed, which makes the task more challenging for this language pair (see Section 6).

Table 4 shows the proportion of words annotated as rationales. The numbers in Table 4 are consistent with the average sentence-level quality, as De-Zh and Ru-De have the lowest and the highest percentage, respectively. This is expected given that lower quality translations should contain a higher number of errors. In general, the proportion of tokens considered relevant for explaining sentence-level ratings is fairly low. This is consistent with the annotation guidelines which stipulate that all and only the words necessary to justify the sentence score must be highlighted. Finally, we observe that, for Et-En and Ro-En, the percentage of annotated tokens is higher for the target than for the source sentences. This can be related to the presence of hallucinations, where the target contains words that do not have a clear correspondence with any part

Src	Pe 20 august , trupele sârbe au început urmărirea austriecilor în retragere .										
PE	On 20 August , the Serbian troops began pursuing the retreating Austrians .										
MT	Serbian	troops	started	pursuing	Austria	on	20	August	in	withdrawal	.
Ann-EXPL	Serbian	troops	started	pursuing	Austria	on	20	August	in	withdrawal	.
Ann-EXPL*	Serbian	troops	started	pursuing	Austria	on	20	August	in	withdrawal	.
Predictions	Serbian	troops	started	pursuing	Austria	on	20	August	in	withdrawal	.
Ann-PE	Serbian	troops	started	pursuing	Austria	on	20	August	in	withdrawal	.
Color scale	0.0			0.5			1.0				

Table 3: Example of the target-side annotation from the Ro-En test set and the output expected from the participants. "Src" stands for the source sentence, "MT" is the MT output, "PE" is the post-edited version of the MT output taken from the MLQE-PE dataset. "Ann-EXPL*" is the mean of the binary scores for each word averaged across the annotators. "Ann-EXPL" corresponds to the binary scores obtained by aggregating individual annotations through majority voting (official gold standard of the shared task). "Ann-PE" is the word-level annotation derived from post-editing. "Predictions" contains the predictions (after min-max normalization) for this sentence from the IST-Unbabel submission to the constrained track.

		Et-En	Ro-En	De-Zh	Ru-De
Ours	Source	0.14	0.09	0.11	0.21
	MT	0.18	0.13	0.12	0.21
MLQE	Source	0.22	0.20	-	-
	MT	0.26	0.22	-	-

Table 4: Percentage of source and MT tokens annotated as rationales. For comparison, the percentage of source and target tokens annotated as errors in the same test partition of the MLQE-PE dataset is provided.

of the source sentence, as well as to typological differences between languages, whereby there tends to be a one-to-many correspondence between the source and target words.

Difference to existing QE datasets with word-level annotation The test set collected for this shared task is different from existing QE datasets with word-level annotation. A popular approach to building QE datasets is based on measuring post-editing effort (Bojar et al., 2017; Specia et al., 2018a; Fonseca et al., 2019; Specia et al., 2020). This can be done at sentence level, by computing the so called HTER score (Snover et al., 2006) that represents the minimum number of edits a human language expert is required to make in order to correct the MT output; or at word level, by aligning the MT output to its post-edited version and annotating the misaligned source and target words. An important limitation of this strategy is that the annotated words do not necessarily correspond to translation errors, as correcting a specific error may involve changing multiple related words in the sentence. This is exacerbated by the limitations of the heuristics used to automatically align the MT and its post-edited version. Indeed, as shown in Table 4, the percentage of error tokens on the same data for Ro-En and Et-En language pairs is considerably higher in the MLQE-PE dataset, where word-level annotation is derived from post-editing.

An alternative approach is the explicit annotation of translation errors by human experts. This is typically done based on fine-grained error taxonomies such as the Multidimensional Quality Metrics (MQM) framework (Lommel et al., 2014b). While such annotations provide very informative labelled data, the annotator agreement for this style of annotation is fairly low (Lommel et al., 2014a) and the annotation is very time-consuming.[6]

The example in Table 3 shows a sample of the annotated data from the Ro-En test set. The first three rows correspond to the source (Src), the MT output (MT), and the post-edited MT output (PE). "Ann-EXPL*" shows the mean of the binary scores assigned by each annotator to a given word. Thus, the words "20" and "August" were included in the rationale by 1 out of 3 annotators for this example, the words "Austria" and "in" were highlighted by 2 out of 3 annotators; finally, the word "withdrawal" was included in the rationale by all 3 annotators. We can interpret this information as an indirect indication of error severity, as the most serious errors are expected to be noted by all of the annotators. "Ann-EXPL" shows the binary scores that

[6]The interest towards MQM has recently increased due to a higher overall quality of MT (Freitag et al., 2021), but the aforementioned issues still remain unsolved.

we obtain through a majority voting mechanism, as described above. These binary scores were used for the official evaluation reported in Section 6. "Predictions" illustrates the predicted scores from one of the participants of the shared task.[7] The predictions almost perfectly correspond to the human rationale, as in both cases the words "Austria" and "withdrawal" receive the highest scores. Finally, for comparison, "Ann-PE" shows the word labels for this sentence taken from the MLQE-PE dataset. In this case all tokens are considered as errors since re-orderings (or "shifts") are not included in the set of possible edit operations used to compute minimum edit distance, from which the alignment between MT output and its PE is derived.

To the best of our knowledge, this test set is the first MT evaluation dataset annotated with human rationales. The proposed annotation scheme has certain advantages for the QE task, as it allows to explicitly annotate translation errors, and at the same time results in higher agreement and less effort than fine-grained error annotation.[8]

2.2 Training and development data

As discussed above, we use the same sentence-level annotation scheme as the one used in the MLQE-PE dataset. Therefore, for Ro-En and Et-En the participants could use the train and development partitions of MLQE-PE to build their sentence-level models. The De-Zh and Ru-De language pairs represent a fully zero-shot scenario where no sentence-level training data is available.

3 Task and Evaluation

The task consisted of building a QE system that (i) predicts the quality score for an input pair of source text and MT hypothesis, (ii) provides word-level evidence for its predictions. An example of the test data used for evaluation is shown in Table 3. The participants were expected to provide explanations for each sentence pair in the form of continuous scores, with the highest scores corresponding to the tokens considered as relevant by human annotators. The participants could submit to either **constrained** or **unconstrained** track. For the constrained track, the participants were expected to use no supervision at word level, while in the unconstrained track they were allowed to use any word-level data for training.

Explanations can be obtained either by building inherently interpretable models (Yu et al., 2019) or by using post-hoc explanation methods which extract explanations from an existing model (Ribeiro et al., 2016; Lundberg and Lee, 2017; Sundararajan et al., 2017a; Schulz et al., 2020), for example by analysing the values of the gradient on each input feature. In this shared task, we provide both sentence-level training data and strong sentence-level models (see the TransQuest-LIME baseline in Section 4), and thus encourage the participants to either train their own inherently interpretable models or use post-hoc techniques on top of our existing sentence-level models.

We accommodate the evaluation scheme to be suitable both for approaches that return continuous scores, and for supervised approaches that can return binary scores. Namely, we use evaluation metrics based on class probabilities that have been previously adapted for assessing the plausibility of rationale extraction methods (Atanasova et al., 2020). Since explainability methods typically proceed on instance-by-instance basis, and the scores produced for different instances are not necessarily comparable, we compute the evaluation metrics for each instance separately and average the results across all instances in the test set. Following Fomicheva et al. (2021), we define the following evaluation metrics to assess the performance of the submissions to the shared task at the word-level:

AUC score For each instance, we compute the area under the receiver operating characteristic curve (AUC score) to compare the continuous attribution scores against binary gold labels.

Average Precision AUC scores can be overly optimistic for imbalanced data. Therefore, we also use Average Precision (AP). AP summarizes a precision-recall curve as the weighted mean of precisions achieved at each threshold, with the increase in recall from the previous threshold used as the weight (Zhu, 2004).

Recall at Top-K In addition, we report the Recall-at-Top-K metric commonly used in information retrieval. Applied to our setting, this metric computes the proportion of words with the

[7] We did not ask the participants to normalize the scores, as we are only interested in the ranking of tokens according to their relevance for sentence-level quality.

[8] As shown by McDonnell et al. (2017), rationales increase the reliability of human annotation when judging the relevance of webpages for information retrieval. In the future, we plan to investigate whether this also applies to MT evaluation and providing word-level explanations increases the consistency of sentence-level assessments.

Team ID	Participating team	
NICT-Kyoto	National Institute of Information and Communications Technology	Rubino et al. (2021)
IST-Unbabel	IST/University of Lisbon & Unbabel	Treviso et al. (2021)
CLIP-UMD	Department of Computer Science, University of Maryland	Kabir and Carpuat (2021)
Gringham	Technical University of Darmstadt	Leiter (2021)
HeyTUDa	Technical University of Darmstadt	Eksi et al. (2021)
CUNI-Prague	Charles University	Polák et al. (2021)

Table 5: Participants of the Eval4NLP Shared Task on Explainable Quality Estimation.

highest attribution that correspond to translation errors against the total number of errors in the MT output. The code for computing the evaluation metrics can be found in the shared task github repository: `https://github.com/eval4nlp/SharedTask2021/tree/main/scripts`. The shared task used CodaLab as the submission platform.

4 Baseline systems

Random baseline is built by sampling scores uniformly at random from a continuous $[0..1)$ range for each source and target token in a given sentence pair as well as for the sentence-level QE score.

Transquest-LIME uses TransQuest QE models described in Ranasinghe et al. (2020) to produce sentence-level scores. TransQuest follows the current standard practice of building task-specific NLP models by fine-tuning pre-trained multilingual language models, such as XLM-Roberta, on task-specific data. For Ro-En and Et-En, the Ro-En and Et-En TransQuest models are used, whereas for the zero-shot language pairs we use the multilingual variant of TransQuest, which was trained on a concatenation of MLQE-PE data. The post-hoc LIME explanation method (Ribeiro et al., 2016) is then applied to generate relevance scores for the source and target words. LIME is a simplification-based explanation technique, which fits a linear model in the vicinity of each test instance, to approximate the decision boundary of the complex model. Since in our sentence-level gold standard higher scores mean better quality, we invert LIME explanations so that higher values correspond to errors.

XMover-SHAP uses the reference-free metric XMoverScore (Zhao et al., 2020) to rate translations and uses the (likewise post-hoc) SHAP explainer (Lundberg and Lee, 2017) to explain the ratings. In particular, given a source-translation pair, XMoverScore provides a real number to indicate the quality of the translation, in terms of its semantic overlapping with the source sentence, using re-mapped multilingual BERT embeddings and a target-side language model.[9] To explain the contribution of each word in the rating, SHAP creates perturbations of the source/translation sentence by masking out some words and estimates the average marginal contribution of each word across all possible perturbations. The source code for all the baseline systems is available at `https://github.com/eval4nlp/SharedTask2021/tree/main/baselines`.

5 Participants

For this first edition of the shared task, we had a total of 6 participating teams listed in Table 5.[10] Below, we briefly describe the submitted approaches.

NICT-Kyoto use synthetic data to fine-tune the XLM-Roberta language model for the QE task. To produce synthetic sentence-level scores, they translate publicly available parallel corpora using SOTA neural MT systems and compute three reference-based metrics: ChrF (Popović, 2015), TER (Snover et al., 2006) and BLEU (Papineni et al., 2002). To simulate word-level annotation, they derive word-level labels from the alignment between the MT outputs and human reference translations. The QE model is then jointly trained to predict the scores from different metrics as well as word-level tags. A metric embedding component is proposed where each metric is represented with a set of learnable parameters. An attention mechanism between the metric embeddings and the input representations is employed to obtain word-level scores as explanations for the sentence-level predictions.

IST-Unbabel participated in the constrained and unconstrained tracks of the shared task. For the constrained track ("IST-Unbabel" in Table 6), they

[9] Note that XMoverScore is an unsupervised reference-free metric, in contrast to the supervised TransQuest QE model.

[10] Initially, there were seven participating teams, but one of them opted out after the competition ended.

used a set of explainability methods to extract the relevance of the input tokens from sentence-level QE models built on top of XLM-Roberta and RemBERT. The explainability methods explored in this work include attention-based, gradient-based and perturbation based approaches, as well as rationalization by construction. The best performing method which was submitted to the competition relies on the attention mechanism of the pretrained Transformers in order to obtain the relevance scores for each token. In addition, scaling attention weights by the L2 norm of value vectors as suggested in Kobayashi et al. (2020) resulted in a further boost in performance.

For the unconstrained track ("IST-Unbabel*" in Table 6), they add a word-level loss to the sentence-level models and train jointly using the annotated data from the MLQE-PE dataset.

HeyTUDa use the TransQuest QE models (Ranasinghe et al., 2020) for sentence-level prediction and a set of explainability techniques to estimate the relevance of each source and target word. Specifically, they explore three perturbation-based methods: LIME, SHAP, and occlusion (Zeiler and Fergus, 2014), as well as three gradient-based methods: DeepLift (Shrikumar et al., 2017), Layer Gradient x Activation (Shrikumar et al., 2016) and Integrated Gradients (Sundararajan et al., 2017b). They further use an unsupervised ensembling method to combine the different explainability approaches.

Gringham use the reference-free metrics XBERTScore (i.e., BERTScore (Zhang et al., 2020) with cross-lingual embeddings) and XMoverScore and make them inherently interpretable by considering the token alignments produced by the models. The intuition is that words that are not well-aligned are most likely erroneous. Specifically, they explore XBERTScore and XMoverScore as sentence-level models and use the corresponding similarity (or distance) matrices to produce token-level scores.

CLIP-UMD propose an ensemble of two approaches: (1) the LIME explanation technique applied to the TransQuest sentence-level model; (2) Divergent mBERT (Briakou and Carpuat, 2020), which is a BERT-based model that can detect cross-lingual semantic divergences. Divergent mBERT is trained using synthetic data where semantic divergences are introduced automatically following a set of pre-defined perturbations. To produce a combination of the two methods, the predictions from each approach are averaged.

CUNI-Prague participated in the unconstrained track. They fine-tune the XLM-R model for word-level and sentence-level QE. To map sentence piece tokenization from XLM-R to Moses tokenization, they ignore all sentence piece tokens corresponding to a given Moses token except the first one.

6 Results

Table 6 shows the results of the shared task. We report the word-level metrics presented in Section 3, as well as Pearson correlation at sentence level. The values of the "Rank" columns are computed by first ranking the participants according to each of the three word-level metrics and then averaging the resulting rankings.[11] First, we note that all of the submissions outperform the three baselines for all the language pairs,[12] which indicates that error detection can indeed be approached as rationale extraction.

Approaches Overall, the submitted approaches vary a lot in the way they addressed the task. The following trends can be identified:

- Following the recent standard in QE and similar multilingual NLP tasks, all the approaches rely on multilingual Transformer-based language models.
- Submissions to the unconstrained track use the SOTA approach to word-level supervision explored previously by Lee (2020).
- The use of synthetic data produced by aligning MT outputs and reference translations from existing parallel corpora proves an efficient strategy to identify translation errors. Supervising the predictions based on Transformer attention weights with the labels derived from synthetic data was used by the winning submission to the shared task.
- The approaches that rely on attention weights to predict human rationales (NICT-Kyoto and IST-Unbabel) achieve the best results for the constrained track.

[11] This ranking is slightly different from the Codalab results, as one of the teams retracted from the competition.

[12] The only exception is HeyTUDa, which is outperformed by XMover-SHAP for De-Zh and by TransQuest-LIME for Et-En and Ro-En.

	Target				Source				Sentence
	Rank	AUC	AP	Rec	Rank	AUC	AP	Rec	Pearson
					Estonian-English				
IST-Unbabel*	1.0	**0.92**	**0.85**	**0.76**	1.3	**0.94**	**0.86**	**0.77**	0.86
CUNI Prague*	2.0	0.92	0.84	**0.75**	3.0	0.93	**0.85**	**0.76**	0.80
NICT Kyoto†	3.0	**0.90**	0.82	**0.73**	1.7	0.93	0.85	**0.77**	0.85
IST-Unbabel	4.3	0.82	0.74	0.63	4.0	0.86	0.76	0.64	0.82
Gringham	4.7	0.84	0.71	0.60	5.0	0.86	0.72	0.59	0.71
CLIP-UMD	6.0	0.74	0.63	0.53	6.0	0.76	0.51	0.45	0.77
Baseline: TransQuest-LIME	7.3	0.62	0.54	0.43	7.0	0.54	0.44	0.31	0.77
HeyTUDa	7.7	0.66	0.52	0.41	10.	N/A	N/A	N/A	0.77
Baseline: XMover-SHAP	9.0	0.62	0.44	0.34	8.0	0.54	0.37	0.23	0.49
Baseline: Random	10.	0.50	0.36	0.25	9.0	0.49	0.34	0.19	-0.03
					Romanian-English				
NICT Kyoto†	1.0	**0.95**	**0.87**	**0.78**	1.0	**0.95**	**0.85**	**0.75**	0.92
IST-Unbabel*	2.0	0.94	0.84	0.75	2.0	0.93	0.81	0.71	0.87
CUNI Prague*	3.0	0.94	0.83	0.73	3.0	0.93	0.81	0.70	0.89
IST-Unbabel	4.0	0.88	0.78	0.68	4.0	0.86	0.73	0.62	0.90
Gringham	5.0	0.87	0.73	0.61	5.0	0.84	0.61	0.45	0.78
CLIP-UMD	6.0	0.73	0.60	0.49	6.0	0.72	0.41	0.37	0.90
Baseline: TransQuest-LIME	7.7	0.63	0.52	0.42	7.7	0.48	0.35	0.24	0.90
HeyTUDa	7.7	0.68	0.50	0.38	10.	N/A	N/A	N/A	0.90
Baseline: XMover-SHAP	8.7	0.67	0.44	0.30	8.0	0.53	0.29	0.15	0.70
Baseline: Random	10.	0.52	0.31	0.19	8.3	0.50	0.28	0.15	0.02
					Russian-German				
NICT Kyoto†	1.0	**0.93**	**0.83**	**0.74**	1.0	**0.92**	**0.80**	**0.71**	0.68
IST-Unbabel*	2.0	0.80	0.64	0.52	2.0	0.85	0.71	0.59	0.67
CUNI Prague*	3.3	0.76	0.61	0.50	3.3	0.80	0.67	0.56	0.61
Gringham	4.3	0.79	0.57	0.46	3.7	0.84	0.67	0.56	0.60
IST-Unbabel	4.3	0.75	0.58	0.47	5.0	0.77	0.63	0.52	0.64
CLIP-UMD	6.0	0.65	0.46	0.36	6.3	0.66	0.41	0.37	0.30
HeyTUDa	7.3	0.54	0.33	0.23	10.	N/A	N/A	N/A	0.50
Baseline: XMover-SHAP	7.7	0.52	0.33	0.23	8.0	0.52	0.36	0.26	0.25
Baseline: Random	9.0	0.49	0.31	0.22	9.0	0.51	0.34	0.24	-0.02
Baseline: TransQuest-LIME	10.	0.40	0.26	0.16	6.7	0.53	0.43	0.32	0.50
					German-Chinese				
NICT Kyoto†	1.0	**0.85**	**0.68**	**0.57**	1.0	**0.85**	**0.64**	**0.51**	0.29
IST-Unbabel	2.3	0.68	0.50	0.37	3.0	0.67	0.47	0.32	0.33
IST-Unbabel*	2.7	0.71	0.47	0.34	2.0	0.73	0.50	0.35	0.27
CUNI Prague*	4.3	0.61	0.44	0.30	5.0	0.62	0.42	0.27	0.25
CLIP-UMD	4.7	0.63	0.40	0.27	6.3	0.61	0.31	0.25	0.50
Gringham	6.3	0.55	0.36	0.22	4.0	0.64	0.42	0.27	-0.04
Baseline: XMover-SHAP	6.7	0.55	0.33	0.22	9.0	0.47	0.29	0.16	0.18
HeyTUDa	8.0	0.51	0.31	0.18	10.	N/A	N/A	N/A	0.34
Baseline: Random	9.0	0.50	0.29	0.17	7.7	0.50	0.30	0.17	0.00
Baseline: TransQuest-LIME	10.	0.46	0.27	0.14	7.0	0.49	0.32	0.20	0.34

Table 6: Official results of the Eval4NLP Shared Task on Explainable Quality Estimation. Submissions to the unconstrained track are marked with *. We mark the NICT Kyoto submissions with a †, as they submitted to the constrained track, but use synthetic data for word-level supervision. Submissions not significantly outperformed by any other submission according to paired t-test for each metric are marked in bold. N/A means that the participating team did not submit the word-level scores for the source sentences.

- Both IST-Unbabel and HeyTUDa explore a wide set of explanation methods. The differences in performance are likely due to the method used for the final submission. While IST-Unbabel submission explores normalized attention weights, HeyTUDa use an ensemble of gradient-based approaches. A possible reason for the inferior performance of HeyTUDa is that the gradient is computed with respect to the embedding layer. As noted by Fomicheva et al. (2021), attribution to the embedding layer in the Transformer-based QE models does not provide strong results for the error detection task since word representations at the embedding layer do not capture contextual information, which is crucial for predicting translation quality.

- Gringham follow an entirely different strategy where they modify an existing reference-free metric to obtain both sentence score and word-level explanations in an unsupervised way. A similar approach is explored in our XMover-SHAP baseline, but the difference is that we apply SHAP explainer on top of XMover, while Gringham makes the XMover-Score inherently interpretable, which leads to better results.

Winners The overall winner of the competition is the submission to the constrained track from NICT-Kyoto, which wins on 3 out of 4 language pairs, according to the source and target ranking. Fine-tuning on large amounts of synthetic data as well as the use of attention mechanism between the evaluation metric embeddings and the contextualized input representations seem to be the key to their performance. We note, however, that they offer a mixed approach with word-level supervision on synthetic data. Among the constrained approaches that do not use any supervision at word level, the best performing submission is IST-Unbabel, which outperforms other constrained submissions for all language pairs, except Ru-De, where they perform on par with Gringham on the target side and are surpassed by Gringham on the source side. For the unconstrained track we received only two submissions, from which IST-Unbabel* performs the best.

Sentence-level correlation is not predictive of the performance of the submissions at detecting relevant tokens. This is due to the fact that submitted approaches vary in the role played by the sentence-level model. In fact, if we look at the submissions that follow comparable strategies, we do observe a correspondence between sentence-level and token-level results. For example, among the approaches that build upon a sentence-level QE model and use post-hoc methods to explain the predictions, IST-Unbabel tends to achieve higher performance both in terms of the token-level results and in terms of the Pearson correlation with sentence ratings, compared to HeyTUDa and the TransQuest-LIME baseline.

The performance on zero-shot language pairs is lower than for Et-En and Ro-En. This is the case for all approaches except NICT-Kyoto on Ru-De, where the performance at word-level is comparable to the results for Et-En and Ro-En, even though the Pearson correlation for sentence scores is inferior. We attribute this outcome to the use of supervision with synthetic data, which helps boost performance for word-level QE when no manually labelled data is available, as has been shown by Tuan et al. (2021). Performance degradation for De-Zh is considerably larger than Ru-De. De-Zh was among the language pairs with the lowest inter-annotator agreement and, in addition, had a different distribution of sentence-level scores, with many high-quality translations, according to the annotators (see Section 2.1).

Limitations of the evaluation settings Our current evaluation settings can be further improved in various ways. First, the submissions were ranked according to the global statistics, i.e. by comparing the mean AUC, AP and Rec-TopK scores of different submissions over a common set of test instances. However, such aggregation mechanisms ignore how many of its competitors a given submission outperforms and on how many test instances. In the future we plan to follow a more rigorous approach suggested by Peyrard et al. (2021) and use the Bradley–Terry (BT) model (Bradley and Terry, 1952), which leverages the instance-level pairing of metric scores.

Second, the metrics used for evaluation are tailored for unsupervised explainability approaches that produce continuous scores, but they do not allow a direct comparison with the SOTA work on word-level QE, which is evaluated using F-score and Matthews correlation coefficient (Specia et al., 2020). One way to address this would be to require the participants to submit binary scores, but we discarded this option in this first edition of the shared task, as it would substantially limit the exploration of the explainability approaches.

Finally, the binary rationales obtained from our pool of annotators through majority voting do not capture the fact that some words are more relevant for sentence-level quality than others. As shown in Table 3, an alternative version of the data can be produced by averaging the scores assigned to each word by individual annotators, as an indication of the severity of translated errors. In the future, we plan to study to what extent such scores agree with the continuous explanation scores produced by the participants. Another limitation of our annotation scheme is that sometimes a word may be missing in the machine translation, which can then not be highlighted (e.g., Russian does often not use determiners and the MT system may wrongly omit it when translating into English or German).

7 Conclusions

In this paper, we presented the findings of the Eval4NLP-2021 shared task on *explainable Quality Estimation (QE)*, where the goal is to not only produce a sentence-level score for an MT output, given a source sentence, but also highlight erroneous words in the target (and source) sentence explaining the score. We detailed the data annotation, involving two novel non-English language pairs, our baselines (post-hoc explanation techniques on top of state-of-the-art QE models), as well as the participants' approaches to the task. These include supervised approaches, training on synthetic data as well as genuine post-hoc and inherent explainability techniques.

The scope for future research is huge: for example, we aim to include new language pairs, especially low-resource ones, address explainability for metrics in other NLP tasks, e.g. semantic textual similarity (Agirre et al., 2016) and summarization (Gao et al., 2020), and identify error categories of highlighted words, ideally in an unsupervised manner.

Acknowledgments

Marina Fomicheva was supported by funding from the Bergamot project (EU H2020 Grant No. 825303). Piyawat Lertvittayakumjorn was supported by a scholarship from Anandamahidol Foundation. We would like to thank Lisa Yankovskaya and Mark Fishel from the University of Tartu for helping organize and monitor the manual quality annotation. We also thank Anton Malinovskiy for adapting the Appraise interface for quality annotation with rationales. Finally, we gratefully thank the Artificial Intelligence Journal (`https://aij.ijcai.org/`) and Salesforce Research for their financial support enabling our human annotations.

References

Eneko Agirre, Aitor Gonzalez-Agirre, Iñigo Lopez-Gazpio, Montse Maritxalar, German Rigau, and Larraitz Uria. 2016. SemEval-2016 task 2: Interpretable semantic textual similarity. In *Proceedings of the 10th International Workshop on Semantic Evaluation (SemEval-2016)*, pages 512–524, San Diego, California. Association for Computational Linguistics.

Pepa Atanasova, Jakob Grue Simonsen, Christina Lioma, and Isabelle Augenstein. 2020. A diagnostic study of explainability techniques for text classification. *arXiv preprint arXiv:2009.13295*.

John Blatz, Erin Fitzgerald, George Foster, Simona Gandrabur, Cyril Goutte, Alex Kulesza, Alberto Sanchis, and Nicola Ueffing. 2004. Confidence estimation for machine translation. In *COLING 2004: Proceedings of the 20th International Conference on Computational Linguistics*, pages 315–321, Geneva, Switzerland. COLING.

Ondřej Bojar, Rajen Chatterjee, Christian Federmann, Yvette Graham, Barry Haddow, Matthias Huck, Philipp Koehn, Varvara Logacheva, Christof Monz, Matteo Negri, Matt Post, Raphael Rubino, Lucia Specia, and Marco Turchi. 2017. Findings of the 2017 conference on machine translation (wmt17). In *Proceedings of the Second Conference on Machine Translation, Volume 2: Shared Tasks Papers*, Copenhagen, Denmark. Association for Computational Linguistics.

Ralph Allan Bradley and Milton E. Terry. 1952. Rank analysis of incomplete block designs: I. the method of paired comparisons. *Biometrika*, 39(3/4):324–345.

Eleftheria Briakou and Marine Carpuat. 2020. Detecting Fine-Grained Cross-Lingual Semantic Divergences without Supervision by Learning to Rank. In *Proceedings of the 2020 Conference on Empirical Methods in Natural Language Processing (EMNLP)*, pages 1563–1580, Online. Association for Computational Linguistics.

Alexis Conneau, Kartikay Khandelwal, Naman Goyal, Vishrav Chaudhary, Guillaume Wenzek, Francisco Guzmán, Edouard Grave, Myle Ott, Luke Zettlemoyer, and Veselin Stoyanov. 2020. Unsupervised cross-lingual representation learning at scale. In *Proceedings of the 58th Annual Meeting of the Association for Computational Linguistics*, pages 8440–8451, Online. Association for Computational Linguistics.

Marina Danilevsky, Kun Qian, Ranit Aharonov, Yannis Katsis, Ban Kawas, and Prithviraj Sen. 2020. A survey of the state of explainable AI for natural language processing. In *Proceedings of the 1st Conference of the Asia-Pacific Chapter of the Association for Computational Linguistics and the 10th International Joint Conference on Natural Language Processing*, pages 447–459, Suzhou, China. Association for Computational Linguistics.

Jacob Devlin, Ming-Wei Chang, Kenton Lee, and Kristina Toutanova. 2019. BERT: Pre-training of deep bidirectional transformers for language understanding. In *Proceedings of the 2019 Conference* of the North American Chapter of the Association for Computational Linguistics: Human Language Technologies, Volume 1 (Long and Short Papers)*, pages 4171–4186, Minneapolis, Minnesota. Association for Computational Linguistics.

Jay DeYoung, Sarthak Jain, Nazneen Fatema Rajani, Eric Lehman, Caiming Xiong, Richard Socher, and Byron C. Wallace. 2020. ERASER: A benchmark to evaluate rationalized NLP models. In *Proceedings of the 58th Annual Meeting of the Association for Computational Linguistics*, pages 4443–4458, Online. Association for Computational Linguistics.

Finale Doshi-Velez and Been Kim. 2017. Towards a rigorous science of interpretable machine learning. *arXiv preprint arXiv:1702.08608*.

Melda Eksi, Erik Gelbing, Jonathan Stieber, and Chi Viet Vu. 2021. Explaining errors in machine translation with absolute gradient ensembles. In *Proceedings of the 2nd Workshop on Evaluation and Comparison for NLP systems*.

Christian Federmann. 2012. Appraise: An open-source toolkit for manual evaluation of machine translation output. *The Prague Bulletin of Mathematical Linguistics*, 98:25–35.

Marina Fomicheva, Lucia Specia, and Nikolaos Aletras. 2021. Translation error detection as rationale extraction.

Marina Fomicheva, Shuo Sun, Erick Fonseca, Frédéric Blain, Vishrav Chaudhary, Francisco Guzmán, Nina Lopatina, Lucia Specia, and André F. T. Martins. 2020. MLQE-PE: A multilingual quality estimation and post-editing dataset. *arXiv preprint arXiv:2010.04480*.

Erick Fonseca, Lisa Yankovskaya, André F. T. Martins, Mark Fishel, and Christian Federmann. 2019. Findings of the WMT 2019 shared tasks on quality estimation. In *Proceedings of the Fourth Conference on Machine Translation (Volume 3: Shared Task Papers, Day 2)*, pages 1–10, Florence, Italy. Association for Computational Linguistics.

Markus Freitag, George Foster, David Grangier, Viresh Ratnakar, Qijun Tan, and Wolfgang Macherey. 2021. Experts, errors, and context: A large-scale study of human evaluation for machine translation.

Yang Gao, Wei Zhao, and Steffen Eger. 2020. SUPERT: Towards new frontiers in unsupervised evaluation metrics for multi-document summarization. In *Proceedings of the 58th Annual Meeting of the Association for Computational Linguistics*, pages 1347–1354, Online. Association for Computational Linguistics.

Yvette Graham, Timothy Baldwin, Alistair Moffat, and Justin Zobel. 2016. Can machine translation systems be evaluated by the crowd alone. *Natural Language Engineering*, FirstView:1–28.

Francisco Guzmán, Peng-Jen Chen, Myle Ott, Juan Pino, Guillaume Lample, Philipp Koehn, Vishrav Chaudhary, and Marc'Aurelio Ranzato. 2019. The FLORES evaluation datasets for low-resource machine translation: Nepali–English and Sinhala–English. In *Proceedings of the 2019 Conference on Empirical Methods in Natural Language Processing and the 9th International Joint Conference on Natural Language Processing (EMNLP-IJCNLP)*, pages 6098–6111, Hong Kong, China. Association for Computational Linguistics.

Sarthak Jain, Sarah Wiegreffe, Yuval Pinter, and Byron C. Wallace. 2020. Learning to faithfully rationalize by construction. In *Proceedings of the 58th Annual Meeting of the Association for Computational Linguistics*, pages 4459–4473, Online. Association for Computational Linguistics.

Tasnim Kabir and Marine Carpuat. 2021. The umd submission to the explainable mt quality estimation shared task: Combining explanation models with sequence labeling. In *Proceedings of the 2nd Workshop on Evaluation and Comparison for NLP systems*.

Marvin Kaster, Wei Zhao, and Steffen Eger. 2021. Global explainability of bert-based metrics by disentangling along linguistic factors. In *EMNLP 2021*, Online. Association for Computational Linguistics.

Goro Kobayashi, Tatsuki Kuribayashi, Sho Yokoi, and Kentaro Inui. 2020. Attention is not only a weight: Analyzing transformers with vector norms. *arXiv preprint arXiv:2004.10102*.

Dongjun Lee. 2020. Two-phase cross-lingual language model fine-tuning for machine translation quality estimation. In *Proceedings of the Fifth Conference on Machine Translation, Volume 2: Shared Tasks Papers*, Online. Association for Computational Linguistics.

Tao Lei, Regina Barzilay, and Tommi Jaakkola. 2016. Rationalizing neural predictions. In *Proceedings of the 2016 Conference on Empirical Methods in Natural Language Processing*, pages 107–117, Austin, Texas. Association for Computational Linguistics.

Christoph Wolfgang Leiter. 2021. Reference-free word- and sentence-level translation evaluation with token-matching metrics. In *Proceedings of the 2nd Workshop on Evaluation and Comparison for NLP systems*.

Arle Lommel, Maja Popovic, and Aljoscha Burchardt. 2014a. Assessing inter-annotator agreement for translation error annotation. In *LREC Workshop on Automatic and Manual Metrics for Operational Translation Evaluation*.

Arle Richard Lommel, Aljoscha Burchardt, and Hans Uszkoreit. 2014b. Multidimensional quality metrics (MQM): A framework for declaring and describing translation quality metrics. *Tradumàtica: tecnologies de la traducció*, 0(12):455–463.

Scott M Lundberg and Su-In Lee. 2017. A unified approach to interpreting model predictions. In I. Guyon, U. V. Luxburg, S. Bengio, H. Wallach, R. Fergus, S. Vishwanathan, and R. Garnett, editors, *Advances in Neural Information Processing Systems 30*, pages 4765–4774. Curran Associates, Inc.

Tyler McDonnell, Mücahid Kutlu, Tamer Elsayed, and Matthew Lease. 2017. The many benefits of annotator rationales for relevance judgments. In *IJCAI*, pages 4909–4913.

Joseph E Mercado, Michael A Rupp, Jessie YC Chen, Michael J Barnes, Daniel Barber, and Katelyn Procci. 2016. Intelligent agent transparency in human–agent teaming for multi-uxv management. *Human factors*, 58(3):401–415.

Myle Ott, Sergey Edunov, Alexei Baevski, Angela Fan, Sam Gross, Nathan Ng, David Grangier, and Michael Auli. 2019. fairseq: A fast, extensible toolkit for sequence modeling.

Kishore Papineni, Salim Roukos, Todd Ward, and Wei-Jing Zhu. 2002. Bleu: a method for automatic evaluation of machine translation. In *Proceedings of the 40th annual meeting of the Association for Computational Linguistics*, pages 311–318.

Maxime Peyrard, Wei Zhao, Steffen Eger, and Robert West. 2021. Better than average: Paired evaluation of NLP systems. In *Proceedings of the 59th Annual Meeting of the Association for Computational Linguistics and the 11th International Joint Conference on Natural Language Processing (Volume 1: Long Papers)*, pages 2301–2315, Online. Association for Computational Linguistics.

Peter Polák, Muskaan Singh, and Ondřej Bojar. 2021. Explainable quality estimation: Cuni eval4nlp submission. In *Proceedings of the 2nd Workshop on Evaluation and Comparison for NLP systems*.

Maja Popović. 2015. chrF: character n-gram F-score for automatic MT evaluation. In *Proceedings of the Tenth Workshop on Statistical Machine Translation*, pages 372–375, Lisboa, Portugal. Association for Computational Linguistics.

Tharindu Ranasinghe, Constantin Orasan, and Ruslan Mitkov. 2020. Transquest at wmt2020: Sentence-level direct assessment. In *Proceedings of the Fifth Conference on Machine Translation, Volume 2: Shared Tasks Papers*, Online. Association for Computational Linguistics.

Marco Tulio Ribeiro, Sameer Singh, and Carlos Guestrin. 2016. "why should i trust you?": Explaining the predictions of any classifier. In *Proceedings of the 22nd ACM SIGKDD International Conference on Knowledge Discovery and Data Mining*, KDD '16, page 1135–1144, New York, NY, USA. Association for Computing Machinery.

Raphael Rubino, Atsushi Fujita, and Benjamin Marie. 2021. Error identification for machine translation with metric embedding and attention. In *Proceedings of the 2nd Workshop on Evaluation and Comparison for NLP systems*.

Karl Schulz, Leon Sixt, Federico Tombari, and Tim Landgraf. 2020. Restricting the flow: Information bottlenecks for attribution. *arXiv preprint arXiv:2001.00396*.

Avanti Shrikumar, Peyton Greenside, and Anshul Kundaje. 2017. Learning important features through propagating activation differences. In *Proceedings of the 34th International Conference on Machine Learning - Volume 70*, ICML'17, page 3145–3153. JMLR.org.

Avanti Shrikumar, Peyton Greenside, Anna Shcherbina, and Anshul Kundaje. 2016. Not just a black box: Learning important features through propagating activation differences. *CoRR*, abs/1605.01713.

Matthew Snover, Bonnie Dorr, Richard Schwartz, Linnea Micciulla, and John Makhoul. 2006. A study of translation edit rate with targeted human annotation. In *Proceedings of the 7th Conference of the Association for Machine Translation in the Americas: Technical Papers*, pages 223–231.

Yurun Song, Junchen Zhao, and Lucia Specia. 2021. SentSim: Crosslingual semantic evaluation of machine translation. In *Proceedings of the 2021 Conference of the North American Chapter of the Association for Computational Linguistics: Human Language Technologies*, pages 3143–3156, Online. Association for Computational Linguistics.

Lucia Specia, Frédéric Blain, Marina Fomicheva, Erick Fonseca, Vishrav Chaudhary, Francisco Guzmán, and André F. T. Martins. 2020. Findings of the WMT 2020 shared task on quality estimation. In *Proceedings of the Fifth Conference on Machine Translation*, pages 743–764, Online. Association for Computational Linguistics.

Lucia Specia, Frédéric Blain, Varvara Logacheva, Ramón F. Astudillo, and André F. T. Martins. 2018a. Findings of the WMT 2018 shared task on quality estimation. In *Proceedings of the Third Conference on Machine Translation: Shared Task Papers*, pages 689–709, Belgium, Brussels. Association for Computational Linguistics.

Lucia Specia, Carolina Scarton, and Gustavo Henrique Paetzold. 2018b. Quality estimation for machine translation. *Synthesis Lectures on Human Language Technologies*, 11(1):1–162.

Mukund Sundararajan, Ankur Taly, and Qiqi Yan. 2017a. Axiomatic attribution for deep networks. In *International Conference on Machine Learning*, pages 3319–3328. PMLR.

Mukund Sundararajan, Ankur Taly, and Qiqi Yan. 2017b. Axiomatic attribution for deep networks. In *Proceedings of the 34th International Conference on Machine Learning - Volume 70*, ICML'17, page 3319–3328. JMLR.org.

Yuqing Tang, Chau Tran, Xian Li, Peng-Jen Chen, Naman Goyal, Vishrav Chaudhary, Jiatao Gu, and Angela Fan. 2020. Multilingual translation with extensible multilingual pretraining and finetuning.

Ehsan Toreini, Mhairi Aitken, Kovila Coopamootoo, Karen Elliott, Carlos Gonzalez Zelaya, and Aad Van Moorsel. 2020. The relationship between trust in ai and trustworthy machine learning technologies. In *Proceedings of the 2020 conference on fairness, accountability, and transparency*, pages 272–283.

Marcos V. Treviso, Nuno M. Guerreiro, Ricardo Rei, and André F.T. Martins. 2021. Ist-unbabel 2021 submission for the explainable quality estimation shared task. In *Proceedings of the 2nd Workshop on Evaluation and Comparison for NLP systems*.

Yi-Lin Tuan, Ahmed El-Kishky, Adithya Renduchintala, Vishrav Chaudhary, Francisco Guzmán, and Lucia Specia. 2021. Quality estimation without human-labeled data. *arXiv preprint arXiv:2102.04020*.

Sarah Wiegreffe and Yuval Pinter. 2019. Attention is not not explanation. In *Proceedings of the 2019 Conference on Empirical Methods in Natural Language Processing and the 9th International Joint Conference on Natural Language Processing (EMNLP-IJCNLP)*, pages 11–20, Hong Kong, China. Association for Computational Linguistics.

Mo Yu, Shiyu Chang, Yang Zhang, and Tommi S Jaakkola. 2019. Rethinking cooperative rationalization: Introspective extraction and complement control. *arXiv preprint arXiv:1910.13294*.

Omar Zaidan, Jason Eisner, and Christine Piatko. 2007. Using "annotator rationales" to improve machine learning for text categorization. In *Human language technologies 2007: The conference of the North American chapter of the association for computational linguistics; proceedings of the main conference*, pages 260–267.

Matthew D. Zeiler and Rob Fergus. 2014. Visualizing and understanding convolutional networks. In *Computer Vision – ECCV 2014*, pages 818–833, Cham. Springer International Publishing.

Tianyi Zhang, Varsha Kishore, Felix Wu, Kilian Q. Weinberger, and Yoav Artzi. 2020. Bertscore: Evaluating text generation with bert. In *International Conference on Learning Representations*.

Wei Zhao, Goran Glavaš, Maxime Peyrard, Yang Gao, Robert West, and Steffen Eger. 2020. On the limitations of cross-lingual encoders as exposed by reference-free machine translation evaluation. In *Proceedings of the 58th Annual Meeting of the Association for Computational Linguistics*, pages 1656–1671, Online. Association for Computational Linguistics.

Mu Zhu. 2004. Recall, precision and average precision. *Department of Statistics and Actuarial Science, University of Waterloo, Waterloo*, 2(30):6.

Developing a Benchmark for Reducing Data Bias in Authorship Attribution

Benjamin Murauer
Universität Innsbruck
b.murauer@posteo.de

Günther Specht
Universität Innsbruck
guenther.specht@uibk.ac.at

Abstract

Authorship attribution is the task of assigning an unknown document to an author from a set of candidates. In the past, studies in this field use various evaluation datasets to demonstrate the effectiveness of preprocessing steps, features, and models. However, only a small fraction of works use more than one dataset to prove claims. In this paper, we present a collection of highly diverse authorship attribution datasets, which better generalizes evaluation results from authorship attribution research. Furthermore, we implement a wide variety of previously used machine learning models and show that many approaches show vastly different performances when applied to different datasets. We include pre-trained language models, for the first time testing them in this field in a systematic way. Finally, we propose a set of aggregated scores to evaluate different aspects of the dataset collection.

1 Introduction

In authorship attribution, various machine learning techniques are used to predict who has written a specific document, given a set of candidate authors. This means that a dataset used for such experiments must be well-controlled for many aspects like topic, length, etc. to ensure that the model detects the writing *style* of an author rather than something else like the topic of the content (Grieve, 2007; Stamatatos, 2009). For example, a model may find it easy to detect the author if each author writes about a single specific topic, and therefore the model would detect topic rather than style. Therefore, a well-controlled dataset should cover only one topic and one genre so that the only difference between the authors can be attributed to their writing style. Consequently, this makes the results of experiments using these well-controlled datasets prone to data bias, and they become difficult to generalize.

One approach to mitigate that bias is to distinguish the style of authors from the content, which allows to use cross-topic datasets. In this subset of tasks, the documents used for training the models are deliberately different from the texts used for validation thereafter. For example, given a set of journalists that write articles in multiple sections, when news articles about politics are used for training and articles about sports written by the same authors are used for testing, the overlap of topical content can be reduced and the model can only detect stylistic features. Similarly, cross-genre datasets take this one step further and require different genres of documents for training and testing (e.g., text messages and scientific essays). These datasets reduce the amount of stylistic information that can be used for each author to a subset that is expressive in both genres. In cross-language datasets, the training and testing data are written in different languages, further reducing this overlap.

Even when using cross-domain (topic, genre, etc.) datasets, the difficulty of generalizing assumptions regarding the authors' writing style remains, as any conclusions can only be stated for the concrete authors in that dataset. This may be sufficient for some applications, in which the style of *specific* authors or well-controlled groups of authors is analyzed. However, statements that claim to hold up more generally require evaluation with multiple and diverse datasets.

In this paper, we present a collection of datasets for authorship attribution which cover a wide variety of aspects, fulfilling these needs. We include datasets with few and many candidate authors, with different numbers of documents per author, with differently sized documents, and cross-topic, cross-genre and cross-language datasets. We provide detailed suggestions on train/test splits and perform evaluation experiments with a wide variety of models to demonstrate how much the choice of the dataset can impact classification results.

We provide exemplary attribution results for all datasets for a wide variety of machine learning

Proceedings of the 58th Annual Meeting of the Association for Computational Linguistics, pages 179–188

https://doi.org/10.26615/978-954-452-056-4_018

models. We specifically include several pre-trained language models, as they have shown great success in different NLP fields over the last years, but a systematic analysis of their performance in the authorship attribution field has not yet been performed to the best of our knowledge.

Lastly, to evaluate how well a model performs for each aspect of the collection, we provide a set of aggregated scores that combines results from different datasets.

Our contributions in this paper are therefore threefold: (1) we present a collection of selected, highly diverse datasets for authorship attribution that are able to better generalize evaluation results, (2) we benchmark several pre-trained language models on these datasets, providing a previously unavailable baseline in the field of authorship attribution, and (3) we provide a set of scores that evaluate a model based on the different aspects of the datasets.

To ensure reproducibility and foster future research, we publish all code online[1]. Thereby, we focus on providing tooling that minimizes the efforts required to expand both the dataset collection as well as the evaluation scores.

2 Related Work

While many previous studies use either only one dataset or don't specifically increase the diversity of the datasets used, they often fail to address this implicit data bias. Even foundational work in this field trying to categorize features in this field in a fundamental way can be prone to this issue. For example, Grieve (2007) measure the effectiveness of 39 different feature types for attribution. They address the importance of the dataset being representative for a language and explicitly explain the characteristics of the texts and authors in great detail, but consequently, by using a single dataset, their findings of feature performances are restricted to those very characteristics. Nevertheless, findings of such fundamental work are often referenced for research that uses completely different datasets.

One idea to mitigate any bias on the content of a dataset is to focus on the separation between *style* and *content*. This can be achieved by explicitly modelling the topic (Sari et al., 2018) or by using cross-topic or cross-domain datasets, where the training data and the test data have a different genre or contain texts about different topics (Stamatatos, 2013; Sapkota et al., 2015; Kestemont et al., 2018). For the latter, the key idea is that by minimizing the topic or genre-specific content contained in the overlap of training and testing data, any performances measured must conclude from the stylistic information from the authors. Nevertheless, for both approaches, the bias towards those authors remains in the evaluation.

Even from within a dataset, the choice of training and testing data can have a large impact on the outcome and additionally varies across languages (Eder and Rybicki, 2012). Additionally, Eder (2013) demonstrated that the amount of text required to reliably attribute an author also depends on the language, and suspects that this result may be depending on the genre of text as well. Similarly, Luyckx and Daelemans (2011) show that while some feature types are more robust to the size of the dataset, the performance of others varies greatly depending on the number of documents per author and the number of authors.

In this paper, we want to showcase a collection of diverse authorship attribution datasets and perform attribution experiments with several widely used exemplary machine learning models. The higher goal of our work is that it should be easy to make evaluation results of authorship attribution research easily comparable and also generalizable.

Using pre-trained language models for authorship attribution has not been researched in great detail. Some approaches use them as part of a larger ensemble model (Fabien et al., 2020) or as a feature extraction step in front of the actual classifier (Barlas and Stamatatos, 2020). However, when it comes to the performance of the unaltered models that are readily available, no overview for comparisons using widely used authorship attribution datasets are available to the best of our knowledge.

3 Datasets

For this benchmark, we have selected a wide variety of authorship attribution corpora. Thereby, we focussed on multiple aspects of datasets that may influence the classification process and try to provide a diverse but controlled set of these aspects:

- Genres: social media comments, business news, novels, reviews, etc.
- Topics: different news article topics, different fan fiction domains, etc.

[1] `https://git.uibk.ac.at/csak8736/authbench`

Dataset	Text type	$\times_T$	$\times_G$	$\times_L$	A	D	Words	$\|d\|$	D/A	Imb
CCAT50	financial/industrial news				50	2,500	1,254.4K	502	50	0.0
CL-Novels	prose	✓		✓	6	144	1,199.1K	8,354	24	11.7
CMCC	multiple	✓	✓		21	630	378.4K	601	30	0.0
Guardian	book reviews, opinions	✓	✓		13	264	276.0K	1,043	20	4.3
IMDb62	movie reviews				62	49,572	16,904.4K	341	800	1.0
PAN18-FF	prose	✓			20 (12)	88	69.7K	796	7	0.0
Reddit	social media comments			✓	45 (28)	2,366	1,259.7K	532	94	83.5

Table 1: Datasets used in this paper. $\times_{T,G,L}$ denote whether the datasets are cross-topic, cross-genre or cross-language, respectively. A denotes the total number of authors. The Reddit and PAN18-FF datasets have sub-problems with disjunct authors, and the number in parenthesis denotes the mean number of authors per sub-problem. D denotes the total number of documents. $|d|$ is the mean length of a document measured in number of words. D/A denotes the average number of documents available for training per author. Imb is the imbalance of the dataset, measured by the standard deviation of the number of documents per author.

- Languages: single-language datasets, multi-language datasets, cross-language datasets
- Dataset sizes: document size, number of documents per author, number of authors

These lead to the selection of seven datasets, which will be described briefly in the following section. An overview of some basic statistics is presented in Table 1.

3.1 Selected Datasets

The CCAT50 dataset (Liu, 2011) is a subset of the Reuters Corpus Volume 1 (Lewis et al., 2004) and contains 5,000 financial news articles from 50 authors, each having 50 training documents and 50 testing documents.

The CL-Novels dataset (Bogdanova and Lazaridou, 2014) contains English novels by 19th-century authors (Jane Austen, Charlotte Brontë, Lewis Carroll, Rudyard Kipling, Robert Louis Stevenson, and Oscar Wilde) and some Spanish (human) translations of their works. Although the novels are split into 500 sentence chunks (as the original authors did), these chunks are still the largest documents in this benchmark (cf. Table 1).

The CMCC dataset (Goldstein-Stewart et al., 2008) contains texts from 21 students about 6 different topics (church, gay marriage, privacy rights, legalization of marijuana, war in Iraq, gender discrimination) in 6 different genres (email, essay, interview transcript, blog article, chat, discussion transcript). This means that depending on how the data is split into train and test parts, it can function as either cross-topic or cross-genre dataset.

The Guardian dataset (Stamatatos, 2013) consists of book reviews and opinion articles written by professional journalists of *The Guardian* newspaper. The documents are categorized into the two genres of book reviews and opinion articles, and the latter is further divided into four topics (politics, society, world, UK). Hence, similar to the CMCC dataset, the choice of the train/test split defines whether this dataset is cross-topic or cross-genre.

The IMDb62 dataset (Seroussi et al., 2010) contains movie reviews written by 62 users of the internet movie database platform[2]. It features by far the most documents per author (1,000).

The PAN18-FF dataset (Kestemont et al., 2018) consists of fan fiction prose texts written by admirers of authors, novels, TV shows, movies, etc. Thereby, the authors invent and create new stories surrounding the original universes, which are called fandoms. The dataset contains authors that have written fiction in multiple fandoms, making it a cross-domain. Furthermore, the dataset is divided into 10 explicit sub-problems, 2 for each of 5 languages (English, Spanish, French, Italian, and Polish). For each problem, training and testing documents are predefined. Note that these problems are single-language problems and the authors don't overlap across different problems, which means that this is a multilingual, but not a *cross*-lingual dataset.

The Reddit dataset (Murauer and Specht, 2019) consists of comments by multilingual users of the Reddit social media platform. It contains five different language pairs for which users have written comments in both languages (English as well as one of German, Spanish, Portuguese, Dutch, and French). Compared to the other datasets, it is the

[2] `www.imdb.com`

Dataset	Splits	Description
CCAT50	2	predefined (50%/50%)
CL-Novels	$*15$	leave-one-novel out
CMCC$\times_G$	6	leave-one-genre-out
CMCC$\times_T$	6	leave-one-topic-out
Guardian$\times_G$	2	leave-one-genre-out
Guardian$\times_T$	4	leave-one-topic-out
IMDb62	5	stratified 5-fold
PAN18-FF	10	predefined
Reddit	10	leave-one-language-out

Table 2: Train/test splits for each dataset. $*$ Evaluations with identical training documents were combined.

most unbalanced dataset, as for some authors far more documents are available than for others (cf. column 'Imb' in Table 1).

3.2 Evaluation Splits

Deciding which parts of a dataset are used for training and testing plays an important role in interpreting the evaluation results, and being able to replicate results. In this section, we explain how these splits are selected for each dataset. Table 2 contains the overview of the train/test splits used in this paper.

The CCAT50 dataset has predefined subsets for training and testing of equal size.

The CL-Novels dataset is evaluated using *leave-one-novel-out*, as suggested by the original authors: Let D be the set of all novels, l_n the language of novel n, and t_n the original English title of both Spanish and English versions of n. Then, for $\forall n \in D$, the model is trained with all novels $\mathbf{m} = \{m \in D | l_m \neq l_n \wedge t_m \neq t_n\}$. The model is then evaluated on n. For example, for the split that has the English version of *Alice in Wonderland* as test data, m consists of training documents that (1) are not English, and (2) are not (a translated version of) *Alice in Wonderland*. Consequently, all n that only appear in one language have the same training documents $\mathbf{m}$. For these splits, the same model has to be trained only once and can be used for evaluation for all of the splits, increasing efficiency.

The CMCC and Guardian datasets contain multiple topics and genres. We adopt both a *leave-one-genre-out* as well as a *leave-one-topic-out* strategy, which is in line with related studies using these resources. Hence, in the experiments, these datasets are listed twice: once as a cross-genre dataset, and once as a cross-topic dataset.

For the homogeneous IMDb62 dataset, we use a stratified 5-fold cross-validation scheme.

The PAN18-FF dataset is divided into 10 subproblems, each with a predefined training and testing part.

Finally, for the Reddit dataset, we use *leave-one-language-out* splits, where all documents of language l_1 are used for testing, and all documents of the respective other language l_2 are used for training. This is repeated for l_1 and l_2 swapped, and for each language pair (sub-problem) in the dataset.

3.3 Availability

For the IMDb62, PAN18-FF, CMCC, and Guardian datasets, permission to use them is required from the original authors. The CCAT50[3] and Reddit[4] datasets are freely available online. We reconstructed the CL-Novels dataset from the information of the original paper (Bogdanova and Lazaridou, 2014) by downloading the appropriate novels from the Project Gutenberg[5]. We removed introduction texts by the hosting platform (which always include the name of the author) and any appendices and notes from translators. The novels are in the public domain and we make the resulting cleaned dataset available for download online[6].

4 Experiment Setup and Models

The purpose of the evaluation experiments in this paper is to show that the performance of different models varies greatly across different datasets. We therefore perform classification experiments with several classification models to provide an impression of how the choice of a dataset influences the evaluation, but don't claim to provide the best possible configurations of those models for the analyzed datasets.

We select several features in combination with a linear support vector machine, as well as several solutions based on pre-trained language models. Important parameters for the models are listed in Table 3.

[3]https://archive.ics.uci.edu/ml/datasets/Reuter_50_50

[4]https://github.com/bmurauer/reddit_corpora

[5]https://www.gutenberg.org/

[6]https://git.uibk.ac.at/csak8736/authbench

Parameter	Value
TF/IDF	
normalization	$L2$
number of features	all
Doc2Vec	
learn rate	0.02
epochs	20
vector size	100
SVM	
C	1.0
penalty	$L2$
loss	squared hinge
multiclass strategy	one-versus-rest
max. iterations	1,000
tolerance	$1e^{-4}$
Language Model *	
BERT	bert-base-cased
DistilBERT	distilbert-base-cased
RoBERTa	roberta-base

Table 3: Parameters of the models used in the experiments. * Models from `https://huggingface.co/models`, accessed July 2021.

4.1 Features with Linear SVM

As a simple baseline, we use tf/idf-normalized frequencies of character 3-grams. They have been shown to be effective in authorship attribution and are capable of capturing both content-related information as well as author-specific stylistic nuances (Sapkota et al., 2015; Stamatatos, 2013, 2017).

We further adopt two syntax-based features. Firstly, we use part-of-speech (POS) tag n-grams. These abstract from the content of the text and focus on the grammatical structure, which has been shown to identify authors in similar settings (Kaster et al., 2005; Bogdanova and Lazaridou, 2014). Secondly, we utilize the DT-grams feature by Murauer and Specht (2021), which uses POS tags, but additionally incorporates dependency grammar information. *Universal* POS tags (Nivre et al., 2016) are a mapping of language-specific tags into a universal, language-independent space, and we utilize them for the experiments on the cross-language datasets. For both syntax-based features, we use language-specific POS tags for the mono-language datasets, and universal POS tags for the cross-language datasets.

Document embeddings have been shown to be effective for authorship attribution (Gómez-Adorno et al., 2018), and we experiment with both character 3-grams and words as tokens.

4.2 Pre-Trained Language Models

We test three transformer-based models: BERT (Devlin et al., 2018), DistilBERT (Sanh et al., 2019), and RoBERTa (Liu et al., 2019). Previous works use this family of models in combination with an ensemble (Fabien et al., 2020) or as a feature extraction stage for further processing (Barlas and Stamatatos, 2020), but no comprehensive analysis has been performed which uses these models without further modifications to the best of our knowledge. We use the parameters suggested by the respective original authors and use a sequence length of 256 tokens. As many documents are longer than that, we use a sliding window approach that extracts samples from the documents that fit into the maximum sequence length of the models.

5 Evaluation Results

For all models presented in Section 4, we perform authorship attribution experiments for all datasets covered in Section 3 (using the train/test splits as discussed in Section 3.2). In Table 4, the results of these classifications is shown, where each score (measured in macro-averaged F1) represents the mean score of the respective model and dataset for all train/test splits for that dataset. For example, the PAN18-FF dataset has 10 explicit subproblems, so each score in the PAN18 column of Table 4 represents the average score of the model for those 10 problems. As described in Section 3.2, the CMCC and Guardian datasets have two different ways of splitting the data (cross-topic and cross-genre).

From these exemplary experiments, different conclusions can be drawn depending on which subsets of the results are analyzed. In the remainder of this section, we focus on the different aspects that the selected datasets feature.

5.1 Sensitivity to Dataset Size

The IMDb62 and CCAT50 datasets are large enough to extract differently sized subsets to analyze the performance of the models. While the Reddit dataset has comparably many documents, we refrained from including it in this experiment due to the imbalance of the dataset. Therefore, we restricted the number of training documents to 5, 10, 15, 20, 30, 40, and 50 documents for each

Model	CCAT50	CL-Novels	CMCC $\times_T$	CMCC $\times_G$	Guardian $\times_T$	Guardian $\times_G$	IMDb62	PAN18	Reddit
char. 3-grams	**0.703**	0.184	**0.614**	**0.685**	0.819	0.534	0.970	**0.493**	0.049
univ. POS 3-grams	0.614	**0.187**	0.544	0.452	0.813	**0.547**	0.922	0.381	0.131
DT-grams	0.534	0.178	0.394	0.295	0.648	0.305	0.874	0.281	0.166
Doc2Vec (char. 3-grams)	0.303	0.094	0.152	0.207	0.410	0.292	0.189	0.375	0.035
Doc2Vec (word 1-grams)	0.406	0.144	0.254	0.283	0.523	0.392	0.560	0.224	0.044
BERT	0.662	0.116	0.535	0.316	**0.847**	0.441	0.979	0.335	0.185
DistilBERT	0.665	0.107	0.482	0.293	0.814	0.442	0.976	0.391	0.126
RoBERTa	0.659	0.157	0.604	0.289	0.835	0.450	**0.979**	0.417	**0.268**

Table 4: Mean macro-averaged F1 scores of all splits for each dataset and tested model. $\times_G$ denotes cross-genre splitting, while $\times_T$ denotes cross-topic splitting of the CMCC and Guardian datasets.

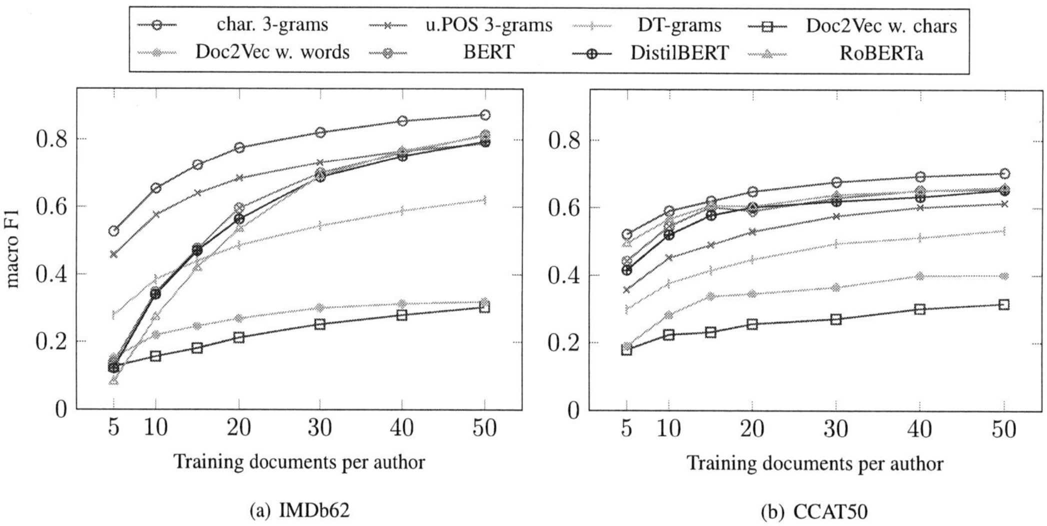

Figure 1: F1 score of subsets of the IMDb62 (left) and CCAT50 (right) datasets with controlled number of documents per author. Note that although the number of authors and document sizes are comparable (cf. Table 1), the performances of the transformer-based models differ significantly, especially when few training samples are available for each author.

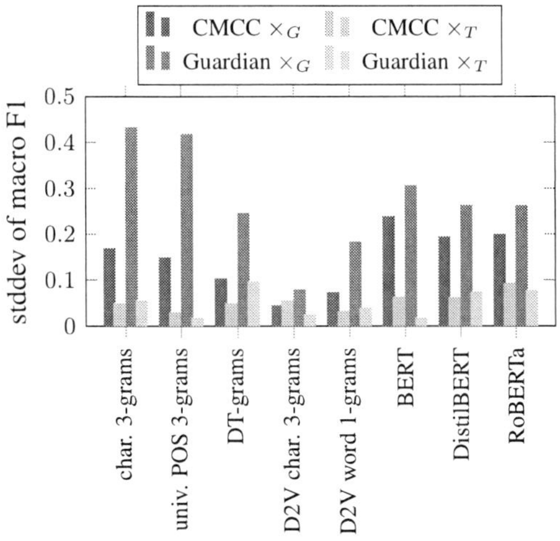

Figure 2: Sensitivity of tested models to cross-genre ($\times_G$) and cross-topic ($\times_T$) splits. The y-axis shows the standard deviation of the F1 score for all splits, high values indicate that the model performed well on some topics/genres and bad on others.

author, while not changing the number of test documents or the number of authors. The sampling of the documents was random, and all experiments were repeated 5 times to mitigate bias. In Figure 1, the F1 score of these sizes is displayed. It can be seen that while the performance for all models rises gradually in the CCAT50 dataset, the transformer-based models have much more trouble with the IMDb62 dataset when provided with fewer training samples, but quickly catch up to the character 3-grams with more training data.

While the reason for this discrepancy remains unanswered by this experiment, it shows that the two datasets exhibit different behaviors when used in combination with transformer-based classifiers. It is likely that other small-scaled datasets also display such incoherences, and it is therefore important to apply any model to multiple datasets to increase the meaningfulness of the evaluation.

In particular, studies along the lines of Luyckx and Daelemans (2011) analyzing comparable problems with varying dataset sizes should also be performed on as many datasets as possible.

5.2 Sensitivity to Genre and Topic

From Table 4, several conclusions can be drawn from the results of the cross-topic/genre datasets. Firstly, we can confirm that cross-genre classification is in general harder than cross-topic classification. Where explicit previous assumptions in this regard use single models and datasets (Stamatatos, 2013; Barlas and Stamatatos, 2020), we affirm this finding with multiple models and datasets. As a single exception, the character 3-grams show a higher performance on the cross-genre version of the CMCC dataset compared to the cross-topic variant.

The table also clearly reflects the difficulty that cross-genre situations impose on the pre-trained language models, which otherwise excel in the cross-topic splits.

Figure 2 shows the standard deviation of the F1 score across the different topics and genres in the CMCC and Guardian datasets. Hence, high values mean that the models perform differently for the topics or genres in the dataset. The figure displays that most models are more sensitive to the genre of the text than they are to the topic, consistently over both CMCC and Guardian datasets. The Doc2Vec model with character 3-grams has a low overall prediction score (cf. Table 4), and shows this effect to a smaller degree.

Note that this does not hold for the average performance over all splits (cf. Table 4): in general, the tested models are performing better on the cross-topic datasets, and do so more consistently for all topics compared to the cross-genre datasets. This result can't be seen from Table 4, and it means that for some cross-genre splits, some models may perform better than the average winner.

5.3 Sensitivity to Language

A surprising overall result for the cross-language datasets in Table 4 is the relatively high efficiency of the pre-trained language models for the Reddit dataset, as they have not been pre-trained using multilingual texts. This performance is not displayed in the other cross-language dataset containing 19th-century novels, which suggest that his behavior could stem from the genre of texts (social media comments), which are more likely to contain words common in multiple languages than documents from the 19th century. However, we suggest that even more datasets are required to answer this specific question.

Cross-language classification problems are defined by two different choices regarding the candidate languages: Firstly, which languages are considered in the classification problem at all, and secondly, which of those languages are used for training and which are used for testing. Figure 3

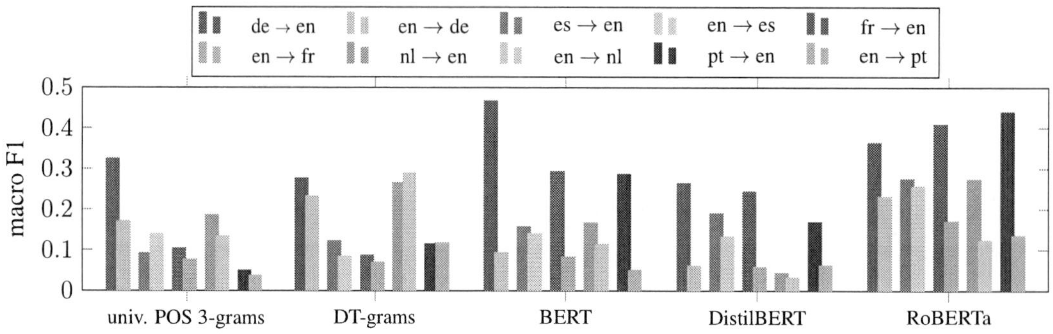

Figure 3: Sensitivity of selected models to the direction of the train/test split for each language pair. de → en denotes the score of the model that was trained with German and tested with English documents.

shows the macro F1 score of two cross-language models (univ. POS tag 3-grams and DT-grams) and the pre-trained language models for the Reddit dataset. The different colors represent the different language pairs of the Reddit dataset, and the two columns of each color represent the classification score (in macro F1) of both train/test directions used for the experiment (thereby, de → en denotes that the model was trained using German documents and tested on English texts).

The performance of the models generally differs across different pairs, which suggests that any cross-language classification approach should use as many language pairs as possible to generalize well. However, cross-language datasets are difficult to compile, as authors writing in more than one language are sparse.

In general, but especially for the language models, the figure also displays that the models perform better when they are fine-tuned using the non-English documents. This suggests that the choice of which language is used for training is an important choice that must be considered and reported by cross-language attribution studies.

6 Scores

The various datasets allow aggregation of the results according to the different aspects described in the previous sections, for which we formulate scores that are listed in Table 5. Each score is calculated by averaging the results from all splits in the respective datasets, weighted by the inverse number of splits in each dataset. Table 6 shows these scores for all models tested in our experiments, while Table 7 shows the standard deviation of each model across the different splits of the respective score. The aim of this separation is to quickly provide an overview of the strengths and weaknesses that a model shows for specifics aspects of the datasets. For example, for the models presented in this paper, it is now more clearly detectable that the character 3-gram features are a very strong baseline, but fail at the cross-language tasks.

Score	Description	Datasets Used
mono	one lang./topic/genre	IMDb62, CCAT50
sm	10 training texts/auth.	IMDb62, CCAT50
ml	mixed languages	PAN18
$\times_T$	cross-topic	CMCC$\times_T$, Guardian$\times_T$
$\times_G$	cross-genre	CMCC$\times_G$, Guardian$\times_G$
$\times_L$	cross-language	Reddit, CL-Novels
avg	mean of all	

Table 5: Scores used to reflect the models performance on the different aspects of the datasets.

The pre-trained language models show promising results for authorship attribution in summary, especially in the unexpected case of cross-language classification. Higher standard deviations indicate that these models are more prone to overfitting to specific fits.

We want to emphasize once more that the aim of this paper is not to provide the best possible results for the tested models, but show how a more expressive evaluation result can be achieved by incorporating multiple datasets into the evaluation process.

7 Limitations and Future Work

The collection of datasets presented in this paper is by no means exhaustive in terms of covered dataset aspects, but it should provide a solid foundation for this purpose. For example, authorship attribution on a larger scale (Narayanan et al., 2012; Tschug-

Model	mono	sm	ml	$\times_T$	$\times_G$	$\times_L$	avg
char. 3-grams	**0.84**	**0.62**	**0.49**	0.70	**0.65**	0.07	**0.56**
u.POS 3-grams	0.77	0.51	0.38	0.65	0.48	0.14	0.49
DT-grams	0.70	0.38	0.28	0.50	0.30	0.17	0.39
Doc2Vec char	0.25	0.19	0.38	0.26	0.23	0.04	0.22
Doc2Vec word	0.48	0.25	0.22	0.36	0.31	0.06	0.28
BERT	0.82	0.45	0.33	0.66	0.35	0.17	0.46
DistilBERT	0.82	0.43	0.39	0.61	0.33	0.12	0.45
RoBERTa	0.82	0.42	0.42	**0.70**	0.33	**0.25**	0.49

Table 6: Aggregated F1 scores reached by the models tested in our experiments.

Model	mono	sm	ml	$\times_T$	$\times_G$	$\times_L$	avg
char. 3-grams	0.19	0.05	0.11	0.12	0.23	0.06	0.13
u.POS 3-grams	0.22	0.09	**0.29**	0.14	0.21	0.09	0.17
DT-grams	**0.24**	0.01	0.16	0.15	0.13	0.08	0.13
Doc2Vec char	0.08	0.05	0.23	0.14	0.06	0.04	0.10
Doc2Vec word	0.11	0.04	0.10	0.14	0.11	0.05	0.09
BERT	0.22	0.14	0.19	0.17	**0.24**	**0.13**	**0.18**
DistilBERT	0.22	0.13	0.19	**0.18**	0.20	0.09	0.17
RoBERTa	0.23	**0.21**	0.13	0.14	0.21	0.11	0.17

Table 7: Aggregated standard deviations of F1 scores reached by the models tested in our experiments.

gnall et al., 2019) requires datasets far beyond the sizes of the presented material, and in general, also requires different methods for evaluation and solving strategies.

From a multilingual standpoint, the dataset collection thus far only contains several European languages, and those are among the smallest datasets in the benchmark. In the long term, our future plans involve including more datasets from as many languages as possible, and ideally also increase the number of cross-language datasets.

As not all models and methods are intended to work with all types of text, we envision well-defined subsets of the benchmark covering the possible application areas for many models. For example, even when a model is only targeted to classify social media text, we aim to provide multiple datasets fulfilling this requirement.

To ensure the continued attribution to this collection, we publish a set of tools[7] which minimize the effort required to add additional datasets to this collection. These tools make it easy to (1) bring the dataset to a common format, (2) define train/test splits that the dataset should be used with, and (3) specify which of these splits contribute to the scores presented in the previous section. Thereby, contributions can be made to existing scores by providing more datasets to reassure them, or add additional scores to the collection. We hope to timely contribute more multilingual datasets to the ml score and expand on different dataset sizes beyond the few thresholds presented by the sm score.

8 Conclusion

In this paper, we present a collection of datasets aimed to increase the expressiveness and generalizability of authorship attribution experiments. The datasets are carefully chosen to include many different aspects of the text, such as document size, number of documents per author, language, genre, or topic. We choose several well-established text classification models and perform attribution experiments on all datasets, for the first time showing results systematically for pre-trained language models in this field. Thereby, we demonstrate the importance of including multiple datasets in any evaluation by showing differences in the classification score for similar datasets and train/test splits. We conclude the paper by suggesting an aggregated score for each of the presented aspects to easily distinguish the strengths and weaknesses of different models.

References

Georgios Barlas and Efstathios Stamatatos. 2020. Cross-domain authorship attribution using pre-trained language models. In *IFIP Advances in Information and Communication Technology*, pages 255–266.

Dasha Bogdanova and Angeliki Lazaridou. 2014. Cross-language authorship attribution. In *Ninth International Conference on Language Resources and Evaluation (LREC'2014)*, pages 2015–2020.

Jacob Devlin, Ming-Wei Chang, Kenton Lee, and Kristina Toutanova. 2018. Bert: Pre-training of deep bidirectional transformers for language understanding.

Maciej Eder. 2013. Does size matter? Authorship attribution, small samples, big problem. *Digital Scholarship in the Humanities*, 30(2):167–182.

Maciej Eder and Jan Rybicki. 2012. Do birds of a feather really flock together, or how to choose training samples for authorship attribution. *Literary and Linguistic Computing*, 28(2):229–236.

Maël Fabien, Esaú Villatoro-Tello, Petr Motlicek, and Shantipriya Parida. 2020. BertAA: BERT fine-tuning for Authorship Attribution. In *Proceedings of the*

[7] `https://git.uibk.ac.at/csak8736/authbench`

17th International Conference on Natural Language Processing.

Jade Goldstein-Stewart, Kerri Goodwin, Roberta Sabin, and Ransom Winder. 2008. Creating and using a correlated corpus to glean communicative commonalities. In *Proceedings of the Sixth International Conference on Language Resources and Evaluation (LREC'08)*. European Language Resources Association (ELRA).

Helena Gómez-Adorno, Juan-Pablo Posadas-Durán, Grigori Sidorov, and David Pinto. 2018. Document embeddings learned on various types of n-grams for cross-topic authorship attribution. *Computing*, 100(7):741–756.

Jack Grieve. 2007. Quantitative authorship attribution: An evaluation of techniques. *Literary and Linguistic Computing*, 22:251–270.

Andreas Kaster, Stefan Siersdorfer, and Gerhard Weikum. 2005. Combining Text and Linguistic Document Representations for Authorship Attribution. In *Working Notes of the 28th Conference on Research and Development in Information Retrieval (SIGIR'2005): Stylistic Analysis of Text for Information Access*, pages 27–35.

Mike Kestemont, Michael Tschugnall, Efstathios Stamatatos, Walter Daelemans, Günther Specht, Benno Stein, and Martin Potthast. 2018. Overview of the Author Identification Task at PAN-2018: Cross-domain Authorship Attribution and Style Change Detection. In *Working Notes Papers of the CLEF 2018 Evaluation Labs*.

David D Lewis, Yiming Yang, Tony Russell-Rose, and Fan Li. 2004. Rcv1: A new benchmark collection for text categorization research. *Journal of machine learning research*, 5(Apr):361–397.

Yinhan Liu, Myle Ott, Naman Goyal, Jingfei Du, Mandar Joshi, Danqi Chen, Omer Levy, Mike Lewis, Luke Zettlemoyer, and Veselin Stoyanov. 2019. RoBERTa: A Robustly Optimized BERT Pretraining Approach.

Zhi Liu. 2011. Reuter 50-50 Dataset. National Engineering Research Center for E-Learning Technology China.

Kim Luyckx and Walter Daelemans. 2011. The effect of author set size and data size in authorship attribution. *Literary and Linguistic Computing*, 26(1):35–55.

Benjamin Murauer and Günther Specht. 2019. Generating cross-domain text classification corpora from social media comments. In *Proceedings of the 20th International Conference of the Cross-Language Evaluation Forum for European Languages (CLEF'2019)*, pages 114–125.

Benjamin Murauer and Günther Specht. 2021. DT-grams: Structured Dependency Grammar Stylometry for Cross-Language Authorship Attribution.

Arvind Narayanan, Hristo Paskov, Neil Zhenqiang Gong, John Bethencourt, Emil Stefanov, Eui Chul Richard Shin, and Dawn Song. 2012. On the feasibility of internet-scale author identification. In *2012 IEEE Symposium on Security and Privacy*. IEEE.

Joakim Nivre, Marie-Catherine De Marneffe, Filip Ginter, Yoav Goldberg, Jan Hajic, Christopher D Manning, Ryan McDonald, Slav Petrov, Sampo Pyysalo, Natalia Silveira, et al. 2016. Universal dependencies v1: A multilingual treebank collection. In *Proceedings of the 10th Int. Conference on Language Resources and Evaluation (LREC'16)*, pages 1659–1666.

Victor Sanh, Lysandre Debut, Julien Chaumond, and Thomas Wolf. 2019. Distilbert, a distilled version of bert: smaller, faster, cheaper and lighter.

Upendra Sapkota, Steven Bethard, Manuel Montes, and Thamar Solorio. 2015. Not All Character N-grams Are Created Equal: A Study In Authorship Attribution. In *Proceedings of the 2015 Conference of the North American Chapter of the Association for Computational Linguistics: Human language Technologies*, pages 93–102.

Yunita Sari, Mark Stevenson, and Andreas Vlachos. 2018. Topic or style? exploring the most useful features for authorship attribution. In *Proceedings of the 27th International Conference on Computational Linguistics*, pages 343–353. Association for Computational Linguistics.

Yanir Seroussi, Ingrid Zukerman, and Fabian Bohnert. 2010. Collaborative Inference of Sentiments from Texts. In *Proceedings of the 18th International Conference on User Modeling, Adaptation and Personalization (UMOD'2010)*, pages 195–206.

E. Stamatatos. 2009. A Survey of Modern Authorship Attribution Methods. *Journal of the American Society for Information Science and Technology*, 60(3):538–556.

Efstathios Stamatatos. 2013. On the Robustness of Authorship Attribution Based on Character N-Gram Features. *Journal of Law & Policy*, pages 421–439.

Efstathios Stamatatos. 2017. Authorship Attribution Using Text Distortion. In *Proceedings of the 15th Conference of the European Chapter of the Association for Computational Linguistics (EACL'2017)*, pages 1138–1149. Association for Computational Linguistics.

Michael Tschuggnall, Benjamin Murauer, and Günther Specht. 2019. Reduce & attribute: Two-step authorship attribution for large-scale problems. In *Proceedings of the 23rd Conference on Computational Natural Language Learning (CoNLL)*, pages 951–960. Association for Computational Linguistics.

Error-Sensitive Evaluation for Ordinal Target Variables

David Z. Chen Maury Courtland Adam Faulkner Aysu Ezen Can
Capital One, Vision and Language Technologies
{david.chen2, maury.courtland, adam.faulkner, aysu.ezencan}
@capitalone.com

Abstract

Product reviews and satisfaction surveys seek customer feedback in the form of ranked scales. In these settings, widely used evaluation metrics including F1 and accuracy ignore the rank in the responses (e.g., 'very likely' is closer to 'likely' than 'not at all'). In this paper, we hypothesize that the order of class values is important for evaluating classifiers on ordinal target variables and should not be disregarded. To test this hypothesis, we compared Multi-class Classification (MC) and Ordinal Regression (OR) by applying OR and MC to benchmark tasks involving ordinal target variables using the same underlying model architecture. Experimental results show that while MC outperformed OR for some datasets in accuracy and F1, OR is significantly better than MC for minimizing the error between prediction and target for all benchmarks, as revealed by error-sensitive metrics, e.g. mean-squared error (MSE) and Spearman correlation. Our findings motivate the need to establish consistent, error-sensitive metrics for evaluating benchmarks with ordinal target variables, and we hope that it stimulates interest in exploring alternative losses for ordinal problems.

1 Introduction

Organizations have a vested interest in ensuring customer happiness. To measure this quantity, analysts often use surveys containing numerical Likert scales addressing various aspects of the customer experience (Allen and Seaman, 2007). One popular question asks customers the likelihood that they will recommend a product or service to others. From these answers, analysts calculate a "Net Promoter Score" (NPS) representing the percentage of customers who will recommend a product or service to others minus those who will recommend against it (Reichheld, 2003). Additionally, many companies are also interested in tracking product reviews (Keung et al., 2020). Collecting, measuring, and analyzing customer feedback is essential to the profitability and long-term success of many companies, but it is prohibitively expensive to survey the entire customer base and even the feedback that a company does receive is often too massive for systematic human evaluation. Therefore, it is important to develop effective machine learning models for predicting customer satisfaction and to maintain consistent and accurate methods and metrics for evaluating their performance.

An important aspect of modeling customer sentiment is the subjective numerical ranking of the customer response. Feedback is often in the form of ranked scales, e.g. rating scales 1-5 or 1-10, or textual "Strongly Agree," "Disagree," etc. Crucially, these Likert scales are ordinal and should not be confused with scalar values: a rating of 5 or "Strongly Agree" is not necessarily 5 times greater than a rating of 1 or "Strongly Disagree" (Allen and Seaman, 2007). To predict ordinal target variables from textual input, we explored a variety of commonplace and cutting-edge NLP techniques, ranging from linear models such as Naive Bayes and Logistic Regression to Transformer-based approaches such as BERT (Devlin et al., 2019) and "Performer" (Choromanski et al., 2021). One of the most striking observations from our experiments was that the most impactful experimental variable was not necessarily the model architecture itself, but rather the loss function employed and classification scheme, i.e. target variable encoding. Specifically, we highlight our use of Ordinal Regression (OR), which is an approach that is underutilized in the field of NLP. This approach has a long history (Frank and Hall, 2001; Graepel and Obermayer, 1999; Gutiérrez et al., 2016; Baccianella et al., 2009)

Proceedings of the 58th Annual Meeting of the Association for Computational Linguistics, pages 189–199

https://doi.org/10.26615/978-954-452-056-4_019

and has recently been applied to deep neural network models predicting ordinal labels (Cao et al., 2020). Here, we extend this framework into the domain of NLP and apply it to train transformer models as a novel application of previous work on OR and transformers. Our results showed that OR produced a distribution of predictions significantly closer to ground truth distributions than Multi-class Classification (MC) for both NPS and survey ratings (i.e. lower K-L divergence), while producing similar accuracies and F1. Additionally, we found that OR improved the correlation between model predictions and ground truth. Our findings highlight that common NLP metrics are insufficient to distinguish the better model(s) for our task, which motivated us to explore and identify error-sensitive metrics more consistent and effective for evaluating models with ordinal target variables.

2 Related work

There has been a longstanding debate (Knapp, 1990; Joshi et al., 2015) within the survey, psychometrics, and crowdsourcing methodology community regarding the use of Likert scales. In particular, a debate on whether the level of measurement in question is interval or ordinal (McCall, 2001) and whether parametric or nonparametric tests should should be used (Kuzon et al., 1996). In a classification setting involving ordinal data, a related question involves the use of multinomial versus ordinal modeling for such data. Intuitively, the inclusion of ordinality in the classification model should improve performance relative to a multinomial approach, as shown in Campbell and Donner 1989. Despite the prevalence of ordinally-scaled tasks in NLP, such as in sentiment analysis (Jiang et al., 2019; Pang and Lee, 2005), stance classification (Sobhani et al., 2015), lexical specificity (Gao et al., 2019), political bias (Baly et al., 2018), and commonsense inference (Zhang et al., 2017), approaches to such tasks have tended to ignore the ordinal nature of the data, treating them as MC tasks. For example, only 2 of 11 participants in subtask C of SemEval 2016 (Rosenthal et al., 2017) (a 5-point-scale twitter sentiment classification task) chose to exploit the ordinal nature of the task in their models. Justifying this choice would involve systematically comparing the use of ordinal versus MC models for these tasks, yet most such comparisons have been reported as an incidental part of experiments for tasks such as sentiment analysis in tweets (Saad and Yang, 2019) and classification of psychiatric symptom severity in clinical notes (Rios and Kavuluru, 2017).

3 Methods

3.1 Datasets

We hypothesize that taking ordinal rankings into account would provide more consistent and better results. To test this, we experimented on 3 common benchmark datasets for sentiment analysis, and 1 additional dataset on Twitter specificity.

Movie Reviews (MR): We used the dataset named "scale dataset v1.0" (Pang and Lee, 2005). It contains full-length movie reviews from 4 authors on RottenTomatoes.com, and we used the 4-class variant, which is obtained by segmenting the ratings from the authors' normalized numerical scale into 4 ranks. Each author a, b, c, and d has 1770, 902, 1307 and 1027 reviews, respectively. The mean number of words per review for each author is 435, 374, 455 and 292, respectively, but the tail is long, with some reviews having 3k words or more. For this dataset, no test data was provided, so we report results on a test set from an 80%/20% train/test split of the dataset.

IMDb: This dataset is titled IMDb Large Movie Dataset, and includes 50k movie reviews written by users on the website IMDb.com (25k train, 25k test) (Maas et al., 2011). Each review had a rating of between 1-4 and 7-10 for low and high sentiment, respectively. Each movie in the dataset is reviewed less than 30 times and no movies reviewed in the training set also appears in the test set. For our experiments, we make use of the fine-grained labels, 1-4 and 7-10, which creates an 8-class classification problem. The reviews vary greatly by length, with some as short as 6 words and others up to 2.4k words.

SST-5: The SST-5 dataset is obtained from Socher et al. 2013, which consists of 215,154 unique phrases parsed from the corpus of 11,855 sentences (averaging 17 words each) from Pang and Lee 2005. Each sentence is labeled by 3 annotators. The labeling interface utilizes a continuous sliding bar with guiding ticks indicating "Very negative," "Negative," "Somewhat negative," "Neutral," "Somewhat positive," "Positive," and "Very positive." For the SST-5 fine-grained sentiment classification version, the slider responses are collapsed down to 5 ranks.

Specificity: This is a corpus of 7,267 tweets that were sampled by taking 2 tweets (excluding re-tweets) from users who have posted at least 4 tweets (3,665 users) (Gao et al., 2019). The specificity annotations were based on a sliding-scale with 5 guiding options: "1 - Very General," "2 - General," "3 - Specific," "4 - Very Specific," and "5 - Extremely Specific," where general refers to posts that do not make references to any specific person, object or event, and specific refers to posts that do. Each tweet was annotated by at least 5 workers on Amazon Mechanical Turk after filtering for low quality labels, with a resulting intra-class correlation coefficient of 0.575. In order to arrive at ordinal labels, we bin and collapse the specificity ratings from a continuous 1-5 scale down to ranks of 1, 2, 3, and 4, where each continuous numerical value, i, is rounded down, i.e. $floor(i)$, in order to reduce class imbalance.

3.2 Model architectures and parameters

All our models share the same underlying architecture in order to minimize differences resulting from model parameterization and feature generation. Model sizes (i.e. # of parameters) differ for each dataset, as the average input sequence lengths are different (e.g. Tweets vs. movie reviews). In general, the model parameters of "sequence length," "embedding dimension," and "feature size" are scaled to the maximum number of tokens contained in any given input text from that particular dataset. Because both the MR and IMDb datasets contain reviews that are longer than typical pre-trained Transformer input sequence sizes, we leverage the "Performer" model architecture (Choromanski et al., 2021) for all models in order to accommodate these inputs without modifying the underlying model architecture. Finally, we train our models without any pre-training and without pre-trained embeddings so that we can have meaningful comparisons between the OR and MC methodologies with fewer confounding variables, as adding pre-training or pre-trained embeddings may change how effectively each methodology learns from the data.

3.3 Loss functions and label encodings

For MC models, we use the Performer architecture with cross-entropy loss. The ordinal labels are encoded as one-hot vectors of length K, where K is the number of classes, i.e. ratings. For OR models, we also use the Performer architecture with cross-entropy, but over $K-1$ classes, where each class represents a threshold decision of whether the rating is predicted to be greater than a value, e.g. is the rating greater than 2. To accommodate the OR loss function, which we adopt from COnsistent RAnk Logits (CORAL) (Cao et al., 2020), we encode the ordinal target variables as vectors, $\boldsymbol{v}$, with length $N-1$, and each index v_k represents a binary indicator of rank threshold, i.e. $v_1 = 1$ if $\hat{y}^1 > 0.5$ and $v_2 = 1$ if $\hat{y}^2 > 0.5$, etc. CORAL seeks to optimize the ordinal rank by penalizing misclassifications of thresholds, and it has theoretical guarantees for rank-consistency (rank-monotonicity), e.g. in order to predict 5 (i.e. >4), the model must also predict >1, >2, >3. This is achieved by allowing the $K-1$ binary thresholds to share the same weight parameters, $\boldsymbol{W}$, but independent biases, b_k. Specifically, we seek to minimize:

$$L(\boldsymbol{W}, \boldsymbol{b}) = -\sum_{i=1}^{N}\sum_{k=1}^{K-1} \lambda^k (\log(\hat{y}_i^k) y_i^k + \log(1-\hat{y}_i^k)(1-y_i^k))$$

where N is the number of training examples, λ^k is the weight associated with the kth rank threshold, and $\hat{y}_i^k = \sigma(g(x_i, W) + b_k)$. Here, $\sigma()$ is the logistic sigmoid function, x_i is the input example, $\boldsymbol{W}$ are the model weight parameters, which are shared for all the binary rank thresholds, and b_k is the independent bias unit for threshold at rank k. In optimizing this loss function, one can prove that the independent bias units will rank order and result in overall rank-monotonicity, i.e. $b_1 \geq b_2 \geq b_3, etc.$ (see Theorem 1 in Cao et al. 2020). Due to this rank-consistency, a model prediction of $\hat{y}^3 > 0.5$ is always accompanied by both $\hat{y}^2 > 0.5$ and $\hat{y}^1 > 0.5$. In other words, for $v_3 = 1$, both

Dataset	Scheme	MSE	Spearman Rho	K-L divergence	Accuracy	F1(macro)	F1(weighted)
MR	MC	0.577	0.611	58.73	50.4	43.9	51.8
	OR	**0.491**	**0.684**	**6.47**	**56.9**	**55.3**	**57.1**
IMDb	MC	3.878	0.719	324.64	**35.0**	**28.1**	**36.4**
	OR	**2.855**	**0.763**	**179.28**	31.2	27.8	30.1
SST-5	MC	2.520	0.308	264.32	**33.2**	**29.9**	**35.2**
	OR	**2.051**	**0.362**	**136.29**	31.3	29.4	31.6
Specificity	MC	0.438	0.502	1057.67	59.5	37.4	62.6
	OR	**0.367**	**0.591**	**18.16**	**64.2**	**50.0**	**65.0**

Table 1: Experimental results for the benchmark datasets comparing OR to MC. Bolded numbers represent higher values except MSE and K-L divergence, where lower is better.

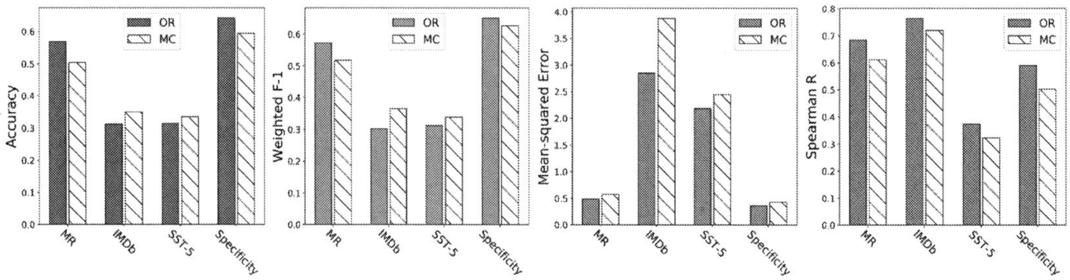

Figure 1: Across datasets, OR outperforms MC on MSE (purple; **lower is better**) and Spearman Rho (blue). The results are mixed for Accuracy (gray) and Weighted-F1 (red).

$v_2 = 1$ and $v_1 = 1$ are also true, and we encode a rating of 4 out of 5 as $\boldsymbol{v} = [1110]$. The model prediction, p, is then the first index at which $v_i = 0$, $argmin(\boldsymbol{v})$, or 5 if $v_i = 1$ for all i in [1..4].

3.4 Parameter tuning

For all experiments, we use existing train/test splits for the benchmark dataset. If no train/test splits exist, we generate a 80%/20% train/test split and randomly select 20% of the training split as a validation split for tuning model parameters and early-stopping. To determine the early-stopping point, we select the training epoch at the inflection point where a 5-epoch moving average of the validation loss no longer improves.

4 Results

Our experiments with MC vs OR classifiers for benchmark datasets (Table 1 and Figure 1) show: 1) Performance, measured in accuracy and F1, varies depending on the underlying dataset, with IMDb and SST-5 favoring MC and MR and Specificity favoring OR. Also, accuracy and F1 are correlated across models and datasets. 2) In contrast, mean-squared error (MSE), Spearman's Rho, and K-L divergence consistently favor OR, with OR achieving the lowest MSE and K-L divergence and highest Spearman Rho across all datasets. Here, MSE could be replaced by mean absolute error (MAE) or root-mean-squared error (RMSE), both of which also select OR as the better methodology over MC (not shown). These observations suggest that typical model evaluation metrics such as accuracy and F1 score, frequently used in benchmarks and leaderboards for sentiment analysis (Ribeiro et al., 2016; Ruder, 2021; Barbieri et al., 2020), may not successfully select the best performing models for classifying ordinal target variables.

For all of our experiments, we determined that our OR models are significantly different from MC models, with OR and MC predictions producing statistically distinct distributions as determined by a paired t-test with p values less than 0.05.

4.1 Dataset benchmarks

While the goal of our experiments is to compare OR vs MC in a baseline setting and not to challenge current state-of-the-art models, we provide our results against benchmarks on the sentiment analysis datasets in order to give additional context to our models' performance.

MR: Benchmarks and leaderboards on this specific dataset are sparse, as most researchers have opted to use the sentence-level polarity dataset from the same authors. The best-performing model we have found is from Bickerstaffe and Zukerman 2010, which achieved author-level accuracies of 65.72%, 52.89%, 66.99%, and 51.87%, respectively (from 10-fold CV). This, on average, out-performed our best-performing OR model, which achieved author-level accuracies of 62.12%, 54.78%, 54.85%, and 52.29%, respectively (from 20% test split). Specifically, Bickerstaffe and Zukerman 2010 out-performed on the majority-authors a and c while OR had a slight edge in the minority-authors b and d. OR out-performed the original models shown in Pang and Lee 2005.

IMDb: There is a lack of available benchmark data on the fine-grained 8-class version of the IMDb dataset, as most researchers opt to experiment on collapsing the labels to a binary classification problem. We obtain 34.98% and 31.19% accuracies for MC and OR, respectively on the fine-grained 8-class task. In an attempt to compare our result with previous work on the binary task, we collapse our predictions into binary format, by mapping predictions 1-4 to 0 and 7-10 to 1. With binary-mapping, we obtain 86.71% and 79.93% accuracies for OR and MC. The OR binary-mapped accuracy is on-par with previous benchmark results on binary IMDb predictions with vanilla CNNs and LSTMs (Camacho-Collados and Pilehvar, 2018). Interestingly, OR outperforms MC for the binary-mapped accuracy while the 8-class accuracy favors MC. This further suggests that OR is more effective at minimizing rank-error compared to MC, as errors in the binary-mapped case represent greater magnitudes than in the 8-class case.

SST-5: Our OR and MC models obtained 31.27% and 33.21% accuracy, respectively. This is substantially lower than baseline results in the literature, which typically achieve >40% accuracy (Socher et al., 2013), with current SOTA in the 50%'s (Khodak et al., 2018). The most comparable model from the literature is the "VecAvg" variant in the original SST-5 paper, which is a word-embedding model that has fine-grained accuracy of 32.7% (Socher et al., 2013). The poor performance exhibited by our OR and MC models on SST-5 might be due to a couple factors: 1) our omitting pre-training in the form of a pre-trained language model or word embeddings, whereas typical protocols for SST-5 train embedding representations on additional data (Khodak et al., 2018) or on the sub-phrases in the SST-5 training set (Socher et al., 2013; Le and Mikolov, 2014), 2) the Performer architecture may not be ideal for modeling very short input sequences, as it was designed to approximate the Attention matrix in order to have favorable time and memory scaling for long input sequences (Choromanski et al., 2021), and 3) 56% of the words in the SST-5 training examples appear only once, which makes pre-training in the form of language models or word embeddings especially important for improving model performance.

Specificity: This dataset is relatively new, and to our knowledge, there has not been any additional published work using this dataset for benchmarking. In addition, it is difficult to compare directly with the authors' results, as they used continuous target values and trained a Support Vector Regression model (Gao et al., 2019).

For our use case of predicting NPS, we greatly value the accuracy of predicted survey ratings not only in absolute class agreement, but also in how closely the predicted ratings distribution matches the actual distribution. For accurate NPS prediction, our model rating distribution needs to reflect the actual distribution of NPS not just in aggregate, but across various business segments. To probe deeper into the performance differences between OR and MC, we examined the predicted distributions of Movie Ratings compared to ground truth.

Overall distributions for the MR and IMDb datasets (Figure 2) show: 1) OR produces more accurate rating distributions, as measured by smoothed K-L divergence (Table 1). 2) MC over-predicts majority classes in both datasets (2s and 3s for MR and 1s and 10s for IMDb) while under-predicting the others (except 2s and 3s in IMDb). These results are in line with the common observation that MC models tend to overfit on the majority classes in im-

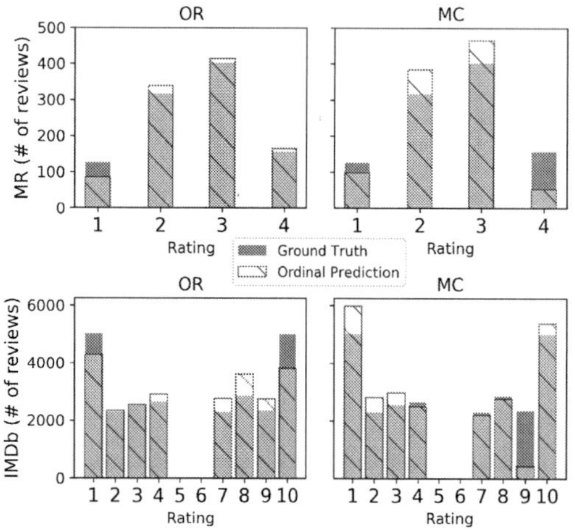

Figure 2: OR (left) outperforms MC (right) with respect to representing whole distributions of movie ratings for MR (top) and IMDb (bottom) datasets as measured by divergence.

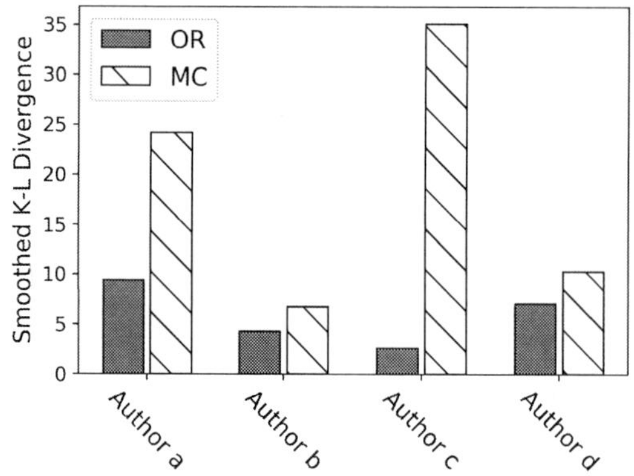

Figure 3: OR outperforms MC across authors in the MR dataset as measured by smoothed K-L divergence (lower is better). This is particularly evident in author c (10x) and author a (2x).

balanced datasets, which motivates the use of "oversampling" or class balancing(Buda et al., 2018; Chawla et al., 2002; Tepper et al., 2020; Gao et al., 2020). OR, in contrast, provides a better fit for MR (slightly under-predicting for 1s), but significantly under-predicts on IMDb majority classes, displaying a much flatter distribution of predictions. 3) Lastly, in MC, for the IMDb distribution, where there are a greater number of classes (8 ratings considered), we observe a tendency to "drop" or ignore a particular class resulting in significant under-prediction, for example the 9s in the bottom right of Figure 2. We observe this throughout training, and, depending on the epoch, have observed the model dropping other minority classes (2's, 3's, 6's, etc.), where we observe a recall less than 3%. This suggests that MC and OR lead to different behaviors with respect to predictive representation, as we discuss later.

To explore the performance of our model with respect to different data subsets, we calculate the smoothed K-L divergence for each of the four authors in the MR dataset (Figure 3). We find that OR greatly out-performs MC: while there are modest improvements in K-L divergence for authors b and d, we observe a two- to ten-fold increase for authors a and c, respectively. We hypothesize that MC is learning associations between review text and ratings as a whole by optimizing for overall accuracy in the predicted ratings, which may resemble learning how an amalgamation (or weighted average) of the 4 authors would rate a given movie. On the other hand, OR appears more sensitive to author-specific language, resulting in far lower K-L divergence values, but this may simply be due to the lower overall K-L divergence in OR calculated over the entire dataset. Lower overall and author-specific K-L divergence may be beneficial for applications with personalized predictions, i.e. in cases where performance on various data segments is important. Notably, authors a and c are the majority segments of the MR dataset, where each author a, b, c, and d has 1770, 902, 1307 and 1027 reviews, respectively. This may partially explain the improved K-L divergence of OR compared to MC for those segments, as there are more training examples for how authors a and c express their opinions on movie ratings.

Table 1 showed that raw accuracy is insufficient to distinguish better performance when distribution fit and error distance are important. In the SemEval-2016 Task for 5-point sentiment analysis of Twitter posts, some contributors used macro-averaged mean absolute error (MAE^M) (Rosenthal et al., 2017), which performs a macroaveraging of absolute errors between prediction and targets across all classes. This metric breaks down the error across target classes and can be better-suited for cases of class imbalance. While MAE^M, MSE, and correlation are all error-sensitive, they do not give

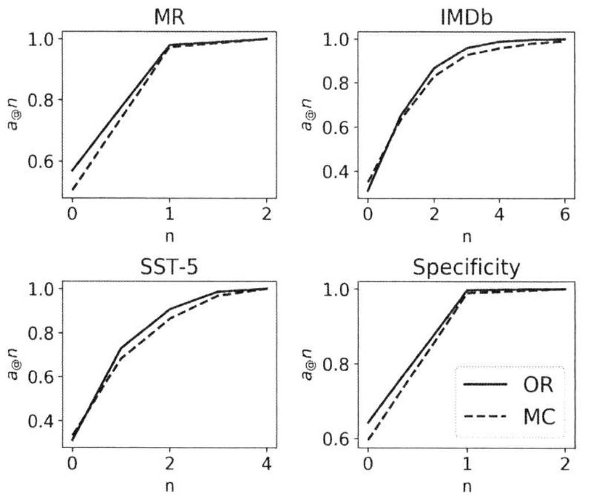

Figure 4: To visualize the impact of optimizing for ordinal rank, we define "accuracy at n" or $a_{@}n$, which considers the closeness of predictions to truth. $a_{@}n$ shows that for all benchmark datasets, OR outperforms MC for $n > 0$, where n is the absolute error.

fine-grained insights into the degree of errors, e.g. how close did we get to the right answer? To show this, we extend MAE^M and MSE with a metric that allows us to visualize degree of error: "accuracy at n" or $a_{@}n$ (Figure 4). $a_{@}n$ calculates the proportion of predictions that are within an allowable absolute error, n (ranging from 0 to $K-1$), from their targets, y. In this metric, $a_{@}0$ represents traditional accuracy. Accordingly, the graphs in Figure 4 begin at the values reported in Table 1 . However, as we increase n, we observe that across the board the $a_{@}n$ for $n > 0$ is higher for OR compared to MC for all datasets. In other words, while MC predicts the exact rating correctly more often than OR for IMDb and SST-5, when OR predicts incorrectly, it generally gets closer to the target than MC. This is highly desirable for tasks where the degree of error is important.

5 Discussion

We have shown that while MC outperformed OR for some datasets in terms of accuracy and F1, OR is significantly better than MC for minimizing error between predictions and targets for all datasets, as revealed by error-sensitive metrics such as mean-squared error and Spearman Rho. This can lead to better performance in terms of representing distributions, as measured by smoothed K-L divergence, and minimizing the magnitude of errors, as shown by $a_{@}n$.

We attribute OR's superiority over MC on MSE and Spearman correlation to the difference in their loss functions. While both MC and OR utilize cross-entropy, the label encodings and model constraints account for major differences. MC assumes that each rating is independent and uses one-hot encodings. OR encodes the ratings as rank thresholds, v, where each index, v_i, represents a binary indicator of threshold, i.e. $v_1 = 1$ if $\hat{y}^1 > 0.5$ and $v_2 = 1$ if $\hat{y}^2 > 0.5$, etc. This encoding combined with shared weight parameters and independent biases enforces rank-consistency, meaning a model prediction of $\hat{y}^3 > 0.5$ is accompanied by both $\hat{y}^2 > 0.5$ and $\hat{y}^1 > 0.5$ because $b_1 \geq b_2 \geq b_3$ (Cao et al., 2020). Consequently, we have not observed rank-inconsistent predictions in our OR models. This rank-consistency places a constraint on the model, forcing it to learn the ordinal information separating different ratings. In terms of bias-variance tradeoff, MC results in a lower bias, higher variance model, while OR produces a higher bias, lower variance model for ordinal target variables. Therefore, OR optimizes for rank-error between prediction and target, leading to lower MSE and higher Spearman correlations compared to MC.

Despite not directly optimizing for raw accuracy, we observe that OR still outperforms MC in accuracy and F1 for the MR and Specificity datasets. We hypothesize that this is related to the independence assumption that MC places during training, which may omit useful ordinal signal. While Likert-like scales can be highly subjective and inconsistent from one reviewer to another (Liang et al., 2020) due to cultural differences (Lee et al., 2002), among other reasons, there is significant overlap in rating schemes among reviewers (e.g. all reviewers should agree that higher ratings are better than lower). This standardization is particularly apparent when ratings are consistently generated, as is the case with MR, where all reviews originate from four authors. Each author, while unique, has a self-consistent way of expressing their reviews, which allows their readers to understand their reasoning for assigning movie ratings. This intra-author consistency may enhance the ordinal signal contained in the MR dataset. The Specificity dataset provides a related explanation. The ranks in the Specificity and MR datasets derive from labeled ratings that were collapsed from a more-continuous scale into 4 ranks. This may help to reduce the variance among the annotators. Additionally, the creators of the Specificity dataset took care to ensure that annotators agreed with one-another, assigning multiple annotators to label each data point (Gao et al., 2019). OR may also benefit from having fewer ranks, as more ranks create more opportunities for inconsistencies among reviewers as to what each rank represents.

The complement to our previous observation is that MC outperforms OR in accuracy and F1 for IMDb and SST-5. For IMDb, we hypothesize that this is related to the granularity of the ranks (8 total classes), and the large number of reviewers (likely tens of thousands). In this case, each person's different notions of ratings introduces considerable noise into the ordinal signal. It seems that OR may be more sensitive to rater inconsistencies compared to MC because OR fits the model on the ordinal signal whereas MC makes a rank-independence assumption. For SST-5, the answer is less clear, as each sentence is annotated by 3 judges, and the labels are collapsed down to 5-classes from a continuous range obtained from a sliding bar. It is possible that OR may struggle to make the generalizations necessary to successfully distinguish different ranks when the input sequences are short, as words may not appear in more than one example. For SST-5, 56% of the words in the training split appear in only one sentence. This may create difficulties in learning to generalize across ranks. It also highlights the impact of pre-training either in the form of language models or word embeddings for performance (Khodak et al., 2018). This pitfall is not apparent in the Specificity dataset, and we hypothesize that it is because the specificity task has significant correlations with the Tweet length itself (Gao et al., 2019), so that learning word associations is less important.

In addition to rank-error minimization, OR avoids the class dropping problem we observe in MC. We hypothesize that MC drops classes because probability mass is shared among all classes via the Softmax activation. This results in a model bias to take probability mass away from minority classes to give to majority classes when it is uncertain, which we observe in MC over-predicting majority classes (Figure 2). This is likely to happen in cases where the model cannot find reliable signal for particular minority class(es). In the extreme case, this leads to nearly no predictions for those minority classes, i.e. class dropping. OR, in contrast, avoids class dropping because its predictions do not share probability mass, i.e. each rank threshold represents its own prediction after Sigmoidal activation, without a Softmax. This builds inherent robustness into the prediction. For example, if the model is quite confident that a review is higher than 2 and less than 5, i.e. $\hat{y}^2 >> 0.5$ and $\hat{y}^5 << 0.5$, but unsure if it is a 3 or a 4, i.e. $\hat{y}^3 \approx 0.5$ and $\hat{y}^4 \approx 0.5$, rather than splitting probability mass between 3 and 4 as in MC (thus making other classes more likely in relation via Softmax), it can adjust the probability mass of v_3 independent of the other thresholds by adjusting b_3. For inputs near the decision boundary for both v_3 and v_4, the model will predict 3 and 4 in roughly equal proportions, avoiding a drop of either rank, whereas for MC, the model's bias towards majority classes coupled with Softmax activation may lead to dropping 3 or 4. Therefore, OR may produce better results in tasks with data imbalance, e.g. with highly-skewed or bi-/multi-modal distributions.

While our results are only empirically demonstrated for OR implemented with CORAL, we expect that our observations would likely generalize to other OR implementations, especially latent-variable models and other variants that produce rank-ordered thresholds, as the salient features would be the same.

6 Conclusion

Common model evaluation metrics such as accuracy, precision, recall, and F1 are insufficient for capturing the degree of error between prediction and target for multi-class prediction where the target is ordinal. Therefore, selecting models based on these traditional metrics may result in selecting an underperforming model. Error-sensitive metrics such as MSE (similarly, MAE and RMSE) and Spearman correlation capture the ordinal error, resulting in selecting models that have more representative distributions and improved generalization across data segments, as measured by K-L divergence. This is particularly important in use cases like predictive NPS, where accurate scores are necessary not just in aggregate, but across time and different customer segments as well. The independence assumption made by MC can remove useful ordinal signal, especially in cases where there is greater consistency across reviewers, their language, or their ratings. For benchmarks involving ordinal target variables, it is important to evaluate the MSE (or a similar error-sensitive metric like MAE, $a_{@}n$, and MAE^M) and Spearman correlations in addition to the usual metrics in determining whether a new model outperforms previous models. We hope to see these metrics included in future benchmarks with ordinal target variables.

Additionally, some of our experimental observations appear to be tied to the Softmax activation used in MC compared to the Sigmoidal activation in OR, such as class dropping in MC and substantially lower author-level K-L divergence in OR. These observations motivate exploration into alternative losses and activations for ordinal problems compared to traditional classification. For example, it would be interesting to compare the MC approach to one that does not involve the Softmax, such as "One-vs-Rest" or "One-vs-One," to observe whether class dropping persists.

References

I. Elaine Allen and Christopher A. Seaman. 2007. Likert scales and data analyses. *Quality Progress.*

Stefano Baccianella, Andrea Esuli, and Fabrizio Sebastiani. 2009. Evaluation measures for ordinal regression. In *Proceedings of the 2009 Ninth International Conference on Intelligent Systems Design and Applications*, pages 283–287, USA. IEEE Computer Society.

Ramy Baly, Georgi Karadzhov, Dimitar Alexandrov, James Glass, and Preslav Nakov. 2018. Predicting factuality of reporting and bias of news media sources. *arXiv preprint arXiv:1810.01765.*

Francesco Barbieri, Jose Camacho-Collados, Leonardo Neves, and Luis Espinosa-Anke. 2020. Tweeteval: Unified benchmark and comparative evaluation for tweet classification. In *Findings of the Association for Computational Linguistics: EMNLP 2020*, pages 1644–1650. Association for Computational Linguistics.

Adrian Bickerstaffe and Ingrid Zukerman. 2010. A hierarchical classifier applied to multi-way sentiment detection. In *Proceedings of the 23rd International Computational Linguistics (Coling 2010)*, pages 62–70. Association for Computational Linguistics.

Mateusz Buda, Atsuto Maki, and Maciej A. Mazurowski. 2018. A systematic study of the class imbalance problem in convolutional neural networks. *Neural Networks*, pages 249–259.

Jose Camacho-Collados and Mohammad Taher Pilehvar. 2018. On the role of text preprocessing in neural network architectures: An evaluation study on text categorization and sentiment analysis. In *Proceedings of the 2018 EMNLP Workshop BlackboxNLP: Analyzing and Interpreting Neural Networks for NLP*, pages 40–46. Association for Computational Linguistics.

M Karen Campbell and Allan Donner. 1989. Classification efficiency of multinomial logistic regression relative to ordinal logistic regression. *Journal of the American Statistical Association*, 84(406):587–591.

Wenzhi Cao, Vahid Mirjalili, and Sebastian Raschka. 2020. Rank consistent ordinal regression for neural networks with application to age estimation. *Pattern Recognition Letters*, 140:325–331.

Nitesh V. Chawla, Kevin W. Bowyer, Lawrence O. Hall, and W. Philip Kegelmeyer. 2002. Smote: Synthetic minority over-sampling technique. *Journal of Artificial Intelligence Research*, 16:321–357.

Krzysztof Choromanski, Valerii Likhosherstov, David Dohan, Xingyou Song, Andreea Gane, Tamas Sarlos, Peter Hawkins, Jared Davis, Afroz Mohiuddin, Lukasz Kaiser, David Belanger, Lucy Colwell, and Adrian Weller. 2021. Rethinking attention with performers. *ICLR.*

Jacob Devlin, Chang Ming-Wei, Lee Kenton, and Toutanova Kristina. 2019. Bert: Pre-training of deep bidirectional transformers for language understanding. In *Proceedings of the 2019 Conference of the North American Chapter of the Association for Computational Linguistics: Human Language Technologies, Volume 1 (Long and Short Papers)*, pages 41710–4186. Association for Computational Linguistics.

Eibe Frank and Mark Hall. 2001. A simple approach to ordinal classification. In *De Raedt L., Flach P. (eds) Machine Learning: ECML 2001.*, volume 2167. ECML 2001. Lecture Notes in Computer Science, Springer, Berlin, Heidelberg.

Yang Gao, Yi-Fan Li, Yu Lin, Charu Aggarwal, and Latifur Khan. 2020. Setconv: A new approach for learning from imbalanced data. In *Proceedings of the 2020 Conference on Empirical Methods in Natural Language Processing (EMNLP)*, pages 1284–1294. Association for Computational Linguistics.

Yifan Gao, Yang Zhong, Daniel Preotiuc-Pietro, and Junyi Jessy Li. 2019. Predicting and analyzing language specificity in social media posts. *Association for the Advancement of Artificial Intelligence.*

T Graepel and K Obermayer. 1999. *Advances in Large Margin Classifiers*, volume 7, chapter Large margin rank boundaries for ordinal regression. The MIT Press.

Pedro Antonio Gutiérrez, María Pérez-Ortiz, Javier Sánchez-Monedero, Francisco Fernández-Navarro, and César Hervás-Martínez. 2016. Ordinal regression methods: survey and experimental study. *IEEE Transactions on Knowledge and Data Engineering*, 28(1):127–146.

Qingnan Jiang, Lei Chen, Ruifeng Xu, Xiang Ao, and Min Yang. 2019. A challenge dataset and effective models for aspect-based sentiment analysis. In *Proceedings of the 2019 Conference on Empirical Methods in Natural Language Processing and the 9th International Joint Conference on Natural Language Processing (EMNLP-IJCNLP)*, pages 6280–6285. Association for Computational Linguistics.

Ankur Joshi, Saket Kale, Satish Chandel, and D Kumar Pal. 2015. Likert scale: Explored and explained. *British Journal of Applied Science & Technology*, 7(4):396.

Phillip Keung, Yichao Lu, György Szarvas, and Noah A. Smith. 2020. The multilingual amazon reviews corpus. In *Proceedings of the 2020 Conference on Empirical Methods in Natural Language Processing (EMNLP)*, pages 4563–4568. Association for Computational Linguistics.

Mikhail Khodak, Nikunj Saunshi, Yingyu Liang, Tengyu Ma, Brandon Stewart, and Sanjeev Arora. 2018. A la carte embedding: Cheap but effective induction of semantic feature vectors. In *Proceedings of the 56th Annual Meeting of the Association for Computational Linguistics (Volume 1: Long Papers)*, pages 12–22. Association for Computational Linguistics.

Thomas R Knapp. 1990. Treating ordinal scales as interval scales: an attempt to resolve the controversy. *Nursing research*, 39(2):121–123.

William Kuzon, Melanie Urbanchek, and Steven McCabe. 1996. The seven deadly sins of statistical analysis. *Annals of plastic surgery*, 37:265–272.

Quoc Le and Tomas Mikolov. 2014. Distributed representations of sentences and documents. In *Proceedings of the 31 st International Conference on Machine Learning*, 32. JMLR.

Jerry W. Lee, Patricia S. Jones, Yoshimitsu Mineyama, and Xinwei Esther Zhang. 2002. Cultural differences in responses to a likert scale. *Research in Nursing and Health*, 25(4):295–306.

Weixin Liang, James Zou, and Zhou Yu. 2020. Beyond user self-reported likert scale ratings: a comparison model for automatic dialog evaluation. In *Proceedings of the 58th Annual Meeting of the Association for Computational Linguistics*, pages 1363–1374. Association for Computational Linguistics.

Andrew L. Maas, Raymond E. Daly, Peter T. Pham, Dan Huang, Andrew Y. Ng, and Christopher Potts. 2011. Learning word vectors for sentiment analysis. In *Proceedings of the 49th Annual Meeting of the Association for Computational Linguistics: Human Language Technologies*, pages 142–150. Association for Computational Linguistics.

Chester H McCall. 2001. An empirical examination of the likert scale: Some assumptions, development and cautions. In *annual meeting of the CERA Conference, South Lake Tahoe, CA.*

Bo Pang and Lillian Lee. 2005. Seeing stars: Exploiting class relationships for sentiment categorization with respect to rating scales. In *Proceedings of the 43rd Annual Meeting of the Association for Computational Linguistics (ACL'05)*, pages 115–124. Association for Computational Linguistics.

Frederick F. Reichheld. 2003. The one number you need to grow. *Harvard Business Review.*

Filipe N. Ribeiro, Matheus Araújo, Pollyanna Gonçalves, Marcos André Gonçalves, and Fabrício Benevenuto. 2016. Sentibench - a benchmark comparison of state-of-the-practice sentiment analysis methods. *EPJ Data Science*, 5(23).

Anthony Rios and Ramakanth Kavuluru. 2017. Ordinal convolutional neural networks for predicting rdoc positive valence psychiatric symptom severity scores. *Journal of biomedical informatics*, 75:S85–S93.

Sara Rosenthal, Noura Farra, and Preslav Nakov. 2017. Semeval-2017 task 4: Sentiment analysis in twitter. In *Proceedings of the 11th international workshop on semantic evaluation (SemEval-2017)*, pages 502–518.

Sebastian Ruder. Nlp-progress: Sentiment analysis [online]. 2021.

Shihab Elbagir Saad and Jing Yang. 2019. Twitter sentiment analysis based on ordinal regression. *IEEE Access*, 7:163677–163685.

Parinaz Sobhani, Diana Inkpen, and Stan Matwin. 2015. From argumentation mining to stance classification. In *Proceedings of the 2nd Workshop on Argumentation Mining*, pages 67–77.

Richard Socher, Alex Perelygin, Jean Y. Wu, Jason Chuang, Christopher D. Manning, Andrew Y. Ng, and Christopher Potts. 2013. Recursive deep models for semantic compositionality over a sentiment treebank. In *Conference on Empirical Methods in Natural Language Processing (EMNLP 2013)*, pages 1631–1642. Association for Computational Linguistics.

Naama Tepper, Esther Goldbraich, Naama Zwerdling, George Kour, Ateret Anaby Tavor, and Boaz Carmeli. 2020. Balancing via generation for multi-class text classification improvement. In *Findings of the Association for Computational Linguistics: EMNLP 2020*, pages 1440–1452. Association for Computational Linguistics.

Sheng Zhang, Rachel Rudinger, Kevin Duh, and Benjamin Van Durme. 2017. Ordinal commonsense inference. *Transactions of the Association for Computational Linguistics*, 5:379–395.

HinGE: A Dataset for Generation and Evaluation of Code-Mixed Hinglish Text

Vivek Srivastava
TCS Research
Pune, Maharashtra, India
srivastava.vivek2@tcs.com

Mayank Singh
IIT Gandhinagar
Gandhinagar, Gujarat, India
singh.mayank@iitgn.ac.in

Abstract

Text generation is a highly active area of research in the computational linguistic community. The evaluation of the generated text is a challenging task and multiple theories and metrics have been proposed over the years. Unfortunately, text generation and evaluation are relatively understudied due to the scarcity of high-quality resources in code-mixed languages where the words and phrases from multiple languages are mixed in a single utterance of text and speech. To address this challenge, we present a corpus (*HinGE*) for a widely popular code-mixed language Hinglish (code-mixing of Hindi and English languages). *HinGE* has Hinglish sentences generated by humans as well as two rule-based algorithms corresponding to the parallel Hindi-English sentences. In addition, we demonstrate the inefficacy of widely-used evaluation metrics on the code-mixed data. The *HinGE* dataset will facilitate the progress of natural language generation research in code-mixed languages.

1 Introduction

Code-mixing is the mixing of two or more languages in a single utterance of speech or text. A commonly observed communication pattern for a multilingual speaker is to mix words and phrases from multiple languages. Code-mixing is widespread across various language pairs, such as Spanish-English, Hindi-English, and Bengali-English. Recently, we observe a boom in the availability of code-mixed data with the inflation of the social media platforms such as Twitter and Facebook.

In past, we witness magnitude of work to address standard code-mixing natural language understanding (NLU) tasks such as language identification (Shekhar et al., 2020; Singh et al., 2018a; Ramanarayanan et al., 2019), POS tagging (Singh et al., 2018b; Vyas et al., 2014), named entity recognition (Singh et al., 2018a), and dependency parsing (Zhang et al., 2019a) along with sentence classification tasks like sentiment analysis (Patwa et al., 2020; Joshi et al., 2016), stance detection (Utsav et al., 2020), and sarcasm detection (Swami et al., 2018). Unlike code-mixed NLU, natural language generation (NLG) of code-mixed text is highly understudied. Resource scarcity adds to the challenge of building efficient solutions for code-mixed NLG tasks. Evaluation of the code-mixed NLG tasks also lacks standalone resources, theories, and metrics.

Recently, we observe a growing interest in the code-mixed text generation task. To generate the code-mixed data various techniques have been employed such as matrix frame language theory (Lee et al., 2019; Gupta et al., 2020; Jain et al., 2021), equivalent constraint theory (Pratapa et al., 2018), pointer-generator network (Winata et al., 2018, 2019; Gupta et al., 2020), Generative Adversarial Networks (GANs) (Gao et al., 2019), etc. The majority of the available datasets (Rijhwani et al., 2017; Solorio et al., 2014; Patro et al., 2017) employed in code-mixed NLG contains noisy code-mixed text collected from social media platforms such as Twitter. These datasets also lack the sanity check for the quality of sentences, making the systems developed on these datasets vulnerable to real-world applicability. To address the challenge of scarcity of high-quality resources for the code-mixed NLG tasks, we propose *HinGE* dataset[1] that will facilitate the community to build robust systems. The dataset contains sentences generated by humans as well as two rule-based algorithms. In Table 1, we compare *HinGE* with three other baseline datasets that can be used in the Hinglish code-mixed text generation and evaluation task.

In addition to the code-mixed NLG, the evaluation of the generated code-mixed text is a challenging task. The widely popular metrics for monolin-

[1] https://sites.google.com/view/vivek-srivastava/resources

Proceedings of the 58th Annual Meeting of the Association for Computational Linguistics, pages 200–208

https://doi.org/10.26615/978-954-452-056-4_020

Dataset characteristics	Banerjee et al. (2018)	Srivastava and Singh (2020)	Gupta et al. (2020)	*HinGE*
Parallel source sentences	Only ES	Only ES	✓	✓
Human-generated code-mixed sentences	✓	✓	✗	✓
Multiple human-generated code-mixed sentences for a parallel sentence	✗	✗	✗	✓
Machine-generated code-mixed sentences	✗	✗	✓	✓
Multiple machine-generated code-mixed sentences for a parallel sentence	✗	✗	✓	✓
Human ratings for the quality of generated code-mixed sentences	✗	✗	✗	✓
Dataset size	6733 UEU, 6549 UHU	13,738	1,561,840 PS, 252,330 MGHS	1,976 PS, 4,803 HGHS, 3,952 MGHS

Table 1: Comparison between the various datasets available for the Hinglish NLG tasks. UEU: Unique English Utterance, UHU: Unique Hinglish Utterance, ES: English Sentences, PS: Parallel Sentences, HGHS: Human-Generated Hinglish Sentences, MGHS: Machine-Generated Hinglish Sentences.

gual languages fail to capture the linguistic diversity present in the code-mixed data, such as spelling variation and complex sentence structuring. The quality ratings of the sentences generated by the rule-based algorithms in *HinGE* dataset will help to develop the metrics and theories for evaluating the code-mixed NLG tasks. Our main contributions are:

- We create high-quality human-generated code-mixed Hinglish sentences corresponding to the parallel Hindi-English sentences. Each pair of parallel sentences has at least two human-generated Hinglish sentences.
- In addition to the human-generated code-mixed sentences, we propose two rule-based algorithms to generate the Hinglish sentences.
- We demonstrate the inefficacy of five widely popular metrics for the NLG task with the code-mixed text.
- To develop efficient metrics for the code-mixed NLG tasks, we provide the human ratings corresponding to the code-mixed sentences generated by the rule-based algorithms.

2 Human-Generated Hinglish Text

The scarcity of high-quality code-mixed datasets limits current research in various NLU tasks such as text generation and summarization. To address this challenge, we create a human-generated corpus of Hinglish sentences corresponding to parallel monolingual English and Hindi sentences. We use the IIT Bombay English-Hindi Parallel Corpus (hereafter *'IIT-B corpus'*) (Kunchukuttan et al., 2018). The IIT-B corpus has 1,561,840 parallel sentence pairs in English and Hindi. The English sentences are written in the Roman script, and the Hindi sentences are written in the Devanagari script. We randomly select 5,000 sentence pairs, in which the number of tokens in both the sentences is more than five to create a human-generated parallel corpus.

To create the gold-standard dataset, we employ five human annotators. Each annotator has expert-level proficiency in writing, speaking, and understanding English and Hindi languages. The objective of the annotation is to generate at least two unique Hinglish code-mixed sentences corresponding to the parallel English and Hindi sentence pairs. The annotators can also generate more than two code-mixed sentences for each sentence pair. We shuffle, pre-process, and share the sentence pairs with the annotators to generate the corresponding Hinglish sentences. A single annotator annotates each sentence pair.

We assign 1,000 unique sentence pairs to each annotator with the following annotation guidelines:

- The Hinglish sentence should be written in Roman script.
- The Hinglish sentence should have words from both the languages, i.e., English and Hindi.
- Avoid using new words, wherever possible, that are not present in both the sentences.
- If the source sentences are not the translation of each other, mark the sentence pair as "#".

Post annotation, we remove the sentence pairs marked as "#" or are missing an annotation. Note that due to the complexity of generating code-mixed sentences, such as the inability to identify two unique Hinglish sentences, complex sentence structuring, and usage of difficult words in monolingual sentences, annotators do not provide two unique sentences Hinglish sentences for each monolingual sentence pair. We obtain 1,978 sentence pairs with two or more unique Hinglish sentences. On average, 2.5 code-mixed sentences are created for each Hindi-English sentence pair. Figure 1 shows an example of two code-mixed sentences generated by the annotator for a given sentence pair.

Qualitative evaluation of the human-generated Hinglish text: To qualitatively evaluate the generated sentences, we adapt the evaluation strategy described in (Srivastava and Singh, 2021). We randomly sample 100 Hinglish sentences generated by humans along with the source parallel monolingual English and Hindi sentences. We employ two human annotators[2] for the qualitative evaluation. We ask the annotators to rate each Hinglish sentence on two metrics:

- **Degree of code-mixing (DCM)**: The code-mixing index (CMI) proposed by (Das and Gambäck, 2014) measures the degree of code-mixing in a text based on language tags of the participating tokens. The objective of DCM follows CMI with an exception of explicit token language identification to measure the degree of code-mixing in the text. The DCM score can vary between 0 to 10. A DCM score of 0 corresponds to the monolingual sentence with no code-mixing, whereas the DCM score of 10 suggests a high degree of code-mixing.
- **Readability (RA)**: RA score can vary between 0 to 10. A completely unreadable sentence due to many spelling mistakes, no sentence structuring, or meaning yields a RA score of 0. A RA score of 10 suggests a highly readable sentence with clear semantics and easy-to-read words.

The average DCM scores by the two human annotators are 8.72 and 8.65. The average RA scores are 8.65 and 8.37. The high average scores demonstrate good quality code-mixed sentence generation. Table 2 shows example ratings provided by the two human annotators to the five Hinglish sentences.

[2]different from the human annotators who generate the Hinglish sentences.

ENGLISH: Choose the version of the Kolab Server you are using.
HINDI: कोलाब संस्करण जो आप इस्तेमाल कर रहे हैं उसे चुनें
HINGLISH 1: Kolab Server version ka jo aap isstemaal kar rahe hai use choose kare.
HINGLISH 2: Kolab Server version ka jo aap isstemaal kar rahe hai use chune.

Figure 1: Example of the code-mixed sentences generated by the annotator for an English-Hindi sentence pair.

3 Machine-Generated Hinglish Text

In addition to the human-generated code-mixed text, we also generate the Hinglish sentence synthetically by following the Embedded-Matrix theory (Joshi, 1982). We propose two rule-based Hinglish text generation systems leveraging the parallel monolingual English and Hindi sentences. In both systems, we use Hindi as the matrix language and English as the embedded language. The matrix language imparts structure to the code-mixed text with tokens embedded from embedded language. We also use several linguistic resources in both generation systems. These resources include:

- **English-Hindi Dictionary**: We curate 77,805 pairs of English words and the corresponding Hindi meanings from two sources[3,4] to construct an English-Hindi dictionary.
- **Cross-lingual Word Embedding**: We leverage multilingual word vectors for English and Hindi tokens. These word-vectors ($dim = 300$) are generated from fastText's multilingual pre-trained model (Bojanowski et al., 2017). We further map these vectors to a common space using VecMap (Artetxe et al., 2018).
- **GIZA++**: GIZA++ (Och and Ney, 2003) learns the word alignment between the parallel sentences using an HMM based alignment model in an unsupervised manner. We train GIZA++ on *IIT-B corpus*.
- **Script Transliteration**: We transliterate the code-mixed sentences containing tokens in the Devanagari script to the Roman script (Mishra, 2019).

[3]http://www.cfilt.iitb.ac.in/~hdict/webinterface_user/index.php

[4]https://jankaribook.com/verbs-list-verb-in-hindi/

Hinglish sentences	Human 1		Human 2	
	DCM	RA	DCM	RA
Media ke exposure ke aadhar par Indian rajyo ki rankings	10	10	8	8
You will be more likely to give up before the 30 minutes, aap logo se jyada he.	7	8	9	8
Shighra hi maansingh british ke saath saude baazi kar rha tha.	8	10	8	8
par there's another way, aur mai aapko bata kar ja rahi hun.	9	10	9	9
"Aren't you a tiny bit andhvishavaasi?"	9	9	9	9

Table 2: Example DCM and RA ratings provided by the two human annotators to the human-generated Hinglish sentences. We color code the tokens in the Hinglish sentence based on the language with the scheme: English tokens with orange, Hindi tokens with blue and language independent tokens with black color.

- **YAKE**: We use YAKE (Campos et al., 2020), an unsupervised automatic keyword extraction method, to extract the key-phrases from the monolingual English and Hindi sentences.

We further extend the English-Hindi dictionary by incorporating parallel sentences in the *IIT-B corpus*. We leverage VecMap's shared representation to identify the closest word in English and the corresponding Hindi sentence. In addition, we also leverage GIZA++ to align the parallel sentences resulting in aligned English-Hindi tokens. Both of these steps extend the initial dictionary from 77,809 to 1,52,821 words and meaning pairs. We use this extended dictionary in the following two code-mixed text generation systems:

- **Word-aligned code-mixing (WAC)**: Here, we align the noun and adjective tokens between the parallel sentences using the extended dictionary. We replace all the aligned Hindi tokens with the corresponding English noun or adjective token and transliterate the resultant Hindi sentence to the Roman script. Figure 2 demonstrates the example Hinglish text generated from the parallel monolingual English and Hindi sentences using the WAC procedure.

- **Phrase-aligned code-mixing (PAC)**: Here, we align the keyphrases of length up to three tokens between the parallel sentences. To identify the keyphrases, we use the YAKE tool. We replace all the aligned Hindi phrases with the corresponding longest matching English phrase and transliterate the resultant Hindi sentence to the Roman script. Figure 3 demonstrates the example Hinglish text generated from the parallel monolingual English and Hindi sentences using the PAC procedure.

It should be noted that the code-mixed sentences generated using the WAC and PAC procedures have added noise (spelling variations, grammatical inconsistencies, etc.) and are not an exact representation of the high-quality code-mixed text generated by humans. This noisy machine-generation of the code-mixed text is intentional such that the efficacy of the evaluation metrics could be studied (see Section 4) for the wide spectrum of sentences and should not be limited to good quality code-mixed sentences.

English sentence: Cannot send message: no recipients defined.

Hindi sentence: संदेश नहीं भेज सकता है: कोई प्राप्तकर्ता परिभाषित नहीं है.

Alignment candidates in English sentence: {message, recipients}

Alignment candidates in Hindi sentence: {संदेश, प्राप्तकर्ता}

Aligned words using extended dictionary: {message→ संदेश, recipients→प्राप्तकर्ता, }

Intermediate code-mixed text: message नहीं भेज सकता है: कोई recipients परिभाषित नहीं है

Romanized code-mixed text: message nahin bhej sakta haia koee recipients paribhasit nahin hai

Figure 2: An example Hinglish code-mixed sentence generated using WAC method.

4 A Study on Evaluation of Code-Mixed Text Generation

In this section, we evaluate machine-generated code-mixed text. This study demonstrates severe limitations of five widely popular NLP metrics in evaluating code-mixed text generation performance. We leverage the following metrics: (i) Bilingual Evaluation Understudy Score (**BLEU**, Papineni et al. (2002)), (ii) **NIST** (Doddington, 2002), (iii) BERTScore (**BS**, Zhang et al.

English sentence: Cannot send message: no recipients defined.

Hindi sentence: संदेश नहीं भेज सकता है: कोई प्राप्तकर्ता परिभाषित नहीं है.

Key-phrases in English sentence: {send message, recipients defined, message, defined, send, recipients}

Key-phrases in Hindi sentence: { संदेश नहीं भेज, भेज सकता है:, है: कोई प्राप्तकर्ता , प्राप्तकर्ता परिभाषित, संदेश, भेज, है:, प्राप्तकर्ता, परिभाषित }

Aligned phrases using extended dictionary: {message→ संदेश, send→ भेज, recipients→प्राप्तकर्ता, defined→परिभाषित, recipient received→प्राप्तकर्ता परिभाषित }

Intermediate code-mixed text: message नहीं send सकता है: कोई recipients defined नहीं है

Romanized code-mixed text: message nahin send sakta haia koee recipients defined nahin hai

Figure 3: An example Hinglish code-mixed sentence generated using PAC method.

(2019b)), (iv) Word Error Rate (**WER**, Levenshtein (1966)), and (v) Translator Error Rate (**TER**, Snover et al. (2006)). Higher BLEU, NIST, or BS values and lower WER or TER values represent better generation performance. We conduct two experiments to evaluate the machine-generated Hinglish text:

- **Human evaluation**: First, we perform coarse-grained qualitative evaluation by randomly sampling 100 English-Hindi sentence pairs and corresponding WAC and PAC generated sentences. We employ two human evaluators[5] who are proficient in English and Hindi languages to evaluate the quality of the generated sentences. We ask evaluators to provide one of the two labels — *Correct* and *Incorrect* — to each of the generated sentences. A sentence is marked *Correct* if it is following the semantics of the parallel sentences and has high readability. Table 3 shows the annotator's agreement on the randomly sampled set of sentences. The coarse-grained qualitative evaluation shows the correct generation in at least 50% of the cases. Table 4 shows the evaluation of the randomly sampled 100 sentences on five metrics. The results show the inefficacy of automatic evaluation metrics to capture the linguistic diversity of the generated code-mixed text due to spelling variations, omitted words, limited reference sentences, and informal writing style (Srivastava and Singh, 2020). We further conduct a fine-grained qualitative human evaluation to measure the similarity between the machine-generated Hinglish sentences and the monolingual pair, the readability, and the grammatical correctness. We employ a new set of eight human evaluators to provide a rating between 1 (low quality) to 10 (high quality) to the PAC and WAC generated Hinglish sentences based on the following three parameters:

  - The similarity between the generated Hinglish and the monolingual source sentences.
  - The readability of the generated sentence.
  - The grammatical correctness of the generated sentence.

  Each generated sentence is rated by two human evaluators. All the evaluators have expert-level proficiency in the English and Hindi languages. Table 5 shows ratings provided to a representative machine-generated Hinglish sentence. Figure 4 shows the distribution of the fine-grained human evaluation scores. For both procedures, the majority (WAC: 82.3% and PAC: 75.2%) of the sentences score in the range 6–9. None of the sentences received a rating score of 1. The results further corroborate our claim that automatic evaluation metrics undermine code-mixed text generation performance. Figure 5 shows the distribution of the disagreement in the human evaluation of the generated sentences. We calculate the disagreement as to the absolute difference between the human evaluation scores. PAC-generated sentences are more prone to high disagreement (>=5) in the human evaluation than WAC. This could be attributed to the fact that PAC-generated sentences are relatively less constrained, which leaves the evaluation to the expertise and interpretation of the Hinglish language by the annotators.

- **Metric-based evaluation**: Next, we analyze the performance of five evaluation metrics on

[5]The evaluators are different from the annotators employed in Section 2).

	WAC		PAC	
	Agree	Disagree	Agree	Disagree
Correct	56	22	55	40
Incorrect	22		5	

Table 3: Annotator agreement on the randomly sampled sentences for WAC and PAC.

	BLEU	WER	TER	NIST	BS
WAC	0.1229	0.8240	0.7830	2.2045	0.857
PAC	0.1202	0.8228	0.7981	2.0497	0.857

Table 4: Automatic performance evaluation of the WAC and PAC procedures on the randomly sampled sentences.

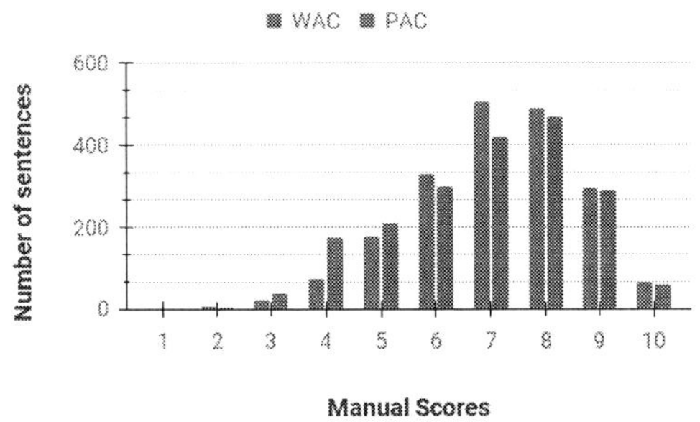

Figure 4: Distribution of human evaluation of the generated Hinglish sentences using WAC and PAC.

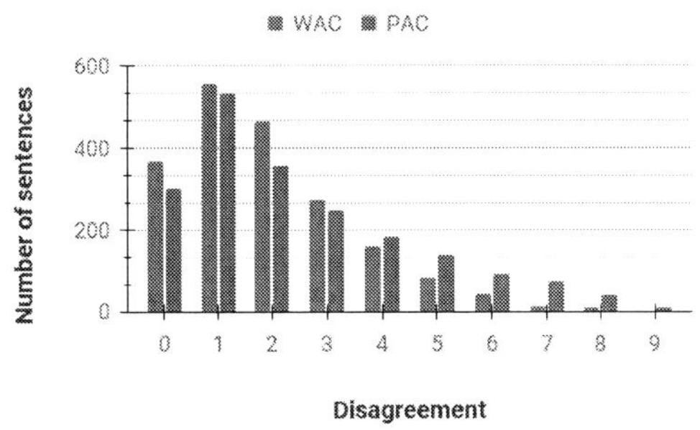

Figure 5: Distribution of the disagreement between human evaluation of the generated Hinglish sentences using WAC and PAC.

the machine-generated code-mixed text. Table 6 shows the average scores for each of the metrics against the corresponding human-provided rating. As evident from the results, the metrics perform poorly on the code-mixed data. We further analyze the correlation[6] of the metric scores with the human-provided ratings for both the text generation procedures. For this task, we divide the human ratings into three buckets:

- Bucket 1: Human rating between 2–10.
- Bucket 2: Human rating between 2–5.
- Bucket 3: Human rating between 6–10.

Table 7 shows the results of the correlation between various metric scores and the human rating to the machine-generated code-mixed sentences using WAC and PAC procedures. Human rating for generated sentences in Bucket 3 is relatively highly correlated with the metric scores compared to Bucket 2. This behavior could be attributed to the fact that low-quality sentences are difficult to rate for the human annotators due to various reasons such as poor sentence structuring and many spelling mistakes.

5 Limitations and Opportunities

In this section, we present a discussion on the various inherent limitations associated with the proposed *HinGE* dataset. We also discuss the various opportunities for the computational linguistic community to build efficient systems and metrics for code-mixed languages. Some of the major limitations with the dataset are:

- Due to the high time and cost associated with the human annotations, the number of samples in the dataset is limited. Because of a similar reason, the other code-mixing datasets (Srivastava and Singh, 2021) suffer from the scarcity of large-scale human annotations.
- The IIT-B parallel corpus does not contain sentences mined from the social media platforms. This potentially reduces the noise in the generated sentences compared to the dataset previously compiled from the social media platforms for various tasks.
- The annotators generating the code-mixed sentences were constrained only to include words from the parallel source sentences. This could potentially limit the observations compared to the real-world datasets collected from social media platforms that are more linguistically diverse due to the presence of a large number of multilingual speakers.
- Due to the high annotation cost and time, the WAC and PAC generated sentences are only rated on a single scale encompassing multiple

[6]We experiment with Pearson Correlation Coefficient. The value ranges from -1 to 1.

English	Hindi	Human-generated Hinglish	WAC	PAC
The reward of goodness shall be nothing but goodness.	अच्छाई का बदला अच्छाई के सिवा और क्या हो सकता है?	The reward of achai shall be nothing but achai. Goodness ka badla goodness ke siva aur kya ho sakta hai. Achai ka badla shall be nothing but achai.	reward ka badla reward ke nothing aur kya ho sakta hai **Rating1**: 7 **Rating2**: 4	reward of goodness goodness ke siva aur kya ho sakta hai **Rating1**: 9 **Rating2**: 7

Table 5: Example human-generated and machine-generated Hinglish sentences from the dataset along with the source English and Hindi sentences. Two different human annotators rate the synthetic Hinglish sentences on the scale 1-10 (low-high quality

Human Score	WAC					PAC				
	BLEU	**WER**	**TER**	**NIST**	**BS**	**BLEU**	**WER**	**TER**	**NIST**	**BS**
2	0.144	0.741	0.667	0.092	0.851	0.126	0.672	0.698	0.176	0.8603
3	0.138	0.735	0.708	0.070	0.852	0.146	0.765	0.696	0.086	0.851
4	0.133	0.695	0.666	0.103	0.849	0.143	0.744	0.703	0.100	0.8464
5	0.135	0.711	0.681	0.110	0.853	0.153	0.726	0.680	0.114	0.8515
6	0.141	0.697	0.670	0.102	0.852	0.164	0.689	0.646	0.124	0.8558
7	0.161	0.663	0.630	0.111	0.856	0.176	0.661	0.618	0.121	0.8581
8	0.177	0.621	0.589	0.127	0.859	0.177	0.639	0.605	0.128	0.8598
9	0.212	0.571	0.538	0.150	0.865	0.184	0.614	0.590	0.129	0.8638
10	0.291	0.509	0.493	0.157	0.878	0.242	0.551	0.543	0.146	0.8731

Table 6: Comparison of various metric scores with the human score for WAC and PAC.

	Bucket 1		Bucket 2		Bucket 3	
	WAC	PAC	WAC	PAC	WAC	PAC
BLEU	0.810	0.910	-0.861	0.878	0.941	0.844
WER	-0.936	-0.822	-0.785	0.457	-0.993	-0.973
TER	-0.891	-0.963	0.000	-0.610	-0.998	-0.970
NIST	0.913	0.127	0.642	-0.559	0.986	0.846
BS	0.844	0.710	0.227	-0.689	0.953	0.937

Table 7: Comparison of correlation between evaluation metrics and human scores for WAC and PAC.

dimensions such as grammatical correctness, readability, etc.

Even with the presence of the above limitations, the *HinGE* dataset could be effectively used for various purposes such as:

- The dataset could be effectively used in developing code-mixing text generation systems. Currently, the dataset supports only one code-mixed language, i.e., Hinglish, but it could be extended using various techniques such as weak supervision and active learning.
- The machine-generated sentences and the corresponding human ratings will be useful in designing metrics and systems for the effective evaluation of various code-mixed NLG tasks. It could also be used to investigate the factors influencing the quality of the code-mixed text.
- The dataset could also be used in investigating the reasoning behind the disagreement in the human scores to the machine-generated sentences.
- The code-mixed text (human or machine-generated) could be useful in the multitude of other code-mixing tasks such as language identification and POS tagging.
- With the recent thrust in code-mixed machine translation, the *HinGE* dataset would be extremely useful in designing and evaluating the machine-translation systems. The multiple code-mixed sentences corresponding to a given pair of parallel monolingual sentences would help to build robust translation systems.

6 Conclusion

In this paper, we present a high-quality dataset (*HinGE*) for the text-generation and evaluation task in the code-mixed Hinglish language. The code-mixed sentences in the *HinGE* dataset are generated by humans and rule-based algorithms. We demonstrate the poor evaluation capabilities of five widely popular metrics on the code-mixed data. Along with the human-generated sentences, the machine-generated sentences (as described in Section 3) and the human ratings of these code-mixed sentences could facilitate building the highly scalable and robust evaluation metrics and strategies for the code-mixed text. The multiple human-generated sentences corresponding to a pair of parallel monolingual sentences will pave the way in designing natural language generation systems robust to adversaries and linguistic diversities such as spelling variation and matrix language.

References

Mikel Artetxe, Gorka Labaka, and Eneko Agirre. 2018. A robust self-learning method for fully unsupervised cross-lingual mappings of word embeddings. In *Proceedings of the 56th Annual Meeting of the Association for Computational Linguistics (Volume 1: Long Papers)*, pages 789–798.

Suman Banerjee, Nikita Moghe, Siddhartha Arora, and Mitesh M Khapra. 2018. A dataset for building code-mixed goal oriented conversation systems. In *Proceedings of the 27th International Conference on Computational Linguistics*, pages 3766–3780.

Piotr Bojanowski, Edouard Grave, Armand Joulin, and Tomas Mikolov. 2017. Enriching word vectors with subword information. *Transactions of the Association for Computational Linguistics*, 5:135–146.

Ricardo Campos, Vítor Mangaravite, Arian Pasquali, Alípio Jorge, Célia Nunes, and Adam Jatowt. 2020. Yake! keyword extraction from single documents using multiple local features. *Information Sciences*, 509:257–289.

Amitava Das and Björn Gambäck. 2014. Identifying languages at the word level in code-mixed indian social media text. In *Proceedings of the 11th International Conference on Natural Language Processing*, pages 378–387.

George Doddington. 2002. Automatic evaluation of machine translation quality using n-gram cooccurrence statistics. In *Proceedings of the second international conference on Human Language Technology Research*, pages 138–145.

Yingying Gao, Junlan Feng, Ying Liu, Leijing Hou, Xin Pan, and Yong Ma. 2019. Code-switching sentence generation by bert and generative adversarial networks. In *Proceedings of the 20th Annual Conference of the International Speech Communication Association, INTERSPEECH 2019*, pages 3525–3529.

Deepak Gupta, Asif Ekbal, and Pushpak Bhattacharyya. 2020. A semi-supervised approach to generate the code-mixed text using pre-trained encoder and transfer learning. In *Findings of the Association for Computational Linguistics: EMNLP 2020*, pages 2267–2280, Online. Association for Computational Linguistics.

Dhruval Jain, Arun D Prabhu, Shubham Vatsal, Gopi Ramena, and Naresh Purre. 2021. Codeswitched sentence creation using dependency parsing. In *2021 IEEE 15th International Conference on Semantic Computing (ICSC)*, pages 124–129, Los Alamitos, CA, USA. IEEE Computer Society.

Aditya Joshi, Ameya Prabhu, Manish Shrivastava, and Vasudeva Varma. 2016. Towards sub-word level compositions for sentiment analysis of hindi-english code mixed text. In *Proceedings of COLING 2016, the 26th International Conference on Computational Linguistics: Technical Papers*, pages 2482–2491.

Aravind Joshi. 1982. Processing of sentences with intra-sentential code-switching. In *Coling 1982: Proceedings of the Ninth International Conference on Computational Linguistics*.

Anoop Kunchukuttan, Pratik Mehta, and Pushpak Bhattacharyya. 2018. The iit bombay english-hindi parallel corpus. In *Proceedings of the Eleventh International Conference on Language Resources and Evaluation (LREC 2018)*.

Grandee Lee, Xianghu Yue, and Haizhou Li. 2019. Linguistically Motivated Parallel Data Augmentation for Code-Switch Language Modeling. In *Proc. Interspeech 2019*, pages 3730–3734.

Vladimir I Levenshtein. 1966. Binary codes capable of correcting deletions, insertions, and reversals. In *Soviet physics doklady*, volume 10, pages 707–710.

Ritwik Mishra. 2019. devanagari-to-roman-script-transliteration. `https://github.com/ritwikmishra/devanagari-to-roman-script-transliteration`.

Franz Josef Och and Hermann Ney. 2003. A systematic comparison of various statistical alignment models. *Computational Linguistics*, 29(1):19–51.

Kishore Papineni, Salim Roukos, Todd Ward, and Wei-Jing Zhu. 2002. Bleu: a method for automatic evaluation of machine translation. In *Proceedings of the 40th annual meeting on association for computational linguistics*, pages 311–318. Association for Computational Linguistics.

Jasabanta Patro, Bidisha Samanta, Saurabh Singh, Abhipsa Basu, Prithwish Mukherjee, Monojit Choudhury, and Animesh Mukherjee. 2017. All that is English may be Hindi: Enhancing language identification through automatic ranking of the likeliness of word borrowing in social media. In *Proceedings of the 2017 Conference on Empirical Methods in Natural Language Processing*, pages 2264–2274, Copenhagen, Denmark. Association for Computational Linguistics.

Parth Patwa, Gustavo Aguilar, Sudipta Kar, Suraj Pandey, PYKL Srinivas, Björn Gambäck, Tanmoy Chakraborty, Thamar Solorio, and Amitava Das. 2020. Semeval-2020 task 9: Overview of sentiment analysis of code-mixed tweets. In *Proceedings of the Fourteenth Workshop on Semantic Evaluation*, pages 774–790.

Adithya Pratapa, Gayatri Bhat, Monojit Choudhury, Sunayana Sitaram, Sandipan Dandapat, and Kalika Bali. 2018. Language modeling for code-mixing: The role of linguistic theory based synthetic data. In *Proceedings of the 56th Annual Meeting of the Association for Computational Linguistics (Volume 1: Long Papers)*, pages 1543–1553, Melbourne, Australia. Association for Computational Linguistics.

Vikram Ramanarayanan, Robert Pugh, Yao Qian, and David Suendermann-Oeft. 2019. Automatic turn-level language identification for code-switched spanish–english dialog. In *9th International Workshop on Spoken Dialogue System Technology*, pages 51–61. Springer.

Shruti Rijhwani, Royal Sequiera, Monojit Choudhury, Kalika Bali, and Chandra Shekhar Maddila. 2017. Estimating code-switching on Twitter with a novel generalized word-level language detection technique. In *Proceedings of the 55th Annual Meeting of the Association for Computational Linguistics (Volume 1: Long Papers)*, pages 1971–1982, Vancouver, Canada. Association for Computational Linguistics.

Shashi Shekhar, Dilip Kumar Sharma, and MM Sufyan Beg. 2020. Language identification framework in code-mixed social media text based on quantum lstm—the word belongs to which language? *Modern Physics Letters B*, 34(06):2050086.

Kushagra Singh, Indira Sen, and Ponnurangam Kumaraguru. 2018a. Language identification and named entity recognition in hinglish code mixed tweets. In *Proceedings of ACL 2018, Student Research Workshop*, pages 52–58.

Kushagra Singh, Indira Sen, and Ponnurangam Kumaraguru. 2018b. A twitter corpus for hindi-english code mixed pos tagging. In *Proceedings of the Sixth International Workshop on Natural Language Processing for Social Media*, pages 12–17.

Matthew Snover, Bonnie Dorr, Richard Schwartz, Linnea Micciulla, and John Makhoul. 2006. A study of translation edit rate with targeted human annotation. In *Proceedings of association for machine translation in the Americas*, volume 200. Cambridge, MA.

Thamar Solorio, Elizabeth Blair, Suraj Maharjan, Steven Bethard, Mona Diab, Mahmoud Ghoneim, Abdelati Hawwari, Fahad AlGhamdi, Julia Hirschberg, Alison Chang, and Pascale Fung. 2014. Overview for the first shared task on language identification in code-switched data. In *Proceedings of the First Workshop on Computational Approaches to Code Switching*, pages 62–72, Doha, Qatar. Association for Computational Linguistics.

Vivek Srivastava and Mayank Singh. 2020. Phinc: a parallel hinglish social media code-mixed corpus for machine translation. *arXiv preprint arXiv:2004.09447*.

Vivek Srivastava and Mayank Singh. 2021. Challenges and limitations with the metrics measuring the complexity of code-mixed text. In *Proceedings of the Fifth Workshop on Computational Approaches to Linguistic Code-Switching*, pages 6–14.

Sahil Swami, Ankush Khandelwal, Vinay Singh, Syed Sarfaraz Akhtar, and Manish Shrivastava. 2018. A corpus of english-hindi code-mixed tweets for sarcasm detection. *arXiv preprint arXiv:1805.11869*.

Jethva Utsav, Dhaiwat Kabaria, Ribhu Vajpeyi, Mohit Mina, and Vivek Srivastava. 2020. Stance detection in hindi-english code-mixed data. In *Proceedings of the 7th ACM IKDD CoDS and 25th COMAD*, CoDS COMAD 2020, page 359–360, New York, NY, USA. Association for Computing Machinery.

Yogarshi Vyas, Spandana Gella, Jatin Sharma, Kalika Bali, and Monojit Choudhury. 2014. Pos tagging of english-hindi code-mixed social media content. In *Proceedings of the 2014 Conference on Empirical Methods in Natural Language Processing (EMNLP)*, pages 974–979.

Genta Indra Winata, Andrea Madotto, Chien-Sheng Wu, and Pascale Fung. 2018. Learn to Code-Switch: Data Augmentation using Copy Mechanism on Language Modeling. *arXiv e-prints*.

Genta Indra Winata, Andrea Madotto, Chien-Sheng Wu, and Pascale Fung. 2019. Code-switched language models using neural based synthetic data from parallel sentences. In *Proceedings of the 23rd Conference on Computational Natural Language Learning (CoNLL)*, pages 271–280, Hong Kong, China. Association for Computational Linguistics.

Meishan Zhang, Yue Zhang, and Guohong Fu. 2019a. Cross-lingual dependency parsing using code-mixed treebank. In *Proceedings of the 2019 Conference on Empirical Methods in Natural Language Processing and the 9th International Joint Conference on Natural Language Processing (EMNLP-IJCNLP)*, pages 996–1005.

Tianyi Zhang, Varsha Kishore, Felix Wu, Kilian Q Weinberger, and Yoav Artzi. 2019b. Bertscore: Evaluating text generation with bert. *arXiv preprint arXiv:1904.09675*.

What is SemEval evaluating? A Systematic Analysis of Evaluation Campaigns in NLP

Oskar Wysocki[1,2], Malina Florea[1], Dónal Landers[2], and André Freitas[1,2,3]

[1]Department of Computer Science, The University of Manchester
[2]digital Experimental Cancer Medicine Team, Cancer Biomarker Centre, CRUK Manchester Institute, University of Manchester
[3]Idiap Research Institute

Abstract

SemEval is the primary venue in the NLP community for the proposal of new challenges and for the systematic empirical evaluation of NLP systems. This paper provides a systematic quantitative analysis of SemEval aiming to evidence the patterns of the contributions behind SemEval. By understanding the distribution of task types, metrics, architectures, participation and citations over time we aim to answer the question on what is being evaluated by SemEval.

1 Introduction

A large portion of the empirical methods in Natural Language Processing (NLP) are defined over canonical text interpretation tasks such as Named Entity Recognition (NER), Semantic Role Labeling (SRL), Sentiment Analysis (SA), among others. The systematic creation of benchmarks and the comparative performance analysis of resources, representations and algorithms is instrumental for moving the boundaries of natural language interpretation. SemEval (May et al., 2019; Apidianaki et al., 2018; Bethard et al., 2017, 2016; Nakov et al., 2015; Nakov and Zesch, 2014; Manandhar and Yuret, 2013; Agirre et al., 2012) is the primary venue in the NLP community for the organisation of shared NLP tasks and challenges. SemEval is organised as an annual workshop co-located with the main NLP conferences and has attracted a large and growing audience of task organisers and participants.

Despite its recognition as a major driver in the creation of gold-standards and evaluation campaigns, there is no existing meta-analysis which interprets the overall contribution of SemEval as a collective effort. This paper aims to address this gap by performing a systematic descriptive quantitative analysis of 96 tasks encompassing the SemEval campaigns between 2012-2019. This study targets understanding the evolution of SemEval over this period, describing the core patterns with regard to task popularity, impact, task format (inputs, outputs), techniques, target languages and evaluation metrics.

This paper is organised as follows: section 2 describes related work; 3 describes the methodology; 4 defines the underlying task macro-categories; 5 and 6 presents the number of tasks and popularity in 2012-2019; 7 discusses SemEval impact in terms of citations; 8 shows targeted languages; then, sections 9, 10, 11 analyse input, output and evaluation metrics; 11 focuses on sentiment analysis architectures and representations; this is followed by a Discussion section; we close the paper with Recommendations and Conclusions.

2 Related work

Each SemEval task is described by an *anthology*, which contains: a summary of previous editions or similar tasks, references to previous works, detailed task description, evaluation methods, available resources, overview of submitted systems and final results of the competition. It is worth noting, there is a variation, or even inconsistency, in the structure and the level of detail in the description. Participants are also encouraged to submit papers with systems architecture explanations. However, there is a lack of overall analysis across different tasks and years in SemEval. There are existing studies on the analysis of specific SemEval tasks. Nakov et al. (2016) focuses on developing Sentiment Analysis tasks in 2013-2015. Sygkounas et al. (2016) is an example of a replication study of the top performing systems, in this case systems used in SemEval Twitter Sentiment Analysis (2013-2015), and focuses on architectures and performance. Evolution and challenges in semantics similarity were described in Jimenez et al. (2015). This is an example of a study on the performance of a given type of architecture across tasks of the same type. There also exist studies on shared tasks in given domain,

Proceedings of the 58th Annual Meeting of the Association for Computational Linguistics, pages 209–229

https://doi.org/10.26615/978-954-452-056-4_021

specially in clinical application of NLP (Filannino and Uzuner, 2018), (Chapman et al., 2011). However, they refer to tasks outside the SemEval and are more result oriented rather than task organization. Some studies discuss ethical issues in the organisation and participation of shared tasks. An overview focusing on task competitive nature and fairness can be found in Parra Escartín et al. (2017). In Nissim et al. (2017) authors also relate to these issues, yet giving the priority to advancing the field over fair competition.

Comparatively, this paper covers a wider range of NLP topics, and compares sentiment analysis and semantic similarity as well as other task types/groups in a systematic manner. To the best to our knowledge this is the first systematic analysis on SemEval.

3 Analysis methodology

We build a corpus based on the ACL anthology archive from the SemEval workshops between the years 2012-2019. Reference material included ACL anthology papers covering the task description, tasks' websites and papers describing the participating systems. All the reference papers included in this analysis are reported in the Appendix B. The pre-processing analysis consisted in manually extracting the target categories for the analysis which includes: task types, input and output types, as well as evaluation metrics, number of teams, languages and system architectures. Tasks were grouped based on the similarity between task types. If the same team took part in several tasks the same year, we considered each participation as distinct. There are four missing tasks in the plotted indexes, due to cancellation (2015-task16, 2019-task11), task-sharing (2013-task6) or lack of supporting task description (2013-task14). Numbers of citations are the numbers returned by Google Scholar, using *Publish and Perish* supporting API (Harzing, 2007). The list of citations were manually validated and noisy entries were filtered out. A final table with all the values extracted from the corpus is included in the Appendix B.

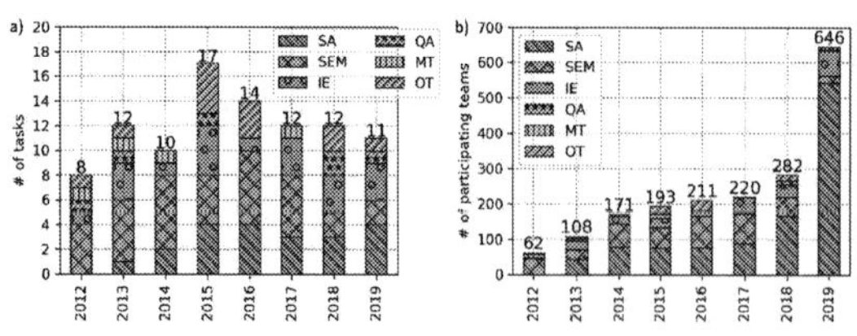

Figure 1: a) # of tasks ; b) # of teams participating in SemEval 2012-2019

4 Task types and groups

Based on task description we group each task within a macro-category. Then, due to a large number of task types, tasks were clustered within 6 groups: *Sentiment Analysis* (**SA**); *Semantic Analysis* (**SEM**): semantic analysis, semantic difference, semantic inference, semantic role labeling, semantic parsing, semantic similarity, relational similarity; *Information Extraction* (**IE**): information extraction, temporal information extraction, argument mining, fact checking; *Machine Translation* (**MT**); *Question Answering* (**QA**); *Other* (**OT**): hypernym discovery, entity linking, lexical simplification, word sense disambiguation, taxonomy extraction, taxonomy enrichment. There are also macro-categories defined by the SemEval organizers, starting from 2015, but we found them not consistent enough for the purpose of this analysis.

5 SemEval tasks in years

Within 8 editions of SemEval, a total of 96 tasks were successfully announced. The number of tasks within one group is roughly similar every year (except for MT), as well as distribution of tasks in each edition. According to Fig.1a, we observe decreasing number of SEM tasks: 5 on average in 2012-2017, and only 2 in 2018-2019. Moreover, there were no machine translation tasks in the last 2 years, and a low number of MT tasks in general (only 4 tasks in 8 years).

Although SA has a relatively limited task complexity when compared to SEM or IE, which reflects a higher variety of task types and an abundance of more specific interpretation challenges, the number of SA tasks each year is high (4, 3, 3 and 4 in years 2016-2019). It is worth mentioning, that there are other 6 SA tasks in the forthcoming SemEval 2020. The absence of some task types may be caused by the emergence of specialized workshops or conferences, e.g. low number of MT tasks in SemEval is caused by the presence a separate venue for MT: the Conference On Machine Translation (Barrault et al., 2019), which attracts more participants than SemEval in this field.

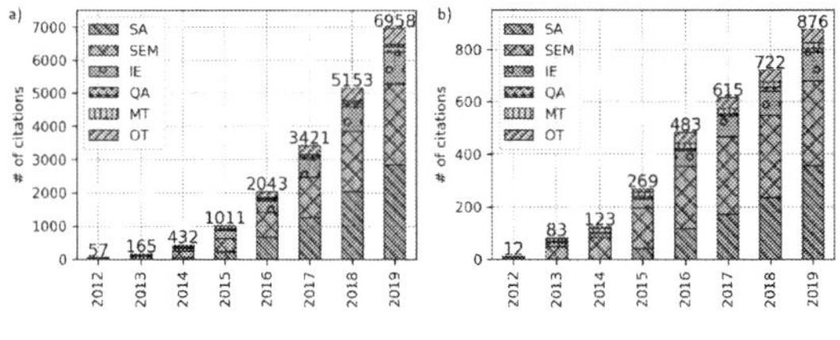

Figure 2: Cumulative number of task citations a) except for citations in SemEval proceedings; b) in SemEval proceedings

6 Task popularity

As a measure of task popularity, we analysed how many teams participated in a given task. As the number of teams signed up to the task is usually much higher than the number submitting a system result, we consider only the latter.

The number of teams increased significantly from 62 in 2012 to 646 in 2019, which shows not only a popularity boost for SemEval, but an increase in the general interest for NLP. So far, a total of 1883 teams participated in this period.

In Fig.1b, we observe a gradual increase in SemEval popularity, 30% on average each year to 2018, with a +129% jump in 2019. This is associated mainly with a dramatic increase of interest for SA: 542 teams (84% of total) in 2019. However, at the same time, number of teams in non-SA tasks decreased from 132 in 2017, to 115 in 2018 and 104 in 2019.

The most popular tasks groups along the years are SA and SEM, which gather more than 75% of teams on average each year. The third most popular is IE, in which total of 235 teams participated in SemEval from 2012 (12% of total). As a contrast, we observe a relatively low interest in QA and OT tasks. Only 41 teams participated in the last 3 years (3% of a total of 1148 in 2017-2019). Especially in OT tasks, which concentrates novel tasks, in many cases including novel formats.

In the last 2 years, SA shows a major increase in popularity (76% of all teams, compared to 40% in 2013-2017). At the same time, in tasks such as 2019-10, 2018-4 and 2018-6, which are mathematical question answering, entity linking on multiparty dialogues and parsing time normalization, respectively, only 3, 4 and 1 teams submitted results. This divergence may be associated with an emergence of easily applicable ML systems and libraries, which better fit to standard classification tasks more prevalent in SA (in contrast to OT, QA nor IE).

7 The impact of SemEval papers

As a measure of the impact of SemEval outcomes in the NLP community, we analysed the numbers of citations per task description in Google Scholar. The task description paper was used as a proxy to analyse the task impact within the NLP community. Papers submitted by participating teams describing systems and methods were not included on this analysis.

We considered the cumulative citations from 2012 to 2019 (Fig.2a), with additional distinction on citations of task description papers published in a given year (Fig.3a). Citations within SemEval proceedings were treated separately, as we focused on the impact both outside (Fig.2a) and inside (Fig.2b) the SemEval community. In other words, citations found in Google Scholar are split into numbers of papers *out* and *in* the SemEval proceedings.

SA and SEM have the highest impact, being the most cited tasks along the years both inside and outside SemEval community, what can be attributed to their high popularity.

Considering the external impact, in 2019 SA and SEM anthologies contributed with 2847 (41%) and 2426 (35%) citations respectively. IE has 985 citations (14%) and QA contributed with 148 citations (2%). The OT group, which consists of less canonical tasks, accumulated 468 citations (7%). The impact of MT papers is noticeably lower - 84 (1%).

In terms of citations within the SemEval community (in all SemEval 2012-2019 proceedings), we observe a similar pattern: 41% and 37% citations in 2019 come from SA and SEM (357 and 322), and for remaining task groups proportions are almost identical as in citations outside community (Chi.sq. *p-value*=0.06).

The number of citations outside is 8 times higher than inside the community. This proves the scientific impact and coverage, which leads to beneficial effect of SemEval on the overall NLP community.

A total of 6958 citations from 2019 are depicted in Fig.3a with distinction on the year in which the task was published (e.g. tasks from 2016 are cited 1682 times (23%)). Similarly, a total of 876 citations in the SemEval proceedings are presented in Fig.3b (e.g. anthologies published in 2015 are cited 163 times in all SemEval proceedings so far). SA tasks from 2016, SEM from 2014 and IE from 2013

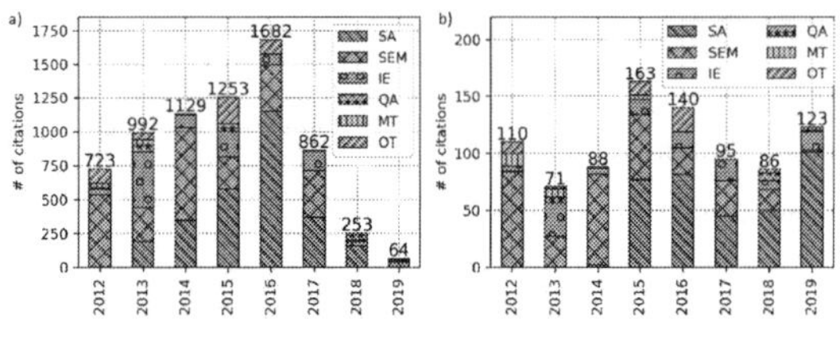

Figure 3: Number of task citations a) published in given year, except for citations in SemEval proceedings; b) from given year in SemEval proceedings

have the highest impact compared within groups (40%, 28% and 42% respectively). One could expect higher numbers of citations for older papers, however, we do not observe this pattern.

8 Languages in tasks

We analysed SemEval in terms of languages used in the tasks (Fig.4). We can distinguish 3 clusters: English-only (except for 3 tasks entirely in Chinese); multi-lingual, which define identical subtasks for several languages; cross-lingual (targeting the use of semantic relation across languages).

In total of 96 tasks, 30 investigated more than one language (multi-lingual and cross-lingual tasks) and 63 tasks were using only English.

The five most popular languages, excluding English are: Spanish (16), French (10), Italian (10), Arabic (8), German (8). Although Chinese is the 1st language in number of speakers, only 4 tasks were organised for Chinese.

Most of multi-lingual or cross-lingual tasks are related to SA (5 in 2016-2018) or SEM (15 in 2012-2019), and obviously on MT tasks (3 in 2012-2014). There were 3 OT tasks, only one QA task, and no IE tasks. Task 11 in 2017 concerning program synthesis, aiming to translate commands in English into (program) code, attracted only one team.

In 2018 and 2019 the interest in other languages is lower compared to previous years. Languages other than English were proposed only 5 and 3 times, respectively, whereas in 2016 and 2017 we observed the occurrence of respectively 10 and 14 times.

9 Input and Output Analysis

In order to better understand the evolution of the semantic complexity of the tasks, we analysed them in terms of the types used to represent input and output data in all subtasks. Based on their descriptions, we devised a list of 25 different abstract types used, then assigning each subtask the most appropriate Input and Output Types.

9.1 Types and Clusters

Taking into consideration both their complexity and purpose, we split the type list into 5 clusters: *cluster 1*: document, text, paragraph, sentence, phrase, word, number; *cluster 2*: score, score real value, score whole value, class label, probability distribution; *cluster 3*: entity, attribute, topic, tree, Directed Acyclic Graph (DAG); *cluster 4*: question, answer, query; *cluster 5*: Knowledge Base (KB), program, time interval, timeline, semantic graph, syntactic labeled sentence.

9.2 Input Types

As expected, types from *cluster 1* (sequential tokens) make up for 76% of overall input types used in all tasks (depicted in the Appendix A, Fig.A.1). Most popular input type is paragraph, for which about 60% of cases represents a tweet. The remaining 24% is split across *clusters 2, 3, 4 and 5*. A subtle divergence towards the right-hand side can be noticed, starting with 2015, driven mostly by tasks from SA and IE task groups. The most dominant Input Types from each cluster are paragraph, class label, entity, question and KB.

9.3 Output Types

As shown in Fig.5, data types from *clusters 2 and 3* are the majority in this case, accounting for 68% of used representations. Class labels are repeatedly employed, especially by SA tasks. *Cluster 1* types are constantly used across the years, fully dependent on the task types given in a certain year, 78% of them coming from SEM, IE and OT. Rarely used are typed from *clusters 4 and 5*, accounting for just 10% of the total, half of which occur in SEM tasks during 2016 and 2017 complex tasks such as Community Question Answering and Chinese Semantic Dependency Parsing. We also found a possible relation between output type and popularity. In 2012-2017 tasks where outputs were in *cluster 4 or 5*, attracted 8.3 teams per task on average, while in *clusters 1-3* 13.9 teams/task. However, despite major increase in SemEval popularity, in 2018-2019 the former attracted only 7 teams/task, and the latter 43.5 teams/task. The group with most type variety is SEM, covering types across all clusters. On the other side of the spectrum, SA has the least variety, despite it being the most popular task group. The most dominant Output Types from each cluster are paragraph, class label, entity, answer and semantic graph.

10 Evaluation Metrics

We counted a total of 29 different evaluation metrics used in SemEval (Fig.6).

At a subtask level, the most frequent metric is F1-score, with 105 usages, followed by recall and precision, with 51 and 49 usages respectively, and accuracy, with 26 usages. F1, recall and precision are frequently jointly used, the last two playing the role of supporting break-down metrics for F1 in 95% of cases. This combination is very popular, especially for IE tasks, almost half of the use coming from this task group.

The top 5 evaluation metrics make up 84% of the total number of metrics used in all years, last 12 (almost half) being only used once. In 89% of cases when rare evaluation metrics (from Kendall's T to the right) are used, they occur in SA and SEM tasks e.g. Jaccard index in Affect in Tweets (2018) or Smatch in Meaning Representation Parsing (2016). Furthermore, 67% of the least used evaluation metrics (only used 3 times or less) appear in 2015-2017, the same period when we could see tasks experimenting the most with input and output types.

10.1 Evaluation Metrics against Output Types

F1, recall and precision (depicted in Appendix A, Fig.A.2) are mostly used for output types such as class label, paragraph and entity (each of which is the top output type from their clusters). Meanwhile, for output types represented by score, most used evaluation metrics are Pearson Correlation, Kendall's T, cosine similarity and Spearman Correlation. MAP, the 6th most used evaluation metric, is mostly used for ranked questions/answers either in recurring tasks such as Community Question Answering. Human judgment was only used twice, in Taxonomy Extraction Evaluation (2016) and Abstract Meaning Representation Parsing and Generation (2017). For further reference, see Appendix A.

11 Zooming in into Sentiment Analysis

11.1 System architectures

The systematic analysis of the prevalent methods and architectures imposed particular challenges with regard to the data extraction process due to the intrinsic complexity of tasks (many systems

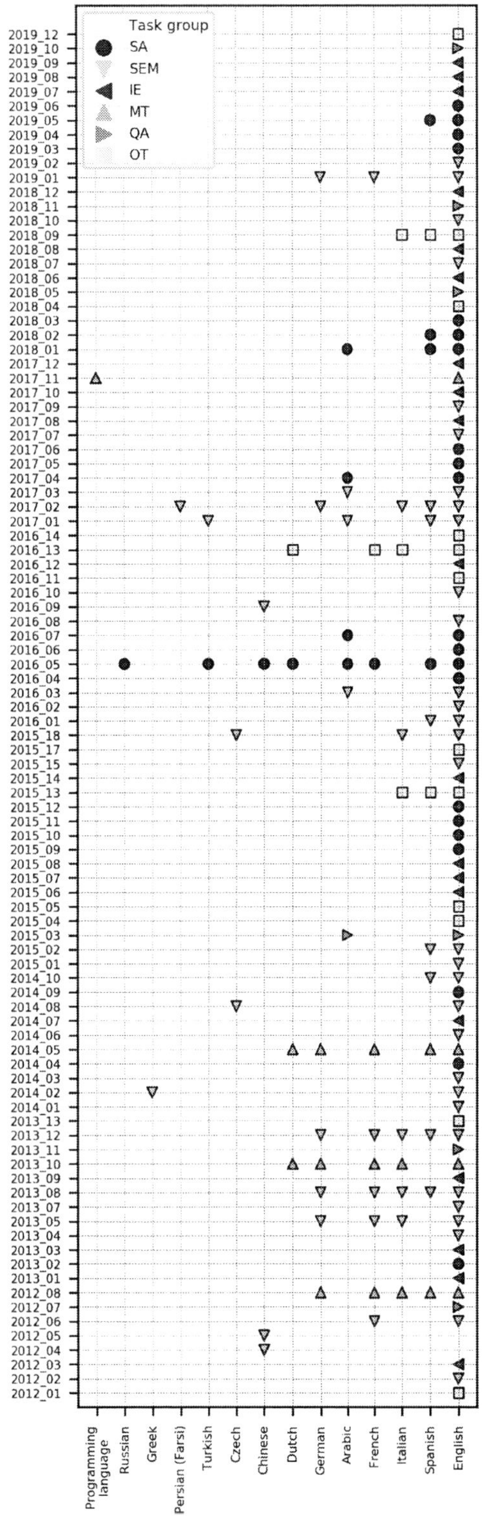

Figure 4: Languages used in SemEval tasks from 2012 to 2019

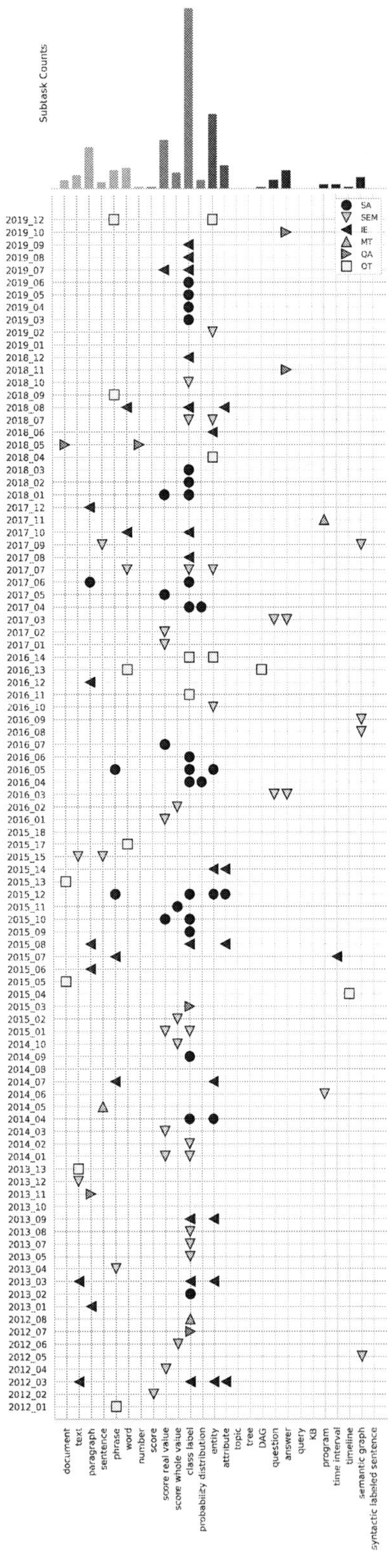

Figure 5: Output Types used in SemEval tasks from 2012 to 2019

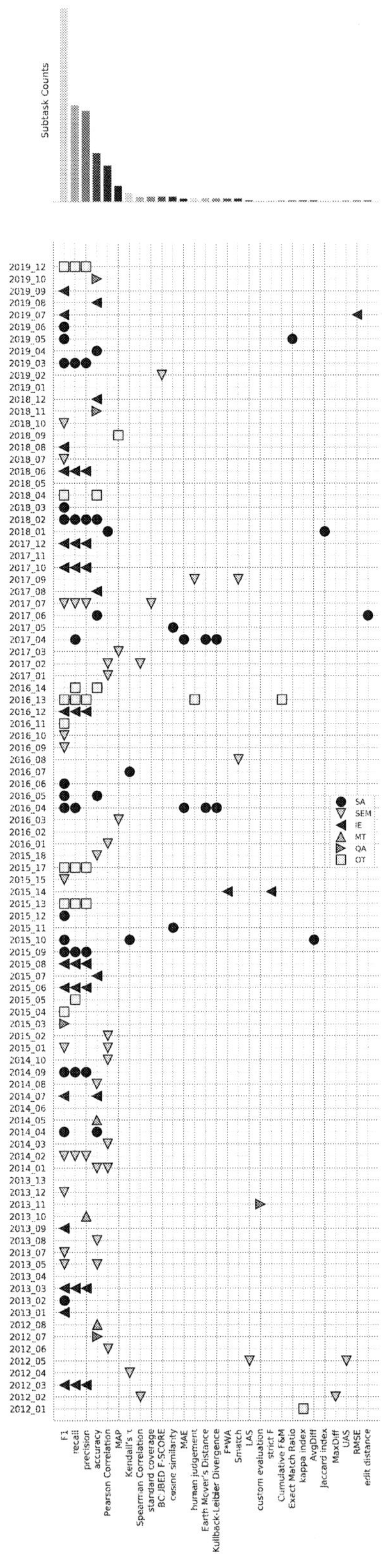

Figure 6: Evaluation Metrics used in SemEval tasks from 2012 to 2019

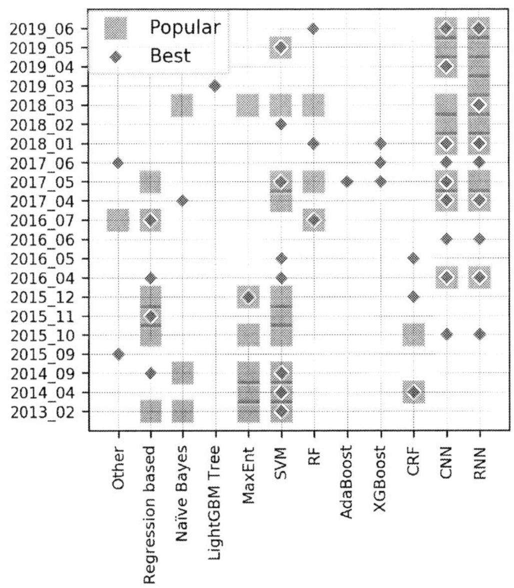

Figure 7: Models used in SA tasks from 2012 to 2019 at SemEval

include the composition of pre-processing techniques, rules, hand-crafted features and combinations of algorithms). Additionally, for the majority of task description papers, there is no systematic comparison between systems within a task, and consequently within group or years.

Due to the consistent presence of SA along all years, we present an overview of the evolution of system architectures used in SA from 2013 to 2019 (Fig.7). In this analysis we focus on the best performing architectures. More than one best model in a task signifies best models in subtasks or that the final system was an ensemble of several algorithms. *Regression based* model encompasses linear, logistic, or Gaussian regression, and *Other* includes all rule-based or heavily hand-crafted models.

We observe a drift in popularity of architectures from ML algorithms (2013-2016) to deep learning (DL) models (2017-2019).

Despite the major adoption of DL models, traditional ML algorithms are consistently in use, both as separate models and as ensembles with DL. This is also true for other types of tasks. In many task description papers from 2018-2019, one can find ML-based systems as top performing participants. SVM-based models are still popular and in some tasks outperforms DL (2018-2, 2019-5).

In the analysis of system architectures one needs to take into account that best system depends not only on the core algorithm but also on the team expertise and supporting feature sets and language resources.

11.2 Representations

The output of the SA related tasks provide an account of the evolution of sentiment and emotion representation in this community from 2013 until 2019 (see Appendix A Fig.A.3).

At a discrete level, the number of maximum class labels representing sentiment intensity grew from 3 in 2013 to 7 in 2019. At a continuous score level, real-valued scores associated with sentiment was first used in 2015; in 2016 it switched to sentiment intensity; in 2017 it was being used as a way to determine the intensity of an emotion component out of 11 emotion types (rather than a single one, or the generic emotional intensity of a sentence). In terms of targeted subject, the tasks grew more granular over time: paragraph/word (2013), aspect terms (2014), sentence topic (2015), person (2016). Additionally, discourse evolved from simpler opinionated text in the direction of figurative language, for example: handling irony and metaphor in SA (2015), phrases comparison/ranking in terms of sense of humor (2017), irony detection (2018) and contextual emphasis (2019).

12 Discussion: What is SemEval evaluating?

The results of the analysis substantiate the following core claims, which summarise some of the trends identified in this paper:

- There is evidence of significant impact of SemEval in the overall NLP community.
- SemEval contributed to the construction of a large and diverse set of challenges with regard to semantic representation, supporting resources and evaluation methodologies and metrics.
- SemEval is becoming heavily biased towards solving classification/regression problems. We observe a major interest in tasks where the expected output is a binary or multiclass label or within a continuous real valued score.
- Sentiment Analysis tasks accounts for a disproportional attention from the community.

- There are two parallel narratives running on SemEval: low entry barrier and state-of-the-art defining. SemEval contains a rich corpus of unaddressed and complex NLP tasks, which are eclipsed by the easier low entry barrier tasks. This points to the double function of SemEval which performs a pedagogical task, serving as an entry point for early career researchers to engage within the NLP community and a state-of-the-art forum for pushing the boundaries of natural language interpretation. With the popularity of NLP applications and Deep Learning, the former function is eclipsing the latter.
- There is a significant trend to decrease the variety in the output and evaluation metrics in the recent years. While in the previous years, tasks focused more on novel and exploratory tasks, recent tasks have explored, probably due to emergence of out-of-the-box DL models, this variety significantly decreased. Consequently, participants focus on easier tasks, which in part dissipates the community potential to address long-term challenges.
- Despite the recent interest in neural-based architectures, there is clear evidence of the longevity and lasting impact of older NLP methods.

13 Recommendations

We believe that this paper can serve as a guideline for the selection and organisation of future SemEval tasks. Based on the analyses performed on this paper, these are the main recommendations:

- Prioritise tasks which have a clear argument on semantic and methodological challenges and novelty.
- Differentiate challenges which have a competition/pedagogical purpose from research tasks.
- Support the systematic capture of task metadata and submission data in a structured manner. This will allow for an efficient comparison between SemEval tasks and deriving insights for future SemEval editions.

14 Conclusions

This paper reported a systematic quantitative analysis of SemEval, which is an important venue for the empirical evaluation of NLP systems. The analysis, which provides a detailed breakdown of 96 tasks in the period between 2012-2019, provided quantitative evidence that:

- SemEval has a significant impact in the overall NLP community
- there is a recent drift towards the direction of Deep Learning classification methods which is eclipsing the research function of SemEval
- there is longevity and impact of older NLP methods in comparison to Deep Learning methods

References

Eneko Agirre, Johan Bos, Mona Diab, Suresh Manandhar, Yuval Marton, and Deniz Yuret, editors. 2012. **SEM 2012: The First Joint Conference on Lexical and Computational Semantics – Volume 1: Proceedings of the main conference and the shared task, and Volume 2: Proceedings of the Sixth International Workshop on Semantic Evaluation (SemEval 2012)*. Association for Computational Linguistics, Montréal, Canada.

Marianna Apidianaki, Saif M. Mohammad, Jonathan May, Ekaterina Shutova, Steven Bethard, and Marine Carpuat, editors. 2018. *Proceedings of The 12th International Workshop on Semantic Evaluation*. Association for Computational Linguistics, New Orleans, Louisiana.

Loïc Barrault, Ondřej Bojar, Marta R. Costa-jussà, Christian Federmann, Mark Fishel, Yvette Graham, Barry Haddow, Matthias Huck, Philipp Koehn, Shervin Malmasi, Christof Monz, Mathias Müller, Santanu Pal, Matt Post, and Marcos Zampieri. 2019. Findings of the 2019 conference on machine translation (wmt19). In *Proceedings of the Fourth Conference on Machine Translation (Volume 2: Shared Task Papers, Day 1)*, pages 1–61, Florence, Italy. Association for Computational Linguistics.

Steven Bethard, Marine Carpuat, Marianna Apidianaki, Saif M. Mohammad, Daniel Cer, and David Jurgens, editors. 2017. *Proceedings of the 11th International Workshop on Semantic Evaluation (SemEval-2017)*. Association for Computational Linguistics, Vancouver, Canada.

Steven Bethard, Marine Carpuat, Daniel Cer, David Jurgens, Preslav Nakov, and Torsten Zesch, editors. 2016. *Proceedings of the 10th International Workshop on Semantic Evaluation (SemEval-2016)*. Association for Computational Linguistics, San Diego, California.

Wendy W Chapman, Prakash M Nadkarni, Lynette Hirschman, Leonard W D'Avolio, Guergana K Savova, and Ozlem Uzuner. 2011. Overcoming barriers to NLP for clinical text: the role of shared tasks and the need for additional creative solutions. *Journal of the American Medical Informatics Association*, 18(5):540–543.

Michele Filannino and Özlem Uzuner. 2018. Advancing the state of the art in clinical natural language processing through shared tasks. *Yearbook of medical informatics*, 27(1):184—192.

A.W. Harzing. 2007. Publish or perish. Available from https://harzing.com/resources/publish-or-perish.

Sergio Jimenez, Fabio A. Gonzalez, and Alexander Gelbukh. 2015. Soft Cardinality in Semantic Text Processing: Experience of the SemEval International Competitions. *Polibits*, pages 63 – 72.

Suresh Manandhar and Deniz Yuret, editors. 2013. *Second Joint Conference on Lexical and Computational Semantics (*SEM), Volume 2: Proceedings of the Seventh International Workshop on Semantic Evaluation (SemEval 2013)*. Association for Computational Linguistics, Atlanta, Georgia, USA.

Jonathan May, Ekaterina Shutova, Aurelie Herbelot, Xiaodan Zhu, Marianna Apidianaki, and Saif M. Mohammad, editors. 2019. *Proceedings of the 13th International Workshop on Semantic Evaluation*. Association for Computational Linguistics, Minneapolis, Minnesota, USA.

Preslav Nakov, Sara Rosenthal, Svetlana Kiritchenko, Saif M. Mohammad, Zornitsa Kozareva, Alan Ritter, Veselin Stoyanov, and Xiaodan Zhu. 2016. Developing a successful semeval task in sentiment analysis of twitter and other social media texts. *Language Resources and Evaluation*, 50(1):35–65.

Preslav Nakov and Torsten Zesch, editors. 2014. *Proceedings of the 8th International Workshop on Semantic Evaluation (SemEval 2014)*. Association for Computational Linguistics, Dublin, Ireland.

Preslav Nakov, Torsten Zesch, Daniel Cer, and David Jurgens, editors. 2015. *Proceedings of the 9th International Workshop on Semantic Evaluation (SemEval 2015)*. Association for Computational Linguistics, Denver, Colorado.

Malvina Nissim, Lasha Abzianidze, Kilian Evang, Rob van der Goot, Hessel Haagsma, Barbara Plank, and Martijn Wieling. 2017. Last words: Sharing is caring: The future of shared tasks. *Computational Linguistics*, 43(4):897–904.

Carla Parra Escartín, Wessel Reijers, Teresa Lynn, Joss Moorkens, Andy Way, and Chao-Hong Liu. 2017. Ethical considerations in NLP shared tasks. In *Proceedings of the First ACL Workshop on Ethics in Natural Language Processing*, pages 66–73, Valencia, Spain. Association for Computational Linguistics.

Efstratios Sygkounas, Giuseppe Rizzo, and Raphaël Troncy. 2016. A replication study of the top performing systems in semeval twitter sentiment analysis. In *The Semantic Web – ISWC 2016*, pages 204–219, Cham. Springer International Publishing.

A Appendix A

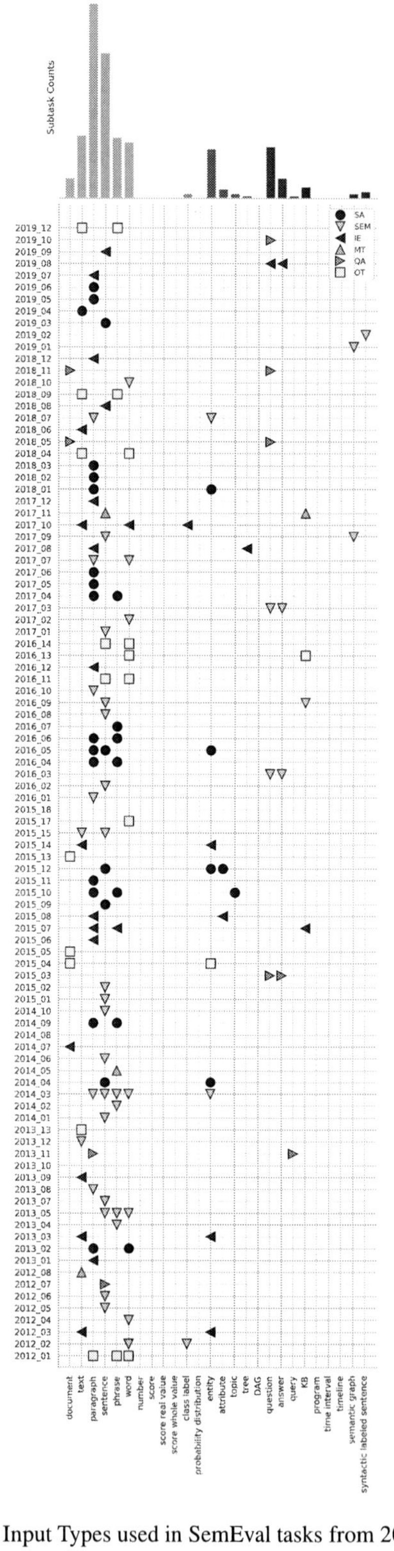

Figure A.1: Input Types used in SemEval tasks from 2012 to 2019

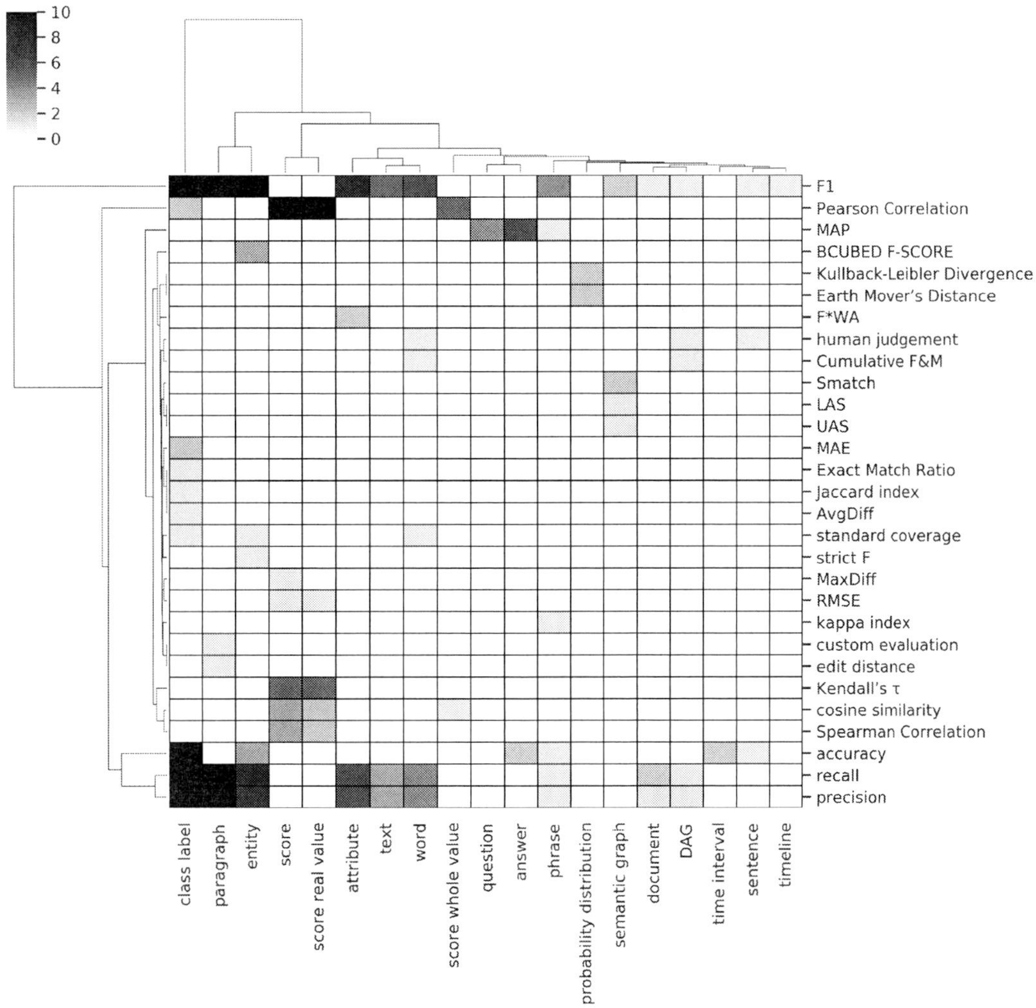

Figure A.2: Heatmap on the Evaluation Metrics and Output Types

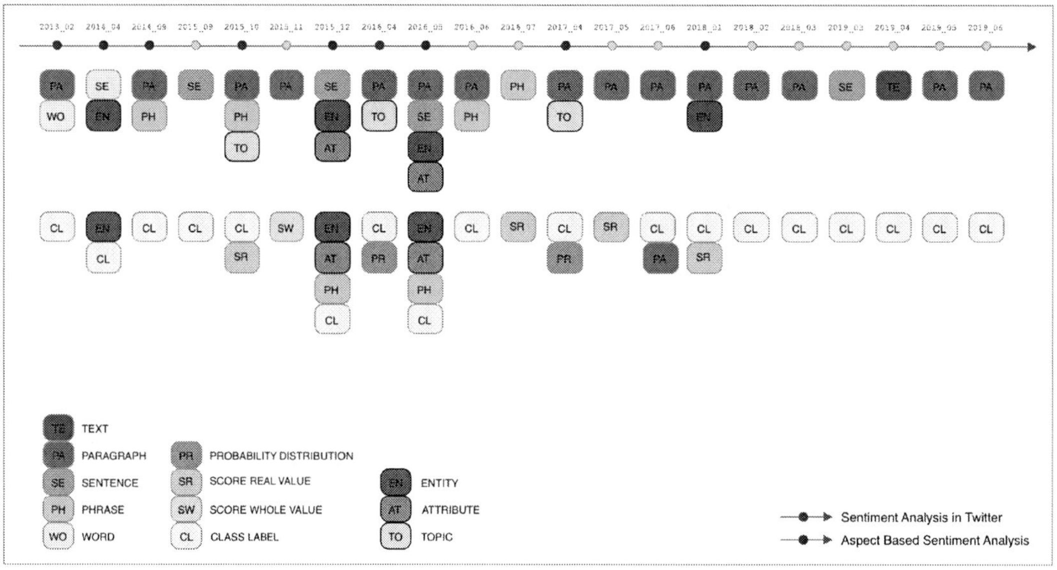

Figure A.3: Timeline of Input Types (upper row) and Output Types (lower row) in Sentiment Analysis tasks at SemEval 2013-2019

Appendix B

Task ID	Full Name	Citations	Task Type	Task Group	Input	Output	Evaluation Metric	Languages	No of Teams
2012_01	1. English Lexical Simplification[1]	103	lexical simplification	OT	word, paragraph, phrase	phrase	kappa index	English	5
2012_02	2. Measuring Degrees of Relational Similarity[2]	122	relational similarity	SEM	word, class label	score	MaxDiff, Spearman Correlation	English	3
2012_03	3. Spatial Role Labeling[3]	39	information extraction	IE	entity, text	entity, attribute, class label, text	recall, F1, precision	English	1
2012_04	4. Evaluating Chinese Word Similarity[4]	35	semantic similarity	SEM	word	score real value	Kendall's τ	Chinese	2
2012_05	5. Chinese Semantic Dependency Parsing[5]	16	semantic parsing	SEM	sentence	semantic graph	LAS, UAS	Chinese	5
2012_06	6. Semantic Textual Similarity[6]	363	semantic similarity	SEM	sentence	score whole value	Pearson Correlation	English, French	35
2012_07	7. COPA: Choice Of Plausible Alternatives An evaluation of commonsense causal reasoning[7]	11	question answering	QA	sentence	class label	accuracy	English	1
2012_08	8. Cross-lingual Textual Entailment for Content Synchronization[8]	34	machine translation	MT	text	class label	accuracy	English, Spanish, Italian, French, German	10

[1] "SemEval-2012 Task 1: English Lexical Simplification - ACL ...." https://www.aclweb.org/anthology/S12-1046. Accessed 28 May. 2020.
[2] "SemEval-2012 Task 2: Measuring Degrees of Relational ...." 7 Jun. 2012, https://www.aclweb.org/anthology/S12-1047.pdf. Accessed 28 May. 2020.
[3] "SemEval-2013 Task 3: Spatial Role Labeling - ACL Anthology." https://www.aclweb.org/anthology/S13-2044. Accessed 28 May. 2020.
[4] "SemEval-2012 Task 4: Evaluating Chinese Word Similarity ...." https://www.aclweb.org/anthology/S12-1049. Accessed 28 May. 2020.
[5] "SemEval-2012 Task 5: Chinese Semantic Dependency Parsing." https://www.aclweb.org/anthology/S12-1050. Accessed 28 May. 2020.
[6] "SemEval-2012 Task 6: A Pilot on Semantic Textual Similarity ...." https://www.aclweb.org/anthology/S12-1051. Accessed 28 May. 2020.
[7] "SemEval-2012 Task 7: Choice of Plausible Alternatives: An ...." https://www.aclweb.org/anthology/S12-1052. Accessed 28 May. 2020.
[8] "Semeval-2012 Task 8: Cross-lingual Textual Entailment for ...." https://www.aclweb.org/anthology/S12-1053. Accessed 28 May. 2020.

2013_01	1. TempEval-3 Temporal Annotation[9]	213	information extraction	IE	paragraph	paragraph	F1	English	9
2013_02	2. Sentiment Analysis in Twitter[10]	195	sentiment analysis	SA	word, paragraph	class label	F1	English	44
2013_03	3. Spatial Role Labeling[11]	29	information extraction	IE	entity, text	entity, class label, text	recall, F1, precision	English	1
2013_04	4. Free Paraphrases of Noun Compounds[12]	30	semantic similarity	SEM	phrase	phrase	?	English	3
2013_05	5. Evaluating Phrasal Semantics[13]	23	semantic inference	SEM	word, sentence, phrase	?, class label	accuracy, F1	English, Italian, French, German	5
2013_07	7. The Joint Student Response Analysis and 8th Recognizing Textual Entailment Challenge[14]	76	semantic inference	SEM	sentence	class label	F1	English	9
2013_08	8. Cross-lingual Textual Entailment for Content Synchronization[15]	10	semantic inference	SEM	paragraph	class label	accuracy	English, Spanish, Italian, French, German	6
2013_09	9. Extraction of Drug-Drug Interactions from BioMedical Texts[16]	170	information extraction	IE	text	class label, entity	F1	English	14
2013_10	10. Cross-lingual Word Sense Disambiguation[17]	42	machine translation	MT	?	?	precision	English, Italian, French, German, Dutch	5
2013_11	11. Evaluating Word Sense Induction & Disambiguation within An End-User Application[18]	48	question answering	QA	query, paragraph	paragraph	custom evaluation	English	5

[9] "SemEval-2013 Task 1: TempEval-3: Evaluating Time ...." 14 Jun. 2013, https://www.aclweb.org/anthology/S13-2001.pdf. Accessed 28 May. 2020.
[10] "SemEval-2013 Task 2: Sentiment Analysis in Twitter." 14 Jun. 2013, https://www.aclweb.org/anthology/S13-2052.pdf. Accessed 28 May. 2020.
[11] "SemEval-2013 Task 3: Spatial Role Labeling - ACL Anthology." https://www.aclweb.org/anthology/S13-2044. Accessed 28 May. 2020.
[12] "SemEval-2013 Task 4: Free Paraphrases of Noun Compounds." https://www.aclweb.org/anthology/S13-2025. Accessed 28 May. 2020.
[13] "SemEval-2013 Task 5: Evaluating Phrasal Semantics - ACL ...." https://www.aclweb.org/anthology/S13-2007. Accessed 28 May. 2020.
[14] "SemEval-2013 Task 7: The Joint Student Response Analysis ...." https://www.aclweb.org/anthology/S13-2045. Accessed 28 May. 2020.
[15] "Semeval-2013 Task 8: Cross-lingual Textual Entailment ... - ACL." https://www.aclweb.org/anthology/S13-2005. Accessed 28 May. 2020.
[16] "SemEval-2013 Task 9 : Extraction of Drug-Drug Interactions ...." https://www.aclweb.org/anthology/S13-2056. Accessed 28 May. 2020.
[17] "SemEval-2013 Task 10: Cross-lingual Word Sense ... - cs.York." https://www.cs.york.ac.uk/semeval-2013/accepted/25_Paper.pdf. Accessed 28 May. 2020.
[18] "SemEval-2013 Task 11: Word Sense Induction and ...." https://www.aclweb.org/anthology/S13-2035. Accessed 28 May. 2020.

2013_12	12. Multilingual Word Sense Disambiguation[19]	107	semantic labeling	SEM	text	text	F1	English, Spanish, Italian, French, German	3
2013_13	13. Word Sense Induction for Graded and Non-Graded Senses[20]	49	word sense disambiguation	OT	text	text	?	English	4
2014_01	1. Evaluation of Compositional Distributional Semantic Models on Full Sentences through Semantic Relatedness and Entailment[21]	374	semantic similarity	SEM	sentence	score real value, class label	accuracy, Pearson Correlation	English	21
2014_02	2. Grammar Induction for Spoken Dialogue Systems [22]	0	semantic similarity	SEM	phrase	class label	recall, F1, precision	English, Greek	3
2014_03	3. Cross-Level Semantic Similarity[23]	42	semantic similarity	SEM	word, phrase, entity, paragraph, sentence	score real value	Pearson Correlation	English	19
2014_04	4. Aspect Based Sentiment Analysis[24]	344	sentiment analysis	SA	entity, sentence	class label, entity	accuracy, F1	English	32
2014_05	5. L2 Writing Assistant[25]	4	machine translation	MT	partial sentence, phrase	sentence	accuracy	English, Spanish, French, German, Dutch	6
2014_06	6. Supervised Semantic Parsing of Spatial Robot Commands[26]	15	semantic parsing	SEM	sentence	program	?	English	6
2014_07	7. Analysis of Clinical Text[27]	96	information extraction	IE	document	entity, phrase	accuracy, F1	English	21
2014_08	8. Broad-Coverage Semantic Dependency Parsing[28]	98	semantic parsing	SEM	?	?	accuracy	English, Czech	8

[19] "SemEval-2013 Task 12: Multilingual Word Sense ...." https://www.aclweb.org/anthology/S13-2040. Accessed 28 May. 2020.
[20] "SemEval-2013 Task 13: Word Sense Induction for Graded and ...." https://www.aclweb.org/anthology/S13-2049. Accessed 28 May. 2020.
[21] "SemEval-2014 Task 1: Evaluation of Compositional ...." 24 Aug. 2014, https://www.aclweb.org/anthology/S14-2001.pdf. Accessed 28 May. 2020.
[22] "Grammar Induction for Spoken Dialogue Systems - ACL ...." https://www.aclweb.org/anthology/S14-2002. Accessed 28 May. 2020.
[23] "SemEval-2014 Task 3: Cross-Level Semantic Similarity - ACL ...." https://www.aclweb.org/anthology/S14-2003. Accessed 28 May. 2020.
[24] "SemEval-2014 Task 4: Aspect Based Sentiment Analysis ...." https://www.aclweb.org/anthology/S14-2004. Accessed 28 May. 2020.
[25] "SemEval 2014 Task 5 - L2 Writing Assistant - ACL Anthology." https://www.aclweb.org/anthology/S14-2005. Accessed 28 May. 2020.
[26] "SemEval-2014 Task 6: Supervised Semantic Parsing of ...." https://www.aclweb.org/anthology/S14-2006. Accessed 28 May. 2020.
[27] "SemEval-2014 Task 7: Analysis of Clinical Text - ACL Anthology." https://www.aclweb.org/anthology/S14-2007. Accessed 28 May. 2020.
[28] "SemEval 2014 Task 8: Broad-Coverage Semantic ... - ACL." https://www.aclweb.org/anthology/S14-2008. Accessed 28 May. 2020.

2014_09	9. Sentiment Analysis in Twitter[29]	3	sentiment analysis	SA	paragraph, phrase	class label	recall, F1, precision	English	46
2014_10	10. Multilingual Semantic Textual Similarity[30]	153	semantic similarity	SEM	sentence	score whole value	Pearson Correlation	English, Spanish	9
2015_01	Task 1: Paraphrase and Semantic Similarity in Tw[31] itter	70	semantic similarity	SEM	sentence	score real value, class label	Pearson Correlation, F1	English	19
2015_02	Task 2: Semantic Textual Similarity, English, Spanish and Pilot on Interpretability[32]	161	semantic similarity	SEM	sentence	score whole value	Pearson Correlation	English, Spanish	29
2015_03	Task 3: Answer Selection in Community Question Answering[33]	56	question answering	QA	question, answer	class label	F1	English, Arabic	13
2015_04	Task 4: TimeLine: Cross-Document Event Ordering[34]	43	temporal analysis	OT	document, entity	timeline	F1	English	4
2015_05	Task 5: QA TempEval[35]	24	temporal analysis	OT	document	document	recall	English	2
2015_06	Task 6: Clinical TempEval[36]	83	information extraction	IE	paragraph	paragraph	recall, F1, precision	English	3
2015_07	Task 7: Diachronic Text Evaluation[37]	31	information extraction	IE	paragraph, KB, phrase	time interval, phrase	accuracy	English	4
2015_08	Task 8: SpaceEval[38]	21	information extraction	IE	attribute, paragraph	attribute, class label, paragraph	recall, F1, precision	English	3
2015_09	Task 9: CLIPEval Implicit Polarity of Events[39]	13	sentiment analysis	SA	sentence	class label	recall, F1, precision	English	2
2015_10	Task 10: Sentiment Analysis in Twitter[40]	252	sentiment analysis	SA	topic, paragraph, phrase	score real value, class label	Kendall's τ, F1, AvgDiff	English	41
2015_11	Task 11: Sentiment Analysis of Figurative Language in Twitter[41]	102	sentiment analysis	SA	paragraph	score whole value	cosine similarity	English	15

29 "SemEval-2014 Task 9: Sentiment Analysis in Twitter - ACL." 24 Aug. 2014, https://www.aclweb.org/anthology/S14-2009.pdf. Accessed 28 May. 2020.
30 "SemEval-2014 Task 10: Multilingual Semantic Textual Similarity." https://www.aclweb.org/anthology/S14-2010. Accessed 28 May. 2020.
31 "SemEval-2015 Task 1: Paraphrase and Semantic Similarity in ...." https://www.aclweb.org/anthology/S15-2001. Accessed 28 May. 2020.
32 "SemEval-2015 Task 2: Semantic Textual Similarity, English ...." https://www.aclweb.org/anthology/S15-2045. Accessed 28 May. 2020.
33 "SemEval-2015 Task 3: Answer Selection in Community ...." https://www.aclweb.org/anthology/S15-2047. Accessed 28 May. 2020.
34 "SemEval-2015 Task 4: TimeLine: Cross-Document Event ...." https://www.aclweb.org/anthology/S15-2132. Accessed 28 May. 2020.
35 "SemEval-2015 Task 5: QA TempEval - Evaluating Temporal ...." https://www.aclweb.org/anthology/S15-2134. Accessed 28 May. 2020.
36 "SemEval-2015 Task 6: Clinical TempEval - ACL Anthology." https://www.aclweb.org/anthology/S15-2136. Accessed 28 May. 2020.
37 "SemEval 2015, Task 7: Diachronic Text Evaluation." https://www.aclweb.org/anthology/S15-2147.pdf. Accessed 28 May. 2020.
38 "SemEval-2015 Task 8: SpaceEval - ACL Anthology." https://www.aclweb.org/anthology/S15-2149. Accessed 28 May. 2020.
39 "SemEval-2015 Task 9: CLIPEval Implicit Polarity of Events ...." https://www.aclweb.org/anthology/S15-2077. Accessed 28 May. 2020.
40 "SemEval-2015 Task 10: Sentiment Analysis in Twitter - ACL ...." https://www.aclweb.org/anthology/S15-2078. Accessed 28 May. 2020.
41 "SemEval-2015 Task 11: Sentiment Analysis of Figurative ...." http://alt.qcri.org/semeval2015/task11/. Accessed 28 May. 2020.

2015_12	Task 12: Aspect Based Sentiment Analysis[42]	214	sentiment analysis	SA	?, attribute, entity, sentence	?, attribute, class label, entity, phrase	?, F1	English	16
2015_13	Task 13: Multilingual All-Words Sense Disambiguation and Entity Linking[43]	85	entity linking	OT	document	document	recall, F1, precision	English, Spanish, Italian	9
2015_14	Task 14: Analysis of Clinical Text[44]	53	information extraction	IE	entity, text	attribute, entity	F*WA, strict F	English	16
2015_15	Task 15: A CPA Dictionary-Entry-Building Task[45]	2	semantic parsing	SEM	text, sentence	?, text, sentence	F1	English	5
2015_17	Task 17: Taxonomy Extraction Evaluation[46]	43	taxonomy extraction	OT	word	word	recall, F1, precision	English	6
2015_18	Task 18: Semantic Dependency Parsing[47]	0	semantic parsing	SEM	?	?	accuracy	English, Italian, Czech	6
2016_01	Task 1: Semantic Textual Similarity, Monolingual and Cross-Lingual Evaluation[48]	150	semantic similarity	SEM	paragraph	score real value	Pearson Correlation	English, Spanish	43
2016_02	Task 2: Interpretable Semantic Textual Similarity[49]	26	semantic similarity	SEM	sentence	score whole value	?	English	9
2016_03	Task 3: Community Question Answering[50]	123	semantic similarity	SEM	question, answer	question, answer	MAP	English, Arabic	18
2016_04	Task 4: Sentiment Analysis in Twitter[51]	436	sentiment analysis	SA	paragraph, phrase	probability distribution, class label	MAE, Kullback-Leibler Divergence, recall, F1, Earth Mover's Distance	English	14
2016_05	Task 5: Aspect-Based Sentiment Analysis[52]	465	sentiment analysis	SA	?, paragraph, entity, sentence	?, class label, entity, phrase	accuracy, F1	English, Spanish, French, Arabic, Dutch, Chinese,	29

[42] "SemEval-2015 Task 12: Aspect Based Sentiment Analysis ...." https://www.aclweb.org/anthology/S15-2082/. Accessed 28 May. 2020.
[43] "SemEval-2015 Task 13: Multilingual All-Words Sense ... - ACL." https://www.aclweb.org/anthology/S15-2049. Accessed 28 May. 2020.
[44] "SemEval-2015 Task 14: Analysis of Clinical Text - ACL ...." https://www.aclweb.org/anthology/S15-2051. Accessed 28 May. 2020.
[45] "SemEval-2015 Task 15: A CPA dictionary-entry-building task." https://www.aclweb.org/anthology/S15-2053.pdf. Accessed 28 May. 2020.
[46] "SemEval-2015 Task 17: Taxonomy Extraction Evaluation ...." https://www.aclweb.org/anthology/S15-2151. Accessed 28 May. 2020.
[47] "SemEval 2015 Task 18: Broad-Coverage Semantic ...." https://www.aclweb.org/anthology/S15-2153. Accessed 28 May. 2020.
[48] "SemEval-2016 Task 1: Semantic Textual Similarity ...." https://www.aclweb.org/anthology/S16-1081. Accessed 28 May. 2020.
[49] "SemEval-2016 Task 2: Interpretable Semantic Textual Similarity." https://www.aclweb.org/anthology/S16-1082. Accessed 28 May. 2020.
[50] "SemEval-2016 Task 3: Community Question Answering - ACL ...." https://www.aclweb.org/anthology/S16-1083. Accessed 28 May. 2020.
[51] "SemEval-2016 Task 4: Sentiment Analysis in Twitter - ACL ...." https://www.aclweb.org/anthology/S16-1001. Accessed 28 May. 2020.
[52] "SemEval-2016 Task 5: Aspect Based Sentiment Analysis ...." https://www.aclweb.org/anthology/S16-1002. Accessed 28 May. 2020.

								Turkish, Russian	
2016_06	Task 6: Detecting Stance in Tweets[53]	209	sentiment analysis	SA	paragraph, phrase	class label	F1	English	28
2016_07	Task 7: Determining Sentiment Intensity of English and Arabic Phrases[54]	39	sentiment analysis	SA	phrase	score real value	Kendall's τ	English, Arabic	5
2016_08	Task 8: Meaning Representation Parsing[55]	28	semantic parsing	SEM	sentence	semantic graph	Smatch	English	11
2016_09	Task 9: Chinese Semantic Dependency Parsing[56]	0	semantic parsing	SEM	KB, sentence	semantic graph	F1	Chinese	3
2016_10	Task 10: Detecting Minimal Semantic Units and their Meanings[57]	23	semantic analysis	SEM	paragraph	entity	F1	English	6
2016_11	Task 11: Complex Word Identification[58]	40	lexical simplification	OT	word, sentence	class label	F1	English	21
2016_12	Task 12: Clinical TempEval[59]	79	information extraction	IE	paragraph	paragraph	recall, F1, precision	English	14
2016_13	Task 13: Taxonomy Extraction Evaluation (TExEval-2)[60]	54	taxonomy extraction	OT	word, KB	word, DAG	human judgement, recall, F1, Cumulative F&M, precision	English, Italian, French, Dutch	5
2016_14	Task 14: Semantic Taxonomy Enrichment[61]	10	taxonomy enrichment	OT	word, sentence	class label, entity	accuracy, recall	English	5
2017_01	Task 1: Semantic Textual Similarity[62]	144	semantic similarity	SEM	sentence	score real value	Pearson Correlation	English, Spanish, Arabic, Turkish	31
2017_02	Task 2: Multi-lingual and Cross-lingual Semantic Word Similarity[63]	56	semantic similarity	SEM	word	score real value	Pearson Correlation, Spearman Correlation	English, Spanish, Italian, German,	17

53 "SemEval-2016 Task 6: Detecting Stance in Tweets - ACL ...." https://www.aclweb.org/anthology/S16-1003. Accessed 28 May. 2020.
54 "SemEval-2016 Task 7: Determining Sentiment Intensity ... - ACL." https://www.aclweb.org/anthology/S16-1004. Accessed 28 May. 2020.
55 "SemEval-2016 Task 8: Meaning Representation Parsing ...." https://www.aclweb.org/anthology/S16-1166. Accessed 28 May. 2020.
56 "SemEval-2016 Task 9: Chinese Semantic Dependency Parsing." https://www.aclweb.org/anthology/S16-1167. Accessed 28 May. 2020.
57 "SemEval-2016 Task 10: Detecting Minimal Semantic Units ...." https://www.aclweb.org/anthology/S16-1084. Accessed 28 May. 2020.
58 "SemEval 2016 Task 11: Complex Word Identification - ACL ...." https://www.aclweb.org/anthology/S16-1085. Accessed 28 May. 2020.
59 "SemEval-2017 Task 12: Clinical TempEval - ACL Anthology." https://www.aclweb.org/anthology/S17-2093. Accessed 28 May. 2020.
60 "SemEval-2016 Task 13: Taxonomy Extraction Evaluation ...." https://www.aclweb.org/anthology/S16-1168. Accessed 28 May. 2020.
61 "SemEval-2016 Task 14: Semantic Taxonomy Enrichment ...." https://www.aclweb.org/anthology/S16-1169. Accessed 28 May. 2020.
62 "SemEval-2017 Task 1: Semantic Textual Similarity ...." https://www.aclweb.org/anthology/S17-2001. Accessed 28 May. 2020.
63 "SemEval-2017 Task 2: Multilingual and Cross-lingual Semantic." https://www.aclweb.org/anthology/S17-2002. Accessed 28 May. 2020.

								Persian (Farsi)	
2017_03	Task 3: Community Question Answering[64]	106	semantic similarity	SEM	question, answer	question, answer	MAP	English, Arabic	23
2017_04	Task 4: Sentiment Analysis in Twitter[65]	307	sentiment analysis	SA	paragraph, phrase	probability distribution, class label	MAE, Kullback-Leibler Divergence, recall, Earth Mover's Distance	English, Arabic	48
2017_05	Task 5: Fine-Grained Sentiment Analysis on Financial Microblogs and News[66]	48	sentiment analysis	SA	paragraph	score real value	cosine similarity	English	32
2017_06	Task 6: #HashtagWars: Learning a Sense of Humor[67]	15	sentiment analysis	SA	paragraph	class label, paragraph	accuracy, edit distance	English	8
2017_07	Task 7: Detection and Interpretation of English Puns [68]	23	semantic parsing	SEM	word, paragraph	word, class label, entity	standard coverage, recall, F1, precision	English	10
2017_08	Task 8: RumourEval: Determining rumour veracity and support for rumours[69]	71	fact checking	IE	tree, paragraph	class label	accuracy	English	8
2017_09	Task 9: Abstract Meaning Representation Parsing and Generation[70]	15	semantic parsing	SEM	semantic graph, sentence	semantic graph, sentence	Smatch, human judgement	English	5
2017_10	Task 10: Extracting Keyphrases and Relations from Scientific Publications[71]	73	information extraction	IE	word, class label, text	word, class label	recall, F1, precision	English	26
2017_11	Task 11: End-User Development using Natural Language[72]	4	machine translation	MT	KB, sentence	program	?	English, Programing language	1
2017_12	Task 12: Clinical TempEval[73]	0	information extraction	IE	paragraph	paragraph	recall, F1, precision	English	11
2018_01	Task 1: Affect in Tweets[74]	98	sentiment analysis	SA	entity, paragraph	score real value, class label	Pearson Correlation, Jaccard index	English, Spanish, Arabic	75

64 "SemEval-2016 Task 3: Community Question Answering - ACL ...." https://www.aclweb.org/anthology/S16-1083. Accessed 28 May. 2020.

65 "SemEval-2016 Task 4: Sentiment Analysis in Twitter - ACL ...." https://www.aclweb.org/anthology/S16-1001. Accessed 28 May. 2020.

66 "SemEval-2017 Task 5: Fine-Grained Sentiment Analysis on ...." https://www.aclweb.org/anthology/S17-2089/. Accessed 28 May. 2020.

67 "SemEval-2017 Task 6: #HashtagWars: Learning a Sense of ...." https://www.aclweb.org/anthology/S17-2004. Accessed 28 May. 2020.

68 "SemEval-2017 Task 7: Detection and Interpretation of English ...." https://www.aclweb.org/anthology/S17-2005. Accessed 28 May. 2020.

69 "SemEval-2017 Task 8: RumourEval: Determining rumour ...." https://www.aclweb.org/anthology/S17-2006. Accessed 28 May. 2020.

70 "SemEval-2017 Task 9: Abstract Meaning Representation ...." https://www.aclweb.org/anthology/S17-2090. Accessed 28 May. 2020.

71 "SemEval 2017 Task 10: ScienceIE - Extracting Keyphrases ...." https://www.aclweb.org/anthology/S17-2091. Accessed 28 May. 2020.

72 "End-User Development using Natural Language - ACL ...." https://www.aclweb.org/anthology/S17-2092. Accessed 28 May. 2020.

73 "SemEval-2017 Task 12: Clinical TempEval - ACL Anthology." https://www.aclweb.org/anthology/S17-2093. Accessed 28 May. 2020.

74 "SemEval-2018 Task 1: Affect in Tweets - ACL Anthology." https://www.aclweb.org/anthology/S18-1001. Accessed 28 May. 2020.

2018_02	Task 2: Multilingual Emoji Prediction[75]	20	sentiment analysis	SA	paragraph	class label	accuracy, recall, F1, precision	English, Spanish	49
2018_03	Task 3: Irony Detection in English Tweets[76]	43	sentiment analysis	SA	paragraph	class label	F1	English	43
2018_04	Task 4: Character Identification on Multiparty Dialogues[77]	2	entity linking	OT	word, text	entity	accuracy, F1	English	4
2018_05	Task 5: Counting Events and Participants within Highly Ambiguous Data covering a very long tail[78]	0	question answering	QA	document, question	number, document	?	English	4
2018_06	Task 6: Parsing Time Normalizations[79]	3	information extraction	IE	text	?, entity	recall, F1, precision	English	1
2018_07	Task 7: Semantic Relation Extraction and Classification in Scientific Papers[80]	26	semantic parsing	SEM	entity, paragraph	class label, entity	F1	English	32
2018_08	Task 8: Semantic Extraction from CybersecUrity REports using Natural Language Processing (SecureNLP)[81]	3	information extraction	IE	sentence	word, attribute, class label	F1	English	9
2018_09	Task 9: Hypernym Discovery[82]	13	hypernym discovery	OT	text, phrase	phrase	MAP	English, Spanish, Italian	11
2018_10	Task 10: Capturing Discriminative Attributes[83]	5	semantic difference	SEM	word	class label	F1	English	21
2018_11	Task 11: Machine Comprehension using Commonsense Knowledge[84]	33	question answering	QA	document, question	answer	accuracy	English	11
2018_12	Task 12: Argument Reasoning Comprehension Task[85]	7	argument reasoning	IE	paragraph	class label	accuracy	English	22
2019_01	Task 1: Cross-lingual Semantic Parsing with UCCA[86]	3	semantic parsing	SEM	semantic graph	?	?	English, French, German	8

75 "SemEval 2018 Task 2: Multilingual Emoji Prediction - ACL ...." https://www.aclweb.org/anthology/S18-1003. Accessed 28 May. 2020.
76 "SemEval-2018 Task 3: Irony Detection in English Tweets ...." https://www.aclweb.org/anthology/S18-1005. Accessed 28 May. 2020.
77 "SemEval 2018 Task 4: Character Identification on Multiparty ...." https://www.aclweb.org/anthology/S18-1007. Accessed 28 May. 2020.
78 "SemEval-2018 Task 5: Counting Events and Participants in ...." 5 Jun. 2018, https://www.aclweb.org/anthology/S18-1009.pdf. Accessed 28 May. 2020.
79 "SemEval 2018 Task 6: Parsing Time Normalizations - ACL ...." https://www.aclweb.org/anthology/S18-1011. Accessed 28 May. 2020.
80 "SemEval-2018 Task 7: Semantic Relation Extraction and ...." https://www.aclweb.org/anthology/S18-1111. Accessed 28 May. 2020.
81 "SemEval-2018 Task 8: Semantic Extraction from ... - ACL." https://www.aclweb.org/anthology/S18-1113. Accessed 28 May. 2020.
82 "SemEval-2018 Task 9: Hypernym Discovery - ACL Anthology." https://www.aclweb.org/anthology/S18-1115. Accessed 28 May. 2020.
83 "SemEval-2018 Task 10: Capturing Discriminative Attributes ...." https://www.aclweb.org/anthology/S18-1117. Accessed 28 May. 2020.
84 "SemEval-2018 Task 11: Machine Comprehension Using - ACL." https://www.aclweb.org/anthology/S18-1119. Accessed 28 May. 2020.
85 "SemEval-2018 Task 12: The Argument Reasoning ... - ACL." https://www.aclweb.org/anthology/S18-1121. Accessed 28 May. 2020.
86 "SemEval-2019 Task 1: Cross-lingual Semantic Parsing with ...." https://www.aclweb.org/anthology/S19-2001. Accessed 28 May. 2020.

2019_02	Task 2: Unsupervised Lexical Semantic Frame Induction[87]	1	semantic labeling	SEM	syntactic labeled sentence	entity	BCUBED F-SCORE	English	13
2019_03	Task 3: EmoContext: Contextual Emotion Detection in Text[88]	11	sentiment analysis	SA	sentence	class label	recall, F1, precision	English	311
2019_04	Task 4: Hyperpartisan News Detection[89]	5	sentiment analysis	SA	text	class label	accuracy	English	42
2019_05	Task 5: HatEval: Multilingual Detection of Hate Speech Against Immigrants and Women in Twitter[90]	15	sentiment analysis	SA	paragraph	class label	F1, Exact Match Ratio	English, Spanish	74
2019_06	Task 6: OffensEval: Identifying and Categorizing Offensive Language in Social Media[91]	13	sentiment analysis	SA	paragraph	class label	F1	English	115
2019_07	Task 7: RumourEval 2019: Determining Rumour Veracity and Support for Rumours[92]	7	fact checking	IE	paragraph	score real value, class label	RMSE, F1	English	22
2019_08	Task 8: Fact Checking in Community Question Answering Forums[93]	4	fact checking	IE	question, answer	class label	accuracy	English	17
2019_09	Task 9: Suggestion Mining from Online Reviews and Forums[94]	3	information extraction	IE	sentence	class label	F1	English	33
2019_10	Task 10: Math Question Answering[95]	0	question answering	QA	question	answer	accuracy	English	3
2019_12	Task 12: Toponym Resolution in Scientific Papers[96]	2	entity linking	OT	text, phrase	entity, phrase	recall, F1, precision	English	8

87 "SemEval-2019 Task 2: Unsupervised Lexical Frame Induction ...." https://www.aclweb.org/anthology/S19-2003. Accessed 28 May. 2020.
88 "SemEval-2019 Task 3: EmoContext Contextual Emotion ...." https://www.aclweb.org/anthology/S19-2005. Accessed 28 May. 2020.
89 "SemEval-2019 Task 4: Hyperpartisan News Detection - ACL ...." https://www.aclweb.org/anthology/S19-2145. Accessed 28 May. 2020.
90 "SemEval-2019 Task 5: Multilingual Detection of Hate Speech ...." https://www.aclweb.org/anthology/S19-2007. Accessed 3 Jun. 2020.
91 "SemEval-2019 Task 6: Identifying and Categorizing Offensive ...." https://www.aclweb.org/anthology/S19-2010. Accessed 28 May. 2020.
92 "SemEval-2019 Task 7: RumourEval, Determining Rumour ...." https://www.aclweb.org/anthology/S19-2147. Accessed 28 May. 2020.
93 "SemEval-2019 Task 8: Fact Checking in Community Question ...." https://www.aclweb.org/anthology/S19-2149. Accessed 28 May. 2020.
94 "SemEval-2019 Task 9: Suggestion Mining from Online ...." https://www.aclweb.org/anthology/S19-2151. Accessed 28 May. 2020.
95 "SemEval-2019 Task 10: Math Question Answering - ACL ...." https://www.aclweb.org/anthology/S19-2153. Accessed 28 May. 2020.
96 "SemEval-2019 Task 12: Toponym Resolution in Scientific ...." https://www.aclweb.org/anthology/S19-2155. Accessed 28 May. 2020.

The UMD Submission to the Explainable MT Quality Estimation Shared Task: Combining Explanation Models with Sequence Labeling

Tasnim Kabir **Marine Carpuat**
Department of Computer Science
University of Maryland, College Park
{tkabir1,marine}@umd.edu

Abstract

This paper describes the UMD submission to the Explainable Quality Estimation Shared Task at the Eval4NLP 2021 Workshop on "Evaluation & Comparison of NLP Systems". We participated in the word-level and sentence-level MT Quality Estimation (QE) constrained tasks for all language pairs: Estonian-English, Romanian-English, German-Chinese, and Russian-German. Our approach combines the predictions of a word-level explainer model on top of a sentence-level QE model and a sequence labeler trained on synthetic data. These models are based on pre-trained multilingual language models and do not require any word-level annotations for training, making them well suited to zero-shot settings. Our best performing system improves over the best baseline across all metrics and language pairs, with an average gain of 0.1 in AUC, Average Precision, and Recall at Top-K score.

1 Introduction

Quality estimation (QE) is the task of predicting the quality of the machine translation (MT) output without reference translation. Predictions can be done at different levels of granularity, such as sentences or words. The explainable QE shared task (Fomicheva et al., 2021a) proposes to frame the identification of translation errors as an explainable QE task, where sentence-level quality judgments are explained by highlighting the words responsible for errors in the MT hypothesis. Given a source sentence and an MT hypothesis, systems are thus asked to provide word-level judgments of translation quality in addition to sentence-level judgments.

Our submission builds on state-of-the-art sentence-level QE models, MonoTransQuest (Ranasinghe et al., 2020a,b). As suggested by the organizers, we rely on the LIME explanation model (Ribeiro et al., 2016) to obtain word-level prediction from the MonoTransQuest model's sentence-level score. We hypothesize that synthetic examples of translation errors can help improve word-level predictions. As a result, we combine the predictions of MonoTransQuest-LIME with those of the Divergent mBERT model which addresses the related task of detecting semantic divergences in bitext (Briakou and Carpuat, 2020). Divergent mBERT model can detect fine-grained differences in bitext by learning to rank synthetic divergence examples of varying granularity. As a result, our approach does not require any word-level labels at training time. Both models are based on multilingual language models and are therefore amenable to zero-shot transfer.

Our submitted system improves over its components and over the official baseline on all tracks and on all language pairs, based on all evaluation metrics (AUC, AP, Recall at Top-K, and Pearson's correlation). Compared to the best baseline system for target languages, it improves AUC by 0.119 for Estonian-English (Et-En), 0.068 for Romanian-English (Ro-En), 0.085 for German-Chinese (De-Zh), and 0.128 for Russian-German (Ru-De). Similarly, for AP score, it has achieved an improvement of 0.095 for Et-En, 0.074 for Ro-En, 0.064 for De-Zh, and 0.13 for Ru-De. For Recall at Top-K score, it has achieved an improvement of 0.103 for Et-En, 0.071 for Ro-En, 0.045 for De-Zh, and 0.13 for Ru-De. For source language word-level scores, it achieves an average gain of 0.18 for AUC, 0.071 for AP and 0.12 for Recall at Top-K score over the average of all languages' baseline scores. Finally, for sentence-level scores, it has achieved an improvement of 0.36 for Et-En, 0.359 for Ro-En, 0.271 for De-Zh, and 0.06 for Ru-De compared to the average of all baseline models for Pearson's correlation.

2 Approach

We first describe the two components of our ensemble and then explain how they are combined.

Proceedings of the 58th Annual Meeting of the Association for Computational Linguistics, pages 230–237

https://doi.org/10.26615/978-954-452-056-4_022

2.1 MonoTransQuest-LIME Model

The first ensemble component is based on one of the baselines provided by the organizers. It uses MonoTransQuest, the state-of-the-art model in the WMT 2020 QE shared task (Ranasinghe et al., 2020a,b), including for mid-resource and high-resource language pairs. This model uses a single XLM-Roberta transformer model (Ranasinghe et al., 2020a,b) trained with data released in WMT quality estimation tasks in recent years. The input of the model is the concatenation of the original sentence x_{source} and its translation x_{target}, separated by the $[SEP]$ token. Therefore, $x = x_{source}, [SEP], x_{target}$ and the model used the embedding of the $[CLS]$ token as the input of a softmax layer, and this layer F predicts the sentence-level score $F(x)$ of the translation at the sentence-level. Mean-squared-error loss is used as the objective function.

For generating word-level scores from the sentence-level scores, the toolkit LIME is suggested by the organizers. LIME explains the predictions of a black-box model by providing a local linear approximation of the model's behavior. For generating an explanation for a prediction, LIME generates neighborhood data by randomly hiding features from the instance and then learns locally weighted linear models on this neighborhood data to explain each of the classes in an interpretable way[1]. Here, LIME treats words in the input sequence as features and thus lets us generate word-level QE scores from the MonoTransQuest sentence-level QE predictions.

We use existing pre-trained MonoTransQuest models. Ranasinghe et al. (2020a,b) note that the QE task can be challenging in the practical environment where the systems have to work in a multilingual setting, so selecting appropriate models for each language pair is key. As summarized in Table 1, for the development languages (et-en, ro-en), we select existing MonoTransQuest models trained on the language pair tested. For the zero-shot test languages (de-zh, ru-de), we select existing MonoTransQuest models trained on language pairs that involve one of the two languages and English (en-zh and en-de, respectively).

2.2 Divergent mBERT

Briakou and Carpuat (2020) introduced the Divergent mBERT model which is a BERT-based model that can detect cross-lingual semantic divergences by ranking synthetic divergences of varying granularity without supervision. Cross-lingual semantic divergence refers to the difference in meaning between sentences written in different languages (Vyas et al., 2018) and therefore might correspond to some adequacy errors observed in MT output.

[1]https://github.com/marcotcr/lime

Task	Model and Training Data
Et-En	TransQuest/monotransquest-da-et_en-wiki
Ro-En	TransQuest/monotransquest-da-ro_en-wiki
De-Zh	TransQuest/monotransquest-da-en_zh-wiki
Ru-De	TransQuest/monotransquest-da-en_de-wiki

Table 1: MonoTransQuest models used for each task.

The Divergent mBERT model is designed to make both sentence-level and word-level predictions. The input of this model is a sequence x generated by concatenating an English sentence x_e and a French sentence x_f with helper delimiter tokens. Therefore, $x = ([CLS], x_e, [SEP], x_f, [SEP])$. Here, the $[CLS]$ token serves as the representative for the sentence-pair x which is passed through a feed-forward network F to get the score $F(x)$ which is converted into the probability that x is equivalent.

For word-level prediction, the final hidden state h_t is passed through a feed-forward layer and a softmax layer for each token y_t in encoded sentence pair x. This produces the probability that the token y_t belongs to the equivalent class. For sentence-level prediction, the model uses margin-loss and for token-level prediction, it uses cross-entropy loss of all tokens. The word-level evaluation on this model found that it outperforms Random Baseline across all metrics. Therefore, this model proves that we can benefit from training even with noisy word-level labels. We can map this task to identifying the error in the word-level QE by marking all divergences as errors.

We made a small change to the original Divergent mBERT model by fine-tuning XLM-Roberta (Conneau et al., 2020) rather than mBERT, and keeping the rest of the model architecture, loss definition, and training data unchanged. As a result, this model is trained on French-English sentence pairs, where positive examples of equivalence are drawn from bitext with a filtering step to ensure that they are not noisy, and negative samples are automatically generated by corrupting the positive samples to introduce meaning mismatches (e.g., by deleting dependency subtrees in one language, substituting words with near-synonyms, or phrases with other phrases that have the same syntactic structure). As a result, this model is used in zero-shot settings for all the test languages of the shared task and does not use any manual QE annotation.

2.3 Ensembling Method

We adopt the approach of Kepler et al. (2019) for building ensemble models for word-level quality estimation, which simply averages the predictions of the ensemble components. While their ensemble had five models, we average the predictions of the two models above, either at the sentence or word level. Given a source sentence (src) and the machine translation hypothesis (mt), Divergent mBERT and MonoTransQuest-LIME produce word-level scores for each word in the MT hypothesis. These are averaged to produce the final word-level score. The same process is used to combine sentence-level predictions. The overall system architecture is shown in Figure 1 for word-level predictions.

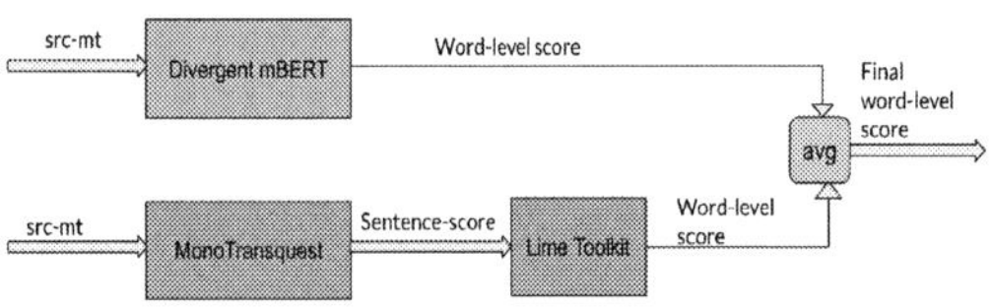

Figure 1: System architecture of the ensemble method. The input src-mt represents the language pair for which the sentence-level and the word-level score are being generated.

3 Datasets

In this section, we describe the data used for training, development, and evaluation.

3.1 Training Data

We use ensemble components that have been pre-trained on different datasets.

MonoTransQuest We use the original models that have been publicly released. They were trained on publicly available datasets from recent WMT sentence-level quality estimation tasks (Specia et al., 2018; Fonseca et al., 2019; Specia et al., 2020). These datasets were collected from Wikipedia and Reddit. In this setup, the Et-En and Ro-En are considered as medium resource language and En-Zh and En-De are considered as high resource language pairs. In Table 1, we can see the lists the training data used to train the original pre-trained MonoTransQuest models. We can note that as there were no De-Zh and Ru-De language pairs used, thus, this model supports prediction in a zero-shot setting.

Divergent mBERT We used the same training data as the original model by Briakou and Carpuat (2020). The training data was the English and French text from WikiMatrix which was normalized with Moses toolkit and tokenized. In our model, we have used "XLMRobertaTokenizer" where the original model used "BERTTokenizer". Similar to the original model, the alignment of English and French bitext was done using Berkeley word aligner. After filtering the noisy samples, the top 5500 samples, ranked by LASER similarity score, were picked, and then the synthetic divergent examples were generated. The synthetic data was generated similar to the original model's synthetic data generation process which is: subtree deletion by deleting a randomly selected subtree in the dependency parse of the English sentence, or French words aligned to English words in that subtree, Phrase Replacement by substituting random source or target sequences by another sequence of words with matching POS tags and lexical substitution by substituting English words with hypernyms or hyponyms from WordNet.

3.2 Development Data

We used the official shared task development data, which is drawn from the Multilingual Quality Estimation and Post-Editing (MLQE-PE) dataset (Fomicheva et al., 2020). There are two language pairs in the development set, with 1000 sentences each: Estonian-English (Et-En) and Romanian-English (Ro-En).

3.3 Test Data

The test data included four language pairs: Estonian-English (Et-En), Romanian-English (Ro-En), German-Chinese (De-Zh), and Russian-German (Ru-De). The first two language pairs are the same as the development set language pairs. German-English (De-Zh) and Russian-German (Ru-De) language pairs are zero-shot languages since they were not available in the development phase. Test set statistics are given in Table 2. Models are evaluated against human annotations by submitting to the official leaderboard.

Language Pair	# of sentences
Et-En	1000
Ro-En	1000
De-Zh	1410
Ru-De	1180

Table 2: Test data statistics.

4 System Configuration

We used the same set of system configurations for all the language pairs in our experiment to ensure consistency among all language pairs.

MonoTransQuest We have used pre-trained MonoTransQuestmodel on the HuggingFace Transformers library (Wolf et al., 2019). We used those pre-trained MonoTranquest models [2]. We have not changed any hyperparameter from those models.

Divergent mBERT For training Divergent mBERT we have used a batch size of 16, Adam optimizer with learning rate $2e^{-5}$ and a linear rate warmup. The model was trained with only training data. The model was trained for five epochs. We have varied the hyperparameter settings: epoch was varied from 3 to 15 epochs, the margin was varied from 5 to 10, the alpha value was varied from 0.2 to 1. Table 3 is the list of the final hyper-parameter settings we used for training in our experiments.

Batch Size	16
Loss Function	Sentence-level: Margin Loss Token-level: Cross Entropy
Optimizer	AdamW
Learning Rate	$2e^{-5}$
Scheduler	Linear Schedule with Warmup
Epoch	5
Margin	5
Alpha	1

Table 3: Divergent mBERT hyperparameters.

5 Evaluation Metrics

This section describes the official evaluation metrics for the shared task. For sentence-level scores, Pearson's correlation is used and for word-level scores, AUC, AP, and Recall at Top-K are used:

- **Pearson's Correlation:** This measures the strength and direction of a linear relationship between the model predicted sentence-level score and human-annotated sentence-level score. Values always range between -1 (strong negative relationship) and +1 (strong positive relationship).

- **AUC Score:** In this shared task, the AUC score between the model predicted output and gold explanation MT score is computed using sklearn[3]. Given a test set of N sentences:

$$AUC = \frac{1}{N} \sum_{n} AUC_n(w_n, a_n^{x^T}) \qquad (1)$$

Here, w_n is a vector representing binary gold word-level labels for each sentence n in the test set and $a_n^{x^T}$ is the vector for the model predicted word-level score for the target words x^T in each target sentence in test set with length T. Equation 1 computes the AUC score to compare the model predicted word-level scores a against binary gold labels (Fomicheva et al., 2021b). Here, AUC_n is the area under the curve generated by plotting the true positive against false positive of the word-level scores of the nth sentence at different thresholds. AUC ranges in value from 0 to 1. A model whose predictions are 100% wrong has an AUC of 0.0; one whose predictions are 100% correct has an AUC of 1.0.

- **AP Score:** AP (Average Precision) evaluates word-level predictions and complements AUC scores which can be overly optimistic for imbalanced data (Fomicheva et al., 2021b). Average precision[4] is defined as:

$$AP = \sum_{n} (R_n - R_{n-1}) P_n \qquad (2)$$

where P_n and R_n are the precision and recall at the nth threshold, where words are assigned to the positive class if the model predicts a score for this word that is higher than the nth threshold.

- **Recall at Top-K:** This metric checks whether the highest predicted values have been assigned to the words corresponding to actual errors. For example, if the gold standard output is $1, 1, 0, 0, 0, 0, 0$ then the recall value

[2]https://huggingface.co/MonoTransQuest

[3]https://developers.google.com/machine-learning/crash-course/classification/roc-and-auc

[4]https://scikit-learn.org/stable/modules/generated/sklearn.metrics.average_precision_score.html

checks whether in the model predicted output, the highest values have been assigned to the first and second word. Specifically this metric computes the proportion of words with the highest attribution corresponding to errors against the total number of errors in the MT output (Fomicheva et al., 2021b):

$$Recall\ at\ Top\text{-}K = \frac{1}{k} \sum_{j \in e_{1:k}} w_j \quad (3)$$

Here, k is the number of errors in the sentence and $e = argsort(a^{x^T})$ is the sequence of highest to lowest sorted indexes of target words according to the attribution scores. The final score is the average over test instances, and ranges from 0 to 1.

6 Results

We describe the performance of our models on the development and test sets using the official shared task metrics.

6.1 Development Set Results

The results achieved by each of the organizers provided baseline systems, Divergent mBERT, and our ensemble method is described in Table 4. This table described the results on the Et-En and Ro-En language pairs of the validation set. Our ensemble model outperforms the baselines, as well as its components according to all metrics.

We can see a consistent improvement for all the language pairs in the development set. In comparison with the average of all baselines, for Et-En language pair, on target word-level scores, our ensemble method achieves an improvement of 0.15 in AUC score, 0.17 in AP score, and 0.17 in Recall at Top-K score. Similarly, for the source language, it achieves an improvement of 0.19 in the AUC score, 0.123 in AP score, and 0.2 in Recall at Top-K score over the average of all baselines. Similarly, For the Ro-En language pair, on target word-level scores, our ensemble method achieves an improvement of 0.15 in AUC score, 0.21 in AP score, and 0.231 in Recall at Top-K score over the average of all baselines. Similarly, for the source language, it achieves an improvement of 0.185 in the AUC score, 0.156 in AP score, and 0.23 in Recall at Top-K score over the average of all baselines.

The Divergent mBERT model has a smaller but consistent advantage over all the baseline models. If we take the average on baselines on Et-En, this model achieves an improvement of 0.126 on AUC, 0.043 on AP, and 0.126 on Recall at Top-K score. Similarly, on the average of all baselines for Ro-En, this model achieves an improvement of 0.152 on AUC, 0.1 on AP, and 0.187 on Recall at Top-K score. Overall, these results suggest that Divergent mBERT and MonoTransQuest have complementary strengths, which benefit the ensemble.

We illustrate the complementarity of the ensemble components with randomly selected examples from the Ro-En development set in Table 5. The Divergent mBERT model predicts better error labels for short sentences than the MonoTransQuest-model. However, MonoTransQuest is more accurate on longer or more complex sentences.

6.2 Word-level Test Results

Table 6 summarizes model performance for all the language pairs in the test set. Consistent with the development set results, the ensemble improves over all the baselines, and outperforms each of its components.

Et-En : For Et-En language pair, on target word-level scores, our ensemble method achieves an improvement of 0.164 in AUC score, 0.186 in AP score, and 0.181 in Recall at Top-K score over the average of all baselines. Similarly, for the source language, it achieves an improvement of 0.236 in the AUC score, 0.13 in AP score, and 0.208 in Recall at Top-K score over the average of all baselines.

Ro-En For Ro-En language pair, on target word-level scores, our ensemble method achieves an improvement of 0.129 in AUC score, 0.173 in AP score, and 0.135 in Recall at Top-K score over the average of all baselines. Similarly, for the source language, it achieves an improvement of 0.22 in the AUC score, 0.102 in AP score, and 0.193 in Recall at Top-K score over the average of all baselines.

De-Zh For De-Zh language pair, on target word-level scores, our ensemble method achieves an improvement of 0.13 in AUC score, 0.1 in AP score, and 0.09 in Recall at Top-K score over the average of all baselines. Similarly, for the source language, it achieves an improvement of 0.123 in the AUC score, 0.01 in AP score, and 0.08 in Recall at Top-K score over the average of all baselines.

Ru-De For Ru-De language pair, on target word-level scores, our ensemble method achieves an im-

Pair	System	Word-level Score						Sentence-level Score
		Target			Source			
		AUC	AP	Recall	AUC	AP	Recall	Pearson's
Et-En	*Random (Baseline 1)*	0.505	0.387	0.284	0.496	0.380	0.249	-0.048
	XMover-SHAP (Baseline 2)	0.583	0.456	0.352	0.513	0.394	0.262	0.415
	TransQuest-LIME (Baseline 3)	0.592	0.510	0.402	-1.00	-1.00	-1.00	0.722
	Divergent mBERT	0.686	0.494	0.472	0.608	0.403	0.357	0.572
	Ensemble	**0.710**	**0.621**	**0.515**	**0.695**	**0.510**	**0.459**	**0.772**
Ro-En	*Random (Baseline 1)*	0.488	0.359	0.239	0.505	0.374	0.254	-0.021
	XMover-SHAP (Baseline 2)	0.638	0.464	0.339	0.541	0.384	0.265	0.638
	TransQuest-LIME (Baseline 3)	0.619	0.552	0.439	-1.00	-1.00	-1.00	0.882
	Divergent mBERT	0.734	0.557	0.526	0.618	0.412	0.372	0.742
	Ensemble	**0.728**	**0.664**	**0.570**	**0.708**	**0.535**	**0.486**	**0.890**

Table 4: Word-level and sentence-level scores on development data. The baseline scores are taken from the leader-board. Best results for each language by any method are marked in bold.

Source Sentence 1	Dobridorul nu este o excepție în ceea ce privește depozitele de
Target Sentence 1	The acquirer is not a deposit exception
Gold word-level label	1 1 0 0 1 1 1
MonoTransQuest label	-0.034 -0.090 -0.043 -0.023 0.006 -0.039 -0.096
Divergent mBERT label	1 1 0 0 0 0 0
Source Sentence 2	Dacă IA este programată pentru „ " obiectivele pot fi induse implicit prin recompensarea unor tipuri de comportament sau prin pedepsirea altora.
Target Sentence 2	This is because if IA is scheduled for another the objectives can be induced implicitly by rewarding some types of behaviour or by punishing others.
Gold word-level label	1 1 1 1 1 1 0 1 0 1 0 0 0 0 0 0 0 0 0 0 0 0 0 0 0 0 0 0
MonoTransQuest label	0.002 0.013 0.040 -0.005 -0.022 -0.017 -0.007 -0.044 -0.023 0.012 -0.007 -0.007 -0.052 -0.027 -0.004 -0.034 -0.02 -0.003 -0.025 -0.006 -0.009 -0.002 -0.020 -0.018 0.001 -0.019 -0.005 0.001
Divergent mBERT label	0 0 0 0 0 0 0 0 0 1 1 0 0 0 0 0 0 0 0 0 0 0 0 0 0 0 0 0

Table 5: Examples of word-level labels for different models.

Pair	System	Training Data	Target			Source		
			AUC	AP	Recall	AUC	AP	Recall
Et-En	*Random (Baseline 1)*	-	0.497	0.358	0.274	0.487	0.339	0.194
	XMover-SHAP (Baseline 2)	Et-En	0.616	0.441	0.338	0.535	0.371	0.231
	TransQuest-LIME (Baseline 3)	Et-En	0.624	0.536	0.424	0.544	0.440	0.309
	Divergent mBERT	En-Fr	0.725	0.536	0.493	0.544	0.440	0.309
	Ensemble Method	Et-En, En-Fr	**0.743**	**0.631**	**0.527**	**0.758**	**0.514**	**0.453**
Ro-En	*Random (Baseline 1)*	-	0.516	0.311	0.187	0.500	0.280	0.150
	XMover-SHAP (Baseline 2)	Ro-En	0.666	0.438	0.295	0.534	0.292	0.148
	TransQuest-LIME (Baseline 3)	Ro-En	0.634	0.523	0.415	0.478	0.351	0.243
	Divergent mBERT	En-Fr	0.717	0.462	0.452	0.478	0.351	0.243
	Ensemble Method	Ro-En, En-Fr	**0.734**	**0.597**	**0.486**	**0.724**	**0.410**	**0.373**
De-Zh	*Random (Baseline 1)*	-	0.496	0.294	0.174	0.500	0.300	0.174
	XMover-SHAP (Baseline 2)	WMT's all language pairs	0.545	0.334	0.220	0.474	0.287	0.159
	TransQuest-LIME (Baseline 3)	WMT's all language pairs	0.460	0.271	0.145	0.486	0.317	0.196
	Divergent mBERT	En-Fr	0.556	0.303	0.238	0.478	**0.351**	0.243
	Ensemble Method	En-Zh, En-Fr	**0.630**	**0.400**	**0.265**	**0.610**	0.311	**0.252**
Ru-De	*Random (Baseline 1)*	-	0.492	0.308	0.216	0.506	0.341	0.237
	XMover-SHAP (Baseline 2)	WMT's all language pairs	0.522	0.328	0.224	0.522	0.356	0.259
	TransQuest-LIME (Baseline 3)	WMT's all language pairs	0.404	0.262	0.164	0.534	**0.427**	0.320
	Divergent mBERT	En-Fr	0.579	0.418	0.321	0.478	0.351	0.243
	Ensemble Method	En-De, En-Fr	**0.650**	**0.458**	**0.354**	**0.658**	0.413	**0.373**

Table 6: Word level results for all language pairs on the test set in terms of AUC, AP and Recall at Top-K. The baseline scores are taken from the leader-board. Best results for each language by any method are marked in bold.

provement of 0.18 in AUC score, 0.16 in AP score, and 0.153 in Recall at Top-K score over the average of all baselines. Similarly, for the source language, it achieves an improvement of 0.14 in the AUC score, 0.04 in AP score, and 0.101 in Recall at Top-K score over the average of all baselines.

Discussion Taken together, these results show that the ensemble method performs similarly for those language pairs that are used in the training phase (Et-En, Ro-En language pairs) and for the zero-shot language pairs (De-Zh, Ru-De). It has an average improvement of 0.15 in AUC, 0.18 in AP, and 0.16 in Recall at Top-K score for those language pairs which is in its training data and an average improvement of 0.16 in AUC, 0.13 in AP, and 0.12 in Recall at Top-K score for those language pairs which it is not trained on. Therefore, we can see we can have a consistent gain for all language pairs with this method without including that particular language pair in the training data. The Divergent mBERT model is effective on all language pairs, even though it is trained on synthetic data generated from English-French bitext: this suggests that the word-level weak supervision provided by the synthetic samples is robust, although it would be interesting to investigate the impact of the choice of training languages further in future work. Secondly, a clear takeaway is that the ensembling of different systems can give large gains, even if some of the subsystems are weak individually and even in zero-shot settings.

6.3 Sentence-level Scores on Test Set

Pair	System	Pearson's
Et-En	*Random (Baseline 1)*	-0.029
	XMover-SHAP (Baseline 2)	0.494
	MonoTransQuest (Baseline 3)	0.772
	Divergent mBERT	0.021
	Ensemble	**0.772**
Ro-En	*Random (Baseline 1)*	0.017
	XMover-SHAP (Baseline 2)	0.695
	MonoTransQuest (Baseline 3)	0.899
	Divergent mBERT	0.661
	Ensemble	**0.899**
De-Zh	*Random (Baseline 1)*	0.000
	XMover-SHAP (Baseline 2)	0.336
	MonoTransQuest (Baseline 3)	0.335
	Divergent mBERT	0.096
	Ensemble	**0.495**
Ru-De	*Random (Baseline 1)*	-0.017
	XMover-SHAP (Baseline 2)	0.252
	MonoTransQuest (Baseline 3)	**0.498**
	Divergent mBERT	0.449
	Ensemble	0.303

Table 7: Results of sentence-level submissions and their performance on the test set. The baseline scores are taken from the leaderboard. Best results for each language by any method are marked in bold.

Table 7 contains the results for the sentence-level submission on the test set. Evaluated on Pearson's correlation, our ensemble method has a consistent improvement of 0.36 for Et-En, 0.359 for Ro-En, 0.271 for De-Zh, and 0.06 for Ru-De compared to the average of all baseline models. However, in a zero-shot setting, Pearson's correlation varies significantly between different language pairs.

We observe that the MonoTransQuest baseline achieves better performance on test language pairs, which is not surprising since it was trained on all the language pairs of WMT. This impacts results on the zero-shot languages: for De-Zh MonoTransQuest outperforms Divergent mBERT by a large margin, but the ensemble still benefits from Divergent mBERT. For Ru-De, the MonoTransQuest achieve the strongest level correlation and Divergent mBERT does not improve over it when added to the ensemble, unlike for word-level predictions.

The Divergent mBERT model has unequal performance across languages. It achieves the highest Pearson Correlation for Ro-En, which is the closest language pair to the one it is trained on (English-French) but performs poorly for Estonian-English and German-Chinese.

7 Conclusion

We described the University of Maryland's contribution to the Eval4NLP 2021 Shared Task on Quality Estimation. Our submission was based on ensembling existing models: (1) the state-of-the-art framework MonoTransQuest model followed by the LIME explanation model, and (2) an mBERT model trained to detect cross-lingual semantic divergences. We show that averaging the prediction of these models outperforms all the baselines and their individual predictions, even though none of the ensemble components are trained with word-level supervision.

Overall, our approach shows the benefits of leveraging pre-trained multilingual LMs to port to multiple language pairs, including in zero-shot settings: the Divergent mBERT component is even trained on a language pair that is not used for any of the test tasks. In the future, training Divergent mBERT with other language pairs can lead to more promising results. This work also shows the complementarity of explanation models and of sequence labelers trained on synthetic data for word-level predictions. In future work, controlled comparison of these approaches on the same languages and data conditions can lead to further insights on their respective strengths and weaknesses.

References

Eleftheria Briakou and Marine Carpuat. 2020. Detecting fine-grained cross-lingual semantic divergences without supervision by learning to rank. In *Proceedings of the 2020 Conference on Empirical Methods* in *Natural Language Processing (EMNLP)*, pages 1563–1580, Online. Association for Computational Linguistics.

Alexis Conneau, Kartikay Khandelwal, Naman Goyal, Vishrav Chaudhary, Guillaume Wenzek, Francisco Guzmán, Edouard Grave, Myle Ott, Luke Zettlemoyer, and Veselin Stoyanov. 2020. Unsupervised cross-lingual representation learning at scale. In *ACL*.

Marina Fomicheva, Piyawat Lertvittayakumjorn, Wei Zhao, Steffen Eger, and Yang Gao. 2021a. The eval4nlp shared task on explainable quality estimation: Overview and results. In *Proceedings of the 2nd Workshop on Evaluation and Comparison of NLP Systems*.

Marina Fomicheva, Lucia Specia, and Nikolaos Aletras. 2021b. Translation error detection as rationale extraction. *arXiv preprint arXiv:2108.12197*.

Marina Fomicheva, Shuo Sun, Erick Fonseca, Frédéric Blain, Vishrav Chaudhary, Francisco Guzmán, Nina Lopatina, Lucia Specia, and André FT Martins. 2020. Mlqe-pe: A multilingual quality estimation and post-editing dataset. *arXiv preprint arXiv:2010.04480*.

Erick Fonseca, Lisa Yankovskaya, André F. T. Martins, Mark Fishel, and Christian Federmann. 2019. Findings of the WMT 2019 shared tasks on quality estimation. In *Proceedings of the Fourth Conference on Machine Translation (Volume 3: Shared Task Papers, Day 2)*, pages 1–10, Florence, Italy. Association for Computational Linguistics.

Fábio Kepler, Jonay Trénous, Marcos Treviso, Miguel Vera, António Góis, M Amin Farajian, António V Lopes, and André FT Martins. 2019. Unbabel's participation in the wmt19 translation quality estimation shared task. *WMT 2019*, page 80.

Tharindu Ranasinghe, Constantin Orasan, and Ruslan Mitkov. 2020a. Transquest at wmt2020: Sentence-level direct assessment. In *Proceedings of the Fifth Conference on Machine Translation*.

Tharindu Ranasinghe, Constantin Orasan, and Ruslan Mitkov. 2020b. Transquest: Translation quality estimation with cross-lingual transformers. In *Proceedings of the 28th International Conference on Computational Linguistics*.

Marco Tulio Ribeiro, Sameer Singh, and Carlos Guestrin. 2016. " why should i trust you?" explaining the predictions of any classifier. In *Proceedings of the 22nd ACM SIGKDD international conference on knowledge discovery and data mining*, pages 1135–1144.

Lucia Specia, Frédéric Blain, Marina Fomicheva, Erick Fonseca, Vishrav Chaudhary, Francisco Guzmán, and André F. T. Martins. 2020. Findings of the WMT 2020 shared task on quality estimation. In *Proceedings of the Fifth Conference on Machine Translation*, pages 743–764, Online. Association for Computational Linguistics.

Lucia Specia, Frédéric Blain, Varvara Logacheva, Ramón Astudillo, and André FT Martins. 2018. Findings of the wmt 2018 shared task on quality estimation. In *Proceedings of the Third Conference on Machine Translation: Shared Task Papers*, pages 689–709.

Yogarshi Vyas, Xing Niu, and Marine Carpuat. 2018. Identifying semantic divergences in parallel text without annotations. In *Proceedings of the 2018 Conference of the North American Chapter of the Association for Computational Linguistics: Human Language Technologies, Volume 1 (Long Papers)*, pages 1503–1515.

Thomas Wolf, Lysandre Debut, Victor Sanh, Julien Chaumond, Clement Delangue, Anthony Moi, Pierric Cistac, Tim Rault, Rémi Louf, Morgan Funtowicz, et al. 2019. Huggingface's transformers: State-of-the-art natural language processing. *arXiv preprint arXiv:1910.03771*.

Explaining Errors in Machine Translation with Absolute Gradient Ensembles

Melda Eksi **Erik Gelbing** **Jonathan Stieber** **Chi Viet Vu**
Department of Computer Science
Technical University of Darmstadt
Germany
{melda.eksi, erik.gelbing, jonathan.stieber, chiviet.vu}
@stud.tu-darmstadt.de

Abstract

Current research on quality estimation of machine translation focuses on the sentence-level quality of the translations. By using explainability methods, we can use these quality estimations for word-level error identification. In this work, we compare different explainability techniques and investigate gradient-based and perturbation-based methods by measuring their performance and required computational efforts[1]. Throughout our experiments, we observed that using absolute word scores boosts the performance of gradient-based explainers significantly. Further, we combine explainability methods to ensembles to exploit the strengths of individual explainers to get better explanations. We propose the usage of absolute gradient-based methods. These work comparably well to popular perturbation-based ones while being more time-efficient.

1 Introduction

Building trustworthy and reliable Machine Translation (MT) systems has been a broad topic in Natural Language Processing (NLP) for the past decade. Advances in research have led to dominant architectures like the BERT transformer models (Devlin et al., 2019; Wolf et al., 2020), which got widely adapted by the NLP community for a variety of tasks, including automated MT. Pretraining models (McCann et al., 2017; Devlin et al., 2019; Liu et al., 2019) on generic corpora has simplified the deployment of performant, yet easily adaptable models, and therefore became a central part of new translation systems which show great progress in terms of their translation quality while maintaining reasonable computational costs (Liu et al., 2020).

Traditionally, estimating the quality of a given translation requires human supervisors who are able to identify weaknesses in the translation, attribute wrongly translated parts and correct them manually (Comparin and Mendes, 2017). Reference-free (i.e. without access to a reference translation) Quality Estimation (QE) tries to solve this costly and time-consuming process by providing models that are able to assign quality-scores automatically (Fomicheva et al., 2020b).

TransQuest (TQ), presented by Ranasinghe et al. (2020), is a quality estimation framework which won the sentence-level direct assessment shared task in WMT 2020, thus we will utilize TQ primarily in this work as our target model to be explained.

This year's 'Explainable Quality Estimation' shared task (Fomicheva et al., 2021) focuses on the evaluation of current QE by using different explainability methods. As the organizers propose, the identification of translation errors therefore should be seen as an explainability problem. Explanations are expected to provide insights into the connection between a given input-output-pair so that humans are able to easily understand the explanation and, if necessary, take action. Further, analyzing a set of predictions of a system with explainability methods helps with comparing the system's decision with human reasoning, ultimately assessing trust in the system (Ribeiro et al., 2016).

In this work, we will compare five explainability techniques on this year's task dataset (Section 3). We experiment with perturbation-based methods as well as gradient-based methods (Section 4) and propose a simple, yet effective ensembling technique to improve the overall classification performance. Our goal is to provide an overview of each approach's capabilities in terms of classification performance, but also in the context of the computational overhead required for each approach.

2 Related work

Explainability is already a key research topic for Computer Vision (CV), but there are many rising efforts to make NLP models explainable as well

[1]Code for this paper is available at `https://github.com/SinisterThaumaturge/MetaScience-Explainable-Metrics`

Proceedings of the 58th Annual Meeting of the Association for Computational Linguistics, pages 238–249

https://doi.org/10.26615/978-954-452-056-4_023

(Pröllochs et al., 2019; Rajani et al., 2019). It can be helpful for different tasks, e.g. automated fact-checking for public health (Kotonya and Toni, 2020). Frameworks for interpretability were already developed for CV, e.g. iNNvestigate or InterpretML (Alber et al., 2019; Nori et al., 2019) but specific ones for NLP are also on the rise, like AllenNLP Interpret (Wallace et al., 2019).

Essential for ensuring trust in models are evaluation metrics that are more aligned with human perception of 'goodness'. For this reason, there are rising efforts in research for the creation of such metrics for various NLP tasks.

Existing popular evaluation metrics for text generation tasks like ROUGE (Lin, 2004) for text summarization and BLEU (Papineni et al., 2002) for MT base their measures on statistical similarity rather than evaluating semantic similarity. Several alternative metrics aim to tackle these shortcomings: unsupervised metrics MoverScore (Zhao et al., 2019) and its reference-free extension XMover-Score (XMS) (Zhao et al., 2020) that generates better aligned cross-lingual embeddings on basis of which translation quality can be measured more similarly to how humans do it.

It should be possible to derive valuable information from sentence-level QE scores for word-level translation error identification. Until now there are no existing approaches for explaining errors in MT based on QE scores that we know of. However, in consideration of the 'Explainable Quality Estimation' shared task that is part of EMNLP 2021, we expect new approaches that address this problem.

3 Data

We conduct our experiments on the Multilingual Quality Estimation and Automatic Post-editing Dataset (MLQE-PE) (Fomicheva et al., 2020a). The training and development data for this shared task consists of Romanian-English (Ro-En) and Estonian-English (Et-En) language pairs where word-level gold labels and sentence-level gold scores are provided in addition to source sentences and MT outputs. Data is shown exemplary in Figure 1.

Our approach is to estimate word-level scores in an unsupervised fashion to show specific errors in translation. Therefore, we use explanations on sentence-level scores to get word-level scores, which are then evaluated with the given gold standard word-level scores in the development set.

The training and development data consists of 7000 and 1000 tokenized sentences respectively for both Estonian-English and Romanian-English. Sentence-level scores range in [0, 100] where higher scores indicate better translations. We predict these with the QE model. Tokens for the sentence quality score (word-level labels) are rated binary, 1 being relevant and thus responsible for low-quality scores and 0 being correct tokens.

Source: Turnul a fost distrus de cutremur , trebuind să fie recunstruit în anii următori .
MT: The earthquake destroyed the pole , having to be reunified in the years to come .
Gold Explanations Source: 1 0 0 0 0 0 1 1 0 0 1 0 0 0 0
Gold Explanations MT: 0 0 0 0 1 1 1 0 0 1 0 0 0 0 0 0
Gold Sentence Level Score: 49.667

Figure 1: Example Romanian-English sentence data from the MLQE-PE training set (Fomicheva et al., 2020a). Highlights show wrongly translated tokens.

Test data consists of further annotated Et-En and Ro-En sentences. Zero-shot test sets for German-Chinese (De-Zh) and Russian-German (Ru-De) language pairs are also provided in addition, which neither contain word- nor sentence-level annotations. We did not use the training set at all as the models were all pre-trained and evaluated the explanations on the development and test set.

4 Methods

4.1 Perturbation-based methods

Methods described in the following section follow a perturbation-based approach. As the name suggests, perturbation-based explainers perturb the inputs randomly, with the goal of observing a changing behavior on the output of the model to be explained, or even on its individual neurons (Shrikumar et al., 2016).

4.1.1 LIME

Ribeiro et al. (2016) propose the usage of Local Interpretable Model-agnostic Explanations (LIME). As a *model-agnostic* explainability technique, LIME quickly gained popularity and acceptance not just in the NLP community. The main goal of LIME is to explain any complex model $f : \mathbb{R}^d \rightarrow \mathbb{R}$ by creating a simple interpretable model $g \in G$

(e.g. a sparse linear model), that is *locally trustworthy*. This means that instead of trying to globally explain the predictions of the model, specific instances $x \in \mathbb{R}^d$ are selected and explained on a local level. While many modern NLP models such as Bidirectional Encoder Representations from Transformers (BERT), Robustly Optimized BERT Pretraining Approach (RoBERTa) or XLM-RoBERTa (XLM-R) (Devlin et al., 2019; Liu et al., 2019; Conneau et al., 2020) rely on word embeddings as their input representation, these representations contradict the expectations we have for interpretable explanations. As explanations should be easily understandable, Local Interpretable Model-agnostic Explanations (LIME) is using a word-level representation that enables humans to understand the influence of each word on the decision of the underlying classifier or regressor. For each instance to be explained, the original input is transformed into an *interpretable representation* $x' \in \{0,1\}^{d'}, d' : number\ of\ words\ in\ a\ sentence$, which holds a binary vector denoting whether a certain component is present or not. To explain a specific instance, the input x' is perturbed randomly (e.g. masking for text classification). The resulting perturbations are weighted by a proximity function π_x (e.g. cosine distance for text classification). The proximity function is a distance measure where an input that has been heavily modified should have a high distance to the original, which means that the explanation will probably also differ more strongly. The weighting process ensures that the resulting explanations are locally faithful, as more similar perturbations have a higher impact on the loss of the objective function and therefore on the overall explanation. Additionally, the resulting perturbations are used to minimize an error function $\xi(x)$, e.g. linear least squares in our case.

Figure 2 shows the LIME explanations for the pre-trained MonoTransQuest (MTQ) estimator on an example translation.

4.1.2 SHAP

Lundberg and Lee (2017) propose SHapley Additive exPlanations (SHAP) which builds upon various existing explainability techniques unified in a class of *additive feature attribution methods*. To explain certain instances, SHAP values are utilized to measure the influence of features towards a certain prediction.

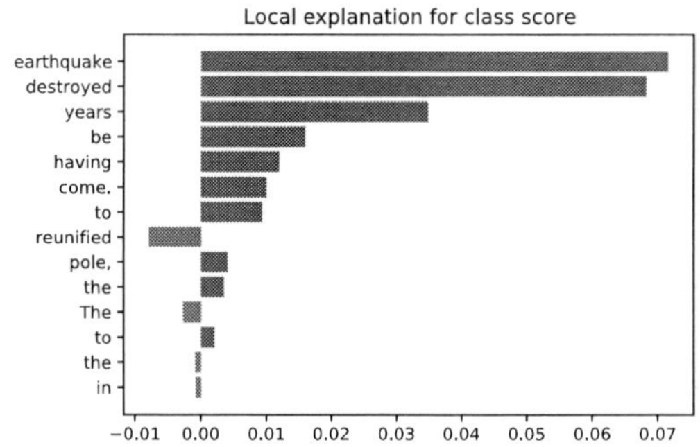

Figure 2: Explanations provided by the LIME Text Explainer (Ribeiro et al., 2016) on our example sentence. As the source sentence is fixed, we are only interested in the explanation of the target sentence. Each word can be seen as an interpretable feature holding a score that denotes its influence on the decision of the estimator.

Additive Feature Attribution Methods are a collection of methodologies that all utilize a linear function as their explanation model:

$$g(z') = \phi + \sum_{i=1}^{M} \phi_i z'_i, \quad (1)$$

The summation of the attributed effect ϕ_i of each feature from z' approaches the original model $f(x)$. Lundberg and Lee (2017) show that various current explainers like LIME or DeepLIFT (Shrikumar et al., 2017; Bach et al., 2015) match the definition in (1) and can therefore be transformed into an additive feature attribution method.

SHAP Values are based on Shapley regression values, Shapley sampling values and Quantitative Input Influence (Lipovetsky and Conklin, 2001; Bach et al., 2015; Strumbelj and Kononenko, 2014). Shapley values provide a measure for the importance of individual features and are utilized in combination with the additive feature attribution methods to derive SHAP values.

Based on these values, the SHAP explainer is able to attribute the impact of each feature to the overall prediction. SHAP conditions on one feature at a time and incrementally adds up the other features to determine ϕ_i. As the calculated effect is often dependant on the order of the features presented to the equation, ϕ_i is computed recursively for all possible orderings of features and then averaged (Shrikumar et al., 2016; Lundberg and Lee, 2017).

4.1.3 Occlusion

Occlusion is a generalization of the sliding window approach presented by Zeiler and Fergus (2014). The algorithm replaces (contiguous) patches of the input with a baseline (in our case: zero-scalar, denoting the presence or absence of a feature). Importance scores are calculated by measuring the effect of the perturbation in form of the difference in the predictions of the output layer. Therefore, we test each feature independently by comparing the output of the model if the feature is enabled (it takes its original value) versus disabling it (replacing the feature with the baseline). The resulting heatmap represents the attributions of each feature. Importance scores of the output are used to propagate their influence back to the inputs.

4.2 Gradient-based methods

Gradient-based explainers (i.e. backpropagation-based explainers) are based on the idea of propagating an importance score measured at an individual output backwards to the network (Shrikumar et al., 2016). We use these methods targeting the embedding layers of the QE model. The scores which we can propagate towards this layer serve as the explanations for individual embeddings and therefore for the overall model. Usually, these methods are more lightweight and thus require less computational overhead.

4.2.1 Layer Gradient X Activation

Layer Gradient X Activation is based on gradient*input which is a very simple explanation technique (Baehrens et al., 2010). Since the gradients represent how, and how strongly the model will behave for each input dimension, they can be seen as an expression of importance. Unfortunately, the gradient is only an accurate representation of importance locally when considering small steps. Layer Gradient X Activation is based on Shrikumar et al. (2016), which is the preceding work to DeepLIFT (Section 4.2.2). We use this approach to compute the element-wise product of gradients and activation, but contrary to regular gradient*input we only apply the method on the hidden embedding layer of the quality estimator, in order to retrieve explanations.

4.2.2 DeepLIFT

DeepLIFT (Learning Important FeaTures) (Shrikumar et al., 2017) is used to explain instances by measuring the effect $C_{\Delta x_i \Delta t}$ of a feature x_i on the overall prediction if set to a predefined reference value compared to its true value. The summation of effects for each input:

$$\sum_{i=1}^{n} C_{\Delta x_i \Delta t} = \Delta t \tag{2}$$

is called the *summation-to-delta* property with t being the reference activation of the output and Δt representing the *difference-from-reference*. Equation (2) conducts that the difference-from-reference can be determined for each x_i in the context of the reference value.

As the authors propose, DeepLIFT uses a set of rules (i.e. Linear, Rescale and RevealCancel) for assigning importance scores which can be seen as approximations of Shapley values (Section 4.1.2). In fact, the linear and rescale rules were presented in an earlier version of their work whereas the reveal-cancel rule was published later as an improved version, avoiding specific pitfalls which they describe in their work in detail. These rules are used to map the contribution scores of neurons to their immediate inputs, and further, to any input for a given target output by utilizing backpropagation.

We used **Integrated Gradients** (IG) (Sundararajan et al., 2017) as an additional gradient-based method during our experiments (see Appendix A), but we will not go into this method further as it does not have any noteworthy performance compared to the other methods.

4.3 Absolute methods

Throughout our experiments, we often observed that wrong words got high positive gradient explanations for the MTQ model. To further investigate this, we propose a different way of using the output of the explainers by just taking the absolute values for each word score. Therefore, we assume that wrong words do not have large negative gradients but instead that their gradient magnitude is higher than those of correctly translated words, leading to the intuition that wrong words have higher deviations in negative, but also positive direction with respect to the gradient. We labeled absolute methods with the prefix *Abs.* in our experiments (Section 5).

4.4 Ensemble methods

To improve our performance of the task dataset, we consider simple, yet effective ensembling techniques of the previously described approaches. In short, we use an unsupervised ensemble method to combine the different explainers. Therefore, we tested combining the individual explanations using the minimum, maximum or mean explanation values of all members in the ensemble. With these simple voting strategies, we were able to find ensembles that outperformed their individual members by a significant margin while maintaining reasonable computational extra costs. Our most successful ensembles are visualized in Figure 4. We report on our results in Section 5.2.1 and 5.2.2 in more detail.

5 Experiments

5.1 Experimental setup

All of our gradient-based methods (Section 4.2) as well as the Occlusion approach (Section 4.1.3) were implemented using the open source *Captum Model Interpretability Library* (Kokhlikyan et al., 2019).

We base our results primarily on the outputs of the MonoTransQuest (MTQ) model but also tried experimenting with XMover-Score (XMS) whenever possible (mentioned in Section 2). Due to difficulties of making the XMover-Score (XMS) model work with Captum, we were only able to retrieve predictions of the quality estimator for LIME and SHAP, for which we used their original implementations published by the authors.

We were presented with two strong baselines by the shared task, XMS+SHAP and MTQ+LIME, as well as a weak baseline of random explanations. We extended the baselines with an all-zero baseline for both language pairs, which serves as another weak baseline where no explanations are used at all. A detailed overview of our results can be found in Table 1 and Table 4. We evaluated each explainer for both language pairs and also used simple unsupervised ensembles of specific explainers.

We conducted our experiments with MTQ using those pre-trained models for the respective language pair. We performed additional tests for the zero-shot language pairs using the any-to-any model, as no specialized pre-trained models were available for these language pairs.

All methods were used with the initial parameters, except for LIME where we explored the difference in using 1000 samples instead of the default 5000 samples.

5.2 Word piece explanations

To receive the gradient-based explanation we use the embedding layer of the MTQ model which uses XLM-RoBERTa word embeddings. This embedding layer raises the problem of WordPiece embeddings (Wu et al., 2016): specific words are not only represented by one word embedding but can consist of multiple WordPiece embeddings where each of them will result in an explanation. The number of explanations will therefore be higher than the actual word counts in most cases (see Figure 3).

Text: Turnul a fost distrus de cutremur , trebuind să fie recunstruit în anii următori . (15)
Embedded text: _Turn, ul, _a, _fost, _distr, us, _de, _cutremur, _, _trebui, nd, _să, _fie, _recu, n, stru, it, _în, _ani, i, _următor, i, _. (23)

Figure 3: WordPiece example. Pieces without a _-prefix show that the corresponding word consists of different word pieces. Numbers in the brackets show the number of words and the number of WordPieces of the text.

In order to overcome this problem, we assume that if one WordPiece is translated wrong, the whole word translation is wrong. For the non-absolute methods specifically (we do not use the absolute explanations here) we take the minimum of the different WordPiece explanations. The underlying assumption is that if one WordPiece has a low score it indicates that this WordPiece and therefore the whole word is translated wrong. For the absolute methods, which assume that wrong words have larger absolute values, we use the maximum of the absolute WordPiece explanations.

We conducted additional experiments with different methods, e.g. using mean or absolute minimum, but the results were not on a par with the abovementioned methods for all explainers.

Since LIME and SHAP are model-agnostic and do not use WordPieces for their explanations, this problem does not occur.

5.2.1 Individual explainers

Our results show that most gradient-based methods are hardly able to compete with the baseline of MTQ+LIME. While gradient-based explainers remain clearly below the baseline's values on both datasets, we could achieve at least comparable results using DeepLIFT or Layer Gradient X Activation (LGXA) with absolute word scores. As it can

	Method	Model	Ro-En AUC	Ro-En AP	Ro-En RC	Et-En AUC	Et-En AP	Et-En RC
	Random Baseline		*0.488*	*0.359*	*0.239*	*0.49*	*0.378*	*0.271*
Gradient	DeepLift	MTQ	0.544	0.458	0.346	0.545	0.460	0.353
	LayerGradientXActivation		0.567	0.463	0.349	0.534	0.441	0.336
	Max. Gradient-based Ensemble		0.599	0.487	0.375	0.574	0.465	0.357
Abs. Gr.	Abs. DeepLift	MTQ	0.675	0.543	0.428	0.621	0.511	**0.404**
	Abs. LayerGradientXActivation		0.645	0.517	0.405	0.589	0.481	0.373
	Max. Abs. Gradient-based Ensemble		**0.682**	**0.552**	**0.440**	**0.622**	**0.509**	0.401
Perturbation	*LIME 5000 Samples*	MTQ	*0.619*	*0.552*	*0.439*	*0.592*	*0.510*	*0.402*
	LIME 1000 Samples		0.618	0.547	0.435	0.587	0.501	0.395
	SHAP		0.589	0.496	0.385	0.571	0.487	0.376
	Occlusion		0.590	0.517	0.405	0.533	0.463	0.352
	LIME 1000 Samples	XMS	0.639	0.489	0.371	0.608	0.467	0.358
	SHAP		*0.638*	*0.464*	*0.339*	*0.583*	*0.456*	*0.352*
	Max. Perturbation-based Ensemble	Both	0.674	0.550	0.435	0.612	0.514	0.407

Table 1: Evaluation results for different explanation methods, models and both language pairs on the development set - MTQ: MonoTransQuest, XMS: XMover-Score, AP: average precision, RC: recall on top 5. This table only shows some of the methods that we implemented. The complete list can be found in appendix A. The underlined scores show the best scores for a method type, the **bold** values show the global maximum and the *italic* values show the baselines.

be seen in Table 1, we can achieve comparable, if not even slightly improved AUC scores for these methods while maintaining mostly equal precision and recall values. In general, our experiments show that the usage of absolute word scores fails across the board for perturbation-based approaches, leading to even worse results than both weak baselines. Considering our initial observation (Section 4.3), this is not a big surprise as it is only valid for gradient-based methods. For precisely those approaches, however, we can see an improvement in every case if we consider just taking the absolute word scores of the respective explainer instead of the signed values. Our best performing approach, Abs. DeepLIFT outperforms MTQ+LIME with a difference of 0.056 in AUC on the Ro-En dataset and 0.029 for Et-En.

The baseline of XMS+SHAP has improved AUC values, but lower precision and recall scores than MTQ+LIME. Comparing our methods to XMS+SHAP reflects these differences, ultimately leading to Abs. DeepLIFT and Abs. LGXA now consequently outperforming the baseline on all measured scores. The AUC values for Abs. DeepLIFT are better than XMS+SHAP by 0.037 for Ro-En and by 0.029 for Et-En.

Across just the perturbation-based methods we can see mostly similar performances close to the XMS+SHAP baseline. Because the runtime of LIME with the default 5000 samples was too high, we only used 1000 samples. This decrease in runtime only reduced the performance marginally. For the language pair Ro-En there was only a decrease in AUC of 0.001 and 0.005 for Et-En. As the word scores for LIME were not available, we needed to calculate the word scores of LIME for our ensembles. Experiments with 1000 samples were sufficient. Occlusion, our additional perturbation-based explainer, performed worse than LIME and SHAP with AUCs of 0.59 for Ro-En and 0.533 for Et-En.

We observe that the results of LIME and SHAP with XMS are better than the MTQ results. Experiments with XMS could thus further improve the explainability performance.

5.2.2 Ensembles

We can see that the simple ensemble methods, described in Section 4.4, are able to improve the explanation score for absolute and non-absolute gradient methods. For the non-absolute method, a maximum ensemble of IG, DeepLift and LGXA results in an AUC score of 0.599 which is an improvement of 0.032 compared to the best single explainer LGXA. We see an improvement of 0.007 in the group of absolute gradient methods with the

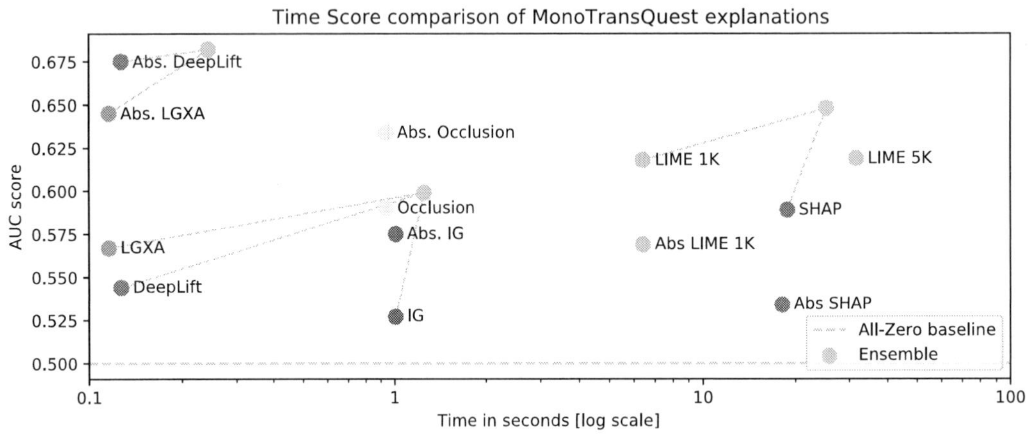

Figure 4: AUC scores on the development set for the MonoTransQuest explanations combined with explanation time of the Ro-En language pair. Notice that we use log scale which indicates that especially the perturbation-based methods LIME and SHAP take much longer compared to the gradient-based methods.

maximum ensemble of Abs. DeepLift and Abs. LGXA, reaching 0.682. There is also an improvement in the values if we use an ensemble of all perturbation-based methods. The maximum ensemble of them was better than the best performing perturbation-based method LIME+XMS by 0.035. Using all the methods and combining them into an ensemble did not increase the performance of the explainers. The all-method ensemble achieves the same AUC score as the ensemble with Abs. DeepLift and Abs. LGXA for the language pair Ro-En, but it was worse in all other metrics. Our best performing explainer is the ensemble consisting of Abs. DeepLift and Abs. LGXA.

5.3 Explanation duration

Figure 4 shows the AUC scores of the models compared to the duration in seconds for generating a single explanation. It can be seen that gradient-based methods have a massive advantage compared to perturbation-based methods in terms of the required computation time. Although we only measured execution times naively, the collected values should be sufficient to obtain a rough picture of how the individual methods compare to each other. Since perturbation-based methods do multiple forward passes while gradient-based methods use only one, we can see that gradient-based methods are much faster than perturbation-based ones overall. While LGXA only takes about 0.1 seconds, LIME with 5000 samples can take more than 30 seconds for a single sentence explanation.

Occlusion proves to achieve worse results than LIME and SHAP but with a faster execution time. However, Occlusion still requires significantly longer execution times than most gradient-based approaches, making it not competitive with the other methods.

Since our ensembles are simple operations, their duration is only the sum of the duration times of each ensemble member. As shown, our ensemble with gradient-based methods is not only significantly faster but also performs better than the baselines of LIME and SHAP.

5.4 Zero-shot explainers

We did further experiments with the provided language pairs De-Zh and Ru-De. The results can be seen in Table 2. We tried using our best-performing method, the maximum ensemble of Abs. DeepLift and Abs. LGXA. By using this setup we could easily include IG into the list of experiments. Surprisingly, absolute methods, except Abs. IG, perform worse than their non-absolute counterparts for De-Zh. The best performing method for De-Zh was the traditional ensemble consisting of all gradient-based methods. With an AUC of only 0.569 the explainer performance is insufficient. We can observe similar performances for the language pair Ru-De where the absolute methods are worse. The exception is Abs. DeepLift with the best performing AUC value of 0.621 and an AP value of 0.511 which is even better than the best score for Et-En. These experiments illustrate that the performances of the explainers vary significantly for each language pair.

	Method	Model	De-Zh			Ru-De		
			AUC	AP	RC	AUC	AP	RC
Gradient	Integrated Gradients [1]	MTQ	0.476	0.334	0.187	0.618	0.311	0.175
	DeepLift [2]		0.453	0.316	0.172	0.614	0.297	0.191
	LayerGradientXActivation [3]		0.500	0.344	0.195	0.500	0.344	0.195
	Max. Gradient-based [E]		**0.569**	**0.421**	**0.321**	0.592	0.332	0.226
Abs. Gr.	Abs. Integrated Gradients [1]	MTQ	0.547	0.386	0.250	0.520	0.405	0.302
	Abs. DeepLift [2]		0.453	0.306	0.214	**0.621**	**0.511**	**0.404**
	Abs. LayerGradientXActivation [3]		0.436	0.321	0.230	0.589	0.481	0.373
	Max. Abs. Gradient-based [E 2,3]		0.467	0.309	0.246	0.555	0.283	0.170

Table 2: Results for the zero-shot language pairs De-Zh and Ru-De on the development set (provided gold standard of 20 annotated sentence pairs). No baselines were provided. - MTQ: MonoTransQuest, [E]: Ensemble of all methods, [E 2,3] ensembles of methods 2 and 3

5.5 Shared task performance

For each language pair we chose methods that performed best on the development sets as our submission methods. Our results are shown in Table 3.

The any-to-any tokenizer had problems with tokenizing Russian and Chinese sentences, which led to the problem of getting less word level explanations than necessary. We solved this by padding the explanations with the default value of 1 as a simple fix.

For the Et-En and Ro-En language pairs, our ensembling approach outperformed the random and XMS+SHAP baselines, while performing on par with MTQ+LIME. On the Ru-De and De-Zh data, our approach hardly shows improvements over the given baselines which probably results due to the weak performance of the any-to-any model on these language pairs.

6 Discussion

The dependency on the performance of QE models is the main limitation of our approaches. Explanations are generated in a pipeline fashion where potential errors will be propagated into the explanation models. MTQ and XMS work quite well already, but there is still room for improvement, especially for language pairs that are not that similar. It is likely that we could achieve better explanations with better QEs.

Another limitation of absolute gradient-based methods is their model-awareness where explainers need access to a QE model's training procedure in order to calculate the gradients. In cases where explanations should be generated in a black-box manner, perturbation-based methods like LIME or SHAP are better suited.

We showed that perturbation-based methods work generally well for predicting errors in MT based on QE and that existing gradient-based methods perform quite poorly in comparison. Our proposed absolute gradient method is a simple extension of those existing methods, but with large performance improvements. However, absolute perturbations seem to worsen the performance of existing perturbation-based methods. Explainer ensembles outperformed single explainers in all cases, where maximum ensembles generally worked best. Absolute explanations also improved gradient-based ensembles.

Our experiments justify the popularity of perturbation-based explainers. Nonetheless, gradient-based methods should not be overlooked. They are not only faster in comparison, but with the extension of absolute explanation ensembles can also perform better for the given task and are hence worth to consider.

7 Conclusion

We showed that absolute gradient-based methods are worthy contenders to perturbation-based methods when it comes to generating plausible word-level explanations for MT. Explainer ensembles also exploit the strengths of their individual members and yield better explanations, be they perturbation-based or gradient-based ones. Gradient-based methods have the potential to be used in online applications given that they are more time-efficient than popular perturbation-based approaches, even as ensembles. Black-box models however are better explained with regular perturbation-based methods.

Language Pair	Method	AUC	AP	RC
Et-En	*MTQ+LIME*	*0.624*	*0.536*	*0.424*
Et-En	Max. Abs. Gradient-based Ensemble (Abs. DeepLift & Abs. LayerGradientXActivation)	0.658	0.516	0.404
Ro-En	*XMS+SHAP*	*0.666*	*0.438*	*0.295*
Ro-En	Max. Abs. Gradient-based Ensemble (Abs. DeepLift & Abs. LayerGradientXActivation)	0.677	0.505	0.381
De-Zh	*XMS+SHAP*	*0.545*	*0.334*	*0.220*
De-Zh	Max. Gradient-based Ensemble (DeepLift & LayerGradientXActivation)	0.513	0.311	0.185
Ru-De	*XMS+SHAP*	*0.522*	*0.328*	*0.227*
Ru-De	Abs. DeepLift	0.543	0.328	0.224

Table 3: Results on the test data of our models that performed best on the development set. All methods use MTQ as their QE model. We include the results of the best performing baseline in terms of AUC score for each language pair for comparison in *italic*.

Future work might explore training QE and explanation methods end-to-end, find better performing (multilingual) QE models, or train models on word-level information. One could also try to solve the given problem with recently proposed explanation methods that try to tackle problems of existing explainers.

Another way of improving the explanation scores might be using supervised ensemble methods on different explainers by using the training dataset to train e.g. a simple decision tree. The training dataset could be also used to finetune the QE models.

Acknowledgement

This work was created in the context of the Meta-Science Seminar at the Technical University of Darmstadt. We thank Steffen Eger for his supervision.

References

Maximilian Alber, Sebastian Lapuschkin, Philipp Seegerer, Miriam Hägele, Kristof T. Schütt, Grégoire Montavon, Wojciech Samek, Klaus-Robert Müller, Sven Dähne, and Pieter-Jan Kindermans. 2019. innvestigate neural networks! *J. Mach. Learn. Res.*, 20:93:1–93:8.

Sebastian Bach, Alexander Binder, Grégoire Montavon, Frederick Klauschen, Klaus-Robert Müller, and Wojciech Samek. 2015. On pixel-wise explanations for non-linear classifier decisions by layer-wise relevance propagation. *PLOS ONE*, 10(7):1–46.

David Baehrens, Timon Schroeter, Stefan Harmeling, Motoaki Kawanabe, Katja Hansen, and Klaus-Robert Müller. 2010. How to explain individual classification decisions. *J. Mach. Learn. Res.*, 11:1803–1831.

Lucia Comparin and Sara Mendes. 2017. Using error annotation to evaluate machine translation and human post-editing in a business environment. *Proceedings of EAMT 2017, Prague, May 29*, 31.

Alexis Conneau, Kartikay Khandelwal, Naman Goyal, Vishrav Chaudhary, Guillaume Wenzek, Francisco Guzmán, Edouard Grave, Myle Ott, Luke Zettlemoyer, and Veselin Stoyanov. 2020. Unsupervised cross-lingual representation learning at scale. In *Proceedings of the 58th Annual Meeting of the Association for Computational Linguistics, ACL 2020, Online, July 5-10, 2020*, pages 8440–8451. Association for Computational Linguistics.

Jacob Devlin, Ming-Wei Chang, Kenton Lee, and Kristina Toutanova. 2019. BERT: pre-training of deep bidirectional transformers for language understanding. In *Proceedings of the 2019 Conference of the North American Chapter of the Association for Computational Linguistics: Human Language Technologies, NAACL-HLT 2019, Minneapolis, MN, USA, June 2-7, 2019, Volume 1 (Long and Short Papers)*, pages 4171–4186. Association for Computational Linguistics.

Marina Fomicheva, Piyawat Lertvittayakumjorn, Wei Zhao, Steffen Eger, and Yang Gao. 2021. The eval4nlp shared task on explainable quality estimation: Overview and results. In *Proceedings of the 2nd Workshop on Evaluation and Comparison of NLP Systems*.

Marina Fomicheva, Shuo Sun, Erick Fonseca, Frédéric Blain, Vishrav Chaudhary, Francisco Guzmán, Nina Lopatina, Lucia Specia, and André F. T. Martins. 2020a. MLQE-PE: A multilingual quality estimation and post-editing dataset. *arXiv preprint arXiv:2010.04480*.

Marina Fomicheva, Shuo Sun, Lisa Yankovskaya, Frédéric Blain, Francisco Guzmán, Mark Fishel, Nikolaos Aletras, Vishrav Chaudhary, and Lucia Specia. 2020b. Unsupervised quality estimation for neural machine translation. *Trans. Assoc. Comput. Linguistics*, 8:539–555.

Narine Kokhlikyan, Vivek Miglani, Miguel Martin, Edward Wang, Jonathan Reynolds, Alexander Melnikov, Natalia Lunova, and Orion Reblitz-Richardson. 2019. Pytorch captum. `https://github.com/pytorch/captum`.

Neema Kotonya and Francesca Toni. 2020. Explainable automated fact-checking for public health claims. In *Proceedings of the 2020 Conference on Empirical Methods in Natural Language Processing, EMNLP 2020, Online, November 16-20, 2020*, pages 7740–7754. Association for Computational Linguistics.

Chin-Yew Lin. 2004. ROUGE: A package for automatic evaluation of summaries. In *Text Summarization Branches Out*, pages 74–81, Barcelona, Spain. Association for Computational Linguistics.

Stan Lipovetsky and Michael Conklin. 2001. Analysis of regression in game theory approach. *Applied Stochastic Models in Business and Industry*, 17(4):319–330.

Yinhan Liu, Jiatao Gu, Naman Goyal, Xian Li, Sergey Edunov, Marjan Ghazvininejad, Mike Lewis, and Luke Zettlemoyer. 2020. Multilingual denoising pretraining for neural machine translation. *Trans. Assoc. Comput. Linguistics*, 8:726–742.

Yinhan Liu, Myle Ott, Naman Goyal, Jingfei Du, Mandar Joshi, Danqi Chen, Omer Levy, Mike Lewis, Luke Zettlemoyer, and Veselin Stoyanov. 2019. Roberta: A robustly optimized BERT pretraining approach. *CoRR*, abs/1907.11692.

Scott M. Lundberg and Su-In Lee. 2017. A unified approach to interpreting model predictions. In *Advances in Neural Information Processing Systems 30: Annual Conference on Neural Information Processing Systems 2017, December 4-9, 2017, Long Beach, CA, USA*, pages 4765–4774.

Bryan McCann, James Bradbury, Caiming Xiong, and Richard Socher. 2017. Learned in translation: Contextualized word vectors. In *Advances in Neural Information Processing Systems 30: Annual Conference on Neural Information Processing Systems 2017, December 4-9, 2017, Long Beach, CA, USA*, pages 6294–6305.

Harsha Nori, Samuel Jenkins, Paul Koch, and Rich Caruana. 2019. Interpretml: A unified framework for machine learning interpretability. *arXiv preprint arXiv:1909.09223*.

Kishore Papineni, Salim Roukos, Todd Ward, and Wei-Jing Zhu. 2002. Bleu: a method for automatic evaluation of machine translation. In *Proceedings of the 40th Annual Meeting of the Association for Computational Linguistics, July 6-12, 2002, Philadelphia, PA, USA*, pages 311–318. ACL.

Nicolas Pröllochs, Stefan Feuerriegel, and Dirk Neumann. 2019. Learning interpretable negation rules via weak supervision at document level: A reinforcement learning approach. In *Proceedings of the 2019 Conference of the North American Chapter of the Association for Computational Linguistics: Human Language Technologies, NAACL-HLT 2019, Minneapolis, MN, USA, June 2-7, 2019, Volume 1 (Long and Short Papers)*, pages 407–413. Association for Computational Linguistics.

Nazneen Fatema Rajani, Bryan McCann, Caiming Xiong, and Richard Socher. 2019. Explain yourself! leveraging language models for commonsense reasoning. In *Proceedings of the 57th Conference of the Association for Computational Linguistics, ACL 2019, Florence, Italy, July 28- August 2, 2019, Volume 1: Long Papers*, pages 4932–4942. Association for Computational Linguistics.

Tharindu Ranasinghe, Constantin Orasan, and Ruslan Mitkov. 2020. Transquest: Translation quality estimation with cross-lingual transformers. In *Proceedings of the 28th International Conference on Computational Linguistics, COLING 2020, Barcelona, Spain (Online), December 8-13, 2020*, pages 5070–5081. International Committee on Computational Linguistics.

Marco Tulio Ribeiro, Sameer Singh, and Carlos Guestrin. 2016. "why should i trust you?": Explaining the predictions of any classifier. In *Proceedings of the 22nd ACM SIGKDD International Conference on Knowledge Discovery and Data Mining*, KDD '16, page 1135–1144, New York, NY, USA. Association for Computing Machinery.

Avanti Shrikumar, Peyton Greenside, and Anshul Kundaje. 2017. Learning important features through propagating activation differences. In *Proceedings of the 34th International Conference on Machine Learning, ICML 2017, Sydney, NSW, Australia, 6-11 August 2017*, volume 70 of *Proceedings of Machine Learning Research*, pages 3145–3153. PMLR.

Avanti Shrikumar, Peyton Greenside, Anna Shcherbina, and Anshul Kundaje. 2016. Not just a black box: Learning important features through propagating activation differences. *CoRR*, abs/1605.01713.

Erik Strumbelj and Igor Kononenko. 2014. Explaining prediction models and individual predictions with feature contributions. *Knowl. Inf. Syst.*, 41(3):647–665.

Mukund Sundararajan, Ankur Taly, and Qiqi Yan. 2017. Axiomatic attribution for deep networks. In *Proceedings of the 34th International Conference on Machine Learning, ICML 2017, Sydney, NSW, Australia, 6-11 August 2017*, volume 70 of *Proceedings of Machine Learning Research*, pages 3319–3328. PMLR.

Eric Wallace, Jens Tuyls, Junlin Wang, Sanjay Subramanian, Matt Gardner, and Sameer Singh. 2019. Allennlp interpret: A framework for explaining predictions of NLP models. In *Proceedings of the 2019 Conference on Empirical Methods in Natural Language Processing and the 9th International Joint Conference on Natural Language Processing, EMNLP-IJCNLP 2019, Hong Kong, China, November 3-7, 2019 - System Demonstrations*, pages 7–12. Association for Computational Linguistics.

Thomas Wolf, Lysandre Debut, Victor Sanh, Julien Chaumond, Clement Delangue, Anthony Moi, Pierric Cistac, Tim Rault, Rémi Louf, Morgan Funtowicz, Joe Davison, Sam Shleifer, Patrick von Platen, Clara Ma, Yacine Jernite, Julien Plu, Canwen Xu, Teven Le Scao, Sylvain Gugger, Mariama Drame, Quentin Lhoest, and Alexander M. Rush. 2020. Transformers: State-of-the-art natural language processing. In *Proceedings of the 2020 Conference on Empirical Methods in Natural Language Processing: System Demonstrations, EMNLP 2020 - Demos, Online, November 16-20, 2020*, pages 38–45. Association for Computational Linguistics.

Yonghui Wu, Mike Schuster, Zhifeng Chen, Quoc V. Le, Mohammad Norouzi, Wolfgang Macherey, Maxim Krikun, Yuan Cao, Qin Gao, Klaus Macherey, Jeff Klingner, Apurva Shah, Melvin Johnson, Xiaobing Liu, Lukasz Kaiser, Stephan Gouws, Yoshikiyo Kato, Taku Kudo, Hideto Kazawa, Keith Stevens, George Kurian, Nishant Patil, Wei Wang, Cliff Young, Jason Smith, Jason Riesa, Alex Rudnick, Oriol Vinyals, Greg Corrado, Macduff Hughes, and Jeffrey Dean. 2016. Google's neural machine translation system: Bridging the gap between human and machine translation. *CoRR*, abs/1609.08144.

Matthew D. Zeiler and Rob Fergus. 2014. Visualizing and understanding convolutional networks. In *Computer Vision - ECCV 2014 - 13th European Conference, Zurich, Switzerland, September 6-12, 2014, Proceedings, Part I*, volume 8689 of *Lecture Notes in Computer Science*, pages 818–833. Springer.

Wei Zhao, Goran Glavas, Maxime Peyrard, Yang Gao, Robert West, and Steffen Eger. 2020. On the limitations of cross-lingual encoders as exposed by reference-free machine translation evaluation. In *Proceedings of the 58th Annual Meeting of the Association for Computational Linguistics, ACL 2020, Online, July 5-10, 2020*, pages 1656–1671. Association for Computational Linguistics.

Wei Zhao, Maxime Peyrard, Fei Liu, Yang Gao, Christian M. Meyer, and Steffen Eger. 2019. Moverscore: Text generation evaluating with contextualized embeddings and earth mover distance. In *Proceedings of the 2019 Conference on Empirical Methods in Natural Language Processing and the 9th International Joint Conference on Natural Language Processing, EMNLP-IJCNLP 2019, Hong Kong, China, November 3-7, 2019*, pages 563–578. Association for Computational Linguistics.

A Appendix

	Method	Model	Ro-En AUC	Ro-En AP	Ro-En RC	Et-En AUC	Et-En AP	Et-En RC
	All-Zero Baseline		0.5	0.251	0.210	0.5	0.285	0.253
	Random Baseline		*0.488*	*0.359*	*0.239*	*0.49*	*0.378*	*0.271*
Gradient	Integrated Gradients [1]	MTQ	0.527	0.407	0.288	0.539	0.422	0.317
	DeepLift [2]		0.544	0.458	0.346	0.545	0.460	0.353
	LayerGradientXActivation [3]		0.567	0.463	0.349	0.534	0.441	0.336
	Mean Gradient-based [E]		0.561	0.465	0.349	0.554	0.461	0.360
	Max. Gradient-based [E]		0.599	0.487	0.375	0.574	0.465	0.357
	Min. Gradient-based [E]		0.505	0.405	0.295	0.518	0.429	0.329
	Mean Gradient-based [E 2,3]		0.559	0.461	0.342	0.544	0.451	0.347
	Max. Gradient-based [E 2,3]		0.577	0.479	0.367	0.560	0.463	0.360
	Min. Gradient-based [E 2,3]		0.538	0.448	0.333	0.523	0.440	0.336
Abs. Gradient	Abs. Integrated Gradients [1]	MTQ	0.575	0.433	0.317	0.520	0.405	0.302
	Abs. DeepLift [2]		0.675	0.543	0.428	0.621	0.511	0.404
	Abs. LayerGradientXActivation [3]		0.645	0.517	0.405	0.589	0.481	0.373
	Mean Abs. Gradient-based [E 2,3]		0.677	0.541	0.526	0.618	0.504	0.393
	Max. Abs. Gradient-based [E 2,3]		**0.682**	0.552	0.440	**0.622**	0.509	0.401
	Min. Abs. Gradient-based [E 2,3]		0.653	0.520	0.399	0.599	0.490	0.384
Perturbation	*LIME 5000 Samples*	MTQ	*0.619*	*0.552*	*0.439*	*0.592*	*0.510*	*0.402*
	LIME 1000 Samples		0.618	0.547	0.435	0.587	0.501	0.395
	SHAP		0.589	0.496	0.385	0.571	0.487	0.376
	Occlusion		0.590	0.517	0.405	0.533	0.463	0.352
	LIME 1000 Samples	XMS	0.639	0.489	0.371	0.608	0.467	0.358
	SHAP		*0.638*	*0.464*	*0.339*	*0.583*	*0.456*	*0.352*
	Mean Perturbation-based [E]	Both	0.627	0.550	0.435	0.585	0.510	0.404
	Max. Perturbation-based [E]		0.674	**0.581**	0.474	0.612	**0.514**	**0.407**
	Min. Perturbation-based [E]		0.571	0.475	0.369	0.535	0.434	0.327
	Mean LIME SHAP [E]		0.648	0.565	**0.462**	0.602	0.502	0.396
	Max. LIME SHAP [E]		0.648	0.557	0.443	0.594	0.504	0.396
	Min. LIME SHAP [E]		0.615	0.492	0.389	0.578	0.460	0.360
Abs. Perturbation	Abs. LIME	MTQ	0.569	0.404	0.283	0.523	0.407	0.306
	Abs. SHAP		0.534	0.377	0.258	0.582	0.445	0.336
	Abs. Occlusion		0.634	0.490	0.365	0.587	0.465	0.363
	Abs. LIME	XMS	0.401	0.311	0.200	0.426	0.334	0.232
	Abs. SHAP		0.365	0.290	0.181	0.418	0.337	0.232
	Mean Abs. Perturbation-based [E]	Both	0.564	0.412	0.288	0.549	0.425	0.327
	Max. Abs. Perturbation-based [E]		0.596	0.457	0.332	0.550	0.436	0.340
	Min. Abs. Perturbation-based [E]		0.453	0.337	0.222	0.468	0.362	0.255
All	Mean All [E]	Both	0.589	0.498	0.387	0.570	0.477	0.371
	Max. All [E]		0.618	0.495	0.381	0.589	0.469	0.360
	Min. All [E]		0.49	0.416	0.307	0.503	0.410	0.306
	Mean Abs. All [E]		0.675	0.542	0.425	0.607	0.494	0.390
	Max. Abs. All [E]		**0.682**	0.546	0.429	0.600	0.485	0.375
	Min. Abs. All [E]		0.461	0.342	0.230	0.475	0.368	0.259

Table 4: Results of various explanation methods for the Ro-En and Et-En language pairs on the development set - MTQ: MonoTransQuest, XMS: XMover-Score, [E]: Ensemble

Explainable Quality Estimation: CUNI Eval4NLP Submission

Peter Polák and **Muskaan Singh** and **Ondřej Bojar**
Institute of Formal and Applied Linguistics,
Faculty of Mathematics and Physics,
Charles University
<polak,singh,bojar>@ufal.mff.cuni.cz

Abstract

This paper describes our participating system in the shared task Explainable quality estimation of 2nd Workshop on Evaluation & Comparison of NLP Systems. The task of quality estimation (QE, a.k.a. reference-free evaluation) is to predict the quality of MT output at inference time without access to reference translations. In this proposed work, we first build a word-level quality estimation model, then we finetune this model for sentence-level QE. Our proposed models achieve near state-of-the-art results. In the word-level QE, we place 2nd and 3rd on the supervised Ro-En and Et-En test sets. In the sentence-level QE, we achieve a relative improvement of 8.86% (Ro-En) and 10.6% (Et-En) in terms of the Pearson correlation coefficient over the baseline model.

1 Introduction

Quality Estimation (QE) or Confidence Estimation (CE) is a task of assessing the quality of machine-translated text given the source without accessing the reference (Blatz et al., 2004; Specia et al., 2009). QE can be assessed on sentence-level, word-level granularity or even document-level (Ive et al., 2018). Sentence-level scores predict what score would a human annotator assign to the whole sentence; most commonly, direct assessment (Graham et al., 2017) or HTER (Snover et al., 2006) serve as the golden standard. Word-level QE indicates word-level errors in machine translation output or incorrectly translated words in the source. While automatic word-level scores are usually continuous, the gold truth is binary: some words are labeled as correct while some are labeled as wrong. This estimation provides an aid in the translation workflow. For instance, it can help to determine if the machine-translated sentence is good enough to be used as-is or if it requires a human translator for post-editing or translating from scratch (Kepler et al., 2019b).

In this paper, we present our submission to the shared task of Explainable quality estimation of 2nd Workshop on Evaluation & Comparison of NLP Systems (Fomicheva et al., 2021).[1] Our solution is based on the XLM-R multilingual pretrained model (Conneau et al., 2020). We first build a word-level quality estimation model. Then we finetune this model for sentence-level QE.

We make our code publicly available.[2]

2 Related Work

In the past decade, most of the quality estimation systems depended heavily on feature engineering, linguistic information, and machine learning algorithms such as support vector machines or randomized decision trees (Specia et al., 2013, 2015). In recent years, emerging neural-based QE have been outperforming earlier approaches on leaderboards of MT quality estimation (Kepler et al., 2019a). For instance, POSTECH (Kim et al., 2017), a purely neural system based on encoder-decoder recurrent neural network (referred to as a predictor) is stacked with bidirectional RNN (referred to as an estimator).

This predictor-estimator QE system was the best-performing one in WMT 2017.[3] It was further extended in DeepQuest architecture (Ive et al., 2018). These systems required extensive pretraining, which makes them dependent on large parallel corpora and computationally expensive. To overcome this problem, cross-lingual embeddings (Ruder et al., 2019) were used to reduce the burden of deep neural network architecture. TransQuest used these cross-lingual embeddings and was the best-performing sentence-level QE model at WMT 2020 QE Shared Task (Specia et al., 2018). For the

[1] https://eval4nlp.github.io/sharedtask.html

[2] https://github.com/pe-trik/eval4nlp-2021

[3] https://www.statmt.org/wmt17/quality-estimation-task.html

Proceedings of the 58th Annual Meeting of the Association for Computational Linguistics, pages 250–255

https://doi.org/10.26615/978-954-452-056-4_024

sentence-level QE task, the model was finetuned on multilingual pre-trained representations. For the word-level QE task, the authors used direct assessment (DA) quality scores from the MLQE-PE dataset. Motivated by this work, we finetune our word-level model to yield sentence-level QE.

Overall, the tremendous progress in the field of quality estimation is achieved thanks to the annual focus of the shared task organized by WMT and thanks to the annotated data released in these tasks, leading to the development of various open-source systems such as QuEst (Specia et al., 2013), QuEst++ (Specia et al., 2015), deepQuest (Ive et al., 2018), OpenKiwi (Kepler et al., 2019b) and TransQuest (Ranasinghe et al., 2020).

3 Task Description

The task consists of building a quality estimation system that (1) predicts the quality score for an input pair of the source text and MT hypothesis, and (2) provides word-level evidence for its predictions.

4 Dataset Description

The dataset for the shared task consists of training, development, and test sets. The training and development sets are Estonian-English (Et-En) and Romanian-English (Ro-En) partitions of the MLQE-PE dataset (Fomicheva et al., 2020). The test set consists of sentence-level quality scores and word-level error annotations for these two language pairs. The goal of the shared task is to estimate the word quality in unsupervised settings (no training data for word-level QE whatsoever). However, participating systems can also be labeled as "unconstrained" and use word-level QE training data.

Additionally, there are zero-shot test sets for two language pairs, i.e., German-Chinese (De-Zh) and Russian-German (Ru-De), where no sentence-level OR word-level annotations were available at training time.

5 Methodology

In the proposed system, we use a pre-trained XLM-R model (Conneau et al., 2020) to obtain representations of input sentences in continuous space. XML-R is trained on large-scale multilingual CommonCrawl datasets. We have two separate models for the word-level and sentence-level quality estimation.

5.1 Data Representation

The pre-trained XLM-R model uses BPE encoding (Sennrich et al., 2016) for input tokenization. In order to input two sentences to the model (i.e., the source and the MT candidate), the sentences are concatenated with two `</s>` tokens[4] between them:

$$\texttt{<s>}\ s_1, ..., s_m\ \texttt{</s></s>}\ t_1, ..., t_n\ \texttt{</s>}.$$

5.2 Word-level QE

In the word-level QE, the task is to predict for each source and target word if it was translated correctly. We use the XLM-R model extended a linear layer on top of the hidden-states output (see Figure 1). We use cross-entropy loss. The BPE encoding might break a word into more tokens; this is especially true for the less frequent or misspelled words (Polák, 2020). E.g., "misstake" (with double s) might be broken down into two tokens: "_miss" and "take". Because we are interested in word-level predictions and not token-level predictions, we label only the first token of each word and put the "ignore" label to others (including the special tokens `<s>` and `</s>`).

We also experiment with an alternative representation: we put a `<cls>` token after each word. In this case, we ignore all labels except for `<cls>`. But as we will document later, this alternative does not bring any improvement.

5.3 Sentence-level QE

For the sentence-level QE, we use the XLM-R model extended with a linear layer on top of the pooled output. We finetune the model with mean square error loss. We normalize the scores to interval [0; 1].

6 Experiments and Results

In all our experiments, we use XLM-R large model[5] using Hugging Face Transformers (Wolf et al., 2020). We run all our experiments on NVIDIA RTX 3090. To find the best parameters, we run a grid search. The optimal hyper-parameters are $2e^{-5}$ learning rate, three epochs, and batch size of 16.

[4]We follow the tokenization procedure in `https://huggingface.co/transformers/model_doc/xlmroberta.html#xlmrobertatokenizerfast`.

[5]`https://huggingface.co/xlm-roberta-large`

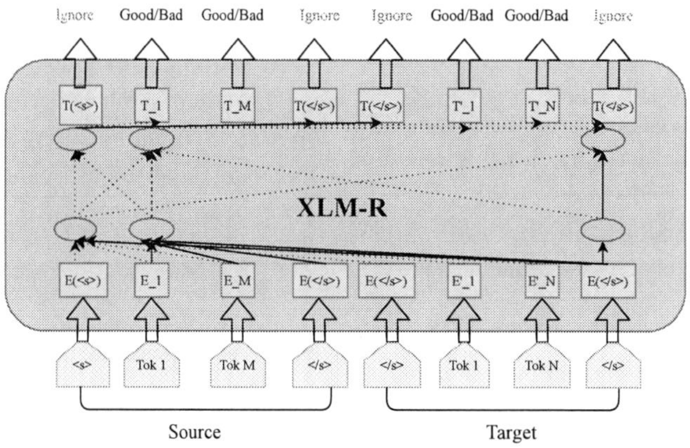

Figure 1: Our model architecture for the word-level quality estimation task.

	AUC	AP	Recall at top-K
ro-en only	0.926	0.840	0.738
ro-en & et-en	**0.933**	**0.861**	**0.770**

Table 1: Models trained on Ro-En data only and all training data performance comparison on Ro-En development set. The score differences are statistically significant (paired t-test with $p < 0.01$).

6.1 Quantitative Analysis

In this section, we provide the analysis across each level of experiments.

6.1.1 Word-level QE

First, we consider having separate models for source and target sentence word-labels prediction. We compared the separate models with a joint one, but we did not find any statistically significant evidence of difference.

We also consider the variant with <cls> token. Again, the model does not perform better. Additionally, we noticed a much larger GPU-memory consumption.

We were also interested in whether to use all training data (Ro-En and Et-En) or to match the test pair (two test sets are supervised with matching language pairs). We found out that it is better to include both language pairs (see Table 1). This suggests the model is learning the tasks independent of language pair and benefits from more training data.

6.1.2 Sentence-level QE

We first tried a simple approach computing the sentence-level QE using the word labels. We defined the score as 1 minus the geometric mean of the word-level scores (i.e., the probability of a word being incorrectly translated). The scores surpassed the shared task author's XMOVER-SHAP (Zhao et al., 2020) baseline with Pearson correlation coefficients of 0.501 and 0.648 compared to 0.415 and 0.638 on Et-En or Ro-En development sets, respectively.

Our second approach is again based on the XLM-R model. We tried to use the vanilla XLM-R pre-trained model as in the word-level QE task. The model failed to converge. To circumvent this, we finetuned the best-performing word-level QE model. This provided much better results (0.776 and 0.880 on Et-En or Ro-En development sets respectively).

6.1.3 Ensembling

To leverage all the models we trained during the hyper-parameter search we employ ensembling. We tried two approaches: (1) weighted geometric mean and (2) weighted arithmetic mean. The former failed to produce results as the number of models was too large (36 models).

We estimate the model weights using Bayesian optimization with target sentence AUC as an objective function. We optimized the parameters on the development sets (for each Et-En and Ro-En separately). For the zero-shot test sets (De-Zh or Ru-De), we averaged the weights obtained for both development sets (Et-En and Ro-En).

Table 2 documents slight improvement using ensembling compared to the best model.

6.2 Qualitative Analysis

We were interested to see, how well the model performed on unseen language pairs. We had no bilingual speaker of the provided language pairs.

		AUC	AP	Recall at top-K
et-en	best model	0.884	0.819	0.722
	ensemble	**0.892**	**0.829**	**0.729**
ro-en	best model	0.933	0.861	0.770
	ensemble	**0.939**	**0.871**	**0.782**

Table 2: Comparison of the best model and ensemble. Results are word-level target side QE on development sets.

	/Salvadorans/	/protested/	/against/	/bitcoin/
1.	Salvádorčania	protestovali	proti	bitcoinu
	0.40	0.02	0.02	0.02
	Salvadorianer	protestierten	gegen	Bitcoin
	0.27	0.01	0.02	0.00
2.	Salvádorčania	protestovali	proti	bitcoinu
	0.49	0.03	0.14	0.04
	Salvadorianer	protestierten	**für** /for/	Bitcoin
	0.44	0.04	0.27	0.02
3.	Salvádorčania	protestovali	proti	bitcoinu
	0.98	0.03	0.03	0.04
	Somalis	protestierten	gegen	Bitcoin
	0.97	0.02	0.02	0.01

Table 3: Examples of unsupervised Slovak-German MT QE. Each number below a word represents a probability of being incorrectly translated generated by our best-performing model. Words in slashes present English translations. Words in bold denote translation errors.

Therefore, we assembled our own Slovak-German test set (we used Google Translate to obtain the translation and we introduced artificial errors). We draw three examples in Table 3. We see the model also works on an unseen language pair (recall the XLM-R model was pre-trained on both languages, but we use different languages for the QE task fine-tuning).

In the first example (a correctly translated sentence), the model labels the words correctly (although we see a bit of uncertainty over the first, less frequent word). The second example changes the meaning (protested *for* instead of protested *against*). We see some hesitation in the third word, still, the predicted probabilities are incorrect. We hypothesize this may be due to the fact the model prefers predicting based on co-occurrences, not necessarily on the meaning (Kim et al., 2019). In the third example, the model correctly detects the first mistranslated word both in the source and target sentence.

6.3 Comparative analysis of our submission with other submissions.

In the shared task, 11 teams from different organizations participated. Out of the 11 different submissions, two teams submitted to the unconstrained track. The rest of the teams submitted to the constrained track as they did not use any supervision at the word level. Our submission was also in the unconstrained category. We report all the results from the leaderboard[6] in Table 4.

7 Conclusion

The paper describes our submission to the shared task, EVAL4NLP, co-located with EMNLP. First, we built a word-level quality estimation model. Then we finetuned it for obtaining sentence-level QE. In the word-level QE, we placed 2nd and 3rd on the supervised Ro-En and Et-En test sets. In the sentence-level QE, we achieved a relative improvement of 8.86% (Ro-En) and 10.6% (Et-En) in terms of the Pearson correlation coefficient over the baseline model.

Acknowledgements

The work was supported by the grant 825303 "Bergamot" of European Union's Horizon 2020 research and innovation programme, 19-26934X "NEUREM3" of the Grant Agency of the Czech Republic, and START/SCI/089 (Babel Octopus: Robust Multi-Source Speech Translation) of the START Programme of Charles University.

References

John Blatz, Erin Fitzgerald, George Foster, Simona Gandrabur, Cyril Goutte, Alex Kulesza, Alberto Sanchis, and Nicola Ueffing. 2004. Confidence estimation for machine translation. In *Coling 2004: Proceedings of the 20th international conference on computational linguistics*, pages 315–321.

Alexis Conneau, Kartikay Khandelwal, Naman Goyal, Vishrav Chaudhary, Guillaume Wenzek, Francisco Guzmán, Edouard Grave, Myle Ott, Luke Zettlemoyer, and Veselin Stoyanov. 2020. Unsupervised cross-lingual representation learning at scale. In *Proceedings of the 58th Annual Meeting of the Association for Computational Linguistics*, pages 8440–8451, Online. Association for Computational Linguistics.

Marina Fomicheva, Piyawat Lertvittayakumjorn, Wei Zhao, Steffen Eger, and Yang Gao. 2021. The

[6]https://competitions.codalab.org/competitions/33038#results

	Source			Target		
	AP	AUC	Recall at top-K	AP	AUC	Recall at top-K
Et-En (supervised)						
Our Submission	0.851	0.928	0.761	0.841	0.917	0.751
Average of all teams	0.496	0.610	0.397	0.651	0.759	0.548
Best of all teams	0.855	0.935	0.771	0.852	0.922	0.762
Ro-En (supervised)						
Our Submission	0.808	0.934	0.696	0.830	0.935	0.730
Average of all teams	0.445	0.603	0.344	0.653	0.788	0.544
Best of all teams	0.851	0.947	0.752	0.869	0.946	0.778
Ru-De (unsupervised)						
Our Submission	0.668	0.802	0.562	0.610	0.759	0.502
Average of all teams	0.421	0.562	0.332	0.494	0.669	0.389
Best of all teams	0.804	0.922	0.709	0.829	0.927	0.736
De-Zh (unsupervised)						
Ours	0.423	0.618	0.268	0.435	0.611	0.303
Average of all teams	0.279	0.468	0.160	0.406	0.603	0.279
Best of all teams	0.645	0.847	0.509	0.679	0.849	0.571

Table 4: Comparative results from the leaderboard. The scores were evaluated against error labels resulting from manual annotation. Missing word errors were ignored in this track. The main metrics for evaluation were AUC and AUPRC scores for word-level explanations.

eval4nlp shared task on explainable quality estimation: Overview and results. In *Proceedings of the 2nd Workshop on Evaluation and Comparison of NLP Systems*.

Marina Fomicheva, Shuo Sun, Lisa Yankovskaya, Frédéric Blain, Francisco Guzmán, Mark Fishel, Nikolaos Aletras, Vishrav Chaudhary, and Lucia Specia. 2020. Unsupervised quality estimation for neural machine translation. *Transactions of the Association for Computational Linguistics*, 8:539–555.

Yvette Graham, Timothy Baldwin, Alistair Moffat, and Justin Zobel. 2017. Can machine translation systems be evaluated by the crowd alone. *Natural Language Engineering*, 23(1):3–30.

Julia Ive, Frédéric Blain, and Lucia Specia. 2018. Deepquest: a framework for neural-based quality estimation. In *Proceedings of the 27th International Conference on Computational Linguistics*, pages 3146–3157. Association for Computational Linguistics.

Fabio Kepler, Jonay Trénous, Marcos Treviso, Miguel Vera, António Góis, M Amin Farajian, António V Lopes, and André FT Martins. 2019a. Unbabel's participation in the wmt19 translation quality estimation shared task. *arXiv preprint arXiv:1907.10352*.

Fabio Kepler, Jonay Trénous, Marcos Treviso, Miguel Vera, and André FT Martins. 2019b. Openkiwi: An open source framework for quality estimation. *arXiv preprint arXiv:1902.08646*.

Hyun Kim, Jong-Hyeok Lee, and Seung-Hoon Na. 2017. Predictor-estimator using multilevel task learning with stack propagation for neural quality estimation. In *Proceedings of the Second Conference on Machine Translation*, pages 562–568.

Hyun Kim, Joon-Ho Lim, Hyun-Ki Kim, and Seung-Hoon Na. 2019. Qe bert: bilingual bert using multi-task learning for neural quality estimation. In *Proceedings of the Fourth Conference on Machine Translation (Volume 3: Shared Task Papers, Day 2)*, pages 85–89.

Peter Polák. 2020. Spoken Language Translation via Phoneme Representation of the Source Language. Master's thesis, Charles University, Faculty of Mathematics and Physics.

Tharindu Ranasinghe, Constantin Orasan, and Ruslan Mitkov. 2020. Transquest at wmt2020: Sentence-level direct assessment. *arXiv preprint arXiv:2010.05318*.

Sebastian Ruder, Ivan Vulić, and Anders Søgaard. 2019. A survey of cross-lingual word embedding models. *Journal of Artificial Intelligence Research*, 65:569–631.

Rico Sennrich, Barry Haddow, and Alexandra Birch. 2016. Neural machine translation of rare words with subword units. In *Proceedings of the 54th Annual Meeting of the Association for Computational Linguistics (Volume 1: Long Papers)*, pages 1715–1725.

Matthew Snover, Bonnie Dorr, Richard Schwartz, Linnea Micciulla, and John Makhoul. 2006. A study of translation edit rate with targeted human annotation. In *Proceedings of the 7th Conference of the Association for Machine Translation in the Americas: Technical Papers*, pages 223–231.

Lucia Specia, Frédéric Blain, Varvara Logacheva, Ramón F. Astudillo, and André F. T. Martins. 2018. Findings of the WMT 2018 shared task on quality estimation. In *Proceedings of the Third Conference on Machine Translation: Shared Task Papers*, pages 689–709, Belgium, Brussels. Association for Computational Linguistics.

Lucia Specia, Gustavo Paetzold, and Carolina Scarton. 2015. Multi-level translation quality prediction with quest++. In *Proceedings of ACL-IJCNLP 2015 System Demonstrations*, pages 115–120.

Lucia Specia, Kashif Shah, José GC De Souza, and Trevor Cohn. 2013. Quest-a translation quality estimation framework. In *Proceedings of the 51st Annual Meeting of the Association for Computational Linguistics: System Demonstrations*, pages 79–84.

Lucia Specia, Marco Turchi, Nicola Cancedda, Nello Cristianini, and Marc Dymetman. 2009. Estimating the sentence-level quality of machine translation systems. In *EAMT*, volume 9, pages 28–35.

Thomas Wolf, Lysandre Debut, Victor Sanh, Julien Chaumond, Clement Delangue, Anthony Moi, Pierric Cistac, Tim Rault, Rémi Louf, Morgan Funtowicz, Joe Davison, Sam Shleifer, Patrick von Platen, Clara Ma, Yacine Jernite, Julien Plu, Canwen Xu, Teven Le Scao, Sylvain Gugger, Mariama Drame, Quentin Lhoest, and Alexander M. Rush. 2020. Transformers: State-of-the-art natural language processing. In *Proceedings of the 2020 Conference on Empirical Methods in Natural Language Processing: System Demonstrations*, pages 38–45, Online. Association for Computational Linguistics.

Wei Zhao, Goran Glavaš, Maxime Peyrard, Yang Gao, Robert West, and Steffen Eger. 2020. On the limitations of cross-lingual encoders as exposed by reference-free machine translation evaluation. In *Proceedings of the 58th Annual Meeting of the Association for Computational Linguistics*, pages 1656–1671, Online. Association for Computational Linguistics.

Association for Computational Linguistics
209 N. Eighth Street
Stroudsburg, Pennsylvania 18360

ISBN 978-1-7138-9183-3

CURRAN ASSOCIATES INC.
proceedings.com